RESPONDING
TO THE OPPRESSION
OF ADDICTION

RESPONDING TO THE OPPRESSION OF ADDICTION

Canadian Social Work Perspectives
Third Edition

Edited by
Rick Csiernik and William S. Rowe

CANADIAN
SCHOLARS

Toronto | Vancouver

Responding to the Oppression of Addiction: Canadian Social Work Perspectives, Third Edition
Edited by Rick Csiernik and William S. Rowe

First published in 2017 by
Canadian Scholars
425 Adelaide Street West, Suite 200
Toronto, Ontario
M5V 3C1

www.canadianscholars.ca

Library and Archives Canada Cataloguing in Publication

Responding to the oppression of addiction : Canadian
social work perspectives / edited by Rick Csiernik and William
S. Rowe. -- Third edition.

Includes bibliographical references and index.
Issued in print and electronic formats.
ISBN 978-1-55130-933-0 (softcover).--ISBN 978-1-55130-934-7
(PDF).--ISBN 978-1-55130-935-4 (ebook)

1. Social work with drug addicts--Canada. 2. Social work with
alcoholics--Canada. 3. Substance abuse--Treatment. 4. Compulsive
behavior--Canada. I. Csiernik, Rick, editor II. Rowe, William S.,
1949-, editor

HV5000.C3R48 2017   362.29'1530971   C2016-908230-X
                                             C2016-908231-8

Text and cover design by Peggy & Co. Design Inc.

17   18   19   20   21   5   4   3   2   1

Printed and bound in Canada by Webcom

MIX
Paper from
responsible sources
FSC® C004071

CONTENTS

Child welfare workers, marital and family counsellors, school social workers, housing and homelessness advocates, trauma workers, criminal justice proponents, mental health workers, medical and psychiatric social workers, community developers, policy analysts, shelter workers, crisis counsellors, people working with refugees and immigrants, and most other social work practitioners all have a portion of their practice that involves clients with addiction issues. However, addiction education is not available for all Canadian social work students and remains primarily an elective offering at institutions that do offer courses in this complex area. Canadian social workers that graduated in the last century may have never even considered addiction as a primary social work practice area, and, typically, addiction-related professional development is not presented by social workers or from a social work viewpoint.

Addiction is a highly interdisciplinary practice area, and social workers work with correctional officers, probation and parole staff, certified alcohol and drug counsellors, EAP practitioners, policy analysts, psychologists, physicians, psychiatrists, nurses, nutritionists, pharmacologists, and related health care and counselling professionals in their work with clients who have a drug dependency. As a result, non-social work authors have dominated the academic and applied literature in the field of addiction and have generally not presented a holistic orientation to the field.

Canada has been both a leader and a follower in the area of addiction practice and policy over the past two centuries. We were among the first Western nations to prohibit alcohol and criminalize heroin and cannabis, yet we resisted the call for another "War on Drugs" during the 1980s. Alcohol advertising is prevalent throughout Canada, and beer imagery is extensively intertwined with our national pastime, yet we were among the first nations to ban smoking advertising and restrict the use of tobacco on planes, in public buildings, and restaurants, and now even outdoors. We readily welcome immigrants and accept refugees from around the world but then restrict the use of psychoactive agents that are readily available and legal in their home nation. Of all known world cultures, the Innu of Labrador and northern Quebec are one of the few to have never used psychoactive agents prior to contact with other cultures, though now drugs threaten to destroy them and other First Nations communities, peoples across Canada. While the tradition of Alcoholics Anonymous is firmly entrenched in our treatment culture, we continue to pursue and develop innovative counselling approaches.

Social workers receive education and training within a context of professional and ethical responsibility to both individuals and the community. This results in social workers having a unique perspective to bring to the multidisciplinary practice area of addiction. Social work views addiction not merely from a clinical perspective but

1

from a more holistic, anti-oppressive orientation, considering the client in relation to his or her environment along with the structural factors that contribute to the use, misuse, and abuse of psychoactive drugs. As Canadians, we too have a different perspective on global problems. Thus, as Canadian social workers, we should also have a unique perspective on addiction. Yet, prior to the first edition of this book, Canadian social workers both directly and indirectly involved in the addiction field, be it in prevention, health promotion, direct practice, or policy development, have not had a uniquely Canadian social work resource.

The first edition of this book, published in 2003, brought together for the first time in one place the voices of over two dozen Canadian social work academics and practitioners discussing this theme. The second edition, published seven years later, provided an expanded version with nine new, six revised, and seven updated chapters, adding 16 new voices to the dialogue. The third edition has 21 new contributors and eight new chapters as our knowledge in the field continues to expand. Also, for the first time, a chapter is included that is not written, at least in part, by a social worker. Thomas' story is a first person narrative that arose after the author read the second edition and was moved for the first time to fully explore his own journey into and out of addiction (Chapter 22).

As may be expected from a profession and nation as diverse as ours, the orientations are varied and the perspectives multidimensional; the topics covered are broad, yet still not exhaustive. The themes discussed include prevention initiatives, program descriptions, discussions of the special needs of different populations, and policy perspectives framed within an anti-oppression standpoint.

The concluding section focuses upon issues typically—and incorrectly—called addictions. While they require unique intervention, treatment systems, and policies, more fundamentally these do not have the same biological issues as those that occur with addiction to psychoactive substances.

We hope that the standpoints in this collection continue to inform and educate you in a unique manner. We also hope they assist you in conceptualizing addiction as oppression and aid you to practice within an anti-oppressive framework. We hope the contents allow you to be the fish that sees the water that you swim in.

At first people refuse to believe that a strange new thing can be done, then they begin to hope it can be done, then they see it can be done—then it is done and all the world wonders why it was not done long before.

FRANCIS HODGSON BURNETT, *THE SECRET GARDEN*

Rick Csiernik and William S. Rowe
September 2016

ACKNOWLEDGEMENTS

We wish to continue to acknowledge and recognize the front-line social workers and their clients who live the drama of addiction every day, struggling to find dignity and fulfillment in their lives.

As well, we wish to thank Dr. Susan Silva-Wayne for her initial and ongoing support of this project along with the staff of Canadian Scholars who make the ideas a reality.

INTRODUCTION

CHAPTER 1

Creating a Holistic Understanding of Addiction

Rick Csiernik and William S. Rowe

That humanity at large will ever be able to dispense with artificial paradises seems very unlikely. Most men and women lead lives at worst so painful, at the best so monotonous, poor and limited that the urge to escape, the longing to transcend themselves if only for a few moments, is and has always been one of the principal appetites of the soul.

—ALDOUS HUXLEY (1952)

Introduction

Psychoactive drugs are used for an almost incomprehensible list of reasons. Not only are drugs taken to reduce pain, suffering, agitation, and anxiety, but also to enhance the normal human state, to increase pleasure, facilitate learning, reduce aggressiveness, and respond to a myriad of mental health concerns. The reasons for drug use, misuse, and abuse vary from drug to drug, person to person, occasion to occasion, and culture to culture. Among the reasons for drug use are:

- curiosity and experimentation
- access and availability
- peer pressure
- escapism
- relaxation
- stress reduction
- the inability to cope with problems
- boredom
- lack of self-esteem
- financial poverty
- spiritual poverty
- increased sociability
- hospitality and friendship
- pleasure
- rebellion
- adolescence
- cultural norms
- societal modelling
- friends/family using
- fun

However, drug use has both a significant personal and societal cost. In 1986 the Addiction Research Foundation of Ontario first calculated the cost of illegal drug use to the province and estimated it to be in excess of $9 billion per year. Among the costs was $250 million for law enforcement, $500 million in reduced labour productivity, and the single greatest cost was $5 billion attributed to alcohol-related problems (Black, 1988). In the mid-1990s the Canadian Centre on Substance Abuse conducted a similar national appraisal on the cost of alcohol, tobacco, and illicit drug use in Canada and placed the total at $18.45 billion (Single, Robson, Xie, & Rehm, 1996). When the national study was repeated in 2002 the revised estimate had more than doubled to $39.8 billion, an annual cost of $1,267 for every child and adult in Canada. The 2002 calculations placed productivity losses at $24.3 billion or 61% of the total, while health care costs were $8.8 billion (22.1%) and the cost for law enforcement was estimated at $5.4 billion (13.6%) (Rehm et al., 2006). Substance use is also directly associated with a broad range of social issues including increased risk of suicide (Schneider, 2009), interpersonal violence (Korcha et al., 2014), gang violence (International Centre for Science in Drug Policy, 2010), homelessness (Forchuk, Csiernik, & Jensen, 2011), and poverty (Amundson, Zajicek, & Hunt, 2014).

A Global Perspective

The United Nations Office on Drugs and Crime (2014) estimates that between 3.5% and 7.0% of the world's population aged 15-64 uses illicit drugs, which represents upwards of 300 million people. Of these, 6 million to 39 million are likely addicted, producing a mortality rate by illegal drugs of 40/million population globally. Overall, global dependency on illicit drugs is responsible for 3.6 million years of life lost through premature death and 20 million years of life lived with disability. Nations with the greatest rate of burden include the United States, United Kingdom, Russia, and Australia (Degenhardt et al., 2013). However, this does not include the two most problematic substances, which are both licit. Alcohol remains directly responsible for approximately 6% of death on the planet, or 3.3 million persons; tobacco produces even more harm, with approximately 5 million deaths annually as a result of smoking and another 600,000 caused by second-hand smoke. The World Health Organization (2012) predicts that without changes in use, the 21st century will see 1 billion deaths attributed to tobacco, primarily in the developing world.

Among illicit drugs, opioids currently produce the most death and disease, just surpassing stimulants. Afghanistan continues to be the world's largest producer of opium with Myanmar (Burma) seeing major areas in cultivated land devoted to this crop. Likewise, drug cartels in Mexico have also begun growing more opium, which has led to record amounts of acreages devoted to this crop, over 300,000 in 2013. In contrast, global coca cultivation, which had been stable, has now dropped to approximately 133,000 hectares, partially because of increasing use of synthetic stimulants, primarily crystal methamphetamine, and other related new products such as bath salts (methyl-enedioxypyrovalerone) and synthetic (JWH-018) and herbal (AM-2201) cannabis that do not have to be imported and can be synthesized locally. Cannabis continues to be grown globally with specific increases in use noted in Uruguay and specific geographic jurisdictions in the United States, both of which have legalized and regulated the sale of the drug, placing cannabis in an increasing unique legal position (United Nations Office on Drugs and Crime, 2014).

While the overall global crime rate related to violent and property crime has decreased since the beginning of the 21st century, this is not the case for drug-related offences. Between 2002 and 2012 the number of persons arrested for possession of illicit drugs for personal use increased 31%. The United Nations Office on Drugs and Crime's (2002) last official estimate of the global sale of illicit drugs was between $450 billion and $750 billion, while in Canada the federal government estimated that it is somewhere in the range of $7 billion to $18 billion (Auditor General of Canada, 2001). African countries facing serious social and infrastructural issues including extreme poverty, political instability, and rampant corruption, in combination with their geographical location, have facilitated the establishment of organized crime linked to the distribution of illicit drugs. Several West African countries now serve as transhipment points and storage for South American cocaine destined primarily for the European market. Cocaine smuggled into transit countries such as Cape Verde, Guinea-Bisseau, the Canary Islands, Ghana, Togo, Benin, Nigeria, Liberia, and Senegal is subsequently shipped to European nations, primarily Spain and Portugal. In 2013 it was estimated that 18 tons was shipped through this region, worth $1.25 billion wholesale. However, African nations are also being targeted by heroin smugglers from Southwest Asia as they seek new routes to ship their product to North American and European markets (United Nations Office on Drugs and Crime, 2013, 2014).

When one examines the profit to be made, it is understandable why the illicit drug trade is a global economic driver. From the point of growing in Colombia to the point of sale in North America, the markup on coffee is 69%. In comparison, the markup on coca from harvest to sale as cocaine in North America is 635%, which indicates why the sale of this psychoactive drug is positive for all involved except the individual consumer. In comparison, from point of growing to individual consumption the mark up for Afghani heroin is 3745%, while on Colombian cocaine it is 6427%, both of which only increase the more it is confiscated (London School of Economics, 2014). However, it is once again legal drugs that remain the most problematic. Estimates for the costs of excessive alcohol use in the United States alone are $232.5 billion annually from health care expenses, motor vehicle incidents, loss of workplace productivity, property damage, and criminal justice costs. Of this, 11% is attributed to underage drinking (Bouchery et al., 2011). Tobacco is even more costly, adding another $300 billion in costs in the United States alone, $170 billion in direct medical costs and $156 billion due to losses in productivity arising from premature death and second-hand smoke (United States Department of Health and Human Services, 2014; Xu et al., 2014).

Recently, the move towards legalization of formerly illicit drugs has gained momentum with cannabis being legalized in Uruguay, eight American states, and Canada, with even more radical decriminalization of drugs having taken place in Portugal and Ghana. The Colorado (2015) government generated over $50 million in revenue from taxes, licences, and fees in the first year cannabis was legalized, which does not even consider the additional income tax paid by employees working in this new field. In Washington State, the first month of legalization resulted in just under $4 million in sales, generating approximately $1 million in new tax revenue. The Washington State Liquor Control Board, which oversees marijuana sales, estimates marijuana tax revenue for 2015 to 2017 will be $122 million, rising to $336 million between 2017 and 2019 as more licences are approved across the state (Henchman, 2014).

Even more controversial was Portugal's move in 2001 to decriminalize all formerly illicit drugs. While not legal, possession for personal use is prosecuted through a distinct judicial process that involves not just lawyers but also psychologists and social workers. Outcomes can range from mandated treatment referrals to simple fines depending upon the individual circumstances, though drug distribution and trafficking continue to be criminal offences with substantive periods of incarceration. Conversely, possession has moved from being a criminal matter to one of public health. While there were grave concerns about this move, particularly among social conservatives inside Portugal and throughout the European Union, the policy shift has not resulted in increased use. The opposite has occurred, as predicted by addiction specialists, with an overall decrease in drug use and decreases in HIV infections and drug overdoses. HIV and sexually transmitted infection rates are among the lowest in Europe, lifetime cannabis use is one quarter of that in North America, and treatment use doubled between 2001 and 2009. This is also in part an outcome of funding that used to be directed towards law enforcement and imprisonment being instead spent on education, prevention, and treatment, as well as users not fearing imprisonment if they seek assistance. However, there still remain jurisdiction issues that slow down the process, as an occasional cannabis user apprehended in a club will go through the same process as a 10-year heroin user (Greenwald, 2009).

Addiction as Oppression

In the United States Black people comprise 13 percent of the US population but 31 percent of those arrested for drug law violations.

　　—DRUG POLICY ALLIANCE, 2016

It is evident that the anti-drug campaigns over the past 20 years have added to the isolation and marginalization of the discarded working-class youth…. In addition to having to overcome their addiction, one of the biggest hurdles they have to face is breaking through the barrier of social exclusion.

    —BUCHANAN & YOUNG (2000, P. 414)

All oppression creates a state of war.

    —SIMONE DE BEAUVOIR (1949, P. 717)

Oppression refers to a mode of unjust human relations that involves economic, social, political, and psychological exploitation, marginalization, and domination between social groups and classes within and between societies. The term *oppression* comes from the Latin "to press down" and relates to the feelings of being both mentally and physically burdened, devalued, and deprived of privileges, and includes the ideas of cultural imperialism and violence. Oppression is a multidimensional, dynamic process that, once it becomes ingrained in a society's institutional order and into its unconsciousness, becomes the norm and is not typically overtly challenged. Oppression bestows power and advantage on one group, who are deemed to be the norm, at the expense of the other because of their otherness (Gil, 1998). Oppression occurs when individuals are blocked from self-development, excluded from full participation in society, and do not have or believe that they do not have certain rights (Mullaly, 2002). Frye (1983) wrote that individuals are oppressed simply by being a member of a group or a category. Oppression transpires when frustrations, restrictions, and pain arise due to a person's membership in this group or category rather than because of the individual's talents, merits, or failings (Mullaly, 2007). Oppression occurs at three distinct levels: the personal, the cultural, and the structural (Figure 1.1) (Thompson, 2006).

This is what it is to be an alcoholic, to be an addict, to be a junkie. Not a person with an addiction or a person with a dependency to alcohol, but rather a label, a thing identified by one behaviour whose entire persona becomes that one attribute—an attribute the majority of society still does not want in their neighbourhood or community, or to openly acknowledge (unless of course the person is a celebrity going into rehab). While the field of addiction has made monumental leaps in the past 50 years, the dominant form of assistance still necessitates a code of anonymity, of not openly declaring one's name and or openly advocating for social change lest the average, non-celebrity member be identified and stigmatized. In North America, the race issue is now openly spoken of, if still far from being resolved, gays and lesbians can openly proclaim love for each other and be married, and individuals do not have to unwillingly leave their employment because they have been alive 65 years, yet a vast majority of people with an addiction still identify themselves only as Rick C. or Bill R., and take pride in announcing their membership in a fellowship of millions only in anonymity.

Figure 1.1 Thompson's Model of Oppression

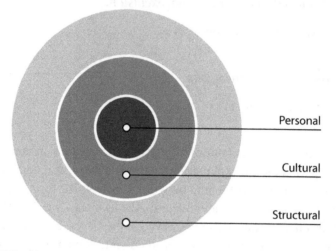

Source: Thompson, 2006, p. 28.

Structural examples of oppression against individuals with an addiction are unfortunately plentiful. In Ontario it took a decade of legal battles and a 3-0 ruling at the Divisional Court level before the province of Ontario would include addiction as a disability classification for social assistance. When the judgment was made in 2009, the general monthly social assistance payments were $536, whereas those made under long-term disability were $959, a 44% difference. The provincial Social Benefits Tribunal initially ruled against the two male claimants. However, in 2006, the Supreme Court of Canada ordered the tribunal to reconsider the case and determine whether the law violated the Human Rights Code (Kari, 2009). Since 1997, Project Prevention (2015) in the United States has paid out $300 to over 5,000 individuals with a confirmed history of drug use who agreed to undertake long-term birth control. Of those participants, 1,757 women and 138 men underwent sterilization procedures so as addicts they would not become parents. Indonesia's Narcotic Act, introduced in 2009, identifies drug addicts as criminals, distinguishing them from drug abusers who are eligible for rehabilitation, without explaining the difference between the two. It also has a provision where parents can be fined or imprisoned if they do not report their children's drug use, and retains the death penalty for drug trafficking (Lembaga, Bantuah, Hukum & Masyarakat, 2009). Likewise, Malaysia's drug treatment system makes no distinction between occasional drug users and those actually dependent on drugs. Any individual can be detained for a period of two weeks and forcibly tested by police on suspicion of drug use. Those testing positive, even in the absence of possession, can be flogged and interned for up to two years in a compulsory drug treatment centre (International Harm Reduction Development Program, 2009).

On a societal level, the classic historic example of addiction as oppression is British–Chinese relations from the 18th century to the 20th century. In the late 1700s, Britain began to import opium to China to offset the trade deficit that developed in part due to the massive civil service Britain required to administer its global empire. The direct result was an increased use of opium in China, which led to further offshore growing, primarily in India, and importation that, in turn, led to increasing social problems throughout China. Eventually the ruling Qing Empire protested and actively opposed the opium trade with Britain. In response to the attempted prohibition, Britain fought two wars over opium, from 1839–1842 and again from 1856–1860, the second with the overt support of France, to allow it to import as much opium as it desired. The British victories led to a free-flowing opium trade and treaties that not only made Hong Kong a British colony and gave other trade benefits to European nations, but also provoked, in China, the largest addiction ever in world history. Eventually, consumption and addiction spurred opium production in China itself with subsequent disastrous social and public health consequences. By 1878 it was estimated that there were 20 million Chinese people addicted to opium, a number that would not decrease until the beginning of the next century. By the turn of the 20th century, opium had caused widespread social dysfunction not only in China but also among Chinese immigrants to Canada and the United States (Lin, Fang, & Wang, 2008; Mandancy, 2001).

The Process of Drug Use

The process from initial contact with a drug to addiction, while not complex, is typically a lengthy progression. Among adult first-time treatment admissions in the United States, an average of 15.6 years elapses between the first use of the primary substance of abuse and treatment entry (Substance Abuse and Mental Health Administration, 2011). Regardless of why a person first tries a drug, initial contact is the entry phase (Figure 1.2). Some users stop after an initial experimentation phase or they stop at the integrated use level. Integrated use is the casual and/or occasional drink, smoke, or toke. Drug use remains at a controlled level. Integrated or experimental use can both, however, lead to excessive use. When a person begins to use a drug at a level that is excessive to her or his physical, psychological, or social well-being, one of four outcomes is possible: (1) the person may stop on his or her own or seek assistance to stop; (2) a return to the integrated phase may occur; (3) the individual might remain at the excessive level of drug use with its associated problems; or (4) an individual can move on to the addicted phase. As in the excessive use phase, four alternatives exist in the addicted phase:

Figure 1.2 Stages in the Process of Drug Use

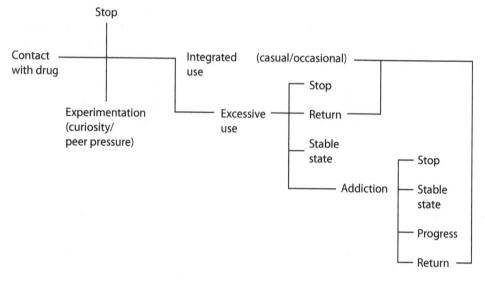

Source: Link, Hachman, & Casey, 1977, p. 126.

1. Stop
2. Remain addicted
3. Progress to the point of an early death
4. Return to a lower level of usage

The scenario is simple. Fully understanding and providing assistance to abate this process is not.

The underlying dilemma is that, as a species, humans have a fascination with any psychoactive agent or behaviour that alters the basic perception of the world. Anthropologists have claimed that a primary reason for the shift from nomadic hunting and gathering to agriculture was to allow for the regular and systematic cultivation of intoxicating beverages. Europeans smoked or inhaled opium and hemp for both ceremonial and intoxicating reasons as early as 4200 BCE, and alcohol use began as early as 3500 BCE (Berridge, 1999; Rudgely, 1995). Intoxicating mushrooms were used by the shamans of Siberia, and Scythians used hallucinogenic cannabis as early as 600 BCE. Roots and berries including belladonna, hemlock, and mandrake were all consumed by ancient civilizations because of their mind-altering and hallucinogenic effects. Many influential writers, such as Elizabeth Barrett Browning and Charlotte Brontë, have described their personal use of intoxicants (Aldrich, 1994; Rudgely, 1995). In the 20th century drugs such as alcohol, marijuana, LSD, cocaine, and ecstasy have been implicated in both socio-political movements and world events. Unfortunately, as earlier discussed, these substances and their associated consequences can have an astronomical cost financially and in terms of human suffering. Despite the discouragement of drug use and continuous attempts at prohibition, psychoactive drugs have become an integral part of culture and it is unlikely that drug use will ever cease. A more realistic and pragmatic goal is a move towards wellness and the reduction of abuse by lessening the extent to which persons are harmed and cause harm to others because of psychoactive drugs.

A Brief Canadian Historic Overview

In Canada drug prohibition laws have been repeatedly introduced and repealed. Alcohol was the first substance banned, followed by opium, alcohol again, cocaine, marijuana, alcohol yet again, and now ecstasy and khat.[1] The first law proclaiming a psychoactive substance illicit other than alcohol was introduced in 1908, subsequent to the growing concern surrounding opium use (Fischer, 1997). The Opium Act of 1908, which later formed the more general Opium and Drug Act of 1911, specifically targeted opium smoking and was passed based on pressure from both moral reformers and a general climate of hostility towards Chinese immigrants in Canada (Giffen, Endicott, & Lambert, 1991). Emerging drug laws were essentially punitive in nature. Possession, trafficking, sale, production, and import of certain psychoactive drugs could result in harsh penalties and extensive imprisonment. Special powers were extended to the police for search and seizure, and there were few options available for treatment and rehabilitation. In many ways addictions to alcohol and other drugs were primarily considered failures of character, willpower, and morality.

The inception of Alcoholics Anonymous in 1935 initiated a more humane approach to addiction and gave rise to the disease model.[2] In the 1950s, drug use in Vancouver was seen as especially problematic and many called for changes in policy. In fact, the first treatment centres were established in 1955 in British Columbia, and the professions of social work, psychiatry, and psychology became more actively if belatedly involved. Nonetheless, the debate continued as to whether or not those with an addiction were curable, whether addiction was contagious, and whether treatment should be mandated. Unfortunately, during the same period, Canadian drug enforcement authorities began to focus primarily on the drug users themselves as opposed to suppliers or producers. The number of drug charges increased from a few hundred to tens of thousands annually by the 1960s (Fischer, 1997). The Narcotic Control Act was introduced in 1961 and drug policy retained its primarily punitive and prohibitive nature. It wasn't until the Le Dain Commission (1969-1973) that strong recommendations were made for the government to redirect its efforts towards health promotion and away from criminalization (Erickson, 1998).

The Le Dain Commission report raised some controversial issues, such as when the Commission wrote, "In every case the test must be a practical one: we must weigh the potential for harm, individual and social, of the conduct in question against the harm, individual and social, which is caused by the application of the criminal law, and ask ourselves whether, on balance, the intervention is justified" (1973, p. 93). By the mid-1970s the number of Canadian drug offences had topped 40,000 annually, and people began to question the efficacy of criminal sanctions as a deterrent. Coincidentally, with the arrival of HIV and later hepatitis C, the health and social costs of illicit drug use were becoming greater and many people began to recognize the need for a more effective solution. During this period treatment programs expanded and harm reduction concepts began to be considered and eventually, and often begrudgingly, funded.[3]

In 1997 Canada passed the Controlled Drugs and Substance Act (CDSA), formerly Bill C-7. This bill clearly demonstrated the ambivalence of lawmakers and politicians concerning drug use, because it reaffirmed the deviant status of illicit drug use and the primacy of criminal justice over public health and social justice alternatives. In fact, Erickson (1998, p. 263) states that the "CDSA is a throwback to the 1920s (it is) a revamped Narcotic Control Act based on myths and preconceptions about illicit drugs and their evil, addictive effects on users, reinforcing the additional policy criminalization." At the same time, policy-makers, responding to calls from advocacy groups and embracing the results of effective programming in Europe and Australia, have pushed for and achieved more public health-oriented approaches. These include the use of marijuana for medical purposes, and a mayoralty election in Vancouver at the beginning of the new century where the successful candidate included safer injection sites as a platform in his campaign.[4] Despite this, the Auditor General of Canada (2001) reported that 95% of Canada's Drug Strategy budget for dealing with illicit drugs remains devoted to measures to reduce the supply.

Despite legislation that remains mired in moral model thinking, new philosophical approaches have emerged in Canada. In 2001, the City of Vancouver adopted a Four Pillars model (MacPherson & Rowley, 2001) that incorporated a focus on treatment with prevention, harm reduction, and law enforcement, along with the integration and coordination of strategies sometimes referred to as "the fifth pillar" with the goal to reduce harm to both individuals and communities (Figure 1.3).

Figure 1.3   Four Pillars Model

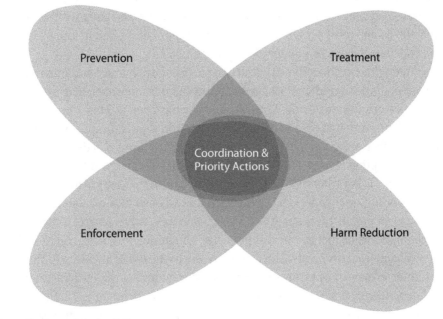

Source: MacPherson & Rowley, 2001

Key Concepts

Prior to being able to define addiction in a social work context, definitions of some key and often misused terms are required. To a pharmacologist, a psychoactive drug is either a chemical not naturally found in the body, or it is a normal body chemical administered in a larger dose than is normal to the body. The chemical is taken by a specific person, via some mode of administration, in a given amount, with a particular periodicity, and for a certain length of time. The drug is administered to produce a change in body functioning, and with psychoactive drugs primarily a change to the central nervous system. The Le Dain Commission (1973) defined a psychoactive drug as any substance, either natural or synthesized, that by its chemical nature alters the structure or function of the body or mind in a living organism.

Psychoactive drugs are substances that alter brain functioning by decreasing (depressants), increasing (stimulants), or disrupting (hallucinogens) central nervous system activity. This in turn produces changes in mood, perception, sensation, need, consciousness, and other psychological functions and ultimately produces changes in behaviour. In addition, these substances may influence a great number of physiological functions mediated by the brain that are outside the realm of conscious control: the peripheral, including the autonomic, nervous system. These may include changes of cardiovascular function, respiration, and hormonal balance, as well as activation of the internal fight-or-flight response. Psychoactive agents are used for both medical and non-medical purposes and are both legal and illicit, social constructs that change over time and by culture. The oldest recorded use of psychoactive drugs is in religious ceremonies. Over time these drugs moved into the secular realm and finally into social use. All societies and most persons have used some type of drug, be it nicotine, caffeine, alcohol, codeine, cocaine, amphetamines, or cannabis.

Associated with psychoactive drugs are the ideas of drug abuse and misuse. *Drug misuse* refers to the periodic or occasional improper or inappropriate use of either a social or a prescription drug. The term *drug abuse* has been used in a broader social context to define any instance of drug administration that is disapproved of by the society in which it occurs. A more consumer-oriented definition of drug abuse limits its use to a description of drug administration that is causing some kind of adverse effect on the individual user rather than on society. According to the medical model, the term *drug abuser* is limited to individuals who persistently consume a substance to such an extent that they impair their quality of life in some way. Adverse effects can include medical complications, behavioural alterations, difficulties with social relationships, and medical and legal problems. Thus, abuse refers to the use of any drug to the point where it interferes with a person's health or with economic or social adjustment.

Drug dependency is the stage following drug abuse. Dependency is actually what most people mean when they use the term *addiction*. When the media discuss a compulsive food, shopping, or sexual behaviour, what they actually mean is dependency, more specifically a psychological dependency or compulsion to engage in a behaviour to a problematic degree. One can be dependent upon almost any activity—Internet use, gambling, sex, and even work—however, addiction has a more complicated and holistic meaning.

Physical dependence is a physiological state of cellular adaptation occurring when the body becomes so accustomed to a psychoactive drug that it can only function normally when the drug is present. Without the drug the user will experience physical disturbances or illnesses, known as withdrawal. Withdrawal symptoms can be prevented or promptly relieved by the administration of a sufficient quantity of the original drug or, often, by one with similar pharmacological activity. The latter case, in which different drugs are used interchangeably to prevent withdrawal symptoms, is called cross-dependence.

The development of physical dependence is important in the maintenance of drug taking, not only because of its negative reinforcement, but also because administration, either to alleviate or to prevent withdrawal, results in additional positive reinforcement. Instead of returning to a neutral state, or homeostasis, there may be an overshooting effect resulting in further positive reinforcement. Physical dependency is typically preceded by serious personal, psychological, social, and even physiological complications. Physical dependence usually occurs with chronic use of most depressants, opioids, and stimulants. Among the hallucinogens, physical dependence has not yet been demonstrated except with long-term use of cannabis products.

The complement to physical dependency is psychological dependency, which is also referred to by some as behavioural or emotional dependence. Psychological dependence occurs when a drug becomes so important to a person's thoughts or activities that the individual believes that he or she cannot manage without it. Psychological dependence may range from a mild wish to a compelling emotional need for a periodic or continuous use of a drug and may include feelings of loss or even desperation if the drug is unavailable. In the case of psychological dependence a person begins to feel, or believe, that he or she needs the drug effect in order to cope with a variety of life situations and eventually all life situations. The feelings of either relaxation or arousal become required because individuals believe that they cannot get through life without these effects. In most instances, the psychological aspects are considerably more important than physical dependence in maintaining chronic drug use. The major problem with dependence is not the physical aspect, as withdrawal can usually be successfully achieved within several days, but the great likelihood that the individual will return to chronic use for psychological reasons. Subtle yet persistent psychological and social factors are enough to maintain the behaviour of drug consumption.

Providing a Social Work Understanding of Addiction

Words are important. If you want to care for something, you call it a "flower";
if you want to kill something, you call it a "weed."

—DON COYHIS, 2002

This brings us to the term *addiction* and a social work understanding of this complex phenomenon. Physical dependency is relatively easy to manage. Non-medical withdrawal management and detoxification centres assist thousands of clients every year in Canada, and only a few with severe alcohol or barbiturate withdrawal require more specialized medical attention. In fact, most people can be physically withdrawn from almost any psychoactive drug in a few days to two weeks, though typically with much discomfort, anxiety, and physical and emotional pain. Psychological dependency is more complicated and intricate and much of this book is devoted to providing insights into how to assist with the management of psychological dependency through different forms of counselling and insights into specific client groups. This, however, still leaves the third dimension of addiction, the one most other professions ignore, but which social work, by the nature of its professional mandate, must address: the social. The neglect of the social and thus the lack of addressing addiction in a holistic manner may explain why the addiction issues of clients of one in six counsellors worsen after beginning treatment (Kraus et al., 2011).

The term *addiction*, itself, has been used so loosely that in daily usage it has become an ineffectual term. The term has been misused and overused not only for medical, political, and economic purposes but also for entertainment and amusement. Addiction derives from the Latin word *addicto*, meaning bound or devoted, or bondage to a practice. Compulsive drug users are typically labelled addicted to their substance, or more frequently, substances of choice without appreciating the entire latitude of the term. The fifth edition of the Diagnostic and Statistical Manual of Mental Disorders (DSM-V) uses neither the term *physical* nor *psychological dependency*, but rather the title "Substance-Related and Addictive Disorders." The focus of the DSM-V is on cognitive, behavioural, and physiological symptoms that indicate continued substance use despite problems arising due to the use of psychoactive drugs (American Psychiatric Association, 2013). In contrast, the American Society of Addiction Medicine (ASAM, 2011), after engaging in its own extensive consultation process, proclaimed that addiction was a primary, chronic disease of brain reward, motivation, memory, and related circuitry. ASAM claims that this definition serves to destigmatize addictive disorders, but then added a list of behaviours that have no disease mechanism, such as gambling, to their list that members of the society should address medically and thus receive financial compensation for.

Sussman and Sussman (2011) reviewed the literature and found five primary themes repeated in discussing the idea of addiction:

1. Feeling different from others who were using the drug
2. Preoccupation with drug use
3. Only temporary satiation before using more
4. Loss of control
5. Negative consequences of using

However, it was a psychologist, Stanton Peele (1983, 1985, 1989), who was the first to openly challenge a purely bio-psycho conceptualization of addiction. He claimed that addiction was not merely a chemical reaction. Addiction, for him, was a social experience that in and of itself could bring about dependency to a substance in an otherwise well person. He claimed that individuals could become dependent to a particular state of body and mind. For Peele, no substance was inherently addictive nor was substance addiction a single phenomenon. He claimed, rather, that addiction occurs along a continuum and even those at the extremes of addictiveness showed the capacity to act outside of typical addiction behaviours under appropriate circumstances.

The most dramatic example of this relates to veterans of the Vietnam War. As early as 1971 there was extensive evidence of widespread and heavy drug use by soldiers in Vietnam. Estimates ranged from 10–15% of lower-ranking enlisted men to upwards of 25% who were addicted to heroin during their tours of duty. Thus, it was anticipated that during the course of the Vietnam War somewhere between 35,000 to 60,000 Americans returned to the United States addicted to heroin. However, upon reaching the United States only a small percentage actually required formal addiction treatment (Brecher, 1972; Robins, Helzer, Hesselbrock, & Wish, 2010; Roffman, 1976; Woodson,

1973). In a probability sample of 898 United States Army enlisted male armed forces personnel returning to the United States after an active tour of duty, 52.2% tested positive for illicit drugs upon leaving Vietnam, with 20% being classified as addicted to heroin. Heroin is generally believed to be the most difficult substance from which to abstain, other than nicotine, once a person becomes dependent. However, one year later only 6% had relapsed and only 1% of the former soldiers were still using heroin. This finding was at first disbelieved, especially because the majority of those returning from Vietnam who tested positive for drugs claimed they had become addicted in Vietnam.

There were a variety of theories offered for this dramatic and completely unexpected decrease in addiction, including the statement that the veterans received more extensive and superior counselling and support services upon returning home than would a typical heroin addict (Price & Copeland, 1993). What was not openly discussed, but is very evident in retrospect, is the considerable impact environmental change has upon addiction. Young men from urban and rural America were suddenly dropped into an environment where they were regularly forced to risk their lives and try to kill an unseen, unknown enemy. They then returned to an environment where the threat of death and risk to life was virtually eliminated. The radical change in the men's environments enabled a radical change in their initial and subsequent drug using behaviour.

This incorporation of the social context of addiction draws from systems and ecological theory and takes into consideration the person-in-environment. By examining addiction as a biopsychosocial phenomenon, social work and other counselling professions, consider not only the pharmacological characteristics of the psychoactive drug and the individual characteristics of the user, but also the social context of use. What are key environmental factors that contribute to the development and maintenance of drug using behaviour? In a social work understanding of addiction, oppression and marginality are brought equally into the equation. Thus, relapse is not merely the failing of a client, or an indication of denial or the fault of an unmotivated user. Neither is addiction viewed merely as a neurobiological phenomenon dependent upon improper serotonin, dopamine, endomorphine, or GABA levels (Graham, Young, Vlach, & Wood, 2008). The larger social circumstances are considered as a component of a treatment plan, when working with the community in dealing with homelessness, or when examining social policies that address the societal value of addiction.

Agar (2001) stated that at the turn of the 20th century middle-class housewives showed the highest rate of opioid addiction in the United States. Primarily young, white, urban, working-class men then abused heroin in the 1920s, and after World War II heroin use became more prominent within the African-American community. Agar claims that the common theme among the three apparently disparate groups is that during the era each group was the greatest user and abuser of heroin they experienced social marginality. Kasl expressed a similar view, stating that "patriarchy, hierarchy and capitalism create, encourage, maintain and perpetuate addiction and dependency" (1992, p. 53). A longitudinal study of babies born during the crack epidemic of the late 20th century in the United States demonstrated that it was not the drug use of the mothers that led to developmental issues throughout childhood and adolescence, but rather issues of poverty. Children from lower socio-economic communities whose mothers had and had not used crack experienced the same cognitive and academic delays compared to national averages. It was not the in utero drug use that was the primary issue, but rather the poverty and disadvantaged social conditions that were greater contributing factors to academic success (Hurt et al., 2005; Hurt et al., 2008). Buchanan (2004) in his work in Liverpool, England, illustrated how stigmatization, marginalization, and social exclusion are components that are regularly excluded in the discussion of addiction, yet are of significance to those who struggle daily with the reality of their psychoactive drug use. To this we add that the majority of helping professions do not consider patriarchy, hierarchy, capitalism, and oppression and, in fact, these issues have historically been and continue to be ignored in any discussion of addiction. Thus, social workers must bring these issues to the forefront and must also appreciate their centrality when working in this field.

Stigma serves as a substantive barrier to help-seeking for those with addiction issues, and the way the individual is described and self-identifies can either perpetuate or diminish stigmatizing attitudes and thus increase or decrease the likelihood of the person seeking to change their situation. This is critical given that those with drug use issues are more stigmatized than individuals with other mental health issues, due in part to the pervasive belief that drug users are to be blamed for their behaviour. This stigma is perceived not only by the general public but also by health care providers and those misusing substances themselves (Hamilton, Mann, & Noh, 2011; Hunte & Finlayson, 2013; Keyes et al., 2010; van Boekel, Brouwers, van Weeghel, & Garretsen, 2014).

A social work understanding of addiction also necessitates examining language, for in social work language is our primary communication tool and the words we use have significant impact. Historically in the addiction field those abusing substances have been called addicts, as opposed to a person with addiction, and this is where the oppression first takes hold. An *addict* is an object, whereas when the term *person with an addiction* is used it is the individual who is misusing substances who is placed first, not one of his/her attributes. While the addiction may be the central organizing principle of the person's life it is still only one of their characteristics and behaviours; it is not the entire person. The dominant societal and media portrayals of addicts rather than people with an addiction further damages and dehumanizes those misusing and abusing drugs, acting as a further barrier to accessing treatment (Cortina, 2013). The individual misusing drugs has many additional qualities and attributes, many of which are strengths that are often ignored rather than acknowledged and built upon in the historic addiction counselling relationship. Thus the person is not a label, she or he is also a sibling, a parent, someone's child, a friend, a colleague, a classmate. While *person with an addiction* is much longer to both type and speak, it is much less oppressing. To use the label *addict* implies a judgment, has a negative connotation, and contributes further to the oppression of these individuals. The language employed when a drug user becomes abstinent is also significant; the person is now labelled *clean,* which, of course, by definition means that those who are not abstinent are dirty. The dominant lens through which addiction is still viewed in Canada and globally is a moralistic one, leading addiction to primarily be considered a criminal issue. Some have moved cautiously forward to claim addiction is a brain disease, though this too still makes the phenomenon an individual's responsibility and failing, be it character defect or body defect; while increasing service, this perspective does not decrease stigma. These views are inadequate, incomplete, and fail to offer holistic responses to the oppression of addiction. These paradigms not only minimize the individual and blame the victim—they also divert our attention away from the social context of use and the environment within which addiction is allowed to exist.

NOTES

1.   See Chapter 25 for a more extensive discussion of Canadian drug policy.

2.   See Chapter 11 for a more extensive discussion of Alcoholics Anonymous.

3.   See Chapter 2 for a more extensive discussion of harm reduction.

4.   See Chapter 3 for a more extensive discussion of supervised injection sites.

REFERENCES

Agar, M. (2001). A trend theory for drug use. *Developments, 21*(5), 2–4.

Aldrich, M.R. (1994). Historical notes on women addicts. *Journal of Psychoactive Drugs, 26*(1), 61–64.

American Psychiatric Association. (2013). *Diagnostic and statistical manual of mental disorders* (5th ed.). Washington, DC: American Psychiatric Publishing.

American Society of Addiction Medicine (2011). *Definition of addiction.* Retrieved from http://www.asam.org/for-the-public/definition-of-addiction

Amundson, K., Zajicek, A., & Hunt, V. (2014). Pathologies of the poor: What do the war on drugs and welfare reform have in common? *Journal of Sociology & Social Welfare, 41*(1), 5–28.

Auditor General of Canada. (2001). *2001 Annual Report.* Ottawa, ON: Auditor General of Canada.

Berridge, V. (1999). *Opium and the people: Opiate use and drug control policy in nineteenth and early twentieth century England.* New York: Free Association Books.

Black, K. (1988). *Report of the task force on illegal drug use in Ontario.* Toronto.

Bouchery, E., Harwood, H., Sacks, J., Simon, C., & Brewer, R. (2011). Economic costs of excessive alcohol consumption in the U.S., 2006. *American Journal of Preventative Medicine, 44*(2), 516–524.

Brecher, E. (1972). *Licit and illicit drugs.* Toronto, ON: Little, Brown and Company.

Buchanan, J. (2004). Tackling problem drug use: A new conceptual framework. *Social Work in Mental Health, 2*(2/3), 117–138.

Buchanan, J., & Young, L. (2000). The War on Drugs: A war on drug users? *Drugs: Education, Prevention and Policy, 7*(4), 409–422.

Colorado. (2015). *Colorado marijuana tax data.* Retrieved from https://www.colorado.gov/pacific/revenue/colorado-marijuana-tax-data

Coyhis, D. (2002). *The red road to Wellbriety: In the Native American way.* Coloroda Springs: White Bison Inc.

Cortina, S. (2013). Stigmatizing harm reduction through language. *Journal of Addiction Nursing,* 24(2), 102–107.

de Beauvoir, S. (1949 [1997]). *The second sex.* Translated and edited by H.M. Parshley. London: Vintage.

Degenhardt, L., Whiteford, H., Ferrari, A., Baxter, A., Charlson, F. Hall, W., Freedman, G., Burstein, R., Johns, S., Engell, R., Flaxman, A., Murray, C., & Vos, T. (2013). Global burden of disease attributable to illicit drug use and dependence: Findings from the Global Burden of Disease Study 2010. *The Lancet, 382*(9904), 1564–1574.

Drug Policy Alliance. (2016). *The Drug War, Mass Incarceration and Race.* Retrieved from http://www.drugpolicy.org/sites/default/files/DPA%20Fact%20Sheet_Drug%20War%20 Mass%20Incarceration%20and%20Race_(Feb.%202016).pdf

Erickson, P. (1998). Neglected and rejected: A case study of the impact of social research on Canadian drug policy. *Canadian Journal of Sociology, 23*(2/3), 263–280.

Fischer, B. (1997). The battle for a new Canadian drug law: A legal basis for harm reduction or a new rhetoric for prohibition? A chronology. In P. Erickson, D. Riley, Y. Cheung & P. O'Hare (Eds.), *Harm reduction: A new direction for drug policies and programs* (pp. 47–68). Toronto, ON: University of Toronto Press.

Forchuk, C., Csiernik, R., & Jensen, E. (2011). *Homelessness, housing and mental health: Finding truths — creating change.* Toronto, ON: Canadian Scholars' Press.

Frye, M. (1983). *The politics of reality: Essays in feminist theory.* Trumansburg, NY: Crossing Press.

Giffen, P., Endicott, S., & Lambert, S. (1991). *Panic and indifference: The politics of Canada's drug laws.* Ottawa, ON: Canadian Centre on Substance Abuse.

Gil, D. (1998). *Confronting injustice and oppression: Concepts and strategies for social workers.* New York, NY: Colombia University Press.

Graham, D., Young, R., Vlach, L., & Wood, A. (2008). Addiction as a complex social process: An action theoretical perspective. *Addiction Research and Theory, 16*(2), 121–133.

Greewald, G. (2009). *Drug decriminalization in Portugal.* Washington, DC: CATO Institute.

Hamilton, H., Mann, R., & Noh, S. (2011). Adolescent immigrant generation and stigmatizing attitudes toward drug addiction. *Addiction Research and Theory, 19*(4), 344–351.

Henchman, J. (2014). Taxing marijuana: The Washington and Colorado experience. *Tax Foundation.* Retrieved from http://taxfoundation.org/article/ taxing-marijuana-washington-and-colorado-experience

Hunte, H., & Finlayson, T. (2013). The relationship between perceived discrimination and psychotherapeutic and illicit drug misuse in Chicago, IL, USA. *Journal of Urban Health, 90*(6), 1112–1129.

Hurt, H., Brodsky, N., Roth, H., Malmud, E., & Giannetta, J. (2005). School performance of children with gestational cocaine exposure. *Neurotoxicology and Teratology, 27*(2), 203–211.

Hurt, H., Giannetta, J., Korczkowski, M., Hoang, A., Tang, K., Beancourt, L., Brodsky, N., Shera, D., Farah, M., & Detre, J. (2008). Functional magnetic resonance imaging and working memory in adolescents with gestational cocaine exposure. *The Journal of Pediatrics, 152*(3), 371–377.

Huxley, A. (1952). The doors of perception. *Mental, 98,* 2–24.

International Centre for Science in Drug Policy. (2010). *Effect of drug law enforcement on drug related violence: Evidence from a scientific review.* Vancouver, BC: International Centre for Science in Drug Policy.

International Harm Reduction Development Program. (2009). *Human rights abuses in the name of drug treatment: Reports from the field.* Retrieved from http://www.opensocietyfoundations. org/sites/default/files/treatmentabuse_20090309.pdf

Kari, S. (2009). Court deems law biased against alcoholics, addicts. *National Post,* April 24.

Kasl, C. (1992). *Many roads, one journey: Moving beyond the 12 steps.* New York, NY: Harper Perennial.

Keyes, K., Hatzenbuehler, M., McLaughlin, K., Link, B., Olfson, M., Grant, B., & Hasin, D. (2010). Stigma and treatment for alcohol disorders in the United States. *American Journal of Epidemiology, 172*(12), 1364–1372.

Korcha, R., Cherpitel, C., Witbrodt, J., Borges, G., Hejazi-Bazargan, S., Bond, J., Ye, Y., & Gmel, G. (2014). Violence-related injury and gender: The role of alcohol and alcohol combined with illicit drugs. *Drug and Alcohol Review, 33*(1), 43–50.

Kraus, D., Castonguay, L., Boswell, J., Nordberg, S., & Hayes, J. (2011). Therapist effectiveness: Implications for accountability and patient care. *Psychotherapy Research, 21*(3), 267–276.

Le Dain Commission. (1973). *Final report of the commission of inquiry into the non-medical use of drugs.* Ottawa, ON: Government of Canada.

Lembaga Bantuan Hukum Masyarakat. (2009). Law on narcotics. *Caveat: Indonesia's Monthly Human Rights Anlaysis, 4*(1), 3–4.

Lin, L., Fang, Y., & Wang, X. (2008). Drug abuse in China: Past, present and future. *Cellular and Molecular Neurobiology, 28*(4), 479–490.

Link, W., Hachman, R., & Casey, E. (1977). *Facts about drug abuse.* Rockville, MD: National Drug Abuse Centre.

London School of Economics. (2014). *Ending the drug wars.* London, UK: LSE Expert Group on Economics of Drug Policy.

MacPherson, D., & Rowley, M. (2001). *A framework for action: A four-pillar approach to drug problems in Vancouver.* Vancouver, BC: City of Vancouver.

Mandancy, J. (2001). Unearthing popular attitudes toward the opium trade and opium suppression in late Qing and early republican Fujian. *Modern China, 27*(4), 436–483.

Mullaly, R. (2002). *Challenging oppression: A critical social work approach.* Don Mills, ON: Oxford University Press Canada.

Mullaly, R. (2007). *The new structural social work* (3rd ed.). Don Mills, ON: Oxford University Press Canada.

Peele, S. (1983). *The science of experience.* Toronto, ON: Lexington Books.

Peele, S. (1985). What treatment for addiction can do and what it can't; What treatment for addiction should do and what it shouldn't. *Journal of Substance Abuse Treatment, 2*(4), 225–228.

Peele, S. (1989). Ain't misbehavin': Addiction has become an all purpose excuse. *The Sciences, 29*(4), 14–21.

Price, R., & Copeland, R. (1993). *Vietnam drug users two decades after Vietnam: A first look at follow-up outcomes.* American Sociological Association.

Project Prevention. (2015). *Statistics.* Retrieved from http://www.projectprevention.org/statistics

Rehm, J., Baliunas, D., Brochu, S., Fischer, B., Gnam, W., Patra, J., Popova, S., Sarnocinska-Hart, A., & Taylor, B. (2006). *The costs of substance abuse in Canada, 2002.* Ottawa, ON: Canadian Centre on Substance Abuse.

Robins, L., Helzer, J., Hesselbrock, M., & Wish, E. (2010). Vietnam veterans three years after Vietnam: How our study changed our view of heroin. *American Journal on Addictions, 19*(3), 203–211.

Roffman, R. (1976). Addiction concepts and the Vietnam experience. *Urban and Social Change Review, 9*(2), 16–18.

Rudgely, R. (1995). *Essential substances: A cultural history of intoxicants in society.* New York, NY: Kodansha America Inc.

Schneider, B. (2009). Substance use disorders and risk for completed suicide. *Archives of Suicide Research, 13*(4), 303–316.

Single, E., Robson, L., Xie, X., & Rehm, J. (1996). *The cost of substance abuse in Canada.* Ottawa, ON: Canadian Centre on Substance Abuse.

Substance Abuse and Mental Health Administration (2011). *Treatment Episode Data Set report: Length of time from first use to adult treatment admission.* Rockville, MD: SAMSHA.

Sussman, S., & Sussman, A. (2011). Considering the definition of addiction. *International Journal of Environmental Research and Public Health, 8*(10), 4025–4038.

Thompson, N. (2006). *Anti-discriminatory practice* (4th ed.). London, UK: Palgrave Macmillan.

United Nations Office on Drugs and Crime. (2002). *Global illict drug trends 2002.* New York: United Nations.

United Nations Office on Drugs and Crime. (2013). *Transnational organized crime in West Africa.* Vienna: United Nations.

United Nations Office on Drugs and Crime. (2014). *2014 world drug report.* Vienna: United Nations.

United States Department of Health and Human Services. (2014). *The health consequences of smoking—50 years of progress: A report of the Surgeon General.* Atlanta, GA: U.S. Department of Health and Human Services, Centers for Disease Control and Prevention, National Center for Chronic Disease Prevention and Health Promotion, Office on Smoking and Health.

van Boekel, L., Brouwers, E., van Weeghel, J., & Garretsen, H. (2014). Comparing stigmatising attitudes towards people with substance use disorders between the general public, GPs, mental health and addiction specialists and clients. *International Journal of Social Psychiatry, 61*(6), 539–549.

Woodson, D. (1973). SOADAP chief resigns after bitter struggle. *Journal of the Addiction Research Foundation, 2*(1), 1.

World Health Organization. (2012). *Mortality attributable to tobacco.* Geneva, Switzerland: World Health Organization.

Xu, X., Bishop, E., Kennedy, S., Simpson, S., & Pechacek, T. (2014). Annual healthcare spending attributable to cigarette smoking: An update. *American Journal of Preventive Medicine, 48*(3), 326–333.

PREVENTION

CHAPTER 2

Prevention as Controversy: Harm Reduction

Rick Csiernik, William S. Rowe, and Jim Watkin

For most drug users harm reduction, not abstinence, is the only chance to survive. Harm reduction relieves them from the humiliating consequences of prohibition. Harm reduction enables them to save their lives and live them free of contempt and humiliation. Harm reduction means to lead a constant fight against people's need to reassure themselves of their superiority by stigmatizing those who deviate from normality.... By fighting for harm reduction, social workers, nurses and doctors lend their voice to those who otherwise do not have anything to say. The quality of a democracy can be judged by the treatment of its weakest members. Harm reduction cares for the weakest. Therefore, the keeping up of the principles of harm reduction is a touchstone for the implementation of freedom, equality and fraternity in a society.

> —JORG GOLZ, HEAD OF THE GERMAN SOCIETY FOR ADDICTION MEDICINE,
> BARCELONA HARM REDUCTION CONFERENCE, 2008

Human rights apply to everyone. People who use drugs do not forfeit their human rights, including the right to the highest attainable standard of health, to social services, to work, to benefit from scientific progress, to freedom from arbitrary detention and freedom from cruel inhuman and degrading treatment. Harm reduction opposes the deliberate hurts and harms inflicted on people who use drugs in the name of drug control and drug prevention, and promotes responses to drug use that respect and protect fundamental human rights.

> —HARM REDUCTION INTERNATIONAL, 2015

Introduction

Historically, treating addiction involved a prohibitionist mindset with an abstinence-based, medical-focused model. Over time, this philosophy has been found wanting and incomplete. A proportion of individuals have greater difficulty than others emerging from the cyclical nature of addiction. These difficulties are reflected in lapsing and relapsing behaviours, drug-seeking behaviours as labelled by the medical profession, and in ongoing conflict with the law. These individuals were typically labelled as being in denial, treatment resistant, or unmotivated. Failure was rarely considered a reflection of the abstinence-based program's function within its narrow and limited treatment paradigm. As a result of perceived weakness or unwillingness to change, an individual's return to drug use sometimes included expulsion from a program and the loss of a newly developed support system.

As social workers and other client centred counselling professionals began to acknowledge the limitations of the abstinence-based approach, a series of alternative strategies evolved that were both more client-centred and derived from a different paradigm (Bigg, 2001; Single, 2001). Members of the established, traditional addiction community have deemed some of these options radical and inappropriate. The result has been the fractioning of the addiction field and the creation of divisions between segments of the addiction treatment sector. To this end, the evolving strategies can become difficult to manage. Social workers have been party to both sides of the debate as we work to support our clients, sometimes clinging to more "professional" medical-based models and shying away from leadership positions supporting alternative treatment options. This chapter identifies some of the more prominent alternate methods of harm reduction and the reasons they are seen as both controversial and successful.

Harm Reduction

The term *harm reduction* has become closely associated with addiction interventions, though this is not its origin. Harm reduction in its most basic form is defined as any strategy or behaviour that an individual uses to reduce the potential harm that may exist for him or her. This type of strategy can been seen in behaviours as simple as washing your hands before preparing a meal for a family or sterilizing a baby's bottle before adding fresh formula or putting your seatbelt on before driving an automobile. In the addiction field, harm reduction is an active process that can be viewed on the continuum of prevention as secondary prevention. It acknowledges that specific risks are associated with substance abuse and that using psychoactive drugs by definition is a high-risk behaviour. However, harm reduction in the addiction field entails a series of activities and options, the intent of which is to minimize or eliminate risks that often arise because of the illegality of certain psychoactive drugs, thus reducing their impact upon individual users and upon society collectively. It is a health-centred approach that seeks to reduce the health and social harms associated with drug use without necessarily requiring users to abstain (Thomas, 2005).

Canadian drug policy has historically focused upon criminalization[1] and abstinence in drug treatment. However, not all countries and governments have consistently stayed on this course in setting social policy. In the Netherlands, the implementation of the Revised Opium Act (1976) reflected the central notion in Dutch social drug policy that drugs are, first and foremost, a public health and welfare issue (Advisory Committee on Population Health, 2001). This Dutch act was the first in the evolution of contemporary harm reduction–based drug policy and it has become a model for strategies throughout the world (Erickson, Riley, Cheung, & O'Hare, 1997). Harm reduction, as it is currently recognized in addiction intervention, came to the forefront internationally in part because of a series of global conferences in response to the success of drug strategies in the Netherlands, but more so as a direct response to AIDS and HIV. Within the realm of addiction work, strategies and theories underwent a radical rethinking due to the awareness and introduction of blood-borne diseases among people injecting drugs. Due to the paradigm-shattering foundation laid by advocates of controlled drinking, a licit behaviour, and as a result of increased understanding of diseases such as HIV/ AIDS, hepatitis B, and hepatitis C (HCV), the importance of reducing individual risk behaviour has slowly become a greater priority for social workers and related addiction and health care workers. This orientation has provided an alternative focus in assisting individuals in addressing their health concerns and struggles with addiction.

While harm reduction was formally incorporated into Canadian policy with the 1987 establishment of Canada's Drug Strategy, it was a meeting of provincial and federal health ministers in 2001 that solidified harm reduction as an integral part of responses to issues of addiction. The ministers set as their formal goals:

- increasing efforts to address the determinants of health and underlying factors associated with drug misuse;
- reducing injection drug-related mortality and morbidity;
- reducing the incidence and prevalence of injection drug use; and
- reducing the costs and related health, social, and economic consequences of injection drug use (Health Canada, 2001).

Harm reduction, as it relates to addiction, can be defined as any policy directed towards reducing or containing adverse health, social, and economic consequences of drug use without necessarily requiring a reduction in consumption or abstinence from substance use or behaviour that an individual uses in their life to reduce the drug-related harm that may exist for them (AADAC, 2001). This definition implies a number of basic interpretations that are necessary for both the social worker and the client in order to maintain an appropriate working relationship:

- all humans have intrinsic value;
- all humans have the right to comprehensive non-judgemental medical and social services;
- licit and illicit drugs are neither good nor bad;
- psychoactive drug users are sufficiently competent to make choices regarding their use of drugs;
- outcomes are in the hands of the client; and
- options are to be provided in a non-judgemental, non-coercive manner (Hagan, 1999).

The harm reduction approach to psychoactive drugs is based on a strong commitment to public health and human rights. It targets the causes of risks and harms. The identification of specific harms, their causes, and decisions about appropriate interventions requires proper assessment leading to targeted responses. The tailoring of harm reduction interventions to address specific risks and harms must also take into account oppressive factors that can render people who use drugs particularly vulnerable, such as age, gender, and incarceration. Harm reduction approaches are pragmatic. They are by definition practical, feasible, effective, and based upon the strongest available evidence. They are typically inexpensive, cost-effective, and easy to implement, with a direct impact on individual and community health. Harm reduction principles encourage open dialogue, consultation, and debate. A wide range of stakeholders must be meaningfully involved in policy development and program implementation, delivery, and evaluation. In particular, people who use drugs and other affected communities should be involved in decisions that affect them (Harm Reduction International, 2015).

Change arising from harm reduction practice is often incremental, which is one reason it remains controversial. It views any positive change as success and thus harm reduction services are designed to meet people's needs where they currently are in their lives. Individuals are much more likely to take multiple smaller steps rather than one or two large leaps at once. Abstinence remains a goal but for many is difficult to achieve immediately. Within a harm reduction paradigm any action that people take to stay alive and minimize the harm of using drugs is appropriate (Harm Reduction International, 2015). Harm reduction approaches have been successful both in lowering risky alcohol use and in reducing injection related morbidity and mortality (Leslie, 2008; Turner et al., 2011).

However, for many people, harm reduction alone is seen as an ineffective treatment strategy. This belief is reflected in the vast majority of Canadian governmental drug policy and in the prominent abstinence-based treatment ideals. For proponents of traditional models, harm reduction remains a rejection of the "Just Say No" approach and some perceived capitulation to drug use. Some view agencies that primarily embrace a harm reduction philosophy as enabling drug use and not acknowledging the struggle that is associated with ending drug-using behaviour. There is also an historic anti-medication bias in North America due to early non-evidence-informed attempts at harm reduction, which included teaching alcohol dependent individuals to substitute beer and wine for spirits, using morphine to treat alcohol, cocaine, and cannabis addiction, and multiple failed alcohol vaccines (White & Coon, 2003). As well, the opinion that harm reduction enables and supports drug use remains based upon a belief system that drug use is strictly a matter of individual choice and that external social and environmental factors are non-existent for people using substances.

Factors such as the pressure from peer groups, which can be a powerful trigger to continue drug-using behaviours, are ignored, as are oppressive social environments that directly support the need to escape temporarily. As well, biological factors such as the extreme prolonged physical withdrawal from the use of opioids, benzodiazepines, cocaine, and alcohol that often lead individuals back to use in order to eliminate the physical symptoms and the pain of their withdrawal are negated by the traditional perspective. This view has also contributed to the development of a primarily non-medical withdrawal management approach throughout much of Canada.

The baseline measure for success in addiction treatment has traditionally been abstinence, a measurement that is quite simple to assess. This is witnessed by the fact that many Canadian treatment programs will expel an individual who is found to be using, even once, while in the recovery program, rather than working more intensively with the client who has experienced a lapse. Some of these programs even regularly drug test their clients to determine if any drug has been ingested. This action is punitive for individuals who are struggling with a cycle of addiction that often results in alternate "dirty and clean" periods and discounts the prominence and learning opportunities that can derive from both lapses and relapses. The view by experts that they know what is best for an individual eliminates the individual's right to choice and self-determination in setting treatment goals or in conjointly establishing a treatment plan. Traditional addiction treatment and public policy reflects the thought that drug use is seen as a threat to human willpower and self-control, especially with respect to the use of illicit drugs (Rubin, 1999), though the notion of licit and illicit is itself a social construct.

Harm reduction is also controversial due to the speed with which individuals may make modifications in their lives. Sometimes within a harm reduction program, individual change can appear to occur at an almost glacial pace. Measurement techniques for change are also controversial. Within traditional recovery programs, change and success are viewed only as "clean time" and this success is dependent upon maintaining this time. However, within a harm reduction treatment plan success can be measured in a variety of ways. These include safer methods of use, reduced drug use, longer periods of time between uses, alternate drugs being used to reduce harm, better family or interpersonal relationships, decreased conflict with the law, the ability to find or maintain employment, and related changes that clients themselves determine to be a measure of success. In fact, the term *clean* for a person not using implies a person who does use is dirty, and thus these terms are themselves oppressive in nature and use.

Another controversy is the measurement of success of harm reduction programs. Unlike traditional programs, harm reduction does not necessarily focus upon an individual's ability to maintain a "clean" lifestyle. The success of any harm reduction strategy depends in large part upon maintaining the previously named principles of harm reduction, as discussed above. When maintaining these principles, a social worker and client are able to develop a trusting, supportive relationship that leads to growth and change at a speed that is comfortable and manageable for the individual. This can be quite difficult to compare with more traditional outcome indicators. In harm reduction, the primary goal is to engage the client. This relationship is often the first significant connection that an individual will make with a social service or health agency. As it develops, this relationship can then lead to self-education, self-efficacy, and the adoption of further harm reduction strategies. In addition, the client may access a broader range of addiction services, including abstinence-based options. By following this approach, agencies using harm reduction strategies have been shown to be effective in reducing the transmission of blood-borne infections (Zaric, Barnett, & Brandeau, 2000). Although harm reduction has been a controversial strategy in addiction since its introduction, the implication of this mode of treatment is that a more holistic, anti-oppressive view of the impact of addiction on individual and public health is necessary and eventually will lead to broader community success. In many parts of the world, harm reduction has been accepted as a valid public health response to substance use (Poulin, 2006).

Harm Reduction Strategies

The first controversial harm reduction strategy to be introduced involved alcohol: controlled drinking, an approach that still leads to great passionate debates. The range of approaches, however, is broad, from drug testing kits to determine if the drug you think you have bought is actually what you have bought, to crack pipes used to decrease the risk of transmitting saliva and blood-borne illnesses, to emergency naloxone overdose response kits that are distributed to opioid users and their allies in case of an accidental overdose. However, when the term *harm reduction* is raised most immediately think of intravenous drug use of heroin and related opioids. Drug dependence that involves opioids is a chronic, relapsing condition with a generally unfavourable prognosis. The characteristic elements include an overpowering drive or compulsion to continue to take the drug for pleasure and to obtain it by any means, and ultimately to avoid the significant and prolonged intense discomfort of withdrawal. Harm reduction strategies that are currently employed in Canada have primarily focused upon opioid drugs. These include needle exchanges, methadone treatment and methadone maintenance programs, supervised injection facilities and, to a limited degree, heroin prescription. However, we should not forget other much less contentious initiatives such as designated driver programs, contract-for-life programs between adolescents and their parents, and fully accepted nicotine drug substitution and replacement strategies are also harm reduction initiatives. The following section focuses primarily upon prevention issues that have created the most controversy for clients, social work, and society.

Needle Exchange

Needle exchange is a service that allows individuals to trade old, used syringes for new, sterile syringes and related injection works. This exchange of needles can occur in fixed sites, in street outreach, or in mobile locations. Needle exchanges in recent years have also begun to offer crack pipes and straws for other modes of drug use, as well as entire kits to allow for the safe preparation of the substance prior to injection. Along with single-use needles a typical kit would include:

- **Cookers:** containers that allow the drug to be mixed with water and heated to better prepare the mixture for injection.
- **Filters:** cotton placed on the tip of the needle to prevent any undissolved particles of the drug, other debris from the crushed drug, or bacteria from being drawn into the syringe and potentially injected into a vein.
- **Ascorbic acid:** added as part of the cooking process to better dissolve the drug to allow for safer injection. Some drugs, such as crack cocaine and heroin, must be converted into a water-soluble form by using acid. Other options are citric and acetic acid.
- **Sterile water:** used to make the solution by a person converting the drug from its powder, solid, or table form into an injectable substance.
- **Alcohol swabs:** used to clean the injection site prior to injection to reduce the risk of bacterial infection, and also to clean the user's fingers of blood or other contaminants.
- **Tourniquets:** used to tie off the vein, to allow additional pressure, increase the blood flow, and make the vein more prominent, thus avoiding problems when a vein is missed while trying to inject. (Strike et al., 2013)

Needle exchange is a harm reduction strategy that has become more prominent as a result of blood-borne infections such as HIV, HCV, and hepatitis B (HBV). These infections transfer readily through the sharing of syringes by injection drug users and ultimately into the general population. Needle exchange in and of itself has been proven to reduce the spread of these blood-borne infections (Urban Health Research Initiative, 2013).

Needle exchange also reduces the significant financial expense involved in caring for individuals who have contracted either HIV or HCV. The costs of medical care for an individual who is living with HIV has been estimated to be upwards of $150,000 (Hanvelt, Copley, Schneider, & Meagher, 1999) over a lifetime, while treatment for hepatitis C is estimated at between $30,000 per course of treatment and $250,000 for a liver transplant (Health Canada, 2001). Needle exchange programs may also be used to create supportive contact between a social service agency and the highly marginalized and oppressed population of injection drug users.

The controversy that surrounds the concept of needle exchange closely follows the controversy of harm reduction itself. Many people working both inside and outside the addiction field believe needle exchange encourages and subsidizes drug use, particularly among young people. The belief is that needle exchanges promote and enable individuals to use injection drugs longer than they would without this intervention, thus prolonging the addiction. Another belief states that distributing needles creates greater access, which then enables more people to begin using illicit drugs. Critics also propose that this program sends a mixed message: while the drugs you use are illegal, we will still legally supply you with the paraphernalia to use the illicit substance. Research has also found that, despite entering into needle exchange programs, some sharing did still occur between program participants, along with the sharing of drug use equipment associated with needle sharing including cotton filters, cookers, and water (Sears, Weltzein, & Guydish, 2001; Valente and Vlahov, 2001).

The concept of a needle exchange clearly does not coincide with the dominant societal standpoint of treatment as abstinence, and the continuing War on Drugs. Many hold this view, as best evidenced by protests from conservative religious groups against fixed-site needle exchanges and street outreach initiatives. As recently as the spring of 2008, a needle exchange program in Calgary could not find a landlord to rent it space after its existing rental agreement expired, with much of the pressure being coordinated through the offices of municipal politicians (MacNeil & Pauly, 2010). As well, in some communities, law enforcement has attempted to disrupt the work of needle exchange programs through surveillance initiatives and client harassment. However, there has been no significant geographic relationship between crime counts and methadone clinics and harm reduction sites. In fact it is far more likely to be a victim of crime the closer you live to a convenience store than to a treatment centre (Boyd et al., 2012).

Despite these concerns, the economic, social, and humanitarian utility of needle exchange programs has been widely documented, highlighting the reduction of new HIV and HCV infections among the drug-using populations (Bluthenthal et al., 2000; Vertefeuille et al., 2000). There are 82 nations that now officially sanction needle exchange as part of their public health programming (Mathers et al., 2010). In New Zealand, upwards of 3 million clean needles have been distributed through 200 outlets, and this program has contributed to the prevalence of HIV/AIDS dropping to 0.3% of the entire population (Henderson, 2012). In neighbouring Australia, needle exchange programs have been documented to be among the most cost-effective national public health initiatives. The first decade of active needle exchange resulted in a reduction in the seroprevalence of HIV among drug users from 50% to 2% (Hagan, 1999). Between 2000 and 2009 needle exchange programs directly averted 32,050 new HIV infections and 96,667 new HCV infections. While the cost to run the program was $243 million (Australian), the estimated return in health care savings was $1.28 billion (Australian), more than five to one without even considering the human suffering that was averted and the additional health constraints avoided (Wilson, Kwon, Anderson, & Thein, 2009).

Supervised Injection Facilities

Overdose from illicit drugs is a prominent preventable cause of premature mortality in North America. Internationally, more than 65 supervised injecting facilities (SIFs), also referred to as supervised injection sites (SIS), where drug users can inject pre-obtained drugs have been opened. Supervised injection facilities are clinics that allow injection drug users to obtain clean needles and sterilized works and provide a clean, private setting to allow them to inject their drugs in a safer setting.[2] This concept is considered by many opponents as yet another means to enable and support drug use rather than rooting it out. The goal of a supervised injection facility is not only to provide individuals a safer environment in which to inject drugs but also to provide related health and social services all in one location (Rowe & Gonzalez, 2010; Wood et al., 2001). Switzerland, Germany, and the Netherlands have adopted the concept of safe rooms, which dates back as early as 1970. This strategy also has the potential to decrease new HIV and HCV infections, reduce the number of overdose-related deaths, provide access to primary and emergency health care, and enable access to a very elusive portion of the population (Drug Policy Alliance, 2002). Currently, only two such programs exist in Canada and this required a Supreme Court ruling (Berthiaume, 2011), though under the Trudeau government there are likely other communities that will now move forward in establishing programs.

An examination of population-based overdose mortality rates over a four-year period before and after the opening of the Vancouver SIF was conducted. Of 290 decedents, 229 (79%) were male with a median age at death of 40. One-third of deaths occurred in city blocks within 500 meters of the facility. After the opening of the facility, the fatal overdose rate in this area decreased by 35%. In contrast, during the same period, the fatal overdose rate in the rest of the city also decreased, but only by 9.3% (Marshall et al., 2011). Pinkerton (2010), in an economic analysis of the lone Canadian program, estimated that if closed the annual number of incident HIV infections among Vancouver injection drug users would increase from 179 to 263. These 84 preventable infections are associated with $17.6 million in lifetime HIV-related medical care costs, greatly exceeding the program's operating costs, which are approximately $3 million per year. Canadian research has also shown that after the opening of a supervised injection facility there is a decrease in public nuisance issues related to drug use including public injecting, discarded syringes, and injection-related litter (Wood, Kerr, Small et al., 2004).

Methadone Treatment and Methadone Maintenance

Methadone is a long-acting synthetic opioid analgesic with properties similar to those of morphine, first synthesized by the Germans just prior to World War II as an alternative to opium-based analgesics to be used on the battlefield. It was discovered post-war to be an effective "treatment" mode for individuals dependent upon heroin, as it produces morphine-like actions and cross-tolerance but does not produce euphoria when administered orally. As well, unlike morphine and heroin, methadone is highly effective in masking pain when administered orally because it is excreted slowly—a single dose is effective for up to 24 hours. Tolerance and withdrawal do occur in methadone users, though its development is much slower than with other opioids. However, without other forms of intervention, regular users do become both psychologically and physically dependent upon methadone.

Both Methadone Maintenance (MM) and Methadone Treatment (MT) consist of an individual drinking a sufficient dose of methadone on a daily basis. This eliminates withdrawal symptoms from any opioid, for contemporary programs have expanded beyond using methadone to substitute for heroin alone. The basic premise for opioid substitution therapy is that a suitable opioid agent that is administered daily by mouth is effective in the suppression of withdrawal symptoms and in the reduction of the use of illicit opioids or excessive use of licit opioids. MM involves determining a correct dose for each individual and providing ongoing health care, while MT programs also entail counselling, social support, mental health services, health promotion, disease prevention, and education along with advocacy and linkages to community-based supports and services such as housing.

A cost analysis conducted in Ontario found that the average cost per day for methadone was $15.48, or $5,651 per year. However, the breakdown is most interesting, for the cost of the methadone itself is only $0.59 (3.8%) per day. In comparison, physicians receive $1.52 (9.8%) for every dose of methadone prescribed, even though they do not see clients daily, while pharmacy costs are $6.17 (39.8%); the most expensive part is drug testing clients, which accounts for nearly half the cost. Thus, if drug testing were eliminated the annual cost would drop to just over $3,000 per annum (Zaric, Brennan, Varenbut, & Daiter, 2012).

As with all forms of harm reduction, controversy follows MT but even more so MM. For many individuals living with opioid addiction, the damage that has occurred to their bodies as a result of prolonged drug use may not allow them to ever withdraw completely from methadone. For others, drug substitution, such as MM, is simply the replacement of one abused psychoactive drug with a safer, more societally sanctioned psychoactive drug. While there are no reports of serious side effects with the therapeutic use of methadone, it still is an addictive substance. As such, a major question arises with the use of methadone: in whose interest is it used, the client's or society's? This is more the case in MM where, unlike MT, there tends not to be ongoing psychosocial supports or goal setting towards reducing and ultimately eliminating the use of methadone. However, for pregnant women addicted to opioids, MM is often recommended as the fetus can be put at risk if withdrawal occurs during a pregnancy. Improved prenatal care and nutrition, decreased criminal activity (including sex work), decreased risk of contracting HIV, and decreased incidence of premature delivery and infant mortality have all been associated with MM programs for pregnant women. As well, the majority of infants exposed to methadone while in utero have been shown to have better outcomes than infants exposed to heroin or other illicit psychoactive substances (Bodnarchuk, Patton, & Broszeit, 2005; Schilling, Dornig, & Lungren, 2006).

Methadone is also controversial since it is as addictive as other opioids, making the treatment process, when followed, much longer in terms of time than typical abstinence-based treatment initiatives. Due to the fact that methadone works strictly for opioid dependence, participants are quite often seen and referred to as "junkies" in every negative sense of the identity and label. Thus, many people both inside and outside of the addiction treatment community do not consider MT an appropriate treatment method, but strictly a substitution of drugs by a more legal method, whereas MM is viewed as a societally sanctioned addiction despite the fact that methadone used alone does not produce euphoria among users.

Despite these concerns, methadone has been documented to assist both individuals and society in many ways. In the 1990s the life expectancy of heroin users in Barcelona, Spain, increased by 21 years, largely due to the expansion of oral methadone mainten-ance clinics, which not only reduced the risk of contracting HIV but also the risk of overdosing from the unregulated drug (Brugal et al., 2005). Merrill (1998) found that after four years, those who had received no treatment were 4.2 times more likely to have seroconverted to HIV positive than were those who had received two or more years of methadone. Studies have consistently found that after beginning a methadone program individuals substantially reduced their risk of HIV infection due to behaviours linked to their drug use. Entering a program was also associated with significant decreases in the total number of persons injecting and the frequency of these injections, but using methadone still does not always preclude the use of other opioids. Reduced use does typically occur immediately and is typically sustained while using methadone. Methadone use is also associated with a significant decrease in the sharing of injecting equipment (Gowing et al., 2011).

Research has demonstrated that opioid-dependent people who receive treatment with methadone:

- use fewer illicit drugs,
- have decreased risk of becoming HIV positive or transmitting the virus,
- have better general health,
- access health care more readily,
- have a greater sense of psychological well-being,
- have a greater ability to acquire and maintain employment,
- are less reliant on public assistance,
- report better domestic relations,
- have less conflict with the law,
- have improved parenting and child care ability, and
- have overall better social functioning and relations (De Maeyer et al., 2011; Methadone Strategy Working Group, 2001; Schilling, Dornig, & Lungren, 2006).

Methadone is considered the "gold standard" internationally and the most commonly used global treatment strategy for opioid dependency, with 70 nations now providing methadone as part of their public health programming (Mathers et al., 2010).

The actual experiences of individuals who have used methadone are also a testament to the life-changing successes these individuals have achieved:

I wish I had kept a diary from just before I started methadone, then every time I am having a difficult time, I could re-read my thoughts and know that I do not want to return to that place. (Adam, age 20, quoted in Maynes, 2008)

Since I started on methadone, I've become a caring involved husband, father and taxpayer. I've found my life's work, and I'm free of the crushing physical and mental burden of having to use opiates. (Jeff, age 42, quoted in Maynes, 2008)

While methadone remains the most widely used substance for opioid substitution, suboxone has emerged as a superior but more expensive option. When administered orally, suboxone is similar in efficacy to methadone even if used less frequently. Users reported more clarity of thinking, greater confidence, and lower stigma compared to those using methadone (Tanner, Bordon, Conroy, & Best, 2011). Suboxone is a combination of buprenorphine, which is a potent opioid, and naloxone, which in an opioid antagonist. Buprenorphine, which is also administered orally, is equivalent in pain-masking ability to methadone but with fewer side effects. When taken a person does not undergo withdrawal. The naloxone is added if a person takes the drug in any way other than intended, such as by snorting it or injecting, and this component of the drug will immediately place a person in very painful opioid withdrawal (Orman & Keating, 2009). However, as with methadone, suboxone is not a cure for addiction and is merely a drug substitute—users remain dependent upon the drug. But as with methadone, suboxone is a safer alternative to injecting.

Heroin Prescription and Heroin-Assisted Treatment (HAT)

Heroin prescription involves a physician providing identified drug users, who have exhausted every other mode of drug treatment without success, with daily prescriptions of medical-grade heroin (Carnwath, 2005). This is not a new idea and was first introduced, long before contemporary harm reduction initiatives, in 1926 in the United Kingdom when the Rolleston Committee of the Royal College of Physicians proposed using either morphine or heroin on an indefinite basis for those addicted to opium in cases where multiple attempts at abstinence had failed. It was acknowledged at that time that HAT was not treatment but that it was both common sense and humane. This practice was retained in England until the 1970s when methadone maintenance replaced heroin maintenance. In this regard England was a world leader in harm reduction initiatives that put the person first (Ashton, 2006).

The idea of heroin-assisted treatment re-emerged in 1992 when the Swiss formally began using it as a maintenance option for persons who had failed other opioid-based treatment initiatives. Soon after, it was re-adopted in the United Kingdom, where 1.5% of people who are addicted to heroin received regular prescriptions (Rihs-Middell, 1997; Stimson, 1995). Contemporary drug trials conducted in Spain, Switzerland, and the Netherlands have also demonstrated that HAT works within a maintenance model framework. In a two-year study involving 515 subjects, participants reported improvements in both physical and mental health as well as decreases in illicit drug use (Verthein et al., 2008). A related study in England compared the risk of relapse between three randomized groups of heroin users: those who received oral methadone, those receiving injectable methadone, and those receiving injectable heroin. The oral methadone group experienced the greatest dropout rate while the supervised injectable heroin group had the lowest levels of lapse, with use of street drugs dropping 75% and program participants committing two-thirds fewer crimes aimed at obtaining drugs compared to before entering the program. However, the program costs were expensive, averaging $22,000 per year, far more than for methadone (Strang et al., 2010).

The North American Opiate Medication Initiative (NAOMI) was initiated in 2004 in Montreal and Vancouver to compare the therapeutic utility of heroin and methadone prescriptions. One component was a randomized control study involving long-term users of injectable heroin who had not remained abstinent after at least two previous attempts at treatment for their addiction including at least one involving methadone. The study involved randomly assigning 111 individuals to receive orally administered methadone and another 115 to receive medical-grade injectable heroin. More members of the heroin cohort completed the study (87.8% versus 54.1%), while also reporting a greater decrease in criminal activity including the use of illicit drugs (67% to 47.7%). As well, there was no increase in community-based problems or increase in crime in the neighbourhoods where the two sites were located. However, 10 members of the heroin group did suffer overdoses, while six had seizures requiring hospitalization, neither of which occurred among those using methadone (Lasnier, Brochu, Boyd, & Fischer, 2010; Oviedo-Joekes et al., 2009).

NAOMI further demonstrated that heroin-assisted therapy was superior to methadone for individuals with chronic, relapsing heroin addiction both in terms of retention in addiction treatment and overall clinical response (Schechter & Kendall, 2011), and was no more costly in the long term due to these factors (Nosyk et al., 2012). Despite this, upon completion of the study the federal government refused to allow those in the study to continue to use medical-grade heroin until the Supreme Court ruled in the users' favour. The federal Conservative government was able to block efforts to establish a permanent clinic to allow non-study participants this treatment option (Chung, 2009). Federal Conservative Health Minister Rona Ambrose publically decried her own department's actions, stating that prescribing heroin "is in direct opposition to the government's anti-drug policy and violates the spirit and intent of the special access program" (Ward, 2013). However, with the change in federal governments, Health Canada announced in May 2016 that a regulatory amendment would allow access to prescription heroin under their special access program for properly screened and assessed individuals.

The controversy attached to this concept and reflected in the Harper government's response reflects the belief that in this harm reduction option otherwise illegal substances are being provided under a doctor's care, as if the drug were no more problematic than an antibiotic. These prescriptions are typically paid for through universal health care funds. The illusion of enabling seems very real when doctors and pharmacists become sanctioned drug distributors. Protocols also necessitate that all injectable doses of heroin be administered under direct medical or nursing supervision, ensuring compliance, monitoring, and safety, and preventing the medication being diverted to the illicit market. However, proponents counter that this strategy enables individuals with the greatest dependencies to regain their lives, receive consistent primary health care without discrimination or harassment, and reduce both the rate of overdose death and the transmission of diseases, such as HIV and HCV; this has led to the initial groundswell of support for controversial harm reduction programs (Small, 2000).

HAT is not considered a first-line treatment, but rather a second-line harm reduction option for hard-to-reach individuals who have not responded to standard treatments including oral methadone maintenance treatment or residential abstinence-focused rehabilitation. However, a German study involving 1,015 participants indicated that individuals with no failed history of methadone maintenance who were provided heroin had fewer lapses and less criminal activity than a comparable group receiving methadone (Eiroa, Haasen, Verthein, & Orosa 2010). Further, in 2009 Germany's parliament voted to allow the prescription of heroin to long-term users who fail to respond to other treatments. Approved by the Bundestag (the lower house) by 349 votes to 198, the measure applies to any individual 23 years of age or older with at least five years of dependency who has undergone at least two unsuccessful rehabilitation attempts.

Controlled Drinking

When first proposed, the idea of controlled drinking was as controversial as any other addiction-related harm reduction option proposed. It created huge rifts within the treatment community and still leads to impassioned cries of ignominy. In essence, controlled drinking is not a true treatment modality, but rather an outcome or treatment goal. Thus, treatment is as much about the functionality of the alcohol as about how much is consumed, how it is consumed, and under what circumstances. Historically, with the broadening view of alcoholism to incorporate the concepts of alcohol dependence, alcohol abuse, and alcohol-related disabilities, a wider range of treatment goals began to be considered. While originally hypothesized to be attainable for any person misusing or abusing alcohol, current formal treatment protocols typically call for the use of controlled drinking only with those persons experiencing low levels of alcohol abuse, though there remains discussion on the utility of using this as a first step towards abstinence of dependent drinkers (Adamson, Heather, Morton, & Raistrick, 2010; McKay, Mcbride, Sumnall, & Cole, 2012). The assessment of the client's level of alcohol dependence is essential in order to properly determine whether a goal of either controlled drinking or total abstinence should be set.

Controlled drinking is a component of the behaviourist school of treatment. Training in drinking skills is based upon the view that excessive drinking is a learned response that has short-term effectiveness for the drinker in specific situations, particularly when the individual lacks effective non-drinking responses or coping options. Drinking skills training is used to teach alcohol misusers to drink in a non-abusive manner as an alternative to abstinence, and usually forms part of a more broad-based treatment program. For these persons, what is missing is a lack of control and not a loss of control (Donovan & O'Leary, 1979; Glatt, 1980; Pendery, Maltzman, & West, 1982).

The first step in controlled drinking is determining whether a client is a problem drinker or an alcohol-dependent individual. This is accomplished by first imposing a two-to-three-week period of abstinence on a potential client. If the person can go without drinking, he or she is moved into the next phase. Those who cannot abstain during this baseline period generally do not qualify for a controlled drinking treatment program and thus are directed to abstinence-based approaches. Those facilitating a program of controlled drinking provide eligible clients with a set of goals and rules to help with their alcohol consumption. A common drinking goal of a set number of standard drinks per week is established with numerous limitations. For a young healthy male approximately six feet tall and 180 pounds, the following regimen may apply:

- no more than two standard drinks per day
- no more than one drink per hour
- sip drinks and avoid carbonated beverages
- drink only on a full stomach
- two days per week must be set aside where no alcohol is consumed
- limit weekly intake to 14 standard drinks (9 for women) (a standard drink is equivalent to a 12-ounce bottle of 5% beer, or a five-ounce glass of 12% wine, or 1.5 ounces of 40% spirits)

Self-management or behavioural self-control training procedures require clients to implement their own treatment. The primary advantage of these procedures is that the individual can maximize the generalization of treatment effects during and after treatment. The main problem with such techniques, however, is that they are likely feasible with only highly motivated individuals. Self-management programs generally consist of the behavioural strategies of self-monitoring, goal setting, changes in drug-using behaviour, rewards for goal attainment, analysis of drug-using situations, and learning alternative coping skills (Hester, Nirenberg, & Begin, 1990).

Reduced drinking may be a viable treatment goal for problem drinkers, individuals not exhibiting levels of alcohol dependence, those who do not have alcohol-related physical damage, and those who have not experienced any serious personal, financial, legal, or employment problems as a result of their drinking. If problem drinkers have no history of unsuccessful attempts at curbing their drinking behaviour, and if they will not accept abstinence as a lifelong goal, they can attempt controlled drinking. Systematic assessment is critical for establishing the severity of a person's alcohol problem and for deciding upon the most appropriate long-term goal. It is also crucial to conduct continued monitoring of the problem drinker's progress to ensure achievement of treatment goals.

The literature attests to the fact that controlled drinking is an attainable and successful goal for problem drinkers who have not established significant degrees of dependence. Abstinence does not have to be the only treatment goal (Miller, 1983). However, disagreement remains among controlled drinking trainers, as some advocates support the use of abstinence as the treatment goal regardless of the level of alcohol dependency.

Conclusion

Harm reduction is applicable in many instances. Whether it relates to social drinkers, casual drug use of the middle class, or the use of more illicit substances by marginalized individuals, harm reduction creates controversy with its acceptance of slow change and the inherent challenges to more established ideals among the professional treatment community and traditional self-help groups. These challenges consistently lead to debate and controversy regarding an approach that, for some individuals, is the most realistic and manageable means for dealing with their addiction. However, harm reduction should not be a controversial approach for social work, for in many ways it reflects social work values. Harm reduction is client-centred. It holds that every individual is worthy and unique, and entitled to justice, to freedom, and to be part of the community. Support for harm reduction initiatives is now part of formal social or health policy in the vast majority of the world, as are needle exchange and drug substitution programs (Cook, 2009).

Practically speaking, the questions become more ethically and morally challenging when the clients are minors, children, or other at-risk populations. For example: to what degree do we teach homeless minors how to do drugs safely? Do we show adolescents involved in the sex industry the safest place to do business? Should we facilitate the development of safe houses so that street youth do not run the risks associated with parks and alleys? These questions illustrate the complexity of the issues and highlight the social work value of client self-determination and the social work maxim to "start where the client is." In some cases, this will create a serious internal struggle for the social worker.

The main principles of harm reduction are pragmatism, respect, and priority of goals (Gleghorn, Rosenbaum, & Garcia, 2001). The main targets of many harm reduction initiatives are often the most marginalized and oppressed people of society: street-engaged youth, the homeless, sex workers, and others in conflict with the law. Thus, the controversial nature of the programs is further intensified, which reinforces the key role social work has to play in promoting ideals and values inherent in harm reduction programs.

NOTES

1. See Chapters 18 and 25.

2. See Chapter 3 for a more detailed discussion of supervised injection facilities.

REFERENCES

AADAC [Alberta Alcohol and Drug Addiction Commission]. (2001). *Alberta Alcohol and Drug Addiction Commission policy on harm reduction.* Edmonton, AB: ADDAC.

Adamson, S., Heather, N., Morton, V., & Raistrick, D. (2010). Initial preference for drinking goal in the treatment of alcohol problems: II. Treatment outcomes. *Alcohol and Alcoholism, 45*(2), 136–142.

Advisory Committee on Population Health. (2001). *Reducing the harm associated with injection drug use in Canada.* Ottawa, ON: Health Canada.

Ashton, M. (2006). The Rolleston legacy. *Drug and Alcohol Findings, 15*(1), 4–5, 20–21.

Berthiaume, L. (2011). U.S. wanted safe injection facility shut down. Retrieved from http://www.vancouversun.com/news/wanted%2Bsafe%2Binjection%2Bfacility%2Bshut%2Bdown/5487910/story.html

Bigg, D. (2001). Substance use management: A harm reduction-principled approach to assisting the relief of drug-related problems. *Journal of Psychoactive Drugs, 33*(1), 33–38.

Bluthenthal, R., Kral, A., Gee, L., Erringer, E., & Edlin, B. (2000). The effect of syringe exchange use on high-risk injection drug users: A cohort study. *AIDS, 14*(5), 605–611.

Bodnarchuk, J., Patton, D., & Broszeit, B. (2005). *Evaluation of AFM's methadone and needle exchange program.* Winnipeg, MB: Addiction Foundation of Manitoba.

Boyd, S., Fang, L., Medoff, D., Dixon, L., & Gorelick, D. (2012). Use of a 'microecological technique' to study crime incidents around methadone maintenance treatment centers. *Addiction, 107*(9), 1632–1638.

Brugal, M., Domingo-Salvany, A., Puig, R., Barrio, G., Garcia de Olalla, P., & De LaFuente, L. (2005). Evaluating the impact of methadone maintenance programmes on mortality due to overdose and aids in a cohort of heroin users in Spain. *Addiction, 100*(7), 981–989.

Carnwath, T. (2005). Heroin prescription: A limited but valuable role. *Psychiatric Bulletin, 29*, 126–127.

Chung, A. (2009, November 23). Pioneer heroin study in jeopardy in Quebec. *Toronto Star.* Retrieved from http://www.thestar.com/life/health_wellness/news_research/2009/11/23/pioneer_heroin_study_in_jeopardy_in_quebec.html

Cook, C. (2009). *Harm reduction policy and practice worldwide: An overview of national support for harm reduction in policy and practice.* London, UK: International Harm Reduction Society.

De Maeyer, J., Vanderplasschen, W., Camfield, L., Vanheule, S., Sabbe, B., & Broekaert, E. (2011). A good quality of life under the influence of methadone: A qualitative study among opiate-dependent individuals. *International Journal of Nursing Studies, 48*(10), 1244–1257.

Donovan, D., & O'Leary, M. (1979). Control orientation among alcoholics: A cognitive social learning perspective. *American Journal of Drug and Alcohol Abuse, 6*(4), 487–499.

Drug Policy Alliance. (2002). *Safe injecting rooms.* Ottawa, ON: Drug Policy Alliance.

Eiroa, C., Haasen, U., Verthein, F., & Orosa, I. (2010). Is heroin-assisted treatment effective for patients with no previous maintenance treatment? Results from a German randomised controlled trial. *European Addiction Research, 16*(3), 124–130.

Erickson, P., Riley, D.M., Cheung, Y.W., & O'Hare, P.A. (1997). *Harm reduction: A new direction for drug policies and programs.* Toronto, ON: University of Toronto Press.

Glatt, M. (1980). The alcoholic: Controlled drinking. *British Journal of Alcohol and Alcoholism, 15*(2), 48–55.

Gleghorn, A., Rosenbaum, M., & Garcia, B. (2001). Bridging the gap in San Francisco: The process of integrating harm reduction and traditional substance abuse services. *Journal of Psychoactive Drugs, 33*(1), 1–7.

Gowing, L., Farrell, M., Bornemann, R., Sullivan, L., & Ali R. (2011). Oral substitution treatment of injecting opioid users for prevention of HIV infection. *Cochrane Database of Systematic Reviews*, Issue 8, Art. No. CD004145.

Hagan, G. (1999). *HIV/AIDS and the drug culture*. New York, NY: The Haworth Press.

Hanvelt, R., Copley, T., Schneider, D., & Meagher, N. (1999). *The economic costs and reSource impacts of HIV/AIDS in British Colombia*. Community Health Resource Project NHRDP Project No. 6610–2372.

Health Canada. (2001). *Reducing the harm associated with injection drug use in Canada*. Ottawa, ON: Health Canada.

Henderson, A. (2012). *New Zealand Needle Exchange Program Annual Report*. Christchurch, NZ: The Centre for Harm Reduction.

Hester, R., Nierenberg, T., & Begin, A. (1990). Behavioural treatment of alcohol and drug abuse. In M. Galanter (Ed.), *Recent developments in alcoholism: Volume 8*, pp. 305–327. New York, NY: Plenum Press.

Harm Reduction International. (2015). A position statement from Harm Reduction International. Retrieved from http://www.ihra.net/what-is-harm-reduction

Lasnier, B., Brochu, S., Boyd, N., & Fischer, B. (2010). A heroin prescription trial: Case studies from Montreal and Vancouver on crime and disorder in the surrounding neighbourhoods. *International Journal of Drug Policy, 21*(1), 28–35.

Leslie, K. (2008). Harm reduction: An approach to reducing risky health behaviours in adolescents. *Paediatric Child Health, 13*(1), 53–56.

MacNeil, J., & Pauly, B. (2010). Impact: A case study examining the closure of a large urban fixed site needle exchange in Canada. *Harm Reduction Journal, 7*(11). Retrieved from http://www.biomedcentral.com/content/pdf/1477-7517-7-11.pdf

Marshall, B., Milloy, M., Wood, E., Montaner, J., & Kerr, T. (2011). Reducing overdose mortality after the opening of North America's first medically supervised safer injecting facility: A retrospective population-based study. *The Lancet, 377*(9775), 1429–1437.

Mathers, B., Degenhardt, L., Ali, H., Wiessing, L., Hickman, M., Mattick, R., Myers, B., Ambekar, A., & Strathdee, S. (2010). HIV prevention, treatment, and care services for people who inject drugs: A systematic review of global, regional, and national coverage, *The Lancet, 375*(9719), 1014–1028.

Maynes, M. (2008). *Methadone maintenance treatment: Client handbook*. Toronto: Centre on Addiction and Mental Health.

McKay, M., Mcbride, N., Sumnall, H., & Cole, J. (2012). Reducing the harm from adolescent alcohol consumption: Results from an adapted version of SHAHRP in Northern Ireland. *Journal of Substance Abuse, 17*(2), 98–121.

Merrill, J. (1998). Evaluating treatment effectiveness. Changing our expectations. *Journal of Substance Abuse Treatment, 15*(3), 175–176.

Methadone Strategy Working Group. (2001). *Countering the crisis: Ontario's prescription for opioid dependence*. Toronto, ON: Methadone Strategy Working Group.

Miller, W. (1983). Controlled drinking: A history and a critical review. *Journal of Studies on Alcohol, 44*(1), 68–83.

Nosyk, B., Guh, D., Bansback, N., Oviedo-Joekes, E., Brissette, S., Marsh, D.C., Meikleham, E., Schecher, M., & Anis, A. (2012). Cost-effectiveness of diacetylmorphine versus methadone for chronic opioid dependence refractory to treatment. *Canadian Medical Association Journal, 184*(6), E317–E328.

Orman, J., & Keating, G. (2009). Spotlight on buprenorphine/naloxone in the treatment of opioid dependence. *CNS Drugs, 23*(10), 899-902.

Oviedo-Joekes, E., Brissette, S., Marsh, D., Lauzon, P., Guh, D., Anis, A., & Schechter, M. (2009). Diacetylmorphine versus methadone for the treatment of opioid addiction. *The New England Journal of Medicine, 361*(8), 777-786.

Pendery, M., Maltzman, I., & West, L.J. (1982). Controlled drinking by alcoholics? New findings and a reevaluation of a major affirmative study. *Science, 217*(2), 169-175.

Pinkerton, S. (2010). Is Vancouver Canada's supervised injection facility cost-saving? *Addiction, 105*(8), 1429-1436.

Poulin, C. (2006). *Harm reduction policies and programs for youth.* Ottawa, ON: Canadian Centre on Substance Abuse.

Rihs-Middell, M. (Ed.). (1997). *The medical prescription of narcotics: Scientific foundations and practical experience.* Bern, Switzerland: Swiss Federal Office of Public Health.

Rowe, W., & Gonzalez, C. (2010). Supervised injection sites: Harm reduction and health promotion. In R. Csiernik & W.S. Rowe (Eds.), *Responding to the oppression of addiction* (2nd ed., pp. 35-46). Toronto, ON: Canadian Scholars' Press.

Rubin, E. (1999). *Minimizing harm: A new crime policy for modern America.* Boulder, CO: Westview Press.

Schechter, M., & Kendall, P. (2011). Is there a need for heroin substitution treatment in Vancouver's Downtown Eastside? Yes there is, and in many other places too. *Canadian Journal of Public Health, 102*(2), 87-89.

Schilling, R., Dornig, K., & Lungren, L. (2006). Treatment of heroin dependence: Effectiveness, costs, and benefits of methadone maintenance. *Research on Social Work Practice, 16*(1), 48-56.

Sears, C., Weltzein, E., & Guydish, J. (2001). A cohort study of syringe exchangers and nonexchangers in San Franciso. *Journal of Drug Issues, 21*(Spring), 445-464.

Single, E. (2001). *Towards a new conceptualization of harm reduction: Making evidence-based decision making a reality.* Ottawa, ON: CCSA National Working Group on Policy.

Small, R. (2000). *Is there a more effective response with respect to the problems of substance misuse in British Colombia?* Vancouver, BC: VANDU.

Stimson, G. (1995). AIDS and injecting drug use in the United Kingdom, 1987-1993: The policy response and the prevention of the epidemic. *Social Science Medicine, 41*(5), 699-716.

Strang, J., Metrebian, N., Lintzeris, N., Potts, L., Carnwath, T., Mayet, S., Williams, H., Zador, D., Evans, R., Groshkova, T., Charles, V., Martin, A., & Forzisi, L. (2010). Supervised injectable heroin or injectable methadone versus optimised oral methadone as treatment for chronic heroin addicts in England after persistent failure in orthodox treatment (RIOTT): A randomised trial. *The Lancet, 375*(9729), 1885-1895.

Strike, C., Hopkins, S., Watson, T., Gohil, H., Leece, P., Young, S., Buxton, J., Challacombe, L., Demel, G., Heywood, D., Lampkin, H., Leonard. L., Lebounga Vouma, J., Lockie, L., Millson, P., Morissette, C., & Nielsen, D., Petersen, D., Tzemis, D., & Zurba, N. (2013). *Best practice recommendations for Canadian harm reduction programs that provide service to people who use drugs and are at risk for HIV, HCV, and other harms: Part 1.* Toronto, ON: Working Group on Best Practice for Harm Reduction Programs in Canada.

Tanner, G., Bordon, N., Conroy, S., & Best, D. (2011). Comparing methadone and suboxone in applied treatment settings: The experiences of maintenance patients in Lanarkshire. *Journal of Substance Abuse, 16*(3), 171-178.

Thomas, G. (2005). *Harm reduction policies and programs for persons involved in the criminal justice system.* Ottawa, ON: Canadian Centre on Substance Abuse.

Turner, K., Hutchinson, S., Vickerman, P., Hope, V., Craine, N., Palmateer, N., May, M., Taylor, A., De Angelis, D., Cameron, S., Parry, J., Lyons, M., Goldberg, D., Allen, E., & Hickman, M. (2011). The impact of needle and syringe provision and opiate substitution therapy on the incidence of hepatitis C virus in injecting drug users: Pooling of UK evidence. *Addiction, 106*(11), 1978-1988.

Urban Health Research Initiative. (2013). *Drug situation in Vancouver.* Vancouver, BC: British Columbia Centre for Excellence in HIV/AIDS.

Valente, T., & Vlahov, D. (2001). Selective risk taking among needle exchange participants: Implications for supplemental interventions. *American Journal of Public Health, 91*(3), 406-411.

Vertefeuille, J., Marx, A., Tun, W., Huettner, S., Strathdee, S., & Vlahov, D. (2000). Decline in self-reported high-risk injection-related behaviours among HIV-seropositive participants in the Baltimore needle exchange programs. *AIDS & Behavior, 4*(4), 381-388.

Verthein, U., Bonorden-Kleij, K., Degkwitz, P., Dilg, C., Kohler, W., Passie, T., Soyka, M., Tanger, S., Vogel, M., & Haasen, C. (2008). Long-term effects of heroin-assisted treatment in Germany. *Addiction, 103*(6), 960-966.

Ward, J. (2013, September 20). Rona Ambrose slams decision to give heroin to certain addicts. *Toronto Star.* Retrieved from http://www.thestar.com/news/canada/2013/09/20/rona_ambrose_slams_decision_to_give_heroin_to_certain_addicts.html

White, W., & Coon, B. (2003). Methadone and the anti-medication bias in addiction treatment. *Counselor, 4*(5), 58-63.

Wilson, D., Kwon, A., Anderson, J., & Thein, R. (2009). *Return on investment 2: Evaluating the cost-effectiveness of needle and syringe programs in Australia.* Canberra, Australia: Australian Government Department of Health and Ageing.

Wood, E., Kerr, T., Small, W., Li, K., Marsh, D., Montaner, J., & Tyndall, M. (2004). Changes in public order after the opening of a medically supervised safer injecting facility for illicit injection drug users. *Canadian Medical Association Journal, 171*(7), 731-734.

Wood, E., Tyndall, M., Spittal, P., Li, K., Kerr, T., Hogg, R., Montaner, J., O'Shaughness, V., & Schechter, T. (2001). Unsafe injection practices in a cohort of injection drug users in Vancouver: Could safer injecting rooms help. *Canadian Medical Association Journal, 165*(4), 405-410.

Zaric, G., Barnett, P., & Brandeau, M. (2000). HIV transmission and the cost effectiveness of methadone maintenance treatment. *American Journal of Public Health, 90*(7), 1100-1111.

Zaric, G., Brennan, A., Varenbut, M., & Daiter, J. (2012). The cost of providing methadone maintenance treatment in Ontario, Canada. *The American Journal of Drug and Alcohol Abuse, 38*(6), 559-566.

CHAPTER 3

Supervised Injection Sites: Harm Reduction and Health Promotion

William S. Rowe and Lisa Rapp

In mental health workers' narratives about people with both mental illness and substance abuse, addiction has traditionally been organized as separate from the mental illness component. I suggest that this separation has not been productive, and that we should instead focus on that which is similar in these experiences: the quest for personal healing.

—SMALL (2004, P. 37)

Introduction

Social workers, in co-operation with other health professionals, have been providing services to people who use injection drugs for decades. Numerous and untold lives have been saved and positively influenced by the advocacy, support, and psychosocial interventions of these professionals. Social workers' involvement in ensuring access to progressive, effective, and compassionate programming has consistently been strong, and the profession has been quick to respond to the immediate and ongoing concerns of drug users. In recent years, social workers have been involved in harm reduction programs to make significant contributions to the health and well-being of their clients.

> Harm reduction is a set of practical strategies and ideas aimed at reducing negative consequences associated with drug use. Harm Reduction is also a movement for social justice built on a belief in, and respect for, the rights of people who use drugs. (Harm Reduction Coalition, 2015)

Harm reduction strategies encompass a wide continuum of possibilities, from safe use to managed use to no use, and supervised injection sites (SIS) are a significant part of the harm reduction and educational strategies for injection drug users (IDU). SIS provide those addicted to drugs with their basic human right to health care. Prior to 2002 it was very challenging to find individuals in positions of power in North America that would publicly support SIS or even admit that the issue of addiction is a health and social issue and not a criminal justice one (Small, Palepu, & Tyndall, 2005). For years the publically stated policy position has been that drug problems should be dealt with through law enforcement, even with the abundant amount of evidence that law enforcement has failed to solve this problem. For over four decades the United States has pushed a "War on Drugs," though it has been more a war on drug users. Unfortunately, this War on Drugs has not lived up to its promise of keeping drugs off the street and stopping people from using them. Instead it has led to overpopulated prisons and an outbreak of HIV/AIDS from contaminated needle sharing (Newman, 2007).

Drug problems have been a major drain on Canada's economy, costing an estimated $9 billion annually through law enforcement, prosecution, and incarceration expenses alone (National Anti-Drug Strategy, 2008). Bula (2008) reported that in 2004 and 2005 73% of the anti-drug budget was spent on enforcement, while only 14% was spent on treatment, and a paltry 3% was spent on prevention and harm reduction. Although there was more focus on drug treatment in 2007, overall budget allocations did not change substantively, with 70% allotted to enforcement, 17% to treatment, and only 4% to prevention and 2% to harm reduction. Further review of the website in 2015 indicated that even though a small percentage was allocated for treatment and prevention, only 67% of that funding had been utilized and the rest had been returned to the Canadian government. In addition, the results from the 2012 Canadian Alcohol and Drug Use Monitoring Survey showed no improvement in harm to those using drugs as far back as 2002 (Health Canada, 2012).

Addicted individuals have historically been stigmatized and viewed as damaged and devalued. Also, people with addictions have historically been judged more harshly than others, including those suffering from mental illness (Small, 2004). Some people believe that addiction services, including SIS, bring those addicted to drugs into their neighbourhoods, encourage and spread addictive behaviour, and keep people on drugs. It is also believed by some that people choose to be addicts and therefore only have themselves to blame for their problems (Rights of drug addicts, 2008; Small, 2004; Small & Drucker, 2005). In Europe, a range of helping professionals, including social workers, and members of general society have begun viewing injection drug users as a legitimate part of contemporary society and a core component of the treatment continuum of care. However, this phenomenon has not yet gained acceptance worldwide. A common treatment belief is that individuals who are addicted should just decide not to take drugs or be mandated to stop taking them through some sort of program (Small, 2004).

Addiction began being viewed more as a public problem requiring public intervention when three related variables were recognized as interacting: a rise in drug overdose deaths, the proliferation of HIV/AIDS, and drug use in public locations (Small & Drucker, 2005). Injection drug use has resulted in the prevalence of infectious diseases and drug overdosing in numerous cities around the world (Wood, Tyndall, Lai et al., 2006). According to Small and Drucker (2007) HIV is the leading cause of death worldwide for the 15-to-49-year-old age group, partly due to intravenous drug use. Drug-related overdose also continues to be a major contributor to the mortality of IDU (Kerr, Small, Moore, & Wood, 2007). SIS were implemented as a response to addiction being viewed as a public health problem and therefore the responsibility of public institutions to provide a solution (Small et al., 2006). Those supporting SIS realize that saving lives is essential, even if there is not agreement with their choices, and people need to be alive in order to find and access services (Small, 2004). Although many SIS can be found in Europe, South Asia, and Australia, Vancouver's SIS, Insite, is the busiest in the world serving at least double the number of clients per day than any other program. Insite has also become a world leader in research, with 80% of all research projects examining SIS done through this Canadian facility.

This chapter provides a general overview of SIS and the main issues relevant to social work. It also examines Canada's first and only supervised injection site, Insite. In addition, it describes how social workers can involve themselves in advocacy, staffing, community organizing, research, and multidisciplinary approaches to these sites, which are an important component of an effective harm reduction strategy and a comprehensive continuum of care.

What Are Supervised Injection Sites?

Supervised injection sites (SIS), also referred to as supervised injection facilities (SIF), are safe places where people can go to inject drugs under the supervision of trained multidisciplinary staff. The staff can provide education regarding safer injection practices, as well as respond appropriately in the event of an overdose. They can also provide information regarding treatment resources should an individual be interested. While each SIS varies in the way it operates, in general injection drug users (IDU) bring pre-obtained illegal drugs to the site, are provided with sterile equipment to use, and inject drugs with nurses and other trained staff nearby (Kerr, Small, Moore, & Wood, 2007). Typically, needles, syringes, candles, sterile water, paper towels, cotton balls, cookers/spoons, ties, alcohol swabs, filters, ascorbic acid, and bandages are available in the injection areas. SIS allow IDU to have their privacy, while also offering the comfort of knowing that trained staff are available to respond in case of an emergency. SIS do not allow the sharing of drugs or equipment and prohibit assisted injection (Canadian Centre on Substance Abuse, 2004). Research studies have consistently demonstrated that supervised injection site use by IDU leads to a reduction in syringe sharing among users, which also reduces the spread of diseases and infections (Kimber et al., 2003; Wood et al., 2005). It is critical to note how SIS differ markedly from the illegal shooting galleries operating in many cities, where drug users must pay a small amount of money for a few minutes in a private or semi-private room. The latter are profit motivated, may be littered with trash and/or needles, violent, controlled by drug dealers, allow participants to share dirty needles, and show little regard for the client's health and safety (Dolan et al., 2000; Newman, 2007). In contrast, SIS attempt to protect and promote the health of injection drug users by employing a non-judgemental, client-centred approach rooted in harm reduction tactics.

The focus of SIS includes reducing individual harm and addressing the concerns of overdosing, spreading diseases, and infections among IDU. Overdosing, contracting HIV and/or hepatitis C, and bacterial infections, such as endocarditis, are common among IDU (Wood, Kerr, Montaner et al., 2004). Drug overdose has become a leading cause of death among IDU in many countries (Kerr, Small, Moore, & Wood, 2007). Also, not only is HIV common among IDU, but injection drug use actually serves as a primary force behind the epidemic in several areas around the world (Wood et al., 2005). It has been recognized that when injections occur in front of health professionals the risk of disease decreases (Rights of drug addicts, 2008). As an injection is supervised, trained professionals can offer medical advice on how to inject without damaging the vein or surrounding tissues and encourage users to inject in less dangerous places on their bodies.

SIS also serve as a referral source by supporting contact between health care services and the population of IDU, which is usually difficult to reach in other settings (Wood et al., 2007). SIS provide IDU with an opportunity to more effectively maximize their health through connections with health care and social services that otherwise might not be available to them, since for many clients this is their first significant engagement with health and social services. In addition to primary care and treatment of diseases or infections, IDU at SIS are also able to access addiction counselling and treatment. Users have access to education about drugs and drug use, information on various treatment and rehabilitation options and primary health care services or referrals. This information can be provided at a level appropriate to the client's needs and state of readiness for change, and reinforced as necessary, in a barrier-free, client-centred manner. Research has shown that there is a positive correlation between IDU that attend SIS and meet with the addiction counsellors on-site and IDU that attend a detoxification program (Wood et al., 2007).

In 2003 Vancouver started operating North America's first legal SIS, known as Insite. Currently, Insite is an integrated part of a community centre called the Portland Hotel Society. Insite is located in the most destitute area in Canada, the Downtown Eastside of Vancouver (Wood et al., 2005). Of the 4,600 persons with an addiction found in the Downtown Eastside 87% are infected with hepatitis C and 17% with HIV (Rights of drug addicts, 2008). It is estimated that eight out of every nine Insite clients are infected with hepatitis C. Insite is open 18 hours a day, seven days a week, and includes 12 individual spaces for injection. Since its opening in 2003, there have been more than 2 million visits, and while there are over 200 overdose events each year no overdose deaths have occurred (Pinkerton, 2010). In 2012, there were on average 1,028 visits each day and staff made 4,564 referrals for other health and social services (Leung, 2013).

The 12 booths in operation are designed so that they are open at the back to a central desk that is always staffed by a nurse. There are five program staff and two nurses on duty at any given time. Peer counsellors are available in the chill out room. There are no security guards at Insite and its management model is bottom-up in order to ensure the best possible approach to services for clients.

Insite provides IDU with critical and life-saving health care, and for many IDU accessing Insite is their primary source of health care services. In addition to wound care and health education Insite users also have access to vaccinations for pneumonia and the flu, as well as HIV testing, tuberculosis screening, and sexual health diagnostics (Marsh & Buchner, 2008). Opioid users tend to come in two to three times per day whereas some cocaine users might come as many as ten to twelve times.

However, as mentioned previously, Insite can only accommodate 12 injections at a time, which means that it is only able to service a small portion of all injections occurring in the IDU population (Wood et al., 2005). Insite is oversubscribed and could easily be opened 24 hours a day. One study noted the main complaint about Insite was the long wait to get in (Jozaghi, 2012). To receive services at Insite, clients need only provide their birthday, though there is no formal checking by staff of the accuracy of the date or year given. Clients are also tracked by ethnicity and gender and while they are asked for additional information they do not have to provide it in order to use the facility.

According to Kerr, Small, Moore, and Wood (2007) when participants in a study were questioned about Insite there was an agreement that using the Insite facility reduces the risk of IDU overdosing because they have more time to measure their drugs and "taste" them for strength before using them. Also, there was a consensus regarding the ability and timeliness of Insite staff to treat IDU in the event of an overdose. Insite does not dispense medication, but if an opioid overdose does occur the facility has staff members that can immediately respond by administering naloxone (narcan) to counteract the effects of respiratory depression and, when necessary, by calling an ambulance for further formal assistance. SIS are seen by IDU as safe alternatives to injecting in a public location and places where an individual does not have to fear overdosing and not receiving treatment, being robbed, or being arrested. Ninety-five per cent of Insite users rate the service as either good or excellent (Petrar et al., 2007).

In September 2007 Insite established a short-term residential detoxification centre in the same building called Onsite. Onsite provides treatment on demand for Insite clients who want to stop using drugs. There are 12 short stay units where clients are able to stay from 1 to 10 days. In addition the program offers a therapeutic day treatment program along with 18 transitional recovery units with a typical stay ranging from one to three months (Marsch & Buchner, 2008).

Internationally, SIS have legally been in operation since the 1970s, when Amsterdam introduced them as one component of a local harm reduction strategy, despite ongoing concerns by the United Nation's International Narcotics Control Board that drug-injection sites are not in line with international drug-control treaties that promote only prevention and treatment (Canadian Centre on Substance Abuse, 2004). Other Dutch cities opened SIS in the early 1980s, and 16 of the sites currently operate in the Netherlands (Dolan et al., 2000). Switzerland established legal injection rooms in 1986 and 17 SIS operate in that country. Germany officially established SIS in 1994 with 13 sites existing in four different major cities. In Switzerland, approximately 100 clients visit each of the country's SIS per day, and an estimated 68,000 legal injections occur per year (Dolan, 1997). Other sites, such as Frankfurt's supervised injection site, may supervise as many as 500 injections per day. Users of these sites report attending the sites primarily to inject in peace, to obtain free injecting equipment, and to obtain medical attention, which is consistent with reports from Insite users. Overseas interest in the sites has grown as injection drug problems exacerbate and the publication of related media reports has increased in frequency. Australia began an 18-month supervised injection site trial in Sydney in May 2001 and evaluated the site to decide if it was an appropriate strategy. The Sydney site has yielded positive research findings similar to that of Insite, the most recent pertaining to overdose-related demand on ambulance services. More than 1,700 overdose cases were treated at the Sydney centre during a five-year period, overdoses that might otherwise have occurred in the immediate vicinity, necessitating ambulance attendance. Thus, as a secondary benefit to the community, the Sydney SIS frees up ambulances allowing them to attend other medical emergencies (Salmon et al., 2010). However, both sites have also been in jeopardy of closing due to changes in governmental leadership (Beletsky, Davis, Anderson, & Burris, 2008).

Social and Community Issues

Harm reduction initiatives, including needle exchange programs, methadone clinics, and supervised injection sites, have caused some degree of public distress and consternation in each country that has implemented them. In many areas, people's concerns tend to be less about the theory or principle of the programs than about their establishment in specific communities. Many people who are supportive of, or indifferent to, the initiatives still maintain that they should not be located in their neighbourhoods (Malatesta, Kubler, Joye, & Hausser, 2000). Former US Office of National Drug Control Policy Director John Walters suggested that the implementation of SIS may escalate HIV transmissions among IDU and cause a migration of IDU to the city (Wood, Kerr, Montaner et al., 2004). A major social and community issue in regard to SIS is the misconception that these sites bring with them an increase in drug dealing, using, and other crimes to the neighbourhood in which they are located. However, the benefits of SIS to public drug use and HIV risk behaviour have not come at the cost of increases in criminal activity (Wood, Tyndall, Lai, Montaner, & Kerr, 2006). In addition, SIS can actually enhance public order through a decrease in public drug use (Petrar et al., 2007).

Wood, Tyndall, Montaner, and Kerr (2006) indicate that initially there were concerns that the opening of Insite would lead to an increase in drug use in IDU and decrease the likelihood for seeking treatment. However, their study demonstrated, as have others before it, that use of SIS actually leads to an increase in addiction treatment and/or detoxification services. There is also no evidence to suggest that the presence of SIS leads to more individuals initiating injection drug use or that using SIS results in an increase in the relapse of injection drug use or the decrease of quitting injection drug use. Research findings also indicate that after the opening of Insite the number of publicly discarded syringes, public drug injection, injection-related trash, and presence of suspected drug dealers in the surrounding area all declined. In addition, the opening of Insite has not been related to any rise in criminal charges for drug dealing or drug-related crimes. As one can observe from the research, initial concerns of residents seem to primarily stem from a fear of the unknown, a feeling of uncertainty, and a lack of knowledge regarding what SIS are and how they operate, rather than actual events or evidence (Fast, Small, Wood, & Kerr, 2008).

Public approval and support is necessary for SIS to stay open and meet their public health mandate. There is some evidence that public support has begun to increase. Strike and colleagues (2014) found increases in the public's belief that SIS help reduce neighbourhood problems, help IDUs contact health and social workers, reduce overdoses and infectious diseases, and encourage safer injections. There are still mixed feelings for many, but a shift has occurred.

To be more accessible supervised injection sites need more funding, as well as co-operation from the police, zoning departments, and health authorities (Small, Palepu, & Tyndall, 2006). Insite is located close to Vancouver's Chinatown, whose merchants initially opposed its opening. However, there is now general support for the program from this group as they report that when Insite is open there are fewer people harassing their customers. At this time Insite has also garnered support from the local police station, which is only one block away, municipal government officials, and the Canadian Medical Association, as well as a local bank that will cash cheques for Insite clients. Vancouver police are now actively encouraging IDU at times to go to Insite, to minimize their risk of overdosing as a result of the unusually strong drugs that can be bought on the streets (Small, Palepu, & Tyndallm, 2006).

In addition, a study conducted by Pinkerton (2010) found that HIV infections have decreased since Insite's opening. Examining data from one year of operation, Pinkerton found a decrease in 84 HIV infections. These infections alone cost approximately $17.6 million (Canadian) in lifetime HIV-related medical care and this does not include the number of individuals infected from these 83.5 cases over time. Considering Insite's budget of about $3 million per year, the cost savings as well as the reduction in personal suffering is clear.

Since its opening, Insite has shown numerous community and public health benefits. The majority of IDU reported a positive difference in their injecting behaviour since attending Insite including a decrease in rushed injecting, less outdoor injecting, a decrease in unsafe syringe disposal, more ease in finding a vein on the first try, using clean water to inject more often, cleaning the injection site more often, a reduction in the reuse of syringes, and not needing help injecting any longer (Fast, Small, Wood, & Kerr, 2008; Petrar et al., 2007). Jozaghi (2012) found from qualitative interviews of Insite clients that they had seen numerous lives saved by the Insite staff, had dramatically changed their sharing behaviours, had better access to care, and had been provided a clean, safe refuge from the dangerous urban area where they lived. Reductions in the number of drug users injecting in public, the number of discarded syringes, and the amount of drug-related litter was found by Wood, Kerr, Small, and colleagues (2004) when they compared the surrounding neighbourhood before and after Insite was opened.

Overall, results indicate that implementing SIS lead to a reduction in public drug use and a decrease in several aspects of unsafe drug injection procedures. Supervised injection sites benefit a hard-to-reach population of IDU by offering services with minimal barriers to access. Contact with these hard-to-reach persons can lead to important social and health referrals and treatment opportunities, which ultimately results in positive social and community opportunities. A study by DeBeck and colleagues (2011) provided evidence that SIS participants increased their utilization of addiction services and increased injection cessation.

Dolan and colleagues (2000) also discussed that client contact with SIS has contributed to individual improvements in health, social functioning, and stabilization. Clients generally ceased to use the sites upon attainment of stable living arrangements. In this way, injection sites can improve the likelihood that IDU can re-integrate into mainstream society. Some SIS offer job skill training, education, and social support groups. There are also suggestions that injection rooms enhance and encourage more positive relationships between law enforcement agents and drug users, as is the case with Insite.

In 2011, The Supreme Court of Canada issued a unanimous ruling granting Insite an extended exemption to operate. It was a short-lived celebration, as soon afterwards, the Respect for Communities Act was introduced by Harper's Conservative government hindering Insite and other proposed facilities with new requirements and cumbersome policies (Zlotorzynska, Wood, Montaner, & Kerr, 2013), though these barriers appear to be lowering under the federal government led by Liberal Prime Minister Justin Trudeau.

The Role of Social Workers

Historically, social workers have been involved in a wide range of professional activities relating to core supervised injection site issues: community health, education and empowerment, HIV prevention and care, drug abuse treatment and prevention, and research and policy. In co-operation with other health professionals social workers have provided services to people who use injection drugs for decades. The role of social workers in prevention and treatment has been recognized as unique. Social workers are well situated to provide specialized care because of their specific experience and training with multi-barrier clients and families (Magura, 1994), and because of the profession's traditional prioritization of social justice, equality, public welfare, and client-centred care (Freeman, 1992; Specht & Courtney, 1994).

Rozier and Laberge (1997) state that an important challenge for social workers is to bridge the gap between the traditional, abstinence-based school of thought and those working from harm reduction frameworks. Social workers may uniquely possess the flexibility of thought, multiple perspectives, and values required to respond effectively to the differing and often conflicting needs of clients, communities, and medical/social professionals. Social workers' involvement in ensuring access to progressive, effective, and compassionate programming for injection drug users has been consistent and strong. Many workers in the profession have been quick to respond to the immediate and ongoing concerns of drug users and those at risk of, or infected with, HIV (Bowlby, 1998).

A major contribution of social workers to the IDU population in SIS comes through addiction counselling onsite and referrals to community resources and offsite addiction treatment. Rehabilitation focuses on changing people, while harm reduction strategies focus on supporting those with addiction issues where they are rather than changing them, which is what they require in the beginning (Small, 2004). Social workers are available to meet those with addiction issues where they are in their lives and support them. Individuals who are addicted to psychoactive drugs require healing that involves recognition of their value as a person. In addition to addiction services, social workers also strive to meet the needs of IDU through community resource referrals for other basic needs such as housing (Wood et al., 2006).

Social workers have been instrumental in lobbying to open SIS and to continue to keep them open. In their involvement with SIS, social workers now have the opportunity to lend further support to injection drug users and their communities and to strengthen efforts to minimize HIV and other public health harms. In doing so, social workers must be active in both multidisciplinary partnerships and in asserting their unique expertise. Additional research and continued action are needed to ensure that client-centred care remains a priority, that controversial projects are evaluated fairly, and that the integration of new policies and programs is optimally beneficial for all involved. Social workers may be called upon to act as a bridge between drug users and their communities, medical and social professionals, the government, and other stakeholders. In this way, social workers may make original and valuable contributions to the debate surrounding supervised injection sites in Canada.

Conclusion

Harm reduction is not an all or nothing approach. As Small and Drucker (2007) report, instead of trying to eliminate addiction, occasionally we have to be content with helping individuals avoid an HIV infection and thus in turn contribute to the overall social and physical health of the community. Supervised injection sites function to save lives through encouraging, instead of deterring, IDU to access health care. While complete abstinence from drug use is ideal, preventing unnecessary deaths due to diseases and overdoses is an excellent and vital starting point. The progress of SIS has been mired in politics, abstinence values, and fear, but as Montreal Mayor Denis Coderre aptly said, "What are we waiting for? People are dying" (Fidelman, 2015). Insite is helping hundreds of IDUs in the Vancouver area, but the need is far greater. With the election of the Trudeau government in 2015, restrictions around SIS establishment were eased and interest in opening sites has been expressed in communities including Victoria, Surrey, Edmonton, Hamilton, Toronto, Ottawa, and Montreal.

Injection drug use has also been a major problem in the United States for several decades. Syringe exchange programs have operated in several cities in the US for many years, indicating the likely success of SIS there. According to the *Seattle Times* (Beekman, 2016), Seattle is currently considering becoming the first city in the United States to house a supervised injection site. Some have suggested that instead of starting a supervised injection site from scratch it would be beneficial to integrate it into an already-established social service program. For a supervised injection site to be successful in the United States it would need political and law enforcement support at the local, state, and national levels (Beletsky, David, Anderson, & Burris, 2008). An HIV outbreak in rural Indiana finally forced then Indiana governor, Mike Pense, to issue an emergency order to overrule a state law to allow syringe swapping in the region. The Centers for Disease Control and Prevention (CDC) had traced the outbreak to Scott County residents who were dissolving and injecting prescription pain medication and sharing needles (CDC, 2015). Sadly it will likely take many more such circumstances to garner the political will to allow supervised injection sites to become an accepted component of the harm reduction continuum in North America.

REFERENCES

Beekman, D. (2016). Heroin, cocaine users in Seattle may get country's first safe-use site. Retrieved from http://www.seattletimes.com/seattle-news/politics/heroin-other-drug-users-may-get-a-safe-use-site-in-seattle/

Beletsky, L., Davis, C., Anderson, E., & Burris, S. (2008). The law (and politics) of safe injection facilities in the United States. *American Journal of Public Health, 98*(2), 231–237.

Bowlby, A. (1998). Care and the context of injection drug use. In W. Rowe & B. Ryan (Eds.), *Social work and HIV: The Canadian experience* (pp. 183–194). Toronto, ON: Oxford University Press.

Canadian Centre on Substance Abuse (2004). *Supervised injection facilities.* Ottawa, ON: Canadian Centre on Substance Abuse.

DeBeck, K., Kerr, T., Bird, L., Zhang, R., Marsh, D., Tyndall, M., Montamer, J., & Wood, E. (2011). Injection drug use cessation and use of North America's first medically supervised safer injecting facility. *Drug and Alcohol Dependence, 113*(2–3), 172–176.

Dolan, K. (1997). No place to go. *Connexions, 12*(10), 18–23.

Dolan, K., Kimber, J., Fry, C., Fitzgerald, J., McDonald, D., & Trautmann, F. (2000). Drug consumption facilities in Europe and the establishment of supervised injecting centres in Australia. *Drug and Alcohol Review, 19*(3), 337–346.

Fast, D., Small, W., Wood, E., & Kerr, T. (2008). The perspectives of injection drug users regarding safer injecting education delivered through a supervised injecting facility. *Harm Reduction Journal, 5*(1), 32.

Fidelman, C. (2015). Coderre wants safe injection sites by this fall in Montreal. *Montreal Gazette.* Retrieved from http://montrealgazette.com/news/local-news/coderre-wants-safe-injection-sites-by-this-fall

Freeman, E. (1992). *The addiction process: Effective social work approaches.* New York, NY: Longman.

Harm Reduction Coalition (2015). *Principles of harm reduction.* Retrieved from http://harmreduction.org/about-us/principles-of-harm-reduction

Health Canada (2012). *Canadian alcohol and drug use monitoring survey.* Retrieved from http://www.hc-sc.gc.ca/hc-ps/drugs-drogues/stat/_2012/summary-sommaire-eng.php

Jozaghi, E. (2012). "A little heaven in hell": The role of a supervised injection facility in transforming place. *Urban Geography, 33*(8), 1144–1162.

Kerr, T., Small, W., Moore, D., & Wood, E. (2007). A micro-environmental intervention to reduce the harms associated with drug-related overdose: Evidence from the evaluation of Vancouver's safer injection facility. *International Journal of Drug Policy, 18*(1), 37–45.

Kimber, J., Dolan, K., van Beek, I., Hedrich, D., & Zurhold, H. (2003). Drug consumption facilities: An update since 2000. *Drug and Alcohol Review, 22*(2), 227–233.

Leung, M. (2013). As InSite turns 10, others fight for supervised drug injection sites across Canada. *CTV News.* Retrieved from http://www.ctvnews.ca/health

Magura, S. (1994). Social workers should be more involved in substance abuse treatment. *Health & Social Work, 19*(1), 3–5.

Malatesta, D., Kubler, D., Joye, D., & Hausser, D. (2000). Between public health and public order: Harm reduction facilities and neighbourhood problems. In J.P. Moatti, Y. Souteyrand, A. Prieur, T. Sandfort, & P. Aggleton (Eds.), *AIDS in Europe: New challenges for the social sciences* (pp. 178–188). New York, NY: Routledge Press.

Marsh, D., & Buchner, C. (2008). *Insite: Treatment and care for people with chronic addiction and complex health issues.* Retrieved from http://www.vch.ca/sis

National Anti-Drug Strategy. (2008). *Drug treatment courts.* Retrieved from http://www.nationalantidrugstrategy.gc.ca/comm-coll/dtc-ttt.html

Newman, T. (2007, May 31). Supervised drug injection sites? New research in Canada shows they reduce HIV, overdose deaths, and even help encourage addicts into treatment. *The Huffington Post.* Retrieved from http://www.huffingtonpost.com/tony-newman/supervised-drug-injection_b_50227.html

Permanent safe injection site for Victoria: Report. (2008, March 31). *Canadian Press.* Retrieved from http://bc.ctvnews.ca/permanent-safe-injection-site-for-victoria-report-1.286148

Petrar, S., Kerr, T., Tyndall, M., Zhang, R., Montaner, J., & Wood, E. (2007). Injection drug users' perceptions regarding use of a medically supervised safer injecting facility. *Addictive Behaviors, 32*(5), 1088–1093.

Pinkerton, S. (2010). Is Vancouver Canada's supervised injection facility cost-saving? *Addiction, 105*(8), 1429–1436.

Rights of drug addicts. (2008, May 29). *Globe and Mail*. Retrieved from http://www.theglobeandmail.com/globe-debate/the-rights-of-drug-addicts/article20384727

Rozier, M., & Laberge, D. (1997). *Rapport d'évaluation: L'implantation de 'Chez Ma Cousine Evelyne.'* Montreal, QC: Collectif de recherche sur l'itinérance, Department de Sociologie, Université du Québec à Montréal.

Salmon, A., Van Beek, I., Amin, J., Kaldor, J., & Maher, L. (2010). The impact of a supervised injecting facility on ambulance call-outs in Sydney, Australia. *Addiction, 105*(4), 676-683.

Small, D. (2004). Mental illness, addiction and the supervised injection facility: New narratives on the Downtown Eastside. *Visions: BC's Mental Health and Addictions Journal: Concurrent Disorders, 2*(1), 37-39.

Small, D., & Drucker, E. (2007). Closed to reason: Time for accountability for the International Narcotic Control Board. *Harm Reduction Journal, 4*(13).

Small, D., Palepu, A., & Tyndall, M.W. (2006). The establishment of North America's first state sanctioned supervised injection facility: A case study in culture change. *International Journal of Drug Policy, 17*(1), 73-82.

Specht, H., & Courtney, M. (1994). *Unfaithful angels: How social work has abandoned its mission.* New York, NY: Free Press.

Strike, C., Jairam, J., Kolla, G., Millson, P., Shepherd, S., Fischer, B., Watson, T., & Bayoumi, A. (2014). Increasing public support for supervised injection facilities in Ontario, Canada. *Addiction, 109*(6), 946-953.

Wood, E., Kerr, T., Montaner, J., Strathdee, S., Wodak, A., Hankins, C., Schechter, M.T., & Tyndall, M. (2004). Rationale for evaluating North America's first medically supervised safer-injecting facility. *Lancet Infectious Diseases, 4*(5), 301-306.

Wood, E., Kerr, T., Small, W., Li, K., Marsh, D., Monatmer, J., & Tyndall, M. (2004). Changes in public order after the opening of a medically supervised safer injecting facility for illicit injection drug users. *Canadian Medical Association Journal, 171*(7), 731-734.

Wood, E., Tyndall, M., Lai, C., Montaner, J., & Kerr, T. (2006). Impact of a medically supervised safer injecting facility on drug dealing and other drug-related crime. *Substance Abuse Treatment, Prevention, and Policy, 1*(13).

Wood, E., Tyndall, M., Montaner, J., & Kerr, T. (2006). Summary of findings from the evaluation of a pilot medically supervised safer injecting facility. *Canadian Medical Association Journal, 175*(11), 1399-1404.

Wood, E., Tyndall, M.W., Stoltz, J., Small, W., Lloyd-Smith, E., Zhang, R., Montaner, J., & Kerr. T. (2005). Factors associated with syringe sharing among users of a medically supervised injecting facility. *American Journal of Infectious Diseases, 1*(1), 50-54.

Wood, E., Tyndall, M., Zhang, R., Montaner, J., & Kerr, T. (2007). Rate of detoxification service use and its impact among a cohort of supervised injecting facility users. *Addiction, 102*(6), 916-919.

Zlotorzynska, M., Wood, E., Montamer, J., & Kerr, T. (2013). Supervised injection sites: Prejudice should not trump evidence of benefit. *Canadian Medical Association Journal, 185*(15), 1303-1304.

CHAPTER 4

The Role of Culture in Prevention

Joe Antone and Rick Csiernik

Introduction

Culture is a set of beliefs, values, and characteristics shared by members of a social group that include common understandings, patterns of beliefs, and expectations. Culture is defined by language, faith, social habits, and also by drug use. Cultural guidelines are the informal yet integrated and respected rules of conduct that reflect the morals and values of a specific population and provide a frame for the group's social behaviour (Jenks, 2004). These guidelines involve how the group identifies itself, how it defines family, its spiritual practices, as well as how the group uses psychoactive agents, which ones, and to what degree. Cultural theories move our understanding of addiction beyond biological and psychological perspectives, incorporating and emphasizing the social context of drug use. In general, cultural theories claim that use of psychoactive drugs is more likely to occur within groups where anxiety is high due to external factors and where there are few alternatives to drinking or drug use to relieve this tension (Csiernik, 2016). During the era when Alcoholics Anonymous was first established, Bales (1946) was outlining how culture influences the use, misuse, and abuse of alcohol in three distinct ways:

1. by the degree to which a culture operates to bring about acute needs for adjustment of inner tensions such as guilt, aggression, conflict, and sexual tension in its members;
2. by the attitudes towards drinking that the culture produces in its members; and
3. by the degree to which the culture provides substitute means of satisfaction beyond substance use in the form of positive alternative lifestyle options.

The use of psychoactive substances exists in all cultures globally. However, what is considered a drug, normal versus problematic alcohol and drug consumption, and beliefs about what manifests addiction are as diverse as the cultures themselves (Bennett, Campillo, Chandrasheker, & Gureje, 1988; Centre for Addiction and Mental Health [CAMH], 2003; Das, Balakrishnan, & Vasudevan, 2006; Mäkinen & Reitan,

2006; Moolasart & Chirawatkul, 2012). Human culture has been shaped to such an extent by psychoactive drugs that it can be argued that drug culture is an integral part of humanity. However, culture also operates as a protective factor limiting drug use. This chapter will examine the role of culture as prevention, including one's ethnic or cultural identity, the role of family in the context of culture, and the function of religion and spirituality in protecting against substance misuse.

The Canadian Context

The lack of clear consensus on appropriate levels of use or even what should be licit or illicit contributes to why drug use is a substantive issue in Canadian society. North American culture in general allows, encourages, and actively promotes the ingestion of drugs for personal use and for the attainment of quick physical and emotional pain relief including self-medication. The use of drugs is poorly integrated into North American society with attitudes towards use being ambivalent and inconsistent (Csiernik, 2016). The diversity of groups throughout Canada has likewise contributed to different patterns of use because of distinct cultural protective factors. Census data reveals that 20.6% or 6,775,800 people living in Canada were foreign born, hailing from over 200 different ethnic origins (Statistics Canada, 2011).

A focus group conducted in Ontario using key informants from the Polish, Portuguese, Punjabi, Russian, Serbian, Somali, and Tamil communities found drastic differences in alcohol consumption patterns, the community's views on alcohol consumption and drinking practices, and what is considered a culturally appropriate health strategy (Agic, Mann, & Kobus-Mathews, 2011). There were some similarities, such as alcohol being used as a coping strategy when dealing with problems and stress, and also the common belief that alcohol is good for one's health. There were also drastic differences, particularly in perceptions of what was considered normal drinking, excessive drinking, and even what a standard drink was. Punjabi participants noted that there was no acceptable level of drinking. A Somali informant described two beers (two standard drinks) as being normal drinking, whereas a Russian informant described a half-litre of vodka as normal (11 standard drinks). In the Serbian and Russian communities, men are expected to drink large amounts of alcohol, and it is indeed associated with masculinity (Hinote & Webber, 2012).

Three of the communities in the focus group ascribed to religions that either prohibit the use of alcohol, as was the case with the Somali and Punjabi groups, or strongly condemn its use, as was the case for the Tamil community. However, even with cultural norms established through religious sanctions put in place, drinking still occurred to varying degrees. Interestingly, other factors that, from an evidence standpoint, have been shown to impact substance use patterns within a cultural context were not addressed by study participants, including sex, age, and family (Agic, Mann, & Kobus-Mathews, 2011; Neumark, Rahav, Teichman, & Hasin, 2001).

As addiction is a cultural construct, and because patterns and motivations for substance use are embedded in a given culture, so too should be efforts in prevention and treatment (Anderson, 1998; Edwards & Arif, 1980). However, what further exacerbates this situation is that there continues to exist a discrepancy between the health system and the needs of members of many cultural communities in Canada that creates conflict. Examples of this disconnect include language barriers, varying conceptions of what is considered addiction, and how individuals from different cultural groups describe, interpret, and manifest symptoms (Kwok, 2010). The conflict is also in part a result of a cultural blindness approach to health service delivery, which asserts that all people are alike, and therefore that all people should be treated equally regardless of colour or culture (Issel, 2004). This method of service delivery has led to a much lower rate of participation in health promotion, prevention, and treatment programs from some cultural communities within Canada (Asanin & Wilson, 2008; Dean & Wilson, 2010; Dunn & Dyck, 2000). These factors can all contribute to discrimination, stigmatization, and mistrust of mainstream service providers, which contributes to the oppression when addiction arises (CAMH, 2003, 2004). This makes an emphasis upon prevention even more important, particularly among groups that do not fully engage with the health care system.

Cultural Protective Factors

Cultural Identity

The concept of cultural or ethnic identity is multidimensional in nature, and includes notions of knowledge and participation in the culture; ethnic attachment, which refers to the sense of belonging and the extent that one labels oneself as belonging to a particular group; and ethnic identification, which involves identifying with friends of similar heritage (Brook et al., 1998). A strong identification with one's culture or ethnicity has shown to be a protective factor against substance use across a number of cultures, including Asian Canadian (Costigan, Koryzma, Hua, & Chance, 2010), African-American (Nasim et al., 2007; Brook & Pahl, 2005), Australian (Gaziz, Connor, & Ho, 2010), Canadian Jewish (Waxman & Csiernik, 2010), Mexican American (Codina, Yin, Zapata, & Katims, 2001), and Puerto Rican (Brook et al., 1998). Maintaining a positive ethnic or cultural identity can help mitigate the increase in substance use that tends to come with acculturating to North American culture in an effort to be similar (Brook et al, 1998).

Among the African-American community, commonly cited cultural norms include identifying as part of a highly interdependent community (Hughes et al., 2006; Meomeka, 1998), being religious/spiritual (Cook & Wiley, 2014; Taylor, 1988), identifying as communal (Boykin & Toms, 1985; Meomeka, 1998), and high levels of social control and abstinence drinking norms (Herd & Grube, 1996). While there is not a large body of research in these areas, the research that exists suggests that these aspects of

African-American cultural identity are, for the most part, protective. It should be noted that while the above aspects are common among different groups of African-Americans, it by no means captures all of what is a complex and culturally diverse population.

Herd and Grube's (1996) study of 1,947 African-American adults found both direct and indirect links between ethnic identity and decreased drinking. Specific reasons included high levels of social involvement with other African-Americans, high African-American social and political awareness, adherence to African-American drinking norms of abstinence, and high levels of religiosity. Wallace, Brown, Bachman, and Laveist (2003) reported that religiosity among this group may function at a community level to promote abstinence messages associated with African-American cultural identity.

Perhaps the most telling example of the protective importance of having a positive identification with one's culture is the impact of what happens when people have no culture to identify with, or when the culture they identify with has been decimated through systemic efforts to destroy it, as is the case with Canada's Indigenous people.[1] The erosion of the continuity of an Indigenous identity through colonization has seen Canada's Indigenous people affected by major health concerns at a rate much higher than non-Indigenous people in Canada, including higher levels of substance abuse and higher instances of illnesses and deaths linked to misuse of alcohol and other drugs. Additionally, this group experiences higher levels of infant mortality; heavier burdens of infectious disease, malnutrition, and stunted growth; shortened life expectancy; and diseases and death associated with cigarette smoking, suicide, obesity, and chronic diseases such as diabetes (National Collaborating Centre on Aboriginal Health, 2013).

> We are constantly developing our identity, from birth to the end of our lives. We build it based on our relationships to relatives, friends, community, geography, language and other social factors. Identity plays a key role in our lives. When a child feels a sense of belonging to family, community and peers he or she is better able to deal with adversity. (National Centre for First Nations Governance, n.d.)

Through the creation of residential schools, the reservation system, the outlawing of cultural practices, and other colonial tools of oppression, generations of Indigenous people that occupy land presently known as Canada in many cases no longer have a cultural identity from which to navigate periods of adversity in their lives. Not wishing to identify with Western culture, a culture that many Indigenous people have come to associate with the attempted destruction of their own, Indigenous people are left in a space where they have no cultural identity, or an identity they are ashamed of (Berry, 1999). Consequently, many turn to the use of substance escape:

> Substance abuse (alcohol, drugs, cigarettes) and gambling were often referred to by participants as an attempt to escape from or deny their cultural identity. As a result of repeated acts of discrimination people felt a diminished sense of

pride and replaced it with a sense of shame. Substance abuse, in particular, provided a means to obliterating these feelings of shame and low self-esteem. One participant shared: "It's really hard to talk about. I came from a family of 17 before residential school. We are now a family of 8 after residential school, through the alcohol, drugs, suicides and suicide attempts. I even tried it and almost succeeded because I didn't know who I was." (Berry, 1999, p. 24)

Family

Family is the foundation of all cultures and provides the cornerstones of living in the society into which a person is born (Alaggia & Csiernik, 2010). The family is where children first learn about and form their opinions regarding alcohol and other psychoactive substance use. Family values in turn are greatly influenced by larger cultural guidelines. If children grow up in an environment where abstinence is a dominant attitude, then they are more likely to adopt abstinence as their own stance when they are presented with choices during adolescence. Likewise, when alcohol is used in a ritualistic manner or only under certain prescribed circumstances, there is a greater likelihood that youth will adopt a more controlled pattern of use themselves. Adolescents do typically care about what their parents think and their reactions to their behaviour, often more so than peer groups, particularly early in adolescence. While the family continues to be the primary learning environment from which adolescents draw when forming opinions on drug use, the influence of peers becomes greater over the course of adolescence and as a young person moves towards adulthood (Gale, Lenardson, Lambert, & Hartley 2012; McBroom, 1994).

Families provide a socialization function and in doing so prepare their children for the stresses and challenges of life more than any other single factor. Thus, young people's families serve as a significant mechanism to assist with coping. Culture significantly contributes to the norms espoused by parents including those regarding alcohol and other drug use. Conversely, when the family structure or family relations are not well established or are in a constant state of change and flux, this can create additional stress for adolescents (Persike & Seiffge-Krenke, 2012). A study of Ontario students indicated that family disruption had a profound effect on their cannabis use as compared to those students that did not report any family disruption. There were similar findings for students that reported poor family relations, while stability in these areas was found to act as a preventative factor against substance use and abuse (Butters, 2002).

The important role family can play in prevention is strongly highlighted in Latino culture. Within this group the concept of *familismo* is characterized by three traits (Gaines et al., 1997):

1. Strong identification and attachment with nuclear and extended families
2. Strong family unity and interdependence among family members
3. High levels of social support

Specific features of *familismo* include loyalty, reciprocity, and solidarity. Numerous studies have identified *familismo* as being a distinctive cultural protective factor against illicit drug use and alcohol misuse as it provides a sense of family obligation, parental monitoring, and family cohesion (Dillon, De La Rosa, Sastre, & Ibanez, 2013; Gallo, Penedo, Espinosa de los Monteros, & Arguelles, 2009; Gil, Wagner, & Vega, 2000; Lac et al., 2011; Mulvaney-Day, Alegría, & Sribney, 2007; Telzer, Gonzalez, & Fuligni, 2014).

Family obligation is defined as the psychological sense that one should help, respect, and contribute to one's family (Hardaway & Fuligni, 2006). It is thought that when Latino adolescents internalize this value, "they feel more connected to and embedded within a supportive family network, which can provide them with a sense of support and structure and help them select effective coping strategies to avoid substance use" (Unger et al., 2002, p. 259). Several studies have associated family obligation values with reduced likelihood of use and delayed onset of use (German, Gonzalez, & Dumka, 2009; Gil, Wagner, & Vega, 2000; Kaplan, Nápoles-Springer, Stewart, and Pérez-Stable, 2001; Ramirez et al., 2004; Telzer, Gonzales, & Fuligni, 2014; Unger et al. 2002).

Parental monitoring, defined as parents keeping track of their child's whereabouts, is another key factor in protecting against substance use in Latino youth. Parental monitoring has been found to be directly related to lower rates of substance use, with the mechanism being the influence of the parent on the child's selection of drug-using versus non-drug-using friends (Sieving, Perry, & Williams, 2000; Simons-Morton & Chen, 2005). Parental monitoring also reduces use by mitigating the negative influences of substance-using peers (Lopez et al., 2009). This approach is also likely aided by the open communication often found in Latino family life, and works in concert with the youth's sense of obligation towards the family, as the respect inherent in the obligation one feels could reduce the engagement in risky activities, knowing they may reflect poorly on the family (German, Gonzalez, & Dumka, 2009).

A third identified protective factor is family cohesion, which is defined as closeness within the family (Behnke et al., 2008). Family cohesion has been associated with lower levels of both alcohol use (Marsiglia et al., 2009) and illicit drugs (Gil, Vega, & Biafora, 1998). It is thought here that the mutual goal setting, enjoyment found in spending time with other family members, and propensity to get support from within the family would result in Latino youth being less likely to seek support from people outside of the family, including peers who engage in delinquent behaviour (Lac et al., 2011).

Gender role also is an important factor, as Latino male lifetime marijuana use was 18.8%, compared to 14.4% among females (Substance Abuse and Mental Health Service Administration, 2010). This difference of 4.4% is even more substantial when compared to differences in Caucasian male and females in the United States, where the difference is only 0.2% (Substance Abuse and Mental Health Service Administration, 2008). This disparity may be the result of the gender roles typically found in Latino family systems. According to Arriagada as cited by Lac and colleagues (2010), "girls are typically socialized to be homebound and to help with household and caretaking duties, whereas boys are given more opportunities for autonomy" (p. 645). Further to this point are the cultural values given to each: the value of "machismo" associated with masculinity, male dominance, sexual prowess, physical strength, and honour (Gonzales et al., 2002; Neff, Prihoda, & Hoppe, 1991), and the value of "marianismo" (emulating the Virgin Mary) that focuses on providing instrumental and emotional support to family members, maintaining family traditions, preserving the integrity of the family, and self-sacrifice (Falicov, 2013). Latino adolescent boys may experiment with drugs as a way of asserting their independence and proving their toughness and masculinity, while for females, the combination of the amount of time spent at home and the discouragement from participating in rebellious behaviours accounts for their comparatively lower use (Lac et al., 2011).

The ideas of loyalty, reciprocity, and solidarity discussed above are seen within other cultural groups (Waxman & Csiernik, 2010), underscoring that while cultures unite groups there are also themes that run between them. For instance, the idea of having a robust relationship between a parent and a child entering into and during adolescence is a protective factor in virtually any cultural context, even if that relationship manifests itself differently.

In many Asian cultures, the notion of filial piety, characterized by obedience to parents, providing financial and emotional support, and avoidance of disgraceful behaviour is a protecting factor (Unger et al., 2002). In Hispanic cultures, obligation to the family including to the parents is protective in developing strategies to avoid use and in delaying the onset (Telzer, Gonzalez, & Fuligni, 2014), which is in itself a strong defense against developing an addiction (Csiernik, 2016). In African-American communities the cultural norms of family cohesion (Duncan, Tildesley, Duncan, & Hops, 2015) and parental monitoring (Clark, Nguyen, Belgrave, & Tademy, 2011; Clark, Shamblen, Ringwalt, & Hanley, 2012) have also been found to be protective against substance misuse.

All this speaks to the importance of the parent-child relationship and highlights that if social workers are to effectively and appropriately respond to the oppression of addiction, understanding how culture shapes family interactions, beliefs, and practices is essential. Interventions should be targeted based on what is appropriate within the culture of focus, whilst always being mindful that each culture in and of itself is rich with difference and that there is heterogeneity even within homogeneous groups.

Religion and Spirituality

Another factor that not only binds cultures but also creates them is their faith beliefs. Faith beliefs can take the form of religion, characterized by formal, doctrinal, structured, and community-oriented practices of that faith, and/or spirituality, referring to what meaning is taken on an individual level from that faith and can be expressed and practiced within a formal religious context, or can be entirely secular (Allen & Lo, 2010). Both concepts, separate but related, have shown to be a protective factor against addiction, evidenced by a systematic review by Chitwood, Weiss, and Leukefeld (2008) showing that 99 of 105 publications on the subject find a significant relationship between religiosity/spirituality and a reduced risk of substance use/misuse.

Examples of protection faith brings ranges broadly, including edicts given to Latter Day Saints, Muslims, and members of the Presbyterian Church in the United States whose doctrines state that alcohol abuse is sin because of the harm its use causes to oneself and to others (Csiernik, 2016). Wills, Yeager, and Sandy (2003) found that religiosity could even be a protective factor at an individual level against smoking. Within the construct of religiosity, there are specific mechanisms that have shown to be protective, including the adoption of specific moral and religious principles, social mechanisms such as social control, social learning, and social support, and psychological mechanisms such as a positive self-concept, control beliefs, and psychological well-being (Ellison & Levin, 1998; Ford & Hill, 2012; George, Ellison, & Larson, 2002; Gorsuch, 1995; Pargament, 1997; Smith 2003; Wallace & Foreman, 1998; Welch, Tittle, & Grasmick, 2006).

While trauma certainly contributes to substance use, a collective historic trauma that befalls a group can also act as a protective factor and discourage drug use, as witnessed among the Jewish community in response to the Holocaust (Waxman & Csiernik, 2010). Students that reported religion as being important in their lives were more likely to abstain from using alcohol and other drugs, regardless of their race or religion, while students with no or little religious affiliation were least likely to abstain from alcohol and other substances (Miller, Davies, & Greenwald, 2000; Wallace, Brown, Bachman, & Laveist, 2003).

The vital importance of spirituality as preventing a return to substance abuse once a person has become addicted can be seen in Alcoholics Anonymous (AA). Arguments can be easily made indicating this group has become a culture in and of itself, and one that accepts those of different ethnic and religious groups openly without question to remain abstinent.[2] Part of the reason for the success of AA is that it draws on the various protective factors of both spirituality and religion. With respect to spirituality, it allows for the person to practice his or her own individual faith beliefs without feeling made to conform to another's beliefs, which many people find empowering when they begin attending. Alcoholics Anonymous also draws on protective factors found in the construct of religion, but not necessarily found in spirituality, and that is the social component. The social support and social learning opportunities afforded to people in organized religion are also present in Alcoholics Anonymous. Here people adopt social networks of sober friends, which expose them to new social learning opportunities around living sober and a network of social supports.

When considering the role of religion and spirituality as a protective factor in responding to the oppression of addiction, it becomes increasingly important to understand the differences between the two concepts, as participation in organized religion, particularly among the young, decreases. Burke and colleagues (2014) reported that the number of people who are non-affiliated religious has increased from 13% to 25% in the United States, and the number of people who identify as spiritual but not religious has increased, especially among younger adults. It is thought that this trend is a consequence of the social turmoil of the 1950s and 1960s (Allen & Lo, 2008), a general disenchantment with the conservative politics of organized religion, and the changing lifestyles and social roles of younger people (Burke et al., 2014). While both religion and spirituality do serve as protective factors against substance abuse, we need to be ever mindful of their potential to also oppress. Creating conditions where the various protective factors of spirituality and religion can be made useful while limiting their potential to oppress is an important consideration for social workers in the addiction field moving forward.

Conclusion

Cultures that have lower rates of addiction tend to have better defined practices regarding the use of psychoactive agents. These collectively understood rules are clear, uniform, and prohibitive. Historically, in cultures where addiction was less of an issue, members tended to be exposed to alcohol or other drugs at an early developmental stage with youth observing adult members of their culture using drugs in moderate or prescribed manners, often in situations that discouraged intoxication, such as during meals or religious ceremonies. Cultures with lower rates of addiction also tend to discourage excessive use of alcohol or drugs including public displays of intoxication (Whitehead & Harvey, 1974). However, Canadian culture, because of its heterogeneity, has not yet had an opportunity to develop a set of cultural norms, and this has left it vulnerable to drug misuse.

It could be that a shift in thinking is necessary in order for social workers to use mechanisms such as culture and religion/spirituality to prevent, protect, and treat addiction. Instead of viewing service delivery from a place of "Canadian culture," which is far too diverse to use as a starting place to effectively design anti-oppressive programming, it is more useful to work at a local level, and use already-proven constructs such as family, spirituality, and cultural identity as they pertain to the culture of that community as starting places for program design.

The idea of a community development model in addiction work is not novel, and is already widely being used with Canada's First Nation, Metis, and Inuit people. Given that Canada has accepted approximately 230,000 immigrants a year since 1990, and the "mismatch between the culture of the health system and the needs of the members of ethno/racial/cultural communities," it is an idea that is gaining acceptance (CAMH, 2003, p. 5). Having more culturally appropriate services will help reduce the barriers that ethno-racial/cultural communities experience that prevent them from accessing services such as language and communication barriers, health messages that differ from their own beliefs and traditions, community-specific stigma associated with mental illness and addictions, and discrimination and mistrust of the health care system (CAMH, 2003).

For example, in order to avoid shame, Asian Canadians may want to avoid outside help, and if they see a loved one suffering from addiction "will try to lock the addict at home hopefully to keep him or her from accessing drugs" (Nguyen, personal communication 2014). A community-oriented approach may involve a more flexible treatment strategy such as a mobile withdrawal management team, made up intentionally of non-Asian people so that the family can avoid the shame associated with struggling with an addiction.

All of this leads to the conclusion that culture matters. It matters when thinking about how addiction manifests, and also how protective variables such as family, identity, and religion and spirituality act to protect against addiction. As social workers and other health care providers, having insight into the differences found within and among cultures is necessary to avoid further oppressing people in our attempts to treat and to prevent.

NOTES

1. See also Chapters 20, 21, and 22.

2. See Chapter 11.

REFERENCES

Agic, B., Mann, R., & Kobus-Mathews, M. (2011). Alcohol use in seven ethnic communities in Ontario: A qualitative investigation. *Drugs: Education, Prevention and Policy, 18*(2), 116–123.

Alaggia, R., & Csiernik, R. (2010). Coming home: Rediscovering the family in addiction treatment in Canada. In R. Csiernik & W.S. Rowe (Eds.), *Responding to the oppression of addiction: Canadian social work perspectives* (2nd ed., pp. 133–150). Toronto, ON: Canadian Scholars' Press.

Allen, T., & Lo, C. (2010). Religiosity, spirituality, and substance abuse. *Journal of Drug Issues, 40*(2), 433–459.

Anderson, T.L. (1998). A cultural-identity theory of drug abuse. *Sociology of Crime, Law, and Deviance, 1*, 233–262.

Asanin, J., & Wilson, K. (2008). "I spent nine years looking for a doctor": Exploring access to health care among immigrants in Mississauga, Ontario, Canada. *Social Science and Medicine, 66*(6), 1271–1283.

Bales, R. (1946). Cultural differences in rates of alcoholism. *Quarterly Journal of Studies on Alcohol, 35*(6), 480–499.

Behnke, A., MacDermid, S., Coltrane, S., Parke, R., Duffy, S., & Widaman, K. (2008). Family cohesion in the lives of Mexican American and European American parents. *Journal of Marriage and Family, 70*(4), 1045–1059.

Bennett, L., Campillo, C., Chandrashekar, C., & Gureje, O. (1988). Alcoholic beverage consumption in India, Mexico and Nigeria: A cross-cultural comparison. *Alcohol Health and Research World, 22*(4), 243–252.

Berry, J. (1999). Aboriginal cultural identity. *The Canadian Journal of Native Studies, 19*(1), 1–36.

Boykin, A., & Toms, F. (1985). Black child socialization: A conceptual framework. In H. McAdoo & J. McAdoo (Eds.), *Black children: Social, educational, and parental environments* (pp. 33–51). Thousand Oaks, CA: Sage Publications, Inc.

Brook, J., & Pahl, K. (2005). The protective role of ethnic and racial identity and aspects of an Africentric orientation against drug use among African American young adults. *The Journal of Genetic Psychology, 166*(3), 329–345.

Brook, J., Whiteman, M., Balka, E., Thetwin, P., & Gursen, M. (1998). Drug use among Puerto Ricans: Ethnic identity as a protective factor. *Hispanic Journal of Behavioral Sciences 20*(2), 241–254.

Burke, A., Van Olphen, J., Eliason, M., Howell, R., & Gonzalez, A. (2014). Re-examining religiosity as a protective factor: Comparing alcohol use by self-identified religious, spiritual, and secular college students. *Journal of Religion and Health, 53*(2), 305–316.

Butters, J. (2002). Family stressors and adolescent cannabis use: A pathway to problem use. *Journal of Adolescence, 25*(6), 645–654.

CAMH [Centre for Addiction and Mental Health]. (2003). *Health promotion programs on mental health/illness and addiction issues in ethno-racial/cultural communities: A literature review.* Retrieved from http://www.camh.ca/en/education/Documents/www.camh.net/education/ethnocult_healthpromores02.pdf

CAMH. (2004). *Culture counts: Best practices in community education in mental health and addiction with ethnoracial/ethnocultural communities: Phase one report.* Retrieved from http://www.camh.ca/en/education/Documents/www.camh.net/education/Resources_communities_organizations/culture_counts_jan05.pdf

Chitwood, D., Weiss, M., & Leukefeld, C. (2008). A systematic review of recent literature on religiosity and substance use. *Journal of Drug Issues, 38*(3), 653–688.

Clark, H., Shamblen, S., Ringwalt, C., & Hanley, S. (2012). Predicting high risk adolescents' substance use over time: The role of parental monitoring. *The Journal of Primary Prevention, 33*(2–3), 67–77.

Clark, T., Nguyen, A., Belgrave, F., & Tademy, R. (2011). Understanding the dimensions of parental influence on alcohol use and alcohol refusal efficacy among African American adolescents. *Social Work Research, 35*(2), 147–157.

Codina, G., Yin, Z., Zapata, J., & Katims, D. (2001). Ethnic identity, risk and protective factors related to substance use among Mexican American students. *Ethnic Studies Review, 24*(1–3), 85.

Cook, D., & Wiley, C. (2014). Psychotherapy with members of African-American churches and spiritual traditions. In P. Richards & A. Bergin (Eds.), *Handbook of psychotherapy and religious diversity* (2nd ed., pp. 373–397). Washington, DC: American Psychological Association.

Costigan, C., Koryzma, C., Hua, J., & Chance, L. (2010). Ethnic identity, achievement, and psychological adjustment: Examining risk and resilience among youth from immigrant Chinese families in Canada. *Cultural Diversity and Ethnic Minority Psychology, 16*(3), 264–278.

Csiernik, R. (2016). *Substance use and abuse: Everything matters* (2nd ed.). Toronto, ON: Canadian Scholars' Press.

Das, S., Balakrishnan, V., & Vasudevan, D. (2006). Alcohol: Its health and social impact in India. *Medicine and Society, 19*(2), 94–99.

Dean, J., & Wilson, J. (2010). "My health has improved because I always have everything I need here…": A qualitative exploration of health improvement and decline among immigrants. *Social Science and Medicine, 70*(8), 1219–1228.

Dillon, F., De La Rosa, M., Sastre, F., & Ibanez, G. (2013). Alcohol misuse among recent Latino immigrants: The protective role of pre-immigration familismo. *Psychology of Addictive Behaviors, 27*(4), 956–965.

Duncan, T., Tildesley, E., Duncan, S., & Hops, H. (1995). The consistency of family and peer influences on the development of substance use in adolescence. *Addiction, 90*(12), 1646–1660.

Dunn, J., & Dyck, I. (2000). Social determinants of health in Canada's immigrant population: Results from the National Population Health Survey. *Social Science and Medicine, 51*(11), 1573–1593.

Edwards, G., & Arif, A. (1980). *Drug problems in the sociocultural context: A basis for policy and programme planning.* Geneva, Switzerland: World Health Organization.

Ellison, C., & Levin, J. (1998). The religion–health connection: Evidence, theory, and future directions. *Health Education and Behavior, 25*(6), 700–720.

Falicov, C. (2013). *Latino families in therapy*. New York, NY: Guilford Publications.

Ford, J., & Hill, T. (2012). Religiosity and adolescent substance use: Evidence from the national survey on drug use and health. *Substance Use and Misuse, 47*(7), 787-798.

Gaines, S., Marelich, W., Bledsoe, K., Steers, W., Henderson, M., Granrose, C., Barajas, L., ... Page, M. (1997). Links between race/ethnicity and cultural values as mediated by racial/ethical identity and moderated by gender. *Journal of Personality and Social Psychology, 72*(6), 1460-1476.

Gale, J., Lenardson, J., Lambert, D., & Hartley, D. (2012). *Adolescent alcohol use: Do risk and protective factors explain rural-urban differences* (Working Paper #48). Portland, ME: University of Southern Maine, Muskie School of Public Service, Maine Rural Health Research Center.

Gallo, L., Penedo, F., Espinosa de los Monteros, K., & Arguelles, W. (2009). Resiliency in the face of disadvantage: Do Hispanic cultural characteristics protect health outcomes? *Journal of Personality, 77*(6), 1707-1746.

Gaziz, N., Connor, J., & Ho, R. (2010) Cultural identity and peer influence as predictors of substance use among culturally diverse Australian adolescents. *Journal of Early Adolescence, 30*(3), 245-368.

George, L., Ellison, G., & Larson, D. (2002). Explaining the relationships between religious involvement and health. *Psychological Inquiry, 13*(3), 190-200.

German, M., Gonzalez, N., & Dumka, L. (2009). Familism values as a protective factor for Mexican-origin adolescents exposed to deviant peers. *Journal of Early Adolescence, 29*(1), 16-42.

Gil, A., Vega, W., & Biafora, F. (1998). Temporal influences of family structure and family risk factors on drug use initiation in a multiethnic sample of adolescent boys. *Journal of Youth and Adolescence, 27*(3), 373-393.

Gil, A., Wagner, E., & Vega, W. (2000). Acculturation, familism, and alcohol use among Latino adolescent males. *Journal of Community Psychology, 28*(4), 443-458.

Gonzales, N., Knight, G., Morgan-Lopez, A., Saenz, D., & Sirolli, A. (2002). Acculturation and the mental health of Latino youths: An integration and critique of the literature. In J.M. Contreras, K.A. Kerns, & A.N. Neal-Barnett (Eds.), *Latino children and families in the United States: Current research and future directions* (pp. 45-74). Westport, CT: Praeger Publishers.

Gorsuch, R. (1995). Religious aspects of substance abuse and recovery. *Journal of Social Issues, 51*(1), 65-83.

Hardway, C., & Fuligni, A. (2006). Dimensions of family connectedness among adolescents with Mexican, Chinese, and European backgrounds. *Developmental Psychology, 42*(6), 1246-1258.

Herd, D., & Grube, J. (1996). Black identity and drinking in the US: A national study. *Addiction, 91*(6), 845-857.

Hinote, B., & Webber, G. (2012). Drinking toward manhood: Masculinity and alcohol in the former USSR. *Men and Masculinities, 15*(3), 292-310.

Hughes, D., Rodriguez, J., Smith, E., Johnson, D., Stevenson, H., & Spicer, P. (2006). Parents' ethnic-racial socialization practices: A review of research and directions for future study. *Developmental psychology, 42*(5), 747-770.

Issel, L. (2004). *Health program planning and evaluation: A practical, systematic approach for community health*. Burlington, MA: Jones & Bartlett Learning.

Jenks, C. (2004). *Culture* (2nd ed.). New York, NY: Routledge.

Kaplan, C., Nápoles-Springer, A., Stewart, S., & Pérez-Stable, E. (2001). Smoking acquisition among adolescents and young Latinas: The role of socioenvironmental and personal factors. *Addictive Behaviors, 26*(4), 531-550.

Kwok, S. (2010). The experiences of Chinese-Canadians in drug treatment programs. In R. Csiernik & W. Rowe (Eds.), *Responding to the oppression of addiction* (2nd ed., pp. 244–255). Toronto, ON: Canadian Scholars' Press.

Lac, A., Unger, J., Basanez, T., Ritt-Olson, A., Soto, D., & Baezconde-Garbaati, L. (2011). Marijuana use among Latino adolescents: Gender differences in protective familial factors. *Substance Use & Misuse, 46*(5), 644–655.

Lopez, B., Wang, W., Schwartz, S.J., Prado, G., Huang, S., Brown, C.H., … Szapocznik, J. (2009). School, family, and peer factors and their substance use in Hispanic adolescents. *Journal of Primary Prevention, 30*(6), 622–642.

Mäkinen, I., & Reitan, T. (2006). Continuity and change in Russian alcohol consumption from the tsars to transition. *Social History, 31*(2), 160–179.

Marsiglia, F., Kulis, S., Parsai, M., Villar, P., & Garcia, C. (2009). Cohesion and conflict: Family influences on adolescent alcohol use in immigrant Latino families. *Journal of Ethnicity in Substance Abuse, 8*(4), 400–412.

McBroom, J. (1994). Correlates of alcohol and marijuana use among junior high school students: Family, peers, school problems, and psychosocial concerns. *Youth and Society, 26*(1), 54–68.

Miller, L., Davies, M., & Greenwald, S. (2000). Religiosity and substance use and abuse among adolescents in the national co-morbidity survey. *Journal of the American Academy of Children and Adolescent Psychiatry, 39*(9), 1190–1197.

Moemeka, A. (1998). Communalism as a fundamental dimension of culture. *Journal of Communication, 48*(4), 118–141.

Moolasart, J., & Chirawatkul, S. (2012). Drinking culture in the Thai-Isaan context of northeast Thailand. *Southeast Asian Journal of Tropical Medicine and Public Health, 43*(3), 795–807.

Mulvaney-Day, N., Alegría, M., & Sribney, W. (2007). Social cohesion, social support and health among Latinos in the United States. *Social Science & Medicine, 64*(2), 477–495.

Nasim, A., Corona, R., Belgrave, F., Utsey, S., & Fallah, N. (2007). Cultural orientation as a protective factor against tobacco and marijuana smoking for African American young women. *Journal of Youth and Adolescence, 36*(4), 503–516.

National Centre for First Nations Governance. (n.d.). *Reclaiming our identity: Band membership, citizenship and the inherent right.* Retrieved from http://fngovernance.org/resources_docs/ReclaimingOurIdentity_Paper.pdf

National Collaborating Centre for Aboriginal Health. (2013). *Setting the context: An overview of Aboriginal health in Canada.* Retrieved from http://www.nccah-ccnsa.ca/Publications/Lists/Publications/Attachments/101/abororiginal_health_web.pdf

Neff, J., Prihoda, T., & Hoppe, S. (1991). "Machismo," self-esteem, education and high maximum drinking among Anglo, Black and Mexican-American male drinkers. *Journal of Studies on Alcohol and Drugs. 52*(5), 458–463.

Neumark, Y., Rahav, G., Teichman, M., & Hasin, D. (2001). Alcohol drinking patterns among Jewish and Arab men and women in Israel. *Journal of Studies on Alcohol and Drugs, 62*(4), 443–447.

Pargament, K.I. (1997). *The psychology of religion and coping: Theory, research, practice.* New York, NY: The Guilford Press.

Persike, M., & Seiffge-Krenke, I. (2012). Competence in coping with stress in adolescents from three regions of the world. *Journal of Youth and Adolescence, 41*(7), 863–879.

Ramirez, J., Crano, W., Quist, R., Burgoon, M., Alvaro, E., & Grandpre, J. (2004). Acculturation, familism, parental monitoring, and knowledge as predictors of marijuana and inhalant use in adolescents. *Psychology of Addictive Behaviors, 18*(1), 3–11.

Sieving, R., Perry, C., & Williams, C. (2000). Do friendships change behaviors, or do behaviors change friendships? Examining paths of influence in young adolescents' alcohol use. *Journal of Adolescent Health, 26*(1), 26–35.

Simons-Morton, B., & Chen, R. (2005). Latent growth curve analyses of parent influences on drinking progression among early adolescents. *Journal of Studies on Alcohol, 66*(1), 5–13.

Smith, C. (2003). Religious participation and network closure among American adolescents. *Journal for the Scientific Study of Religion, 42*(2), 259–267.

Statistics Canada. (2011). *Immigration and ethnocultural diversity in Canada*. Retrieved from https://www12.statcan.gc.ca/nhs-enm/2011/as-sa/99-010-x/99-010-x2011001-eng.cfm

Substance Abuse and Mental Health Service Administration. (2008). *The 2007 national survey on drug use and health: Public use file codebook*. Rockville, MD: Office of Applied Studies.

Substance Abuse and Mental Health Service Administration. (2010). Marijuana use in lifetime, past year, and past month among persons aged 12 to 17, by demographic characteristics: Percentages, 2007 and 2008. Retrieved from http://www.oas.samhsa.gov/NSDUH/2k8NSDUH/tabs/Sect1peTabs1to46.htm#Tab1.25B

Taylor, R. (1988). Structural determinants of religious participation among Black Americans. *Review of Religious Research, 30*(2), 114–125.

Telzer, E., Gonzales, N., & Fuligni, A. (2014). Family obligation values and family assistance behaviors: Protective and risk factors for adolescent substance use. *Journal of Youth and Adolescence, 43*(2), 270–283.

Unger, J., Ritt-Olson, A., Teran, L., Huang, T., Hoffman, B., & Palmer, P. (2002). Cultural values and substance use in a multiethnic sample of California adolescents. *Addiction Research and Theory, 10*(3), 257–279. Wallace, J., Brown, T., Bachman, J., & Laveist, T. (2003). The influence of race and religion on abstinence from alcohol, cigarettes and marijuana among adolescents. *Journal of Studies on Alcohol, 64*(6), 843–848.

Wallace, J., & Forman, T. (1998). Religion's role in promoting health and reducing risk among American youth. *Health Education & Behavior, 25*(6), 721–741.

Waxman, M., & Csiernik, R. (2010). *Culture as prevention: A case study of urban Canadian Jewish male students*. In R. Csiernik & W. Rowe (Eds.), *Responding to the oppression of addiction* (2nd ed., pp. 47–59). Toronto, ON: Canadian Scholars' Press.

Welch, M., Tittle, C., & Grasmick, H. (2006). Christian religiosity, self-control and social conformity. *Social Forces, 84*(3), 1605–1623.

Whitehead, P., & Harvey, C. (1974). Explaining alcoholism: An empirical test and reformulation. *Journal of Health and Social Behaviour, 15*(1), 57–64.

Wills, T., Yeager, A., & Sandy, A. (2003). Buffering the effect of religiosity for adolescent substance abuse. *Psychology of Addictive Behaviors, 17*(1), 24–31.

PART 2

PROGRAMS

CHAPTER 5

Coming Home: Rediscovering the Family in Addiction Treatment in Canada

Ramona Alaggia and Rick Csiernik

Introduction

After a history of relative neglect, an increasing amount of research has been conducted upon family-based approaches in addiction treatment and this work has uniformly demonstrated that family involvement is strongly indicated for increasing the effect-iveness of treatment and relapse prevention (Austin, MacGowan, & Wagner, 2005; Becker & Curry, 2008; French, 1987; Merikangas, Dierker, & Fenton, 1998; Moore, 2005; O'Farrell & Fals-Stewart, 2000; O'Farrell, Murphy, Alter, & Fals-Stewart, 2008). Since the first edition of this book in 2003 there has been substantive growth in the practice and research literature showing the development of an evidence base for family systems and couple therapy in addiction treatment. Views have continued to evolve and the field has advanced in its thinking regarding how the family should be involved in the treatment and recovery of those with addiction issues, the impact of the person with an addiction's behaviour on family dynamics, and the mutually influencing relationships within the family. A shift in the addiction field has occurred where "those who work in the field of drug treatment and prevention increasingly consider the family to be a key resource in harm avoidance and treatment effectiveness strategies" (Madill Parker Research & Consulting, 2006, p. 7). This shift has resulted in programming that is slowly beginning to include a family focus. Despite this, situations such as in the United Kingdom where less than 1% of the drug treatment budget is spent supporting the families of those using psychoactive drugs (Addaction, 2009) remain the norm.

The addiction field has historically viewed and approached the role of the family in treatment and recovery with mixed responses that have varied depending upon the theoretical orientation of specific services, and according to the developmental stage of the person with an addiction at the time the individual seeks or is referred for help. The field has used biopsychosocial-ecological explanatory frameworks for understanding and developing interventions, with individual programs usually favouring one of these aspects in their delivery of services. The family has traditionally been considered to the degree that each individual program recognizes the value of the family's involvement in ongoing treatment, which prior to this century was minimal.

The term *alcoholic* did not enter our vocabulary until introduced by Swedish public health physician Magnus Huss in 1849 (Csiernik, 2016). Counselling individuals with alcohol and other drug-related problems is a relatively new phenomenon with a contemporary history dating back only to 1935. Historically, alcohol and drug abuse intervention has appropriately placed the individual at the centre of treatment as the primary client. However, this positioning has included purposefully isolating the drug user from his or her family unit. Until recently, families, when considered at all, have at best been viewed as secondary systems (French, 1987; Kaufman & Kaufman, 1979; Nichols & Schwartz, 2007). It should be noted though that the mutual aid program Alcoholics Anonymous (AA) early in its development established a parallel program—Al-Anon—for family members, though it was primarily attended by wives while their husbands went to AA meetings (Timko, Young, & Moos, 2012). This occurred in recognition of the impact of the behaviour of the person with an addiction upon family functioning, the value of family involvement in recovery, and to help ameliorate contributing factors to relapse within the family.

Alcohol and other substances of abuse[1] have a powerful effect on family relations and are recognized as a significant family stressor. By the time most individuals who are abusing psychoactive substances are referred to treatment, their drug use has touched not only themselves but also their entire family and social structure. Thus, one individual's behaviour and addiction can reach out to his or her partner, the couple's children, and the user's parents and siblings (Campbell, Masters, & Johnson, 1998; Cowley & Godon, 1995; Fleming et al., 1998; Hall, Henggeler, Ferreira, & East, 1992; O'Farrell, 1991; Taylor, Toner, Templeton, & Velleman, 2008; Usher, Jackson, & O'Brien, 2007). This is not surprising as the family is still the primary biological, economic, social, legal, and historical unit of our society. The family provides us with four cornerstones of living: our initial self worth, how to communicate, the rules of living, and our links with society. Research indicates that each person with an addiction seriously influences the lives of four to six other people (Abbott, 2000). Grant's (2000) study indicated that one in four children in the United States lives in a family that has a history of alcohol abuse, while the *Sydney Morning Herald* reported on October 21, 2008, that one-third of Australian families were "blighted" by drinking (Stark, 2008). The negative consequences of alcohol abuse that children in these families face range from economic hardship to violence to a greater propensity for alcohol or other drug abuse themselves.

Children of alcoholics are at greater risk for alcohol dependence and other drug abuse than are children of a non-alcohol-abusing parent, and they also consistently score lower in tests of cognitive verbal abilities. This attribute is correlated with impeded school performance, poorer peer relationships, and the inability to develop and sustain intimate relationships, including having lower levels of trust. A Canadian study found that children exposed to parental addiction have 69% greater odds of developing depression in adulthood compared to their peers with non-addicted parents. The relationship between parental addictions and depression does not vary by gender. These findings further underscore the intergenerational consequences of addiction. (Fuller-Thomson et al., 2013). Simply put, children raised in families where at least one parent is abusing drugs, including alcohol, have substantially different life experiences than do their peers (Addaction, 2009; Bijttebier, Goethals, & Ansoms, 2006; Jones & Houts, 1992; Nurco & Lerner, 1996). Finally, abusive use of substances may in turn lead to separation and divorce, and is strongly correlated with violence in the family (Brown, Werk, Caplan, & Seraganian, 2010).

Two significant areas that have received considerable attention in regards to the family have been in adolescent substance abuse treatment and in marital therapy. The role of families in education, prevention, and treatment has been seen as significant in understanding adolescent drug misuse and pivotal in subsequent treatment involvement. There continues to be much written on family involvement in adolescent treatment for substance abuse (Austin, MacGowan, & Wagner, 2005; Becker & Curry, 2008; Hendriks, van der Schee, & Blanken, 2011; Szapocznik, Zarate, Duff, & Muir, 2013; Rigter et al., 2013), and some significant reviews have identified an evidence base for the use of specific family-based treatments, which include brief strategic family therapy (BSFT) (Briones, Robbins, & Szapocznik, 2008; Austin, MacGowan, & Wagner, 2005; Robbins & Szapocznik, 2000) and multidimensional family therapy (MDFT) (Liddle et al., 2001; Szapocznik, Zarate, Duff, & Muir, 2013).

Family-based treatments for adults with addiction issues have also advanced in the field of marital family therapy where significant research has been conducted (Fletcher, 2013). Behavioural couples therapy (BCT) (O'Farrell & Clements, 2012; Shadish & Baldwin, 2005) and behavioural marital therapy (BMT) have gained a reputation as effective treatment interventions (Barber & Gilbertson, 1996; Morgenstern & McKay, 2007; O'Farrell & Fals-Stewart, 2000; O'Farrell, Murphy, Alter, & Fals-Stewart, 2008). In Fletcher's (2013) systematic review of 18 scientific studies, the author states that "BCT is arguably the relational approach to treating substance dependence most based on evidence." (p. 344). This model showed effectiveness with both heterosexual and same-sex couples by enhancing relationship satisfaction and reducing substance reliance.

Contextualizing Family Treatment and Addiction Counselling

Once substance abuse problems have developed and become incorporated into a family's functioning, the nature of family homeostasis can inadvertently maintain the dysfunctional behaviour without specialist intervention. Thus, if the individual seeks treatment and the substance abuse ceases, everyone within the nuclear family, and often members of the extended family, may become vulnerable to the unbalanced family system. This disequilibrium, created by the positive act of addiction treatment, can make the family seem and feel dysfunctional as family members no longer know how to act or behave with the newly sober person as part of their system. The family system may have become organized around behaviour exhibited by the person with an addiction, such as keeping secrets, coercive behaviour, and covert communication, for a significant period of time. One outcome that can occur to alleviate this family uneasiness is for the family to attempt to return to the previous homeostatic or steady state. This return to the status quo can inadvertently result in eroding treatment gains and impeding the ongoing recovery process. If this unbalancing is not dealt with effectively with early family intervention, long-term problems can set in and risk for lapse and relapse increases. Thus, applying a family systems framework enables social workers to recognize and acknowledge that problems both influence and are influenced by the family.

Historically, family treatment and addiction counselling have been compartmentalized, from a paradigmatic perspective and in terms of service provision. Berg and Reuss (1998) observed that even amongst family therapists there was a tradition of systems thinking in which family members are believed to be "afraid of the positive changes the client is making and are prone to 'sabotage' the effort of recovery" (p. 102). Family therapy models are driven by systems theory, which maintains that the whole is greater than and different from the sum of its parts, and that change in one part of the system can produce change in other parts (Andreae, 1996; Payne, 2014). This is a departure from psychodynamic/psychopathological and group approaches typically used in treating the individual for substance abuse wherein the individual is treated in isolation from his or her family. In addition, family therapy is more commonly practiced in agencies servicing children and where children are referred for problems related to a parental substance abuse problem, but not necessarily identified as such, or within the adolescents themselves. In many of these cases, the substance abuse problems are still in the secrecy or pre-contemplative phase of family functioning and have not been disclosed to professionals. On the other hand, addiction interventions aimed at individuals are delivered under the auspices of adult services where family interventions are not fully, if at all, integrated.

Treatment for addiction is not a straightforward proposition. There are numerous potential pathways for identification that lead to referral for assessment, including:

- Health care providers for physical health–related issues arising from addiction
- Child protection services due to child maltreatment/neglect concerns
- Legal channels, police or courts, after-legal intervention for driving under the influence, assault charges such as a domestic violence incident, public disruption, or custody and access disputes
- Children's mental health services for child emotional or behavioural problems due to parental addiction

- Family support, family intervention, or pressure from family members
- Self-referral.

Identification and assessment will be either voluntary or mandated depending on how the addiction is identified. This can result in a referral to an outpatient clinic with weekly counselling, or a short-term inpatient program (21–35 days), or a longer-term rehabilitation centre, where treatment may take several months to a year. In some cases an immediate detoxification process might also be necessary, requiring attendance at a withdrawal management centre which would last three to ten days before commencement of formal treatment.

Often, unfortunately, if a referral to an addiction assessment program is not made right away, a non-specialist is solicited for the assessment and this usually leads to under or misdiagnosing serious problems, and making an inappropriate or no referral unless the generalist has had some training in addiction assessment and treatment. Further, most publically funded addiction treatment systems typically have extensive waiting lists, even for withdrawal management. Clients with extended health care plans or incomes that can afford private care can access the increasing number of fee-for-service clinics, though there remains no regulatory body overseeing this sector and thus no assurance of the quality of care that is provided. As well, an issue with both the public and private sector is there is often little attention on the family system in the addiction treatment process.

Treatment approaches for adults can generally be summarized into programs that deal first with the addicted person as an individual, and second indirectly with the family as a whole. Others are parent programs with mostly mothers that sometimes include children but rarely partners. Yet other programs more fully integrate a family support component. It is being recognized that supportive people in a person's life, such as family of origin and extended family, can play pivotal roles with a recovering family member. Often it is a family member who has initiated a referral or has precipitated someone to refer themselves or connect with a referral agent. Willing family members are integral in providing information during the completion of a comprehensive biopsychosocial assessment, especially as they are often needed supports throughout the recovery process. Supportive partners, extended family members, or concerned significant others (CSO) can play a role in supporting persons during recovery. Current partners, extended family members, close friends, and CSOs need to be aware of the differences between outpatient care and more intensive residential programming. They need to be aware that their participation in family programming, when it is available, is crucial for the person with an addiction's successful recovery. The inclusion of family programming enhances the effectiveness of treatment as it more fully addresses the holistic nature of addiction.

Compounding this, of the family programs that have been developed only a few have been empirically tested and are very different in their philosophy and approach. The community reinforcement and family training (CRAFT) model, Al-Anon/Nar-Anon for family members, and the Johnson Institute intervention have each been examined for treatment engagement, though unfortunately not for treatment effectiveness. CRAFT is an engagement model designed for treatment-resistant clients with alcohol addiction (Meyers, Villanueva, & Smith, 2005). It is family systems focused and makes use of family members or CSOs to encourage the person with the addiction into treatment. It differs from Al-Anon and Nar-Anon in that it is a formal treatment approach and not a mutual aid program. Al-Anon and Nar-Anon are peer-led voluntary meetings where participants are encouraged to demonstrate loving detachment from their family member who is labelled an alcoholic or addict. Family members are taught that they are powerless over the addict. The locus of change is with the person with the addiction while family members provide a conducive environment. The program provided by Al-Anon and Nar-Anon view the behaviour change lying with the person with the addiction and that family members need to practice self-care and resist in engaging in co-dependent and/or enabling behaviours. AA was the first support for those with addiction issues while Al-Anon was the first for family members. Their contribution to the addiction field has been invaluable; however, these programs have stayed virtually unchanged over the decades due to their early success.

In further contrast is the Johnson Institute intervention model, which is a professional model and has family members/CSOs take a highly active role in staging an intervention in a confrontation with the person with the addiction to convince them to enter treatment. Like AA, this has arisen out of the disease model philosophy of addiction and is neither evidence-informed nor founded in a holistic biopsychosocial orientation. In fact, Clark (2012) claims that as clinical psychology in the United States was actively questioning the utility of treating maladjusted individuals for the sake of preserving the nuclear family, formal addiction intervention was being popularized by the producers of popular media doing exactly that, using the nuclear family as a source of drama, countering empirically supported findings.

CRAFT is a treatment package that requires specialized training of therapists and close supervision. It operates on behavioural theory broadly defining CSOs as intimate partners, extended family, close friends, and significant others who act as motivators combined with environmental contingencies to create the conditions for promoting the substance abusing individual to enter treatment (Roozen, de Waart, & van der Kroft, 2010). Al-Anon and Nar-Anon are based on the 12-step recovery model. The person with the addiction attends regular AA/NA support meetings and has a sponsor, while family members attend separate meetings for their support as CSOs. These family supports were not intended to act as motivators for treatment engagement of the family member with the addiction. The Johnson intervention is a rigidly orchestrated confrontation staged as a meeting of family, relatives, and close friends who urge the person with the addiction to seek treatment. Blunt testimonials are given by caring support people as to the direct personal harm that has been done to them and also to the addict due to their substance abuse. In a carefully staged intervention, arrangements to take their loved one to a facility have been pre-planned so that this can occur almost immediately. This intervention is used in cases of highly treatment-resistant people and should only be undertaken by a specialist who is trained in this procedure (Johnson, 2009).

The Family and Addiction Programming

Contemporary work with the family potentially moves us away from a therapeutic model focused exclusively upon individual pathology and acknowledges the need for concurrent individual intervention with family members. On the micro level of addiction treatment there are three potential targets. The primary target remains, and needs to remain, the individual with the substance abuse issue. The second level of intervention is the substance user as located within his or her family unit. Third, it is also feasible, valuable, and necessary to work with individual non-abusing members of the family unit, just as we intervene with individual substance abusers. The addiction field has become quite adept at working with people who abuse substances. This same approach and expertise has not, however, been used extensively or consistently in Canada with members of the whole family unit whose lives have been directly and indirectly altered by the abuse of substances and the accompanying behaviours. Family work in addiction varies in intensity depending upon what the mandate of the treatment program is. The four primary approaches (Boudreau, 1997) are:

1. Family Orientation: this involves informing family members about the rehabilitation program upon which the identified client is embarking. It is used to enlist family support in the client's treatment.
2. Family Education: this approach is used to inform family members about family-relation issues and how they may be relevant to substance abuse and the substance abuser.
3. Family Counselling: this is employed to bring about the resolution of problems identified by family members as related to the substance abuse.
4. Family Therapy: this method is employed to bring about significant and permanent changes to intractable areas of systemic family dysfunction related to the substance abuse.

Family treatment has a variety of interpretations, though in general using this approach emphasizes the process of interaction, communication, and conflict resolution within the family, rather than focusing exclusively upon the member who is substance dependent. Family treatment typically evolves around the following interactional issues:

- all couples and families have problems, but substance abuse prevents resolution of these problems and creates new and more complex ones;
- no individual can force another to change;
- personal change comes through accepting responsibility for one's own behaviour;

- all members of the family are involved in the problem and all have a responsibility to find some form of resolution;
- removal of drugs and/or alcohol from the family system represents a necessary beginning in the recovery process, yet is incomplete in itself; and
- dysfunctional communication and ineffective conflict resolution in the family inadvertently maintains substance abuse problems and substance-abusing behaviour.

Family intervention is by no means a straightforward activity. The underlying family structure is the primary concern of therapists. When abstinence/sobriety is achieved in a family system that has been organized around addiction behaviours, a vulnerable period in family functioning is to be expected. While collective relief may be an initial response, this vulnerable period is also marked by chaos, stress, and uncertainty. Notwithstanding these complex dynamics, the family is best recognized as an important source of support and integral to maintaining gains in the recovery process. After all, the person with an addiction will return to and continue to be a member of their family and everyone involved should be prepared for the recovering person's re-entry into the family.

Case Example

Jim (34) recently returned from a 30-day treatment program for alcohol abuse. His marriage had dissolved over the past year and he was unemployed. He had no choice but to return to live temporarily with his father. Jim's father, a heavy drinker himself, chose not to be involved in Jim's aftercare and tended to minimize the extent of Jim's alcohol abuse. He did not see the value of Jim attending his AA meetings regularly. He viewed AA as "cult-like." Jim relapsed within 26 days.

In Jim's case, stressors around his impending divorce, diminished financial status, and his children refusing to visit him began to erode his self-confidence. His father was invited for psychoeducational family sessions during Jim's treatment stay and to attend Al-Anon after his discharge, both of which he declined to participate in. Clearly, Jim returned to an environment that could not support his sobriety and eventually he returned to using alcohol as a means of dealing with the stressors in his life.

There are a variety of methods of family counselling, with valid theoretical foundations. The most significant approaches historically have been structural, strategic, multigenerational, and behavioural (Boudreau, 1997; Bowen, 1991; Haley, 1982; O'Farrell & Fals-Stewart, 2000; Robbins & Szapocznik, 2000; Stanton, Todd, & Associates, 1982). Recently, a new era of family therapy models have been ushered in. Rooted in social constructionism and focusing upon family strengths, these conceptualizations attempt to bridge the divisions between addiction treatment for the individual and family treatment for the entire system (Berg & Reuss, 1998; Diamond, 2000; O'Farrell & Fals-Stewart, 2000). Brief, solution-focused, and cognitive-behavioural therapies are contemporary models that can be tailored to families dealing with addiction issues and that have demonstrated effectiveness (Barber & Gilbertson, 1996; Berg & Reuss, 1998; Diamond, 2000; Hendriks, van der Schee, & Blanken, 2011; O'Farrell, Murphy, Alter, & Fals-Stewart, 2008; Rigter et al., 2013; Szapocznik, Zarate, Duff, & Muir, 2013). The common thread underpinning each approach is that the family is treated as a whole system and the member with the substance abuse problem is not viewed in isolation. However, when the substance abuser chooses not to enter treatment or is unable to complete a rehabilitation program, it remains appropriate and prudent to provide assistance to the other members of the family. The following case example illustrates how behavioural-cognitive and multidimensional systems models aid working with adolescents who abuse substances.

Case Example

Jordan (16) and his family were referred to a children's mental health service due to Jordan's increasing marijuana use. His parents were unclear whether this was typical adolescent experimenting or if something more serious was manifesting. Initially Jordan was seen alone for individual counselling to be evaluated for depression. He soon dropped out of the counselling because he did not view himself as depressed. His parents later re-contacted the agency because he had become isolated from his peers and had stopped going to school. Their complaints were that he had become lethargic, belligerent, and was caught "smoking up" in their home and stealing money from them. A family therapist was assigned and soon assessed that they were dealing with a more serious substance abuse issue. Initially Jordan refused to attend sessions, however his parents continued with their therapy. Eventually they were able to convince Jordan to be assessed for his substance use, and he was subsequently referred to an adolescent group with a harm reduction focus. Jordan's parents concurrently attended a group for parents of teens dealing with addiction issues, with occasional family sessions to contract for basic house expectations, including abstinence, attending school or work, and respecting others' property.

In Jordan's case, the therapist used:

- Effective joining interventions to stress family strengths: Jordan's parents were commended for identifying the problems early and engaging in therapy before Jordan was ready, and Jordan was later praised for trying out the teens group.

- Diagnosis: The therapist and parents worked together to encourage Jordan to participate in a thorough substance abuse assessment and Jordan joined a group with other teens like him in an open and non-judgemental environment.
- Restructuring: Family contracting put the parents in a clear parental position to set limits without becoming punitive.

As well, other important systems in the family were enlisted, such as school involvement and accessing community resources, to promote prosocial activities.

Brief, solution-focused approaches view the family as a resource for helping the member with the dependency issues maintain positive changes. Therapists who employ brief, solution-focused approaches also encourage a parallel process for family members, and may, when it is an appropriate match, support them in attending Al-Anon and Al-Ateen, while embarking on family work for the entire family system. This model is one of the few family therapy approaches that has also adapted to a harm reduction approach versus taking an abstinence-only position (Berg & Reuss, 1998; Miller & Berg, 1996).

Case Example

Meena, 28, was hospitalized for a cocaine overdose, which resulted in a 90-day stay in an inpatient treatment centre for women. Meena and her husband had "dabbled" in cocaine use at parties, but while her husband could walk away from it, Meena developed a serious addiction and also became dependent on alcohol. Upon discharge, Meena was relieved to be freed from her two addictions but was apprehensive about maintaining a sober lifestyle. Meena and her husband started couples' counselling focused upon striking a sobriety contract, which entailed his abstinence as well as hers, with regular sessions to maintain positive couple communication.

Meena and her husband received a course of behavioural couples treatment where one person has acknowledged an addiction. This course of treatment included them mutually giving up friends who were using drugs and staying away from risky environments. Together they embarked on this journey, with Meena attending Women for Sobriety meetings as her ongoing relapse prevention.

Another contemporary example is that of narrative family therapy, which emphasizes immediately beginning family treatment. While the family member with the substance abuse problem is being treated individually either on an inpatient or outpatient basis, the remaining family is viewed as worthy of treatment (Diamond, 2000). Main objectives of this approach are to assist the family in uncovering the meaning and impact of the addiction for each member, exploring the history of addiction through the family genogram, and avoiding blaming interactions while still having the member with the addiction take responsibility. In meeting these objectives, the person who is drug and/or alcohol dependent is encouraged to seek appropriate treatment to control or completely stop the destructive behaviours. Those with the addiction issue are expected to honour their commitment to deal honestly with their substance-abusing behaviour (see also Chapter 9).

These models also emphasize identifying and capitalizing on family strengths. For example, while acknowledging the serious, wide-ranging negative effects of substance abuse, the proponents of these models maintain that many children coming from households where addiction is an issue demonstrate great resilience. They are viewed as having the potential to overcome the legacies of ongoing addiction and to become fully functioning adults (Berg & Reuss, 1998; Diamond, 2000). Children of alcoholics are not automatically presumed to go on to repeat traumatic family dynamics with their own children. This notion is particularly important in multigenerational family work. Unfortunately, because brief, solution-focused, and narrative family therapies are in formative stages of development, there is minimal research evaluating their long-term effectiveness.

Mutual Aid/Self-Help Initiatives

The most prominent mutual aid/self-help initiative in the addiction field derives from the 12 steps conceived by the early members of Alcoholics Anonymous over 80 years ago (Alcoholics Anonymous, 2005). The importance of 12-step programs to addiction counselling has been documented in detail (Csiernik, 2000, 2002). Many of the principles adapted from 12-step programs correspond with the principles of a family systems approach, including helping family members differentiate from each other and break out of dysfunctional patterns (Nichols & Schwartz, 2007).

Al-Anon is a 12-step mutual aid program initiated by Lois Wilson, the wife of the founder of AA, to assist those living with an alcohol abuser, and from it has arisen several related programs: Al-Ateen, Adult Children of Alcoholics (ACoA), and Nar-Anon. Unfortunately, there has been minimal research conducted as to the value of Al-Anon despite the fact that there are over 14,000 meetings every week throughout the United States and Canada (Al-Anon, 2015), though what has been published has overall been supportive of this form of self-help activity (Fernandez, Begley, & Marlatt, 2006). Friedemann (1996) compared the family functioning of 39 family members who participated in Al-Anon while their partner received treatment, to the family functioning of a group of 21 controls. Members of the control group all had their partners enrolled in an inpatient program receiving rehabilitation services; however, the family members received no formal or informal support. One month after treatment was completed family members attending Al-Anon had a higher rating of family effectiveness than did members of the control group. Three months after treatment was completed 39% of subjects who had a family member attending Al-Anon had relapsed compared with 61% of those in the control group. Involvement with Al-Anon has been shown to enhance social support (Lander, Howsare, & Byrne, 2013; Timko, Young, & Moos, 2012), coping skills (Rychtarik, Carstensen, Alford, & Schlundt, 1988), quality of life (Timko et al., 2013) and marital adjustment (Keinz, Schwartz, Trench, & Houlihan, 1995; Timko et al., 2014) while reducing personal problems (Barber & Gilbertson, 1996; Dittrich & Trapold, 1984). Attendance at Al-Anon by one family member does not necessarily correlate with improvements in the alcohol abuser (Barber & Gilbertson, 1996; Miller, Meyers, & Tonigan, 1999), however, Miller, Meyers, and Tonigan (1999) also report that those attending Al-Anon meetings benefitted from this form of mutual aid regardless of the amount of improvement by the substance abuser. Documented benefits by those who attended Al-Anon meetings included reductions in depression, anger, and family conflict as well as improvements in family cohesion. Likewise, attendance at meetings of Adult Children of Alcoholics has been reported to increase the self-esteem of regular attendants (Kingree, 2000).

In addition, addiction treatment has borrowed from family counselling in another significant manner. The typology of Adult Children of Alcoholics, proposed by Wegscheider-Cruse in 1985, of hero, scapegoat, lost child, and mascot was adapted from the ideas of family roles proposed earlier by Virginia Satir (1972).

Research Findings

The idea of working with families in addiction has substantive empirical support, particularly in the areas of engagement and relapse reduction. Over three decades ago Stanton, Todd, and Associates (1982) published their landmark article on the value of family counselling with individuals addicted to heroin. In one of the most methodologically sound studies involving family counselling, this group of researchers focused upon structural-strategic family therapy. They demonstrated, in a controlled experiment, how family counselling led to marked improvement over non-family treatments on several drug-related outcome measures, both at the termination of treatment and at follow-up intervals. The specific importance of this study lies in the fact that individuals addicted to heroin have among the greatest rate of relapse, and yet family involvement was able to make a significant impact upon lapsing and relapsing events as well as on overall family functioning.

Recent research in the area of family-based interventions has demonstrated positive advancements in families with adolescents and in couples counselling. Evidence-based interventions are being identified in approaches that use cognitive-behavioural theory, ecological theory, developmental theory, and family systems theory as a framework for intervening with couples and families dealing with addiction issues. In recent reviews of the research literature (Austin, Macgowan, & Wagner, 2005; Becker & Curry, 2008; Morgenstern & McKay, 2007), behavioural couples treatment (BCT), multidimensional family therapy (MDFT), and brief strategic family therapy (BSFT) have all been identified as being evidence-based and are recommended for use with couples and adolescents. However, even though these findings have demonstrated effectiveness they still need to be interpreted with caution due to the use of small samples and the lack of follow-up studies.

In behavioural couples treatment (BCT), the couple starts sessions directly after the partner with the addiction ceases use of substances. A sobriety contract is struck where persons with an addiction commit to and follow through on sobriety on a daily basis, and their partners affirm and praise their abstinence. This behavioural contract is followed carefully while at the same time sessions focus upon decreasing negative communication patterns that are associated with lapse and relapse. Controlled studies on BCT have found increased abstinence and relationship satisfaction, as well as decreased domestic violence. The results of these most recent studies (Austin, et al 2005; Becker & Curry, 2008; Morgenstern & McKay, 2007), support Edwards and Steinglass' (1995) earlier review of the literature, a meta-analysis of 21 studies of family-involved treatment for alcoholism. They identified that two prominent factors associated with successful outcomes for family treatment were investment in the relationship and perceived support from the partner for abstinence. This finding brought empirical support to the long-held belief by certain sectors of the addiction field that family treatment was an effective support intervention.

The most recent systematic review of couple therapy treatments for substance use disorders examined 18 studies of behavioural couples therapy (BCT) (O'Farrell & Clements, 2012); alcohol behaviour couple therapy (ABCT), a variation of BCT (Epstein & McCrady, 1998); and one study of brief couple therapy/systemic couple therapy. The results of the review showed BCT to be the most effective in improving couple communication, thus contributing positively to relapse prevention (Fletcher, 2013). As indicated in earlier studies, BCT remains the preferred evidence-informed model that involves the person with the addiction and their partner actively in treatment. It is a very specific model with a detailed protocol involving contracting for sobriety and recovery to rebuild trust within the couple unit and improve communication to lower the relapse occurrences (O'Farell & Clements, 2012; O'Farrell & Schein, 2011).

In use with adolescents, multidimensional family therapy (MDFT) operates at multiple domains of functioning and intervenes with youth, their family, and the youth's support network. Based upon family systems theory, developmental psychology, ecosystems theory, and resilience theory, the treatment is provided on an outpatient basis over the length of time needed by the youth and family. MDFT has shown associations with statistically significant decreases in youth drug use. Brief strategic family therapy (BSFT) is a time-limited intervention composed of joining, diagnosis, and restructuring (Robbins & Szapocznik, 2000; Szapocznik, Zarate, Duff, & Muir, 2013). This approach is based upon child development and family systems principles to meet the diverse needs of families. Over a brief period of time, typically 10 to 12 sessions, the family is seen and interactions are focused upon addressing problematic adolescent behaviours. The intervention can be applied conjointly and with whichever caregiver is available. Community and neighbourhood resources are identified and employed in a comprehensive treatment plan. Clinical trials of BSFT using comparison treatments have shown significant levels of reduction in drug use among adolescents.

Several systematic reviews have also found that couples therapy is superior to individual counselling and peer-group therapy (Cottrell & Boston, 2002; Fletcher, 2013; Powers, Vedel, & Emmelkamp, 2008; Stanton & Shadish, 1997). Family counselling was also demonstrated to be an effective mechanism in dealing with adolescent drug users by Lewis, Piercy, Sprenkle and Trepper (1990) and by Joanning, Quinn, Thomas, and Mullen (1992). Pidock and Fischer (1998) in a study of 928 university students found that students with parents in recovery from addiction had less problematic behaviours than those students whose parents were still using. This included decreased substance abuse and dependency and fewer eating disorders.

Roozen and colleagues (2010), in a systematic review, analyzed studies comparing three approaches for treatment engagement of adults with addiction issues and found community reinforcement and family training (CRAFT) to be significantly more effective than Al-Anon/Nar-Anon or the Johnson Institute intervention; CRAFT was also assessed to be more effective in treatment engagement of the addicted person by Miller, Meyers, and Tonigan (1999). According to the review findings CRAFT showed significant improvement of CSO functioning in anger, depression, family cohesion, and relation satisfaction. Improvements were irrespective of interpersonal engagement (Roozen, de Waart, & van der Kroft, 2010). However, only a meagre four studies met the inclusion criteria for quality and some of the sample sizes were small. Questions are also raised by the review authors about the suitability of collapsing some programs for alcohol addiction with programs for drug addiction in two of the studies. Clearly more studies are needed in order to establish a strong evidence base for any of these approaches.

However, of these models that attempt to be inclusive in their approaches to treating the family as a whole, outcome research is still needed. Empirical studies of brief, solution-focused models have targeted individual treatment for addictions and are poorly designed, while narrative approaches have been limited to single-case evaluations and anecdotal accounts (Diamond, 2000; Gingerich & Eisenhart, 2000). While promising, these approaches need investigative attention to determine their effectiveness for families dealing with issues of substance abuse. Additionally, the scientific literature almost exclusively examines how the family can support the member who is dealing with substance abuse. As such, little formal research has been conducted on the needs of non-alcohol- or non-drug-abusing family members, either in conjunction with or independent of the substance abuse treatment intervention for the individual.

Conclusion

The common definition of neglect is a lack of attention. Indeed, historically there has been a lack of attention paid to both the theory and practice of family treatment in addiction in Canada. The Canadian addiction field continues to need to pay attention to the emerging evidence that treatment of substance abuse, for both adults and adolescents, clearly shows improved outcomes when the entire family is engaged. This neglect of family treatment appears to be the result of a "silo" structure often produced in Canadian service-delivery systems due to idiosyncratic funding arrangements created among municipal, provincial, and federal levels of government that form barriers to delivering evidence-based treatments. The programs that have been cited as showing effectiveness are largely unavailable through publically funded services. Family treatment is still not a focus of the majority of addiction treatment resources in Canada at present, despite increased attention to the area and development and evaluation of creative new models of family treatment.

A family systems point of reference provides a comprehensive and meaningful approach to addressing underlying issues related to substance abuse. It is an integrated approach that acknowledges the complex interplay and effects of substance abuse and the family. As demonstrated in ongoing investigations, family treatment, when incorporated with other counselling approaches, significantly increases the level of improvement observed at both short-term and long-term follow-up intervals (Austin, MacGowan & Wagner, 2005; Becker & Curry, 2008; Kolezon & Green, 1985; Lebell, 1986; Moore, 2005; O'Farrell & Fals-Stewart, 2000; O'Farrell, Murphy, Alter, & Fals-Stewart, 2008; Thomas, 1989). The lack of availability of this form of assistance is an issue that requires continuing attention and integration. Even when an individual is not successful or is not interested in receiving treatment, active involvement with the remaining family members is still possible and should be offered. In circumstances when the person with an addiction is unable or unwilling to seek treatment, family intervention becomes an even more vital component of the continuum of care.

In closing, an important caveat: matching and assessment are crucial processes in every phase of the addiction treatment. When working with families it also needs to be ascertained if one of the triggers for drug use is the family itself. While support from the family can be integral there will be situations where disengaging from the family system is necessary in order for the client to begin the recovery process.

NOTE

1. Throughout the addiction literature the terms *alcoholism, alcohol and drug dependency, chemical dependency, drug abuse* and *substance use/abuse* are used frequently and sometimes interchangeably even though clinically these are distinctly different phenomena. In this chapter we attempt to use terms specifically related to the theoretical and research issues we are addressing, although at times we refer specifically to "substance abuse" rather than the broader term "addiction."

REFERENCES

Abbot, A. (2000). *Alcohol, tobacco and other drugs.* Washington, DC: National Association of Social Workers Press.

Addaction. (2009). *Trouble and love: The impact of drugs on family life.* London, UK: Addaction.

Al-Anon. (2015). *Al-Anon family groups background.* Retrieved from http://al-anon.org/media-files

Alcoholics Anonymous. (2005). *Alcoholics Anonymous.* New York: AA World Services.

Andreae, D. (1996). Systems theory and social work treatment. In F.J. Turner (Ed.), *Interlocking theoretical approaches: Social work treatment* (4th ed., pp. 601–616). New York: The Free Press.

Austin, A., MacGowan, M., & Wagner, E. (2005). Effective family based interventions for adolescents with substance use problems: A systematic review. *Research on Social Work Practice, 15*(2), 67–83.

Barber, J., & Gilbertson, R. (1996). An experimental study of brief unilateral intervention for the partners of heavy drinkers. *Research on Social Work Practice, 6*(3), 325–336.

Becker, S., & Curry, J. (2008). Out-patient interventions for adolescent substance abuse: A quality of evidence review. *Journal of Consulting and Clinical Psychology, 76*(4), 531–543.

Berg, I., & Reuss, N. (1998). *Solutions step by step: A substance abuse treatment manual.* New York: W.W. Norton & Co.

Bijttebier, P., Goethals, E., & Ansoms, S. (2006). Parental drinking as a risk factor for children's maladjustment: The mediating role of family environment. *Psychology of Addictive Behaviors, 20*(2), 126–130.

Boudreau, R. (1997). Addiction and the family. In S. Harrison and V. Carver (Eds.), *Alcohol and drug problems: A practical guide for counselors* (2nd ed). Toronto, ON: Addiction Research Foundation.

Bowen, M. (1991). Alcoholism as viewed through family systems theory and family psychotherapy. *Family Dynamics of Addiction Quarterly, 1*(1), 94–102.

Briones, E., Robbins, M., & Szapocznik, J. (2008). Brief strategic family therapy: Engagement and treatment. *Alcoholism Treatment Quarterly, 26*(1–2), 81–103.

Brown, T., Werk, A., Caplan, T., & Seraganian, P. (2010). Violent substance abusers in domestic violence treatment. In R. Csiernik & W.S. Rowe (Eds.), *Responding to the oppression of addiction* (2nd ed., pp. 184–196). Toronto, ON: Canadian Scholars' Press.

Campbell, J., Masters, M., & Johnson, M. (1998). Relationship of parental alcoholism to family-of-origin functioning and current marital satisfaction. *Journal of Addictions and Offender Counseling, 19*(1), 7–14.

Clark, C. (2012). Tough love: A brief cultural history of the addiction intervention. *History of psychology, 15*(3), 233–246.

Cottrell, D., & Boston, P. (2002). Practitioner review: the effectiveness of systemic family therapy for children and adolescents. *Journal of Child Psychology and Psychiatry, 43*(5), 573–586.

Cowley, D., & Godon, C. (1995). Assessment of family history of alcoholism in sons of alcoholic fathers. *Journal of Addictive Diseases, 14*(2), 75–81.

Csiernik, R. (2000). *Twelve-step orientated residential treatment programs: A review.* Toronto, ON: Twelve-Step Working Group.

Csiernik, R. (2002). Determining the value of Alcoholics Anonymous. *Canadian Social Work, 4*(1), 14–22.

Csiernik, R. (2016). *Substance use and abuse: Everything matters.* Toronto, ON: Canadian Scholars' Press.

Diamond, J. (2000). *Narrative means to sober ends: Treating addiction and its aftermath.* New York: Guilford Press.

Dittrich, J., & Trapold, M. (1984). A treatment program for the wives of alcoholics: An evaluation. *Bulletin of the Society of Psychologists in Addictive Behaviors, 43*(1), 91–102.

Edwards, M., & Steinglass, P. (1995). Family therapy treatment outcomes for alcoholism. *Journal of Marital and Family Therapy, 21*(4), 475–509.

Epstein, E., & McCrady, B. (1998). Behavioral couples treatment of alcohol and drug use disorders: Current status and innovations. *Clinical Psychology Review, 18*(6), 689–711.

Fernandez, A., Begley, E., & Marlatt, G. (2006). Family and peer interventions for adults: Past approaches and future directions. *Psychology of Addictive Behaviors, 20*(2), 207–213.

Fleming, J., Mullen, P., Sibthorpe, B., Attwell, R., & Bammer, G. (1998). The relationship between childhood sexual abuse and alcohol abuse in women: A case control study. *Addiction, 93*(12), 1787–1798.

Fletcher, K. (2013). Couple therapy treatments for substance use disorders: A systematic review. *Journal of Social Work Practice in the Addictions, 13*(4), 327–352.

French, S. (1987). Family approaches to alcoholism: Why the lack of interest among marriage and family professionals? *Journal of Drug Issues, 17*(4), 359–368.

Friedemann, M. (1996). Effects of Al-Anon attendance on family perceptions of inner-city indigents. *American Journal of Drug and Alcohol Abuse, 22*(1), 123–134.

Fuller-Thomson, E., Katz, R., Phan, V., Liddycoat, J., & Brennenstuhl, S. (2013). The long arm of parental addictions: The association with adult children's depression in a population-based study. *Psychiatry Research, 210*(1), 95–101.

Gingerich, W., & Eisengart, M. (2000). Solution-focused brief therapy: A review of the outcome research. *Family Process, 39*(4), 477–498.

Goldenberg, I., & Goldenberg, H. (1980). *Family therapy: An overview*. Monterey, CA: Brooks-Cole.

Grant, B. (2000). Estimates of US children exposed to alcohol abuse and dependence in the family. *American Journal of Public Health, 90*(1), 112–115.

Haley, J. (1982). *Heroin my baby: A clinical model*. In M.D. Stanton, T. Todd, & Associates (Eds.), *The family therapy of drug abuse and addiction* (pp. 154–189). New York: Guilford Press.

Hall, J., Henggeler, S., Ferreira, D., & East, P. (1992). Sibling relations and substance use in high risk female adolescents. *Family Dynamics of Addiction Quarterly, 2*(1), 44–51.

Hendriks, V., van der Schee, E., & Blanken, P. (2011). Treatment of adolescents with cannabis use disorder: Main findings of a randomized controlled trial comparing multidimensional family therapy and cognitive behavioral therapy in the Netherlands. *Drug and Alcohol Dependence, 119*(1), 64–71.

Joanning, H., Quinn, W., Thomas, F., & Mullen, R. (1992). Treating adolescent drug abuse: A comparison of family systems therapy, group therapy and family drug education. *Journal of Marital and Family Therapy, 18*(4), 345–356.

Johnson, V. (2009). *Intervention: How to help someone who doesn't want help*. Center City, MN: Hazelden Publishing.

Jones, D., & Houts, R. (1992). Parental drinking, parent-child communication, and social skills in young adults. *Journal of Studies on Alcohol, 53*(1), 48–56.

Kaufman, E., & Kaufman, P. (1979). *Family therapy of drug and alcohol abuse*. New York: Gardner Press.

Keinz, L., Schwartz, C., Trench, B., & Houlihan, D. (1995). An assessment of membership benefits in the Al-Anon program. *Alcoholism Treatment Quarterly, 12*(4), 31–38.

Kingree, J. (2000). Predictors and by-products of participation in a mutual help group for adult children of alcoholics. *Alcoholism Treatment Quarterly, 18*(2), 83–94.

Kolezon, M.S., & Green, R.G. (1985). *Family therapy models: Coverage and divergence*. New York: Springer Publishing.

Lander, L., Howsare, J., & Byrne, M. (2013). The impact of substance use disorders on families and children: From theory to practice. *Social Work in Public Health, 28*(3–4), 194–205.

Lebell, R. (1986). Treating alcoholics and their spouses: A family-systems centred approach. *Canadian Family Physician, 32*, 1295–1297.

Lewis, R., Piercy, F., Sprenkle, D., & Trepper, T. (1990). Family-based intervention for helping drug-abusing adolescents. *Journal of Adolescent Research, 13*(1), 35–44.

Liddle, H.A., Dakof, G.A., Parker, K., Diamond, G.S., Barett, K., & Tejeda, M. (2001). Multidimensional family therapy for adolescent drug abuse: Results of a randomized clinical trial. *American Journal of Drug and Alcohol Abuse, 27*(4), 651–688.

Madill Parker Research & Consulting. (2006). *Identifying the role of families within treatment*. London, UK: Madill Parker Research & Consulting.

Merikangas, K., Dierker, L., & Fenton, B. (1998). Familial factors and substance abuse: Implications for prevention. In R. Ashery, E. Robertson, & K. Kumpfer (Eds.), *Drug abuse prevention through family interventions*. Rockville, MD: National Institute of Drug Abuse.

Meyers, R., Villanueva, M., & Smith, J.E. (2005). The community reinforcement approach: History and empirical validation. *Journal of Cognitive Psychotherapy, 19*, 251–264.

Miller, S.D., & Berg, I.K. (1996). *The miracle method: A radically new approach to problem drinking*. New York: W.W. Norton.

Miller, W., Meyers, R., & Tonigan, J. (1999). Engaging the unmotivated in treatment for alcohol problems: A comparison of three strategies for intervention through family members. *Journal of Consulting and Clinical Psychology, 67*(5), 688–697.

Moore, B. (2005). Empirically supported family and peer interventions for dual disorders. *Research on Social Work Practice, 15*(4), 231–245.

Morgenstern, J., & McKay, J. (2007). Rethinking the paradigms that inform behavioural treatment research for substance use disorders. *Addiction, 102*(9), 1377–1389.

Nichols, M., & Schwartz, R. (2007). *Family therapy: Concepts and methods* (6th ed.). Boston, MA: Allyn and Bacon Publishers.

Nurco, D., & Lerner, M. (1996). Vulnerability to narcotic addiction: Family structure and functioning. *Journal of Drug Issues, 26*(4), 1007–1025.

O'Farrell, T. (1991). Using couples therapy in the treatment of alcoholism. *Family Dynamics of Addiction Quarterly, 1*(4), 39–45.

O'Farrell, T., & Clements, K. (2012). Review of outcome research on marital and family therapy in treatment for alcoholism. *Journal of Marital and Family Therapy, 38*(2), 122–144.

O'Farrell, T., & Fals-Stewart, W. (2000). Behavioral couples therapy for alcoholism and drug abuse. *Journal of Substance Abuse Treatment, 18*(1), 51–54.

O'Farrell, T., Murphy, M., Alter, J., & Fals-Stewart, W. (2008). Brief family treatment intervention to promote continuing care among alcohol-dependent patients in inpatient detoxicification: A randomized pilot study. *Journal of Substance Abuse Treatment, 34*(3), 363–369.

O'Farrell, T., & Schein, A. (2011). Behavioral couples therapy for alcoholism and drug use. *Journal of Family Psychotherapy, 22*(2), 193–215.Payne, M. (2014). *Modern social work theory: A critical introduction* (4th ed.). Toronto, ON: Lyceum Books.

Pidock, B., & Fischer, J. (1998). Parental recovery as a moderating variable of adult offspring problematic behaviours. *Alcoholism Treatment Quarterly, 16*(4), 45–57.

Powers, M., Vedel, E., & Emmelkamp, P. (2008). Behavioral couples therapy (BCT) for alcohol and drug use disorders: A meta-analysis. *Clinical Psychology Review, 28*(6), 952–962.

Rigter, H., Henderson, C.E., Pelc, I., Tossmann, P., Phan, O., Hendriks, V., Schaub, M., & Rowe, C.L. (2013). Multidimensional family therapy lowers the rate of cannabis dependence in adolescents: A randomised controlled trial in Western European outpatient settings. *Drug and Alcohol Dependence, 130*(1), 85–93.

Robbins, M.S., & Szapocznik, J. (2000). Office of Juvenile Justice and Delinquency Prevention. *Brief Strategic Family Therapy.* Retrieved from http://www.ojjdp.ncjrs.org/pubs/alpha.html

Roozen, H.G., de Waart, R., & van de Kroft, P. (2010). Community reinforcement and family training: An effective option to engage treatment-resistant substance-abusing individuals in treatment. *Addiction, 105*(10), 1729–1738.

Rychtarik, R., Carstensen, L., Alford, G., & Schlundt, D. (1988). Situational assessment of alcohol-related coping skills in wives of alcoholics. *Psychology of Addictive Behaviors, 2*(2), 66–73.

Satir, V. (1972). *Peoplemaking.* Palo Alto, CA: Science and Behavior Books.

Shadish, W.R., & Baldwin, S.A. (2005). Effects of behavioural marital therapy: A meta-analysis of randomized control trials. *Journal of Consulting and Clinical Psychology, 73*(1), 6–14.

Stanton, D., Todd, T., & Associates (1982). *The family therapy of drug abuse and addiction.* New York: Guilford Press.

Stanton, M., & Standish, W. (1997). Outcome attribution and families/couple treatment for drug abuse: A meta-analysis and review of the controlled and comparative studies. *Psychological Bulletin, 122*(2), 170–191.

Stark, J. (2008). *One-third of families blighted by drinking.* Retreived from http://www.smh.com.au/news/national/onethird-of-families-blighted-by-drinking/2008/10/20/1224351155150.html

Szapocznik, J., Zarate, M., Duff, J., & Muir, M. (2013). Brief strategic family therapy: Engaging drug using/problem behaviour adolescents and their families in treatment. *Social Work in Public Health, 28*(3/4), 206–223.

Taylor, A., Toner, P. Templeton, L., & Velleman, R. (2008). Parental alcohol misuse in complex families: The implications for engagement. *British Journal of Social Work, 38*(5), 843–864.

Timko, C., Cronkite, R., Kaskutas, L., Laudet, A., Roth, J., & Moos, R.H. (2013). Al-Anon family groups: Newcomers and members. *Journal of Studies on Alcohol and Drugs, 74*(6), 965–976.

Timko, C., Cronkite, R., Laudet, A., Kaskutas, L., Roth, J., & Moos, R.H. (2014). Al-Anon family groups' newcomers and members: Concerns about the drinkers in their lives. *American Journal on Addictions, 23*(4), 329–336.

Timko, C., Young, L., & Moos, R. (2012). Al-Anon family groups: Origins, conceptual basis, outcomes, and research opportunities. *Journal of Groups in Addiction & Recovery, 7*(2–4), 279–296.

Thomas, J. (1989). An overview of marital and family treatments with substance abusing populations. *Alcoholism Treatment Quarterly, 6*(3/4), 91–102.

Usher, K., Jackson, D., & O'Brien, L. (2007). Shattered dreams: Parental experiences of adolescent substance abuse. *International Journal of Mental Health Nursing, 16*(6), 422–430.

Wegscheider-Cruse, S. (1985). *Choicemaking for co-dependents, adult children and spirituality seekers.* Pompano Beach, FL: Health Communications.

CHAPTER 6

Perinatal Drug Dependency Disorders

Cecilia M. Jevitt and William S. Rowe

Introduction

The issues of substance use, abuse, and dependency during pregnancy have legal, moral, and biopsychosocial consequences. While the biological and health concerns have become increasingly clear, this is less the case with the legal, moral, and psycho-social issues. In Canada the statutes are clear that the mother's rights are paramount until the fetus is viable outside the body. Section 223 of the Criminal Code of Canada (1985) states that a fetus is a "human being ... when it has completely proceeded, in a living state, from the body of its mother whether or not it has completely breathed, it has an independent circulation or the navel string is severed." This was tested in 1996 when a woman from Winnipeg who was using inhalants was ordered into an addiction treatment facility for the remainder of her pregnancy by a judge responding to an appeal by child welfare authorities. However, the Supreme Court of Manitoba overturned this decision because the mother's rights superseded those of the fetus. To date, no American state has enacted a law that criminalizes specific behaviour during pregnancy; nonetheless, it has been estimated that at least 200 women in the United States have been criminally prosecuted or arrested under existing child abuse statutes for allegedly bringing about harm in-utero through their conduct during pregnancy (Center for Reproductive Rights, 2000).

Addiction to nonnutritive substances during pregnancy ranges from tobacco smoking to intravenous heroin use. Tobacco smoking remains very common during pregnancy with approximately 25% of women using tobacco at the time of conception. Marijuana remains a commonly used substance during pregnancy throughout North America, with perinatal use prevalence rates from maternal self-reports ranging from 3 to 30% in varied American populations. Canada has not collected separate data on marijuana use during pregnancy but the 2008 Perinatal Health Report found that 5% of Canadian women used illegal drugs while pregnant (Canadian Centre on Substance Abuse [CCSA], 2015; Metz & Stickrath, 2015). Illicit drug use in teens contributes to unprotected sex and higher numbers of unplanned pregnancies in this age group.

The views of Canadian and American health care providers, law enforcement, courts, and policy-makers range from drug use as criminal activity to drug dependency as a multifactorial medical and mental health problem. Treatment is particularly difficult because two lives are intertwined and involved in the addiction: the mother and the fetus. Potentially addiction-producing substances ingested by the mother cross the placenta, causing varying levels of harm to the fetus depending on the maternal dose and other maternal health variables. Many mothers will stop the use of harmful substances once they know they are pregnant; however, a pregnancy may not be obvious for six to eight weeks, exposing the embryo to harmful chemicals during its most vulnerable stages of formation. Effective help for pregnant women with drug addiction must include medical, psychiatric, and social support from a team of skilled clinicians that might include physicians, midwives, advanced practice nurses, social workers, psychologists, and psychiatrists.

Signs of Drug Dependency

Signs of dependency can be overt, such as the odour of alcohol and slurred speech, or subtle, such as women who complain of intractable back pain and frequently ask for opioid (narcotic) pain relief. Cannabis dilates pupils while opioid use constricts pupils. Injectable drug use leaves round, discoloured marks at the injection site, sometimes with discoloration over a portion of the vein. Use of unclean needles may cause small abscesses or cellulitis at the injection site. Cocaine and amphetamine use increase blood pressure and pulse. In contrast, cannabis and opioid use lower blood pressure, pulse, and respirations. Long-term methamphetamine users and crack cocaine smokers have dental disease, including visible plaque and tooth decay. Poor memory is characteristic of all chronic drug and alcohol abuse. Unfortunately, most of these signs will never be seen during prenatal care because women with drug dependencies tend to avoid prenatal care.

Semi-structured interviews and focus groups conducted by Roberts and Pies (2011) in California found that women physically dependent on illegal substances avoided prenatal care to avoid detection and consequences that can range from loss of child custody to incarceration for detoxification. Additionally, the drug lifestyle imposed barriers on accessing prenatal care. One mother said, "By the time I found out I was pregnant, I had zero dollars, zero friends, a car that I couldn't drive. I didn't have Internet, I didn't have telephone." Many North American communities do not have specialized treatment resources needed during pregnancy. In another study of alcohol and drug using women, mistrust of health care providers was identified as a barrier to continuing to participate in prenatal care activities. Women reported that health care providers covertly attempting to identify drug use and report this to child protective services was an ongoing issue. Women additionally expected to feel harsh judgment from providers, reinforcing their own feelings of maternal failure. To avoid these negative feelings and additional scrutiny, they disengaged from prenatal care (Roberts & Nuru-Jeter, 2010).

Testing for Drug Dependency Disorders

Screening Tools

All health care organizations recommend that pregnant women be screened for drug use at the first prenatal visit. A number of validated screening tools exist for this purpose, such as the T-ACE (Tolerance, Annoyance, Cut down, Eye-opener) and the 4Ps Plus (Parents, Partner, Past, Pregnancy) (Young & Martin, 2012). However, prenatal care providers usually see these as tools for use by mental health providers. Prenatal health histories completed at the first prenatal visit all contain questions about tobacco, alcohol, and drug use, however, since most women with dependency disorders avoid prenatal care, these questions have limited usefulness in identifying women needing help.

Laboratory Testing

Psychoactive drugs can be identified through blood or urine samples but a drug test has to be requested specifically. Many laboratories have panels that test one sample for up to a dozen substances. However, the standard of care does not dictate screening all women for substance abuse. Samples for testing can be obtained covertly while the numerous blood and urine samples analyzed during pregnancy are obtained; however, this violates principles of informed consent. Many women in treatment or with histories of drug dependency treatment will volunteer to have urine analyzed monthly during pregnancy. Assuming the specimens remain negative for drugs, clients with a history of addiction can build a sober profile that children's aid networks and the courts can review while deciding custody and placement of the newborn (Table 6.1).

However, maternal specimens that test positive for prescription drugs need to be compared to the mother's medical history and record. A woman might be using opioids intermittently for chronic pain use following a severe back injury and not OxyContin recreationally. In another example, a mother might be seen in a hospital for a labour exam. If her labour is not advanced, she might be sent home after receiving morphine or meperidine to stop pain and allow for sleep. These medications may be detected in the newborn days later and will indicate opioid use as well. Newborn urine and stool (meconium) can also be tested to ascertain maternal drug use. Meconium testing has the advantage of documenting up to 20 weeks of maternal ingestion.

Table 6.1   Drugs Detectable in Blood, Urine, or Meconium Samples

Drug Class	Substances
Amphetamines	amphetamine, MDA, MDMA, methamphetamine
Barbiturates	amobarbital, butalbital, pentobarbital, phenobarbital, secobarbital
Benzodiazepines	alprazolam, ativan, diazepam, lorazepam, oxazepam
Buprenorphine	buprenorphine, norbuprenorphine
Cannabinoids	carboxy-THC
Cocaine	benzoylecgonine, cocaethylene, cocaine, meta-hydroxybenzoylecgonine
Meperidine	normeperidine
Methadone	EDDP, methadone
Oxycodone	oxycodone
Phencyclidine	phencyclidine (PCP)
Propoxyphene	norpropoxyphene
Tramadol	tramadol

Legal Issues with Drug Testing

Covertly obtaining drug screens and confronting women with positive results erodes client confidence in a provider and drives women out of prenatal care. As with all encounters, open-ended, non-judgemental questions with time given for the mother to talk helps women to reveal their drug use and enables the provider to request screening tests more openly. Women may be more agreeable to testing if they understand that positive results help with the development of effective treatment plans and that negative tests demonstrate self-care.

Specimens that will be eligible to be used in court must be "chain of custody" specimens. In chain of custody specimens, obtaining the specimen must be directly observed, thereby necessitating an informed consent–producing conversation with the mother about drug testing. For example, a woman must be accompanied to a toilet to give a urine specimen. She must be observed to have no bag or full pockets and she must hand the specimen to the observer. Then observer and the subsequent specimen handlers all sign for the specimen so that it can be tracked, proving that there was no substitution of another's urine. While this follows best practice drug testing guidelines it is not at all conducive to building a therapeutic alliance.

Newborn urine or stool can easily be tested if providers suspect that a mother has a drug dependency disorder. Box 6.1 lists the medical indications for drug testing in newborns. Many hospitals in areas of high drug use routinely test all newborn urine, reporting positive results to child protective services. Some hospitals routinely request that mothers sign permission for newborn drug testing. The newborn of any mother who refuses permission for drug testing for herself is routinely tested in a variety of

North American jurisdictions. New York State is one of 17 American states that define maternal drug use as child neglect. A single positive drug screen in some of these states removes the child from maternal custody (Guttmacher Institute, 2015). Women in Tennessee convicted of drug use are charged with child assault and may be sentenced to up to 15 years in prison. Many health care organizations, including the American Medical Association and the American College of Obstetricians and Gynecologists (ACOG), object to punitive prenatal anti-drug laws, arguing that "incarceration and threat of incarceration have proved to be ineffective in reducing the incidence of alcohol or drug abuse (ACOG, 2014).

Box 6.1   Medical Indications for Newborn Drug Testing

- History of maternal illicit drug use
- Unexplained agitation or altered mental status in mother
- No prenatal care
- Placental abruption
- Unexplained neurological complications in the newborn such as altered mental status or intracranial hemorrhage
- Symptoms of drug withdrawal in the newborn: tachypnea, hypertonicity, jitteriness, excessive crying, lethargy, excessive stooling or secretions
- Poor feeding behaviour, uncoordinated or frenzied sucking

Sources: Farst, Valentin, Whit Hall (2011); Mactier (2013)

Effect of Drug and Alcohol Use on Perinatal Health

The potential effects of drug use on pregnancy are numerous. However, assigning drug causation for poor pregnancy outcomes is difficult as mothers can use a variety of drugs along with tobacco to cope with their physical and mental symptoms. Opioids, barbiturates, and amphetamines can be potent appetite suppressants causing mothers to eat insufficient calories or nutrients for appropriate fetal growth. Marijuana, a potent appetite stimulant, used daily could cause excessive weight gain in some mothers. Intoxicated mothers may be unable to sustain employment, with resultant poverty pushing them to homelessness and hunger. Women may trade sex for drugs, exposing themselves and their newborns to the dangers of sexually transmitted infections, including HIV. Illegal drug use is often associated with underlying mental health issues. This complicates a woman's ability to organize her day-to-day life and participate in treatment. Numerous cases of drug-dependent women who were victims of childhood physical or sexual abuse have been documented (CCSA, 2013; Hiebert-Murphy

& Woytkiw, 2010). Determining the exact impact of drug use on a pregnancy is made difficult due to frequent comorbid physical and psychological conditions.

Drug use treatment during pregnancy must balance the health of the mother and that of the fetus. The optimal treatment is for a woman to seek treatment and be drug free at the time of conception. Problematic aspects of drug or alcohol use include poorer judgment and increasing impulsivity, thereby reducing the effectiveness of some contraceptive methods and leading to unplanned pregnancies. Sober women are often six to eight weeks into a pregnancy before they realize they are pregnant. The altered cognition of chronic drug or alcohol use may further delay pregnancy recognition, thwarting the benefits of early prenatal care.

Cessation of cocaine, methamphetamine, marijuana, and alcohol use as soon as pregnancy is diagnosed provides the best protection for both mother and fetus. The most successful withdrawals occur with medical supervision and may include gradual tapering of the substance, medications to treat co-existing psychiatric illness or depression, and non-psychoactive medications to treat withdrawal symptoms such as vomiting or diarrhea. Pregnancy-safe doses of cannabis or alcohol have not been determined; therefore total abstinence from these substances is advised. In the case of opioids drug cessation can lead to spontaneous abortion given the extreme pain associated with withdrawal and thus drug substitution using methadone is often a typical course of action (CCSA, 2015; Metz & Stickrath, 2015).

The effects of drug dependency during pregnancy can last decades beyond birth. Addiction stresses family and other supportive relationships and the costs of ongoing drug use can impoverish a family. However, children taken away from drug-dependent mothers may not have the most supportive parenting and care from their guardians. Forty years ago, newborns went through detoxification following birth and providers assumed that the infant had a clean start to life. High substance abuse rates in those born to drug-using mothers were thought to be due to a home environment where drug use was ongoing. Newer epigenetic research has revealed that neurological and metabolic changes occur at the gene level in utero, with fetuses exposed to drugs in utero potentially primed for subsequent drug seeking. Even supposedly milder drugs like marijuana are increasingly implicated in adverse childhood cognitive development, hyperactivity, impulsivity, and increased likelihood of substance abuse and delinquency (CCSA, 2015).

Table 6.2 summarizes the effects of selected drugs on pregnancy and the newborn.

Dependency-Producing Drugs

Opioids (Narcotics)

Opioids are a large class of medications including buprenorphine, butorphanol (stadol), fentanyl, heroin, hydrocodone (codeine), methadone, morphine, oxycodone and pethidine (Demerol, meperidine). Opioids can be ingested orally, via mucous

Table 6.2   Effects of Selected Drugs on Mother and Fetus in Pregnancy

Drug	Effect on Mother	Effect on Fetus
Alcohol	• Increased risk of damage to all organs • Miscarriage • Preterm birth	• Intrauterine growth restriction • Low birth weight • Fetal Alcohol Spectrum Disorders
Amphetamines	• Premature birth	• Low birth weight • Fetal death in utero
Cannabis	• Decreased fertility • Miscarriage • Preterm birth	• Intrauterine growth restriction • Low birth weight • Fetal death
Cocaine	• Miscarriage • Premature birth • Placental abruption	• Intrauterine growth restriction • Fetal death in utero • Low birth weight • Neonatal abstinence syndrome (NAS)
Opioids	• Miscarriage • Premature birth • Placental abruption	• Low birth weight • Fetal death in utero • Respiratory difficulty at birth • Neonatal abstinence syndrome (NAS)
PCP, MDMA, LSD	• Miscarriage	• Low birth weight • CNS irritability

Sources: CCSA, 2013, 2015; Farst, Valentine, & Whit Hall, 2011; Mactier, 2013; Stewart et al., 2013; Wright, Schuetter, Tellei, & Sauvage, 2015; Young & Martin, 2012

membrane, or injected. Diversion and street sale of prescription narcotics has been a growing problem in both Canada and the United States during the 21st century. Opioid ingestion is followed by analgesia, anxiety reduction, and sleepiness. Opioids readily cross the placenta but have not been linked with patterns of birth defects (Young & Martin, 2012). However, opioid use in pregnancy may restrict fetal growth, particularly as maternal appetite can be suppressed. Opioids relax the uterine muscle and prolong the early stages of labour. Additionally, analgesia from opioid use may mask symptoms of early labour so that mothers are ready for birth at hospital admission or accidentally give birth outside the hospital. Children exposed to opioids during pregnancy have shown neurocognitive delay and behavioural problems (Mactier, 2013; Young & Martin, 2012).

There are two choices for management of opioid addiction in pregnancy: gradual staged detoxification or maintenance with methadone, buprenorphine (Subutex), or buprenorphine plus naloxone (Suboxone). While some research indicates increased risks of miscarriage, premature birth, and intrauterine fetal demise with prenatal detoxification from opioids, other studies did not report these types of outcomes. Nonetheless, the potential risks are the primary reason many physicians encourage women dependent on opioids to use a maintenance program until birth (Stanhope, Gill, & Rose 2013). Additionally, pregnancy is a time of new stressors for mothers, adding to the risk of lapse and relapse. Cycles of relapse, intoxication, and withdrawal can cause interruptions in maternal oxygenation and placental blood flow, leading to fetal hypoxia, acidosis, and permanent brain damage. Acute withdrawal can stimulate miscarriage or preterm labour, additional reasons to assist pregnant women with enrolling in a maintenance program (Young & Martin, 2012). However, neither methadone nor buprenorphine are associated with fetal anomalies and can be administered once daily in directly observed therapy.

Unfortunately, newborns born to opioid users are addicted and must undergo detoxification treatment. The symptoms of newborn withdrawal or newborn abstinence syndrome (NAS), which begin at 24 to 72 hours of life depending on the mother's last drug dose, include lethargy or jitteriness, constant crying, hypertonicity, poor sleep duration, tremors, frequent yawning, sneezing, vomiting, excessive stooling or oral secretions, and uncoordinated sucking, becoming increasingly evident on post-partum days two and three (Stanhope, Gill, & Rose, 2013). Detoxification is achieved by increasing weight-adjusted doses of oral morphine or methadone, sometimes with the addition of phenobarbital, until withdrawal symptoms are controlled for 48 hours. Then those medications are gradually tapered over seven to ten days (Mactier, 2013).

As well, opioids are secreted into breast milk. Hydrocodone use during breastfeeding has been linked to newborn deaths as concentrations in breast milk may reach 9% of maternal serum levels (American Academy of Pediatrics, 2013). In contrast, methadone is concentrated into breast milk at 2% of maternal levels and is considered safe for breastfeeding with no reports of infant sedation. However, methadone in breast milk alone is insufficient to control the symptoms of NAS. Breast milk remains superior to manufactured formula even when the mother uses maintenance-dose levels of methadone. This is in part because breastfeeding produces oxytocin, a hormone that relaxes mothers and enhances bonding. However, mothers are typically discharged from hospital care at 24-72 hours postpartum while newborns remain hospitalized to complete their detoxification.

Cocaine

Cocaine (blow, coke, crack, nose candy) can be smoked, snorted, injected, or taken orally or rectally. Cocaine use in pregnancy causes episodes of hypertension along with euphoria and hyper-alertness. Hypertension reduces uterine blood flow and causes uterine contractions, most likely responsible for the increased first trimester miscarriage rate and the 8% increase in stillborn babies among cocaine abusers (CCSA, 2013). High doses of cocaine cause placental abruption, a prenatal emergency as the newborn loses placental circulation. Emergency Cesarean may save the life of the fetus during a placental abruption.

Newborns born to cocaine-addicted mothers and those ingesting breast milk containing cocaine exhibit intoxication, seizures, irritability, vomiting, diarrhea, and tremulousness (AAP, 2013). Thus, cocaine-using mothers should be counselled not to breastfeed. Long-term follow-up of children exposed to cocaine in utero shows delayed cognition and poor school performance (Mactier, 2013), though there is confounding data that links this to an impoverished childhood as much as to in utero issues.

Amphetamine

Amphetamines (bennies, beans, uppers), like cocaine, are a central nervous system stimulant and likewise produce euphoria, hyperactivity, hyper-alertness, and insomnia. Methamphetamine (chalk, crank, glass, crystal meth, ice, speed), the strongest of the amphetamines, can be manufactured inexpensively from easily obtained precursors such as pseudoephedrine. It can be smoked, injected, snorted, or ingested orally or via mucous membrane. Methamphetamine users often have uncontrollable sensations of itching or crawling on their skin that is scratched until raw, with lesions covering face, trunk, and extremities, along with severe tooth decay. Long-term methamphetamine use causes insomnia, anxiety, depression, memory loss, violent behaviour, and psychosis, with structural changes in the brain areas responsible for emotions and memory demonstrated on brain imaging studies (ACOG, 2011).

Despite this, amphetamines are not associated with a pattern of congenital anomalies even when used in the first trimester; some studies suggest infant and childhood neurobehavioural abnormalities may arise, but again this is difficult to distinguish from environmental factors (ACOG, 2012). Amphetamine reduces breast milk production and is then concentrated in breast milk at two to seven times the level of maternal plasma. Newborns receiving amphetamines through breast milk are irritable and agitated and thus amphetamine-using mothers should be discouraged from breastfeeding (AAP, 2013; Mactier, 2013).

Cannabis

Cannabis sativa (doobie, marijuana, Mary Jane, weed) is a commonly used drug during pregnancy. With cannabis use not only being decriminalized in Canada but increasingly used as medication, women will likely increasingly view it as a safe substance. Cannabis can be smoked or ingested orally. In states where recreational use is legal, products such as cannabis-containing cookies and lollipops further add to its image as a safe product.

Cannabinoid compounds are produced in the brain and mediate pleasure, anxiety, and satiety states. The main cannabinoid in marijuana is delta-9-tetrahydrocannabinol (THC). It has a half-life of 20–36 hours in occasional users, though non-psychoactive THC metabolites may persist for up 30 days during heavy use. THC binds to cannabinoid type 1 receptors (CB1) in the brain, reducing anxiety, producing lethargy and feelings of pleasure, and simultaneously stimulating appetite.

THC crosses the placenta with fetal plasma levels being approximately 10% of maternal levels (ACOG, 2015). CB1 receptors are present in the fetus by 14 weeks, allowing for the fetus to be affected by the exogenous cannabinoids. However, at this time, no research has linked cannabis use with fetal malformations (ACOG, 2015; CCSA, 2015). However, one study of pregnant women who used marijuana and smoked cigarettes found that they had twice the rate of fetal deaths in utero and stillbirths as mothers who used neither substance (Varner et al., 2014), though the results are somewhat confounded by maternal tobacco use. Studies in laboratory rats have shown disruptions in normal brain development and function following in utero exposure to exogenous cannabis. Several studies have demonstrated lower test scores on visual problem solving, visual-motor coordination, and visual analysis, along with decreased attention spans and behavioural problems, in children who were exposed to cannabis in utero than in those who were not exposed (ACOG, 2015; CCSA, 2015). A longitudinal study of lower socio-economic status urban children showed poorer reading and spelling scores among those with perinatal cannabis exposure (Goldschmidt, Day, & Richardson, 2000).

THC has been found in breast milk. With no safe dose of THC established in pregnancy, pregnant women, even those who have been using medical marijuana, and breast-feeding mothers should be encouraged to stop cannabis use (ACOG, 2015; CCSA, 2015).

Alcohol

Chronic alcohol use in pregnancy has long been known to be teratogenic, causing the manifestations of Fetal Alcohol Spectrum Disorder (FASD) (Table 6.3). As these symptoms are irreversible, prevention is the key. Although damage seems to be related to dose, no safe dose of alcohol has been identified for pregnancy and current recommendations are that women avoid alcohol use entirely during pregnancy (CCSA, 2013; Centers for Disease Control [CDC], 2015).

The Centers for Disease Control (2015) estimate the prevalence of FASD to be 1–9 per 1,000 births, with as many as 20 to 50 affected children per 1,000 in some communities. The Canadian Center on Substance Abuse estimates that 1–2 per 1,000 Canadian births are affected by FASD (2013). Up to 25% of children with Fetal Alcohol Spectrum Disorder will have an intellectual disability and learning problems (CCSA, 2013).

Table 6.3 Manifestations of Fetal Alcohol Spectrum Disorder

Newborn Symptoms	Childhood Symptoms
• Abnormal facial features, such as a smooth ridge between the nose and upper lip, flattened nasal bridge and wide set eyes • Small head size • Low body weight with growth restriction • Jitteriness, tremors, frequent crying • Uncoordinated suck • Heart, kidney, and bone malformations	• Poor coordination • Hyperactive behaviour • Difficulty with attention • Poor memory • Learning disabilities or low IQ • Speech and language delays • Poor reasoning and judgment skills • Vision or hearing problems

Alcohol freely passes into breast milk and can have a sedating effect on the infant. Its effect to relax the mother along with B vitamins contained in European stouts has led to alcohol being recommended to increase milk production in the past. Recent research indicates that alcohol reduces milk production and that frequent alcohol ingested through breast milk can negatively affect infant neuro-cognitive development (Menella, 2015) and as such, regular alcohol use during breastfeeding should be discouraged.

Postpartum and Beyond

The social worker is a vital member of the health care team during the postpartum period when mothers transition from medical recovery to parenting and providing for the newborn. If the mother has a current drug dependency, the social worker needs to inform the woman of the role of the local assessment centre and support her in attending the intake interview. Additionally, social workers in community health clinics can serve as the liaison between the mother, family, and child protective services while safe placement of the newborn is determined.

Ideally, the new mother will receive assistance in selecting a birth control method that can help her delay future pregnancies until her dependencies are controlled and she has the capacity to parent. The mother may also need assistance with housing, food, and job services to support safe parenting. Many communities now have specific community-based programs to support dependent mothers and their newborns, where women can learn parenting skills, receive maintenance or tapered withdrawal therapy, and assistance with job placement.

Ongoing research continually produces new knowledge concerning drug use and dependency during pregnancy. Researchers, medical and mental health providers, social workers, and policy-makers must apply these new findings to medical and mental health therapies and assistance for mothers and newborns. Helping mothers find treatment for their dependencies and assisting children with the sequelae of neonatal abstinence syndrome and other perinatal drug exposures will help communities see drug dependency less as an unconquerable curse and more as a complex, biopsychosocial problem that can be ameliorated with the compassionate assistance of a health care team.

REFERENCES

American Academy of Pediatrics (AAP). (2013). *The transfer of drugs and therapeutics into human breast milk: An update on selected topics.* Retrieved from http://pediatrics.aappublications. org/content/early/2013/08/20/peds.2013-1985.full.pdf

American College of Obstetricians and Gynecologists (ACOG). (2011). *Methamphetamine abuse in women of reproductive age. Committee Opinion #479.* Retrieved from http://www.acog. org/-/media/Committee-Opinions/Committee-on-Health-Care-for-Underserved-Women/ co479.pdf?dmc=1&ts=20150619T1355220173

American College of Obstetricians and Gynecologists (ACOG). (2012). *Opioid abuse, dependence, and addiction in pregnancy. Committee Opinion # 524.* Retrieved from http://www.acog. org/Resources-And-Publications/Committee-Opinions/Committee-on-Health-Care -for-Underserved-Women/Opioid-Abuse-Dependence-and-Addiction-in-Pregnancy

American College of Obstetricians and Gynecologists (ACOG). (2014). *Substance abuse reporting and pregnancy: The role of the obstetrician-gynecologist. Committee Opinion #473.* Retrieved from http://www.acog.org/Resources_And_Publications/ Committee_Opinions/Committee_on_Health_Care_for_Underserved_Women/ Substance_Abuse_Reporting_and_Pregnancy_The_Role_of_the_Obstetrician_Gynecologist

American College of Obstetricians and Gynecologists (ACOG). (2015). *Marijuana use during pregnancy and lactation. Committee Opinion #637.* Retrieved from http://m.acog.org/ Resources-And-Publications/Committee-Opinions/Committee-on-Obstetric-Practice/ Marijuana-Use-During-Pregnancy-and-Lactation

Canadian Centre on Substance Abuse (CCSA). (2013). *Licit and illicit drug use during pregnancy: Maternal, neonatal and early childhood consequences.* Retrieved from http://www.ccsa.ca/ Resource%20Library/CCSA-Drug-Use-during-Pregnancy-Report-2013-en.pdf

Canadian Centre on Substance Abuse (CCSA). (2015). *Clearing the smoke on cannabis: Maternal cannabis use during pregnancy.* Retrieved from http://www.ccsa.ca/Resource%20Library/ CCSA-Cannabis-Maternal-Use-Pregnancy-Report-2015-en.pdf

Center for Reproductive Rights. (2000). *Punishing women for their behavior during pregnancy.* Retrieved from http://www.reproductiverights.org/sites/default/files/documents/pub_bp_ punishingwomen.pdf

Centers for Disease Control (CDC). (2015). *Fetal Alcohol Spectrum Disorders.* Retrieved from http://www.cdc.gov/ncbddd/fasd/data.html

Criminal Code of Canada. (1985). *Justice laws website.* Retrieved from http://laws-lois.justice. gc.ca/eng/acts/C-46/section-223.html

Fasrt, K., Valentine, J., & Whit Hall, R. (2011). Drug testing for newborn exposure to illicit substance in pregnancy: Pitfalls and pearls. *International Journal of Pediatrics*, Article ID 951616, doi:10.1155/2011/951616.

Goldschmidt, L., Day, N., & Ricahrdson, G. (2000). Effects of prenatal marijuana exposure on child behavior problems at age 10. *Neurotoxicology and Teratology, 22*(3), 325-336.

Guttmacher Institute. (2015). *Substance abuse in pregnancy: State policies in brief.* Retrieved from http://www.guttmacher.org/statecenter/spibs/spib_SADP.pdf

Hiebert-Murphy, D., & Woytkiw, L. (2010). A model for working with women dealing with child sexual abuse and addiction: The Laurel Centre. In R. Csiernik & W. Rowe (Eds.), *Responding to the oppression of addiction* (2nd ed., pp. 74-87). Toronto, ON: Canadian Scholars' Press.

Mactier, H. (2013). Neonatal and longer term management following substance misuse in pregnancy. *Early Human Development, 89*(11), 887-892.

Menella, J. (2015). *Alcohol's affect on lactation.* National Institute on Alcohol Abuse and Alcoholism. Retrieved from http://pubs.niaaa.nih.gov/publications/arh25-3/230-234.htm

Metz, T., & Stickrath, E. (2015). Marijuana use in pregnancy and lactation: A review of the evidence. *American Journal of Obstetrics and Gynecology, 213*(6), 761-778.

Roberts, S., & Nuru-Jeter, A. (2010). Women's perspectives on screening for alcohol and drug use in prenatal care. *Women's Health Issues, 20*(3), 193-200.

Roberts, S., & Pies, C. (2011). Complex calculations: How drug use during pregnancy becomes a barrier to prenatal care. *Maternal and Child Health Journal, 15*(3), 333-341.

Stanhope, T., Gill, L., & Rose, C. (2013). Chronic opioid use during pregnancy. *Clinics in Perinatology, 40*(3), 337-350.

Stewart, R., Nelson, D., Adhikari, E., McIntire, D., Roberts, S., Dashe, J., & Sheffield J. (2013). The obstetrical and neonatal impact of maternal opioid detoxification in pregnancy. *American Journal of Obstetrics and Gynecology, 209*(3), 267(e1-e5).

Varner, M., Silver, R., Hogue, C., Willinger, M., Parker, C., Thorsten, V., ... Eunice Kennedy Shriver National Institute of Child Health (2014). Association between still birth and illicit drug use and smoking during pregnancy. *Obstetrics and Gynecology, 123*(1), 113-125.

Wright, T., Schuetter, R., Tellei, J., & Sauvage, L. (2015). Methamphetamines and pregnancy outcomes. *Journal of Addiction Medicine, 9*(2), 111-117.

Young, J., & Martin, P. (2012). Treatment of opioid dependence in the setting of pregnancy. *Psychiatric Clinics of North America, 35*(2), 441-460.

CHAPTER 7

The Treatment of Adolescent Substance Abuse

Chris Stewart, William S. Rowe, and Tara Bruno

Case Studies

Kevin

Kevin is a 16-year-old African-Canadian male. He was asked to participate in counselling by his mother because of trouble in school and church. His mother reports that his grades have been falling over the past two semesters and she is worried that Kevin's chances for attending college may be in jeopardy. She also states that neither she nor Kevin's father have any significant use or treatment history. Kevin had consistently achieved a low B average and never had any trouble before he "started hanging out with those other kids." Kevin's mother fears that he may be developing an addiction problem. The greatest concern for Kevin's mother is that he stopped attending some church activities, which is an important part of the family's life. His mother reports, "He only goes to youth group on Tuesday nights but won't go to Wednesday or Sunday services." She is also embarrassed because the pastor caught Kevin drinking during a youth group activity. Kevin's mother also reports that Kevin has begun to fight more with his younger brother, who is 11 years old.

Kevin denies any problems with alcohol. He reports that he has been angry since his parents started fighting the last few months. He admits using marijuana "once in a while" with his friends at the youth group. In addition, he drinks occasionally. Kevin speaks of his new friends with excitement and his demeanor visibly changes as he describes their activities. He states that he can "drink his friends under the table."

Lisa

Lisa is a 17-year-old white female. She was referred for treatment from the juvenile justice system. Lisa has had a long criminal history beginning with an arrest for shoplifting at age 13. Her most recent arrest was for assault when she was fighting with another student at school. Lisa did well in elementary school but has achieved poor grades since she entered high school. Lisa is currently in danger of not being able to graduate. Her social history reports that she has no knowledge of her father and lives with her mother. Lisa states that her mother "is always working" and that she rarely has occasion to see her. She also reports that she is often drunk and becomes angry, often throwing things before she "passes out." Her sister, who is 28 years old, has a significant drug history with many treatment episodes. Her younger brother, age 12, is doing well in school with no current substance use issues. Lisa reports that she is concerned about her brother stating, "He'll probably end up just like the rest of us." Lisa states that she began smoking cigarettes at age nine, had her first drink at about the same time, and has tried "most everything." Lisa sarcastically states that, "I've been in more treatment centers than you." She reports that she uses ecstasy at least twice a week and drinks almost every day. She smokes marijuana at least four times weekly. "I'd use more if I could get it, it's my best thing," she reports.

Epidemiology

Adolescent substance use and misuse is an important issue to examine for treatment providers, individual users, and society alike. Gore and colleagues (2011) examined data from the World Health Organization's 2004 Global Burden of Disease study and found that tobacco, alcohol, and illicit drug use during adolescence are important risk factors for disabilities, injuries, and diseases later in life. According to a 2013 report from the Centers for Disease Control and Prevention, substance use disorders are among some of the most significant mental health issues youth experience, which is further complicated by co-existing mental health disorders, such as ADHD, depression, or conduct disorder.

Information from the Canadian Centre on Substance Abuse (CCSA) (2007) suggests that, although the overall rate of youth substance use has stabilized or is in decline across Canada, current use of substances remain at levels comparable to those in the late 1970s, when they were at an all-time high. Interestingly, the rates of tobacco use among the youth have begun a fairly dramatic decline. The latest estimates suggest that 11% of Canadian youth (defined as ages 15–19) are current tobacco users, the lowest rate measured since Health Canada began tracking smoking patterns in the population (Statistics Canada, 2015). Although there have been significant declines in smoking over the past decade, likely due to rising public disapproval and cost, these declines have slowed over the past several years with a corresponding increase in the smoking of cannabis. Alcohol use has also shown a slow decrease in both overall use and binge drinking.

Nonetheless, alcohol use is still widespread among the adolescent population in Canada with approximately 60% of 15- to 19-year-olds having used alcohol in the past year. Approximately 20% of youth drinkers exceeded the chronic risk guidelines recommended by the CCSA, while 15% exceeded the acute risk guidelines (Statistics Canada, 2015). The intention behind developing low-risk guidelines for drinking is to identify thresholds where long-term problems or situational risks are more likely to emerge. However, these guidelines are often unknown to or ignored by youth. Over 40% of Canadian youths between the ages of 15 and 19 reported binge drinking at least once in the past year, and 25% of those between 12 and 19 having binged 12 or more times over the past year (CCSA, 2007).

Alcohol is the most widely consumed substance amongst Canadian youth after caffeine. Cannabis use is still far less prevalent than alcohol use among adolescents. According to Statistics Canada (2015), approximately 22% of youth reported using cannabis in 2013, a rate that was unchanged from the previous year. As for other psychoactive substances, less than 1% of 15- to 19-year-olds reported using such substances as cocaine, hallucinogens, ecstasy, or methamphetamines, rates that also remained stable from previous years.

Demographically, the estimates for illicit drug use in general indicate a clear difference between youth aged 15 to 24 and adults 25 years and older. Youth are significantly more likely to use and abuse illicit substances than adults (Statistics Canada, 2015), though by definition almost all psychoactive agents are illicit to part of this age group. The gender gap, referring to the historic difference in use between males and females, still persists for several different categories of substances. While males tend to be more likely to use tobacco, alcohol, and most illicit drugs, females are actually reporting greater use of psychoactive pharmaceutical drugs. Use, abuse, and dependence all pose concerns for adolescents due to issues ranging from amotivational syndrome to disinhibition and, with drugs such as crystal methamphetamine, atypical aggression.

Assessment

There are two central themes when addressing the substance use practices of youth. One centres on problematizing youth substance use, while the other focuses on the normalization of youth substance use. These conceptualizations are important as they also direct policy and practice. Indeed, Canada's National Anti-Drug Strategy, set out by the Harper Conservative government in 2008, clearly illustrates how youth drug and alcohol use continue to be defined as problematic in contemporary society. Using abstinence-based advertising and educational programs targeted mainly to youth, the anti-drug strategy resorts primarily to fear messages to deter those who consider using drugs or alcohol. Moreover, the advertisements and educational programs aimed at parents further encourage adults to be alarmed and proactive at the first suspicion that a child or youth may be using drugs. However well intentioned, the imagery and messages in media representations of youth substance use, along with ongoing government campaigns aimed at not just discouraging but totally preventing any substance use among youth, contribute to the perception that youth substance use is a serious social problem (Government of Canada, 2011).

From a clinical standpoint, adolescent substance use presents unique issues. The first involves the rather normative use of substances. Available evidence suggests that the majority of adolescents have experimented with both socially defined legal and illegal substances. Some have suggested that because these substances, including alcohol and tobacco, are illegal for adolescents to use, any use also implies abuse. This stance directly implies that any adolescent using substances requires interventions for substance abuse. Rather than considering the pattern and severity of use, a problem is strictly defined by this legal definition, which fails to account for a wide variety of reasons for initiation of use, use patterns, and possible consequences of that use. From a social justice perspective, we may be disadvantaging youth by applying legalistic criteria versus a clear assessment of the impacts of use, excessive use, or dependence on personal and social functioning.

While prevention is an important aspect of drug education and treatment, previous research has indicated that abstinence-based, one-size-fits-all approaches attempting to scare and coerce youth are ineffective (Csiernik, 2016; Midford, 2006). Moreover, such approaches may actually increase substance use by youth because they fail to address the situational and interactive nature of youthful decision-making (West & O'Neal, 2004). Thus, rather than attempt to abolish all substance use through law-enforcement scare tactics and abstinence-based education, prevention strategies should also acknowledge that opportunities for substance use are a normal part of growing up for most youth, and consider more inclusive harm reduction approaches that educate *about* drugs, rather than against them (Csiernik, 2016; Erickson, 1997).

Also, problems arise when the traditional DSM-V criteria are applied to the adolescent population. The main diagnostic criteria can manifest differently with adolescents, causing some misdiagnoses. For example, tolerance will undoubtedly occur as a normal developmental phenomenon and may not necessarily indicate a problem of dependence. Further, there is the fairly common situation among adolescents of the "diagnostic orphan," which delineates a situation in which the adolescent presents one or two dependence symptoms but no abuse symptomology (Winters, Latimer, & Stinchfield, 2001). These issues tend to allow adolescents to be both under- and over-diagnosed in the abuse or dependence categories.

One attempt to create a more comprehensive approach to understanding adolescent use of substances was a cycle of use created by the American Academy of Pediatrics (Martin & Winters, 1998) (Table 7.1). This cycle allows for normative developmental issues and takes into account psychosocial factors in assessing use patterns. The use of such a cycle also provides some protection against attributing behaviour to the use of psychoactive substances when it may be either a fairly normal developmental factor, or perhaps a symptom of some other issue, such as health or mental health.

In an effort to eliminate misdiagnoses and address assessment issues, including both developmental and environmental factors, Winters, Latimer, and Stinchfield (2001) have suggested three main areas of foci in assessing adolescents for substance use problems (Table 7.2). This matrix allows for a more complete clinical assessment of the adolescent by simultaneously addressing factors relevant to adolescent substance use.

Table 7.1   Cycle of Adolescent Substance Use

Abstinence	Experimental Use	Early Abuse	Abuse	Dependence	Recovery
• No use	• Minimal use • Recreational use • Limited substances (e.g., just alcohol)	• Established use pattern • Multiple substances • Beginning of personal consequences of use	• Regular and frequent use • Continuing consequences of use	• Tolerance develops • Continued use despite growing consequences • Change in lifestyle to accommodate substance use	• Return to abstinence

Source: Martin & Winters, 1998

Table 7.2   Adolescent Assessment Factors

Problem Severity	Risk Factors	Cognitive Factors

• Pattern of use:
  • Age at initiation (younger more problematic)
  • Current use (continuity, change, and desistance)
  • Duration (longer greater risk)
• Preferred drug(s) (risks and harms vary)
• DSM symptoms (consequences of use)
	• History of family abuse or dependence
	• Family treatment history
	• Family use
	• Deviant behaviour and legal issues
	• Comorbid psychopathology
	• School issues
	• Community or environmental factors (i.e., crime, poverty, peers)
		• Reasons for use:
		  • Peer influence
		  • Relieve anxiety
		  • Stress or other mental health disorders
		  • Curiosity
		  • Relationship conflict
		• Expectancies: pros and cons of using versus not using
		• Readiness for change
		• Self-efficacy

	Protective Factors	
	• Psychological well-being • Problem solving or coping skills • Academic achievement • Social connectedness to adults • Non-using peers • Religious involvement	

Source: Winters, Latimer, & Stinchfield, 2001

Utilization of these factors has the advantage of a broader multidimensional or inter-sectional perspective. It then becomes possible to accurately screen for those adolescents that may not currently fit the criteria for either abuse or dependence. Similarly, it is also possible to refer those adolescents who have a significant problem to a higher level of care, such as an inpatient program, though in many parts of Canada these are rare and have long waiting lists. To assist with accurate assessments, several screening and assessment measures are available. However, there is no standardized assessment tool for youth, even amongst the most highly regarded treatment facilities (Gans, Falco, Schackman, & Winters, 2009). Thus, there is no guarantee of the validity and reliability of the assessments being used. While not exhaustive, some youth-based measures with good psychometric properties are listed in Table 7.3.

Table 7.3   Assessment Measures for Adolescents

Measure	Source	Type	Length	Subject
Problem Oriented Screening Questionnaire (POSIT)	(Rahdert, 1991)	Screening, self-report	139 items	Drug severity, psychosocial factors
Drug Use Screening Inventory (DUSI-R)	(Tarter, Laird, Bukstein, & Kaminer, 1992)	Screening, self-report	159 items	Drug severity, psychiatric comorbidity, psychosocial factors
Client Substance Index-Short (CSI-S)	(Thomas, 1990)	Screening, self-report	15 items	Drug severity
Teen Severity Index (T-ASI)	Kaminer, Bukstein, & Tarter, 1991)	Comprehensive interview	Varies with severity of use	Drug severity, psychiatric comorbidity, psychosocial factors
Diagnostic Interview Schedule for Children (DISC)	(Costello, Edelbroch, & Costello, 1985)	Comprehensive interview	Varies with severity of use	Drug severity, psychiatric comorbidity, psychosocial factors

Case Study Assessments

The two cases presented earlier offer different clinical issues. Kevin appears to have little significant family use history or other patterns of use. While there is clearly the development of tolerance, that alone does not indicate dependence. Further, there may be several protective factors, such as parental support and possible faith involvement, that may help in the treatment process. The most significant contributing factors to use and progressive risks may be parental fighting, but it would be important to assess the interactive nature of parental fighting with adolescent use. Peers may also have a significant influence in Kevin's case. Given that his peers are connected to his religious involvements, this should also be taken into consideration when assessing his case. In contrast, Lisa's situation suggests a different clinical scenario. There is an early age at onset, other social and interpersonal conflicts, and a significant family history of substance use. Further, there appear to be several risk factors and few protective factors. While little is known about the reasons for use, the available information suggests a much more serious developmental problem than outlined with Kevin.

Both cases also require the use of a multidimensional framework that includes relevant cultural factors. Both adolescents are part of populations that require some consideration in assessment. Culture may have some impact for Kevin as an African-Canadian. Issues of race can be important and may exacerbate any particular problem as well as provide important cultural sources of strength. For instance, healthy mother-adolescent relationships are particularly important for adolescents of African ancestry (Clark, Belgrave, & Abell, 2012). Further, gender may be an important factor for Lisa. It is possible that trauma issues or relational patterns may be uniquely experienced by adolescent women and may, directly or indirectly, have a role in the use of substances (Svensson, 2003). Information on patterns of use, peer use, and other psychosocial factors would be important in determining the best clinical interventions in both of these cases.

Treatment

While the general substance abuse treatment literature is growing, there is still a significant lack of knowledge concerning treatment and the adolescent population (Gans, Falco, Shackman, & Winters, 2009; Kaminer & Bukstein, 2005; Levy, 2014). Several factors have been found to be important in determining successful treatment outcomes (Calabria, Shakeshaft, & Havard, 2011; Deas & Thomas, 2001; Sheidow & Henggeler, 2008; Winters, Botzet, & Fahnhorst, 2011). Severity of substance use, quality of family involvement, and association with non-using peers all significantly contribute to both successful completion of treatment and successful outcomes in post-treatment follow-ups. It was also found that the length of time in treatment and positive relationships with treatment staff were of considerable influence, which directly supports the important conclusion that participation in treatment is better than no treatment (Kaminer & Bukstein, 2005).

Adolescents presenting for treatment, because of unique developmental and social situations, can present a complex clinical picture. One nationwide study conducted in the United States found that 63% of adolescents admitted for substance abuse treatment also carried a DSM-IV-TR disorder (Hser et al., 2001). In a comprehensive province-wide study of outpatient, inpatient, and community-based treatments in Ontario, Rush and Koegl (2008) found that approximately 24% of young people aged 16–24 have co-occurring mental health and substance use disorders. This rate was higher than the older age groups captured in the study. Similarly, family problems, issues at school, and negative peer influence have also been found to be common among adolescents presenting for treatment (Kaminer & Bukstein, 2005; Sanjuan & Langenbucher, 1999). Further, these factors have also been associated with increased rates of relapse post-treatment.

Given these complexities of adolescent lives, there are several guidelines that increase the chance of successful treatment (Sanjuan & Langenbucher, 1999). Firstly, treatment plans should be multidimensional and address not only substance use, but also those comorbid factors that contribute to attitudinal and behaviour problems. This would suggest that common issues such as psychiatric issues, whether or not related directly to the substance, and family issues should be conceptualized and treated interactively and holistically rather than as separate entities with separate outcomes (Kimberly & Osmond, 2010). Treatment elements that have demonstrated importance in achieving successful outcomes, such as relationship with staff and parental involvement, would be beneficial to include whenever possible in treatment planning (Catalano et al., 1991; Toumbourou et al., 2007; Williams, & Chang, 2000).

The level of care needs to be determined through a thorough assessment on an individual basis of severity, but it is thought that outpatient care is preferable due to the possible stigmatizing nature of inpatient treatment. Of course, adolescents with extensive histories of failed treatment, severe psychiatric comorbidity, or other issues where a change of or controlled environment are deemed beneficial might require an inpatient setting, when readily accessible. The length of treatment, regardless of setting, should be of sufficient length and duration to completely address all of the targeted objectives, which is another issue as the length of time allotted for residential treatment has steadily decreased over the past 20 years in many provinces. An optimal approach, as occurs in many American settings in an effort to provide the best treatment in a cost-effective manner, utilizes a step-down approach where the adolescent begins with, for example, an inpatient stay sufficient to establish behaviour patterns, and is then transitioned to intensive outpatient treatment. The intensity of the treatment gradually decreases as treatment goals are achieved. This approach allows for the maximum length of treatment to be achieved, which has been found to be critical, thus increasing the chances for success.

Although these general principles have been found to be effective, there is relatively little evidence to suggest that one particular modality is superior (Kaminer & Bukstein, 2005; Toumbourou et al., 2007). Again, because of the strong multidimensional presentation of problems and risks in adolescents treatment success is more likely to be achieved with a multimodal approach. There has been some research into specific modalities with promising, albeit not conclusive, results. Family therapies, including multidimensional family and functional family therapies, and forms of cognitive-behavioural therapy have demonstrated positive outcomes with adolescents exhibiting substance use problems. Motivational interviewing has also been shown to be beneficial, while the Minnesota 12-Step Model has had mixed results with this population. While inpatient treatment based upon this approach has evidence to suggest efficacy, participation in follow-up groups has yet to demonstrate significant results for adolescents. In Canada there still exists comparatively few addiction treatment programs aimed specifically at young users (Knudsen, 2009).

Treatment Considerations of the Case Studies

In considering the treatment options for Kevin it is important to review the information gathered at assessment. If standardized measures were used, as is done in Ontario, then these can be included in treatment planning. Given the lack of obvious family history and the lack of a serious pattern of use, Kevin probably falls into either Early Abuse or Abuse as categorized in Table 7.1. It is likely that Kevin's substance use may be one of several subjects of intervention. He may also be experiencing depression or require some intervention for anger and interactive patterns of affect, the severity of which should also be assessed in addition to the substance use. The relationship with his new peers will be an important consideration in any planned behaviour or attitudinal change.

Kevin also has several strengths that might be appropriate in designing treatment objectives. He continues to have some involvement with his church and that may prove helpful in the future. Family involvement with their church was, at least at one time, an important part of their lives. It may be worthwhile to investigate the reason(s) for Kevin's withdrawal from family church activities and investigate the possibility of using this resource in further interventions. Further, and perhaps most importantly, his mother appears to be involved and her participation would definitely improve the chances for a positive outcome. It would also be relevant to determine the possibility of other family members' involvement in the treatment process. The more cohesive and integrated the approach, regardless of treatment modality, and the more resources available to support the needed change and sustained gains, the greater the chances for a successful outcome.

While the choice of treatment modality may be made through practical con-siderations—for example, if only one type is available—there are several that may be helpful. First, it is unlikely that an inpatient setting would be required. Family ther-apy may be relevant given that the origin of at least some of Kevin's problem(s) may stem from a change in family dynamics, particularly the conflict between his parents. Further, it is likely that some cognitive-behavioural approach would be useful with his personal issues.

The case of Lisa appears more complex, with greater risk and potential for harm. Her early onset, long history, rather developed pattern of use, and extensive treatment history suggest that her substance abuse problems have reached a critical point. It is probable that she he would be in the dependence category (see Table 7.1) and most likely has some fairly significant genetic and possibly developmental components. Also, the lack of any family support and criminal justice involvement suggest that there may be some underlying psychological issues that would need to be addressed simultaneously for a greater chance of success. Investigation of trauma should be a priority. Assessment measures and diagnostic interviews would be helpful in ascer-taining exactly which issues exist and to what severity. As well, real time observation in group or family therapy may also help to refine the assessment of Lisa's strengths and needs (Werner-Wilson, 2001).

The best way to proceed may be an inpatient setting. Motivational interviewing might help create some internal motivation for Lisa, as she most likely is not interested in either behavioural or attitudinal change. Depending upon the issues involved, a cognitive-behavioural or even simply behavioural approach may also help with the underlying issues related to the substance abuse. There would need to be some effort in establishing some support system and a fairly detailed discharge plan to ensure that the challenges of the environment do not completely derail any treatment gains.

Conclusion

The primary difficulty in assessing and treating adolescent substance abuse and dependence, as exemplified by the case studies, is the wide variety of presentation of symptoms, risk, harm, and etiology. Successful outcomes will depend upon a thorough assessment, including all of the relevant areas, such as family and trauma, and a comprehensive treatment approach. Utilization of assessment procedures and treatment planning that incorporate all relevant factors will give the practitioner the proper information for dealing with the complex issues interacting with their adolescent clients.

REFERENCES

Calabria, B., Shakeshaft, A.P., & Havard, A. (2011). A systematic and methodological review of interventions for young people experiencing alcohol-related harm. *Addiction, 106*(8), 1406–1418.

Canadian Centre on Substance Abuse. (2007). *Substance abuse in Canada: Youth in focus.* Ottawa: Canadian Centre on Substance Abuse.

Catalano, R., Hawkins, J., Wells, E., Miller, J., & Brewer, D. (1991). Evaluation of the effectiveness of adolescent drug abuse treatment, assessment of risks for relapse and promising approaches for relapse prevention. *International Journal of the Addictions, 25*(S9–S10), 1085–1140.

Centers for Disease Control and Prevention. (2013). Mental health surveillance among children-United States, 2005–2011. *Morbidity and Mortality Weekly Report, 62*(2), 1–38.

Clark, T., Belgrave, F., & Abell, M. (2012). The mediating and moderating effects of parent and peer influences upon drug use among African American adolescents. *Journal of Black Psychology, 38*(1), 52–80.

Costello, E., Edelbroch, C., & Costello, A. (1985). Validity of the NIMH Diagnostic Interview Schedule for Children: A comparison between psychiatric and pediatric referrals. *Journal of Abnormal Child Psychology, 13*(4), 570–595.

Csiernik, R. (2016). *Substance use and abuse: Everything matters* (2nd ed.). Toronto, ON: Canadian Scholars' Press.

Deas, D., & Thomas, S. (2001). An overview of controlled studies of adolescent substance abuse treatment. *American Journal of Addictions, 10*(2), 178–189.

Erickson, P. (1997). Reducing the harm of adolescent substance use: Editorial. *Canadian Medical Association Journal, 156*(10), 1397–1399.

Gans, J., Falco, M., Schackman, B., & Winters, K. (2009). An in-depth survey of the screening and assessment practices of highly regarded adolescent substance abuse treatment programs. *Journal of Child & Adolescent Substance Abuse, 19*(1), 33–47.

Gore, F., Bloem, P., Patton, G., Ferguson, J., Joseph, V., Coffey, C., Sawyer, S., & Mathers, C. (2011). Global burden of disease in young people aged 10–24 years: A systematic analysis. *The Lancet, 377*(9783), 2093–2102.

Government of Canada. (2011). *National anti-drug strategy.* Retrieved from nationalantidrugstrategy.gc.ca

Hser, Y., Grella, C., Hubbard, R., Hsieh, S., Fletcher, B., Brown, B., & Anglin, M. (2001). An evaluation of drug treatment for adolescents in 4 U.S. cities. *Archives of General Psychiatry, 58*(7), 689–695.

Kaminer, Y., & Bukstein, O. (2005). Treating adolescent substance abuse. In R. Frances, S. Miller, & A. Mack. (Eds.), *Clinical textbook of addictive disorders* (pp. 559–587). New York: Guilford Press.

Kaminer, Y., Bukstein, O., & Tarter, R. (1991). The Teen-Addiction Severity Index: Rationale and reliability. *International Journal of the Addictions, 26*(2), 219–226.

Kimberley, M., & Osmond, M. (2010). Concurrent disorders and social work interventions. In R. Csiernik & W.S. Rowe (Eds.), *Responding to the oppression of addiction* (2nd ed., pp. 274–293). Toronto, ON: Canadian Scholars' Press.

Knudsen, H. (2009). Adolescent-only substance abuse treatment: Availability and adoption of components of quality. *Journal of Substance Abuse Treatment, 36*(2), 195–204.

Levy, S. (2014). Brief interventions for substance use in adolescents: Still promising, still unproven. *Canadian Medical Association Journal, 186*(8), 565–566.

Martin, C., & Winters, K. (1998). Diagnosis and assessment of alcohol use disorders among adolescents. *Alcohol Health Research World, 22*(1), 95–106.

Midford, R. (2006). Why is drug education popular? *Issues, 74*, 41–42.

Rahdert, R. (1991). *The adolescent assessment/referral system manual.* DHHS Publication No. ADM 91-1735. Rockville, MD: National Institute on Drug Abuse.

Rush, B., & Koegl, C. (2008). Prevalence and profile of people with co-occurring mental and substance use disorders within a comprehensive mental health system. *Canadian Journal of Psychiatry, 53*(12), 810–821.

Ryglewicz, H., & Pepper, B. (1996). *Lives at risk: Understanding and treating young people with dual disorder.* New York: The Free Press.

Sanjuan, P., & Langenbucher, J. (1999). Age-limited populations: Youth, adolescents, and older adults. In B. McCrady & E. Epstein (Eds.), *Addictions: A comprehensive guidebook* (pp. 477–498). New York: Oxford University Press.

Sheidow, A., & Henggeler, S. (2008). Multisystemic therapy for alcohol and other drug abuse in delinquent adolescents. *Alcoholism Treatment Quarterly, 26*(1–2), 125–145.

Statistics Canada. (2015). *Canadian tobacco, alcohol and drugs survey (CTADS): Summary of results for 2013.* Retrieved from http://healthycanadians.gc.ca/science-research-sciences-recherches/data-donnees/ctads-ectad/summary-sommaire-2013-eng.php

Svensson, R. (2003). Gender differences in adolescent drug use. *Youth & Society, 34*(3), 300–329.

Tarter, R., Laird, S., Bukstein, O., & Kaminer, Y. (1992). Validation of the Adolescent Drug Use Screening Inventory: Preliminary findings. *Psychology of Addictive Behaviors, 6*(4), 322–326.

Thomas, D. (1990). *Substance abuse screening protocol for the juvenile courts.* Pittsburgh, PA: National Center for Juvenile Justice.

Toumbourou, J., Stockwell, T., Neighbors, C., Marlatt, G., Sturge, J., & Rehm, J. (2007). Interventions to reduce harm associated with adolescent substance use. *The Lancet, 369*(9570), 1391–1401.

Werner-Wilson, R. (2001). *Developmental-systemic family therapy with adolescents.* New York: Routledge/Haworth.

West, S., & O'Neal, K. (2004). Project D.A.R.E. outcome effectiveness revisited. *American Journal of Public Health, 94*(6), 1027–1029.

Williams, R.J., & Chang, S.Y. (2000). A comprehensive and comparative review of adolescent substance abuse treatment outcome. *Clinical Psychology: Science and Practice, 7*(2), 138–166.

Winters, K., Botzet, A., & Fahnhorst, T. (2011). Advances in adolescent substance abuse treatment. *Current Psychiatry Reports, 13*(5), 416–421.

Winters, K., Latimer, W., & Stinchfield, R. (2001). Assessing adolescent substance use. In E. Wagner & H. Waldron (Eds.), *Innovations in adolescent substance abuse interventions* (pp. 1–29). New York: Elsevier Science.

CHAPTER 8

A Model for Working with Women Dealing with Child Sexual Abuse and Addiction

Diane Hiebert-Murphy and Lee Woytkiw

Introduction

The experience of child sexual abuse is increasingly recognized as a significant risk factor for subsequent development of adjustment difficulties. A growing body of research has documented the negative effects of child sexual abuse on adult functioning (Beitchman et al., 1992; Furniss, 2013; Gladstone et al., 2004; Polusny & Follette, 1995). Women who have experienced sexual abuse in childhood are more likely to experience a variety of other difficulties, including anxiety (Maniglio, 2013), depression (Pérez-Fuentes et al., 2013), a negative self-image (Herman, 1981), homelessness (Hadland et al., 2012), post-traumatic stress (Brown, 2000), sexual difficulties (Briere & Runtz, 1988), and suicidal ideation and attempts (Briere & Runtz, 1986; Marshall, Galea, Wood, & Kerr, 2013). There is also considerable evidence that women with histories of child sexual abuse are more likely than women without child sexual abuse histories to experience substance abuse problems (Roesler & Dafler, 1993; Simons et al., 2003; Teusch, 2001; Wilsnack, Bogeltanz, Klassen, & Harris, 1997), including intravenous drug use (Hadland et al., 2012).

Along with the growing recognition of the negative effects of child sexual abuse has been the attempt to develop treatment strategies to address the needs of women who are dealing with this issue. A variety of approaches have been suggested to deal with the impact this trauma has on women (Briere, 1992; Brown, Rechberger, & Bjelajac, 2005; Finkelstein & Markoff, 2005; Veysey et al., 2005), particularly the unique needs of women who are dealing with both sexual abuse and substance abuse (Chiavaroli, 1992; Fallot & Harris, 2005; Jean Tweed Centre, 2013; Simmons, Sack, & Miller, 1996; Wadsworth, Spampneto, & Halbrook, 1995). Attention to both issues is seen as critical for a successful treatment outcome.

While giving attention to both trauma and addiction issues when working with women dealing with both issues is clinically sound, the integration of these two approaches to treatment presents a conceptual challenge. The treatment of sexual abuse has evolved out of the feminist movement, which points to patriarchy and the abuse of power as key elements. Empowerment of the survivor is seen as fundamental to the resolution of the trauma. As such, survivors are encouraged to find a voice in expressing the violence that has been perpetrated against them and are encouraged to believe that the difficulties they encounter are not their fault, rather, they are the result of being the victim of another's abuse of power. Addiction treatment was historically based on a distinctly different conceptualization. The medical model has had and continues to have a profoundly powerful impact on the addiction field. Despite arguments that approaches such as 12-step programs, which are based on this model, are limiting (Ferri, Amato, & Davoli, 2006; Kasl, 1992), the medical model remains a dominant approach to addiction treatment. From this perspective, addiction is viewed as an illness over which the individual is powerless. The dilemma for the treatment of women who are dealing with both child sexual abuse and addiction is the development of models that provide a convergence of these two distinct approaches to intervention.

Several authors have described treatment approaches to work with women dealing with child sexual abuse and addiction. For example, Bollerud (1990) describes a treatment program for women victims of trauma who become hospitalized for treatment of addiction. This program consists of patient education, individual psychotherapy, and group psychotherapy and is followed by outpatient aftercare. Harris (1996) also describes a program of treatment for women experiencing mental health symptoms, substance abuse, homelessness, and sexual abuse. This approach includes supportive group therapy, cognitive reframing, and social skills training. While providing useful descriptions of treatment programs, the theoretical models underlying these interventions are not well articulated, though Najavits' (2002, 2004) work with addiction and post-traumatic stress has been much more thoroughly developed.

However, few models have been well developed to fully guide clinical practice in this area. Barrett and Trepner (1991) describe one model based upon a multiple systems model of incest. Their model has three stages: (a) creating a context for change in which denial is addressed and the dysfunctional sequences leading to substance abuse are identified; (b) challenging behaviours and expanding alternatives; and (c) consolidation. However, this inpatient treatment for addiction still relied on 12-step programs and did not incorporate language from the transtheoretical model of change (DiClemente, 2007; Prochaska, 2008)

Evans and Sullivan (1995) developed a second theoretical model. Their treatment model was based on an integration of therapeutic approaches with a 12-step approach to the treatment of addiction. They proposed a five-stage model for treatment of survivors of childhood abuse who are chemically dependent that included crisis work, skills building, education, integration, and maintenance. While this model makes an important contribution, it too is based upon a medical view of addiction as an illness and depends upon the clients' acceptance of a 12-step approach to treatment. Although this approach may fit with the needs and perspectives of some clients, there are others for whom this approach is not congruent. Simmons, Sack, and Miller (1996) acknowledge the limitations of the traditional 12-step approach and have suggested that certain substantive modifications are required if the approach is to be effective with survivors of sexual abuse.

The purpose of this chapter is to describe the development of an alternative treatment model for women dealing with sexual abuse who are affected by addiction. This model attempts to bridge the gap between the often-divergent views of treatment that is evident in the trauma recovery literature and the addiction literature. It represents the integration of a trauma recovery model (Herman, 1992) with a feminist approach to practice. The model is based on the knowledge and practice experience of clinicians working at the Laurel Centre in Winnipeg, a community-based agency that provides services to this group of women. The process by which the treatment model was developed is outlined, the treatment model is presented, and a case study is provided to exemplify the application of the model.

Description of the Agency[1]

The Laurel Centre was established in 1985 as a service for women who are survivors of sexual abuse in childhood or adolescence and who have been affected by addiction. The mission of the Centre is to enable the provision of counselling services for women who have experienced childhood or adolescent sexual victimization and want to resolve the long-term effects of abuse. The agency recognizes addiction as one of the long-term consequences related to unresolved trauma. As well, the Centre addresses the issue of society's lack of acknowledgement of the seriousness and prevalence of the problem of childhood sexual abuse and the detrimental long-term effects, one of which is addiction.

The Laurel Centre staff believe that it is important for women to have control over their lives, that decisions about problems to be dealt with in the counselling sessions must be in accordance with the client's wishes, and that identification with the feelings and experiences of other women is integral to the counselling and the resolution of the trauma. Therapeutic interventions are provided on an outpatient basis and include individual counselling, parenting and sexuality groups, and couple counselling. A Youth Program exists to address the specific needs of women aged 16 to 24. Each treatment plan is tailored to the needs of the individual woman and is developed jointly by the women clients and the clinical staff. Staff at the Laurel Centre work with approximately 300 clients per year, with an average length of service of one year. Clients are referred by a variety of community agencies or are self-referred and typically have a long history of seeking help from providers of addiction and mental health services.

The Clinical Model

A child who has been sexually abused has been traumatized. This interrupts the normal human developmental process and results in immediate and long-term effects, such as terror, nightmares, flashbacks, psychosomatic symptoms, identity confusion, interpersonal difficulties with family members, depression, and low self-esteem. Women who were sexually abused as children develop numerous ways of coping with the aftermath of trauma. Some of these coping strategies lead to the resolution of the trauma. Other coping strategies enable the women to cope with the traumatic environment but do not facilitate resolution and can become problematic later in life. Addiction and other compulsive behaviours are common examples of problematic coping strategies. The Laurel Centre recognizes that there is a complex link between addiction, compulsive behaviours, and child sexual abuse. Effective intervention requires attention to all of these factors. Women who were sexually abused as children require an environment and relationships that foster a healing process. When the trauma of the abuse is unresolved, therapy provides a context in which healing can occur. Based on the understanding of this client group and trauma resolution theory, the Laurel Centre developed a therapeutic intervention involving five distinct stages. These stages recur and overlap throughout the therapeutic process with this process being either continuous or episodic.

Engaging and Assessing

This opening stage is about beginnings. The goals are to establish rapport and to assess the fit between the client's needs and the agency's resources. It is a mutual process that enables a determination of client goals and the negotiation of the therapeutic contract. Critical is the establishment of the roles and boundaries of the therapeutic alliance.

To accomplish the goals of this stage of intervention, the social worker is involved in clarifying, normalizing, and validating the client's experience. The abuse experienced by the client is acknowledged. Information is gathered and shared, facilitating the assessment of both the long-term effects of the abuse and the client's strengths, coping skills, and internal and external resources. The social worker's sharing of information empowers the client to give informed consent for therapy.

This stage also involves an exploration of the effects of addictive behaviour on the client and/or significant others and the extent to which the client uses psychoactive drugs as a coping strategy. The social worker and client acknowledge addiction issues and determine the initial focus of treatment. The social worker facilitates the client's explanation of her own perspectives/beliefs/understanding of the addiction process. An assessment of strategies to address addiction, both formal and informal, also occurs. The client is educated about addiction, including the link between addiction and trauma. All of these interventions are important in joining with the client.

Creating Safety

The second stage focuses on safety. Safety in the therapeutic relationship and in the client's life are central to the therapeutic process and are long-term, ongoing issues. The social worker works to develop trust, solidify the alliance between herself and the client, and create emotional safety in the therapeutic relationship. The competence of both the client and the counsellor must be established and the power issues in the relationship addressed. Appropriate boundaries must be established, identified, and maintained if there is to be safety in the therapeutic relationship. To help the client achieve safety in her life, the social worker and client must address high-risk behaviour. This may involve dealing with addiction and helping the client understand how the use of psychoactive drugs compromises safety. The client is made aware of the possibility of substituting addiction for another compulsive behaviour and is assisted in identifying and utilizing appropriate supports for facilitating a change in behaviour. This stage may also involve looking at abusive relationships in the client's life. Feelings related to making change, such as confusion, anxiety, and fear, are closely examined.

Throughout this process the social worker may challenge coping responses that put the client at risk. Current safety concerns must be identified and addressed. The goal is to decrease the client's vulnerability. The client is encouraged to develop a range of different coping methods. The social worker works with the client to build and strengthen the client's resources: social, psychological, physical, and emotional.

In accomplishing these goals, the counsellor works in a manner that decreases fear, anxiety, and shame. The social worker uses language that is respectful and non-blaming to facilitate disclosure. The social worker also pays attention to body language and is attentive to the pacing of interventions. There is an increase in awareness of abuse and consciousness-raising begins.

Intense Debriefing

This third stage of intervention involves the processing of the child sexual abuse and its context. The multiple effects of abuse—sensory, cognitive, behavioural, physical, and emotional—are all addressed. This processing facilitates a shift in understanding of the meaning of the abuse and helps the client begin to define self. There is a linking of past experiences and messages with present behaviours, beliefs, and responses. The client is assisted in recognizing her personal power. She is supported in grieving the losses associated with child sexual abuse and other childhood traumas and is helped to let go of fantasies about the way things "should" have been. During this stage, the client is also encouraged to talk about losses that have occurred as a result of the addiction and is helped to deal with the grief over the emotional loss of the drug of choice. The flood of emotion resulting from no longer suppressing emotion with addictive behaviour is monitored and healthier resources, skills, and supports are reinforced.

Integrating

This stage involves working towards aligning behaviour, affect, and cognition to achieve congruency. Changes made earlier in the therapeutic process are solidified. The client is encouraged to develop a sense of competence in new behaviours and skills. She is assisted in developing new or changed relationships based on new information and understanding. The reorganization and synthesis of various aspects of the self is facilitated. The client is helped to begin developing a positive future orientation with realistic expectations. She is assisted in placing her experiences within the broader socio-political environment that includes misogyny, sexism, racism, heterosexism, and other forms of oppression. As well, to assist in managing the addiction, new coping skills are entrenched. The client is helped to develop a heightened self-awareness and deeper understanding of past patterns that better enable her to access new skills.

Moving On

This final stage facilitates a shift in priorities so that the abuse is no longer the central feature of a client's identity. The client's accomplishments are celebrated and the client is helped to make desired changes in goals, roles, career, and/or lifestyle. Her sense of holistic health is heightened.

During this phase, the client's independence is highlighted and there is a gradual de-emphasizing of the counsellor's role. The client is encouraged to develop herself as a primary resource to continue her healing. She is also urged to increase her use of informal social supports and resources. She is engaged in reflection and evaluating the therapy. This stage involves closure of the therapeutic relationship and involves recognizing and processing the loss. There is a strengthening of social supports that encourage a lifestyle of minimizing self-harming behaviour and that encourage behaviours that create a balanced lifestyle. The client is encouraged to self-monitor behaviours, thoughts, and emotional states that may indicate increased risk of returning to previous addictive behaviour. She is helped to anticipate and prepare for future difficulties.

An Application of the Model

The following case describes the involvement of Jane, a 35-year-old woman, with the Laurel Centre. Jane initially made contact with the agency when she had abstained from cocaine for three months and was having difficulty attending family functions where her uncle, who had sexually abused her, was also in attendance. Jane was able to maintain employment and despite having few financial resources she was able to provide for herself and her two children. There was no history of involvement with child protection authorities and Jane appeared to be meeting the needs of her children.

The process of the treatment is described as it occurred, thereby illustrating the cyclical nature of the intervention.

Engaging and Assessing

At the point of intake, Jane's current situation and treatment needs were assessed. Her ability to stop using cocaine and her recognition of the negative effects of drug abuse were highlighted as strengths. Despite experiencing ongoing negative emotions and thoughts of resuming drug use, Jane was coping with her situation. Jane was informed that there was a 10- to 12-month waiting list before she could receive service. The intake worker supplied Jane with a contact for Cocaine Anonymous and gave her the number for a crisis service. Jane was encouraged to call in the intervening months between being placed on the waiting list and receiving counselling to check her place on the list. This was a strategy to help Jane remember that help was on the way. A letter was sent to Jane confirming that she was on the waiting list. The letter suggested some written resources and once again gave Jane the number for the crisis service.

After 11 months, a therapist contacted Jane and informed her that there was an opening in the pre-counselling group program, and she could begin group counselling. Jane contacted the agency six times during her wait, at times when she was beginning to feel that help would never come. The brief contacts provided enough encouragement for Jane to continue to wait for service.

The facilitators for the pre-counselling group met with Jane prior to starting the group and explored what she needed from the group. She was informed of the goals of the group and the expectations of the members. Together they identified Jane's goals for the group. Jane's primary goal was to get information on how to deal with her memories and her family. Jane made the commitment to attend the 12-week group.

Creating Safety, Intense Debriefing, and Moving On

The primary focus of the pre-counselling group was to provide information and create safety. Through the group process, Jane learned some rudimentary breathing techniques for managing intense emotions. She also found it helpful to develop a concrete plan for managing her affect. For example, Jane identified three people she could call when she was feeling overwhelmed.

Having become somewhat comfortable with managing intense emotional states, Jane readily participated in a group session that dealt with an introduction to the topic of sexual abuse. However, two days after the session, Jane called one of the group leaders in crisis. The therapist intervened with the goal of helping Jane maintain safety. They identified Jane's need to take a break from the stressors in her life. Jane identified a friend who could provide child care for her for a few hours to give her some time off. Jane decided that on her next day off she would go for a drive to a nearby lake, an activity she found relaxing. Jane also decided to take a 10-minute walk during her lunch break at work. Jane returned to the next group session feeling less distressed.

Jane was actively involved in planning the final group session. She wrote a poem as a contribution to the final session. She exchanged phone numbers with two of the other group members and made a commitment to contacting these women. Jane also confided her difficulties with a co-worker and felt positive about the support she received.

Engaging and Assessing

After participating in the pre-counselling group, Jane moved on to individual work. This work was done with another therapist who had not led the group. In the initial session of individual work, the new therapist encouraged Jane to identify what had been helpful about the group and areas that she felt she needed to change. Jane identified that she wanted to decrease her anger and to feel less overwhelmed when she thought about the abuse.

In the first several sessions, the therapist talked with Jane about her current situation and her reasons for seeking therapy. Jane identified areas of difficulty that she had experienced, her use of drugs, current stressors, and her desire to change her life. While she was abstaining from cocaine use, she reported periodic abuse of non-prescription drugs. The therapist also explored and validated Jane's areas of strength. After attending three therapy sessions, Jane did not attend her next two scheduled sessions. Upon returning to therapy, Jane was relieved to know that despite having "messed up" and not cancelling her appointments, the therapist was willing to continue to see her. The therapist addressed Jane's ambivalence about treatment. She reflected to Jane that sometimes women have mixed feelings when attending therapy, and that while there are feelings of relief associated with going to therapy, many people also feel very scared about talking about painful issues. Jane reported feeling relieved that the therapist had understood her and not "written her off." Trust, respect, control, and the boundaries of the therapeutic relationship were issues being explored. In anticipation of her eventually moving on, the therapist spent time in the first sessions discussing with Jane how she would know that she no longer needed to be in therapy. Although she was unable at that time to answer the question, Jane was beginning to be empowered by having the therapist identify that she was in control of the goals of the therapy and was an active collaborator in the therapeutic process.

Creating Safety

Jane maintained close contact with her sister, Tracy, who had first introduced Jane to cocaine. Tracy often offered to "score" for Jane. Tracy also told Jane that she thought too much about the past and was no longer any fun to be around. She wanted Jane to stop therapy. Jane was helped to see that her relationship with Tracy was complex. When they were children, Tracy had protected Jane, often running interference with their stepfather when he was about to hit Jane. However, Tracy refused to talk about what had happened in the family and had ongoing contact with the uncle who had sexually abused Jane. After having contact with her sister, Jane reported feeling suicidal. She acknowledged a recent relapse involving cocaine use after a visit. After several weeks, Jane was able to see that, while Tracy cared for her, she was currently getting in the way of Jane making necessary changes. The contact was identified as an important risk factor for Jane returning to drug use. Jane began to refuse to go to Tracy's apartment and talked to Tracy about always pressuring her to use "coke." Tracy became angry and did not speak to Jane for two months. During the break in contact, Jane noticed that she had less suicidal ideation and spent less time thinking about using drugs, both of which decreased her risk for drug use. However, Jane reported feelings of guilt and disloyalty associated with Tracy's absence. These feelings were identified as increasing her risk for relapse. To decrease the risk, Jane began to call one of the women she met through the pre-counselling group.

Engaging and Assessing

In the early stages of individual therapy, Jane disclosed that she was feeling that she was not a good parent and wanted to take better care of her children. Jane was referred to the parenting program and attended this at the same time as attending individual therapy. Through her involvement in this program she learned some new skills that enhanced her parenting. She also began to see her strengths as a parent as well as areas in which change was needed. She appreciated the opportunity to be with other mothers and perceived that she benefited greatly from their ideas and validation.

Intense Debriefing

Jane began to have nightmares abut her uncle shortly after Tracy disconnected from her. She began to talk for the first time about the sexual abuse by her uncle, disclosing that the abuse began when she was 5 and continued until she ran away at age 17. Jane felt that the abuse was her fault because she had initially liked the attention he had given her. Her uncle had often taken her out for ice cream and walks prior to the day he began touching her "down there." Even after her uncle had started the sexual touching, Jane still wanted to go for ice cream with him. Jane stated that she felt that by maintaining contact with her uncle she had agreed to what he had done. She referred to herself as a "little slut" who had wanted it. After reporting these thoughts about herself, Jane recalled her uncle telling her, "You want this don't you Janey, you like this don't you." Jane remembered further that her uncle had said this despite the fact that she had cried and asked him to stop. She began to remind herself that she had not liked what her uncle had done to her.

Integrating

Over the course of therapy, Jane began to see that there were a number of things in her childhood over which she had no control. The therapist helped Jane look at the fact that at the time of the abuse, Jane's mother was very involved in caring for Jane's alcoholic father, who was dying. Tracy, who was six years older, was spending a great deal of time with her friends from school. Jane's uncle had come along when Jane was feeling very alone and vulnerable. Jane began to understand how feelings of sadness and aloneness were risk factors for cocaine use and other problematic coping behaviours.

During her involvement in individual therapy, Jane participated in a time-limited therapy group for women in treatment at the agency. This group helped her experience that she was not alone in dealing with sexual abuse. She began to see herself as belonging to a group of women with similar life experiences who were also struggling to cope. She developed an awareness of the enormity of the problem of violence against women and children and began to see her experiences as part of a larger social problem. This helped to challenge Jane's feelings of aloneness and clarified her thinking around issues of blame and responsibility. She also reported that she benefited from a safe environment in which to talk about her concerns regarding sexuality and intimacy. Overall, Jane's participation in the various groups enhanced her interpersonal skills and contributed to improvement in her self-esteem. Recognizing that she could be a support and help to other women gave Jane a different view of herself.

Moving On

After 14 months of individual therapy, Jane reported that she no longer had nightmares and no longer felt she was a bad person. She felt that she had identified and addressed issues that increased her risk to use drugs. Her interpersonal relationships also improved. After several months of no communication, Tracy contacted Jane. They made an agreement involving Tracy not offering drugs and Jane not talking about the past. Although not ideal, this arrangement allowed the two to remain in contact while defining some parameters for their relationship. Jane developed a supportive friendship with a co-worker who was in Alcoholics Anonymous (AA) and, through her, connected with other people dealing with addiction-related issues. While Jane did not want to attend AA, she found that she could call many of these new people in her life when she was having a difficult time. She made arrangements to call one of these individuals after attending a family gathering. Jane found that knowing that there were people she could talk to made it easier to leave family functions when she was feeling overwhelmed. Jane was supported in her desire to better her financial situation; she enrolled in a course to get her high school diploma and began to look at ways of getting a new job that would be more suited to her skills and interests. She continued to feel more positively about her parenting and had some people in her support network that could provide her with tangible help as well as emotional support in parenting.

Jane reported that she no longer felt her anger was out of control and felt that she no longer needed to come for therapy. Termination involved talking about what Jane had accomplished, identifying challenges that she was likely to face, and talking about the loss of the therapeutic relationship. Jane reported that she was afraid to end therapy, just in case "something else came up." The therapist assured Jane that she was free to come back, should she assess the need for further support.

Discussion

The Laurel Centre model represents the practices of staff working with women deal-ing with sexual abuse and affected by addictions. Unlike Barrett and Trepper's (1991) model, which is based upon a multiple systems model of sexual abuse, this model is strongly influenced by the trauma recovery model proposed by Herman (1992). While the stages of the model are similar to those described by Evans and Sullivan (1995), this model does not rely on a 12-step approach to addiction treatment, yet clients can still reach out to 12-step groups as an ancillary resource. However, the primary emphasis is on the resolution of the trauma, which includes addressing addiction issues, and assumes a cyclical process of recovery. It deals with the divergent views of underlying trauma therapies and addiction treatment by conceptualizing addiction as a coping mechanism aimed at managing the negative effects of child sexual abuse.

The model does not preclude the use of any one approach to addiction; rather, it enables an integration of various addiction treatment models depending upon the needs of the client. The model can be adapted for use with clients who wish to involve themselves in other addiction programs, such as membership in a 12-step group or acute detoxification programs. As illustrated by the case description, the model can be used to integrate a relapse prevention model (Sanchez-Craig, 1996) with the trauma recovery model. Social workers remain flexible in helping clients discover ways of coping with addiction that fit their situation and world view. Ideally, social workers using this model are knowledgeable about different treatments for addiction, and during the assessment phase develop a treatment plan that fits with the needs and views of the client.

Inherent in the model is the recognition of women's rights to control their lives and to be active collaborators in treatment. Although the difficulties the women experi-ence are not minimized, the strengths they demonstrate in coping with challenging life circumstances are acknowledged. Validation of the client's experiences occurs; this includes not only the experiences of abuse that are part of the women's lives, but also the ongoing life issues with which women are confronted. The trauma and addiction issues are viewed from a perspective that encompasses the entire context of the women's lives.

There is a conscious effort to be aware of the role of the therapist and the power issues that exist in all human relationships. Acceptance of this knowledge and experience of the therapist is balanced with respect for the woman and her strengths as well as her right to control the process of her treatment. This is reflected in the client's control of the pacing of therapy, an acknowledgment that the process is not linear, and an acceptance that treatment may be episodic. The women are given an active role in therapy and encouraged to exercise their power in the therapeutic relationship. There is recognition, however, that abuse can make trust and assertion in interpersonal relationships difficult. Throughout treatment, the relationship evolves as the client moves towards health and wellness.

Consistent with a feminist approach to practice, women's difficulties are seen as embedded in a socio-political context; clients are thought to benefit from seeing their problems linked to broader social forces. While not forcing a particular ideology, the therapeutic process is aimed at providing opportunities for the development of a different understanding of the abuse and other difficulties the clients have experienced. As well, therapists encourage the development of support among women through the strengthening of formal and informal support networks.

The Laurel Centre approach provides a framework for working with child sexual abuse and addiction that enables the integration of various addiction treatment models with the trauma recovery model. The emphasis is upon resolving the trauma of child sexual abuse while addressing addiction issues from an approach that fits with the views and needs of the client. Therapists using the model must be knowledgeable about addiction treatment and flexible in their use of various treatment approaches. While a challenging model to implement, its strength lies in its adaptability for use with a wide range of clients. Furthermore, the emphasis upon empowerment of women, and upon women's oppression, provides a useful base from which to address issues related to both addiction and child sexual abuse.

NOTE

1. For more information on the Laurel Centre please visit http://www.thelaurelcentre.com

REFERENCES

Barrett, M., & Trepper, T. (1991). Treating women drug abusers who were victims of childhood sexual abuse. In C. Bepko (Ed.), *Feminism and addiction* (pp. 127-146). New York: Haworth Press.

Beitchman, J., Zucker, K., Hood, J., daCosta, G., Akman, D., & Cassavia, E. (1992). A review of the long-term effects of child sexual abuse. *Child Abuse and Neglect, 16*(1), 101-118.

Bollerud, K. (1990). A model for the treatment of trauma-related syndromes among chemically dependent inpatient women. *Journal of Substance Abuse Treatment, 7*(2), 783-787.

Briere, J. (1992). *Child abuse trauma: Theory and treatment of the lasting effects.* Newbury Park, CA: Sage Publications.

Briere, J., & Runtz, M. (1986). Suicidal thoughts and behaviors in former sexual abuse victims. *Canadian Journal of Behavioural Science, 18*(4), 413-423.

Briere, J., & Runtz, M. (1988). Post sexual abuse trauma. In G. Wyatt & G. Powell (Eds.), *Lasting effects of child sexual abuse* (pp. 85-99). Newbury Park, CA: Sage.

Brown, P. (2000). Outcome in female patients with both substance use and post-traumatic stress disorders. *Alcoholism Treatment Quarterly, 18*(3), 127-135.

Brown, V., Rechberger, E., & Bjelajac, P. (2005). A model for changing alcohol and other drug, mental health, and trauma services practice. *Alcoholism Treatment Quarterly, 22*(3), 81-94.

Chiavaroli, T. (1992). Rehabilitation from substance abuse in individuals with a history of sexual abuse. *Journal of Substance Abuse Treatment, 9*(4), 349-354.

DiClemente, C. (2007). The transtheoretical model of intentional behaviour change. *Drugs and Alcohol Today, 7*(1), 29-33.

Evans, K., & Sullivan, J. (1995). *Treating addicted survivors of trauma.* New York: Guildford Press.

Fallot, R., & Harris, M. (2005). Integrated trauma services teams for women survivors with alcohol and other drug problems and co-occurring mental disorders. *Alcoholism Treatment Quarterly, 22*(3), 181–199.

Ferri, M., Amato, L., & Davoli, M. (2006). Alcoholics Anonymous and other 12-step programmes for alcohol dependence. *Cochrane Database of Systematic Reviews, 19*(3), CD005032.

Finkelstein, N., & Markoff, L. (2005). The women embracing life and living (WELL) project: Using the relational model to develop integrated systems of care for women with alcohol/drug use and mental health disorders with histories of violence. *Alcoholism Treatment Quarterly, 22*(3–4), 63–80.

Frankel, S., Frankel, H., & Tabisz, E. (1995). *Sexual abuse survivorship and substance abuse: Intervention and recovery (Study Series No. 12546)*. Winnipeg, MB: Faculty of Social Work, University of Manitoba, Child and Family Services Research Group.

Furniss, T. (2013). *The multiprofessional handbook of child sexual abuse: Integrated management, therapy, and legal intervention*. New York: Routledge.

Gladstone, G. Parker, G., Mitchell, P., Malhi, G., Wilhelm, K., & Austin, M. (2004). Implications of childhood trauma for depressed women: An analysis of pathways from childhood sexual abuse to deliberate self-harm and revictimization. *American Journal of Psychiatry, 161*(8), 1417–1425.

Hadland, S., Werb, D., Kerr, T., Fu, E., Wang, H., Montaner, J., & Wood, E. (2012). Childhood sexual abuse and risk for initiating injection drug use during adolescence and young adulthood: A prospective cohort study. *Journal of Adolescent Health, 50*(2), S1.

Harris, M. (1996). Treating sexual abuse trauma with dually diagnosed women. *Community Mental Health Journal, 32*(4), 371–385.

Herman, J. (1981). *Father-daughter incest*. Cambridge, MA: Harvard University Press.

Herman, J. (1992). *Trauma and recovery*. New York: Harper Collins.

Jean Tweed Centre. (2013). *Trauma matters: Guidelines for trauma-informed practices in women's substance use services*. Toronto, ON: Jean Tweed Centre.

Kasl, C. (1992). *Many roads, one journey*. New York: Harper Perennial.

Maniglio, R. (2013). Child sexual abuse in the etiology of anxiety disorders: A systematic review of reviews. *Trauma, Violence, & Abuse, 14*(2), 96–112.

Marshall, B., Galea, S., Wood, E., & Kerr, T. (2013). Longitudinal associations between types of childhood trauma and suicidal behavior among substance users: A cohort study. *American Journal of Public Health, 103*(9), e69–e75.

Najavits, L. (2002). *Seeking safety: A treatment manual for PTSD and substance abuse*. New York: Guilford Press.

Najavits, L.M. (2004). Treatment of posttraumatic stress disorder and substance abuse. *Alcoholism Treatment Quarterly, 22*(1), 43–62.

Pérez-Fuentes, G., Olfson, M., Villegas, L., Morcillo, C., Wang, S., & Blanco, C. (2013). Prevalence and correlates of child sexual abuse: A national study. *Comprehensive Psychiatry, 54*(1), 16–27.

Polusny, M., & Follette, V. (1995). Long-term correlates of child sexual abuse: Theory and review of the empirical literature. *Applied and Preventative Psychology, 4*(3), 143–166.

Prochaska, J. (2008). Decision making in the transtheoretical model of behavior change. *Medical Decision Making, 28*(6), 845–849.

Roesler, T., & Dafler, C. (1993). Chemical dissociation in adults sexually victimized as children: Alcohol and drug use in adult survivors. *Journal of Substance Abuse Treatment, 10*(6), 537–543.

Sanchez-Craig, M. (1996). *A therapist's manual: Secondary prevention of alcohol problems*. Toronto, ON: Addiction Research Foundation.

Simmons, K., Sack, T., & Miller, G. (1996). Sexual abuse and chemical dependency: Implications for women in recovery. *Women and Therapy, 19*(1), 17–30.

Simons, L., Ducette, J., Kirby, K., Stahler, G., & Shipley Jr., T. (2003). Childhood trauma, avoidance coping, and alcohol and other drug use among women in residential and outpatient treatment programs. *Alcoholism Treatment Quarterly, 21*(4), 37–54.

Teusch, R. (2001). Substance abuse as a symptom of childhood sexual abuse. *Psychiatric Services, 52*(11), 1530–1532.

Veysey, B., Andersen, R., Lewis, L., Mueller, M., & Stenius, V. (2005) Integration of alcohol and other drug, trauma and mental health services, *Alcoholism Treatment Quarterly, 22*(3), 19–39.

Wadsworth, R., Spampneto, A., & Halbrook, B. (1995). The role of sexual trauma in the treatment of chemically dependent women: Addressing the relapse issue. *Journal of Counseling and Development, 73*(4), 401–406.

Wilsnack, S., Vogeltanz, N., Klassen, A., & Harris, T. (1997). Childhood sexual abuse and women's substance abuse: National survey findings. *Journal of Studies on Alcohol, 58*(3), 264–271.

CHAPTER 9

Narrative Therapy Ideas and Practices for Working with Addiction

Laura Béres

Introduction

Narrative therapy, as developed by Michael White and David Epston (1990), although steadily growing in popularity in counselling and community settings, continues to be considered a relatively new approach to practice, and particularly new in relation to when addiction counselling first began. It is sometimes referred to as a post-modern or post-structuralist therapy, influenced by certain anthropologists (Bruner, 1986a; Myerhoff, 1986) and philosophers (Derrida, 1973; Foucault, 1965). Narrative therapy has philosophical and political underpinnings that contribute to its commitment to moving away from totalizing and pathologizing accounts of those people who come and consult us (White, 1995). These commitments can be viewed as being in direct opposition to certain approaches to working with addiction that use a disease model framework and expect people to label themselves as addicts or alcoholics for their entire lives.

This revised chapter for the third edition of *Responding to the Oppression of Addiction* will review and update some key ideas related to narrative therapy that are particularly important for narrative therapists to keep in mind when working with people attempting to gain control over addiction in their lives.[1] These ideas are contextualized using a case example, privileging Becky's descriptions of her journey through an inpatient rehabilitation program, various eclectic social work interventions, attendance of Alcoholics Anonymous (AA) meetings, and finally a combination of AA and individual narrative therapy conversations with this author as her primary social worker. Becky provides insights as to how she has been able to supplement her AA support with what she calls the more empowering and liberating ideas she has received from narrative practices that do not limit her identity to that of an addict, or recovering addict, but rather provide further choices regarding her story and her future. She describes how this has not been experienced as contradictory, but rather as hopeful.

Ideas Related to Narrative Therapy

Moving Away from Totalizing and Pathologizing Accounts

White (2007a) points out that people who seek counselling often believe that the problems in their lives are due to some problem associated with their identity. They may
begin to believe that their problems are "internal to their self or the selves of others—that
they or others are in fact the problem" (p. 9). White worked against these tendencies
for people to see themselves as the problem by developing a method of interacting with
people that he described as an externalizing conversation. The process of engaging in
an externalizing conversation "makes it possible for people to experience an identity
that is separate from the problem; the problem becomes the problem, not the person ...
the problem ceases to represent the 'truth' about the (person's identity), and options
for successful resolution suddenly become visible and accessible" (p. 9).

Conversations that externalize the problem from someone's internalized account
of their identity also involve externalizing internalized discourses to a certain degree
(White, 1995). In describing discourses, Healy (2000) has presented a useful definition:

> Discourses are structures of knowledge, claims and practices through which
> we understand, explain and decide things. In constituting agents they also
> define obligations and determine the distribution of responsibilities and
> authorities for different categories of persons such as parents, children,
> social workers, doctors, lawyers and so on.... They are frameworks or grids of
> social organization that make some social actions possible while precluding
> others. (p. 39)

An internalized discourse, therefore, acts as a framework of understanding the world
and how to behave in it that has been incorporated and become "taken-for-granted,"
thereby also becoming almost invisible and difficult to notice, like the air we breathe.
These internalized discourses can be externalized through the use of externalizing
conversations so that people can reflect upon where they have learned these ways of
being, and make decisions about whether they wish to continue to be influenced in
these ways. Many discourses are supported and circulated through popular cultural
texts with which people engage (Bennett, Mercer, & Woolacott, 1986; Béres, 1999, 2002).

Hari, in his 2015 book *Chasing the Scream: The First and Last Days of the War on
Drugs*, presents an in-depth analysis of the development of the discourses associated
with addiction, and the devastating effects of prohibition, beginning with a war on
alcohol and continuing with the ongoing War on Drugs. He unpacks many of today's
taken-for-granted assumptions about the dangers of drugs and shaming attitudes and
language used to describe those using drugs, such as addicts and alcoholics, as having
been purposefully developed by the leaders of the Department of Prohibition, which
was then replaced by the Federal Bureau of Narcotics in the United States. Reporting
on three years of interviews with people around the world, Hari presents a perspective

that is oddly consistent with the political and philosophical commitments of narrative therapy. He suggests, in much the same way a narrative practitioner would, that it is necessary to move away from shaming, labelling, and fearing people with addictions and to begin to become more aware of the broader social contexts in which addictions develop and are then supported and maintained.

There are therapeutic discourses as well as cultural, political, and popular-cultural discourses that influence how we interact. White, influenced by Foucualt (1965), also made visible and challenged the normative practices that have developed over the last 300 years in Western culture that have contributed towards the objectification, totalization, and pathologizing of modern-day subjects. Foucault pointed out that psychologies and psychotherapies have also contributed to the reproduction of these tendencies that arose with scientific classification and labelling through disorders and dysfunctions, as occurs when an individual is given a DSM diagnosis (White, 1995). White states, "we can render transparent many of the taken-for-granted practices of the culture of psychotherapy that are reproductive of problematic aspects of the dominant culture" (p. 46) and he provides methods of interacting with people in a more transparent manner. It is this aspect of narrative practice that I believe is the most congruent with anti-oppressive social work, which seeks to provide alternative approaches to working with people other than the mainstream expert-driven approaches that can inadvertently reinforce current power structures within society.

A person is objectified, totalized, and patholgized when she is labelled, or referred to, as a "victim" or even a "survivor," as "depressed" or as an "alcoholic" since each of these terms has the tendency to limit the person's identity to only that one descriptor. These labels and diagnoses are also more apt to suggest individual causes and effects and less likely to fully examine the social aspects of the problem. Having worked for many years with adult survivors of childhood sexual abuse and also with people who had experienced the effects of intimate partner violence, I was struck by the fact that many people with histories of being abused would often commence counselling feeling as though they were merely victims, would move to a point of viewing themselves as survivors, but would then move on to a position of not wanting to think of themselves in relation to their history of abuse at all, so not as victims or survivors, but just as people with far richer lives than either of these identities can imply.

Due to my experiences of realizing the importance of moving away from totalizing and pathologizing accounts in relation to childhood sexual abuse and intimate partner violence, I was particularly careful about the use of language in my work with people struggling with addiction that could label them in these ways. Although there is a history of AA expecting people to take responsibility for their lives by saying, "I am an alcoholic," I have been worried by the possibility of this approach limiting people's options and preferences in their lives. I was interested in asking Becky how she was able to manage this difference in our work together versus her experiences with AA. Becky reported that she has found it much more empowering to be able to begin to introduce herself at her regular AA meetings as someone who has struggled with addiction, rather than as an addict, since this frees her to be more than just an addict.

Re-authoring from Dominant to Alternative Storylines

White and Epston (1990), building on the work of Bruner (1986a), Geertz (1986), and Gergen and Gergen (1984), began considering the "proposal that persons give meaning to their lives and relationships by storying their experience, and that in interacting with others in the performance of these stories, they are active in shaping their lives and relationships" (White & Epston, 1990, p. 13).

Accepting the notion that a story is made up of a series of events, linked over time according to a plot or theme, White and Epston (1990) went on to build upon Goffman's (1961) idea that there are "unique outcomes," or events in peoples' lives that may have been ignored, which fall outside of the dominant problem storyline that can be built upon to develop a new or preferred storyline. This process of moving from a problem or dominant storyline to an alternative or preferred storyline is described by White (2007a) as a "re-authoring" (p. 61) conversation.

When people begin counselling they usually then go on to tell the history of their problem, telling the story of the series of events that have happened over time that prove their problem. When Becky began counselling with me, for example, she told me she had been clean and sober for a few years but that she was still struggling with low self-esteem and relationship difficulties. She labelled herself as an alcoholic and told me of the series of events over the course of her life that when strung together could be labelled as having the plot of alcoholism and low self-esteem. She had met with several therapists and trainee therapists who believed in the importance of uncovering the details of these painful experiences in order for her to understand herself better, deal with her emotions, and not make the same mistakes again. In beginning a new therapeutic relationship with me, she indicated that she was worried that she would be required to go over everything with me again and that she was never going to be better and able to move on from these events.

Although it is not necessary to explain the theory of re-authoring conversations to people in order to assist them in moving into a preferred storyline, I decided to explain this idea to Becky in one of her later sessions with me. I explained that people often think of themselves and describe themselves to others in a storyline format. I also pointed out that of all the events that have occurred in a person's life only a fraction of those events are given enough importance to be linked together in the story. Becky had spent many years thinking of all those painful events over the course of her life and all those times when she smoked pot and drank beer to excess and lost control. She had thought and spoken of those events and that story as having the overriding theme of "addiction." Each time she told that story again to herself or a new therapist she reinforced and further solidified that story. Despite those events and that problem storyline, there are many more events in Becky's life that may have previously seemed insignificant, that had not been privileged (given any attention), and that had not become part of a story. When she is able to look at those events when she has been taking care of herself, enjoying her time with her son, reading and journaling and generally feeling relaxed and happy, she can see that there is more than one truth about herself or storyline in her life. If she steps into the re-authoring of her life, looking for those events that can be linked together into a preferred and healthier storyline, she is better able to make choices about her future life that are consistent with her preferred storyline rather than consistent with the problem storyline.

When I first began working from a narrative framework with people who requested counselling I would become excited when we discovered a unique outcome or event that stood outside of the problem storyline and showed a victim of sexual abuse, for example, that she was not only a victim but also a survivor. I was initially disappointed by the fact that finding this event did not make as much of a positive impact as I might have hoped. It took a while for me to truly comprehend that it takes more than one event to make a new story; it takes a series of events over time to make a story. One unique outcome or event is susceptible to being argued away as being a coincidence or fluke. The more events that can be discovered that fit into the preferred storyline and the more details that can be shared about those events and story, the more robust the story will be and more able to have ongoing positive effects in the person's life. Since the problem storyline has usually become strengthened by many retellings, it is useful to spend time assisting the person in adding as much detail as possible to the newer, preferred storyline in order to also strengthen it.

The idea that people make meaning of their lives by storying the events, and that there are multiple stories available and possible from the multitude of events in a person's life, are consistent with Foucauldian, post-modern, and post-structuralist thinking. Irving (1999) points out that "Foucault draws us away from enlightenment ideas of a universal history, atemporal truth, and human nature that is fixed and timeless. He looks to pluralities, provisional truths, and many changing practices of knowledge" (p. 43). Healy (2000) points out that while post-structuralists highlight the power of language and discourses they also "are concerned to move away from the notions of 'essential' meanings or beliefs in a fixed, singular, logical order" (p. 39). This encourages us in moving away from assessing and labelling someone as an alcoholic, which can be experienced as totalizing and limiting alternate possibilities, and towards a curiosity in the multiple possibilities present in the person's experiences and in their interpretations. This is not to be misunderstood as a relativist stance, as if "anything goes" or "it just depends on your point of view." It is a truth that a victim of sexual abuse was victimized and it is true that someone has experienced negative effects from alcoholism. What is important to hold on to, however, is that these are not the only truths in peoples' lives. They have also resisted, survived, and been sober at other times.

Values, Hopes, Preferences

The re-authoring conversation, as described above, also involves what White (2007a) describes as two distinct landscapes. He developed the re-authoring conversation in such a way that it can be visualized or "mapped" over time from remote history, distant history, or recent history to the present and imagined into the near future. As well as involving this timeline, the conversation also zigzags back and forth between what he has called the "landscape of action" and the "landscape of identity" (2007a, p. 81). White's use of these "landscapes" has been influenced by Bruner (1986b). Asking "what," "when," "where," and "who" questions within the landscape of action would elicit concrete details of things that have occurred ("just the facts"). Asking questions in the landscape of identity involves inquiring about the person's understandings, meaning-making, preferences, and hopes, which involves asking "how" and "why" questions. By being careful to ask questions in both landscapes a richer and more complex story is developed. Thinking about a favourite novel or film, it is possible to think about the richness of details, motives, and hopes that contribute to the development of an engaging story beyond merely a list of events. These are the details that could be considered as beginning to move an initial assessment meeting with someone beyond a simple checklist with tick boxes and towards an engaging conversation that is characterized by curiosity and interest.

I believe that one of the unique contributions of narrative therapy to the field of counselling is its focus upon people's values and preferences. Not only does the re-authoring conversation involve discussions with people about their hopes, values, and meaning-making through questions in the landscape of identity; most of the conversational maps that White (2007a) has developed also include a component of asking why a person has judged something a certain way. This is done in order to centre and privilege the client's beliefs, interpretations, and judgements over the therapist's assessment as to whether the effects of a behaviour are good or bad.

I have also begun to realize that narrative practices are particularly well-suited to incorporating discussions about the role of spirituality in people's lives (Béres, 2013a, 2013b, 2014). Spirituality can be described as "the human quest for personal meaning and mutually fulfilling relationships among people, the non-human environment, and, for some, God" (Canda, 1988, p. 243). If spirituality is defined and understood as that which gives people a sense of meaning and purpose in their lives, whether or not it has anything to do with organized religion or God, then we do a disservice to people if we are unwilling to discuss spirituality with them. Many social work students and practitioners express discomfort with this proposition for a variety of reasons, yet using the narrative conversational maps as a framework for interactions with people provides a method of including questions about meaning-making, hopes, values, and preferred ways of being without having to worry about how to begin to talk about something so ethereal as spirituality.

As Jarusiewicz (2000) points out, other than in AA approaches to responding to addictions, spirituality has rarely been incorporated into mainstream treatment methods beyond asking about any religious affiliation. She speculates that this may be due to the non-religious and non-spiritual stance of much of the medical and scientific communities. Based upon her research that shows the strong correlation between spirituality and recovery, she suggests that treatment approaches must become more responsive to the spirituality of people who are requesting assistance with overcoming their addictions.

Galanter (2006) also points out that "the paradigms on which contemporary psychiatry are based do not readily lend themselves to the consideration of spirituality as an empirically validated component of mental function" (p. 287). He adds that Freud's orientation of viewing religion as a mass delusion did not leave space for much interest in spirituality. Not surprisingly, Galanter describes the manner in which William James, who also influenced White's narrative therapy practices, derided medical materialism as falling short of explaining people's engagement with religion and spirituality. He explains that both James and Jung "were influential in legitimizing the role of spirituality embodied in Alcoholics Anonymous. Bill W., AA's co-founder, had read James and corresponded with Jung; both of his predecessors had emphasized that alcoholics were seekers, usually of God or serenity, in attempting to relieve emotional distress" (p. 288). He moves on to also describe the manner in which meaning-making and hope can be integrated into treatment approaches that are more secular in nature. He describes the importance of personal meaning, which is associated with humanism and also Zen Buddhism, and so suggests that treatment approaches can be tailored to be respectful of various cultures and subcultures.

As social workers drawing upon what we have observed in other people struggling with addictions, it might seem sensible to make a value judgment and assume that alcoholism is "bad" and has negative effects in someone's life. This would perhaps lead us to assist a person in problem solving a way out of the problem of alcoholism or addiction. This can inadvertently be an act of silencing the person's own meaning-making as the therapists judge what is best for the person. If a person struggling with an addiction is asked to think about and describe why they have judged the effects of their addiction as negative, and what that therefore means they give value to, then the person is better able to develop more individualized strategies for developing behaviours that are in-line with their own preferences, values, and dreams. White (2007a) has suggested that this can lead to "problem dissolving" versus "problem solving." Sometimes peoples' preferences for their lives are influenced by their beliefs about spirituality, so highlighting and supporting those beliefs in therapeutic conversations can be another method of supporting the person's self-determination and experience-based knowledge. This helps de-centre the therapist's knowledge and centres the knowledge of the person coming to consult the therapist.

Re-membering Conversations

Re-membering conversations contain a particular structure within narrative practices (Russell & Carey, 2004; White, 1995, 2007a) that allow for conversations with those people who consult us that focus on the impact of other people in their lives. White developed re-membering conversations based upon the "conception that identity is founded upon an 'association of life' rather than on a core self" (White, 2007a, p. 129). He has also described this "association of life" as a club, as if our club of life is made up of many members. We can review membership of our club of life and make choices regarding revoking membership from those people who are not supporting our preferences, and perhaps giving honorary life membership to those who have been particularly significant in positively shaping who and what we are.

My experience with re-membering conversations with many people, with a range of presenting problems, is that they are profoundly moving. The steps of re-membering conversations (see Russell & Carey, 2004, or White, 2007a, for a fuller description) provide people with the opportunity to closely examine and richly describe not only other peoples' contributions to their lives and identity, but also their own contributions back to those people.

This idea of examining the effects of people in someone's life and making changes so that people will support sobriety versus addiction is not new. What is new about this within narrative practices is how these re-membering conversations focus upon how people affect one another's identity (White, 2007a). This focus allows for the people consulting us to reflect upon how they in turn have shaped the identity of the people who have been so supportive of them. For those people who cannot remember any positive person in their life, these conversations can be based upon people whom they admire from a distance, fictional characters, pets, and even toys. These conversations would flow into discussions of how the client imagines how the other person might be affected if he or she knew of their importance to the client.

Re-membering conversations are facilitated for a number of reasons. They can be facilitated when someone is grieving the loss of someone they love, and so be used to examine the importance of that relationship and how the effects of that relationship will continue. They may be facilitated when people talk about how much they admire and respect someone who is helping them, so that they can see that they also are contributing something to the other's life and identity. They can also be used when there is a new tentative skill, like sobriety or abstinence, developing and we ask who might support the person in continuing to develop this new skill, or ask about who would be least surprised to know that this new skill was an important development.

In one of my earlier conversations with Becky, she was telling me about how important her current sponsor was to her. Going through the steps of the re-membering conversation, I asked her about those activities that they had pursued together and then had her explore how those events and activities had contributed to how she thought of herself and the development of her identity. However, the final two steps of the conversation involved having Becky recall and describe in detail how she had contributed to her sponsor's life and then how she imagined she would have impacted her sponsor's sense of self. These last steps of the conversation need to be prefaced with a comment about how difficult it often is for people to answer these types of questions, because we are not usually asked to reflect in this way. Answering such questions as, "How do you guess your acceptance of your sponsor's help has affected how she thinks about herself and her purpose in life?," "How has knowing you, and you being part of her life, enriched her life and what she holds dear?" and "The fact that you have continued with her as your sponsor—what is your guess about how that has reinforced what she values?" all brought about a shift in thinking for Becky where she was able to begin to think of her own value as well as her sponsor's value. She left the session telling me that this was a completely different conversation from any she had previously experienced and could be the beginning of building back some of her self-esteem.

The Absent but Implicit

Michael White (2007b) has spoken about the fact that he wished he had previously stressed the importance of what he called an "absent but implicit" conversation. He said that he had begun to think it was one of the most useful conversation maps, and he intended to write about it extensively.[2]

The development of this way of thinking about conversations with people who come to counselling with many complaints about life, and about other people in their lives, was deeply influenced by White's reading of philosophers like Derrida. Wyschogrod (1989) has described some of Derrida's contributions to the notion of the absent but implicit when stating, "representation conceals, while pretending to reveal" (1989, p. 191). It is, in other words, important as practitioners not to limit ourselves to only the surface meaning of the words people use, but to explore the fullness of what might be meant by the words, and what is also implied by those words. This should not be confused as reading between the lines or "reading into" from a place of expertise; it is about assisting the other person in uncovering what is implied by, or underneath, their statements. Wyschogrod goes on to explain:

> For Derrida ... each element acquires meaning only through a play of differences, the intersignificative relationship to one another of elements which themselves lack self-present meaning. Each element is so interwoven with every other that it is constituted only by the traces within it of the other bits in the chain or system. There are no independent meanings but only traces of traces. (1989, p. 192)

When a person is attempting to describe complex emotions, thoughts, and reactions, it becomes even more important to be cognizant of the multiple and fluid meanings of the words used. A single word, after all, is not complex enough on the surface to describe the fullness of a person's experience. The word *sad*, for example, will mean something different to each person using it, based on a range of experiences, and the meanings will also change over time.

Derrida describes each word as involving both a description of what it is attempting to represent (the "signified") and also a description of its opposite (or what it is not). Derrida referred to this idea of a word containing a comparison of what it is attempting to represent as *différance*. In relation to social work and counselling conversations, if people have always been sad and listless and despairing, they may not complain about the condition because they have had no other experience against which to compare it.

Becky spoke at one point in the course of her therapy about how unloved she felt and, after past experiences of types of therapy that focused on looking for causes, she began to wonder about how she had developed into an unloveable person. This, clearly, also reinforced themes of self-blame. Attempting to incorporate what I had been learning about what is *implied* by complaints, although otherwise *absent* from clear descriptions, I asked her how it was that she had come to think of herself as unloveable. My assumption was that she must have experienced feeling loved at some point in her life for her to be able to compare this current situation and describe it as feeling unloved. So, I asked her if there was a time in her life when she had felt different and what that had been like. She then began speaking about times in her childhood when she was in the car with her father and he was driving and she felt very much connected to him and loved by him. This memory presented itself like a unique outcome that could be the start of a preferred storyline about feeling loved. As this alternative storyline developed the events in that storyline also reminded her of memories of experiences against which she could compare new experiences in relationships.

Therapeutic Documents

White and Epston (1990), as part of their commitment to ensuring that people did not become overly reliant on therapists and formal ongoing therapy, developed the practice of incorporating therapeutic documents into their work. In their work with children they wrote lists of insights children had gained in sessions and provided these lists to parents and children to review in between sessions. They also made certificates of accomplishment to provide to children as they finished sessions. However, they also began writing letters to adults that focused on the elements of preferred storylines, new skills and initiatives, and the way in which they appeared to be moving towards their hopes and dreams. In a tongue-in-cheek nod to research, White and Epston asked recipients of these letters what they thought of the usefulness of these letters, and when they indicated they were very useful in supporting new developments, White and Epston asked them if they could suggest how useful they were in comparison to one good therapy session. They reported that people answered that each good therapeutic document was worth at least as much as six good therapy sessions.

Epston (2012) has continued to use therapeutic documents in his work and inter-acts with people extensively through carefully worded email communication, where he makes use of narrative questioning approaches. Speedy (2005) has described the manner in which she has written poetic therapeutic documents from the notes she keeps as she has conversations with people. Using the words that jump from the page and sparkle with new meaning and insight, and developing poems from those words, has been powerfully moving for people and often results in them commenting that they had not realized they could be so insightful and poetic.

In my work with Becky, I did write her one letter when I had a planned absence for a few weeks and was unable to meet with her. I focused in that letter on what we had recently been talking about in sessions and the significance to her of having recently been asked to consider becoming a sponsor for others at AA. I asked some questions in the letter about who would be least surprised to know about this new development and what this invitation meant others were seeing in her. When I returned and met with her she expressed that this had been such a unique and empowering letter to receive and she had never experienced anything quite like it before. She indicated it had added to her growing confidence and assisted in bridging our counselling sessions. At a later period in our work together I put together a poem made up of words she had used during our session, quickly stringing them together in the shape of a poem, and handed it over to her as she was leaving the session. Again she indicated this was a profoundly moving celebration of her insights and she said she planned to put this poem on a wall at home where she could reread it often, reminding herself of her own knowledge and insights.

Weegman (2010), in describing his narrative practices with people in recovery from addiction, comments on his use of therapeutic documents as he writes to people, but also as he engages them in sessions in writing themselves. He suggests that when using the metaphors of stories and storylines it is possible for people to also think about chapters, or episodes, in their lives. This can assist people in more fully seeing how they have not always been the same way and that if things in their lives have changed before they can change again.

Becky's Story: Experiences of Narrative Conversations while Also Attending AA

Becky has chosen to use her true name for the purposes of this chapter, because she is proud of her healing process and wants to take credit for telling her story and helping others to develop their skills in working with people struggling with addiction. She consented to be audiotaped while she was interviewed about her story of healing for the purposes of this chapter and then later read and approved the written version that is included here. She was given the opportunity to make changes and corrections.

* * *

Becky first realized she might have a problem with addiction and alcoholism shortly after the death of her mother. She noticed she was drinking a lot. She was seeing a social worker at that time who suggested that she try to slow down the amount she drank, by drinking a glass of water in between each alcoholic beverage. Becky says this seemed to reduce her hangovers, but did not slow down her alcohol consumption.

She then decided to attend an addiction treatment centre. They told her she was an alcoholic but that she should be able to drink socially. They were hesitant to give her a list of local AA meetings because they did not encourage the AA approach. They made a follow-up appointment for her two months later, but she cancelled it because she did not think they were going to be able to help her. She continued to drink for another one-and-a-half years.

When a friend of hers at work told her about how her husband had attended a residential treatment centre for addiction and alcoholism she realized she needed to also look for more serious treatment and assistance. She went to her general practitioner to ask for a referral and was told that only 10% of alcoholics and addicts can recover (a totally incorrect fact), but that she should start by attending a "detox" centre. She went to the withdrawal management centre, not knowing what to expect, and was told that she would have to stay for a week right away. She found the staff rude and unpleasant and unwilling to assist her in juggling her work responsibilities, and so she left.

At this point Becky was given the name and number of a doctor who specialized in assisting people in preparing for withdrawal symptoms who referred her to the residential setting. She was given the time necessary to negotiate with her employer in order to have the 21 days necessary to move in to the residential program setting.

She found the residential program very helpful. The first week provided her with time to "dry out," and she was expected to begin attending three AA or NA meetings each week. She remembers being physically sick and also struggling with "paranoia" in her second week there.

Becky says that the hardest part of the program was the daily morning check-in groups when each person was expected to talk about how they were feeling at that moment. She says this was a very great struggle for her. Her 21-day program became a 28-day program since she was having difficulty sharing her emotions in the group setting. She says she ended up staying for six weeks because she was nervous about leaving and going home where there was no one to support her in her new sobriety.

Becky describes the residential program as having promoted healthy living and a routine that could support health. They were encouraged to eat breakfast, lunch, and dinner regularly, to walk, and to attend recreational groups as well as the therapeutic groups. She says the therapy groups were similar to AA groups but facilitated by a professional counsellor.

After the six weeks in the residential setting, she was offered a nine-month aftercare program that involved attending a counsellor-led group each week. Although she was also encouraged to attend AA meetings five to seven times each week during this time she remembers "lapsing" several times during the nine months of the aftercare program.

About one-and-a-half years after completing the residential and aftercare program she met her son's father. This was a difficult relationship and during this time a cousin of Becky's, who was working as a social worker, suggested she begin individual counselling. At this point she began receiving individual counselling at a small counselling agency and she says that this, combined with AA, "saved her."

Becky says that she greatly values the one-on-one professional environment that individual counselling provides. She says that as many as 25 people may attend her usual AA meeting, and there is not time for everyone to talk and share their feelings and thoughts each week. As well, she finds there can be concerns regarding trust at times within these AA meetings.

Becky met with three different social workers in individual counselling appointments prior to being referred to me. Two of these three were social work students. She says that she would describe this time as a time of "having to go back to move forward." Each time she was transferred to another social worker, she says she would spend lots of time again looking at the history of her problem. She says she believes that she learned to be flexible during this time as she was transferred from one person to another.

* * *

At the time of first writing this chapter Becky had been attending individual appointments with me for approximately two years. She scheduled appointments about once every three weeks, attended weekly AA meetings, and also had begun to attend church regularly. She said this is what she found the most supportive of her at that time. Since the completion of the first version of this chapter for the second edition of this book, Becky reported that she no longer believed she needed ongoing counselling. She knows that she can reconvene at any time, but she has reported that she is moving beyond former limitations that she had experienced in her life.

I asked Becky to describe her reactions to working with me and the approach I use. She says that it feels natural and that what she has understood from my approach is that she has several stories, whereas for so many years it felt like there was only one story, which was of addiction. She says she has found it freeing to be able to pick out the more positive ways of being. In more mainstream counselling approaches she was told she had to go over the painful parts of her past in order to try and figure it out and make it better. This seemed to her to be consistent with step four in the AA 12 steps, where she had to make an inventory of everything, including all the hurts to herself and others. She says this can be quite engaging and emotionally involving if you do it right, but the idea is to move on, and she has found that a narrative approach to counselling has helped her more with the moving on.

As far as Becky can see, having to say, "Hi, I'm an alcoholic," is helpful for many people in AA, perhaps because it helps people become more accepting of themselves. It seems to make people think of themselves as always being an alcoholic and so helps people stay committed and involved in AA. However, Becky reports that it also feels very good within narrative conversations to begin to feel separate from the alcoholism and to think of herself as having a relationship with the alcoholism versus being an alcoholic. These types of externalizing conversations do not in any way minimize the seriousness of the effects of alcoholism. Becky and I continued to have discussions about how "sneaky" alcohol and pot can be in her life. They still have the power to try and convince her that just one joint or just one drink won't hurt her, but having had a recent lapse she knows the effects of giving in and knows that she and her son are both much healthier and happier when she continues to choose healthy routines.

What Becky suggested in her final comments was that the group and community aspects of AA are extremely helpful, even though she has moved away from embracing all of AA's practices. She was interested in the possibility of narrative therapy being able to provide group support and said that she would be able to fill a group with interested people should we ever want to begin such a narrative therapy group for people wanting to take control over their addiction.

Reflections

It is interesting that Becky suggested that a narrative therapy group would have been a welcome alternative to AA group meetings. Garte-Wolfe (2011) has written about the use of narrative therapy in group work with chemically dependent people with HIV/AIDS. Gardner and Poole (2009) have also written about the usefulness of narrative therapy and narrative group work with older adults with addiction issues. Narrative practices can easily be integrated into group work of all kinds, and given the usefulness of social support in recovery from addictions, this makes perfect sense in this field.

Becky's stories also raise interesting general considerations for working in the area of addiction. She has attempted various treatment options and has found the greatest success from a combination of approaches. We cannot argue that one approach is the best approach. Becky has also experienced the frustration of lapses, but these seem to be shorter and less dramatic than her experiences with drugs and alcohol prior to initiating treatment. Perhaps this implies we examine more carefully our preconceived ideas about what success and health look like. Success does not have to be based upon never having a lapse or a relapse. It can be based upon constantly moving forward, having fewer lapses, and making more choices that fit within a person's preferences for her life. It is useful to have these discussions with people, so that they are prepared for the challenges and for what they will need to do to help themselves move back into their preferred storyline. This would be consistent with White and Epston's (1990) use of van Gennep's "rite of passage" (p. 7) metaphor. This "rite of passage" describes a change process made up of a separation phase, a liminal or betwixt-and-between phase, and a reincorporation phase. White has also described this as a "migration of identity," where we can use this metaphor to describe the process by which someone separates from understanding themselves in one way (for example, as an alcoholic) and sets sail into the unknown towards a new way of thinking of themselves. The migration can begin with hope but often involves rough waters and a time of readjustment in the new world of sobriety or abstinence. If we prepare people for what this journey can entail they will be better able to cope with the challenges.

Although Becky had not used drugs for many years, and had recently been baptized and become more involved in a local church, which she reports as a significant positive change in her life, when her sponsor told her that she thought she was ready to begin dating again, Becky jumped at this suggestion. She says that she had been happy as a single mom, raising her son alone, and focusing on her and her son's health, but became distracted by this suggestion. At that point she says she thought she might not need to continue individual counselling for very much longer, since things appeared to be going so well in her life. However, she became very excited by her sponsor's suggestion, and began using a telephone dating service, and met and attempted beginning relationships with a couple of men. This did not go well and negatively affected her self-esteem again, which prompted a short relapse, which also affected her self-esteem. In the last few appointments we had together, we examined how her use of the telephone dating service mirrored some of the other negative thinking. The telephone dating service can be as "sneaky" as the alcoholism, attempting to convince her that "just one" call, or "just one more" meeting with a man, may bring her great happiness.

In one of our last sessions together, Becky and I examined her alternative storyline again, looking at how a recent holiday with her son, when she was not tempted by addiction, fit within her preferences and hopes. She was able to step into the alternative and preferred storyline and begin to imagine what types of small changes she might bring about if she could hold on to her values and preferences.

Just as Becky was beginning to feel far more confident in her abilities to manage her addiction and the oppressive discourses that would have labelled her as an addict, it would seem as though she was challenged by another set of discourses that suggested she needed a man in her life in order for her to be fulfilled. As discussed previously, narrative practices are positioned to examine internalized discourses, and although our earlier conversations were focused on externalizing those internalized discourses that labelled Becky as an alcoholic, narrative practices keep open the space for shifting conversations and can later focus upon externalizing other discourses. Our conversations were then also able to focus upon gender and heterosexual romance discourses and the effects of these in her life. For instance, where do any of us learn that alcohol and drugs might give some release from stress in our lives, and where do we learn that a relationship will bring further happiness?

Conclusions

In a book regarding narrative practices with people resisting anorexia and bulimia, Maisel, Epston, and Borden (2004) state their work is not a "how to" therapy manual, since anorexia and bulimia "is too cunning a problem for any one-size-fits-all approach. It is a moving target, sidestepping your shot and returning fire. Furthermore, blanket prescriptions, even if well-intentioned, often end up mirroring the prescriptive nature of a/b itself" (p. 2). In much the same way, it is important to maintain flexibility in work with addiction because addiction, particularly alcoholism, has long been called both cunning and baffling.

The premise of this book is that addiction creates oppression. Narrative therapists would argue that many various discourses, whether about addiction or about therapeutic practices, contribute towards the oppression of people. Given some of the commonalities between anorexia, bulimia, disordered eating, and alcoholism, I have been struck by Maisel, Epston, and Bordern's (2004) comments about how narrative practices can be seen as anti-oppressive. Maisel describes himself as having been drawn to narrative practices because of his "long-standing desire to see psychotherapy used to address social injustice ... (White's) work illustrates how power can operate in an oppressive way in the therapist-client relationship" (p. 7). Borden goes on to say that "narrative therapy's focus on the external 'forces' which shape people's lives was far more in line with (her own) sense of justice than the therapies which viewed problems as merely arising within families or in individual minds. Narrative therapy called upon (her) desire to not stand idly by but to actively challenge cultural discourses, including those of the culture of psychotherapy" (p. 9).

Narrative practices have provided me with an approach that is sensitive to the effects of discourses in the lives of the people, like Becky, who consult me. The problem storyline of addiction or alcoholism may have been what initiated Becky's search for counselling, but "solving" or even "dissolving" that one problem does not necessarily mean she is immune to the effects of other discourses in her life. As Maisel, Epston, and Borden (2004) suggest, it is important for narrative therapists to also be involved in a type of practice that does not recreate oppressive interactions between therapists and clients, and that provides opportunities to deconstruct all the discourses that contribute to social injustice in a person's life.

I am particularly drawn to narrative practices because of their commitment to assisting people in reflecting upon the effects of internalized discourses that contribute to social injustice and the maintenance of problem storylines. Becky's story is one example, however, of how useful it is to have a range of approaches available for people when they are attempting to free themselves from the effects of alcohol and addiction. Her concluding remarks point out that she has appreciated the liberating aspects of narrative practices and she leaves us with the challenge to incorporate narrative thinking within more mainstream supports like AA.

NOTES

1. For those interested in developing practice skills in this area see Béres, 2014; Russell & Carey, 2004; White, 2007a.

2. After White's death in April 2008, it was left to those of us who had spoken with him about this type of conversation to begin practicing and writing about the manner in which this way of working with people could be integrated into narrative practices (see Béres, 2014; Carey, Walther, & Russell, 2009).

REFERENCES

Bennett, T., Mercer, C., & Woolacott, J. (Eds.). (1986). *Popular culture and social relations.* Milton Keynes, UK: Open University Press.

Béres, L. (1999). Beauty and the beast: The romanticization of abuse in popular culture. *European Journal of Cultural Studies, 2*(2), 191–207.

Béres, L. (2002). Negotiating images: Popular culture, imagination, and hope in clinical social work practice. *Affilia: Journal of Women and Social Work, 17*(4), 429–447.

Béres, L. (2013a). Celtic spirituality and postmodern geography: Narratives of engagement with place. *Journal for the Study of Spirituality, 2*(2), 170–185.

Béres, L. (2013b). The conversational maps of narrative practice as structures of ethical engagement: Privileging people's values, hopes, and dreams. A Narrative Future for Health Care. Narrative Medicine Conference, London, England.

Béres, L. (2014). *The narrative practitioner.* Basingstoke, UK: Palgrave MacMillan.

Bruner, E. (1986a). Ethnography as narrative. In V. Turner & E. Bruner (Eds.), *The anthropology of experience* (pp. 139 –155). Chicago: University of Illinois Press.

Bruner, J. (1986b). *Actual minds, possible worlds.* Cambridge, MA: Harvard University Press.

Canda, E.R. (1988). Afterword: Linking spirituality and social work: Five themes for innovation. In E.R. Canda (Ed.), *Spirituality in social work: New directions* (pp. 97–106). New York: Haworth Press.

Carey, M., Walther, S., & Russell, S. (2009). The absent but implicit: A map to support therapeutic enquiry. *Family Process, 48*(3), 319–331.

Derrida, J. (1973). *Speech and phenomena and other essays on Husserl's theory of signs.* Evanston, IL: Northwestern University Press.

Epston, D. (2012, October 9–11). *Master class.* Sponsored by Re-authoring Teaching: Creating a Collaboratory, Waltham, Vermont, US.

Foucault, M. (1965). *Madness and civilization: A history of insanity in the age of reason.* New York: Random House.

Galanter, M. (2006). Spirituality and addiction: A research and clinical perspective. *American Journal on Addictions, 15*(4), 286–292.

Gardner, P., & Poole, J. (2009). One story at a time: Narrative therapy, older adults, and addictions. *Journal of Applied Gerontology, 28*(5), 600–620.

Garte-Wolfe, S. (2011). Narrative therapy group work for chemically-dependent clients with HIV/AIDS. *Social Work with Groups, 34*(3–4), 330–338.

Geertz, C. (1986). Making experience, authoring selves. In V. Turner & E. Bruner (Eds.), *The anthropology of experience* (pp. 373–380). Chicago: University of Illinois Press.

Gergen, M., & Gergen, K. (1984). The social construction of narrative accounts. In K.J. Gergen & M.M. Gergen (Eds.), *Historical social psychology* (pp. 173–189). Hillsdale, NJ: Lawrence Erlbaum Associates.

Goffman, E. (1961). *Asylums: Essays in the social situation of mental patients and other inmates.* New York: Doubleday.

Hari, J. (2015). *Chasing the scream: The first and last days of the war on drugs.* New York: Bloomsbury Publishing.

Healy, K. (2000). *Social work practices: Contemporary perspective on change.* London, UK: Sage Publications.

Irving, A. (1999). Waiting for Foucault: Social work and the multitudinous truth(s) of life. In A.S. Chambon, A. Irving, & L. Epstein (Eds.), *Reading Foucault for social work* (pp. 27–50). New York: Columbia University Press.

Jarusiewicz, B. (2000). Spirituality and addiction: Relationship to recovery and relapse. *Alcoholism Treatment Quarterly, 18*(4), 99–109.

Maisel, R., Epston, D., & Borden, A. (2004). *Biting the hand that starves you: Inspiring resistance to anorexia/bulimia.* New York: W.W. Norton.

Myerhoff, B. (1986). Life not death in Venice: Its second life. In V. Turner & E. Bruner (Eds.), *The anthropology of experience* (pp. 261–286). Chicago: University of Illinois Press.

Russell, S., & Carey, M. (2004). *Narrative therapy: Responding to your questions.* Adelaide, Australia: Dulwich Centre Publications.

Speedy, J. (2005). Using poetic documents: An exploration of poststructuralist ideas and poetic practices in narrative therapy. *British Journal of Guidance & Counselling, 33*(3), 283–298.

Weegman, M. (2010). Just a story? Narrative approaches to addiction and recovery. *Drugs and Alcohol Today, 10*(3), 29–36.

White, M. (1995). *Re-authoring lives: Interviews and essays.* Adelaide, Australia: Dulwich Centre Publications.

White, M. (2007a). *Maps of narrative practice.* New York: W.W. Norton.

White, M. (2007b, December 10–15). *Level 2 narrative therapy training.* Sponsored by the Dulwich Centre, Adelaide, Australia.

White, M., & Epston, D. (1990). *Narrative means to therapeutic ends.* New York: W.W. Norton.

Wyschogrod, E. (1989). Derrida, Levinas, and violence. In H.J. Silverman (Ed.), *Continental philosophy II: Derrida and deconstruction* (pp. 182–200). New York: Routledge.

CHAPTER 10

Impact of Addiction on Parenting Post-Separation

Rachel Birnbaum

Introduction

In Canada, more than 70,000 couples divorce every year and over a third of all divorces involve children (Statistics Canada, 2008). These numbers are conservative since they do not account for other intimate domestic relationships that end in separation, in particular cohabiting unmarried couples who have children and separate. As of 2012, the number of divorced Canadian families increased, leaving many children in lone parent households: 1,200,295 with lone mothers and 327,545 with lone fathers (Statistics Canada, 2015).

In Canada, 16% of fathers and 20% of mothers have an addiction issue (Langlois & Garner, 2013). Despite this, the prevalence of addiction and substance abuse issues in family law disputes is an area that has received little attention, despite the research data that reports one in five Canadians will experience a mental health or addiction problem in any given year (Smetanin, Stiff, Briante, & Khan, 2011). Saini, Black, Fallon, and Marshall (2013) report that children involved in custody disputes have a higher proportion of emotional harm allegations reported to child welfare agencies compared to children not involved in their parents' custody dispute. In their secondary data analysis of the 2008 *Canadian Incidence Study of Reported Child Abuse and Neglect* (CSI), they found that parental alcohol abuse was significantly higher (19%) in child welfare investigations involving a child custody dispute, compared to 15% without a child custody dispute. Moreover, based on a sample of 6,163 substantiated child welfare investigations across Canada, alcohol abuse accounted for 21% and drug/solvent abuse accounted for 17% of all investigations of the primary parent risk factor (Public Health Agency of Canada, 2008). There is a correlation between parents abusing alcohol or drugs and a range of negative socio-emotional and behavioural outcomes for children (MacMillan et al., 1997). The *Quebec Incidence Study of Reported Child Abuse, Neglect, Abandonment, and Serious Behavioural Problems* (Tourigny et al., 2002) reported using data from 1998 that in substantiated cases of child neglect, children were living in families that struggled with:

- both drug and alcohol abuse (45%);
- substance abuse and domestic violence (42%);
- substance abuse and criminal activity (32.2%); and
- substance abuse and mental health problems (31.3%).

The researchers reported that children living with a parent with substance abuse were more likely to have had previous child welfare involvement, been taken into care, exhibited delayed development, and were more likely to be referred for placement out of home compared to neglected children living in families where substance abuse was not observed.

This is concerning given that children of disputing parents are at risk of poor parenting as a result of one or both of their parents' addiction-related problems (Gregoire & Schultz, 2001; Horvath, Logan, & Walker, 2002). Equally concerning is that the lack of inquiry about addiction and the subsequent impact on parenting post-separation has received little attention by mental health professionals engaged in making parenting recommendations to the court (Schleuderer & Campagna, 2004).[1]

The purpose of this chapter is twofold: to describe the purpose and nature of a child custody and access assessment to provide context to a differentiated approach focusing on addiction, and also to describe the framework for a differentiated child custody assessment when one or both parents has an addiction issue and is involved in a child custody dispute. An ecological framework will be used that draws on the work of Heise (1998), Belsky (1980), Bronfenbrenner (1979, 1986), and Germain and Gitterman (1996) to understand how addiction and different systems—including the individual, family, community, and broader social structures—impede and enhance parenting, and interact with one another in separating and divorcing families. Ecological theory seeks to understand the human experience and behaviour within a "person-in-environment" framework, thereby demonstrating the complex interplay of many factors (Bronfenbrenner, 1986). Typically, addiction has been viewed through the lens of the psychological model that focuses on the individual and pathology (Baker, Piper, McCarthy, Majeskie, & Fiore, 2004) or a neurobiological model that focuses on reward, learning, and stress pathways (Robinson & Berridge, 2003) without understanding the intersection of the individual, community, and broader social structures that can impact on the family, particularly on parenting post-separation (Gruber & Taylor, 2006). The author argues that all three lenses, biological, psychological, and social, must be brought to bear on the family when examining addiction in post-separated families.

The relationship between stress and high conflict in litigating families has long been known to increase vulnerability to addiction and plays an important role in the parenting of addicted individuals (Chaplin & Sinha, 2013). Separated parents are not only in the midst of loss of their intimate relationship but also a loss of their parental role.

These types of stressors are cumulative and can potentially damage the parent-child relationship post-separation. Therefore, it is imperative that mental health professionals engaged with separated families understand that while addiction has a distinct biological component, parents with psychoactive drug issues require a thorough and

---

Box 10.1   Example of a Court Judgment

The following child custody dispute before the court involved a father seeking access to his seven-year-old child that he had not seen in three years. The dispute before the court highlights the number of systems involved with this family and their child (child welfare, Office of the Children's Lawyer, criminal and family justice, and mental health) and the impact that domestic violence and drug abuse problems have during times of separation that go beyond simply numbers and descriptions. The following paragraphs from *Scarlett v. Farrell*, 2015 ONCJ 35, eloquently portray how the father's lack of insight and understanding about his drug problems and abusive behaviour towards the mother and their child lead to an order of no access to the child.

[116] The father also has a history of drug-related incidents, including his most recent conviction in 2014.

[117] What all of this reveals is that the father has a demonstrated history of skirting around the edges of socially and criminally acceptable behaviour and, sometimes, piercing through those edges into flagrant criminal misconduct. When he was asked on cross-examination what steps he has taken to address his long-standing drug abuse problem, he responded simply that he hasn't been to treatment since that last conviction.

[145] Justice Sherr then referred to *Jennings v. Garrett, supra*, quoting Justice Blishen at paragraph 135 of her judgment, as setting out a number of "useful factors that have led courts to terminate access" [my emphasis]:

1. Long term harassment and harmful behaviours towards the custodial parent *causing that parent and the child stress and or fear.*
2. History of violence; unpredictable, uncontrollable behaviour, alcohol, drug abuse which has been witnessed by the child and/or presents a risk to the child's safety and well-being.
3. Extreme parental alienation which has resulted in changes of custody and, at times, no access orders to the former custodial parent.
4. Ongoing severe denigration of the other parent.
5. Lack of a relationship or attachment between *noncustodial parent and child.*
6. Neglect or abuse to a child on the access visits.
7. Older children's *wishes and preferences to terminate access.*

Source: Scarlett v. Farrell, 2015 ONCJ 35 (CanLII), 2015. Retrieved from http://canlii.ca/t/gg33n.

comprehensive systems-level assessment that focuses not just on the challenges of each parent's addiction but also on their strengths, to assist the court in their decision-making about the children's best interests.

Child Custody Assessments Post-Separation for Addiction

There are many excellent textbooks on conducting child custody and access assessments[2] (Ackerman, 2006; Birnbaum, Fidler, & Kavassalis, 2008; Drozd, Olesen, & Saini, 2013; Gould & Martindale, 2007; Melton, Petrila, Poythress, & Slobogin, 1997, 2007; Stahl, 1994, 1999) and guidelines and standards of practice in conducting them. For example, the Association of Family and Conciliation Courts, Model Standards of Practice for Child Custody Evaluation (Martindale, Martin, Austin, Drozd, Gould-Saltman, et al. 2007) includes guidelines and standards on how to prepare custody and access assessments for all mental health professionals, social workers, psychologists, and psychiatrists who are members of this international organization.[3] For social workers, in particular, there are several regulatory colleges and associations across Canada that have guidelines and/or standards of practice related to custody and access assessments. In British Columbia, the Board of Registration for Social Workers produced Standards of Practice in Child Custody and Access Assessments (2002) while in Saskatchewan, the Saskatchewan Association of Social Workers (2001) produced Standards in Custody/Access for Registered Social Workers. In Ontario, the Ontario College of Social Workers and Social Service Workers (OCSWSSW, 2009) has also produced custody and access guidelines for social work members. All of these various guidelines have been accepted by the regulatory colleges and/or associations for social workers and psychologists to be a useful set of guidelines for those professionals conducting custody and access assessments for the courts (Birnbaum, Fidler, & Kavassalis, 2008). Yet, unlike the growing body of literature on post-separation domestic violence (Hardesty, Haselschwerdt, & Johnson, 2012; Jaffe, Johnston, Crooks, & Bala, 2008), children who resist visiting with a parent (Fidler, Bala, & Saini, 2012), supervised access (Birnbaum & Alaggia, 2006; Birnbaum & Chipeur, 2010), and high conflict families post-separation (Birnbaum & Bala, 2010), few, if any, texts specifically address how the social science and empirical literature addresses addiction and its impact on parenting post-separation.

Child custody and access assessments are often complex and time-intensive, involving the need to review all relevant documents and reports, contact personal and professional collateral sources, use proper interviewing techniques with adults and children, and conduct home and office visits that culminate in written parenting recommendations. The parenting recommendations essentially make judgments about parental competencies, parenting strengths and weaknesses, and how the children's needs have been met by each parent prior to, during, and post-separation. The parenting recommendations made by assessors can significantly impact families, including who, where, when, and how children will continue to maintain their parent-child relationship post-separation. Therefore, assessors must be competent and qualified in many different areas such as child development and attachment; family systems and the impact of separation and divorce; high conflict disputing families; the many forms of domestic violence; alcohol and other drug use, misuse, and abuse; child maltreatment; interviewing skills with both children and adults; and knowledge of relevant legal standards and procedures, to name a few (Geffner, Geis, & Aranda, 2006).

In addition to understanding the strengths and limitations of the fifth edition of the Diagnostic and Statistical Manual of Mental Disorders (DSM-V)[4] in regards to the diagnostic criteria for substance use disorders, it is equally important for the assessor to have a working knowledge of the empirical research in separation and divorce over the last three decades, specifically related to addiction and the impact on parenting post-separation. The reason for this is that methodologies and research designs (self-report measures, mixed method studies, quantitative and qualitative studies) have significantly grown in the child custody area, and more specifically theoretical frameworks (Kelly & Ramsay, 2009; Loughran, 2006; Stimmel, 2009) and treatment approaches continue to change in relation to addiction (Forrester & Harwin, 2011; Niccols et al., 2012). In child custody in general, there has also been an increase in empirical studies that compare results of a large number of studies, using both meta-analyses and systematic reviews while focusing on the strengths and limitations of the methods, and scoping reviews that describe and explore studies of a population over time to examine common themes. In addition, long-term studies now focus on disentangling the effects of pre- and post-separation variables and the effects of the pre-separation family environment on children's adjustment; these studies have eclipsed the cross-sectional data, examining only one point in time, when drawing conclusions about parent-child relationships (Kelly, 2012). Moreover, exploring and understanding risk and protective factors, a child's age at divorce, gender, pre- and post-separation experiences, marital conflict, types of parenting arrangements, mediating variables between conflict, and child adjustment have all been at the centre of the growing research. Therefore, it is important to unpack the myths from the realities about what is in a child's best interest, particularly when addiction is present. The assessor must be able to separate aspirational parenting recommendations from realistic ones.

Generally Accepted Methodology and Procedures

There are six key data gathering components that assessors typically follow that have demonstrated a high degree of reliability and validity in the social science literature. These are:

1. Defining the scope of the assessment
2. Interview protocols
3. Self-report measures and checklists

4. Psychological testing, drug testing,[5] and medical testing
5. Direct behavioural observations
6. Collateral interviews and record reviews (Birnbaum, Fidler, & Kavassalis, 2008; Fidler & Birnbaum, 2006; Galatzer-Levy, Kraus, & Galatzer-Levy, 2009; Gould, 1998, 1999; Melton, Petrila, Poythress, & Slobogin, 1997; Pezzot-Pearce & Pearce, 2004; Pickar & Kaufman, 2013; Schleuderer & Campagna, 2004).

With respect to psychological, drug, and medical testing it is important to highlight the range of different tests and their strengths and limitations given their perceived high objectivity and scientific reliability when used for court purposes. Having said this, there are no psychological tests that have predictive validity relating to parenting capacity, adaption of parenting time schedules, and the different types of custodial arrangements post-separation (Birnbaum, Fidler, & Kavassalis, 2008). More significantly, there is no psychological test that can reliably test for addiction (Schleuderer & Campagna, 2004). Psychological tests may only rule in or out individual psychopathology and personality functioning.

Some of the most commonly used psychological tests are the Minnesota Multiphasic Personality Inventory (MMPI-2) (Austin, 1994), which helps to identify general personality characteristics; the Ackerman-Schoendorf (1994) Scales for Parent Evaluation of Custody used in child custody and access disputes; and Bricklin's Perception-of-Relationships Test (Bricklin & Halbert, 2004), most often given to children. To address addiction-related concerns, there is the Substance Abuse Subtle Screening Inventory (SASSI-III) (Miller, 1997), the Michigan Alcohol Screening Test (MAST) (Selzer, 1971) and the Alcohol Use Inventory (AUI) (Horn, Wanberg, & Foster, 1987).

There is also medical information that an assessor can request from each parent when addiction is raised as a concern. For example, physical tests tend to infer the presence or absence of substance abuse in the parent. However, the ability to make that inference is limited by excretion rates that are individually determined by the drug or alcohol, their use, body type, weight, tolerance, and other individual biological variables. All that the blood and urine tests can do is rule out presence of the substance at the time of testing and detection levels of the test. As noted by Schleuderer and Campagna (2004), testing cannot distinguish between a parent using alcohol or other drugs for recreational purposes and an addiction to one or both, nor if it affects parenting capacity.

While many of these psychological, drug, and medical tests may provide some helpful information on degree of credibility of parental concerns, malingering, impulse control, anxiety and depression, self-esteem, sociability, paranoia, coping mechanisms, and response to rules and authority, the tests still need to be situated in the context of all of the other information gathered during a child custody and access assessment. In other words, they are only a piece of the puzzle and not the determining factor about addiction and parenting post-separation. Flens (2005) notes that, "evaluators should focus their attention and assessment efforts on functional abilities that bear directly upon attributes, behaviours, attitudes and skills that published research suggests are reliably associated with effective parenting and co-parenting" (p. 15).

Assessors also detail and demonstrate how the child's best interest addresses:

- the child's adjustment emotional/behavioural, social, and academic
- the quality of relative parenting capacity, and parenting strengths and challenges
- the psychological adjustment and health of each parent and the impact of these, if any, on parenting and the parent-child relationship
- the quality of the parents' relationship with each other, and the nature and extent of conflict and co-operation, abuse, and violence
- the quality of the child's relationship with each parent, including the "fit" between the child and parent, taking into account any special needs that the child might have
- the quality of the parent's relationship with any new partner or spouse
- the quality of the child's relationship with other relevant family members
- the child's preferences (if any), perceptions, and views, where they can be reasonably ascertained (Birnbaum, Fidler, & Kavassalis, 2008; Fidler, Bala, Birnbaum, & Kavassalis, 2008; Gould, 1998, 1999; Melton, Petrila, Poythress, & Slobogin, 1997; Pickar & Kaufman, 2013; Pezzot-Pearce & Pearce, 2004).

Information is also gathered from interviews with the parents and children, observations of the parents and children, and interviews with individual children and observing siblings together over multiple times. The focus is on examining each parent regarding the following:

- How co-operative is each parent?
- How does each parent communicate with the other parent?
- How child-focused is each parent, looking at strengths, limitations, child support, and parenting style?
- What did parenting involvement look like pre-, during, and post-parental relationship?
- What is the quality of the parental relationship pre- and post-separation in terms of level of conflict and respect of the other's parenting abilities?
- What is the quality of the extended family support network; is it hostile, undermining, or supportive?
- What are the reasons provided by each parent about one parenting time arrangement over another?
- What do the children have to say about parenting time arrangements?

Collateral information is gathered from both personal (friends, neighbours, family members) and professional (employer, teachers, doctors, therapists, coaches) collateral contacts until sufficient information is gathered that rules in or out hypotheses made during the assessment to formulate parenting recommendations on behalf of the children.

Implicit in gathering personal and professional collateral information is an analysis of the information obtained, the context in which it was collected, who the reporter is and their relationship to each parent, and that each parent is informed about the information obtained and allowed an opportunity to address any concerns raised (Kirkland, 2005).

While every area listed above is important to assess and understand both from an empirical and clinical perspective, how parenting is assessed will vary considerably based on how information is collected and reported and, more significantly, how information about addiction is examined from a systems perspective. Parenting abilities are obtained not just from each parent, but also from collateral sources, and compared and contrasted for hypothesis testing throughout the assessment process. It is important that common responses in a particular population, such as addiction, are not compared to families that are experiencing domestic violence or neglect and child abuse matters, even though some families may be experiencing all of these issues as a result of a parent's addiction-related problems. Collecting specific and detailed information on areas of discipline and parenting approaches, aspirations for their children, responses to typical parenting stress, perceptions of children's adjustment pre- and post-separation, and empathy for and understanding of children's special needs are all part of the information gathering; this information is then used to differentiate parenting abilities and the impact on parent-child relationships when addiction is the issue before the court.

In addition to the above questions and areas that the assessor explores, several other key questions need to be examined with each parent and child to understand the impact, if any, the addiction has had on parenting. For example, the following are all important questions to explore (Schleuderer & Campagna, 2004):

- the frequency and history of usage, including first usage and most recent usage
- the type of drug or alcohol preferred, the frequency of usage, and the context in which substances are taken
- the desired effect of usage, both positive and negative
- examining each family member's reaction to the use and the impact it has had
- work absences or illnesses, social contacts, and/or social isolation
- the history of automobile accidents, speeding, and other driving-related offences.

All these questions are meant to investigate not only the drug use of the parent, but more importantly the impact that it might have on parenting post-separation.

Addiction, like domestic violence, child neglect, and abuse, is a serious concern and is challenging for the courts when raised by one parent or the other. It is equally challenging for a child custody assessor, as parental addiction is a complex multi-systemic issue that involves the individual, the partner of the addicted individual, and their children, as well as the broader system including employment, criminal and family court systems, public health, and mental health. Therefore, it is essential to use a differentiated approach to assessing, treating, and providing an individualized parenting plan for the family.

Framework for a Differentiated Assessment for Addiction Post-Separation

The blueprint for a differentiated multidisciplinary approach to assessing addiction in post-separated families involves not only a systems level analysis of the parent, the pre- and post-parental relationship, and the parent-child relationship, but also an analysis of systems at the individual, social, and legal levels. Figure 10.1 illustrates this approach.

Figure 10.1   Framework for a Differentiated Assessment for Addiction Post-Separation

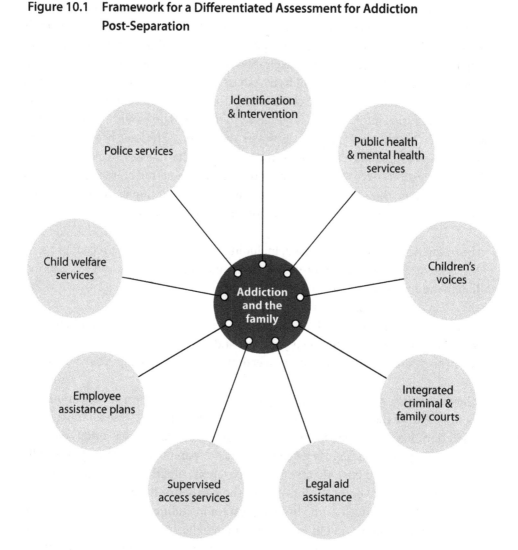

While the assessment process begins with the identification and examination of the addiction and its impact on parenting there are overlapping issues that the assessor must also understand. It is this differentiated systems approach that includes the community and broader societal levels that also needs to be integrated into the assessment process. Public health and mental health services, police services, child welfare services, legal aid services, integrated criminal and family courts, supervised access services, employee assistance programs—and hearing directly from children about the extent and impact of the addiction—is part and parcel of a differentiated assessment process. While it is often argued that addiction to alcohol or other drugs is a chronic illness and that both public and private services are required, there needs to be a greater focus on highlighting the strengths of the family dynamics, rather than just the limitations and challenges imposed by the addiction on the family, maximizing the chances of successful post-separation parenting in spite of addiction.

NOTES

1. A search of Quicklaw and Westlaw legal databases captured over 1,000 child custody and access disputes that involved alcohol and drug abuse concerns post-separation across Canada (last accessed August 6, 2015). It should be noted that legal databases only provide case law for disputed matters before the court. Therefore, there can be many more child custody cases that have been settled, mediated, or arbitrated by lawyers or mental health professionals involving one or both parents with addiction-related problems.

2. The term *assessment* is being used interchangeably with the American term *evaluation* or *forensic evaluation*.

3. http://www.afccnet.org/resources/standards_practice.asp

4. See Jones, Gill, & Ray (2012) for a review of the changes to the DSM-V regarding substance abuse disorders.

5. The Ontario government has begun an inquiry into the Motherisk program on drug testing using hair analysis. See http://news.ontario.ca/mag/en/2014/11/ontario-initiates-review-of-motherisk-hair-analysis.html, and also Chapter 26.

REFERENCES

Ackerman, M.J. (2006). *Clinician's guide to child custody evaluations* (3rd ed.). Hoboken, NJ: John Wiley & Sons.

Ackerman, M.J., & Schoendorf, K. (1994). *Aspect: Ackerman-Schoendorf Scales for Parent Evaluation of Custody: Manual*. Torrance: Western Psychological Services.

Austin, J. (1994). Minnesota Multiphasic Personality Inventory (MMPI-2). *Measurement and Evaluation in Counseling and Development, 27*(3), 178–185.

Baker, T.B., Piper, M.E., McCarthy, D.E., Majeskie, M.R., & Fiore, M.C. (2004). Addiction motivation reformulated: An affective processing model of negative reinforcement. *Psychological Review, 111*(1), 33–51.

Belsky, J. (1980). Child maltreatment: An ecological integration. *American Psychologist, 35*(4), 320–335.

Birnbaum, R., & Alaggia, R. (2006). Supervised visitation: A call for a second generation of research. *Family Court Review, 44*(1), 119–134.

Birnbaum, R., & Bala, N. (2010). Towards the differentiation of "high conflict" families: An analysis of social science research and Canadian caselaw. *Family Court Review, 3*, 403–416.

Birnbaum, R., & Chipeur, S. (2010). Supervised visitation in custody and access disputes: Finding legal solutions for complex family problems. *Canadian Family Law Quarterly, 29*, 79–94.

Birnbaum, R., Fidler, B.J., & Kavassalis, K. (2008). *Child custody and access assessments: A resource guide for legal and mental health professionals.* Toronto, ON: Thomson Carswell Publishing.

Bricklin, B., & Halbert, M. (2004). Perception-of-Relationships Test and Bricklin Perceptual Scales: Validity and reliability issues, part II of two parts. *The American Journal of Family Therapy, 32*(3), 189–203.

British Columbia Board of Registration for Social Workers. (2002). *Standards of practice in child custody and access assessments.* Vancouver: British Columbia Board of Registration for Social Workers.

Bronfenbrenner, U. (1979). *The ecology of human development.* Cambridge, MA: Harvard University Press.

Bronfenbrenner, U. (1986). Ecology of the family as a context for human development: Research perspectives. *Developmental Psychology, 22*, 723–742.

Chaplin, T.M., & Sinha, R. (2013). Stress and parental addiction. In N. Shuman, M. Pajulo, & L. Mayes (Eds.), *Parenting and substance abuse: Developmental approaches to intervention* (pp. 24–43). New York: Oxford University Press.

Drozd, L., Olesen, N., & Saini, M. (2013). *Parenting plan & child custody evaluations: Increasing evaluator competence & avoiding preventable errors.* Sarasota, FL: Professional Resource Press.

Fidler, B., Bala, N., Birnbaum, R., & Kavassalis, K. (2008). *Challenging issues in child custody assessments: A guide for legal and mental health professionals.* Toronto: Thomson Carswell.

Fidler, B., Bala, N., & Saini, M. (2012). *Children who resist postseparation parental conflict: A differential approach for legal and mental health professionals*: New York: Oxford University Press.

Fidler, B., & Birnbaum, R. (2006). *Child custody disputes: Public and private assessments. Canadian Family Law Quarterly, 25*(2), 137–167.

Flens, J.R. (2005). The responsible use of psychological testing in child custody evaluations: Selection of tests. *Journal of Child Custody, 2*(1), 3–30.

Forrester, D., & Harwin, J. (2011). *Parents who misuse drugs and alcohol: Effective interventions in social work and child protection.* Hoboken, NJ: Wiley-Blackwell.

Galatzer-Levy, R.M., Kraus, L., & Galatzer-Levy, J. (2009). *The scientific basis of child custody decisions.* Hoboken, NJ: John Wiley & Sons, Inc.

Geffner, R., Geis, K., & Aranda, B. (2006). Family violence allegations in child custody evaluations: The overlap of family and forensic psychology. *The Family Psychologist, 22*(2), 9–14.

Germain, C.B., & Gitterman, A. (1996). *The life model of social work practice: Advances in theory and practice* (2nd ed.). New York: Columbia University Press.

Gould, J.W. (1998). *Conducting scientifically crafted child custody evaluations.* Thousand Oaks, CA: Sage Publications.

Gould, J.W. (1999). Scientifically crafted child custody evaluations: Part one: A model for interdisciplinary collaboration in the development of psycho-legal questions guiding court-ordered child custody evaluations. *Family and Conciliations Courts Review, 37*, 64–73.

Gould, J.M., & Martindale, D.A. (2007). *The art and science of child custody evaluations.* New York: Guilford Press.

Gregoire, K.A., & Schultz, D.J. (2001). Substance-abusing child welfare parents: Treatment and child placement outcomes. *Child Welfare, 80*, 433–452.

Gruber, K., & Taylor, M. (2006). A family perspective for substance abuse: Implications from the literature. *Journal of Social Work Practice in the Addictions, 6*(1/2), 1–29.

Hardesty, J.L., Haselschwerdt, M.L., & Johnson, M.P. (2012). Domestic violence and child custody. In K. Kuehnle & L. Drozd (Eds.), *Parenting plan evaluations: Applied research for the family court* (pp. 442–475). New York: Oxford Press.

Heise, L.L. (1998). Violence against women: An integrated, ecological framework. *Violence Against Women, 4*, 262–290.

Horn, J.L., Wanberg, K.W., & Foster, F.M. (1987). *Alcohol use inventory.* Minneapolis, MN: National Computer Systems.

Horvath, L., Logan, T., & Walker, R. (2002). Child custody cases: A content analysis of evaluations in practice. *Professional Psychology, Research and Practice, 33*, 557–565.

Jaffe, P.G., Johnston, J.R., Crooks, C.V., & Bala, N. (2008). Custody disputes involving allegations of domestic violence: Toward a differentiated approach to parenting plans. *Family Court Review, 46*(3), 500–522.

Jones, D., Gill, C., & Ray, S. (2012). Review of the proposed DSM-5 substance use disorder. *Journal of Addictions & Offender Counselling, 33*(2), 115–123.

Kelly, J.B. (2012). Risk and protective factors associated with child and adolescent adjustment following separation and divorce: Social science applications. In K. Kuehnle & L. Drozd, *Parenting plan evaluations: Applied research for the family court* (pp. 49–84). New York: Oxford Press.

Kelly, R.F., & Ramsey, S.H. (2009). Child custody evaluations: The need for systems-level outcome assessments. *Family Court Review, 47*(2), 286–303.

Kirkland, K. (2005). Use of collateral contacts in child custody evaluations. *Journal of Child Custody, 2*(1), 95–110.

Langlois, K.A., & Garner, R. (2013). *Trajectories of psychological distress among Canadian adults who experienced parental addiction in childhood.* Ottawa, ON: Statistics Canada.

Loughran, H. (2006). Alcohol problems, marriage, and treatment: Developing a theoretical timeline. In S. Strausser & C. Fewell (Eds.), *Impact of substance abuse on children and families: Research and practice implications* (pp. 31–48). New York: Haworth Press.

MacMillan, H.L., Fleming, J., Trocmé, N., Boyle, M., Wong, M., Racine, Y., ... Offord, D. (1997). Prevalence of child physical and sexual abuse in the community: Results from the Ontario health supplement. *Journal American Medical Association, 278*(2), 131–135.

Martindale, D.A., Martin, L., Austin, W.G., Drozd, L., Gould-Saltman, D., Kirkpatrick, H.D., ... & Siegel, J. (2007). Model standards of practice for child custody evaluation. *Family Court Review, 45*(1), 70–91.

Melton, G., Petrila, J., Poythress, N., & Slobogin, C. (1997). *Psychological evaluations for the courts: A handbook for mental health professionals and lawyers.* New York: Guilford Press.

Melton, G., Petrila, J., Poythress, N., & Slobogin, C. (2007). *Psychological evaluations for the courts: A handbook for mental health professionals and lawyers* (3rd ed.). New York: Guilford Press.

Miller, G. (1997). *SASSI-3: Adult Form.* Springville: SASSI Institute.

Niccols, A., Milligan, K., Sword, W., Thabane, L., Henderson, J., & Smith, A. (2012). Integrated programs for mothers with substance abuse issues: A systematic review of studies reporting on parenting outcomes. *Harm Reduction Journal, 9*(14), DOI: 10.1186/1477-7517-9-14.

Ontario College of Social Workers and Social Service Workers (OCSWSSW). (2009). *Practice guidelines for custody and access assessments.* Retrieved from http://ocswssw.org/wp-content/uploads/2015/01/PG-Custody-and-Access-Assessments.pdf

Pezzot-Pearce, T., & Pearce, J. (2004). *Parenting assessments in child welfare cases: A practical guide.* Toronto, ON: University of Toronto.

Pickar, D.B., & Kaufman, R.L. (2013). The child custody evaluation report: Toward an integrated model of practice. *Journal of Child Custody, 10*, 17–53.

Public Health Agency of Canada. (2008). *Canadian Incidence Study of Reported Child Abuse and Neglect: Major Findings.* Retrieved from http://cwrp.ca/sites/default/files/publications/en/CIS-2008-rprt-eng.pdf

Robinson, T., & Berridge, K. (2003). Addiction. *Annual Review of Psychology, 54*, 25–53.

Saini, M., Black, T., Fallon, B., & Marshall, A. (2013). Child custody disputes within the context of child protection investigations: Secondary analysis of the Canadian Incidence Study of Reporting Child Abuse and Neglect. *Child Welfare, 92*(1), 115–137.

Saskatchewan Association of Social Workers. (2001).*Standards in Custody/Access for Registered Social Workers in Saskatchewan.* Regina: Saskatchewan Association of Social Workers.

Scarlett v. Farrell, 2015 ONCJ 35 (CanLII). (2015). Retrieved from http://canlii.ca/t/gg33n.

Schleuderer, C., & Campagna, V. (2004). Assessing substance abuse questions in child custody evaluations. *Family Court Review, 42*(2), 375–383.

Selzer, M.L. (1971). The Michigan Alcoholism Screening Test: The quest for a new diagnostic instrument. *American Journal of Psychiatry, 127*(12), 1653–1658.

Smetanin, P., Stiff, D., Briante, C., & Khan, M. (2011). *The life and economic impact of major mental illnesses in Canada: 2011–2041.* RiskAnalytica, on behalf of the Mental Health Commission of Canada.

Stahl, P.M. (1994). *Complex issues in child custody evaluation.* New York: Sage Publications.

Stahl, P.M. (1999). *Conducting child custody evaluations: A comprehensive guide.* Thousand Oaks, CA: Sage Publications.

Statistics Canada. (2008). *Divorces, by province and territory.* CANSIM, tables 053-0002 and 101-6501. Retrieved from http://www.statcan.gc.ca/tables-tableaux/sum-som/l01/cst01/famil02-eng.htm

Statistics Canada. (2015). *Age group of child (13), census family structure (7) and sex (3) for the children in census families in private households of Canada, provinces, territories, census divisions and census subdivisions, 2011 census.* Retrieved from http://www12.statcan.gc.ca/census-recensement/2011/dp-pd/tbt-tt/Rp-eng.fm?LANG=E&APATH=3&DETAIL=1&DIM=0&FL=A&FREE=0&GC=0&GID=0&GK=0&GRP=1&PID=102075&PRID=0&PTYPE=101955&S=0&SHOWALL=0&SUB=0&Temporal=2011&THEME=89&VID=0&VNAMEE=&VNAMEF=

Stimmel, B. (2009). From addiction to abstinence: Maximizing the chance of success. *Family Court Review, 47*(2), 265–273.

Tourigny, M., Mayer, M., Wright, J., Lavergne, C., Helie, S., ... Trocme, N. (2002). *Étude sur l'incidence et les caractéristiques des situations d'abus, de négligence, d'abandon et de troubles de comportement sérieux signalées à la direction de la protection de la jeunesse au Québec (ÉIQ).* Montreal, QC: Centre de liaison sur l'intervention et la prévention psychosociale.

CHAPTER 11

Is Alcoholics Anonymous of Value for Social Work Practitioners?

Rick Csiernik and Blanka Jordanov

Introduction

That alcohol misuse and abuse contributes to premature death is an empirical fact. Longitudinal studies indicate that those addicted to alcohol die on average 10 to 15 years earlier than do members of the general population. However, research also indicates that abstinence has a positive effect on the overall survival of those who had been dependent upon alcohol. Those labelled as being alcohol dependent who were able to abstain from use of that drug showed reduced mortality rates and increased longevity compared with those who relapsed and returned to regularly consuming alcohol (John et al., 2013; Miller, 1999). With the introduction of a greater range of empirically supported treatment options, and with an increasing emphasis on harm reduction approaches (Bigg, 2001; Watkin, Rowe & Csiernik, 2010), the initial and at one time most prominent form of assistance in the addiction field, Alcoholics Anonymous (AA), has had its value questioned (Kownacki & Shadish, 1999; Terra et al., 2008; Walters, 2002). One cannot, however, deny AA's survival and growth through the years. William White wrote, "whether one looks to AA through the eyes of a grateful and adoring member or through the eyes of the most rabid AA critic, one fact is unarguable: Alcoholics Anonymous is the only widely available alcoholic mutual aid society in American history that has outlived its founding generation" (p. 15, White, 2001). The fact of AA's survival is in itself evidence of its usefulness and hopefulness for those who utilize it as a component of their recovery.

Alcoholics Anonymous introduced not only the idea that those dependent upon alcohol could be helped, but also spawned the contemporary mutual aid/self-help social movement, one of the core social pillars of the 20th century. From AA arose Narcotics Anonymous, Nicotine Anonymous, Gamblers Anonymous, Overeaters Anonymous, Cocaine Anonymous, Sex and Love Addicts Anonymous, and other similar 12-step recovery groups. Alcoholics Anonymous and related mutual aid/self-help groups are unique as they not only offer social support and serve as to substitute low-risk behaviour, but also because for many they are a new cultural experience. In communities where there are few or no addiction-specific services, there is still likely to be a 12-step group. In larger communities AA groups meet seven days a week, with meetings at different times throughout the day. Membership is voluntary and fees are based on a "pass-the-hat," pay-what-you-can format (Alcoholics Anonymous, 2010). Yet there has been criticism of AA for a range of reasons, of which a lack of empirical support for its claims of effectiveness is the most significant (Boeving, 2011; Bufe, 1997; Burns, 1992; Dodes & Dodes, 2014; Peele, 1990; Ragge, 2005; Sanders, 2011).

There are few social workers whose practice does not include clients with alcohol-related problems. However, much has changed in both the addiction field and in the social work profession since AA began in 1935. With the emergence of empirically based methods of counselling, a schism developed between university-educated social workers and counsellors who had found sobriety through AA but who only had their own stories as a source of validation for this approach. There has, however, been an increasing amount of research conducted to assist in determining the value of Alcoholics Anonymous.

Research Findings

In 1977 Edwards and his colleagues claimed that participation in AA alone, without any formal treatment support, was able to keep approximately 10% of all alcohol abusers abstinent. Subsequent research studies reported positive correlations between AA attendance and abstinence (Alford, 1980; Chi et al., 2009; Tonigan, 2001). The results of two different meta-analyses on earlier AA literature (Emrick, 1987; Emrick, Tonigan, Montgomery, & Little, 1993) also found that there was a positive relationship between drinking outcome and AA involvement, especially when AA involvement arose out of a formal counselling program. This is a finding that has become regularly reported in the literature (Blonigen, Timko, & Moos, 2013; Florentine & Hillhouse, 2000; Gossop, Stewart, & Marsden, 2008; Kaskutas et al., 2005; Moos & Moos, 2005; Timko & Debenedetti, 2007; Timko, Moos, Finey, & Lesar, 2000; Tonigan, Miller, & Connors, 2000; Witbrodt, Bond, & Kaskutas, 2007).

Emrick (1987) discovered that of alcohol-dependent persons who become long-term, active AA members, upwards of 50% enjoyed several years of total abstinence, with approximately two-thirds improving to some extent, drinking less or not at all during their participation in the group. Those who combined AA with other forms of treatment also seemed to do as well as, or better than, those who only attended AA meetings. When AA is combined with clinical work individuals are helped to cope with the transition in their lives to sobriety and are given help to work through loss and grief issues. Bereavement can accompany any major changes in our lives; and changes to drinking habits and lifestyle can create the same fears and negative emotions as any transition or loss. Viewing treatment in these terms broadens treatment possibilities. Using reframing and strength-based approaches in treatment tackles individual issues of substance abuse with a different perspective on the utility of the 12 steps (Streifel & Servanty-Seib, 2006).

Involvement in Alcoholics Anonymous that occurs concurrently at the onset of treatment entry is beneficial to the long-term goal of abstinence (Katkutas, Bond, & Weisner 2003). While research suggests better treatment results when clients attend AA meetings (Manning et al., 2012), Emrick (1987) found that attendance at AA prior to attending a treatment program was not always related to outcome, but when a relationship was observed it was positive. Important to the eventual abstinence of these persons was the introduction of clients to a self-help group by professional counsellors. Emrick did, however, add a caution in his conclusion that highlights the importance of appropriate matching. He found that Alcoholics Anonymous was unsuitable and not recommended for groups of drinkers with low rates of dependency who wished to adopt the harm reduction approach of controlled drinking.

Johnson and Jerringer (1993) examined the relationship between abstinence rates among 50 former inpatients of a substance treatment facility and the ongoing use of 12-step supports. Not surprisingly, they too discovered that attendance at aftercare or AA/NA meetings was significantly related to post-treatment abstinence. What was surprising, however, was that the use of self-help was more significant in maintaining abstinence than was family support. It was also reported that the greater the number of supports the person in recovery had, the greater the likelihood of not returning to alcohol or other drug abuse. In another study examining differences between 733 residential and day hospital treatment participants, the location of treatment was seen as secondary to participation in AA meetings. However, the best predictor of sobriety six months post-treatment was not just attending AA meetings as part of the treatment protocol but rather how active individuals were in attending AA meetings on their own time and own initiative (Zemore & Kaskutas, 2008). Twelve-step programming is also useful in long-term continuing care with adolescents, with daily to weekly attendance being positively correlated with abstinence (Chi et al., 2009). However, proportionately fewer adolescents use this resource compared to their adult counterparts. Attendance by youth is also typically less intensive and discontinues sooner (Kelly, Yeterian, & Meyers, 2008). A subsequent study indicated that both AA and NA could also benefit less severe substance users in outpatient community treatment if participants were linked with community sponsors (Kelly & Urbanoski, 2012).

Humphreys and Moos (1996) followed 200 individuals dependent upon alcohol in San Francisco for a three-year period. One hundred and thirty-five of the study's participants attended AA while sixty-five attended professional outpatient aftercare counselling. Those who attended AA had lower incomes and education, and more severe drinking experiences. At both one- and three-year follow-ups, the AA attending group had lower health care costs than those who only attended professional aftercare groups. Both Dupont and Shiraki (1994) and Miller (1995) in their evaluations found that 12-step programs played an essential and integral role in assisting in the recovery from substance abuse disorders for many clients. DuPont and Shiraki (1994) also highlighted the fact that there was no cost to the health care system when individuals used a 12-step group as a means of aftercare. Humphreys and Noke (1997) added that 12-step involvement after formal treatment assisted individuals in developing new friendships outside of their previously established drug-using circles. Attending AA can help improve moods and fight symptoms of depression (Kelly et al., 2010).

Despite contraindications of the utility of AA among women who have suffered trauma, internal surveys indicate that one-third of AA members are now women. Men are still more likely to maintain abstinence as a function of attending AA than are women. However, active female members appear to benefit from AA attendance during times of sadness or depression, which are prominent relapse triggers. For women, finding healthier ways to cope with negative emotions is an outcome of AA participation, while for men its effectiveness is maximized by aiding in avoiding high-risk social situations in which drinking is the main event, such as at sporting events (Kelly & Hoeppner, 2013).

Majer (1992) examined the relationship between AA, NA, and logotherapy. While Majer was only able to use 29 persons in his study, he did find that the longer the commitment clients made to a 12-step group, the greater the likelihood of the person finding meaning in life. Thus, he concluded, while persons who undergo addiction treatment experience some level of anxiety, unease, and even suffering, their perception of this pain may tend to be altered in a more meaningful way the stronger their commitment to AA's founding principles, especially considering the underlying spiritual dimension of the fellowship. Likewise, Gomes and Hart (2009) in assessing 76 residents from a treatment program two years post-discharge found those remaining abstinent were characterized by lower rates of depression and a stronger conviction that life has meaning and purpose. The study supports a belief that AA involvement reinforces existential well-being, which improves quality of life and emotional wellness.

However, other studies have found that the spiritual components of AA have reverse effects and can contribute to increasing dropout rates (Kelly, Kahler, & Humphreys, 2010). Oakes (2008) found that purpose in life did not have a causal relationship with long-term sobriety. Several reasons were given for this, one of which points to the need for clearer distinctions between the motivation and spiritual constructs of individuals and their involvement with AA. Kurtz (2002) points to alcoholism being a multidimensional phenomenon—bio, psycho, and social, as well as being spiritual. While AA's emphasis on the spiritual is vital and necessary, discussing alcoholism only within a disease framework does not meet the holistic needs of many.

Among the most difficult-to-reach groups for any type of social issue are immigrant, newcomer, and minority populations. Barriers of access, culturally appropriate counselling, and having people new to Canada understand the culture of helping are concerns to social workers regardless of their field of practice. Research indicates that Alcoholics Anonymous is able to reach and assist a wide range of ethnic and religious groups. AA has been able to bring acceptability to seeking external supports as a legitimate action and not a sign of weakness (Caetano, 1993). Self-help is viewed by some as a way to empower the individual and hence community and society at large (Pretto & Pavesi, 2012). Sanders (2006) found that even in the male-dominated culture of 12-step programs, some women became empowered, despite having to give up their power as part of the process, and made positive changes in their lives that led to a spiritual path and a healthier sense of self.

One prominent reason AA has become so accessible is that the literature has been translated into 38 languages and groups exist around the world. Chappel and DuPont (1999) claim that Alcoholics Anonymous has now spread well beyond the confines of the white male, Anglo-Saxon, Protestant, middle-class originators of the 12 steps. Miller and Berinis's research (1995) support this belief, for they found that abstinence-based treatment featuring AA involvement worked as well for unemployed African-Americans as it did for those with more favourable economic characteristics. Kingree and Sullivan (2002) stated that despite its origins, the underlying philosophy of AA—its focus on spirituality and sharing, open to all who have as their goal to stop drinking—and that it is free and does not discriminate against those without health insurance makes it appealing to many African-Americans. Sutro (1989), in his work with Mexican Indigenous groups, found that key elements of 12-step groups have cross-cultural applicability there as well. This cultural transferability is also evident in Master's (1989) report of Jewish alcoholics regularly attending AA meetings in the United States, and Ronel's (1997) work with 21 Jewish members of a Narcotics Anonymous group in Tel Aviv, Israel. Ronel commented that the reason an American-originating, Christian-based program may have universal appeal is because personal suffering from addiction is a universal domain and reality. Bjerke's (2006-2007) analysis of global membership of online AA groups suggests members easily identify with each other, despite cultural differences, by recognizing the common ground of alcohol dependency as a global phenomenon. However, Naegle, Ng, Barron, and Lai (2002) reported that peer-based approaches need to be modified if working with Asian-Americans, as this population finds it very difficult to disclose personal information in group settings, often because they view it as bringing shame onto themselves and their families. The 12-step recovery program has also successfully been modified based upon Islamic principles for the Muslim community in the United States (Millati Islami World Services, 2010).

Concurrent disorder clients are another population with which it is often difficult to engage. The work of Katz (1999), Laudet, Magura, Vogel, and Knight (2003), and Bogenschutz, Geppert, and George (2006) have all indicated that for persons with less severe mental health disorders, 12-step groups provided a positive benefit. Kelly, Kahler, and Humphreys (2010) suggest that concurrent disorder groups that are 12-step based may be helpful for those needing to take medications to manage psychiatric disorders. Prior to those reviews, Schartzer (1992) had supported incorporating AA principles into clubhouse work with mental health consumer survivors, while Kramer and Hoisington (1992) similarly urged increased use of AA and NA with individuals who have acquired brain injury. Kramer and Hoisington stated that the social support network offered by these types of self-help resources is of invaluable assistance with this hard-to-serve clinical subgroup.

Impulsivity has also been shown to decrease with ongoing AA attendance. In turn, decreases in impulsivity lead to fewer legal problems, better ability to manage drinking, and improved psychosocial behaviour (Blonigen et al., 2013). Bogenshutz's (2005) work with one group of 10 individuals with significant mental health issues using a modified version of the 12 steps indicated that while abstinence was not able to be maintained by most group members their overall alcohol and other drug use did decrease.

Despite the growing empirically supported literature on the value of AA, there remains a critique of its effectiveness (Ferri, Amato, & Davoli, 2006). Much of this critique is valid, particularly when applied to how AA is used compared to how it was intended to be used. AA is based upon a disease model of addiction rather than a more holistic biopsychosocial orientation. Some participants can interpret the 12 steps and 12 traditions of Alcoholics Anonymous very rigidly, which leaves little room for personal choices for other members. It can also appear that the philosophy of Alcoholics Anonymous punishes participants for relapses and lapses by deducting credit from their accumulated abstinence time, rather than viewing lapses and relapses as learning opportunities. For this reason and related concerns, such as having to give oneself up to a higher power in order to succeed, AA's philosophy of recovery has been interpreted as disempowering (Kaskutas, 1989; Nevels, 1997; Peele, 1989, 1990).

However, it is difficult to disregard this form of helping, not only because of its historic significance but also due to its massive popularity. Since 1935 estimated membership has grown from two members in the United States to over 2 million members and over 115,000 groups internationally (Alcoholics Anonymous, 2014). The first reported AA chapter in Canada began in 1943 and was organized by two clergy who brought together six men in a restaurant on Bay Street in Toronto to discuss their common issue. The group grew to 15 and, by the end of 1943, they held a banquet attended by 80 men. By the end of World War II, groups had been established in Hamilton, London, Windsor, Ottawa, Montreal, and Winnipeg with every province in the country having at least one active AA group by 1949 (Shrier, 1993). The first AA membership survey to include data on groups in Canada was conducted in 1951 and at that time there were 399 reported groups across the country. That grew to over 1,000 groups by 1963 with just over 15,000 members. By 1972 there were over 2,000 groups with nearly 33,000 participants. The 2014 membership survey indicated that there were 5,129 groups in Canada with approximately 93,000 active members. Historically, the membership survey had indicated that over half of a groups' membership had been part of the fellowship for five or more years (Alcoholics Anonymous, 2008). This is an important finding because it illustrates the ongoing support AA provides its members, and also because frequency of participation has been correlated with a higher likelihood of remaining abstinent (Moos & Moos, 2004).

However, dropout rates remain a significant issue (Kelly, Kahler, & Humphreys, 2010; Laudet, Stanick, & Sands, 2007). In a large American study, 40% of 2,778 males who joined AA after completing a formal treatment program were no longer attending after one year. Interestingly, fewer dropped out who had been introduced to AA during their formal treatment program than those who sought it out on their own after completing treatment (Kelly & Moos, 2003). In a Brazilian study of 300 people between the ages of 20 and 60 (275 of whom were male), less than one-fifth continued to attend AA meetings six months after treatment was completed. Of those who did continue to use AA just over half attended regularly. This led the study's authors to conclude that "AA is inappropriate and ineffective for the majority of patients with the diagnosis (alcohol dependency)" (Terra et al., 2008, p. 52).

Critical to keep in mind in the context of all these findings that at times appear to be contradictory is that the fundamental principle of all forms of self-help is choice: wanting to be there. One of AA's strengths is in its ability to provide self-regulated help according to the individual's perceived need (Kelly, Magill, & Stout 2009). The organizing principle of all forms of mutual aid is voluntary membership. Improvement occurs on one level because people choose to attend and become active in the program, for attendance alone does not indicate involvement or working to change. As well, coerced involvement, such as through court- or workplace-mandated attendance, not only undermines personal initiative, but also establishes different goals and motivation than the foundation of self-help (Fortney et al., 1998; Hester & Miller, 1995; Kownacki & Shadish, 1999).

Conclusion

Involvement with and participation in Alcoholics Anonymous has led to large numbers of formerly alcohol-dependent individuals becoming abstinent for extended periods of time (Emrick, 1987; Humphreys et al., 2004). However, Alcoholics Anonymous and related 12-step programs are definitely not for everyone with an alcohol or addiction issue. The reality of addiction counselling is that not all clients benefit from individual counselling, thrive in a group environment, or benefit from harm reduction options, though this has not stopped clients from having the choice to participate in these alternative forms of counselling. Alcoholics Anonymous represents one pole of the treatment continuum, with the harm reduction approach of controlled drinking representing the other. AA alone is often not enough to help people with alcohol-related problems, and a combination of professional counselling and self-help involvement is usually more efficacious in maintaining abstinence than either option alone. Not everyone requires AA affiliation and participation after their professional treatment regimen has been completed, and not everyone with an addiction problem benefits from, or should be forced to use, self-help as part of their recovery. However, without self-help supports a significant number of people would not be able to establish or maintain their sobriety (Emrick, Tonigan, Montgomery, & Little, 1993).

For some who could benefit from self-help involvement but for whom the principles of AA are overly rigid, other self-help groups have emerged in the addiction field: Women for Sobriety (WFS), a group emphasizing empowerment for its participants; Secular Organization for Sobriety (SOS), which places no emphasis upon a higher power; Rational Recovery (RR), with its cognitive-behavioural approach to self-help; SMART Recovery, an offshoot of RR to support quality of life; and Moderation Management (MM), a self-help group with a harm reduction orientation. The emergence of these alternatives further underscores the value of incorporating self-help with social work practice for addiction, as well as the importance of matching clients to the most appropriate referral option available.

Thus, introduction to Alcoholics Anonymous or an alternative form of self-help during addiction treatment should remain an option regardless of the treatment philosophy of the individual social worker or agency. This is even more important for those persons who come from rural or smaller communities without ready access to the entire continuum of professional intervention and follow-up. In these circumstances self-help becomes the primary means for relapse prevention. The empirical research in this area indicates that early introduction to AA while participating in a formal counselling program makes it more likely that Alcoholics Anonymous will be used later in the recovery cycle (Borkman et al., 1998; Shepard, Larson, & Hoffmann, 1999; Smith 1985, 1986). As well, unlike most social work counselling that has quite specific timelines, self-help support can be indefinite, with no additional cost to the health care system and limited additional cost for individual clients (Kelly, Magill, & Stout, 2009).

While having great potential, Alcoholics Anonymous is no panacea. Its proliferation needs to be examined in context, for it has not been demonstrated to be superior to formal treatment conducted by professional counsellors. The use of self-help for some can be a justification for the curtailing of services, which increases the risk of poorer clients being shunted off to self-help groups, while more affluent individuals receive professional services. Self-help can also become a dumping ground where social workers and other counselling professionals refer hard-to-resolve problems, or for cases where insurance- and/or employer-financed counselling conclude, yet more assistance is required. Thus, AA and related 12-step groups can easily become an inappropriate referral, replacing required and useful professional counselling. As well, AA has always been limited by the anonymity of its approach. Its helping philosophy forces its members to de-emphasize larger societal issues and not advocate for system changes, such as providing adequate financial support for the entire addiction continuum of care.

As well, the idea, associated with anonymous groups, of having to hit rock bottom before recovery from an addiction can begin can create even poorer self-esteem and self-image in some participants. For some an overemphasis on self has the possibility of leading to escapism and narcissism, with the potential to foster dependence and the need for a lifelong commitment instead of "getting better" and moving forward. As well, a lack of formal social work group leadership allows some members to dominate groups while others become lost, even if they continue to attend. If a participant fails to return to the group there is no process for follow-up or to assess what type of support the person may need. Thus, those attending meetings may get participation but not necessarily assistance. Twelve-step groups have also been accused of dealing with problems only at the symptom level, looking at small-scale solutions and providing only marginal alternatives to larger environmental issues (Gartner & Riessman, 1977). However, Miller, in his summary of Alcoholics Anonymous, concluded that:

> Treatment outcome research thus far confirms that there exists a large variety of treatment methods that appear to work in the short run (weeks or months) ... [yet] only one method of treatment appears to be effective and to consistently work in the long run (years to lifetimes), namely abstinence based treatment when combined with regular, continuous and indefinite attendance at Alcoholics Anonymous meetings. (1995, p. 18)

Johnson (1996) stated that affiliation with AA allows for broader solutions for many social problems that are either partially or wholly caused by social disintegration. Twelve-step group participation had distinct impacts on participants' behaviour, as it provides alternatives to drinking or drugging by providing a new group of peers to regularly associate with, a different use of time, and new leisure opportunities. Participation also introduces or reintroduces the idea of spirituality for many, and for many participation instills hope (Gomes & Hart, 2009; Katkutas, Bond, & Weisner, 2003; Magura et al., 2003; Vaillant, 2005). However, the greatest value of AA remains its immense flexibility, and that is what makes it a valuable resource for social workers. For a select few it is not only their primary but also their exclusive method of obtaining sobriety. As well, AA can be used as an adjunct to primary counselling and also as a follow-up and relapse prevention resource. While there is great value in the use of AA by social work practitioners as a community resource, this should not lead to the lack of investment in or a devaluing of social work practice in the addiction field.

REFERENCES

Alcoholics Anonymous. (2008). *Alcoholics Anonymous recovery outcome rates: Contemporary myth and misinterpretation*. New York: AA World Services.

Alcoholics Anonymous. (2010). *Alcoholics Anonymous* (75th anniversary commemorative edition). New York: AA World Services.

Alcoholics Anonymous. (2014). *Estimates of A.A. groups and members*. Retrieved from http://www.aa.org/assets/en_US/smf-53_en.pdf

Alford, G. (1980). Alcoholics Anonymous: An empirical study. *Addictive Behaviours*, 5(4), 359-370.

Bigg, D. (2001). Substance use management: A harm reduction-principled approach to assisting the relief of drug-related problems. *Journal of Psychoactive Drugs*, 33(1), 33-38.

Bjerke, T. (2006-2007). Cross-cultural gateway to recovery: A qualitative study of recovery experiences in international AA online groups. *International Journal of Self Help and Self Care, 5*(1), 73-104.

Blonigen, D., Timko, C., & Moos, R. (2013). Alcoholics Anonymous and reduced impulsivity: A novel mechanism of change. *Substance abuse, 34*(1), 4-12.

Boeving, N.G. (2011). Is addiction really a disease? A challenge to twelve-step programs. *Tikkun, 26*(4), 22-46.

Bogenschutz, M. (2005). Specialized 12-step programs and 12-step facilitation for the dually diagnosed. *Community Mental Health Journal, 41*(1), 7-20.

Bogenschutz, M., Geppert, C., & George, J. (2005). The role of twelve-step approaches in dual diagnosis treatment and recovery. *American Journal of Addictions, 15*(1), 50-60.

Borkman, T., Kaskutas, L., Room, J., Bryan, K., & Barrows, D. (1998). An historical developmental analysis of social model programs. *Journal of Substance Abuse Treatment, 15*(1), 7-17.

Bufe, C. (1997). *Alcoholics Anonymous: Cult or cure?* Tucson, AZ: See Sharp Press.

Burns, C. (1992). *Alcoholics Anonymous unmasked: Deceptions and deliverance.* Shoppensburg, PA: Destiny Image Press.

Caetano, R. (1993). Ethnic minority groups and Alcoholics Anonymous: A review. In B. McCrady & W. Miller (Eds.), *Research on Alcoholics Anonymous: Opportunities and alternatives.* New Brunswick, NJ: Rutgers Centre of Alcohol Studies.

Chappel, J., & DuPont, R. (1999). Twelve-step and mutual-help programs for addictive disorders. *Psychiatric Clinics of North America, 22*(2), 425-446.

Chi, F., Kaskutas, L., Sterling, S., Campbell, C., & Weisner, C. (2009). Twelve-step affiliation and 3-year substance use outcomes among adolescents: Social support and religious service attendance as potential mediators. *Addiction, 104*(6), 927-939.

Dodes, L., & Dodes, Z. (2014). *The sober truth: Debunking the bad science behind 12-step programs and the rehab industry,* Boston. MA: Beacon Press.

DuPont, R., & Shiraki, S. (1994). Recent research in 12-step programs. In N. Miller (Ed.), *Principles of addiction medicine.* Chevy Chase, MD: American Society of Addiction Medicine.

Edwards, G., Orford, J., Egert, S., Guthrie, A., Hensman, C., Mitcheson, M., Oppenheimer, E., & Taylor, C. (1977). Alcoholism: A controlled trial of "treatment" and "advice." *Journal of Studies on Alcohol, 38*(5), 1004-1031.

Emrick, C. (1987). Alcoholics Anonymous: Affiliation processes and effectiveness as treatment. *Alcoholism: Clinical and Experimental Research, 11*(5), 416-423.

Emrick, C., Tonigan, J., Montgomery, H., & Little, L. (1993). Alcoholics Anonymous: What is currently known. In B. McCrady & W. Miller (Eds.), *Research on Alcoholics Anonymous: Opportunities and alternatives.* New Brunswick, NJ: Rutgers Centre of Alcohol Studies.

Ferri, M., Amato, L., & Davoli, M. (2006) Alcoholics Anonymous and other 12-step programmes for alcohol dependence. *Cochrane Database of Systematic Reviews, 19*(3), CD005032.

Fiorentine, R., & Hillhouse, M. (2000). Drug treatment and 12-step program participation: The additive effects of integrated recovery activities. *Journal of Substance Abuse Treatment, 18*(1), 65-74.

Fortney, J., Booth, B., Zhang, M., Humphrey, J., & Wiseman, E. (1998). Controlling for selection bias in the evaluation of Alcoholics Anonymous as aftercare treatment. *Journal of Studies in Alcohol, 59*(6), 690-697.

Garntner, A., & Riessman, F. (1977). *Self-help in the human services.* Washington, DC: Jossey-Bass.

Gomes, K., & Hart, K. (2009). Adherence to recovery practices prescribed by Alcoholics Anonymous: Benefits to sustained abstinence and subjective quality of life. *Alcoholism Treatment Quarterly, 27*(2), 223-235.

Gossop, M., Stewart, D., & Marsden, J. (2008). Attendance at Narcotics Anonymous and Alcoholics Anonymous meetings and substance use outcomes after residential treatment for drug dependence: A five-year follow up study. *Addiction, 103*(1), 119–125.

Hester, R., & Miller, W. (1995) *Handbook of alcoholism treatment approaches* (2nd ed.). Toronto, ON: Allyn and Bacon.

Humphreys, K., & Moos, R. (1996). Reduced substance-abuse-related health care costs among voluntary participants in Alcoholics Anonymous. *Psychiatric Services, 47*(7), 709–713.

Humphreys, K., & Noke, J. (1997). The influence of post-treatment mutual help group participation on the friendship networks of substance abuse patients. *American Journal of Community Psychology, 25*(1), 1–16.

Humphreys, K., Wing, S., McCarty, D., Chappel, J., Gallant, L., Haberle, B., Horvath, T., Kaskutas, L., Kirk, T., Kivlaham, D., Laudet, A., McCarthy, B., McLellan, T., Morgenstern, J., Townswend, M., & Weiss, R. (2004). Self-help organization for alcohol and drug problems: Toward evidence-based practice and policy. *Journal of Substance Abuse Treatment, 26*(3), 151–158.

John, U., Rumpf, H., Bischof, G., Hapke, U., Hanke, M., & Meyer, C. (2013). Excess mortality of alcohol-dependent individuals after 14 years and mortality predictors based on treatment participation and severity of alcohol dependence. *Alcoholism: Clinical and Experimental Research, 37*(1), 156–163.

Johnson, E., & Jerringer, L. (1993). A note on the utilization of common support activities and relapse following substance abuse treatment. *Journal of Psychology, 127*(1), 73–77.

Johnson, J. (1996). Addiction and recovery for individuals and society. In J. Chesworth (Ed.), *The ecology of health: Identifying issues and alternatives*. Thousand Oaks, CA: Sage Publications.

Kaskutas, L. (1989). Women for sobriety: A qualitative analysis. *Contemporary Drug Problems, (16)*, 177–199.

Kaskutas, L., Ammon, L., Delucchi, K., Room, R., Bond, J., & Weiser, C. (2005). Alcoholics Anonymous careers: Patterns of AA involvement five years after treatment entry. *Alcoholism: Clinical and Experimental Research, 29*(11), 1983–1990.

Kaskutas, L., Bond, J., & Weisner, C. (2003). The role of religion, spirituality and Alcoholics Anonymous in sustained sobriety. *Alcoholism Treatment Quarterly, 21*(1), 1–16.

Katz, R. (1999). The addiction treatment unit: A dual diagnosis program at the California medical facility: A descriptive report. *Journal of Psychoactive Drugs, 31*(1), 41–46.

Kelly, J., & Hoeppner, B. (2013). Does Alcoholics Anonymous work differently for men and women? A moderated multiple-mediation analysis in a large clinical sample. *Drug and Alcohol Dependence, 130*(1), 186–193.

Kelly, J., Kahler, C., & Humphreys, K. (2010). Assessing why substance use disorder patients drop out from or refuse to attend 12-step mutual-help groups: The "REASONS" questionnaire. *Addiction Research & Theory, 18*(3), 316–325.

Kelly, J., Magill, M., & Stout, R. (2009). How do people recover from alcohol dependence? A systematic review of the research on mechanisms of behavior change in Alcoholics Anonymous. *Addiction Research & Theory, 17*(3), 236–259.

Kelly, J., & Moos, R. (2003). Dropout from 12-step groups: Prevalence, predictors, and counteracting treatment influences. *Journal of Substance Abuse Treatment, 24*(3), 241–250.

Kelly, J., Stout, R., Magill, M., Tonigan, J., & Pagano, M. (2010). Mechanisms of behavior change in Alcoholics Anonymous: Does Alcoholics Anonymous lead to better alcohol use outcomes by reducing depression symptoms? *Addiction, 105*(4), 626–636.

Kelly, J., & Urbanoski, K. (2012). Youth recovery contexts: The incremental effects of 12-step attendance and involvement on adolescent outpatient outcomes. *Alcoholism: Clinical and Experimental Research, 36*(7), 1219–1229.

Kelly, J., Yeterian, J., & Myers, M. (2008). Treatment staff referrals, participation expectations, and perceived benefits and barriers to adolescent involvement in twelve-step groups. *Alcoholism Treatment Quarterly, 26*(4), 427–449.

Kingree, J., & Sullivan, B. (2002). Participation in Alcoholics Anonymous among African-Americans. *Alcoholism Treatment Quarterly, 20*(3/4), 175–186.

Kownacki, R., & Shadish, W. (1999). Does Alcoholics Anonymous work? The results from a meta-analysis of controlled experiments. *Substance Use and Misuse, 34*(13), 1897–1916.

Kramer, T., & Hoisington, D. (1992). Use of AA and NA in the treatment of chemical dependencies of traumatic brain injury survivors. *Brain Injury, 6*(1), 81–88.

Kurtz, E. (2002). Alcoholics Anonymous and the disease concept of alcoholism. *Alcoholism Treatment Quarterly, 20*(3/4), 5–39.

Laudet, A., Magura, S., Vogel, H., & Knight, E. (2003). Participation in 12-step-based fellowships among dually diagnosed persons. *Alcoholism Treatment Quarterly, 21*(2), 19–39.

Laudet, A., Stanick, V., & Sands, B. (2007). An exploration of the effect of on-site 12-step meetings on post-treatment outcomes among polysubstance-dependent outpatient clients. *Evaluation Review, 31*(6), 613–646.

Magura, S., Knight, E., Vogel, H., Mahmood, D., Laudet, A., & Rosenblum, A. (2003). Mediators of effectiveness in dual-focus self-help groups. *American Journal of Drug and Alcohol Abuse, 29*(2), 301–322.

Majer, J. (1992). Assessing the logotherapeutic value of 12-step therapy. *International Forum for Logotherapy, 15*(2), 86–89.

Manning, V., Best, D., Faulkner, N., Titherington, E., Morinan, A., Keaney, F., Gossop, M., & Strang, J. (2012). Does active referral by a doctor or 12-step peer improve 12-step meeting attendance? Results from a pilot randomised control trial. *Drug and Alcohol Dependence, 126*(1–2), 131–137.

Master, L. (1989). Jewish experience of Alcoholics Anonymous. *Smith College Studies in Social Work, 59*(2), 103–199.

Millati Islami World (2010). *Islamic 12 step program: What is Millati Islami and how did it start?* Retrieved from http://www.millatiislami.org/Welcome/islamic-12-step-program

Miller, N. (1995). *Treatment of the addictions: Applications of outcome research.* Binghamton, NY: Haworth Press.

Miller, N. (1999). Mortality risks in alcoholism and effects of abstinence and addiction treatment. *Psychiatric Clinics of North America, 22*(2), 371–383.

Miller, N., & Berinis, J. (1995). Treatment outcome for impoverished alcoholics in an abstinence based program. *International Journal of the Addictions, 30*(6), 753–763.

Moos, R., & Moos, B. (2004). Long-term influence of duration and frequency of participation in Alcoholics Anonymous on individuals with alcohol use disorder. *Journal of Consulting and Clinical Psychology, 72*(1), 81–90.

Moos, R., & Moos, B. (2005). Paths of entry into Alcoholics Anonymous: Consequences for participation and remission. *Alcoholism: Clinical and Experimental Research, 29*(10), 1858–1868.

Naegle, M., Ng, A., Barron, C., & Lai, T. (2002). Alcohol and substance abuse. *Western Journal of Medicine, 76*(4), 259–263.

Nevels, B. (1997). AA, constructivism and reflecting teams. *Substance Use and Misuse, 32*(14), 2185–2191.

Oakes, K. (2008). Purpose in life: A mediating variable between involvement in Alcoholics Anonymous and long-term recovery. *Alcoholism Treatment Quarterly, 26*(4), 450–463.

Peele, S. (1989). Ain't misbehavin'—Addiction has become an all-purpose excuse. *The Sciences, 29*(4), 14–21.

Peele, S. (1990). Research issues in assessing addiction treatment efficacy. *Drug and Alcohol Dependence, 25*(2), 179–182.

Pretto, A., & Pavesi, N. (2012). Empowerment in the self-help/mutual aid groups: The case study of Alcoholics Anonymous in Italy. *Journal of US-China Administration, 9*(8), 943–952.

Ragge, K. (2005). *The real AA: Behind the myth of 12 step recovery* (2nd ed.). Tucson, AZ: See Sharp Press.

Ronel, N. (1997). The universality of a self-help program of American origin: Narcotics Anonymous in Israel. *Social Work in Health Care, 25*(3), 87–101.

Sanders, J. (2006). Women and the twelve steps of Alcoholics Anonymous. *Alcoholism Treatment Quarterly, 24*(3), 3–29.

Sanders, J. (2011). Feminist perspectives on 12-step recovery: A comparative descriptive analysis of women in Alcoholics Anonymous and Narcotics Anonymous. *Alcoholism Treatment Quarterly, 29*(4), 357–378.

Schartzer, J. (1992). Dealing with substance abuse behaviour in the clubhouse. *Psychosocial Rehabilitation Journal, 16*(2), 107–110.

Shepard, D., Larson, M., & Hoffmann, N. (1999). Cost-effectiveness of substance abuse services: Implications for public policy. *Psychiatric Clinics of North America, 22*(2), 385–404.

Shrier, H. (1993). AA celebrates 50 years in Canada. *The Journal*, August, 1.

Smith, D. (1985). Evaluation of a residential AA program for women. *Alcohol and Alcoholism, 20*(3), 315–327.

Smith, D. (1986). Evaluation of a residential AA program. *International Journal of the Addictions, 21*(1), 33–49.

Streifel, C., & Servanty-Seib, H. (2006). Alcoholics Anonymous. *Alcoholism Treatment Quarterly, 24*(3), 71–91.

Sutro, L. (1989). Alcoholics Anonymous in a Mexican peasant-Indian village. *Human Organization, 48*(2), 180–186.

Terra, M., Barros, H., Stein, A., Figueira, I., Palermo, L., Athayde, L., Goncalves, M., & da Silveira, D. (2008). Do Alcoholics Anonymous groups really work? Factors of adherence in a Brazilian sample of hospitalized alcohol dependents. *American Journal of Addictions, 17*(1), 48–53.

Timko, C., & Debenedetti, A. (2007). A randomized controlled trial of intensive referral to 12-step self-help groups: One-year outcomes. *Drug and Alcohol Dependence, 90*(2–3), 270–279.

Timko, C., Moos, R., Finney, J., & Lesar, M. (2000). Long-term outcomes of alcohol use disorders: Comparing untreated individuals with those in Alcoholics Anonymous and formal treatment. *Journal of Studies on Alcohol, 64*(4), 529–540.

Tonigan, J. (2001). Benefits of Alcoholics Anonymous attendance. *Alcoholism Treatment Quarterly, 19*(1), 67–77.

Tonigan, J., Miller, W., & Connors, G. (2000). Project MATCH client impressions about Alcoholics Anonymous. *Alcoholism Treatment Quarterly, 18*(1), 25–41.

Valliant, G. (2005). Alcoholics Anonymous: Cult or cure? *Australian and New Zealand Journal of Psychiatry, 39*(6), 431–436.

Watkin, J., Rowe, W.S., & Csiernik, R. (2010). Prevention as controversy: Harm reduction. In R. Csiernik & W.S. Rowe (Eds.), *Responding to the oppression of addiction: Canadian social work perspectives* (2nd ed., pp. 19–36). Toronto, ON: Canadian Scholars' Press.

Walters, G. (2002). Twelve reasons why we need to find alternatives to Alcoholics Anonymous. *Addictive Disorders & Their Treatment, 1*(2), 53–59.

White, W. (2001). Pre-AA alcoholic mutual aid societies. *Alcoholism Treatment Quarterly, 19*(2), 1–21.

Witbrodt, J., Bond, J., & Kaskutas, L. (2007). Day hospital and residential addiction treatment: Randomized and nonrandomized managed care clients. *Journal of Consulting and Clinical Psychology, 75*(6), 947–959.

Zemore, S., & Kaskutas, L.A. (2008). Services received and treatment outcomes in day-hospital and residential programs. *Substance Abuse Treatment, 35*(3), 232–244.

CHAPTER 12

How Open Is the Meeting?
Attending AA in a Wheelchair[1]

Melissa Brideau and Rick Csiernik

Introduction

Nearly 4 million Canadians self-identify as having some form of ability issue (Statistics Canada, 2013). However, despite the notable progress that has been made in both the disability and addiction fields, significant gaps in the treatment continuum remain in instances where the two intersect. Individuals with ability issues continue to face a multitude of attitudinal (Koch, Nelipovich, & Sneed, 2002; Robertson et al., 2009), programming (Guthmann & Graham, 2004; Koch, Nelipovich, & Sneed, 2002), and environmental barriers (Substance Abuse and Mental Health Services Administration, 1998; Voss, Cesar, Tymus, & Fiedler, 2002; West, Graham, & Cifu, 2009a, 2009b; West, Luck, & Capps, 2007) when attempting to access appropriate substance abuse treatment. To reduce such barriers, professionals and peer helpers in both the disability and addiction fields need to place a priority on examining practices at the individual, agency, and policy levels of service to identify both existing and potential barriers that may inhibit the ability of those with ability issues to access care that is both supportive and holistic in nature. The mutual aid movement was responsible for the most significant paradigm shift in the addiction field (Csiernik, 2016) and has been identified as one of the significant social movements of the 20th century (Room, 1993). A question arising, then, is if the treatment system continues to lag in meeting the recovery needs of individuals with these intersecting issues, is the mutual aid movement in a position to lead?

Mobility Issues among Canadians

In Canada, there are more than 200,000 persons self-reported as living with *mobility impairments* (Statistics Canada, 2006), a term used when discussing individuals who have difficulty using their extremities or those individuals who demonstrate a lack of strength to walk, grasp, or lift objects. However, in the broader population study just under 2 million Canadians indicated that their mobility was limited (Statistics Canada, 2013). As a result, the use of devices such as a wheelchair, crutches, cane, or walker may be required to assist with mobility. Due to increased awareness and recent legislative changes, attempts have been made to reduce many of the barriers commonly experienced by this population on a daily basis. The limited studies in this field indicate low rates of treatment participation among individuals with ability issues. A study conducted by West, Graham, and Cifu (2009c) revealed that within the province of Ontario, addiction treatment providers had served only 235 individuals with various disabilities during a one-year period. Further, the study also highlighted the fact that out of the 235 individuals with ability issues who participated in treatment, only 6 (2.6%) reported a mobility impairment. The low rate of formal treatment participation among this population has been identified as primarily being due to the fact that many treatment centres are inaccessible to those with mobility impairments despite claims of accessibility. Pritzlaff and colleagues (2002) assessed the perceived versus actual physical accessibility of substance abuse treatment centres. In a telephone interview, 30 of 32 facilities surveyed reported that they were wheelchair accessible; however, an on-site follow-up visit to 15 of the facilities revealed significant differences between what was perceived by the managers to be accessible and those facilities that actually followed legislative guidelines designed to reduce barriers for those with mobility impairments. During the visits, several components of each treatment facility, including the exterior and interior of the building as well as policies and procedures, were examined to determine the actual accessibility of these programs for those with mobility impairments. Inspection by qualified experts familiar with accessibility standards revealed that only 9 of the 15 sites surveyed had an entrance door that met the width guidelines to accommodate individuals in wheelchairs, and only two had washroom facilities that met the appropriate guidelines. In terms of overall accessibility, while 93% of staff indicated in a phone survey that their facility was physically accessible for those with mobility impairments, completion of on-site surveys showed that only 13% of the facilities actually met all accessibility requirements.

Although it has been documented that those with mobility impairments experience lower rates of treatment participation than others in the general population, less is known about these individuals and their involvement in self-help groups due to the anonymity of such programs; it is not only impossible to identify the number of people with mobility impairments who attend meetings in person, but it is also impossible to know how many have been unable to access this vital source of support as a result of barriers that inhibit effective treatment participation. There is also no information found in the literature examining how accessible locations for self-help group meetings were for those with mobility concerns, or if accessibility was a consideration when determining the location for a group to meet.

The Context: Attending an AA Meeting as an Educational Requirement

Education in the field of addiction attracts two dichotomous groups: those with a recovery history and those without. Historic issues in the under-professionalization of the field (Csiernik & McGaghran, 2013) have led to the development of competencies to bring a baseline level of knowledge and practice to those who wish to work in this field (Graves, Csiernik, Foy, & Cesar, 2009). Those entering the addiction field without a recovery history have typically never attended a self-help meeting, and thus, in professional schools, primarily social work, attending an open meeting has become not just a critically important activity in creating competency, but an assigned and graded activity. Fuller (2002) wrote of his experience attending a meeting as part of his bachelor's of social work program. He highlighted his trepidation about getting to the meeting, about his concern that those in attendance would think he was them—an alcoholic, of which he writes, "of course I was not"—and then about the transformation he experienced watching participants interact, share, and trust.

In Social Work 4430: Introduction to Addiction, taught at King's University College at Western University in London, Ontario, students have been required to attend at least one open mutual aid meeting of their choice for the 17 years the course has been a component of the curriculum. Students have until the midpoint of the course to attend a meeting, at which time one three-hour class is entirely devoted to discussing their experiences during the open meeting. The vast majority of students elect to attend an Alcoholics Anonymous (AA) meeting, though over the years, some have attended Narcotics Anonymous, Adult Children of Alcoholics, and on only one occasion a Sex Addicts Anonymous meeting. As with Fuller's (2002) published discussion, their experiences typically run the gamut of uncertainty and even fear prior to attending the meeting and developing an understanding of what it means to label oneself an alcoholic. In addition, by attending such meetings, students are given the opportunity to witness the unconditional support that arises within a group framed in a highly structured format. However, all experiences are not positive; over the years, a minority of students has not felt welcomed for a variety of reasons. Some have had their presence at an open meeting questioned; two female students during the course of the 17 years have been approached after a meeting by male members wishing to provide them with greater details of what AA is about; and two other students had a police escort into a meeting when they were observed driving around lost in a neighbourhood watch community by an on-duty police officer. However, in 2011, the first person to have a mobility issue necessitating the use of a wheelchair enrolled in Social Work 4430, and her experience was unique from the more than 300 students who had completed this assignment before her.

Attending AA in a Wheelchair: A First-Person Narrative

As I opened my eyes on the bright and sunny Tuesday morning, suddenly it hit me. Today was the day I was going to attend my very first AA meeting. Along with this realization, I began to feel slightly anxious and fearful of what to expect from this new experience. Thoughts such as "I wonder how many people will be there," "Will they know I'm the new one?" and "What am I going to say if I'm asked to speak?" were replaying over and over in my head. On top of worrying about events that were going to occur during the meeting, I also had an additional set of concerns that were related to my ability to physically get to the meeting: I have been driving a motorized wheelchair now for 21 years, so I am more than well aware of the fact that just because a building is said to have wheelchair access, it does not necessarily mean that this is the case. However, to rid myself of this extra stress, I chose to go to the meeting that was being held at the main campus of the university I attend, as that was a building with which I was very familiar and I believed that I would have no problem navigating my way around. Upon arriving at the centre, I went to use the elevator, as the meeting was going to be taking place on the third floor, but once I was inside the elevator of the university building, it froze and would not move. I was able to maneuver myself out and access another elevator to reach the third floor, only to discover that the room where the meeting was supposed to be located was actually an equipment storage area. At this point, if I had gone alone, like so many people do to their first AA meeting, I probably would have already left, but because I had gone with somebody else, while still awkward, it made it easier to ask for directions from a person in an office on the same floor. My support and I were directed to where the anonymous meeting was actually to be held, although not as anonymous as I had thought and hoped after all. To access the meeting, we still had to travel down a very narrow corridor that seemed even smaller given the size of my wheelchair. Once we found the room, an overall feeling of relief washed over me as I made it to the right location and realized that all I had to do now was just concentrate on the meeting. However, when we tried to enter the meeting room from the corridor, we discovered that the door was locked and we had to wait in the corridor until the chair of the meeting arrived and let us inside. The waiting period was very uncomfortable because not only did I feel out of place, but also, given the size of my wheelchair, I was certainly not inconspicuous or in any way anonymous as people had to squeeze past me to get further down the corridor to other rooms. When I finally was given access to the room, I was forced to sit right in front of the door as there was a table that spanned the entire length of the room and made it impossible for me to maneuver anywhere else.

However, once everyone was seated inside the room, the attitudes of the older members were very welcoming and friendly. Each individual took the time to say hello and introduce themselves. Before I fully realized what was occurring, the meeting was under way. To begin, three pieces of paper were passed around and people took turns reciting aloud what was on the sheets. The first was the 12 steps, the second was the Serenity Prayer, and finally, there were the traditions, which I was asked to read. This was a very strange moment for me as I was under the impression that my participation in the meeting was completely voluntary and that I would not be asked to speak, but only invited. In addition, when reading the traditions, I encountered another barrier as I realized that the print was too small and close together for me to read. However, the person who had accompanied me noticed my difficulties and assisted me by helping me to keep track of my place on the page. It was at this particular moment in time that I felt very embarrassed and uncomfortable, which does not occur very often as I am quite used to dealing with a number of challenges on a daily basis. Nonetheless, it was an experience that left me feeling very uneasy—like an outsider, like the other.

Next, the chair of the meeting explained the purpose of the chips and everyone was invited to take one if he or she wished. After what seemed liked the most formal part of the meeting, the chair then welcomed the discussion of three topics, which included rigorous honesty, enablers, and stress. As each member began to discuss these topics in relation to their drinking, the mood in the room completely changed. It was a true transformation as these men went from very business-like, matter-of-fact attitudes to attitudes of a much softer nature, which helped to foster an environment that provided an opportunity for each member to experience non-judgemental support and understanding—something that they do not receive outside of the group on a regular basis. In addition, although I was aware that I was the only member of the group with an ability issue that did not entail the use of alcohol, what struck me at this moment was the fact that, other than my colleague, I was the only woman in the room as well.

Once everyone in the group was given the opportunity to speak, we all gathered in a circle joining hands and said the Lord's Prayer. I felt very awkward holding the hand of someone I had just met, and I was not even able to reach properly to finish off the circle as the table created a barrier for me. This was very unfortunate because one of the goals of a mutual aid group is to develop an atmosphere of inclusiveness where one does not have to worry about barriers such as this. This barrier, which was significant to me, remained invisible to other members of the group who had used this space for years to meet together for mutual aid, personal growth, and social support. I had encountered so many challenges in this hour that upon reflecting on my experience at this meeting, I became very saddened and then angered. This was not because of what I had personally gone through, but rather because I kept thinking of all the others who have decided to take the courageous step of going to their first meeting who are met with so many unexpected barriers that they decided the process was not worth all of this extra stress. I imagined how much more vulnerable other newcomers with an ability issue, visible or hidden, would feel, especially if they, like me, felt like an outsider and because of this, ended up not coming back or, worse, never making it to the other elevator, to the correct room, past the staring eyes, and past the too-large table to experience the wonder that a mutual aid self-help meeting can be. It was very disheartening for me to think of how many individuals there may be in my city, my province, my country, and globally who may never get the opportunity to reach out for assistance that could be potentially valuable, simply as a result of barriers such as the ones described. It is only when others in the community, such as students, families, professionals, and colleagues, begin to communicate and collaborate that each of us can unite together and work towards a substance abuse treatment strategy that is effective in providing assistance that is both holistic and supportive in nature, regardless of an individual's abilities or disabilities.

Discussion

Although the evolution of AA was not by happenstance, the theoretical foundations pertaining to group work of which we are now aware certainly were not consciously drawn upon in creating this social movement. The underpinnings upon which group work in addiction functions, both peer and professional, entail providing a space that includes opportunities to experience, share, and strengthen one's social support; knowledge through information sharing and education; identity formation; affiliation within a community; and finally personal growth and transformation (Csiernik, 2016). In terms of social support, it has become increasingly apparent that this occurs almost immediately after an individual has arrived at their first group or self-help meeting. People are typically very welcoming and are genuinely pleased when a new member attends, which is conveyed through their willingness to introduce themselves and make the new member feel as comfortable as possible. In addition, for many people, groups such as AA offer a type of social support that may not be available in other aspects of their lives, particularly if they have had a lifetime of oppression due to a disability. Johnson and Jerringer (1993) reported that participation in aftercare groups, either professionally or peer-led, contributed to maintaining abstinence rates for those who had previously completed a residential treatment program. The authors claimed that the use of self-help groups was even more significant in sustaining abstinence than was family support. However, for this to occur, a person must be present, which, considering the case described in the previous section, may be an extremely difficult task for those with mobility impairments given the many barriers that continue to inhibit the effective treatment participation of those with ability issues.

Addiction treatment and mutual aid groups can provide substantive education and information sharing if consideration of the needs of the other occurs. For many people struggling with issues of ability and the process of addiction, it is easy to feel alone and isolated with respect to one's own experience. However, psychoeducational and self-help groups can both provide a forum where individuals are invited to share experiences in dealing with addiction and where their individual experience is valued. As a result of this mutual sharing of experience, individuals may have an opportunity to normalize others' thoughts, feelings, and behaviours surrounding addiction, their disability, and themselves. This process can be extremely beneficial as this information sharing and education allow an individual to realize that they are not alone in dealing with their particular intersecting challenges, which is one reason why groups have a worldwide appeal (Ronel, 1997).

Education and information sharing within groups are central aspects of aiding individuals to address their addiction. However, here too extra time and consideration is needed to ensure that the specific needs of those with ability issues are recognized and incorporated into the group session. This can not only aid in enhancing other group members' understanding of these two issues and how they intersect, but also may be the only opportunity where an individual who is contending with a mobility impairment feels comfortable enough to share his or her experiences and concerns without fear of judgment.

Addiction treatment and mutual aid groups also assist individuals with the task of identity formation, which is a substantive issue for many struggling with issues of ability. This is because the substance abuse issue and the disability often come to constitute the entirety of one's identity. Unfortunately, one of the major errors when working with individuals who have a mobility impairment and a coexisting substance use issue occurs when only one facet of the individual's identity, the intersection of addiction and ability, is observed, while other important aspects of the person's life are ignored. Using labels such as "cripple" has the potential to create an atmosphere where assumptions, stereotypes, and ideas of what someone should or should not be are given free reign and the uniqueness and diversity that exists within the human experience is stifled. These are issues that must be addressed within the group process in creating a new identity not centred on limits, but rather upon possibilities and abilities. Thus, it is important to ensure that the group environment is not only physically accessible for all participants, but also emotionally accessible to allow for open, honest communication among all members of the group. While identity formation is a critical component of professional addiction treatment and mutual aid groups, it is also equally important to assist individuals in their goals of personal growth and transformation as well as to create an increased sense of community and affiliation. When members participate in a group setting, they are given the opportunity to invest their time and energy into contributing to and participating in communal supportive activities rather than drug-using behaviours. Everyone should have a valued voice, and each member brings a unique perspective that enhances the life of the group. This sharing of perspectives sets the stage for each member's sense of community and affiliation to emerge. It is through this sense of community and affiliation that personal growth and transformation can occur. Addiction groups should be designed for the specific purpose of gaining strength and hope by learning from the experiences of others, and their construction must be considered for inclusion of the other (Csiernik, 2016). Thus, time must be allocated to allow for all of those with various ability issues to have the opportunity to actively participate.

In addition, the fact that self-help groups are self-supporting sends a message about the value of independence to its members by saying no one supports us, but we can support each other. This is very empowering for many individuals who have lived their entire lives with issues of ability, as this allows for the development of an alternative narrative about how their presence and participation can influence others in the group, which in turn fosters personal growth and a sense of community (Csiernik, 2016). Therefore, although it is crucial that a member experience personal growth as well as a sense of affiliation and community, they must also utilize the skills and abilities that have been learned within the confines of the group to further contribute to their own development, health, and well-being so that they can eventually learn to live independently.

There are inherent issues in using a case study as a sole source of knowledge. Being only one anecdotal example, there is limited generalizability. Thus, to enhance the generalizability of this case study, it needs to be tested again in not only the same setting, but also in a number of different environments. This is also required to further open the doors to both self-help and professional treatment in the addiction field. By participating in group meetings and critically reflecting upon the basic theories and principles that are the foundation of such groups, individuals with intersecting issues of ability and addiction can become better equipped to not only deal with their addiction issues, but also respond to seeing themselves as the other. Thus, it becomes imperative for all those involved in the addiction community, be it in a professional or mutual aid capacity, to become aware of the other and to work to ensure their group environment is not only accessible, but also inviting, so that the other is not turned away before they can even begin their recovery journey.

AA led a paradigm shift that welcomed alcohol-dependent individuals to a new experience, a new way to see themselves. The question every member of a self-help group needs to ask him or herself is whether their meeting is open to those who are not like them but who have a need to be in the room. If 12-step groups can take the lead here, perhaps we professionals might again follow.

NOTE

1. This chapter was originally published as Brideau, M. & Csiernik, R. (2014). How open is the meeting? Attending AA in a wheelchair. *Journal of Groups in Addiction and Recovery*, 9(1), 4–13.

REFERENCES

Csiernik, R. (2016). *Substance use and abuse: Everything matters*. Toronto, ON: Canadian Scholars' Press.

Csiernik, R., & McGaghran, C. (2013). Meeting professional competencies through specialized distance education: The McMaster University Addiction Studies Program. *Journal of Teaching in Social Work*, 33(4), 566–577.

Fuller, R. (2002). "I'm a social work student and I'm here to observe an AA Meeting." *Journal of Social Work Practice in the Addictions*, 2(1), 109–111.

Graves, G., Csiernik, R., Foy, J., & Cesar, J. (2009). An examination of Canadian social work program curriculum and the addiction core competencies. *Journal of Social Work Practice in the Addictions, 9*(4), 400–413.

Guthmann, D., & Graham, V. (2004). Substance abuse: A hidden problem within the D/deaf and hard of hearing communities. *Journal of Teaching in the Addictions, 3*(1), 49–64.

Johnson, E., & Jerringer, L. (1993). A note on the utilization of common support activities and relapse following substance abuse treatment. *Journal of Psychology, 127*(1), 73–77.

Koch, S.D., Nelipovich, M., & Sneed, Z. (2002). Alcohol and other drug abuse as coexisting disabilities: Considerations for counselors serving individuals who are blind or visually impaired. *Re: View: Rehabilitation and Education for Blindness and Visual Impairment, 33*(4), 151–159.

Robertson, S., Davis, S., Sneed, Z., Koch, D., & Boston, Q. (2009). Competency issues for alcohol/other drug treatment counselors. *Alcoholism Treatment Quarterly, 27*(3), 265–279.

Ronel, N. (1997). The universality of a self-help program of American origin: Narcotics Anonymous in Israel. *Social Work in Health Care, 25*(3), 87–101.

Room, R. (1993). Alcoholics Anonymous as a social movement. In B. McCrady & W. Miller (Eds.), *Research on Alcoholics Anonymous: Opportunities and alternatives* (pp. 167–187). New Brunswick, NJ: Rutgers Center of Alcohol Studies.

Statistics Canada. (2006). *Participation and activity limitations survey*. Ottawa, ON: Statistics Canada.

Statistics Canada. (2013). *Canadians in context: People with disabilities*. Retrieved from http://well-being.esdc.gc.ca/misme-iowb/.3ndic.1t.4r@-eng.jsp?iid=40

Substance Abuse and Mental Health Services Administration. (1998). *Substance use disorder treatment for people with physical and cognitive disabilities* (PMID 22514835. SMA 98-3249). Rockville, MD: U.S. Center for Substance Abuse Treatment.

Voss, C., Cesar, K., Tymus, T., & Fiedler, I.G. (2002). Perceived versus actual accessibility of substance abuse treatment facilities. *Topics in Spinal Cord Injury Rehabilitation, 7*(3), 47–55.

West, S., Graham, C., & Cifu, D. (2009a). Physical and programmatic accessibility of British alcohol/other drug treatment centers. *Alcoholism Treatment Quarterly, 27*(3), 294–304.

West, S., Graham, C., & Cifu, D. (2009b). Prevalence of persons with disabilities in alcohol/other drug treatment in the United States. *Alcoholism Treatment Quarterly, 27*(3), 242–252.

West, S., Graham, C., & Cifu, D. (2009c). Rates of persons with disabilities in alcohol/other drug treatment in Canada. *Alcoholism Treatment Quarterly, 27*(3), 253–264.

West, S., Luck, R., & Capps, F. (2007). Physical inaccessibility negatively impacts the treatment participation of persons with disabilities. *Addictive Behaviors, 32*(7), 1494–1497.

CHAPTER 13

Maintaining the Continuum of Care: Arguing for Community-Based Residential Addiction Treatment Programs

Rick Csiernik

Introduction

Many controversies exist within the addiction field. Among the most historic is which is "better," residential inpatient care or outpatient (community-based) counselling (Annis, 1984; 1985; Day & Strang, 2011; Hays et al., 2001; McKay et al., 1997; Sherk, 1997). Psychoactive drug abuse treatment in Canada is currently delivered by a diverse network of programs with administrative and fiscal linkages to government ministries, public institutions, private organizations, and lay groups. Alcohol dependency counselling in North America was initially organized, promoted, and governed by lay groups of recovering alcohol-dependent persons responding to neglect by social workers and other helping professionals. The initial addiction counselling programs to emerge in North America, after Alcoholics Anonymous created an environment enabling the provision of assistance to those with alcoholism, were inpatient residential treatment facilities (Chappel & DuPont, 1999; Csiernik, 2016).

In the 1950s, a highly structured program at Willmar State Hospital in Minnesota was created and became known as the Minnesota Model. It includes seven core components:

1. integration of professional staff with trained recovering alcohol-dependent persons, as social workers and other counsellors knew little of alcohol dependency;
2. focus upon the disease concept of alcohol dependency with a linkage to 12-step-related (Alcoholics Anonymous) fellowships;
3. family involvement;
4. abstinence from all psychoactive substances;
5. emphasis upon patient and family education;

6. individualized treatment plans; and

7. sustained 12–step–based aftercare (Chappel & DuPont, 1999).

Originally this treatment regimen lasted from 28 to 42 days, though average length in Canada has now generally been reduced to 21 days and as little as 18 as a result of decreased government support for substance abuse residential programs. These sanatoriums or rehabilitation farms were originally used as much for treatment as to sequester those addicted to alcohol from their environments and also away from the general public. They offered a respite for clients from their harmful environments and the opportunity to obtain more intense and focused treatment. Residential programs ultimately developed in two distinct directions: hospital-based, medical-oriented programs or community-based, social model programs. While both initially tended to use the principles of Alcoholics Anonymous (AA) as their foundation, hospital-based programs employed medical personnel, while social model programs used those recovering from alcohol dependency as counsellors. Social model programs also differed from purely medical model programs in terms of physical environment, staff role, basis of authority, view of recovery, governance, and community orientation. Generally, social workers were not actively involved in the early development of either of these two treatment options (Chappel & DuPont, 1999; Galanter, 1987).

Beginning in the late 1960s, research began to demonstrate that not only was residential programming more costly than outpatient counselling, it was also not necessarily the most efficient method of assisting substance abusers. This was in an era prior to assessment and matching where individuals would attend a program they were familiar with or which was close to them geographically. The first studies to empirically examine this issue were conducted at the Maudsley Hospital in London, England (Edwards & Guthrie, 1966, 1967; Edwards et al., 1977). A one-year follow-up study of men dependent on alcohol reported that there was no significant difference in outcome between those who had received community-based counselling and those who had received several months of inpatient treatment. Helen Annis (1984) of the Ontario Addiction Research Foundation, now the Centre for Addiction and Mental Health, conducted an extensive international literature review and examination of the inpatient versus outpatient debate. She concluded that outcomes studies indicated that in-hospital alcohol treatment programs of a few weeks to a few months in duration showed no higher success rates than did periods of brief hospitalization of a few days. She also reported that partial hospitalization, or day treatment programs, produced outcomes equal to or superior to those produced through inpatient hospitalization at one-half to one-third the cost. Likewise, Miller and Hester (1986) concluded that residential programs were not associated with superior outcomes relative to community-based outpatient programs. However, while this was a major outcome study using a randomly assigned sample, complicated concurrent disorder clients were not included. Studies like these led Canadian provincial governments through the 1980s and 1990s to place a much greater emphasis on outpatient resources, with residential programming playing a lesser role in the continuum of care. This has led to a concern among those working in this branch of addiction treatment (Twelve Step Working Group, 2000), particularly as psychoactive substance abusers are a heterogeneous group, necessitating different types of counselling methods and options.

Research Findings

Despite the perceived limitations of residential programming in the addiction field, studies examining social model programs are relatively limited in the literature. Alford, Koehler, and Leonard evaluated a residential program using a 12-step treatment philosophy in 1991. Their study consisted of 98 male clients and 59 female adolescents and young adult clients, aged 13 to 29, who were chemically dependent. The researchers discovered that those who completed the program had higher rates of abstinence six-months post-completion than those who had dropped out. Also of interest was that female subjects were more likely to be abstinent one and two years post-completion than were male subjects.

Stanley (1999) reviewed the outcomes of a residential program that served over 3,000 patients over the course of two years. It combined a primary care health unit with a residential addiction treatment program, including AA involvement, for patients with an addiction to psychoactive drugs and either a chronic medical or psychiatric diagnosis. This residential service served clients who fell outside traditional treatment programs. Stanley found that positive changes occurred across all client groups, including those categorized as "hard to serve."

The largest single addiction study ever conducted in North America, Project MATCH (1997), spent $47 million dollars examining alcohol dependency treatment in the United States. Among the conclusions made by the researchers was that short-term inpatient treatment was an important means through which clients become aware of and oriented to 12-step groups, their primary source of aftercare and relapse prevention. These studies support earlier research findings from Australia. Smith (1985, 1986), using a quasi-experimental design, studied both men and women with a dependence upon alcohol. He compared those in a residential program featuring AA involvement and staff with a recovery history to those in a hospital-based detoxification centre. After 14 to 19 months, 79% of the treated women and 62% of the treated men remained abstinent while only 3% of the women and 5% of the men who only used the detoxification services were still abstinent.

Shepard, Larsen, and Hoffman (1999) stated that for clients with low or moderate severity of substance abuse, short-term residential counselling was no more effective than outpatient models and was, as expected, costlier. However, when it came to those clients who scored in the high range of substance abuse severity, regular and intensive outpatient treatment programs were considerably less successful in creating abstinence. It was the short-term residential programs that produced over a one-third higher success rate, with success being defined as ongoing abstinence. As well, short-term residential counselling produced the best outcomes of any of the program options for severely dependent clients. In their analysis, which used abstinence rate divided by cost of program, short-term residential counselling was not only the most cost-effective programming option for high severity substance abusers, it also had the third best cost-effectiveness ratio of the 15 treatment options presented in the analysis. Short-term residential programming consistently ranked ahead of intensive outpatient options as well as long-term residential rehabilitation programs.

A study comparing the effectiveness and costs of day hospital versus inpatient rehabilitation for cocaine dependence included 111 inner-city, lower socio-economic, primarily African-American male veterans who assessed as being cocaine dependent (Alterman et al., 1994). Fifty-six participants were randomly assigned to one month of outpatient care consisting of 27 hours of treatment weekly, while the remaining 55 were inpatient clients who participated in 48 hours of scheduled treatment weekly. Outpatient costs were roughly one-half that of inpatient costs but a significantly greater proportion of residential participants (89.1%) completed treatment than did outpatient subjects (53.6%). At the seven-month post-treatment mark significant improvements in substance use, psychosocial functioning, and health status were found in both groups, but there was little evidence of differential improvement between groups. Thus, for those completing treatment there was little difference in outcomes with residential being much more expensive but also being much more likely to retain clients (Alterman et al., 1994).

Tiet and colleagues (2007) followed nearly 2,000 individuals across 50 United States Department of Veterans Affairs settings through their addiction treatment process. They too found that those with more substantive abuse issues experienced better addiction-related outcomes when they attended a residential program versus out-patient counselling. The greater a client scored on the Addiction Severity Index, the greater the likelihood that they would have superior outcomes if they attended an inpatient rather than an outpatient program. Rychtarik and colleagues (2000) found that the more severe the client's problems were prior to entering treatment, the poorer the outcome was when measured in days of abstinence. However, there was greater abstinence reported among those who sought help through a residential program than through a community-based outpatient treatment program.

Hays' group (2001) matched 146 residential clients to 292 outpatient clients under-going smoking cessation treatment on age, sex, education, marital status, and number of cigarettes smoked. Twelve months post-treatment twice as many participants who had undertaken the residential program (45%) remained abstinent compared to those who received outpatient, community-based counselling (23%). Bayer (1995) conducted a small study of 37 employed individuals who sought treatment for their addiction issue with a goal of abstinence through their organization's Employee Assistance Program (EAP). Each employee was given the choice of what type of assistance to seek. After 18 months, 15 (41%) remained abstinent while the majority (n=22, 59%) remained dependent despite all initially voluntarily seeking assistance. Thirteen employees chose only EAP counselling with only two (15.4%) remaining abstinent after 18 months. Eleven individuals voluntarily selected outpatient treatment with again only two (18.2%) remaining abstinent 18 months post-treatment. Of the six that opted for inpatient treatment, five (83.3%) were abstinent while four (80%) of the five who undertook both an inpatient and outpatient program were not drinking 18 months after the conclusion of their treatment. Interestingly, two chose no professional assistance and attended only Alcoholics Anonymous meetings, with both reporting maintaining their sobriety at the 6- and 18-month follow-ups.

Another American workplace-based study that examined whether abstinence-based, inpatient addiction treatment produced significant improvements in work-related absenteeism, tardiness, and productivity followed 154 participants for six months post-treatment. Employees involved in the study reported significant improvements in all three outcome variables regardless of substance of choice or employer involvement (Arbour et al., 2014).

A national review of health care services in the United Kingdom in 2009 stated that providing inpatient detoxification/stabilization and residential rehabilitation interventions, referred to as Tier 4 services, were found to be effective responses to the needs of those with the most severe drug problems. Tier 4 services were reported to allow those misusing drugs to move towards long-term abstinence when appropriate. Inpatient drug treatment in the United Kingdom typically entails short-term hospital-based medical treatment. Medical detoxification is the norm followed by residential rehabilitation services to support clients in moving towards abstinence with an emphasis upon coping strategies and life skills (National Treatment Agency for Substance Misuse, 2009).

French (1995, 2000) argued that, in general, techniques for identifying and measuring treatment outcomes vary depending upon program objectives and the terms used to define a successful outcome. Many programs that may appear cost-effective in fact have hidden costs associated with re-admission and relapse, especially when there is inappropriate or inadequate follow-up and community support. As previously noted, Annis (1984), in her groundbreaking work, demonstrated that lengthy hospital stays were no more effective than shorter hospital stays in producing abstinence. However, this has been misinterpreted by some to indicate that all forms of residential programming in the addiction field are financially inappropriate. In fact, non-medical residential facilities following the social model program approach have made the claim that they are the most cost-effective residential alternative for appropriately assessed and matched clients (Borkman et al., 1998). French (2000) states that the value of non-hospital-based services have been poorly analyzed and should not be included when critiquing hospital-based residential programs. Even Barnett and Swindle's (1997) work that supports reducing inpatient residential programming to 21 days only examined hospital-based programs, which are inherently more expensive. In fact, 21-day hospital programs can be considerably more expensive than 28-day social model programs. Thus, all residential programs should not and cannot be lumped together for cost-effectiveness analysis.

Borkman and colleagues (1998), Rychtarik and colleagues (2000), Shepard, Larsen, and Hoffman (1999), Tiet and colleagues, (2007), Witbrodt, Bond, and Kaskutas (2007), and the Twelve Step Working Group (2000) have all stated that community-based residential addiction treatment programs remain the best match for substance abusers with substantial functional impairment and physical dependency—the most needy and the least promising. Cost-outcome studies report that outpatient addiction care is less costly than is residential programming (French, 2000; Mojtabai & Graff Zivin, 2003). However, short-term residential counselling not only produces positive outcomes with properly matched clients (French, 2000), but also emerges significantly ahead of other options on several criteria, including financial, for those with more significant addiction issues such as being in conflict with the law (McCollister & French, 2003), engaging in self-injurious behaviour (Ilgen, Tiet, Finney, & Harris, 2005), or being homeless (Schumacher et al., 2002).

Discussion

It is likely that any social worker providing casework services will have a portion of her or his clients whose presenting, contributing, or underlying problems relate to a drug dependency or addiction. For many clients, addiction-specific counselling is an important component of the treatment plan, but what type of counselling is best? It was once tempting to assume that more treatment is better treatment, and that longer or more intensive interventions will yield superior outcomes. It subsequently became both tempting and fashionable to claim that time-limited, outpatient treatment is better because it could be shown to be the most fiscally prudent. However, neither absolute is totally accurate or correct. It is essential that in the assessment, process time is taken to match the client to the most appropriate resource, as both outpatient and residential programs have strengths and limitations.

Residential treatment produces positive outcomes for appropriately matched clients (Huang & Ryan, 2011; Mills, Pepler, & Cribbie, 2013). This, along with the acknowledgement that there should be a continuum of care (Government of Ontario, 2010; MacPherson & Rowley, 2001), necessitates supporting and properly funding the entire continuum of care from withdrawal management to relapse prevention programming. Until clients with substance dependency problems become a homogeneous population, we, as social workers, need to advocate for the presence and maintenance of the entire continuum of care to enable the widest possible range of services for those with whom we work. It serves no purpose to fight amongst ourselves for the artificially limited treatment dollars available, when the loss of any component diminishes the entire continuum. No one technique stands out as the panacea for substance dependency treatment, and thus, we remain best served by providing an integrated continuum of care for the continuum of Canadians in need. The research discussed illustrates that, while apparently more costly, community-based residential addiction treatment programs not only serve a specific population extremely well, they actually do it more cost-effectively than can other inappropriately matched resources, particularly for clients with the greatest needs who have the fewest social and environmental supports. While certainly not required for all clients, community-based residential addiction treatment programs are beneficial for many and need to remain an integral aspect of the comprehensive integrated treatment continuum. A balance should be maintained between community and institutional treatment, and outpatient and inpatient counselling, so that our clients' needs remain first on the agenda.

REFERENCES

Alford, G., Koehler, R., & Leonard, J. (1991). Alcoholics Anonymous/Narcotics Anonymous model inpatient treatment of chemically dependent adolescents: A 2-year outcome study. *Journal of Studies on Alcohol, 52*(2), 118–126.

Alterman, A., O'Brien, C., McLellan, A., August, D., Snider, E., Droba, M., Cornish, J., Hall, C., Ralpheson, A., & Schrade, F.X. (1994). Effectiveness and costs of inpatient versus day hospital cocaine rehabilitation. *The Journal of Nervous and Mental Disease, 182*(3), 157–163.

Annis, H. (1984). Is inpatient rehabilitation of the alcoholic cost effective? Con position. *Advances in Alcohol and Substance Abuse, 5*(1–2), 175–190.

Annis, H. (1985). *Is inpatient rehabilitation of the alcoholic cost effective? A reply to Douglas L. Tate.* Toronto, ON: Addiction Research Foundation.

Arbour, S., Gavrysh, I., Hanbley, J., Tse, A., Ho, V., & Bell, M. (2014). Addiction treatment and work-related outcomes: Examining the impact of employer involvement and substance of choice on absenteeism, tardiness, and productivity. *Journal of Workplace Behavioral Health, 29*(1), 73–90.

Barnett, P., & Swindle, R. (1997). Cost-effectiveness of inpatient substance abuse treatment. *Health Services Research, 32*(5), 615–629.

Bayer, D. (1995). Results: A comparison of chemical dependency treatment outcomes when clients are given full choice. *Employee Assistance Quarterly, 10*(4), 53–65.

Borkman, T., Kaskutas, L., Room, J., Bryan, K., & Barrows, D. (1998). An historical developmental analysis of social model programs. *Journal of Substance Abuse Treatment, 15*(1), 7–17.

Chappel, J., & DuPont, R. (1999). Twelve-step and mutual-help programs for addictive disorders. *Psychiatric Clinics of North America, 22*(2), 425–446.

Csiernik, R. (2016). *Substance use and abuse: Everything matters* (2nd ed.). Toronto, ON; Canadian Scholars' Press.

Day, E., & Strang, J. (2011). Outpatient versus inpatient opioid detoxification: A randomized controlled trial. *Journal of Substance Abuse Treatment, 40*(1), 56–66.

Edwards, G., & Guthrie, S. (1966). A comparison of inpatient and outpatient treatment of alcohol dependence. *Lancet,* February 26, 467–468.

Edwards, G., & Guthrie, S. (1967). A controlled trial of inpatient and outpatient treatment of alcohol dependency. *Lancet,* March 11, 555–559.

Edwards, G., Orford, J., Egert, S., Guthrie, S., Hensman, C., Mitcheson, M., Oppenheimer, E., & Taylor, C. (1977). Alcoholism: A controlled trial of "treatment" and "advice." *Journal of Studies on Alcohol, 38*(5), 1004–1031.

French, M. (1995). Economic evaluation of drug abuse treatment programs: Methodology and findings. *American Journal of Alcohol Abuse, 21*(1), 111–135.

French, M.T. (2000). Economic evaluation of alcohol treatment services. *Evaluation and Program Planning, 23*(1), 27–39.

Galanter, M. (1987). Peer-directed self-help treatment for alcoholism. *Alcoholism: Clinical and Experimental Research, 11*(5), 413–415.

Government of Ontario. (2010). *Navigating the journey to wellness: The Comprehensive Mental Health and Addictions Action Plan for Ontarians.* Select Committee on Mental Health and Addictions final report. Toronto, ON: Government of Ontario.

Hays, J., Wolter, T., Eberman, K., Croghan, I., Offord, K., & Hurt, R. (2001). Residential (inpatient) treatment compared with outpatient treatment for nicotine dependence. *Mayo Clinic Proceedings, 76*(2), 124–133.

Huang, H., & Ryan, J.P. (2011). Trying to come home: Substance exposed infants, mothers, and family reunification. *Children and Youth Services Review, 33*(2), 322–329.

Ilgen, M., Tiet, Q., Finney, J., & Harris, A. (2005). Recent suicide attempt and the effectiveness of inpatient and outpatient substance use disorder treatment. *Alcoholism: Clinical and Experimental Research, 29*(9), 1664–1671.

MacPherson, D., & Rowley, M. (2001). *A framework for action: A four-pillar approach to drug problems in Vancouver.* Vancouver, BC: City of Vancouver.

McCollister, K., & French, M. (2003). The relative contribution of outcome domains in the total economic benefit of addiction interventions: A review of first findings. *Addiction, 98*(12), 1647–1659.

McKay, J., Cacciola, J., McLellan, T., Alterman, A., & Wirtz, P. (1997). An intial evaluation of the psychosocial dimensions of the American Society of Addiction Medicine criteria for inpatient versus outpatient substance abuse rehabilitation. *Journal of Studies on Alcohol, 58*(3), 239–252.

Miller, W., & Hester, R. (1986) In-patient alcoholism treatment: Who benefits? *American Psychologist, 41*(7), 794–805.

Mills, L., Pepler, D., & Cribbie, R. (2013). Effectiveness of residential treatment for substance abusing youth: Benefits of the Pine River Institute program. *Residential Treatment for Children & Youth, 30*(3), 202–226.

Mojtabai, R., & Graff Zivin, J. (2003). Effectiveness and cost-effectiveness of four treatment modalities for substance disorders: A propensity score analysis. *Health Services Research, 38*(1), 233–259.

National Treatment Agency for Substance Misuse. (2009). *Improving services for substance misuse. Diversity, and inpatient and residential rehabilitation services.* London, UK: Commission for Healthcare Audit and Inspection.

Project MATCH Research Team. (1997). Matching alcoholism treatments to client heterogeneity: Project MATCH post-treatment drinking outcomes. *Journal of Studies on Alcohol, 58*(1), 7–29.

Rychtarik, R., Connors, G., Whitney, R., McGillicuddy, N., Fitterling, J., & Wirtz, P. (2000). Treatment settings for persons with alcoholism: Evidence for matching clients to inpatient versus outpatient care. *Journal of Consulting Clinical Psychology, 68*(2), 277–289.

Schumacher, J.E., Mennemeyer, S.T., Milby, J.B., Wallace, D., & Nolan, K. (2002). Costs and effectiveness of substance abuse treatments for homeless persons. *Journal of Mental Health Policy and Economics, 5*(1), 33–42.

Shepard, D., Larsen, M., & Hoffman, N. (1999). Cost-effectiveness of substance abuse services. *Psychiatric Clinics of North America, 22*(2), 385–404.

Sherk, C. (1997). *Addiction treatment services restructuring: A draft plan.* Toronto, ON: Ontario Ministry of Health.

Smith, D. (1985). Evaluation of a residential AA program for women. *Alcohol and Alcoholism, 20*(3), 315–327.

Smith, D. (1986). Evaluation of a residential AA program. *International Journal of the Addictions, 21*(1), 33–49.

Stanley, A. (1999). Primary care and addiction treatment: Lessons learned from building bridges across traditions. *Journal of Addictive Diseases, 18*(2), 65–82.

Tiet, Q., Ilgen, M., Byrnes, H., Harris, A., & Finney, J. (2007). Treatment setting and baseline substance use severity interact to predict patients' outcomes. *Addiction, 102*(3), 432–440.

Twelve Step Working Group. (2000). *Twelve-step orientated residential treatment programs in Ontario.* Cambridge, ON: Twelve Step Working Group.

Witbrodt, J., Bond, J., & Kaskutas, L. (2007). Day hospital and residential addiction treatment: Randomized and nonrandomized managed care clients. *Journal of Consulting and Clinical Psychology, 75*(6), 947–959.

PART 3

POPULATIONS

CHAPTER 14

Patterns of Intimacy and Sexual Expression in Interaction with Addictions

Louise Osmond and Dennis Kimberley

This cruel exploitation of the childish eagerness for pleasure is, of course, possible only among a certain type of forlorn city children who are totally without standards and into whose colorless lives a visit to the amusement park brings an acme of delirious excitement.... It is horribly pathetic to learn how far a nickel or quarter will go towards purchasing the virtue of these children.

—JANE ADDAMS (1912)

Historical Context

Social workers have been concerned with addiction problems (Straussner, 2001), problems of intimacy and sexual expression, and concomitant problems (Addams, 1912) since the beginnings of the profession. In the late 1800s, early social work concerns included sexual exploitation of juveniles for purposes of prostitution (Pappenheim, 1924) as well as related inebriety. Early child therapists in the 1940s were puzzled by the indiscriminate and developmentally premature sexualized expression of some children (Freud & Burlingham, 1943, 1944). With professionalization at the turn of the 20th century, social workers had increased community sanction to be involved in marriage preparation, marriage counselling, promoting temperance, promoting mental hygiene, and undertaking assessment and social casework including what was substance use assessment (Richmond, 1917/1944) and would be considered today as addiction assessment and counselling. As well, social workers challenged child sexual abuse and juvenile prostitution; the latter clearly associated with mood modifying substances (Addams, 1912). In short, since the turn of the 20th century, social workers have been aware of, and worked with, the links among addiction, intimacy, and sexual expression and associated personal and social problems, including trauma and complex trauma (Kimberley & Parsons, 2016).

Overview

The intersection of addiction and sexual expression has become an even greater issue with the increased access to a host of Internet and cyber sources (see Chapter 28). This chapter will focus on integration of links between substance use and intimacy and sexual expression as well as examining net and non-net access to modern expressions of more indiscriminate sexuality and eroticization (Hall, 2011; James, 2012; Maltz & Maltz, 2008; Riemersma & Sytsma, 2013). The complex links between attachment, affect regulation, complex trauma, psychosexual and relational development, and addiction will also be examined. The position of the authors is that:

- biopsychosocial interactional analysis and assessment respects the complexities of the lives of clients and supports personal and social change oriented social work practices;
- transtheoretical holistic perspectives, which reflect integrative and intersecting contextually relevant practices, respecting the complexity of lives as lived within social environments, are in the best interest of the client;
- there are known common social relational (creating safety and active presence of relationship) and common structural dimensions (ensuring safety and inclusivity of the helping space) that account for most intervention influence and support influence on needed, required and desired, and personal and social change;
- short-term therapies would not be treatments of choice in addressing such lived complexity and uncertainty; and
- reliance only on narrow cognitive-behavioural theories of intervention, or goal attainment imperatives, would be unjustly limiting in this area of practice (Kimberley & Osmond, 2016).

Substance Use and Sexual Expression

Sexual expression may be described succinctly as a biopsychosocial-spiritual phenomenon that includes development of age-stage appropriate sexual potential; sexual sensations and generalized sex interest; orientation towards preferred sex objects, such as males, females, children, animals, and inanimate objects; attraction to and desire for specific sex objects;[1] sexual desire and sexual arousal by direct physical stimulation through touch or through indirect stimulation in the form of mental imagery; sexual activity and sexual performance that reflect species common and culturally diverse expressions; excitement, climax-orgasm, resolution, and post-resolution intimacy; and existential realities of sex and attachment, including sex and intimacy with and without meaning, sex and intimacy fused with alienation, and sex and detachment (Mikulincer & Shaver, 2016). Each phase may be influenced by biopsychosocial interactions, among which those in the following analysis are included. As a contextual note, in the clinical experience of the authors, it is not uncommon for substance-abusing clients to report that they have seldom engaged in a shared sexual experience that was not mediated by the use of a mood-modifying substance.

There are fundamental biochemical and biophysical realities of human physiology. These interact with substance use, addiction, intimacy, and sexual expression. For example, hormone levels, erotic body sensations, concentrations of psychoactive substances such as alcohol or ecstacy (3,4 methylendioxy-methamphetamine, MDMA) in the blood, and lifestyle patterns converge to increase interest or arousal. However, if central nervous system depressants such as benzodiazepines or barbiturates are administered, a corresponding decrease in sexual performance often occurs (Fuller, 1984; Winick, 1992) and can create orgastic dysfunction (Clayton & Montejo, 2006). Depressed and medicated clients often experience a reduction in sex interest. In contrast, central nervous system stimulants, specifically cocaine or crystal meth, may increase erotic sensation and may also increase latency to orgasm in men and women, depending on patterns of administration such as rubbing the drug on the head of one's penis in the case of cocaine hydrochloride, which also has anesthetic effects (McKay, 2005). Stimulants are frequently used to enhance sex interest and arousal.

Within addictive experiences, there is a great likelihood that a background of biochemical and bioneurological factors interact with biochemical processes (Begun & Brown, 2014), some of which may influence sexual expression. Among these are included inherited addictive risk factors associated with nicotine, alcohol, marijuana, and cocaine; chromosomes that are associated with both increased addiction risks and increased protections; and family histories that are observed, increasingly, as significant in association with biological determinants of risk. Begun and Brown conclude: "The truth seems to lie in a combination of both general and specific genetic vulnerability and resilience related to substance abuse and dependence.... [T]here are genetic influences on neuroanatomy and neuro-chemistry" (p. 41). They also advise that the amygdala area of the brain "has been found to play a central role in alcohol and other drug abuse, in part because it is also responsible for determining which experiences related to pleasure and pain will be encoded in the memory" (p. 44). Psychoactive substances and sexual activity may be used to enhance pleasure; substances may be used to enhance sexual performance and pleasure; substances may be used to numb the psychic and physical pain of undesired sexual activity; and sexual activity may be used to create pleasurable sensations when substance use or abuse is not having the desired effect or when the person with an addiction is experiencing withdrawal.

Individuals commonly experience and express affects that interact with substance use, addiction, intimacy, and sexual expression. Feelings of attraction and disinhibition may increase with compulsive sexual activity and the use of alcohol, marijuana, or ecstasy. Some drugs such as MDA and MDMA can give the person the sensate experience of warmth and a feeling of cosmic connection with the world. Apprehension and anxiety may increase with the use of amphetamines, and in large doses may be associated with loss of feelings of arousal. Persons who are depressed and sad may elevate their mood through self-medication with a stimulant with one of the intended or unintended consequences being the return of sexual desire. Persons who are addicted to heroin have reported that the orgiastic qualities of the drug effect may replace sex interest and sex arousal (Leiblum, 1984; McKim & Hancock, 2013; Winick, 1992). In general, persons who use illicit drugs and live related unhealthy lifestyles, with the possible exception of those with anti-social personality disorders, are likely to exhibit some type of sexual disorder (Johnson, Phelps, & Cottler, 2004). As well, rape associated with date-rape drugs such as GHB, rophynl, or ketamine also typically seriously compromise cognitive functioning and capacity for intimacy and shared sexuality (Jansen & Theron, 2006).

A person's cognitive functioning, orientation to time, place, and self, as well as perception, memory, and attention all interact with substance use, addiction, intimacy, and sexual expression, independent of mental health issues. Impaired perception and judgment are affected by substance use, misuse, or abuse. For example, ecstasy can impair judgment and support intense feelings of bond or intimacy with a stranger (McKim & Hancock, 2013), while opioids (Fentanyl, methadone, morphine, Oxycontin) may reduce a person's perception of personal need for sexual expression (Hartman, 1984; Winick, 1992). Compulsive behaviours and impulse control disorders, such as compulsive Internet use (Beard, 2008), pathological gambling (Blume, 2004; Schreiber, Potenza, & Grant, 2016), and compulsive sexual behaviour (Goodman, 2004; Logan, 1992) may also impair judgment and perception. Some compulsive behaviours are also associated with neurological changes and biochemical changes that parallel substance addiction (Hall, 2011; Laier, Schulte, & Brand, 2013). Concurrent disorders may have interactive effects with cognitive functioning associated with decreased sexual functioning (depression and alcohol use), or with temporarily increased sexual functioning (mania and cocaine use).

Cognitive content, in terms of beliefs, attitudes, values, expectations, and related cognitive scripts concerning substance use and intimacy may support or block intimacy and sexual expression. The person who expects to be unattractive and a poor performer sexually may have sex interests, but may define sexual vulnerability as too much of a risk. That same person under the influence of alcohol, cannabis, or low doses of amphetamine may define him or herself as more able and more risqué in terms of both intimacy and sexual expression. That same person under the influence of cocaine or ecstasy may feel higher levels of arousal and dismiss negative self-talk about performance because the subjective experience of performance may be one of increased ability and authenticity of intimacy (Braun-Harvey, 2009; Mikulincer & Shaver, 2016; Winick, 1992). Expectation effects with respect to the impact of substance use on sexual expression may contribute to patterns of sexual activity or its avoidance; cognitive scripts such as "I need a few drinks if I am really going to let go" may motivate sexual expression or its avoidance. Sex trade workers may purposely use any substance that may support an expectation effect of sexual performance under conditions of lack of sex and erotic interest (cocaine, MDA) and help in taking care of business (Farley, 2003). Some addicted persons may exchange sex for risky substances (cocaine, crack and/or heroin) where the expectation is the benefit of the drug (Sharpe, 2005).

Interpersonal relationship dynamics interact with substance use, addiction, intimacy, and sexual expression. Within the context of typical paths to sexual expression identified above and from a developmental point of view, one of the most important dynamics supporting safe and healthy intimacy linked with sexual expression appears to be a person's ability to trust and to attach and bond with some depth of relationship (Feeney, 1999; Mikulincer & Shaver, 2016; Mohr, 2008). Anxious attachments and loneliness as well as avoidant attachments have been observed to be linked to relationally compromised human development, sometimes associated with parenting deficits or trauma precursors, all of which contribute to both addiction risks as well as clinically significant compromises in expressions of intimacy and sexuality. Additionally, a person might wish to be able to self-protect from intimacy and sexual expression associated with power, control, and coercion (Turner & Colao, 1985). Substance use, misuse, or abuse may act paradoxically and enable a cautious person to trust and connect with a safe sex object, through the use of alcohol, or may enable an otherwise cautious person to succumb to coercion by defining a risky stranger as trustworthy and then having congruent feelings of trust, through the use of MDA or MDMA.

There are several other social dimensions that are interactive with normative healthy and normative risky sexual expression. Socio-economic stability and safety help prevent sexual exploitation and enable more genuine consent under conditions of interest and attraction (Apter-March, 1984). Social structures that support, at best, and tolerate, at least, sexual minorities, such as homosexual and bisexual persons, increase safer self-expression as a sexual entity, though some report needing a disinhibiting substance such as alcohol or cannabis to enable "coming out." (Finnegan & McNally, 1989; Ziebold & Mongeon, 1985). Social situations or contexts in which a person finds him or herself having a lack of privacy may contribute to inhibiting expression in some way (Cupchik & Poulos, 1984), while being addicted may impair sex arousal and performance even if interest is still present. Small amounts of alcohol may disinhibit sexual expression when social situations typically may have been inhibiting. Socio-legal issues abound, even within the context of normative sexual expression; for example, in some jurisdictions, public nudity on a beach is a breach of the law; substance use may impair judgment and contribute to risking law-breaking even when the sexual expression is not clinically pathological or harmful. As part of assessment and treatment, it is important to reduce oppressive barriers to normative intimacy and sexual expression within the context of age-stage appropriateness (Holleran & Novack, 1989).

For some, both spirituality and the spiritual dimensions of interpersonal relationships contribute to the meaning and depth of intimacy and sexual expression (Whitfield, 1984). Some may feel a monogamous commitment, while others may define their partner as a "soulmate," indicating the depth and intensity of intimacy in the attachment. Moral attitudes support safe and responsible sexual expression with a balance of concern for the other and the self. On the other hand, some spiritual beliefs and religious rules may promote guilt and anxiety with respect to intimacy, or marginalize forms of sexual expression and identity, or require oppressive acts of faith such as female genital mutilation. Substances have been found to be facilitative in reducing sexual inhibitions derived from religious imperatives; they have also contributed to subjective experiences of a religious or metaphysical nature (e.g., mescaline, psilocybin).

Developmental history, transgenerational, and relational history, with special attention to attachment and psychosexual development, all have an impact on each person and her or his sexual relationship: human, non-human, and inanimate. It is within the developmental experience and the fabric of the historical narrative of each relationship that some of the pathways to healthy and normative intimacy and sexual expression as well as to problematic sexual expression, detachment, and deviant thoughts and actions are found (James, 2012; Mikulincer & Shaver, 2016). Life cycle and social history also create pathways to normative use of substances and also to addiction (Fewell, 1985), including compulsive sexual behaviour (Carnes, 2001). James summarizes (2012): "Women can develop relationships with their substances if those substances consistently provide positive rewards, take away emotional pain, and serve as surrogate partners" (p. 195). Paradoxically, when one considers the bio-psychosocial development of a partnership or marriage, one may observe a marriage dependent on substances to mask relational issues and thus sexual expression may be assisted; subsequently substance abuse may be associated with a deterioration in intimacy and sexual expression, which even in recovery may be associated with substance-induced sexual dysfunction (Pascoe, 2001). Flores (2004) has suggested that compromised attachments are so dominant in addiction that addiction may itself be viewed as an attachment disorder.

The dimensions described above interact with and contribute to self-development throughout the life cycle within the context of life experiences and psychosexual development, both of which contribute to self-concept, self-worth, self-esteem, self-confidence, and the development of a stable and integrated self. A person has the developmental task of integrating the sexual self into self-development and self-definition (Lolli, 1961). A sense of an addicted self may be disintegrating in terms of self-definition, but paradoxically, if the person has a negative sexual definition, for example as a sex trade worker, and a negative self-definition such as "crack ho," then integration may be in the form of an ill, pathological, deviant, and/or addicted self (the best "crack ho") (Kuttner & Lorincz, 1970; Sharpe, 2005). The sexually abused person may add a self-definition of "damaged self," often within a context of an interaction between trauma and addiction (Dayton, 2000) and trauma and compromised attachments (Brisch, 2012; Kimberley & Parsons, 2016). The synthesis of multiple experiential and defining factors contribute to the uniqueness of each individual's identity as well as the common human elements that make some systematic assessment and intervention possible. From an intervention perspective, the fields of trauma, addiction, and sexuality have been focusing on the interactions among developmentally compromised attachments and developmental deficits in affect regulation, such as an anxious and insecure pursuit of social bonds (Mikulincer & Shaver, 2016); complex trauma-compromised attachments (Kimberley & Parsons, 2016); compounded biopsychosocial deficits in affect regulation (Schore & Schore, 2008); apprehensive and compromised intimacy and sexual expression associated with attachment issues at best (Crocker, 2015); and attachment issues compounded with sexual trauma (Brisch, 2012; Kimberley & Parsons, 2016; Mikulincer & Shaver, 2016). These complexities have some practice theorists concluding that the dynamics that contribute to compulsive behaviours and to sustained substance use arise in order to not only regulate affect, but also to create dissociation effects to enable the person to defend against overwhelming feelings associated with trauma and/or failed attachments.

Case Study: Substance Use and Relatively Normative Psychosexual Development[2]

John, age 16, appeared at the school social worker's office without an appointment. He was awkward and red-faced as he approached her. He requested a "man counsellor" because he needed to talk and he was shy. The female social worker engaged him and made him feel more comfortable to talk, assured privacy, and explained that she was the only counsellor available for three schools. Over three sessions, John described himself as having recently begun to go steady with Mary, age 15, and reported that she had expectations that he do "sexual things" with her to demonstrate that his feelings were genuine. He felt guilty because he found her sexually attractive, he masturbated to his fantasies about seeing her naked, and he had erections and wet discharge when they danced. John explained that part of his guilt was related to his religious upbringing, and he also feared getting her pregnant because it would hurt his parents as well as his girlfriend. He described how he had had some beer before three of their dates and he felt more relaxed and at ease about touching her and letting her touch him, sexually, with little guilt. He added that after their last date with heavy petting and mutual masturbation, he felt guilty about both drinking and sex; he wasn't sure if he would have "gone that far" if he wasn't drinking. He wondered if he was too sexual for his age.

The social worker undertook psychosocial education related to sex and relationships, and substance use, combined with sexuality counselling emphasizing normalization, anxiety, and guilt reduction, and responsible sex norms. A focus on the risks to clear thinking and judgment, and risks of disinhibition of actions through substance use, as well as empowerment of self-expression and genuine consent not mediated by alcohol or other drugs were also explored. She also explained that he would be more aware of his true thoughts and genuine feelings if his sexual experiences where not clouded (mediated) through substance use.

Interactions of Substance Use and Abuse with Sexual Disorders

Substance use and abuse has a paradoxical effect on patterns of intimacy and sexual expression. On the one hand, the use of some substances, typically at low doses, may enhance some aspect of intimacy and sexual expression, and may even erode the symptoms of some sexual disorders. On the other hand, particularly at higher doses and with chronicity, substance use and abuse may "cause" addiction-related sexual disorders or sexual function failures, under conditions where sexual expression is desired (Karacan & Hanusa, 1982; McKay, 2005; Price & Price, 1983; Winick, 1992). In most cases, treatment would include integrated addiction and sexuality counselling (James, 2012; Pascoe, 2001). Sexual well-being and intimacy are also important as part of the addictions recovery process (Braun-Harvey, 2009). Where sexual expression problems appear to be primarily precipitated by substance use and abuse, addiction counselling may be emphasized in the beginning of treatment. When problems of sexual expression are compounded by impulse control disorders such as distressed gambling, compulsive Internet use, or compulsive sexual behaviour or use of pornography, then treatment is more complex. Within a concurrent disorder context, addiction and trauma issues, including sexual trauma and potential interactions, are often best approached in an integrated manner. Some of the common problems with sexual intimacy and sexual expression (Hyde & DeLamater, 2007) are subjected to a paradoxical analysis below. The reader should recall that though there may be psychological and psychosocial factors that recreational drugs moderate, many sexual disorders also have biochemical, biophysical, or biomedical determinates, such as diabetes. One factor that should be ruled out early is the effect of medications, including those used to treat high blood pressure, depression, or diabetes, as well as any opioid-based products or alcohol use, as any of these may precipitate iatrogenic impacts that include sexual dysfunction (Winick, 1992).

Premature ejaculation is characterized by feelings of not being able to control ejaculation and experiencing ejaculation too quickly. This pattern may be moderated by central nervous system depressant use such as alcohol or anti-anxiety medication, in low dosages, which helps the male experience the subjective feeling of relaxation, including the impacts of central nervous system (CNS) depression. Paradoxically, higher doses of alcohol may be associated with precipitating retarded ejaculation; at times that may mean that a male will not have any ejaculation, though aroused. Before heavy use has an impact on sexual dysfunction, stimulants including cocaine and crystal meth may increase agitation and the subjective feeling of sex anxiety, increase latency to orgasm, or be associated with the subjective experience of more arousal and prolonged sexual pleasure. It is important to note that sexual performance problems may be misassessed when a man is gay but is in a heterosexual relationship and has yet to "come out." (Powell, 1984). Relational distancing associated with lack of interest or arousal could also be misjudged as either alienation or attachment disorder based on a narrow focus on the detached behaviour.

Anorgasmia is characterized by many women as having sex interest and even being aroused but not being able to have an orgasm. Some women may have never experienced an orgasm and these problems may be interactive with drug effects. Alcohol or benzodiazepine use may enable the woman to relax sufficiently that performance anxiety, relational anxiety, or sex guilt are reduced, while a stimulant may result in a subjective feeling of increased erotic focus and arousal. In women who do not have a problem with anorgasmia, heavier use of alcohol or another CNS depressant may decrease arousal and intensity of orgasm, but paradoxically be associated with more subjective sense of pleasure (Covington & Kohen, 1984; Winick, 1992).

Female arousal disorder is associated with little or no response to sexual stimulation. This too may interact with drug effects, with some drugs, like alcohol and cannabis, being associated with more relaxation and disinhibition, and some drugs, such as cocaine and ecstasy, being associated with more sexual arousal (though the crack variant of cocaine may be associated with sexual dysfunction in women) (McKay, 2005). As well, in the practice of the authors, some women are embarrassed by the fact that they are more aroused by adult erotica in the form of X-rated videos or Internet content, which if used could help increase sexual responsiveness. As with men, arousal disorder problems may be misassessed when a woman is gay but is in a heterosexual relationship and has yet to "come out." Relational distancing associated with lack of interest or arousal, by a yet-to-be-out woman, could also be misjudged as either alienation or attachment disorder based on a narrow focus on the detached behaviour.

Dyspareunia, or painful intercourse, in men and women decreases a person's pleasure and increases apprehension. Alcohol and marijuana may reduce anxiety, and opioids such as oxycodone may numb the person to subjective emotional pain as well as physical pain, the latter sometimes reported by sex workers. Persons who engage in compulsive sexual behaviour and who masturbate excessively may experience pain as well. Heavy drug use may also increase dyspareunia. Those active in a club drug scene and group sex parties may use lubricants to reduce the risk of dyspareunia; also this is a social context where the inhibitions for safe sex practices may be reduced due to the combined disinhibition effect of peer expectations and substances used.

Vaginismus, or contraction of the vagina such that penetration is difficult to impossible, not uncommon in women who have experienced sexual trauma, is sometimes reduced by alcohol, benzodiazepines, or marijuana. Any substance that increases anxiety or promotes paranoidal feelings may contribute to maintaining the problem (PCP and/or large doses of potent cannabis). Some medications or hormonal shifts may be associated with increased difficulty with natural sex lubrication, even when sex interest and attraction are normative.

Hypoactive sexual desire ranges from no feeling or no interest to low interest by both men and women (Kaplan, 1995). If part of the problem is related to anxiety and guilt, then a relaxant and disinhibitor like alcohol may help. If anxiety and guilt are not mediating factors and the person needs to experience more stimulation to have more desire and pleasure, then a chemical stimulant may be self-reported as improving both sexual response and performance (McKay, 2005; Winick, 1992). Contrarily, large dosages of most types of psychoactive drugs reduce desire, or interest, with little ability to perform sexually, and little or no sexual pleasure or satisfaction.

In sum, low doses of some recreational drugs, including power drinks, may be defined by some clients as a helpful adjunct to sex therapy. On the other hand, larger doses associated with substance addiction may reinforce impaired sexual functioning in the person who desires more self and partner fulfillment. Prescribed medications should also be ruled out as contributing factors to problems with intimacy and sexual expression. A range of sex therapy techniques should be more helpful with most of the problems described above, but arousal problems, common in persons chronically using psychoactive drugs, are often difficult to treat and should be left until the client has built more confidence through other treatment successes. For men, there are medications to help with erectile dysfunction, but if intimacy problems are partly relational then, paradoxically, even erection and orgasm may not be associated with meaningful pleasure and may even be associated with increased alienation. Women may experience parallels without their experiences being mediated by performance medications. As well, non-chemical dependencies such as gambling may reduce sex interest, while others such as compulsive Internet use may actually increase sex interest, at times to risk levels such as with viewing child pornography or excessive amounts of adult pornography.

Case Study: Substance Use and Abuse and Sexual Dysfunction

Ruth came from a family with a pattern of low-level attachment and bond. She was in her mid-30s, and while attracted to men and women, gay women referred to her as a "girly girl." However, Ruth defined herself as not very attractive, especially undressed, and self-defined as "addicted to shopping for clothes and shoes." She presented as glamorous and as if erotic, but experienced low sex interest, low arousal when interested (typically achieved through reading erotic stories), few orgasms when aroused (other than through infrequent masturbation), as well as some vaginal pain when she did have intercourse with on-again, off-again "boyfriends." With one male who was very supportive, who interested her the most and for whom she had a subjective feeling of more passion, she still experienced periodic vaginismus, even with higher levels of arousal. Ruth was uncomfortable with orgasm brought on through oral sex as it made her feel "dirty and out of control." She concluded that when she "got drunk," or "stoned on pot," she had more fun sexually and didn't mind not having an orgasm, and didn't feel the pain; when "drunk" she would tell her partner to "push" in order to penetrate, even when she was experiencing significant vaginismus.

The therapist suggested that Ruth contract, at least for a short period, to stop using alcohol and other drugs, that she agree to begin with a program of non-genital and/ or non-penetration sexual exploration and erotic development and that she evaluate her sexual orientation—heterosexual, bi, and lesbian—before including her current boyfriend in sex therapy. She was also introduced to the likely possibility of integrating substance use counselling if she continued to feel a compulsion to drink or use drugs to support sexual or other social activity, or if she felt any cravings for mood modifying substances.

Interactions of Substance Use and Abuse with Sex Offending and Deviations

When a person at risk for sexual abuse of age-stage inappropriate sex partners, or at risk for date rape, partner rape, or stranger rape, is under the influence of any psychoactive substance, often even at low dosages, then the likelihood of the sex abuse or assault being acted out is increased (Marshall, Laws, & Barbaree, 1990; Turner & Colao, 1985). Drugs such as cocaine and crystal meth are associated with aggression, including sexual aggression. Some drugs such as ecstasy, MDA, and ketamine may be used for date-rape purposes, though it is the use of alcohol that still most commonly places women at risk (Jansen & Theron, 2006). Alcohol, MDMA, crack, potent opioids like heroin may be used to ready the victim for abuse or for prostitution (Farley, 2003; Sharpe, 2005; Winick, 1992). In the extreme, some pimps provide heroin to children, youths, or adults to increase subjective pleasure, reduce resistance to providing sexual services, and to dull the emotional and physical pain—a form of dissociation with detachment. As well, for those who wish to experiment with, or to experience, more deviant sexual experience such as bestiality, the use of a substance may help with disinhibition at one stage of activity and management of guilt thereafter. To be clear, the drugs do not cause the sexual pathology, sex deviation, or victimization, they are just one factor that may increase risk through disinhibition and reduce protective factors, namely clear judgment and reasoning, for both the perpetrators and the victims.

Of note in some practice experience of the authors is what we have termed *late onset incest* related to parental addiction. The dynamic pattern that we have noted most is the estrangement and detachment of the female parent from the male partner, only to be replaced by a female child as a surrogate mate to the male parent with an addiction problem. The female child then becomes more bonded with the male parent and takes on some patterns of "partner" support such as "cleaning up after dad and getting him to bed." The new age-stage inappropriate partnership dynamics and parentification of the child progresses to more intimate exchanges such as sharing a drink and a dance together and then, often to the surprise of both, progresses to a sexual transaction that may be repeated. With late onset and post-pubescent incest, sexual attraction may be mutual.

Independent of addiction to psychoactive drugs, but sometimes interactive with substance-related addiction, is compulsive sexual activity (Braun-Harvey, 2009; Carnes, 1992, 2001; Earle & Earle, 1995; Goodman, 2004; Logan, 1992). Sex offenders and those who engage in deviant sex practices are overrepresented by those assessed as sexually "addicted." The reason why the psychological domain of the addiction paradigm applies to sexual expression is that patterns of excessive sexual behaviour are linked with feelings of craving and impulsive actions, the development of psychological tolerance, psychological feelings of withdrawal, chronic risks or "binge" patterns, increases in deviant sex interest to enhance arousal, and impaired personal and social functioning that is defined as a problem to self and others. In addition, compulsive sexual behaviour and pornography viewing are associated with developmental patterns of compromised attachments, neurological changes found in substance use and abuse, issues of affect regulation, and the use of pornography and sexual activity in dissociative patterns. As well, child sex abuse histories are overrepresented in most addicted populations (Braun-Harvey, 2009; Briere & Scott, 2015; James, 2012; Laier, Schulte, & Brand, 2013; Mikulincer & Shaver, 2016; Riemersma & Sytsma, 2013). In the practice of the authors, some sexually compulsive persons have exhibited concurrent disorders (see Chapter 24). For others, the sexual activity becomes a substitute for a chemical dependency that has been under control. It is not uncommon to observe individuals with compulsive sexual activity to be heavy users of Internet pornography, including child pornography.

Treatment of sexual deviation, compulsive sexual behaviour, and sex offenders is a complex area that requires multidimensional, complex, integrated, and long-term treatment, which still leads to uncertain and inconsistent results (Barbaree & Marshall, 1998; Kimberley & Osmond, 2003).

Case Study: Substance Use and Abuse and Sexual Deviations

Tom was a male in his 30s with a female partner and two female children, aged five and eight. He came to the attention of children's protection services because of his Internet activities that included downloading child pornography and exchanging family photos. Police investigation determined that there was also a warrant for his arrest on suspicion of having sex with an underage teen female. During social work assessment, it was determined that Tom had been sexually abused by a female babysitter, an adult female relative, and a teen male friend. Tom disclosed that as a child he was a voyeur. As a highly sexualized and eroticized male in his mid-teens, he was attractive to adult females who continued his intense and varied "sex education." With respect to his current situation, Tom found sexual relations with his wife, while quite normative, insufficient. He had intercourse daily and masturbated 6 to 12 times per day. He could spend 5 to 12 hours in a day on the Internet, largely looking at adult erotica and child pornography. His pattern was to extend gratification by delaying ejaculation—sometimes for hours. He had a local cyber sex female friend who also spent about 35 hours a week on the net, on chat lines, and sex sites, and who would "show" herself using a webcam. She informed Tom in a private chat room that she drank heavily, in part to help deal with the guilt and shame. When not on the net, Tom could (actively) sustain sexual fantasies for hours; one of the most troublesome to him was a *ménage à trois* with himself, an adult female, and a female child or teen—sometimes with him as a voyeur in the erotic fantasy script.

As assessment continued and treatment began, Tom described a long history of substance abuse that included alcohol, cigarettes, cocaine, and prescription drugs including benzodiazepines, Oxycontin, and codeine, as well as excessive caffeine, all of which appeared to be used as self-medication when he felt depressed or as an exciting substitute for sex. While he no longer had a craving for alcohol, he still craved cocaine and "Oxys."

Tom alerted the social worker to attachment and bond issues when he noted that he could become intensely attracted to women and female children, and then would "disconnect" (detach) quickly. He added that he felt lonely in the presence of others, including his wife and children.

His problems, risks, and needs converged in multiple problems in personal and social functioning, but his strength of motivation and insight, as well as the support of his wife, enabled intensive work towards recovery. Treatment areas included substance abuse, substance use risks with respect to reoffending, sexuality counselling and therapy with a focus on his compulsive sexual acts, deviant sex interest, eroding pedophilic orientation, and victim-survivor issues. Counsellors must keep in mind that for persons with deviation, pathology, and/or offence risks, low-level use of a disinhibiting psychoactive drug, even as little as two or three standard drinks for an adult male, may result in a significant increase in risk for self and others. Family therapy included work on family reunification as well as attachment and bond issues and child protection needs. Some more existential issues that were addressed later in treatment included spirituality and meaning in life that transcended being obsessed with sexual matters. For Tom to sustain his gains and to keep his risks to self and others reduced, he and his therapist agreed to long-term multilevel integrated therapy, with a minimum of two individual sessions per month but more as needed.

Interactions of Substance Use and Abuse with Sex Abuse and Sexual Trauma

Substance use and abuse is often woven in a complex pattern through narratives of sex abuse, sexual assault, and sexual exploitation, as well as the fusion of sex and aggression. It is not uncommon for the offender to be a person who uses and abuses chemicals, and who may be under the influence of substance use effects, including solvents, when victimizing women, men, or children. It is not uncommon that the victim of abuse or assault will have used or administered alcohol or some other substance such as ecstasy or GHB. Victims and survivors are overrepresented among persons at risk for substance-based addiction, concurrent disorders, indiscriminate sex, and sex work (Evans & Sullivan, 1995; Farley, 2003; Harrison, Edwall, Hoffman, & Worthen, 1990; Sharpe, 2005). Women with abuse and assault backgrounds, and associated post-trauma sequelae, often enter treatment through mental health facilities where their addiction problems and risks may be largely ignored. Parents who fail to protect their children may pose serious re-victimization risks associated with parental addictions and mental health problems (Kimberley, 2015). Additionally, abused persons are at high risk for concurrent disorders (Dayton, 2000). It is important to advocate for survivor therapy, post-trauma therapy, other mental health counselling, and addiction counselling as part of an integrated and holistic approach.

Case Study: Substance Use and Abuse and Sexual Victimization

Jane was a woman in her mid-20s. As a child she was sexually abused by a male relative. As a teen she was promiscuous and blamed herself for being date raped at the age of 14. She defined herself as the "fallen daughter" in a family with two female children and one male child. As an adult she was physically and emotionally abused and was subjected to multiple marital rapes. Once divorced, she lived with another male who ended up raping her with a handgun in her mouth. She decided to live alone even though her new apartment was in a very "rough" part of town. One night a stranger came to her door because his "car had broken down"; he raped her. In the latter case the police did not believe that she was raped, yet again, until medical-forensic evidence was brought forward that supported her allegations. With low self-esteem and low self-worth and hour-long periods of dissociation, she increased alcohol, street drug, and prescription drug use in parallel with a life, from teen to adult, of indiscriminate sexual relations. She recalls waking up in hotel rooms "naked, stoned, and full of semen," not remembering how she got there or what she had done; she did not define the latter as rape. She recalls exchanging sex for drugs and "feeling like a whore."

Treatment began with creating a sense of safety of relationship and therapeutic space, post-trauma and survivor treatment, with gradual reduction of alcohol and drug use. Integrated therapy also included strengths building, self-confidence building, lifestyle changes, as well as support and preparation for court testimony. Once stabilized, she was able to set goals for improved social functioning including safe sex and more discriminating mate selection.

Links Between Non-Substance Compulsive Behaviours and Intimacy and Sexual Expression

Problem or distressed gambling may be interactive with both substance use and abuse and concomitant problems such as depression, which can have an impact on sex drive and sexual performance (Blume, 2004; Gaudia, 1992). Problem gamblers often maintain public social functioning, such as workplace performance, for years, but social functioning in home and marriage may deteriorate more rapidly. The addiction paradigm applies in part to this impulse control disorder due to the development of excessive behaviour, psychological tolerance, and psychological perceptions of withdrawal when not gambling, and craving to return, as well as pervasive deterioration in personal and social functioning. Suicide risk is high, including through overdose of drugs.

Compulsive Internet use follows a similar pattern (Beard, 2008). Those persons who exhibit patterns that fit the psychosocial component of the addiction paradigm are also at risk for substance abuse and for impulsive sexual behaviour, including cyber sex encounters, compulsive use of pornography, and pornography creep with a special risk regarding hidden child pornography interests. Net creep and compulsive Internet and pornography use have been observed to be related to reduced interest in established relationships, reduced interest in normative and available sex partners, the development of deviant sex interests, and problems with personal and social functioning at home and at work or school. Some have severe sleep disorder problems that are secondary to compulsive Internet use. Compulsive behaviours have also been found to be associated with attachment and affect regulation difficulties.

Case Study: Problem Gambling and Intimacy and Sexual Expression

As Jenny gambled more and more, she lost interest in sex, and was not regularly available as a sex partner. She described being more interested in the rush of winning; it was "orgiastic." As she lost more and more material things, got into debt, and could not pay her credit cards, she felt hopeless, depressed, and sometimes suicidal. She began to drink more when gambling to soothe the pain and fear, but was not yet dependent upon alcohol. Her depression became so severe that she lost interest in things she used to enjoy, had no interest in sex, unless her husband joined her in gambling and "they" had a big win. When her husband gave up on being out with her and stayed home to be with the children, and she continued to lose money and feel more depressed, she contemplated suicide. When she was taken to court on credit card fraud, she could no longer deny her problem and entered into treatment.

The treatment was approached from a co-occurring disorder model and Jenny's husband was included in therapy, initially within the context of couple counselling. As their lives stabilized and as Jenny "stayed clean," counselling addressed gradual and comfortable return to intimacy, without intercourse being either a demand or an expectation in the beginning. As addiction problems may be derived in part from attachment problems (Thorberg & Lyvers, 2006; Vungkhanching, Sher, Jackson, & Parra, 2004), counselling also explored ways to increase attachment and bond and authentic intimacy communications, both verbally and non-verbally. Progression to alcohol addiction was monitored as a potential but low risk.

Summary and Conclusions

There are complex links among substance use and abuse problems, and/or non-substance use behaviours and problems with intimacy and sexual expression. Assessment must address sexual development and normative functioning, sexual disorder, sexual deviation, and pathology, as well as sexual exploitation and sexual victimization as they interact with substance use, misuse, abuse, and addiction, impulse control disorders, and compulsive behaviours. From a social work perspective, the fundamental concern is with impacts on personal and social functioning and risks to family and children. Integrated assessment and treatment is in order in the majority of cases, with the social worker left to make a refined judgment about concurrent or sequential treatment. An additional critical note to be cognizant of that was not discussed in the chapter is the importance of recognizing the association between addiction and increased risk for HIV infection and other sexually transmitted diseases, as one common effect of alcohol and other drugs is to disinhibit safer sex practices (Lowinson, Ruiz, Millman, & Langrod, 1997).

As social work progresses, social workers are going to be expected to have more knowledge regarding trauma and the links between trauma, addiction, and compromised sexual expression, including increased attachment-informed practice (Crocker, 2015; Joseph & Murphy, 2014; Knight, 2015; Schore & Schore, 2008). Given the relational issues that dominate addiction and sexuality practices, couple and family therapy must be applied in integrated ways to addiction (Kaufman, 2016). Given the limitations of unitary practice theories and narrow visions of practice, practice-based evidence suggests that social workers learn more about the common bases of influence in therapy (Sprenkle, Davis, & Lebow, 2009). Integrative thinking in practice appears to be in the best interests of clients with complex problems.

NOTES

1. The term *sex object* is used in the dynamic clinical sense, not in the political sense.

2. Names and identifying information in the following and subsequent case examples have been changed in the interest of confidentiality. The exemplars are real cases, though they may reflect the merging of facts from similar cases. There is no intention by the authors to stereotype, stigmatize, marginalize, or oppress any social subgroup for which a case example may be representative. The examples are not intended to make any biased gender, racial, or ethnic statement.

REFERENCES

Addams, J. (1912). *A new conscience and an ancient evil*. New York: The Macmillan Company (1972 Reprint by Arno Press and the New York Times).

Apter-March, M. (1984). The sexual behaviour of alcoholic women while drinking and during sobriety. *Alcoholism Treatment Quarterly, 1*(3), 35-48.

Barbaree, H., & Marshall, W. (1998). Treatment of the sexual offender. In R. Wettstein (Ed.), *Treatment of offenders with mental disorders* (pp. 265-238). New York: Guilford Press.

Beard, K.W. (2008). Assessment and treatment of Internet addiction. In J.B. Allen, E.M. Wolf, & L. VandeCreek (Eds.), *Innovations in clinical practice: A 21st century sourcebook*. Sarasota, FL: Professional Resource Press.

Begun, A., & Brown, S. (2014). Neurobiology of substance use disorders and implications for treatment. In S.L.A. Straussner (Ed.), *Clinical work with substance-abusing clients* (3rd ed., pp. 39-66). New York: Guilford Press.

Blume, S.B. (2004). Pathological gambling. In J. Lowinson, P. Ruiz, R. Millman, & J. Langrod (Eds.), *Substance abuse: A comprehensive textbook* (4th ed., pp. 488-497). Baltimore, MD: Williams & Wilkins.

Braun-Harvey, D. (2009). *Sexual health in drug and alcohol treatment: Group facilitator's manual.* New York: Springer Publishing.

Briere, J., & Scott, C. (2015). *Principles of trauma therapy: A guide to symptoms, evaluation, and treatment* (2nd ed.). Los Angeles: Sage.

Brisch, K. (2011). *Treating attachment disorders: From theory to therapy* (2nd ed.). New York: Guilford Press.

Carnes, P. (1992). *Don't call it love: Recovery from sexual addiction.* New York: Bantam Books.

Carnes, P. (2001). *Out of the shadows: Understanding sexual addiction* (3rd ed.). Centre City, Minnesota: Hazelden Information & Educational Services.

Clayton, A., & Montejo, A.L. (2006). Major depressive disorder, antidepressants and sexual function. *Journal of Clinical Psychiatry, 67*(Suppl. 6), 33-37.

Covington, S., & Kohen, J. (1984). Women, alcohol and sexuality. *Advances in Alcohol and Substance Abuse, 4*(1), 41-56.

Crocker, M. (2015). Out-of-control sexual behavior as a symptom of insecure attachment in men. *Journal of Social Work Practice in the Addictions, 15*(4), 373-393.

Cupchik, G.C., & Poulos, C.X. (1984). Judgements of emotional intensity in self and others: The effects of stimulus, context, sex and expressivity. *Journal of Personality and Social Psychology, 46*(2), 431-439.

Dayton, T. (2000). *Trauma and addiction.* New York: Guilford Press.

Earle, R., & Earle, M., with Osborne, K. (1995). *Sex addiction: Case studies and management.* New York: Brunner/Mazel.

Evans, K., & Sullivan, J. (1994). *Treating addicted survivors of trauma.* New York: Guilford Press.

Farley, M. (2003). *Prostitution, trafficking, and traumatic stress.* New York: Routledge.

Feeney, J.A. (2008). Adult romantic attachment: Developments in the study of couple relationships. In J. Cassidy & P.R. Shaver (Eds.), *Handbook of attachment: Theory, research and clinical applications* (2nd ed), pp. 456-481. New York: Guilford Press.

Fewell, C. (1985). The integration of sexuality into alcoholism treatment. *Alcoholism Treatment Quarterly, 2*(1), 47-56.

Finnegan, D., & McNally, E. (1989). The lonely journey: Lesbians and gay men who are co-dependent. *Alcoholism Treatment Quarterly, 6*(1), 121-134.

Flores, P. (2004). *Addiction as an attachment disorder.* New York: Jason Aronson.

Freud, A., & Burlingham, D.T. (1943). *War and children.* New York: Ernst Willard.

Freud, A., & Burlingham, D.T. (1944). *Infants without families: The case for and against residential nursuries.* New York: International University Press.

Fuller, R.W. (1984). Assessment of sexual functioning. *Alcoholism Treatment Quarterly, 1*(3), 49-64.

Gaudia, R. (1992). Gambling: Reframing issues of control. In E. Freeman (Ed.), *The addiction process: Effective social work approaches* (pp. 237-248). New York: Longman.

Goodman, A. (2004). Sexual addiction: Nosology, diagnosis, etiology, and treatment. In J.H. Lowinson, P. Ruiz, R.B. Millman, & J.G. Langrod (Eds.), *Substance abuse: A comprehensive textbook* (4th ed., pp. 504-539). Baltimore, MD: Williams & Wilkins.

Hall, P. (2011). A biopsychosocial view of sex addiction. *Sexual and Relationship Therapy, 26*(3), 217-228.

Harrison, P., Edwall, G., Hoffman, N., & Worthen, M. (1990). Correlates of sexual abuse among boys in treatment for chemical dependency. *Journal of Adolescent Chemical Dependency, 1*(1), 53-67.

Hartman, L. (1984). Attention, focus, sexual responding and metacognitions. *The Journal of Sex Research, 21*(2), 211–217.

Holleran, P., & Novak, A. (1989). Support choices and abstinence in gay/lesbian and heterosexual alcoholics. *Alcoholism Treatment Quarterly, 6*(2), 71–83.

Hyde, J.S., & DeLamater, J.D. (2007). *Understanding human sexuality* (7th ed.). Madison, WI: McGraw-Hill.

James, R. (2012). *Sexuality and addiction: Making connections, enhancing recovery.* Santa Barbara, CA: Praeger.

Jansen, K., & Theron, L. (2006). Ecstacy (MDMA), methamphetamine, and date rape (drug-facilitated sexual assault): A consideration of the issues. *Journal of Psychoactive Drugs, 38*(1), 1–12.

Johnson, S., Phelps, D., & Cottler, L. (2004). The association of sexual dysfunction and substance use among a community epidemiological sample. *Archives of Sexual Behaviour, 33*(1), 55–63.

Joseph, S., & Murphy, D. (2014). Trauma: A unifying concept for social work. *British Journal of Social Work, 44*(5), 1094–1109.

Kaplan, H.S. (1995). *The sexual desire disorders: Dysfunctional regulation of sexual motivation.* New York: Taylor & Francis.

Karacan, I., & Hanusa, T.L. (1982). The effects of alcohol relative to sexual dysfunction. In E. Pattison & E. Kaufman (Eds.), *Encyclopedic handbook of alcoholism* (pp. 686–695). New York: Gardner Press.

Kaufman, E. (2016). Family therapy approaches. In A. Mack, K. Brady, S. Miller, & R. Frances (Eds.), *Clinical textbook of addictive disorders* (4th ed., pp. 612–628). New York: Guilford Press.

Kimberley, D. (2015). Compromised cognitive functioning in concurrent disordered parents: Implications for Aboriginal children, foster care, mental health and addictions. In R. Neckoway & K. Brownlee (Eds.), *Child welfare in rural remote areas with First Nations Peoples: Selected readings* (pp. 16–43). Thunder Bay, ON: CERPYD, Lakehead University.

Kimberley, D., & Parsons, R. (2016). Trauma-informed social work treatment and complex trauma. In F. Turner (Ed.), *Social work treatment: Interlocking perspectives* (6th ed.). Toronto, ON: Oxford University Press.

Kimberley, M.D., & Osmond, M.L. (2003). Night of the tortured souls: Integration of group therapy and mutual aid for treated male sex offenders. In J. Lindsay, D. Turcotte, & E. Hopmeyer (Eds.), *Crossing boundaries and developing alliances through group work* (pp. 75–97). New York: The Haworth Press.

Knight, C. (2015). Trauma-informed social work practice: Practice considerations and challenges. *Clinical Social Work Journal, 43*(1), 25–37.

Kolodny, R.C. (1985). The clinical management of sexual problems in substance abusers. In T. Bratter, G. Forrest, & H.M. Annis (Eds.), *Alcoholism and substance abuse: Strategies for clinical intervention* (pp. 594–622). New York: Simon & Schuster.

Kovach, J.A. (1986). Incest as a treatment issue for alcoholic women. *Alcoholism Treatment Quarterly, 3*(1), 1–16.

Kuttner, R., & Lorincz, A.B. (1970). Promiscuity and prostitution in urbanized Indian communities. *Mental Hygiene, 54*(1), 79–91.

Laier, C., Schulte, F., & Brand, M. (2013). Pornographic picture processing interferes with working memory performance. *Journal of Sex Research, 50*(7), 642–652.

Leiblum, S. (1984). Alcohol and human sexual response. *Alcoholism Treatment Quarterly, 1*(3), 33–44.

Logan, S.M.L. (1992). Overcoming sex and love addiction: An expanded perspective. In E. Freeman (Ed.), *The addiction process: Effective social work approaches* (pp. 207–221). New York: Longman.

Lolli, G. (1961). The taboo on tenderness. In G. Lolli (Ed.), *Social drinking: The effects of alcohol* (pp. 68-84). New York: Collier Books.

Lowinson, J.H., Ruiz, P., Millman, R.B., & Langrod, J.G. (2004). *Substance abuse: A comprehensive textbook* (4th ed.). Baltimore, MD: Williams & Wilkins.

Maltz, W. (1991). *The sexual healing journey: A guide for survivors of sexual abuse.* New York: Harper Perennial.

Maltz, W., & Maltz, L. (2008). *The porn trap: The essential guide to overcoming problems caused by pornography.* New York: Harper.

Marshall, W.L., Laws, D.R., & Barbaree, H.E. (Eds.). (1990). *Handbook of sexual assault: Issues, theories, and treatment of the offender.* New York: Plenum Press.

McKay, A. (2005). Sexuality and substance use: The impact of tobacco, alcohol, and selected recreational drugs on sexual function. *SIECCAN Newsletter, 40*(1), 47-56.

McKim, W., & Hancock, S. (2013). *Drugs and behaviour* (7th ed.). Upper Saddle River, NJ: Pearson.

Mikulincer, M., & Shaver, P. (2016). *Attachment in adulthood: Structure, dynamics, and change* (2nd ed.). New York: Guilford Press.

Mohr, J.J. (2008). Same-sex romantic attachment. In J. Cassidy & P. Shaver (Eds.), *Handbook of attachment: Theory, research and clinical applications* (2nd ed., pp. 482-502). New York: Guilford Press.

Morton, R., & Hartman, L. (1985). A taxonomy of subjective meanings in male sexual dysfunction. *The Journal of Sex Research, 21*(3), 305-321.

Pappenheim, B. von. (1924). *Sisyphus-Arbeit.* Balkan Peninsula: P.E. Linder.

Pascoe, W. (2001). Restoration of intimacy and connection in the treatment of couples with substance issues. *Journal of Couples Therapy, 10*(3/4), 33-49.

Powell, D. (1984). Treatment of impotence in male alcoholics. *Alcoholism Treatment Quarterly, 1*(3), 65-83.

Price, J., & Price, J. (1983). Alcohol and sexual functioning: A review. *Advances in Alcohol and Substance Abuse, 2*(4), 43-56.

Richmond, M.E. (1917/1944). *Social diagnosis.* New York: Free Press.

Riemersma, J., & Sytsma, M. (2013). A new generation of sexual addiction. *Sexual Addiction & Compulsivity, 20*(4), 306-322.

Schore, J., & Schore, A. (2008). Modern attachment theory: The central role of affect regulation in development and treatment. *Clinical Social Work Journal, 36*(1), 9-20.

Schreiber, L., Potenza, M., & Grant, J. (2016). Gambling disorder and other "behavioral" addictions. In A. Mack, K. Brady, S. Miller, & R. Frances (Eds.), *Clinical textbook of addictive disorders* (4th ed., pp. 327-349). New York: Guilford Press.

Sharpe, T. (2005). *Behind the eight ball: Sex for crack cocaine exchange and poor black women.* New York: Haworth Press.

Sprenkle, D., Davis, S., & Lebow, J. (2009). *Common factors in couple and family therapy: The overlooked foundation for effective practice.* New York: Guilford Press.

Straussner, S. (2001). The role of social workers in the treatment of addictions: A brief history. *Journal of Social Work Practice in Addictions, 1*(1), 3-9.

Thorberg, F., & Lyvers, M. (2006). Attachment, fear of intimacy and differentiation of self among clients in substance disorder treatment facilities. *Addictive Behaviours, 31*(4), 732-737.

Turner, S., & Coloa, F. (1985). Alcoholism and sexual assault: A treatment approach for women exploring both issues. *Alcoholism Treatment Quarterly, 2*(1), 91-104.

Vungkhanching, M., Sher, K., Jackson, K., & Parra, G. (2004). Relation of attachment style to family history of alcoholism and alcohol use disorders in early adulthood. *Drug and Alcohol Dependence, 75*(1), 47–53.

Whitfield, C. (1984). Stress management and spirituality during recovery: A transpersonal approach: Part 1: Becoming. *Alcoholism Treatment Quarterly, 1*(1), 3–55.

Winick, C. (1992). Substances of use and abuse and sexual behaviour. In J. Lowinson, P. Ruiz, R. Millman, & J. Langrod (Eds.), *Substance abuse: A comprehensive textbook* (2nd ed., pp. 772–833). Baltimore, MD: Williams & Wilkins.

Young, K. (1999). Evaluation and treatment of Internet addiction. In L. Vandecreek & T. Jackson (Eds.), *Innovations in clinical practice: A source book* (pp. 19–32). Sarasota, FL: Professional Resource Press.

Ziebold, T., & Mongeon, J. (Eds.). (1985). *Alcoholism and homosexuality*. New York. Haworth Press.

CHAPTER 15

The Use of Prescribed Psychotropic Drugs by Working Women

Pauline Morissette and Nicole Dedobbeleer,
with Rick Csiernik and Emma Wilson

Introduction

Psychotropic drugs are one of the most commonly prescribed categories of drugs in industrialized countries (Currie, 2003, 2005). There has also been an increase in the number of people who are being prescribed more than one antidepressant at a time (Mojtabai & Olfson, 2010). This in turn increases the risk of drug-drug interactions for substances whose long-term use has been historically identified as both a public health problem (Medawar, 1992) and a social problem (Saibil, 2005). However, individuals who use psychotherapeutic drugs often experience a different societal response from other drug users as these substances are legally prescribed and, in the case of many working people, paid for by the employer through health benefit plans, which has also contributed to a steady increase in their use (Blum & Straccuzi, 2004). Numerous studies have indicated that women consume psychotropic prescribed drugs at approximately twice the rate of men (Cormier, Dell, & Poole, 2003; Hser, 2007) and are more likely to use them on a long-term basis and use more than two simultaneously (Poole & Dell, 2005). Contributing to this is that physicians are more likely to diagnose depression in women compared with men, even when they have similar scores on standardized measures of depression or present with identical symptoms (Silverstein, 2002).

Valium (diazepam) emerged on the market as "mother's little helper" during the 1960s to assist women with the increasing stresses and pressures of modern life (Herzberg, 2006). While the early 1990s witnessed a decline in the use of benzodiazepines after the introduction of the selective serotonin reuptake inhibitors (SSRIs) such as Paxil and Prozac, serotonin-norepinephrine reuptake inhibitors (SSNRIs) such as Cymbalta and Effexor, and norepinephrine-dopamine reuptake inhibitors (NDRIs) including Wellbutrin and Zyban (Hermann, 2002), it did not mark the end of benzodiazepine use. Between 1996 and 2002 benzodiazepine use still increased by

11%, while antidepressant use increased by 73% over the same period of time (Currie, 2003). Canadians are among the heaviest consumers of psychotropic medication in the world, spending $15 billion on prescriptions drugs in 2003 alone, an increase of 14.5% over 2002 (Weekes, Rehm, & Mugford, 2007).

Reasons Associated with Benzodiazepine Use

Historically, women have received more psychiatric designations than have men. In the early 1900s, women's mental illnesses were more likely to be classified by male psychiatrists as disordered thinking or hysteria (Chesler, 1971). In treating hysteria, it was believed that women needed to be confined, moved out of the workplace, and domesticated. During the earlier part of the 20th century as psychotherapeutic drugs became more commonly employed to treat mental illness it was still believed that women were unreliable for intellectual work and incapable of physical work (Bondi & Burnman, 2001).

Benzodiazepines do have therapeutic value and continue to be used to treat anxiety and insomnia, as well as panic attacks (Kirkley, 2005). However, they are just as likely to be prescribed to aid women coping with difficult life circumstances, such as stress both at home and at work, grief, physical pain, acute or chronic illness, or adjustment to a major life change, rather than to relieve severe clinical symptoms. Christine Kitteringham, clinical manager of the Aurora Centre, an addiction treatment facility in the British Columbia Women's Hospital, states that during the 1970s the makers of Valium published an advertisement in medical journals of a woman standing in front of a sink in curlers with bars across the picture. The caption read, "You can't set her free, but you can help her cope." Today the image may have shifted to a woman behind an executive desk with incoming emails and faxes, but the message remains the same (Hermann, 2002).

In 2002, a University of British Columbia study found that benzodiazepines, such as Xanax and Ativan, were being prescribed to thousands of British Colombia residents in amounts 10 times greater than recommended, despite the risk of harm and minimal evidence of any benefit for many of the conditions. Although it is recommended that most people take no more than 100 pills a year, UBC researchers found that 4.2% of the province's population, approximately 170,000 people, received more than 100 pills in 2002. Of the 4.2%, approximately 10,000 people were prescribed more than 1,000 pills. Of those who received these prescriptions, 7.1% were men while 12.2% were women, a considerable gender gap. The study indicated that women are not only prescribed benzodiazepines more frequently than men, but are also more likely to be prescribed them for longer periods of time (Kirkley, 2005). One in three status First Nations women over 40 in Western Canada were prescribed benzodiazepines in 2000, an increase of one-quarter from 1996. First Nations women were also almost twice as likely to receive a benzodiazepine prescription as were First Nations men.

British Colombia's Provincial Health Officer, Dr. Perry Kendall, stated that one reason benzodiazepines were being used in such large quantities was to numb the physical and mental pain of poverty (Hermann, 2002).

For over 40 years, it has been documented that benzodiazepines begin to produce addiction and have profound effects on the body and the brain at therapeutic doses if regularly used for more than four weeks (Csiernik, 2014). While Health Canada recommends daily use of the drug be limited to four weeks, the Ontario Centre for Addiction and Mental Health cautions that dependency can begin in as little as two weeks depending upon the dosage, frequency, type of benzodiazepine prescribed, and the physiological and psychological attributes of the user (Kirkley, 2005). As well, many users are unaware when first prescribed a benzodiazepine that when they do stop using, they can expect to have withdrawal effects that can include anxiety, tremors, confusion, and insomnia, with insomnia being the most common. Thus, the withdrawal symptoms mirror the issues for which the drug was initially prescribed. This in turn can contribute to the misdiagnosis of symptoms as chronic disorders. These symptoms can also last for weeks or months and often result in continued use of the drug (Csiernik, 2014; Hermann, 2002). It has also been extensively documented that women are more vulnerable to the physical effects of these drugs and therefore are at greater risk of developing health-related problems that occur with their chronic use (Poole & Dell, 2005).

Helman (1986) examined the symbolic role that drugs play in the lives of long-term users. He showed that drugs have three functions—tonic, fuel, or food—depending upon the extent of control that users felt they had over their lives. Tonic referred to control over one's life, fuel to a need to function "normally," and food to survival. In relation to this, Ettorre (1992) found that "any woman's use of an 'acceptable' prescribed drug masks their invisible desire to be an 'acceptable woman in society'" (p. 68).

The Latest Wonder Drugs: SSNRIs, NDRIs, and SSRIs

The use of psychotherapeutic drugs is socially condoned, and within the last decade an increasing number of these have been sanctioned for use. SSNRIs, NDRIs, and SSRIs are all psychoactive drugs intended for use with individuals who are diagnosed with depression but are also widely used to treat other issues including insomnia and anxiety. However, in excessive amounts the brain chemical norepinephrine can produce increased strain on the cardiovascular system as well as anorexia, while excessive amounts of serotonin are associated with delusions and those who have excessive amounts of dopamine levels in their brains display symptoms of psychosis (Csiernik, 2014).

Between 1981 and 2001 the use of antidepressants has risen by 345% (Currie, 2005). Of the over 15 million prescriptions for antidepressants written, two-thirds were for women (Saibil, 2005). Depression has become the fastest rising diagnosis made by

Canadian office-based physicians. Visits for depression have almost doubled since 1994 with two-thirds of general practitioner office visits for depression in 2004 being made by women. Eighty-one percent of these visits concluded with an antidepressant recommendation (Currie, 2005).

The societal definition of depression is broadening, which is a predominant factor accounting for the increase in psychotherapeutic drug prescriptions. Saibil (2005) states that there is no question that severe clinical depression is a real physical disease in which antidepressants may be a benefit. However, mild emotional discomforts among women continue to be viewed as illnesses that also require medical treatment. Mood swings, anxiety, and mild depression are not new to women. What is relatively new is that, over the last several decades, sadness, mild depression, and anxiety have come to be labelled as medical disorders requiring psychoactive drugs.

In 2003, the Canadian Women's Health Surveillance Report found that the predictive factors for diagnosing depression among women were previous depressive episodes, feelings of being out of control or overwhelmed, chronic health problems, traumatic events in childhood or young adulthood, lack of emotional support, and a low sense of mastery. Women who were lone parents or who had chronic pain were the most likely to fit these criteria for depression (Currie, 2005). Currie also argues that there is another prominent factor for women receiving more prescriptions for antidepressants than men: for the past 50 years pharmaceutical companies have promoted the concept that emotional distress experienced by women in reaction to normal or traumatic life events is actually a biological disorder requiring treatment by mood-altering drugs.

The literature on the effects of the new antidepressants indicates that, despite claims of safety, the adverse reactions to them are not only quite diverse and common among users, but they can also be quite harmful. A review of spontaneous adverse drug reaction found that during a 10-year period after Prozac was first introduced more hospitalizations, deaths, and other serious adverse effects were reported to the FDA pertaining to this drug than any other prescribed medication in the United States (Moore, 1998). Neurological, psychiatric, gastrointestinal, and dermatological problems all commonly occurred with use of SSRIs. As well, women experienced a higher rate of the most harmful effects from SSRIs than did men (Anderson et al., 2012). There is the possibility that some who use the new generation of antidepressants develop agitated depression, and in March 2004, a drug advisory was issued in the United States stating that patients on SSRIs should be monitored for worsening depression and suicidality. This advisory also identified other adverse drug reactions from antidepressants including anxiety, agitation, panic attacks, insomnia, irritability, and mania (Currie, 2005).

One of the common side effects of using antidepressants is sexual dysfunction, and as more women are prescribed these drugs than are men, more women experience sexual dysfunction. As antidepressants use can lead to a worsening of depression, emotional blunting or detachment, reduced emotional activity, and memory loss and confusion, these effects, in conjunction with sexual dysfunction, can negatively affect intimate relationships. As well, there is evidence that SSRIs can be harmful to pregnant women and their babies. In 2004, Health Canada issued an advisory warning for pregnant women taking SSRIs during the third trimester of pregnancy that their newborns may experience withdrawal problems. The advisory states that some new-borns whose mothers took SSRIs during pregnancy had developed complications at birth requiring prolonged hospitalization, breathing support, and tube feeding (Currie, 2005). Rebound depression, withdrawal, dizziness, fatigue, weakness, headaches, muscle pain, and tingling sensations have been associated with the use of these drugs (Csiernik, 2014). Hodges (2003), a leading theorist within the anti-psychiatry move-ment, a movement encouraging alternative response to psychiatric interventions, argues that psychotherapeutic drugs are extremely risky. She claims that these drugs are hardly better when compared to placebo effects, produce physical dependency, and can permanently change the brain's structure.

Theoretical Foundations

Gender is a critical determinant of mental health and mental illness (Dennerstein, Astbury, & Morse, 1993; Gabe, 1991; Rogers & Pilgrim, 2014) with female gender roles and status being negatively correlated with health (Spitzer, 2005). Different theories have been used as a guide to obtain a better understanding of women's consumption practices of psychotropic drugs. The sex role theory is one of the first models used to examine the reasons for long-term consumption. In this theory emphasis is placed on behavioural differences during the medical consultation process and doctors' stereotypes. Copperstock (1971) presented four hypotheses pertaining to long-term tranquilizer use:

1. Women are permitted greater freedom to explore their feelings than men and hence are more likely to recognize emotional problems in themselves.
2. Women feel freer than men to bring their perceived emotional problems to the attention of a doctor.
3. Doctors, and especially male doctors, expect women patients to be more emotionally expressive than men.
4. Doctors are therefore more likely to encourage such expressiveness from women patients and to prescribe them tranquilizers.

Gender roles, norms, and responsibilities that have been socially determined for women often place them in situations in which they have little control or power in decisions concerning their lives. For example, in many settings women are made principle care-givers, while giving them less social support to perform this function, leading to low morale and high stress levels.

In contrast to this doctor-centred perspective, a patient-centred approach has appeared. Here the concern is the meaning of medication in people's everyday life. The term *meaning*, in this context, refers to the interpretation a person gives to an object or event in her life. From a conceptual point of view, the use of psychotropic drugs is perceived as a resource that is available to a person in managing everyday life activities and in assisting decision-making processes (Gabe, 1991; Gabe & Thorogood, 1986).

Reale and Sardelli (1997) discussed the mental health consequences of violence and the responses of the health sector. They highlighted that oppression linked to the female role is the main risk factor for women's health. Two critical factors that contribute to this oppression are the burden and stress connected with a maternal role and the violent pressures exerted by the social and family environment. Violence is a common reality of women's lived experiences and can assume various forms, such as sexual violence in the form of rape; physical violence and threats; and verbal and psychological violence such as insults, humiliation, and denial of autonomy. This violence, denigration, and insult forms a powerful and specific risk factor for depression. The feelings of fear and anxiety eventually are disconnected from the woman's unbearable condition of life, which she considers unchangeable. These feelings then become symptoms, signs of an illness and a discomfort that is totally disconnected from the woman's life. Most often, physicians cannot understand the reasons behind the woman's feelings of tiredness, sadness, fear, or lack of motivation, and only confirm or certify to her that she does in fact suffer from depression and anxiety. A diagnosis is made and typically a psychotropic drug is prescribed. Reale and Sardelli argue that the woman's suffering is converted into a pathology that prevents the recognition of its real nature and impedes any change in the woman's lifestyle.

Another model is related to social control and involves the medicalization of everyday life. Large numbers of people who visit physicians show signs of a social problem but are treated in a biological manner for anxiety rather than examining if, in their social circumstance, anxiety is an appropriate response to the environmental risk the person is experiencing. These individuals, who are predominantly female, are treated through the primary means available to physicians: drugs. Within this theoretical model there are two primary reasons contributing to this pharmacological response to a social issue: promotion of drugs by pharmaceutical companies, and doctors' lack of time to fully explore a person's problems. Treatment models based exclusively on biomedical perspectives are inadequate as they ignore cultural, social, and economic factors that play a role in women's distress (Frances, 2013).

Cafferata, Kasper, and Berstein (1983) believe that apart from the sex role theory we need to consider the social support theory and the social stress experienced by drug users to understand the reasons behind long-term psychotropic use. Women are more likely to publically present being negatively affected by stressful family circumstances than are men. Thus, women's social roles and the role of their environments are necessary variables that need to be explored in order to understand the prescribed psychotropic drug consumption of working women. The social roles of large numbers of women have changed over the past few decades. While it was once possible to divide women into the categories of mother or worker, it is now more usual to define women as both mothers and workers. The expanding role of women brings more responsibilities that put additional pressure upon them. Women are thus placed in a position where they are at greater risk for the consumption of prescribed substances. In this context, the effects of the work environment also must be examined.

Role of the Work Environment

Compared to men, women still occupy lower positions in the workplace social structure, they have lower salaries even for identical work, and have less advantageous working status and conditions (Ash, Carr, Goldstein, & Freidman, 2004; Chatterji, Mumford, & Smith, 2007; Weichselbaumer & Winter-Ebmer, 2005). Even if they are also breadwinners, they remain predominantly responsible for children's education and housework (Hook, 2010). Canadian, American, and European studies have all pointed out that women invest more hours than men in family activities (Gutek, Searle, & Klepa, 1991; Lachance-Grzela & Bouchard, 2010; Roos, Lahelma, & Rahkonen, 2005; Sayer, 2005).

Various studies at the conclusion of the 20th century suggested that work was a major influence on the consumption of drugs prescribed to women (Ettore, Klautta, & Riska, 1994; Jacquinet-Salord et al., 1993; Lennon, 1994). Likewise, at the beginning of this century a clear association was displayed in a Belgian study between self-reported use of benzodiazepines and a high-strain job compared to a low-strain job, particularly amongst women (Pelfrene et al., 2004). Other studies have demonstrated that the social context, the quality of social climate, and the cognitive, material, or emotional support from supervisors or colleagues in which a person must assume her or his professional role is a critical element in employees' physical and mental wellness (Constable & Russell, 1986; Csiernik, 2005; Greenglass, 1991; Henderson & Angyle, 1985; Repetti, 1987; Repetti, Matthews, & Waldron, 1989).

Due to the potential impact of substance use on the work and health of female workers, it is crucial to examine substance use patterns in relation to the work environment. Psychoactive substances are drugs that act upon the central nervous system and modify the way a person thinks, feels, and acts. The negative influence of the substance is accentuated if the quantity is wrong or length of consumption is too long. It has thus been observed that the consumption of benzodiazepines and antidepressants can harm memory and concentration, lead to poor judgment and emotional instability, bring people to withdraw from work relationships, and lessen motivation (Hindmarch, 2005). Women who suffer from issues with addiction have unique characteristics, some of which result from their participation in various business and professional roles. Women working in male-dominated occupations have been found to abuse alcohol and other substances to a greater extent (Hser, 2007).

Additionally, in a study by Lallukka and colleagues (2013), it was found that women who had family problems that affected work and in turn reported worry, irritability, lack of energy, and lack of time for relaxation as a source of strain had a greater use of sleep-inducing drugs. Conversely, the same conflicts could not be confirmed as an antecedent to men's use of sleep aids as there was no association between family-to-work conflicts and the use of sleeping medication, suggesting men's stress comes from other sources that are not family related.

Feminist theorists argue that at the beginning of the feminist movement, benzo-diazepines were responsible for numbing women, suppressing their engagement in the burgeoning women's movement. Currently, new generation antidepressants are used to make women more efficient at work and not only endure untenable work/life conditions but also to make them optimistic, energetic, and efficient in these situations (Blum & Stracuzzi, 2004).

Women, Work, and Psychotherapeutics: A Canadian Study

A cross-sectional Canadian study on unionized white-collar workers and professional working women was undertaken in the Montreal area (Morissette, 1993). A questionnaire was mailed to 2,500 potential participants with 1,120 responses (44.8%). Ninety-five percent of the women in the original sample were professionals, teachers, nurses, social workers, or professional government employees, while 5% were office workers, semi-professionals, or technicians. Approximately three-quarters held a permanent job while the others were either hired on a temporary basis (12%) or on contract (11%). Most were working full time (72%). The users and non-users of psycho-tropic drugs did not differ on aspects such as having children at home, professional status, or seniority. They did differ on age, children's age, and living arrangements. Users were more often older, more likely to have children above age 13 living with them when they had children at home, and more likely to live alone or to live with a partner only.

Results showed that 15% of the respondents did use psychotropic prescribed drugs during the 12 months before the survey. Of these, 4.3% reported a high level of drug consumption. A majority of the drug-using women (75%) reported that they used drugs prescribed by their doctor, but there were other sources. About 22% of users obtained benzodiazepines from their friends or relatives while 8.4% obtained them without a prescription.

The use of drugs was an occasional solution for some of the women but a permanent one for others. One user out of five consumed these psychoactive drugs every day while 15% used them four to six times a week. Two users out of five reported using psychotropics for a period equal to or exceeding seven months during the 12-month period preceding the survey. The study's results also indicated that 40% of women who reported using or having used antidepressant drugs during the 12-month period covered by the survey consumed them for seven months or more. As well, more than

20% of the respondents who mentioned consuming one of the three types of drugs investigated in this survey also reported combining them with alcohol, and nearly one-quarter consumed more than one drug. However, results indicated that such consumption was not a habit for the majority.

Survey respondents reported that they took or were taking these drugs often because they felt under pressure or because a personal situation affected them (Table 15.1). In both cases, the percentages exceeded 20% when the two greatest frequencies of consumption ("rather often" and "very often") were combined. Also, more than 10% of the users reported that they took tranquilizers "often" to stay calm in a difficult professional situation, to do a day's work, and to appear calm at work. Moreover, results indicted that 16% of users reported having taken sleeping pills often for difficulties linked to work. Difficulties linked to personal life were reported as a frequent reason for consumption by approximately the same percentage of women (Table 15.2).

Benzodiazepines were prescribed for multiple reasons including tiredness, anxiety, and nervousness, while antidepressant drugs were primarily prescribed for depression. In regard to the time of day the tranquilizers were taken, 25% of respondents reported consuming them in the morning, 21% in the afternoon, 23% upon returning home from work, and 14% before lunch.

Table 15.1 Reasons for and Frequency of Benzodiazepine Consumption during 12-Month Period before Survey

Frequency	To appear calm at work (N=108)		To stay calm when in a difficult professional situation (N=105)		Feeling under pressure (N=110)		To do a day's work (N=104)		Because a personal situation affected me (N=108)	
	%	N	%	N	%	N	%	N	%	N
Never	79.6	86	71.0	74	58.0	64	73.0	76	44.4	48
Very seldom	6.5	7	8.5	9	11.0	12	7.5	8	16.7	18
On occasion	1.9	2	10.0	10	11.0	12	4.5	5	17.6	19
Rather often	5.6	6	4.0	5	12.0	13	6.0	6	9.3	10
Very often	6.5	7	6.5	7	8.0	9	9.0	9	12.0	13

Table 15.2   Reasons for and Frequency of Sleeping Pill Consumption during 12-Month Period before Survey

Frequency	Difficulties linked to work (N=62)		Difficulties linked to personal life (N=62)	
	%	N	%	N
Never	47.0	29	44.0	27
Very seldom	16.5	10	18.5	11
On occasion	21.0	13	20.5	13
Rather often	8.0	5	11.0	7
Very often	7.5	5	6.0	4

Discussion

Few studies have looked at the influence of work upon long-term use of psychotropic prescribed drugs, particularly among women. Results of a Canadian study showed that about 15% of working women consumed psychotropic drugs during the 12 months before the survey and that 5% were high-consumers. This study also revealed that some users adopt health-damaging behaviours such as combining different drugs or drugs and alcohol (20%). The results indicated that 22% of the women obtained psychotropic drugs from friends and/or relatives. The study also revealed that working women have a tendency to maintain consumption practices in line with their doctor's prescription.

Results suggest that certain aspects of users' professional lives have influenced their consumption. First, "feeling under pressure" clearly ranked number one among the reasons given by tranquilizer users (42%). Second, sleeping pill users (53%) reported "problems linked to work." Third, a certain percentage of users reported that they were taking or took tranquilizers often to look calm at work, to stay calm when a professional situation affected them, or to get through a day's work. Finally, the time of day for consumption suggests that a percentage of women often go to work under the influence of tranquilizers with 23% consuming in the morning and 13% in the afternoon. The Canadian study's results also suggest that users faced with difficulties in their professional life have adopted either the permanent consumption of drugs, characterized by daily usage over a long period of time, or a temporary solution that involves occasional consumption or consumption for a few days per week over a few weeks.

Women's social problems continue to be treated with drugs focusing on biological symptoms rather than causative factors. Many users in the Canadian study reported that they had psychotropic drugs prescribed to them to fight tiredness, nervousness, or anxiety, but none reported that such drugs were prescribed for an organic reason. Frances (2013) and Maxwell (2005) both claim that this pattern of drug prescription points to the medicalization of everyday life and the lack of time for doctors to explore a patient's problems fully, only treating symptoms without considering underlying causes.

Although it is not recommended to consume the drugs examined in this research for a long period, a notable percentage of our users were in that situation: approximately 40% of users of each drug had been consuming for seven months or more. In this regard, the use of antidepressant drugs is more alarming because it may hide the symptoms and does not change any of the professional problems that women may have. All these results indicate the need to further investigate the relationship between female workers and doctors. What is the condition of female workers to whom drugs are prescribed over a period of several months? Why are they taking them? While women used tranquilizers to enable them to endure their role within the home, do female workers accept taking drugs or making long-term use of them to sustain themselves in their occupational role or dual role of mother and employee?

REFERENCES

Anderson, H., Pace, W., Libby, A., West, R., & Valuck, R. (2012). Rates of 5 common antidepressant side effects among new adult and adolescent cases of depression: A retrospective US claims study. *Clinical Therapeutics, 34*(1), 113–123.

Ash, A., Carr, P., Goldstein, R., & Friedman, R. (2004). Compensation and advancement of women in academic medicine: Is there equity? *Annals of Internal Medicine, 141*(3), 205–212.

Blum, L., & Stracuzzi, N. (2004). Gender in the Prozac nation: Popular discourse and productive femininity. *Gender and Society, 18*(3), 269–286.

Bondi, L., & Burman, E. (2001). Women and mental health: A feminist review. *Feminist Review, 68*(1), 6–33.

Cafferata, G., Kasper, J., & Berstein, A. (1983). Family roles, structure and stressors in relation to six differences in obtaining psychotropic drugs. *Journal of Health and Social Behaviour, 24*(2), 132–143.

Chatterji, M., Mumford, K., & Smith, P. (2007). *The public-private sector wage differential: Gender, workplaces and family friendliness.* University of Dundee Discussion Papers in Economics.

Chesler, P. (1971). Women as psychiatric and psychotherapeutic patients. *Journal of Marriage and Family, 33*(4), 746–759.

Constable, J., & Russell, D. (1986). The effect of social support and the work environment upon burnout among nurses. *Journal of Human Stress, 12*(1), 20–26.

Cooperstock, R. (1971). Sex differences in the use of mood modifying drugs: An explanatory model. *Journal of Health, Sociology and Behaviour, 12*(3), 238–244.

Cormier, R., Dell, C., & Poole, N. (2003). *Women and substance use problems.* Women's Health Surveillance Report. Ottawa ON: Canadian Institute for Health Information.

Csiernik, R. (2005). *Wellness and work.* Toronto, ON: Canadian Scholars' Press.

Csiernik, R. (2014). *Just say know: A counsellor's guide to psychoactive drugs.* Toronto, ON: Canadian Scholars' Press.

Currie, J.C. (2003). *Manufacturing addiction: The over-prescription of benzodiazepines and sleeping pills to women in Canada.* Vancouver, BC: British Columbia Centre of Excellence for Women's Health.

Currie, J.C. (2005). *The marketization of depression: The prescribing of SSRI antidepressants to women.* Toronto, ON: Women and Health Protection.

Dennerstein, L., Astbury, J., & Morse, C. (1993). *Psychosocial and mental health aspects of women's health.* Geneva, CH: World Health Organization.

Ettorre, E. (1992). *Women and substance use.* New Brunswick, NJ: Rutgers University Press.

Ettorre, E., Klaukka, T., & Riska, E. (1994). Psychotropic drugs long-term use, dependency and the gender factor. *Social Science and Medicine, 39*(12), 1667–1673.

Frances, A. (2013). *Saving normal: An insider's revolt against out-of-control psychiatric diagnosis, DSM-5, big pharma and the medicalization of ordinary life.* New York: Harper Collins.

Gabe, J. (1991). Personal troubles and public issues: The sociology of long-term tranquillizer use. In J. Gabe (Ed.), *Understanding tranquillizer use: The role of social sciences* (pp. 31–48). London, UK: Routledge.

Gabe, J., Gustafsson, U., & Bury, M. (1991). Mediating illness: Newspaper coverage of tanquilizer dependence. *Sociology, Health and Illness, 13*(4), 332–353.

Gabe, J., & Thorogood, N. (1986). Prescribed drug use and the management of every day life: The experiences of black and white working class women. *Sociology Review, 34*(4), 737–772.

Greenglass, E. (1991). Burnout and gender: Theoretical and organizational implications. *Canadian Psychology, 32*(4), 562–572.

Gutek, B., Searle, S., & Klepa, L. (1991). Rational versus gender role explanations for work-family conflict. *Journal of Applied Psychology, 76*(4), 560–568.

Helman, C. (1986). "Tonic," "Fuel" and "Food": Social and symbolic aspects of the long-term use of psychotropic drugs. In J. Gabe & P. Williams (Eds.), *Tranquillizers: Social, psychological and clinical perspectives* (pp. 199–226). London, UK: Tavistock.

Henderson, M., & Angyle, M. (1985). Social support by four categories of work colleagues: Relationship between activities, stress and satisfaction. *Journal of Occupational Behavior, 6*(3), 229–239.

Hermann, Q. (2002). *Addiction by prescription: Why are we still getting caught in the old tranquilizer trap?* Victoria, BC: Victoria Times.

Herzberg, D. (2006). "The pill you love can turn on you": Feminism, tranquilizers, and the Valium panic of the 1970s. *American Quarterly, 58*(1), 79–103.

Hindmarch, I. (2005). Effects of prescribed and over the counter drugs on work performance. In H. Ghodse (Ed.), *Addiction at work.* Surrey, BC: Gower Publishing Limited.

Hodges, K. (2003). The invisible crisis: Women and psychiatric oppression. *Off Our Backs, 33*(7), 12–15.

Hook, J. (2010). Gender inequality in the welfare state: Sex segregation in housework, 1965–2003. *American Journal of Sociology, 115*(5), 1480–1523.

Hser, Y. (2007). The life course perspective on drug use. *Evaluation Review, 31*(6), 515–547.

Jacquinet-Salord, M., Lang, T., Fouriaud, C., Nicoulet, I., & Bingham, A. (1993). Sleeping tablet consumption, self reported quality of sleep, and working conditions. Group of Occupational Physicians of APSAT. *Journal of Epidemiology and Community Health, 47*(1), 64–68.

Kirkley, S. (2005). *British Columbia overdoses on tranquilizers.* CanWest News.

Lachance-Grzela, M., & Bouchard, G. (2010). Why do women do the lion's share of housework? A decade of research. *Sex roles, 63*(11–12), 767–780.

Lallukka, T., Arber, S., Laaksonen, M., Lahelma, E., Partonen, T., & Rahkonen, O. (2013). Work-family conflicts and subsequent sleep medication among women and men: A longitudinal registry linkage study. *Social Science and Medicine, 79*(1), 66–75.

Lennon, M.C. (1994). Women, work & well-being: The impact of work condition. *Journal of Health and Social Behavior, 35*(3), 235–247.

Maxwell, M. (2005). Women's and doctors' accounts of their experiences of depression in primary care: The influence of social and moral reasoning on patients' and doctors' decisions. *Chronic Illness, 1*(1), 61–71.

Medawar, C. (1992). *Power and dependence: Social audit on the safety of medicines.* Bath, UK: Bath Press.

Mojtabai, R., & Olfson, M. (2010). National trends in psychotropic medication polypharmacy in office-based psychiatry. *Archives of General Psychiatry, 67*(1), 26–36.

Moore, T. (1998). *Prescription for disaster.* New York: Dell Publishing.

Morissette, P. (1993). *La solitude professionnelle et privée et la consommation d'alcool et de médicaments chez les femmes au travail.* Rapport final remis au Conseil québécois de la recherche sociale.

Ogur, B. (1986). Long day's journey into night: Women and prescription drug abuse. *Women & Health, 11*(1), 99–115.

Pelfrene, E., Vlerick, P., Moreau, M., Mak, R., Kornitzer, M., & De Backer, G. (2004). Use of benzodiazepine drugs and perceived job stress in a cohort of working men and women in Belgium. Results from the BELSTRESS-study. *Social Science and Medicine, 59*(2), 433–442.

Poole, N., & Dell, C. (2005). *Girls, women and substance abuse.* Ottawa, ON: Canadian Centre on Substance Abuse.

Reale, E., & Sardelli, V. (1997). *European strategies to combat violence against women: The mental health consequences of violence and the responses of the health sector.* Copenhagen, Denmark: World Health Organization.

Repetti, R.L. (1987). Linkages between work and family roles. *Journal of Marriage and Family, 34*(1), 98–127.

Repetti, R., Matthews, K., & Waldron, I. (1989). Employment and women's health: Effects of paid employment on women's and mental physical health. *American Psychologist, 44*(11), 1394–1401.

Rogers, A., & Pilgrim, D. (2014). *A sociology of mental health and illness* (5th ed.). London, UK: McGraw-Hill Education.

Roos, E., Lahelma, E., & Rahkonen, O. (2005). Work-family conflicts and drinking behaviours among employed women and men. *Drug and Alcohol Dependence, 83*(1), 49–56.

Saibil, D. (2005). *SSRI antidepressants: Their place in women's lives.* Ottawa, ON: Government of Canada: Women and Health Protection.

Sayer, L. (2005). Gender, time and inequality: Trends in women's and men's paid work, unpaid work and free time. *Social Forces, 84*(1), 285–303.

Silverstein, B. (2002). Gender differences in the prevalence of somatic versus pure depression: A replication. *American Journal of Psychiatry, 159*(6), 1051–1052.

Spitzer, D.L. (2005). Engendering health disparities. *Canadian Journal of Public Health/Revue Canadienne de Sante'e Publique,* s78–s96.

Weekes, J., Rehm, J., & Mugford, R. (2007). *Prescription drug abuse FAQs.* Ottawa, ON: Canadian Centre on Substance Abuse.

Weichselbaumer, D., & Winter-Ebmer, R. (2005). A meta-analysis of the international gender wage gap. Journal of Economic Surveys, *19*(3), 479–511.

CHAPTER 16

Understanding the Violent Substance Abuser: Issues in Intimate Partner Violence

Tanielle O'Hearn and Rick Csiernik

Introduction

Significant in terms of its prevalence and consequences, intimate partner violence (IPV) is a national public health concern. Statistics Canada (2011) reported a total of 97,500 victims of IPV in one year, 80% of whom were female. Furthermore, female victims of IPV were three times as likely as males to experience disruptions to their daily lives, twice as likely to be physically injured by their partner, and seven times more likely to fear for their lives. Between 2001 and 2011 there were a reported 344 murder-suicides in Canada, over 77% of which were family related. Of these, 97% were male. However, the consequences of IPV are not only directly felt by those who experience it first-hand, but also indirectly through its economic ramifications on a societal level. It is estimated that the costs of IPV against women are approximately $5 billion annually (Statistics Canada, 2013).

There is also an undeniable relationship between substance abuse and violence. "The relationship is profound, costly, and culturally non-specific" (Hoaken et al., 2012, p. 467). The magnitude of this relationship is demonstrated through the plethora of epistemology studies and global statistics. From these studies we know that approximately 3 million victims of violent assault report that the perpetrator was under the influence of alcohol in the United States annually alone (Beck & Heniz, 2013). Furthermore, the United States has seen a general increase in the number of alcohol-related murders over the last 50 years. In Australia there were 24,581 cases of alcohol-related IPV and 69,433 cases of alcohol-attributed assaults on police record in 2008. Alarmingly, this study also reported that 1,294,500 people identified themselves as being negatively affected "a lot" by the drinking of a relative, friend, or household member (World Health Organization, 2011). In 2010/2011 there were 220,000 reported violent crimes reported in Scotland, 63% of which were documented as having been committed under the influence of alcohol (Institute of Alcohol Studies, 2013). The following year it was indicated that approximately half (917,000) of the violent offences committed in England and Wales involved the use of alcohol.

If we narrow our scope from violent offences to those regarding the co-occurrence of substance abuse and IPV exclusively, as well as shift from a global context to a Canadian one, we find that the prevalence and severity of these occurrences remain relatively unchanged. In intimate partner homicides (not ending in suicide), more than two-thirds (67%) of those accused were found to be under the influence of either drugs or alcohol (Statistics Canada, 2011). Regarding intimate partner murder-suicides, 41% of those accused were found to have ingested alcohol or drugs prior to committing the crime. According to the Centre for Addiction and Mental Health (2010), an esti-mated two-thirds of domestic/intimate partner violence is associated with alcohol. These statistics indicate that the co-occurrence of substance abuse and IPV is indeed a public health concern that demands greater understanding, attention, and action. This chapter explores the instances of IPV where the perpetrator was a substance abuser, considering the relationship between substance abuse and violent/aggressive behaviour, and acknowledges the benefits, risks, and challenges of treatment options as documented in the literature.

Co-occurrence in Prior Studies

Chermack and Blow (2002) studied 250 individuals who had recently been enrolled in a substance abuse treatment facility and found that in the three months prior to treatment, 85% reported a significant conflict situation, and over 32% reported an incident of physical violence. Additionally, their study found that individuals who used cocaine and alcohol in higher amounts reported greater levels of violence sever-ity. Consistent with prior studies, conflict-day alcohol and cocaine consumption, as well as general use patterns were determined to have a dose-dependent relationship to the severity of aggression (Brown, Werk, Caplan, & Seraganian, 2010; Leonard & Quigley, 1999; Martin & Bachman, 1997). A recent experimental investigation tested the level of aggression in students who had been randomized to receive either alcohol, a placebo, or no alcohol (Stappenbeck & Fromme, 2014). The results from this study indicated that both intoxicated women and men expressed more verbal and physical aggression than those who had not received any alcohol.

A study examining the rates of expressed partner and non-partner violence reported by individuals in the 12 months prior to entering treatment for substance abuse showed significantly high (75% reported moderate-severe) rates of violence (Chermack, Fuller & Blow, 2000). These rates were considerably greater than those found in a corres-ponding community sample. Similarly, a study conducted by Thomas, Bennett, and Stoops (2013) found that individuals who committed violent acts against their partner who do so while consuming a psychoactive substance were more likely to perpetrate more severe levels of both psychological and physical violence when compared to those who did not use substances. The results of a study comparing 30 female spouses of alcohol-dependent men with spouses of non-drinkers found that the spouses of alcohol-dependent men were not only subjected to an increased amount of painful and aggressive sexual experiences, but were also specifically subjected to more biting of body surfaces and longer lasting body marks in more areas (Maharajh & Akleema, 2005).

Substance use during the occurrence of IPV is also a recurring theme within the literature. It has been hypothesized that incidents of IPV would be more likely to occur either during or shortly after the intoxication of a substance abuser. In his longitudinal study, Fals-Stewart (2003) examined the diaries of men who were entering either domestic violence treatment or alcoholism treatment and through their research offered an understanding of how alcohol contributed to violence on a daily basis. He found that female partners of alcohol-dependent men were more than 19 times more likely to be victims of IPV on days their partner was drinking heavily. Additionally, he found that the odds of men who were entering domestic violence treatment were eight times more likely to perpetrate physical aggression on days that included drinking than on days that did not. In comparison, men entering an alcoholism treatment program were 11 times more likely to perpetrate IPV on days that included drinking. Substance abusing perpetrators of IPV are seven times more likely to be intoxicated during the episode of violence (Kraanen, Scholing, & Emmelkamp, 2010). Thomas, Bennett, and Stoops (2013) compared 274 perpetrators of IPV that were identified as substance abusers with 524 IPV perpetrators that were not. They concluded that the individuals that abuse substances were significantly more violent, demonstrated more severe levels of violence, reported higher levels of trauma and anger, and were more prone to using substances during an occurrence of IPV than those who were not substance abusers. These recent empirical studies demonstrate the current and continued validity and existence of the substance abuse and IPV relationship.

Theoretical Background

The nature of the relationship between substance abuse and violent/aggressive behaviour is one that has been widely debated within the literature. Leonard and Quigley (1999) proposed three conceptual models to assist in the explanation of the association between substance abuse and IPV. The first of these is referred to as the *spurious model* and postulates that the relationship between substance abuse and IPV only appears to be related because of their association with a common third variable, when in fact they are not. For example, an individual who abuses substances might also have a certain personality characteristic that is also associated with interpersonal violence perpetration (Fals-Stewart, 2003). The *indirect effects model* states that substance abuse creates interrelationship conflict, marital dissatisfaction, and other problematic variables that in turn cause IPV. Therefore, it is not the substance that causes IPV, but rather the indirect effects of substances on a relationship. Lastly, according to the *proximal model*, substance abuse has a direct and causal relationship to IPV by means of the psychopharmacological effects of the substances on cognitive functioning. IPV, according to this model, is caused directly by intoxication and therefore suggests, as does the indirect model, that to remove the substance abuse from the dyadic relationship would eliminate IPV (McCollum, Stith, Miller, & Ratcliffe, 2011). Although there have been studies that have found proximal relationships between substance abuse and IPV (Fals-Stewart, 2003) there are substantial practical and ethical limitations to proving a definitive causal relationship. How we understand the relationship between substance abuse and IPV has direct practical implications as it determines how practitioners approach the matter of treatment (McCollum, Stith, Miller, & Ratcliffe, 2011). If these two variables are considered unrelated, the spurious model, then both IPV and substance abuse would require separate individual treatments, and the reduction of one variable would have no effect on the other. However, if we consider the position of the causal or indirect model, treatment of substance abuse would have a direct effect on reducing the occurrence of IPV.

Psychopharmacological theory, which includes the proximal model, remains one of the most predominant theoretical perspectives used to explain the relationship between substance abuse and IPV. Theories that have their foundation in psychopharmacological theory assert that it is the properties of a substance, and the direct physiological effects of those properties on an individual's cognitive functioning, that cause violent/aggressive behaviour. For example, Graham's disinhibition hypothesis (as cited by Beck and Heinz, 2013) suggests that when an individual is under the influence of alcohol disinhibition occurs because the area of the brain that is associated with behaviour, control, and inhibition is severely affected. Therefore, the individual's ability to process information, make decisions, maintain attention, and self-regulate is compromised. Alcohol myopia theory postulates that alcohol intoxication can create a myopic "narrowing" effect on the intoxicated individual's focus, lending them likely to misread social cues or misinterpret events, such as someone casually bumping into them, as threats. Furthermore, this myopic effect also constrains an individual's ability to fully process or give attention to the negative consequences of their actions. As a result, the likelihood of making an impulsive action is increased (Quigley & Leonard, 2006).

Why Do Some Substance Abusers Become Violent and Not Others?

If psychoactive substances have universal psychopharmacological effects on the executive functioning of our brains as some theories hypothesize, why then are only some substances abusers violent, and not all? While there are many variables that have been found to increase the probability of a substance abuser engaging in IPV or other forms of violent/aggressive behaviour, the theoretical position of expectancy explanations can aid our understanding of these discrepancies. Quigley and Leonard (2006) explain that there are two dominant variants of expectancy explanations. One of these variants is rooted in social learning theory and the other in anthropology.

The first variant of this perspective is founded in social learning theory. It claims that individuals may act in an aggressive manner when they are under the influence of substances if they hold the belief that those substances will cause aggressive behaviour. These beliefs can be learned from a variety of sources, which include, but are not limited to, personal experiences, family, friends, and the media. The second variant is referred to as the "deviance-disavowal theory" and explains that individuals might act aggressively and/or violently while using substances as they believe that their actions while intoxicated will not be held to the same formal and social sanctions as they would if they were sober. Critchlow (as cited in Quigley & Leonard, 2006) explains that periods of alcohol consumption could be considered by society as a "time out" for the individual from social rules. In terms of IPV, this theory suggests that implicit permission is given to a husband to be aggressive towards his partner when he is under the influence of alcohol.

A conclusive understanding of the relationship between substance abuse and violent behaviour is one that continues to be evasive. Despite the accumulation of identified influential variables through the conduction of empirical studies, the complexity of this relationship demands the continuance of its analysis. Hoaken and colleagues (2012) argued that to assume direct pharmacological mechanisms as the solitary means of understanding the relationship between drugs and violence is to grossly oversimplify the complexity of addiction. As structural social workers we maintain that in order to effectively assist our clients it is essential to employ an appreciation of persons within the entirety of their contexts. Therefore, to deepen our comprehension of the relationship between substance abuse and violence, our approach to knowledge acquisition should be rich in perspectives and theories from various aspects of human functioning and the social context of behaviour.

Biological Factors

The Role of Serotonin

Our brain is a complex organ composed of billions of neurons that are connected by synapses and release chemicals known as neurotransmitters. These neurotransmitters act as communicators throughout our brain and body. Serotonin is a neurotransmitter that is considered to be associated with mood regulation and has been undisputedly linked to aggression (Badawy, 2003). Serotonin has also been documented as having a vital role in many other aspects of human functioning.

Serotonin dysfunction is generally expressed as low levels of the serotonin metabolite 5-hydroxyindole-3-acetic acid (5-HIAA) within an individual's cerebrospinal fluid (CSF). A study conducted by Roy, Adinoff, and Linnoila (1988) found a strong negative correlation between the urge to act out hostility and CSF levels of 5-HIAA. Significantly lower concentrations of CSF 5-HIAA were also found by Lidberg and colleagues (1985) in male subjects that had been convicted of homicide, as well as males that had attempted suicide, when compared to a control group. Recently, Berglund and colleagues (2013) conducted the first study to look at the relationship between central serotonergic dysfunction and self-reported childhood maltreatment in alcohol-dependent men. These researchers found that there was a dramatic reduction, over 90%, of serotonergic function in individuals who had self-reported experiences of childhood maltreatment, particularly emotional abuse. According to Badawy (2003), acute alcohol intake causes, among other changes to the brain, depletion of serotonin, which in turn induces aggressive behaviour. Although it has been verified through clinical studies that there is a relationship between alcohol dependency, serotonergic dysfunction, and violent/aggressive behaviour, further research is required to accurately determine if the serotonergic dysfunction is a consequence of long-term alcohol consumption, or if the condition is pre-existing.

Neurological Vulnerabilities

For eight years the Amen Clinic extensively studied cerebral perfusion using a technology referred to as brain SPECT imaging. Through their investigations they concluded that individuals might be more prone to abusing substances if they have neurological vulnerabilities in different areas and systems of the brain. Moreover, lesions, physical damage, or abnormalities in specific regions of the brain were found to have a positive correlation with violent/aggressive behaviour. As a result of their findings, it was concluded that an individual who has neurological damage or abnormalities might abuse substances as a method of self-medication to offset the effects of these abnormalities. However, SPECT imaging studies also found that long-term substance abuse could result in cerebral abnormalities, which can then lead to aggressive behaviour. Discussed in this study was the importance of screening both substance abuse clients as well as those in IPV treatment for past head injuries, even minor ones, as brain dysfunction is often considered too late in the treatment process (Amen et al., 1997).

Psychological Factors

Personality Traits

The possession of certain personality traits have been identified within the literature as increasing the likelihood of becoming aggressive/violent while under the use of substances. Godlaski and Giancola (2009) observed that high levels of underlying irritability in males increased the probability and severity of aggression exhibited while intoxicated. Anger has also been found to have a substantial impact on not only substance-related violence, but also on the likelihood of recovery and/or relapse. Kelly and colleagues (2010) found substantially elevated levels of anger within a clinical trial group of alcohol-dependent adults participating in Alcoholics Anonymous meetings compared with the general population (98th percentile). The findings of this study also indicated that attendance in Alcoholics Anonymous is not sufficient for the alleviation of anger or the subsequent risks.

Impulsivity-related issues have been verified to predict IPV perpetration in both women and men (Shorey, Brasfield, Febres, & Stuart, 2011). In studying the relationship between hazardous drinking and intimate partner aggression, it was found that impulse control difficulties were both an important predictor and actor in both psychological and physical aggression (Watkins, Maldonado, & DiLillo, 2014). However, it was found to be an individual's inability to control their impulses specifically when they experienced a negative emotion that most accurately predicted aggression severity, not impulsivity in general. Gender differences in this study found that difficulties controlling impulses upon the onset of a negative emotion predicted the occurrence and severity of physical partner aggression in males, and only psychological partner aggression in females. Similarly, individuals who are present-focused are also significantly more aggressive when intoxicated as opposed to those who are future-focused. Interestingly, aggression levels of future-focused individuals do not change after consuming alcohol.

Social Factors

Intergenerational Transmission Processes and Childhood Maltreatment

The coexistence of violent behaviour and substance abuse in family systems, as well as the link between childhood exposure to parental substance abuse and violence and later emotional and behavioural complications in adulthood, has been well documented (Brown, Werk, Caplan, & Seraganian, 2010; Daisy & Hien, 2014; Francis, Alaggia, & Csiernik, 2010; Maalouf & Campello, 2014). While studying a group of men seeking treatment at a domestic violence program (n=74), Corvo and Carpenter (2000) discovered that childhood abuse was a stronger predictor of the severity of the current violent behaviour than the observation of parental violence. Interestingly, substance abuse in the family of origin was as strong of a predictor of current domestic violence as childhood exposure to parental violence. "Domestic violence in adulthood may not emerge entirely from social learning processes but from a complex of family of origin conditions where violence, abuse of alcohol and drugs, and other problematic conditions intertwine to produce a devil's brew of problems in adulthood" (p. 133).

When compared with other community-based samples, a study of alcohol-dependent inpatients (n=196) demonstrated to have higher rates of both physical and sexual childhood abuse (Huang et al., 2012). The results of this study also indicated that the prevalence of an alcohol-dependent patient having experienced at least two types of childhood maltreatment was significantly high. Furthermore, alcohol-dependent individuals with a history of childhood physical abuse were found to be at an increased risk of self-destructive and impulsive behaviours while intoxicated or during a relapse episode. Alcohol-dependent clients that conjointly experienced physical and sexual abuse in childhood have also been shown to be at a greater risk for generalized anxiety disorder, suicide attempts, major depression, and dysthymic disorder (Windle, Windle, Scheidt, & Miller, 1995).

Other Environmental Factors

The connection between IPV and marijuana use/abuse is much stronger for individuals of minority status, as well as those who are of lower socio-economic status (Stalans & Ritchie, 2008). A high level of stress due to oppressive factors commonly faced by people of minority status such as discrimination, difficulty finding meaningful employment, and being a recipient of welfare has been theorized as one explanation for this connection. Walton, Chermack, and Blow (2002) found that the need for housing, health care, income, and related resources were expressed by both perpetrators and victims of IPV, which led them to conclude that high stress environments and low socio-economic status may create situations that are conducive to IPV. This study also found that substance abusers that perpetrated IPV were more likely to live in environments where leisure activities and social networks involved the use of substances. Females who were young, unemployed, had a higher level of psychiatric distress, and had more baseline drug consequences were at the highest risk for experiencing IPV.

Treatment

Although the co-occurrence of IPV and substance abuse, as well as the consequences of their relationship, is well established, the question of how to respond continues to be debated. Bennett (2008) suggested three approaches to treatment that would service both issues conjointly. The first of these is referred to as serial treatment, wherein an individual first receives treatment for substance abuse, followed by an IPV treatment program. The second approach is concurrent treatment, which seeks to address both issues in either separate facilities or in separate programs at the same time. Lastly, integrated treatment aims to construct a single treatment program wherein both substance abuse and IPV treatment is conducted. There have been several benefits and challenges of each of these models documented (McCollum, Stich, Miller, & Ratcliffe, 2011). While the effectiveness of each approach remains debated, the most promising results have been demonstrated by integrated approaches.

Easton and colleagues (2007) evaluated the effectiveness of a cognitive-behavioural group therapy for alcohol-dependent males with co-occurring interpersonal violence, comprising 12 sessions. They concluded that participants had a significantly increased number of initial days abstinent from alcohol, when compared to men in a traditional 12-step facilitation group, while also experiencing greater reductions in the frequency of physical violence. However, the six-month post-treatment follow-up showed no significant differences in the frequency of physical violence or the percentage of days abstinent from alcohol. However, the addition of one private 90-minute substance abuse session with a therapist integrated into a 40-hour court-mandated IPV program did result in greater short-term improvements in both alcohol consumption and violence than those in a standard IPV program. Furthermore, men that had received the additional substance abuse session were found to have a more significant reduction in their drinking at both three-month and six-month post-treatment intervals. Despite the reductions in both substance abuse and IPV the overall rates of both variables were still too high post-treatment and suggested the implementation of booster sessions throughout the year following treatment to support the initial treatment gains. Kraanen, Vedel, Scholing, and Emmelkamp (2013) randomly assigned individuals who had entered substance abuse treatment and had disclosed having perpetrated IPV into either an integrated program or a cognitive-behavioural substance abuse program that included a session dedicated to IPV. In terms of substance abuse reduction, both treatment programs were equally as successful. Moreover, both programs were also successful in a significant reduction of IPV. Due to the complexity of trying to implement an integrated program into a treatment facility, and the lack of variation between the success rates of the two programs, these authors concluded that a CBT program with the addition of an IPV-focused session would be sufficient to treat individuals with co-occurring IPV and substance abuse issues. However, despite these findings, substance abuse treatment and IPV interventions typically continue to be delivered independently at different agencies and utilizing separate methodologies (McCollum, Stith, Miller, & Ratcliffe, 2011).

Conclusion

The co-occurrence of substance abuse and IPV continues to be an issue that demonstrates a magnitude of complexities, which we continual strive to understand. It is a classic example of intersecting oppressions that affect both the person experiencing the violence and the perpetrator. Although the exact inner workings of this relationship remain debated, what is evident are the ramifications of such a relationship's continuation. As integrated treatments begin to increase in their validity and reliability, further research needs to be conducted to study the effectiveness of various types of integrated models. Furthermore, the issue of how to successfully implement these programs and models into existing treatment frameworks is critical in order to respond to the oppression of addiction affecting these individuals.

REFERENCES

Amen, D., Yantis, S., Trudeau, J., Stubblefield, M., & Halverstadt, J. (1997). Visualizing the firestorms in the brain: An inside look at the clinical and physiological connections between drugs and violence using brain SPECT imaging. *Journal of Psychoactive Drugs, 29*(4), 307-319.

Badawy, A., (2003). Alcohol and violence and the possible role of serotonin. *Criminal Behaviour and Mental Health, 13*(1), 31-44.

Beck, A., & Heinz, A. (2013). Alcohol-related aggression: Social and neurobiological factors. *Deutsches Ärzteblatt International, 110*(42), 711–715.

Bennett, L. (2008). Substance abuse by men in partner abuse intervention programs: Current issues and promising trends. *Violence and Victims, 23*(2), 236–248.

Berglund, K., Balldin, J., Berggren, U., Gerdner, A., & Fahlke, C. (2013). Childhood maltreatment affects the serotonergic system in male alcohol-dependent individuals. *Alcoholism: Clinical and Experimental Research, 37*(5), 757–762.

Brown, T., Werk, A., Caplan, T., & Seraganian, P. (2010). Violent substance abusers in domestic violence treatment. In R. Csiernik & W.S. Rowe (Eds.), *Responding to the oppression of addiction* (2nd ed., pp. 184–196). Toronto, ON: Canadian Scholars' Press Inc.

Centre for Addiction and Mental Health. (2010). *Alcohol*. Retrieved from http://www.camh.ca/en/hospital/health_information/a_z_mental_health_and_addiction_information/alcohol/Pages/alcohol.aspx

Chermack, S., & Blow, F. (2002). Violence among individuals in substance abuse treatments: The role of alcohol and cocaine consumption. *Drug and Alcohol Dependence, 66*(1), 29–37.

Chermack, S., Fuller, B., & Blow, F. (2000). Predictors of expressed partner and non-partner violence among patients in substance abuse treatment. *Drug and Alcohol Dependence, 58*(1), 43–54.

Corvo, K., & Carpenter, E. (2000). Effects of parental substance abuse on current levels of domestic violence: A possible elaboration of intergenerational transmission processes. *Journal of Family Violence, 15*(2), 122–135.

Daisy, N., & Hien, D. (2014). The role of dissociation in the cycle of violence. *Journal of Family Violence, 29*(2), 99–107.

Easton, C., Mandel, D., Hunkele, K., Nich, C., Roundsaville, B., & Carroll, K. (2007). Cognitive behavioural therapy for alcohol-dependent domestic violence offenders: An integrated substance abuse-domestic violence treatment approach (SADV). *The American Journal on Addictions, 16*(1), 24–31.

Fals-Stewart, W. (2003). The occurrence of partner physical aggression on days of alcohol consumption: A longitudinal diary study. *Journal of Consulting and Clinical Psychology, 71*(1), 41–52.

Francis, A., Alaggia, R., & Csiernik, R. (2010). Multiple barriers: The intersection of substance abuse in the lives of women disclosing and seeking help for intimate partner violence. In R. Csiernik & W.S. Rowe (Eds.), *Responding to the oppression of addiction* (2nd ed., pp. 117–125). Toronto, ON: Canadian Scholars' Press.

Godlaski, A., & Giancola, P. (2009). Executive functioning, irritability, and alcohol-related aggression. *Psychology of Addictive Behaviours, 23*(3), 391–403.

Hoaken, P., Hamill, V., Ross, E., Hancock, M., Lau, M., & Tapscott, J. (2012). Drug use and abuse and human aggressive behaviour. In J.C. Verster, K. Brady, M. Galanter, & P. Conrod (Eds.), *Drug abuse and addiction in medical illness: Causes, consequences and treatment* (pp. 467–477). New York: Springer Publishing.

Huang, M., Schwandt, M., Ramchandani, V., George, D., & Heilig, M. (2012). Impact of multiple types of childhood trauma exposure on risk of psychiatric comorbidity among alcoholic inpatients. *Alcoholism: Clinical and Experimental Research, 36*(6), 1099–1107.

Institute of Alcohol Studies. (2013). *United Kingdom alcohol-related crime statistics*. Retrieved from http://www.ias.org.uk/Alcohol-knowledge-centre/Crime-and-social-impacts/Factsheets/UK-alcohol-related-crime-statistics.aspx

Kelly, J., Stout, R., Tonigan, J., Magill, M., & Pagano, M. (2010). Negative affect, relapse, and Alcoholics Anonymous (AA): Does AA work by reducing anger? *Journal of Studies on Alcohol and Drugs, 71*(3), 434–444.

Kraanen, F., Scholing, A., & Emmelkamp, P. (2010). Substance use disorders in perpetrators of intimate partner violence in a forensic setting. *International Journal of Offender Therapy, 54*(3), 430–440.

Kraanen, F., Vedel, E., Scholing, A., & Emmelkamp, P. (2013). The comparative effectiveness of integrated treatment for substance abuse and partner violence (I-StoP) and substance abuse treatment alone: A randomized trial. *BMC Psychiatry, 13*(189), 1-14.

Leonard, K., & Quigley, B. (1999). Drinking and marital aggression in newlyweds: An event-based analysis of drinking and the occurrence of husband marital aggression. *Journal of Studies on Alcohol, 60*(4), 537-545.

Lidberg, L., Tuck, J., Asberg, M., Scalia-Tomba, G., & Bertilsson, L. (1985). Homicide, suicide and CSF 5-HIAA. *Acta Psychiatrica Scandinavica, 71*(3), 230-236.

Maalouf, W., & Campello, G. (2014). The influence of family skills programmes on violence indicators: Experience from a multi-site project of the United Nations Office on Drugs and Crime in low and middle income countries. *Aggression and Violent Behavior, 19*(6), 616-624.

Maharajh, H., & Akleema, A. (2005). Aggressive sexual behaviour of alcohol-dependent men. *Alcoholism Treatment Quarterly, 23*(4), 101-106.

Martin, S., & Bachman, R. (1997). The relationship of alcohol to injury in assault cases. *Recent Developments in Alcoholism, 13*(1), 41-56.

McCollum, E., Stith, S., Miller, M., & Ratcliffe, G. (2011). Including a brief substance-abuse motivational intervention in a couples treatment program for intimate partner violence. *Journal of Family Psychotherapy, 22*(3), 216-231.

Quigley, B., & Leonard, K. (2006). Alcohol expectancies and intoxicated aggression. *Aggression and Violent Behaviour, 11*(5), 484-496.

Roy, A., Adinoff, B., & Linnoila, M. (1988). Acting out hostility in normal volunteers: Negative correlation with 5HIAA in cerebrospinal fluid. *Psychiatry Research, 24*(2), 187-194.

Shorey, R., Brasfield, H., Febres, J., & Stuart, G. (2011). The association between impulsivity, trait anger, and the perpetration of intimate partner and general violence among women arrested for domestic violence. *Journal of Interpersonal Violence, 26*(13), 2681-2697.

Stalans, L., & Ritchie, J. (2008). Relationship of substance use/abuse with psychological and physical intimate partner violence: Variations across living situations. *Journal of Family Violence, 23*(1), 9-24.

Stappenbeck, C., & Fromme, K. (2014). The effects of alcohol, emotion regulation, and emotional arousal on the dating aggression intentions of men and women. *Psychology of Addictive Behaviours, 28*(1), 10-19.

Statistics Canada. (2011). Family violence in Canada: A statistical profile 2011. *Component of Statistics Canada catalogue no. 85-002.* Retrieved from http://www.statcan.gc.ca/pub/85-002-x/2013001/article/11805-eng.pdf

Statistics Canada. (2013). Measuring violence against women: Statistical trends. *Component of Statistics Canada catalogue no. 85-002.* Retrieved from http://www.statcan.gc.ca/pub/85-002-x/2013001/article/11766-eng.pdf

Thomas, M., Bennett, L., & Stoops, C. (2013). The treatment needs of substance abusing batterers: A comparison of men who batter their female partners. *Journal of Family Violence, 28*(2), 121-129.

Walton, M., Chermack. S., & Blow, F. (2002). Correlates of received and expressed violence persistence following substance abuse treatment. *Drug and Alcohol Dependence, 67*(1), 1-12.

Watkins, L., Maldonado, R., & DiLillo, D. (2014). Hazardous alcohol use and intimate partner aggression among dating couples: The role of impulse control difficulties. *Aggressive Behaviour, 40*(4), 369-381.

Windle, M., Windle, R., Scheidt, D., & Miller, G. (1995). Physical and sexual abuse and associated mental disorders among alcoholic patients. *American Journal of Psychiatry, 152*(9), 1322-1328.

World Health Organization. (2011). *Global status report on alcohol and health.* Retrieved from http://www.who.int/substance_abuse/publications/global_alcohol_report/msbgsruprofiles.pdf

Multiple Barriers: The Intersection of Substance Abuse in the Lives of Women Disclosing and Seeking Help for Intimate Partner Violence

Anna Francis, Ramona Alaggia, Rick Csiernik, and Tanielle O'Hearn

Introduction

Both intimate partner violence (IPV) and substance abuse are serious issues in the lives of women in Canada. Being considered a normative part of the female experience, violence against women continues to invade the lives of many women on both a national and international scale (Stenius & Veysey, 2005; World Health Organization, 2013). Recognized as a public health concern, IPV against women also remains a current critical human rights issue (Wortham, 2014; Yok-Fong, 2014; Yuen-Ha Wong, Yee-Tak Fong, Lai, & Tiwario, 2014).

In 2013, the World Health Organization (WHO) released a report on the health effects and prevalence of IPV against women internationally. Among its alarming results, this report found that 35% of women worldwide have experienced sexual and/or physical partner violence or non-partner sexual violence. In Canada, IPV devastates the lives of over 100,000 individuals annually (Statistics Canada, 2010). Furthermore, of the 89 reported spousal homicides reported in Canada in 2011, 76 victims (85%) were female (Statistics Canada, 2011). This statistic converts into one woman being killed by her intimate partner every six days in Canada. A report released by the Canadian Women's Foundation in 2014 showed that since the age of 16, half of Canada's women have reported experiencing at least one incident of physical or sexual violence. Furthermore, this report revealed that 67% of Canadians stated that they personally know a woman who has been abused. While these statistics are significant and alarming, there remains an understanding within the literature that IPV is vastly underreported (Canadian Women's Foundation, 2014; Statistics Canada, 2010; Watts & Zimmerman, 2002).

Thus, we could postulate that the true prevalence of IPV against women is likely much greater than the reported figures. What makes this even more critical is that in a global sense Canada is comparatively "safe" for women.

Despite the efforts to bring IPV into the public sphere to highlight its seriousness and potentially life-threatening consequences, women's experiences of abuse continue to be considered a "taboo" topic: a private matter to be left behind closed doors (Fox, 2013; Petersen, Moracco, Goldstein, & Clark, 2004). Women continue to be criticized, judged, and even blamed for their experiences of IPV. Throughout the literature, the negative consequences of IPV on women are documented extensively (Anderson, Renner, & Danis, 2012). These consequences can have a substantial negative impact on both a woman's physical health (Black, 2011; Ruiz-Perez, Plazaola-Castano, & del Rio-Lozano, 2007; Sharps, Laughon, & Giangrande, 2007) and mental health (Arokach, 2006; Shim Lee & Hadeed, 2009; Stephenson, Winter, & Hindin, 2013; Tadgee, 2008). According to Jones, Hughes, and Unterstaller (as cited in Anderson, Renner, & Danis, 2012), 31% to 84% of IPV survivors exhibit symptoms of post-traumatic stress disorder (PTSD). Lastly, the children of women who survive IPV can experience physical injury as a result of abuse, as well as a host of other psychosocial problems (Dumont et al., 2005; Morrow, 2002). Women's experiences of IPV also need to be understood in relation to their social context, taking into account significant systemic influences, structural issues and barriers, and societal norms and values. This includes critical, often intersecting, factors of class, race, age, ability, and sexual orientation (Bograd, 1999; Fox, 2013).

Addiction influences women's lived experiences physically, psychologically, and socially through the stigma associated with being a female substance user (Ad Hoc Working Group on Women, 2006; Greaves, 2006). The unique needs and challenges faced by women have largely been ignored in the treatment field, in part because much of the research and interventions for drug and alcohol use have been created for men, by men (Bush, 2005). This stigmatization manifests in being viewed as weak, deficient, mentally ill, and for women who have children, inadequate mothers, and raises questions: Is the stigma associated with female addiction similar to what is experienced by women in abusive relationships? How do substance abuse and IPV interact in the lives of women? How does one impact upon the other?

What We Know: Theoretical Frameworks

There has been substantial support for the existence of a relationship between woman's substance abuse and intimate partner violence within the literature (Gatz et al., 2007; Humphreys, Regan, River, & Thiara, 2005; Macy, Renz, & Pelino, 2013; Macy & Goodbourn, 2012; Martin et al., 2008; Najavits, Sonn, Walsh, & Weiss, 2004; Schumacher & Holt, 2012; Stene, Dyb, Jacobsen, & Schei, 2010; Ullman, Relyea, Peter-Hagene, & Vasquez, 2013; Walsh et al., 2014). It must be emphasized that alcohol, or any other psychoactive drug, is not the cause of violence, however alcohol working as a disinhibiting agent interacts with existing factors such as an aggressive personality, a predisposition to the use of violence, and the circumstances surrounding a given situation (Statistics Canada, 2005). Almost one-half of women (44%) in current or previous violent relationships reported that their partner had been drinking at the time of the violence (see also Chapter 16).

The complexity and mutually reinforcing nature of the relationship between drug and alcohol use and female victims of IPV continues to be a focus of investigation in the addiction and IPV fields, as evidenced by a number of significant studies (Burke et al., 2005; James, Johnson, & Raghavan, 2004; Martino, Collins, & Ellickson, 2005; Smith, Homish, Leonard, & Cornelius, 2012). Although the relational direction of these co-occurring issues remains debated, many studies have suggested it to be cyclical in nature. Research within the literature is raising important questions about the relationship between substance abuse and IPV: Does a history of substance abuse make women more vulnerable to IPV in relationships? Or is substance abuse a method of dealing with the effects of IPV? The aim of the study and focus of this chapter is to investigate the role of addiction in women's disclosure of IPV, and whether they are able to effectively seek help for IPV when addiction is a factor in their lives.

From a "substance abuse leads to victimization" framework, the understanding is that psychoactive substance use and the impact of its accompanying lifestyle increases a woman's vulnerability and exposure to assailants (Beydoun et al., 2012; Burke et al., 2005). Impaired judgment, intensified emotional states (James et al., 2004), and misinterpretation of social cues (El-Bassel, Gilbert, Schilling, & Wada, 2000) are linked to substance use, which may in turn increase the risk for victimization for women. An alternative approach used to describe the relationship between IPV and substance use involves looking at substance abuse as a method of coping with experiences of abuse or trauma in women's lives. The use of psychoactive substances has been described as "self-medicating," a mechanism to reduce the physical and emotional pain of being abused (Bliss et al., 2008; Burke et al., 2005; Kilpatrick et al., 1997; La Flair et al., 2012; Stuart et al., 2002).

A further explanation for the relationship between substance abuse and IPV, specifically in relation to experiencing trauma, is that these experiences are connected in a mutually reinforcing negative spiral pattern (Najavits, 2002). A traumatic experience, such as childhood abuse or IPV, may lead women to use substances, possibly to help self-medicate the emotional pain, and by using substances, women may be in a position of increased risk to experience further victimization by a partner. This continued victimization may lead to increased substance use as a way to "cope," and this cycle continues in an ongoing downward spiral pattern.

Although these frameworks are helpful in describing the association between IPV and substance use on an individual level, there is little emphasis on the contextual and societal factors that influence the lives of these women. By focusing solely upon the characteristics of the female being abused, we are essentially creating a "victim-blaming" model: ignoring the ways that IPV is embedded within social contexts and cultures (Fox, 2013; Liang, Goodman, Tummala-Narra, & Weintraub, 2005; Morrow, 2002). With the stigma attached to women in abusive situations, compounded by the judgments imposed by society on women with addiction issues, how are victims of abuse able to disclose the violence in their lives and seek help, especially when substance abuse is an active element in their situation?

In turning to the literatures that have evolved in the areas of both IPV and substance abuse, models have been developed and proposed to create an understanding of how individuals make changes in their lives, specifically the process of help seeking for IPV and the stages-of-change model for addiction (Prochaska & DiClimente, 1983). The IPV help-seeking literature focuses upon the wide array of strategies women use to stop, prevent, or escape violence in their lives (Grauwiler, 2008; Liang, Goodman, Tummala-Narra, & Weintraub, 2005; Moe, 2007). Theories that relate to women's responses to violence vary from women being depicted as passive in their response to violence, such as a learned helplessness approach (Walker, 1979), to seeing women as active in creating safety for themselves and their families, such as the survivor stage (Gondolf & Fisher, 1988; Lempert, 1996) and social entrapment models (Alaggia, Jenney, Mazzuca, & Redmond, 2007; Grauwiler, 2008; Moe, 2007; Ptacek, 1999). Disclosure has been described as an important step in the process of seeking help for abuse (Petersen, Moracco, Goldstein, & Clark, 2004). A woman's decision to disclose her experiences of abuse and seek help for her situation can be viewed as a process (Omarzu, 2000; Liang, Goodman, Tummala-Narra, & Weintraub, 2005), with progression through the stages of disclosure being influenced by a variety of factors: individual, interpersonal, and socio-cultural. These stages are not necessarily linear in nature, and women may move back and forth within the disclosure process before moving ahead in their own help seeking.

One of the first stages of disclosure identified is women's growing recognition of abuse, and defining it as a problem in their lives (Liang, Goodman, Tummala-Narra, & Weintraub, 2005). Women in this pre-contemplative stage may not identify that they are in an abusive relationship and are therefore unlikely to disclose. After recognizing abuse, women then move to a further stage where they make the decision to disclose their abuse and seek help (Omarzu, 2000). At this point they are weighing the risks and benefits of the decision to disclose and seek help. In this second stage, women are seen to move from the private to public sphere, using more informal help-seeking strategies, such as turning to family or friends, to more formal helping forums, such as community agencies (Goodman, Dutton, Weinfurt, & Cook, 2003). Within both these stages, barriers have been identified for women in the disclosure process. Some of these barriers include fear of retribution (Acierno, Resnick, & Kilpatrick, 1997; Fugate et al., 2005), fear of losing children (Alaggia, Jenney, Mazucca, & Redmond, 2007; Fugate et al., 2005), shame (Petersen, Moracco, Goldstein, & Clark, 2004; Wolf, Ly, Hobart, & Kernic, 2003) and previous negative reporting experiences (Liang, Goodman, Tummala-Narra, & Weintraub, 2005). Women's help-seeking behaviours for substance abuse have also been discussed in the literature. Similarly, both external barriers—such as resistance from family and friends or shelter regulations mandating sobriety prior to entry—and internal barriers, such as shame, stigma, and not recognizing problems exist may prevent women from seeking help for their addiction (Beckman, 1994; Copeland, 1997; Jessup, Humphreys, Brindis, & Lee, 2003; Poole & Isaac, 2001; Wu & Ringwalt, 2014).

In attempting to understand the stages of change process, the Transtheoretical Model of Change (TTM) has been used as a framework for promoting behavioural shifts (Prochaska & DiClimente, 1983). TTM proposes that readiness to change is a process that occurs in a series of stages. Individuals are seen to move back and forth between these stages in a spiral manner before being able to maintain a particular behaviour change. However, unlike Najavits' (2002) negative downward spiral, this is an upward positive change. This model, originally developed to understand smoking cessation (Prochaska, DiClemente, & Norcross, 1992), has gradually been adopted in other areas including for women in abusive relationships (Bliss et al., 2008).

What has been less articulated in the literature is the disclosure/help-seeking process for women with co-occurring issues of IPV and substance abuse. Research has identified that there are current gaps in service provision for women with these co-occurring conditions, and that there may be additional barriers in the help-seeking process (Galvani, 2006). To this end, it has been thoroughly documented within the literature that there remains a lack of appropriate and integrated services for women who have coexisting issues of IPV and substance abuse (Building Bridges, 2008; Greaves, Chabot, Jategaonkar, Poole, & McCullough, 2006; Harm Reduction International, 2013; Martin et al., 2008; Rogers et al., 2003; VAWCC, 2013).

This qualitative study's aim was to explore how the intersection of substance abuse and IPV is experienced in the lives of women and how this impacts upon their disclosure of abuse and help-seeking behaviours. Ten women that had both previous experiences of IPV and substance use, as well as three professionals who work in the intersecting areas of IPV and substance abuse, were recruited to participate in this study. The two specific research questions addressed were the following:

1. From the perspective of women experiencing IPV and substance abuse issues, what impedes or facilitates the disclosure process?
2. What do helping professionals in the fields of substance abuse and IPV identify as barriers and/or facilitators for women disclosing intimate partner violence?

Method

The research tradition used for this qualitative study was a grounded theory approach, guided by feminist principles. Grounded theory, initially developed by Glaser and Strauss (1967), is a qualitative means to "generate or discover" a theory, that which is ınded" in data from the field (Strauss & Corbin, 1990). In this study data from the ̶was the actual women's stories. A feminist lens to the research sought to expose ̶alidate women's lived experiences. The trustworthiness and authenticity of this ̶ative study, or the ability to establish confidence in the findings, was ensured ̶ablishing the following criteria: credibility, transferability, dependability, and ̶mability (Creswell, 1998). Persistent observation, reflexivity, and peer debriefing ̶oted authenticity of the data. Persistent observation was achieved through sub-̶al contact with the study participants and rich description garnered through the ̶iew process. Reflexivity and peer debriefing occurred through discussions with ̶chers and practitioners in the field expanding interpretations of findings, and ̶sting various avenues of explanation. Further, dependability of these data was ̶ed through the verbatim transcription of the interviews. Transcripts were coded ̶endently by two research team members. The use of multiple coders and NVivo ̶̶̶̶̶̶ed in reducing researcher bias. Quotes are provided to confirm that findings are grounded in the data.

In line with grounded theory methodology, theoretical sampling was conducted so that women included in the study were drawn from a population with specific "fixed" variables: women over the age of 18 with previous experiences of IPV and substance abuse, but also held diverse characteristics. The experience of substance abuse could include both illicit drugs, such as cocaine or opioids, and licit drugs including alcohol and prescription opioids or sedative hypnotics. Only women who were in "recovery" for their substance abuse issues, and not actively using substances, were recruited to participate. This decision was made in order for women to be fully able to provide informed consent to participate and to reduce any risk that could result in participating. The definition of recovery for this research was women who were currently receiving or had previously received some form of addiction-specific treatment. Treatment ranged from abstinence-based residential programs to voluntarily attending a 12-step group to participating in a community-based harm reduction program. As one of the research goals was to hear how women experience substance abuse and IPV, the definition of recovery was left to the participants to self-define in their lives. The timing of the experience of IPV and substance use was also left open-ended to the participants to specify. This information was used to understand the mutually reinforcing relationship between IPV and substance use and to identify any patterns in the temporal sequence of the experiences.

Data collection occurred through in-depth semi-structured interviews with women that lasted approximately 45 to 90 minutes in length. The interviews contained open-ended questions that addressed the experiences of women with IPV and substance abuse issues, specifically looking at the process of disclosure, seeking help with formal/informal agencies, helpful/harmful aspects of previous service provision, and ways to improve practice for the future. The interviews were audiotaped and then transcribed by the researcher. Ethical considerations were made throughout the research process and the study was approved through the University of Toronto Ethics Review Board.

Data analysis followed grounded theory principles based upon theoretical sampling, whereby as data collection occurs, the sample is refined to determine under which conditions the theory holds true. NVivo, a qualitative data analysis computer program, was used to help interpret the findings and apply the coding frameworks used in the process. During the first stage, the interviews were open coded manually, and this initial coding framework was imported into NVivo. In the axial coding process, interrelationships between different categories of information within the framework were identified and highlighted. Constant comparisons were used to compare the data between each of the individual interviews with women along with the themes and categories emerging from within each interview (Strauss & Corbin, 1990). These comparisons were made between women with or without children, and between women who had or did not have experiences of trauma in their childhoods. In the final stage of the grounded theory process, selective coding, predominant themes were identified and highlighted for further analysis.

Results

Ten women participated in this study with an age range of 21 to 57 years and a mean age of 36 years. Seven women identified themselves as Caucasian, two as being of First Nations ancestry, and one as African-Canadian. Six of the ten women reported having children, though of these women, none of them were currently living with their children. Five of the ten women reported experiencing abuse in their childhoods including physical, emotional, sexual, and institutional abuse and neglect. Two women who did not report childhood abuse reported that they had witnessed intimate partner violence between their caregivers.

The type of substance use reported by the participants fell into three broad categories: alcohol; illicit drugs including crack, cocaine, marijuana, ecstasy, and other hallucinogens and opioids; and prescription medication, such as anti-anxiety agents and anti-depressants, Oxycontin, and Adderol, a Ritalin-like stimulant. The length of substance use varied with each participant, depending upon the substance involved. For instance, some women reported using certain substances only a few times, while one participant reported using psychoactive drugs including alcohol for 41 years.

The women in this study spoke openly and freely about their experiences, which led to six main themes emerging from their stories. Although these themes will be discussed separately and are presented as distinct, it should be noted that they are overlapping and interconnected in many ways.

The Role of Substance Abuse in Abusive Relationships
The first theme that emerged was the complex role of substance abuse in abusive relationships. Some women reported that they were using substances prior to entering into

a relationship, and that substance use increased their vulnerability to abuse. Further, women spoke about experiences of using with their partner while in a relationship and that this was their "point of connection." One woman described the connection with her partner as a "drug relationship":

> [We] were just feeding each other I guess, in our substances and in our needs to party and be with someone while we're partying.

Use of substances was also reported as a response to living with IPV. Some women explained that substance use helped them cope with the relational abuse they were experiencing, by helping distance them from the abuse temporarily, and allowing them to relax. This enabled them to briefly escape from their situations, and to put on a facade for others, masking their painful experiences. Some women described the use of drugs or alcohol as "self-medication," in order to "kill the pain" of current and previous experiences of abuse. Several women spoke about turning to substances as a way of dealing with IPV: "Can't cope, take a pill. Or take a pill anyways."

Substance Abuse and Loss of Control/Means of Control

The second theme that emerged centred around issues of control, both in terms of losing control through using substances, but also using substances as a means of control in their situations. Several participants described that their reliance upon drugs was used by their partners as a means to further isolate them, resulting in loss of control. One woman described this feeling of powerlessness:

> I felt like I was in one of those old 1950s movies where someone gets locked away in an insane asylum and they're not crazy, you know? It was just a nightmare.

Often the women's partners were also the ones receiving and supplying drugs, which increased their dependence on the relationship. One woman described being completely isolated while under the influence of drugs, as her partner was the only person who could "ground" her while coming out of the drug experience, further fostering a dysfunctional dependency upon her partner. There were some women who also reported that using substances while in abusive relationships made them feel more in control of their situations. One woman explained that substance use made her feel like "superwoman," and that she was able stand up to her partner.

> I get more brazen.... I didn't give a shit what he'd say, even though I knew there would be consequences when I got home, on the way home, or even right there. You know, it gave me my nerve to say "I'm really tired of you fucking beating me up."

Cultural, Familial, and Social Influences

A third theme that emerged related to how women's world view of abuse, through cultural messages, and familial and social influences, contributed to their views of their experience of IPV and addiction. One woman described how she believed men justified their abuse towards women, and that women are treated as "subservient." For some of the participants, violence against women and children felt sadly normalized: abuse was "all around" and accepted. Some women described how within certain cultures gender roles were reinforced and abuse was tolerated.

> Women are kind of, they don't have the same rights as men do. I wouldn't justify him or anything, but I would say maybe those were some of the reasons why he was acting that way because a lot of people in that culture do act that way, they feel that men are superior to women.

Other women spoke about the culture of drug use, in which relational abuse was just "part and parcel" with the lifestyle and that "the whole culture is based upon abuse, is based on power and control." Many of the women who shared their stories spoke of being marginalized as a result of their experiences, by family, friends, and professionals. One woman spoke poignantly about being taken to hospital for injuries related to IPV and receiving the message, "Oh, it's her again."

Double Stigma

Related to the previous theme, stigmatization and the intersecting oppression of addiction and IPV emerged clearly. Social stigma associated with female substance abuse co-occurring with IPV reinforced this feeling. One woman summed this up:

> I didn't want to put myself in that category ... well with mental health even, that I have issues, that I'm an alcoholic, that I'm a victim, even just the title victim, I think at that time, now I'm not worried about what it would stereotype me as or not, but at that time it was an issue for me. I didn't want to be looked at as an addict, or as a victim, or as a dysfunctional family even. Like all those words, I didn't want to associate to my life.

The societal view of substance abuse as a "lifestyle choice" also elicited responses such as "what do you expect? You're addicted, you're an addict," when women reported their experiences of abuse to others.

This double stigma was further exacerbated when some of the participants who were mothers shared their experiences. Women with children reported feeling that they were often labelled as incompetent and inadequate as mothers when addiction and IPV intersected in their lives. One woman reported the following after disclosing abuse to her physician:

Because there was the alcohol factor involved, and you know, from my perspective anyway, I felt that she didn't take it [IPV] all that seriously to be honest, now that I'm thinking about it.... Like I feel there's a part of her that looks at me as like an alcoholic mother.... It's just kind of like this is part and parcel to, this happened because of this.... I came away feeling like it was my fault basically.

Many of the study participants in general reported that they felt judged by those who otherwise should have been significant social supports in their lives: family, friends, and professionals.

Substance Abuse as a Barrier to Disclosing and Seeking Help

Another theme that emerged from the study data was how for many of the women substance abuse acted as a barrier to disclosing and seeking help for experiences of abuse. Some women reported how their use of substances prevented them from recognizing the level of danger they were in with their relationships. Other women stated that they were reluctant to seek help for their experiences of IPV because they were using substances at the time and did not want to have to give up using. One woman described being both addicted to her abusive partner and the drugs she was using, making it difficult for her to leave the partner:

Hell. Hell, but I was so addicted to the drug, so, sort of makes you addicted to the person. I guess that's co-dependence you know? I guess that would be the epitome of co-dependence for a drug relationship ... you know, cause you can't leave, even though you want to. It's hard to go, especially if you know, they've got skills in getting drugs and stuff like that ... and you are a team in working at getting drugs.

Substances allowed some women to manage their feelings, and for one woman substance use was considered a substitution for talking to someone or seeking help:

As long as I had [alcohol], I didn't have to get help ... because in my warped mind, it was helping me, because that's all I knew. That's what you rely on when, when the going gets rough, you have a drink.... It replaced anything I needed ever.

Finally, the compounded stigma for women with both experiences of IPV and addiction made it difficult for some women to disclose their experiences: "So [a woman] is already going to feel silenced and judged around the substance use and let alone to talk about this [abuse] too that women already feel silenced about."

Supportive Services

The final theme that was highlighted throughout the women's stories was the reports of services women found helpful throughout their experiences of seeking help, and the recommendations they had for change. Three broad areas in which both the key informants and the women made recommendations for change included:

- making services more accessible for women;
- integrating IPV and substance abuse interventions; and
- creating opportunities for women to have more control over their care and service provision.

Both the key informants and the women who participated spoke of the need for agencies to be more prepared to work with women who have both experiences of abuse and addiction in order to prevent compartmentalizing women's concerns. Participants called for systems to work with women's experiences together, and not separate them. For example, one woman stated

> [I would like to see] the issues be dealt with together. Because ... a lot of women are still using because they can't deal with the abuse issues. Because they can't deal with the drama. Because it keeps coming back up. Because they keep going back and they don't know why. So I have a ton of recovery tools, but I've got no trauma tools, I've got no flashback tools.... I don't have a trauma toolkit, or an abuse toolkit.... Because a lot of people think that "Ok.... I'll get some help for the drug addiction and then everything else will go away. Everything else will be fine." But ... they coincide, they step together.

Both the women and professionals involved in this study stressed the importance of women having more control in how they receive services. One worker spoke about respecting women in their own recovery process and "not hurrying [women] through [programs] and get healed on this, get healed on that." One woman stated that she would like to "see programs that are tailored to the whole person, not just the broken parts of the person," therefore emphasizing strengths rather than deficits and weaknesses.

Integrating the Findings

The women's narratives highlighted the considerable challenges faced in disclosing IPV and help-seeking actions, the role of substance abuse in that process, and the obstacles they had to overcome to secure safety for themselves and often their children. Some of the findings in this study are consistent with what has been identified in previous research looking at women's experiences of IPV. In particular, the mutually reinforcing relationship between substance abuse and IPV (Burke et al., 2005; James, Johnson, &

& Raghavan, 2004; Martino, Collins, & Ellickson, 2005) was evidenced throughout the narratives of the women in this study, specifically substance use increasing women's risk for victimization by partners and the use of substance as a coping mechanism for abuse. As well, the women's narratives articulated their movement through the process of seeking help for both IPV and substance abuse. They identified stigma, shame, and cultural influences as obstacles (Acierno, Resnick, & Kilpatrick, 1997; Dietrich & Schuett, 2013; Do, Weiss, & Pollack, 2013; Liang, Goodman, Tummala-Narra, & Weintraub, 2005; Petersen, Moracco, Goldstein, & Clark, 2004). There were, however, some unique findings that emerged from the narratives that have not been previously discussed in the literature, specifically the process of disclosure of IPV, the role of substance abuse in this process, and the impact of substance abuse on help seeking for IPV.

These study data identify women's substance use as an additional, and problematic, dimension in setting the stage for change and taking action in their abusive situations. We used these data to lend further understanding to this complex process as it applies to the first two stages of the Transtheoretical Model (TTM) of Change (Prochaska and DiClemente, 1983)—pre-contemplation and contemplation. The women's narratives bring to light how their use of substances affect their help-seeking behaviours in two distinct ways, by acting as a disclosure suppressant, and also by acting as another means of isolation either through manipulation by their partners or through the stigmatization of the substance use itself. Women's inability to recognize both relational and substance abuse as a problem is viewed as the pre-contemplation state. Women's identification of substance abuse and IPV as problematic, and their decision to disclose, signals their movement into the contemplation stage. Processes described by the study participants help to understand the early stages of pre-contemplation and contemplation when substance abuse and IPV are both present. First, women go "back and forth" in the spiral of change before they are able to make significant decisions and actions. The presence of substance abuse and IPV make this spiral even more complex in nature, as these data suggest the recognition of abuse and the decision to disclose is inextricably linked to women's level of dependency upon psychoactive substances. Second, within this pre-contemplation stage women's use of substances cloud their ability to recognize abusive aspects of their relationship. Some women reported that they used substances to seemingly escape from their situations, but that this masking of emotions prevented recognition of relational abuse. The use of substances made it difficult to form accurate judgments of risk within their intimate relationships, and not surprisingly problem recognition was impeded as a result of the drug use. The present study results point to the role of substance abuse in minimizing IPV and directly contributing to suppression of IPV disclosure, which in turn affects women's help-seeking action.

Further, women in the study spoke of substance use as a coping mechanism, and for periods of time used it as a solution, though one that would eventually become as problematic as the IPV. The unintended positive benefits that substance use temporarily provided to women was to allow them to cope with and stay in their relationships, which in the short term outweighed the negative consequences of disclosing and leaving the abusive relationship. Although substance use typically started as a coping mechanism for women, it eventually interfered in the assessment of the risks and benefits of making the decision to disclose, impairing women's judgment of their level of safety and potentially leading to physical and psychological dependency.

Indeed, participants in this study spoke of how the control and isolation they felt as a result of their substance use acted as a barrier for disclosing their experiences of relational abuse. By this time, however, they had difficulty breaking free of their substance use and regaining control, because of their addiction to the drug. The same substances that initially enabled them to have positive experiences, even acting to regulate their emotions, became barriers to escaping their violent relationships. Some women described how their partners had control over what substances were used, when they were used, and with whom they were used. Studies have also noted how men can isolate women from their social networks through substance use, as they become the only person the woman can rely on for maintaining her drug use, increasing her dependency on the perpetrator and decreasing her supports, leading to a "vicious cycle" (Covington & Surrey, 1997; Logan, Walker, Cole, & Leukefeld, 2002). The present study further supports this but also details how this evolved during the early stages of change. Clearly, this increased isolation prevents future disclosure of abuse as women may become more physically and emotionally disconnected from sources of positive support.

Substance use thus impacts women's movement through the help-seeking process, acting as an additional barrier for change. It is therefore important for professionals working with women with experiences of IPV to be able to recognize the influence that substance abuse has in the decision-making process for disclosure, and to routinely ask women whether they are using substances. The complex nature of the relationship between substance abuse and IPV also makes it difficult to separate or disentangle these issues in treatment settings.

Implications for Practice and Policy

With an increased understanding of the mutually reinforcing relationship between substance abuse and IPV, and the negative impact of substance abuse on disclosure and help-seeking for IPV, comes the need to create more services in Canada that will address these co-occurring issues and reduce the fragmented nature of service delivery for women. Integration of services is necessary from initial assessment of women when they first present to an agency until service completion. Depending upon whether women access an agency specifically addressing issues of violence or a substance abuse agency, there needs to be systematic screening processes that identify the presence of IPV and/or substance abuse, with adequate corresponding resources and training to provide appropriate services. Without proper training, there is a risk that professionals could provide services that are unsafe, inadvertently colluding with the abuser or not responding to tentative disclosures appropriately (Galvani, 2006). IPV must be included in the addiction assessment process as it can be a trigger for lapse and relapse. A woman's use of substances to manage the anxiety and/or flash-backs of unaddressed trauma can be easily misunderstood as a lack of commitment to sobriety. Social workers and other helping professionals will be unable to fully support women in the change process, in finding other ways to manage these symptoms, and in addressing the negative effects of IPV without this perspective on the relationship between violence and drug use (Moses, Reed, Mazelis, & D'Ambrosio, 2003). There is likewise a need for professionals to understand the dynamic nature of the disclosure and help-seeking process with women's readiness to change and the influence that substance use has on decision-making within the stages of change. Professionals need to tailor their intervention to reflect which stage of change a woman is in. Thus, IPV and addiction services need to build bridges of collaboration in order to be able to provide fully integrated services to women. This collaboration is made more difficult, however, when there are agency differences in treatment philosophies, confidentiality procedures, and competition for funding.

As was explained by the participants in this study, IPV and substance abuse in the lives of women need to be recognized by society as serious and potentially life-threatening conditions. Women's experiences of trauma and violence need to be brought into the public sphere, openly discussed, and validated. Social workers need to advocate in agencies to ensure that the issue of IPV becomes more visible and that these women become more visible themselves and obtain the specific support they require to change their behaviour. Women's stories need to be heard, understood and appropriately responded to rather than being silenced by the traditional belief that the woman could just leave or stop using at any time, that it is her choice—and worse, her fault—for not simply stopping her drinking or drug use and staying in the abusive relationship. "What kind of mother can she be?"

REFERENCES

Acierno, R., Resnick, H.S., & Kilpatrick, D.G. (1997). Health impact of interpersonal violence 1: Prevalence rates, case identification, and risk factors for sexual assault, physical assault, and domestic violence in men and women. *Behavioural Medicine, 23*(2), 53-64.

Ad Hoc Working Group on Women, Mental Health, Mental Illness and Addictions. (2006). *Women, mental health and mental illness and addiction in Canada: An overview.* Retrieved from http://www.cwhn.ca/PDF/womenMentalHealth.pdf

Alaggia, R., Jenney, A., Mazucca, J., & Redmond, M. (2007). In whose best interest? A Canadian case study of the impact of child welfare policies in cases of domestic violence. *Journal of Brief Therapy and Crisis Intervention*, 1-16.

Anderson, M.K., Renner, M.L., & Danis, S.F. (2012). Recovery: Resilience and growth in the aftermath of domestic violence. *Violence Against Women, 18*(11), 1279-1299.

Arokach, A. (2006). Alienation and domestic abuse: How abused women cope with loneliness. *Social Indicators Research, 78*, 327-340.

Beckman, L.J. (1994). Treatment needs of women with alcohol problems. *Alcohol Health and Research World, 18*(3), 206-211.

Beydoun, H., Beydoun, M., Kaufman, J., Lo, B., & Zonderman, A. (2012). Intimate partner violence against adult women and its association with major depressive disorder, depressive symptoms and postpartum depression: A systematic review and meta-analysis. *Social Science & Medicine, 75*(6), 959-975.

Black, C.M. (2011). Intimate partner violence and adverse health consequences: Implications for clinicians. *American Journal of Lifestyle Medicine, 5*(5), 428-439.

Bliss, M.J., Ogley-Oliver, E., Jackson, E., Harp, S., & Kaslow, N.J. (2008). African American women's readiness to change abusive relationships. *Journal of Family Violence, 23*(3), 161-171.

Bograd, M. (1999). Strengthening domestic violence theories: Intersections of race, class, sexual orientation, and gender. *Journal of marital and family therapy, 25*(3), 275-289.

Building Bridges. (2008). *Linking women abuse, substance use and mental ill health.* Retrieved from http://www.bcwomens.ca/NR/rdonlyres/8D65CADE-8541-4398-B264-7C28CED7D208/28333/BuildingBridges_ExecutiveSummary_Final.pdf

Burke, J.G., Thieman, L.K., Gielen, A.C., O'Campo, P., & McDonnell, K.A. (2005). Intimate partner violence, substance use, and HIV among low-income women. *Violence Against Women, 11*(9), 1140-1161.

Bush, F.S. (2005). *Barriers to treatment: An ethnographic study of substance-dependent women seeking treatment.* Doctoral dissertation, University of Pittsburgh.

Canadian Women's Foundation. (2014). *Fact sheet: Moving women out of violence.* Retrieved from http://www.canadianwomen.org/sites/canadianwomen.org/files//FactSheet-StopViolence-ACTIVE_0.pdf

Copeland, J. (1997). A qualitative study of barriers to formal treatment among women who self managed change in addictive behaviours. *Journal of Substance Abuse Treatment, 14*(2), 183-190.

Covington, S.S., & Surrey, J.L. (1997). The relational model of women's psychological development: Implications for substance abuse. In R.W. Wilsnack & S.C. Wilsnack (Eds.), *Gender and alcohol: Individual and social perspectives* (pp. 335-351). New Brunswick, NJ: Rutgers Center of Alcohol Studies.

Creswell, J.W. (1998). *Qualitative inquiry and research design: Choosing among five traditions.* Thousand Oaks, CA: Sage Publications.

Dietrich, D.M., & Schuett, J.M. (2013). Culture of honor and attitudes toward intimate partner violence in Latinos. *Sage Open, 3*(2), DOI: 10.1177/2158244013489685.

Do, K.N., Weiss, B., & Pollack, A. (2013). Cultural beliefs, intimate partner violence, and mental health functioning among Vietnamese women. *International Perspectives in Psychology: Research, Practice, Consultation, 2*(3), 149-163.

DuMont, J., Forte, T., Cohen, M.M., Hyman, I., & Romans, S. (2005). Changing help-seeking rates for intimate partner violence in Canada. *Women & Health, 41*(1), 1-19.

El-Bassel, N., Gilbert, L., Schilling, R., & Wada, T. (2000). Drug abuse and partner violence among women in methadone treatment. *Journal of Family Violence, 15*(3), 209-228.

Fox, V. (2013). Historical perspectives on violence against women. *Journal of International Women's Studies, 4*(1), 15-34.

Fugate, M., Landis, L., Riordan, K., Naureckas, S., & Engel, B. (2005). Barriers to domestic violence help seeking: Implications for intervention. *Violence against Women, 11*(3), 290-310.

Galvani, S. (2006). Safety first? The impact of domestic abuse on women's treatment experience. *Journal of Substance Abuse, 11*(6), 395-407.

Gatz, M., Brown, V., Hennigan, K., Rechberger, E., O'Keefe, M., Rose, T., & Bjelajac, P. (2007). Effectiveness of an integrated trauma-informed approach to treating women with co-occurring disorders and histories of trauma: The Los Angeles site experience. *Journal of Community Psychology, 35*(7), 863-878.

Glaser, B., & Strauss, A.L. (1967). *The discovery of grounded theory: Strategies for qualitative research.* London: Transaction publishers.

Gondolf, E.W., & Fisher, E.R. (1988). *Battered women as survivors: An alternative to treating learned helplessness.* Lexington, MA: Lexington Books.

Goodman, L., Dutton, M.A., Weinfurt, K., & Cook, S. (2003). The intimate partner violence strategies index: Development and application. *Violence against Women, 9*(2), 163-186.

Grauwiler, P. (2008). Vocies of women: Perspectives on decision making and the management of partner violence. *Children and Youth Services Review, 30,* 311-322.

Greaves, L. (2006). Mental health and addictions in women. Mergers and acquisitions: Making them work for women. *Centers for Excellence in Women's Health Research Bulletin, 5*(1), 1-3.

Greaves, L., Chabot, C., Jategaonkar, N., Poole, N., & McCullough, L. (2006). Substance use among women in shelters for abused women and children. *Canadian Journal of Public Health, 97*(7), 388-392.

Harm Reduction International. (2013). *Briefing paper on violence against women who use drugs and access to domestic violence shelters.* Retrieved from http://www.ihra.net/files/2013/03/19/Briefing_Paper_-_Access_to_Shelters

Humphreys, C., Regan, L., River, D., & Thiara, R.K. (2005). Domestic violence and substance use: Tackling complexity. *British Journal of Social Work, 35,* 1303-1320.

James, S.E., Johnson, J., & Raghavan, C. (2004). "I couldn't go anywhere": Contextualizing violence and drug abuse: A social network study. *Violence against Women, 10*(9), 991-1014.

Jessup, M.A., Humphreys, J.C., Brindis, C.D., & Lee, K.A. (2003). Extrinsic barriers to substance abuse treatment among pregnant drug dependent women. *Journal of Drug Issues, 33*(2), 285-304.

Kilpatrick, D.G., Acierno, R., Resnick, H., Saunders, B., & Best, C. (1997). A two-year longitudinal analysis of the relationships among assault and alcohol and drug abuse in women. *Journal of Consulting and Clinical Psychology, 65*(5), 834-847.

La Flair, L., Bradshaw, C., Storr, C., Green, K., Alvanzo, A., & Crum, R. (2012). Intimate partner violence and patterns of alcohol abuse and dependence criteria among women: A latent class analysis. *Journal of Studies on Alcohol and Drugs, 73*(3), 351.

Lempert, L.B. (1996). Women's strategies for survival: Developing agency in abusive relationships. *Journal of Family Violence, 11*(3), 269-289.

Liang, B., Goodman, L., Tummala-Narra, P., & Weintraub, S. (2005). A theoretical framework for understanding help-seeking processes among survivors of intimate partner violence. *American Journal of Community Psychology, 36*(1/2), 71-84.

Logan, T.K., Walker, R., Cole, J., & Leukefeld C. (2002). Victimization and substance abuse among women: Contributing factors, interventions, and implications. *Review of General Psychology, 6*(4), 325-397.

Macy, R.J., & Goodbourn, M. (2012). Promoting successful collaborations between domestic violence and substance abuse treatment service sectors: A review of the literature. *Trauma, Violence, & Abuse, 13*(4), 235-250.

Macy, R.J., Renz, C., & Pelino, E. (2013). Partner violence and substance abuse are intertwined: Women's perceptions of violence-substance connections. *Violence Against Women, 19*(7), 881-902.

Martin, S.L., Moracco, K.E., Chang, J.C., Council, C.L., & Dulli, L.S. (2008). Substance abuse issues among women in domestic violence programs. *Violence Against Women, 14*(9), 985-997.

Martino, S.C., Collins, R.L., & Ellickson, P.L. (2005). Cross-lagged relationships between substance use and intimate partner violence among a sample of young adult women. *Journal of Studies on Alcohol, 66*(1), 139–148.

Moe, A.M. (2007). Silenced voices and structured survival: Battered women's help seeking. *Violence against Women, 13*(7), 676–699.

Morrow, M. (2002). *Violence and trauma in the lives of women with severe mental illness: Current practices in service provision in British Columbia.* British Columbia Centre for Excellence in Women's Health. Retrieved from http://www.bccewh.bc.ca/PDFs/violencetrauma.pdf

Moses, D.J., Reed, B.G., Mazelis, R., & D'Ambrosio, B. (2003). *Creating trauma services for women with co-occurring disorders: Experiences from the SAMHSA women with alcohol, drug abuse and mental health disorders who have histories of violence study.* Retrieved from http://www.criaw-icref.ca/indexFrame_e.htm

Najavits, L.M. (2002). *Seeking safety: A treatment manual for PTSD and substance abuse.* New York: Guilford Press.

Najavits, L.M., Sonn, J., Walsh, M., & Weiss, R.D. (2004). Domestic violence in women with PTSD and substance abuse. *Addictive Behaviors, 29*, 707–715.

Omarzu, J. (2000). A disclosure decision model: Determining how and when individuals will self-disclose. *Personality and Social Psychology Review, 4*(2), 174–185.

Petersen, R., Moracco, K.E., Goldstein, K.M., & Clark, K.A. (2004). Moving beyond disclosure: Women's perspectives on barriers and motivators to seeking assistance for intimate partner violence. *Women & Health, 40*(3), 63–76.

Poole, N., & Isaac, B. (2001). *Apprehensions: Barriers to treatment for substance-using mothers.* British Columbia Centre of Excellence for Women's Health. Retrieved from http://www.bccewh.bc.ca/PDFs/apprehensions.pdf

Prochaska, J.O., & DiClemente, C. (1983). Stages and process of self-change in smoking: Towards an integrative model of change. *Journal of Consulting and Clinical Psychology, 51*(3), 390–395.

Prochaska, J.O., DiClemente, C.C., & Norcross, J.C. (1992). In search of how people change: Applications to addictive behaviours. *American Psychologist, 47*(9), 1102–1114.

Ptacek, J. (1999). *Battered women in the courtroom: The power of judicial responses.* Boston: Northeastern University Press.

Rogers, B., Mcgee, G., Vann, A., Thompson, N., & Williams, O.J. (2003). Substance abuse and domestic violence. *Violence against Women, 9*(5), 590–598.

Ruiz-Perez, I., Plazaola-Castano, J., & del Rio-Lozano, M. (2007). Physical health consequences of intimate partner violence in Spanish women. *European Journal of Public Health, 17*(5), 437–443.

Schumacher, J., M., & Holt, D.J. (2012). Domestic violence shelter residents' substance abuse treatment needs and options. *Aggression and Violent Behavior, 17*(3), 188–197.

Sharps, W.P., Laughon, K., & Giangrande, K.S. (2007). Intimate partner violence and the childbearing year. *Trauma, Violence, & Abuse, 8*(2), 105–116.

Shim Lee, Y., & Hadeed, L. (2009). Intimate partner violence among Asian immigrant communities: Health/mental health consequences, help-seeking behaviors, and service utilization. *Trauma, Violence & Abuse, 10*(2), 143–170.

Smith, P., Homish, G., Leonard, K., & Cornelius, J. (2012). Intimate partner violence and specific substance use disorders: Findings from the National Epidemiologic Survey on Alcohol and Related Conditions. *Psychology of Addictive Behaviors, 26*(2), 236.

Statistics Canada. (2005). *Family violence in Canada: A statistical profile 2005.* Retrieved from: http://www.statcan.gc.ca/pub/85-224-x/85-224-x2005000-eng.pdf

Statistics Canada. (2010). *Family violence in Canada: A statistical profile.* Retrieved from http://www.statcan.gc.ca/pub/85-002-x/2012001/article/11643-eng.pdf

Statistics Canada. (2011). *Homicides in Canada, 2011.* Retrieved from http://www.statcan.gc.ca/pub/85-002-x/2012001/article/11738-eng.pdf

Stene, E.L., Dyb, G., Jacobsen, G.W., & Schei, B. (2010). Psychotropic drug use among women exposed to intimate partner violence: A population-based study. *Scandinavian Journal of Public Health, 38*(5), 88–95.

Stenius, V.M.K., & Veysey, B.M. (2005). "It's the little things": Women, trauma, and strategies for healing. *Journal of Interpersonal Violence, 20*(10), 1155–1174.

Stephenson, R., Winter, A., & Hindin, M. (2013). Frequency of intimate partner violence and rural women's mental health in four Indian states. *Violence Against Women, 19*(9), 1133–1150.

Strauss, A., & Corbin, J. (1990). *Basics of qualitative research: Grounded theory procedures and techniques.* Newbury Park, CA: Sage.

Stuart, G.L., Ramsay, S.E., Moore, T.M., Kahler, C.W., Farrell, L.E., Recupero, P.R., & Brown, R.A. (2002). Marital violence victimization and perpetration among women substance abusers: A descriptive study. *Violence against Women, 8*(8), 934–952.

Tagee, D.A. (2008). The mental health consequences of intimate partner violence against women in Agaro Town, southwest Ethiopia. *Tropical Doctor, 38*(4), 228–229.

Ullman, S.E., Relyea, M., Peter-Hagene, L., & Vasquez, A.L. (2013). Trauma histories, substance use coping, PTSD, and problem substance use among sexual assault victims. *Addictive Behaviors, 38*(6), 2219–2223.

VAWCC. (2013). *Provincial VAWCC newsletter: Fall 2013.* Retrieved from http://www.learningtoendabuse.ca/sites/default/files/BBW%20Newsletter%20-%20Fall%202013.pdf

Walker, L. (1979). *The battered woman.* New York: Harper & Row.

Walsh, K., Resnick, H.S., Danielson, C.K., McCauley, J.L., Saunders, B.E., & Kilpatrick, D.G. (2014). Patterns of drug and alcohol use associated with lifetime sexual revictimization and current posttraumatic stress disorder among three national samples of adolescent, college, and household-residing women. *Addictive Behaviors, 39*(3), 684–689.

Watts, C., & Zimmerman, C. (2002). Violence against women: Global scope and magnitude. *Lancet, 359*(9313), 1232–1237.

Wolf, M.E., Ly, U., Hobart, M.A., & Kernic, M.A. (2003). Barriers to seeking police help for intimate partner violence. *Journal of Family Violence, 18*(2), 121–129.

World Health Organization. (2013). *Global and regional estimates of violence against women: Prevalence and health effects of intimate partner violence and non-partner sexual violence.* Retrieved from http://apps.who.int/iris/bitstream/10665/85239/1/9789241564625_eng.pdf?ua=1

Wortham, T.T. (2014). Intimate partner violence: Building resilience with families and children. *Reclaiming Children and Youth, 23*(2), 58–61.

Wu, L.T., & Ringwalt, C.L. (2014). Alcohol dependence and use of treatment services among women in the community. *American Journal of Psychiatry, 161*(10), 1790–1797.

Yok-Fong, P. (2014). Risk and resilience of immigrant women in intimate partner violence. *Journal of Human Behavior in the Social Environment, 24*(7), 725–740.

Yuen-Ha Wong, J., Yee-Tak Fong, D., Lai, V., & Tiwario, A. (2014). Bridging intimate partner violence and the human brain: A literature review. *Trauma, Violence, & Abuse, 15*(1), 22–33.

CHAPTER 18

Drug Use, Addiction, and the Criminal Justice System

Amber Kellen, Lois Powers, and Rachel Birnbaum

There is little doubt the community and families of both the victim and offender can justifiably find fault with the system. Within the system, from social workers, to the court, every hand along the way contributed, in part, to the tragedies surrounding this case. We, within the system, cannot deny our responsibility. We must learn from our failures. But the failures that led to this crime do not pile up only at the door of the agencies and professionals involved. The family of the offender, his immediate and larger community can also not deny their responsibility and must try to learn from this case.

—THE HONOURABLE JUSTICE BARRY STUART UPON
SENTENCING MARCELLUS JACOB[1]

A Collective Responsibility

The use of drugs in Canada is synonymous with law enforcement and criminalization. Canadian society, through legislation including various prohibitions, historic and contemporary, has indicated which drugs and what forms of substance use will be tolerated and to what extent. The 1996 Controlled Drugs and Substances Act (Government of Canada, 2015a) contains eight schedules, each including a list of specific psychoactive substances. Controlled substances are those that are listed in schedules I–V. It is an offence for anyone, except as authorized under the Regulations, to possess any of the substances that are listed in schedules I–III or obtain substances found in schedules I–IV. Those whose choices contradict these exclusions face the reality that their drug-taking behaviours may result in criminal charges. However, First Nations, Inuit, and Metis peoples, individuals with mental health conditions, those living in poverty, the homeless, immigrants, and visible minority groups who are disproportionately marginalized and oppressed are more likely to face incarceration as a result of being involved with drug use (Fazel & Danesh, 2002).

Also operating within this context are many formal and informal committees, coalitions, and networks working to effect positive drug policy changes. External from government, these groups attempt to provide politicians and the public with necessary education on drug policy issues, while advocating for the adoption and implementation of evidence-based drug policies. Among these groups are:

- The Canadian Foundation for Drug Policy (http://www.cfdp.ca)
- Canadian HIV/AIDS Legal Network (http://www.aidslaw.ca)
- The John Howard Society of Canada (http://www.johnhoward.ca)
- Canadian Harm Reduction Network (http://www.canadianharmreduction.com)
- Law Enforcement Against Prohibition (http://www.leap.cc)

Despite the best efforts of these groups, Canadian correctional facilities continue to primarily warehouse some of the poorest, most addicted and drug-affected persons in our country (Singer, 2008).

Drugs and the Correctional System

The Criminal Justice System

Stringent laws, spectacular police drives, vigorous prosecution, and imprisonment of addicts and peddlers have proved not only useless and enormously expensive as means of correcting this evil (prohibition), but they are also unjustifiably and unbelievably cruel in their application to the unfortunate drug victims. Repression has driven this vice underground and produced the narcotic smugglers and supply agents, who have grown wealthy out of this evil practice and who, by devious methods, have stimulated traffic in drugs. Finally, and not the least of the evils associated with repression, the helpless addict has been forced to resort to crime in order to get money for the drug which is absolutely indispensable for his comfortable existence.

    —AUGUST VOLLMER, PRESIDENT OF THE INTERNATIONAL ASSOCIATION
    OF CHIEFS OF POLICE, 1936

To begin a discussion regarding addiction and the criminal justice system, one must first understand the inner workings of the prison system, and accept that, in general, our prisons mirror the most unjust and neglected aspects of society. These aspects are commonly magnified and then hidden behind the costly concrete tombs and barbed wire fences that act more to dehumanize, punish, and disgrace than to treat or rehabilitate. The Canadian prison system is divided into two parts: the provincial system and the federal system, as in Canada there are no municipally operated jails. Within the federal system, men and women are housed for two years or more while those receiving sentences of two years less a day are housed within the provincial correctional system. The provincial system also houses those awaiting trial who have been charged but not yet convicted. In addition, federal inmates may end up in provincial jails if they are on parole and are non-compliant with their parole restrictions.

Different types of facilities exist in each of the two systems and vary in terms of their security levels. Decisions to send inmates to a facility that has a certain security level is based, to some degree, upon the crimes that they have committed, the level of risk that they are perceived to have, their daily behaviour, and the amount of time that they have already spent serving their sentence. Classification and movement from one security level to the next is complicated, and is frequently reviewed during an inmate's sentence.

Drugs in the System

Canada's prohibitionist, criminalization approach to drug use has resulted in the incarceration of thousands of drug users. Canadian national prevalence data reports that 7 out of 10 offenders in the prison system have been involved with both alcohol and drugs at least one year prior to their incarceration (Canadian Centre on Substance Abuse, 2004; Thomas, 2005). Most research on the topic of crime and addiction points to the co-occurrence of drugs, including alcohol, in a substantial proportion of criminal cases, thereby connecting substance use with criminality (Bean 2014; Brochu, Cournoyer, Motiuk, & Pernanen, 1999; McClelland & Teplin, 2001). In one Canadian study it was found that between 40 to 50% of crimes were related to psychoactive substances, and in particular, intoxication at the time that the crime was committed or having committed the crime to obtain alcohol or other drugs (Pernanern, Cousineau, Brochu, & Sun, 2002). Another study of 8,598 federal prison inmates in Canada from 1993 to 1995 found that prisoners typically consumed large amounts of alcohol or illicit drugs at some point in their lives (95.1%), while nearly two-thirds were regular users of alcohol. More significant was the finding that four out of every five prisoners had used illicit drugs at some time in their lives, while just over half reported using psychoactive drugs regularly. Among the study participants, 79% of alcohol users and 77% of drug users stated that they believe that they would not have committed the offence in question had they not been impaired. Cocaine was the drug most commonly reported being used on the day of a crime. According to data collected using the Alcohol Dependence Scale (ADS) and the Drug Abuse Screening Test (DAST), 7% of respondents showed signs of alcohol dependency, 22% showed signs of drug dependency while 6% showed signs of both (Brochu, Cousineau, & Gillet, 2001).

Drug use, drug addiction, and high levels of drug-related morbidity are a reality of the Canadian prison system (Johnson et al., 2012; Lines, 2002). In fact, the prevalence of substance abuse and drug dependence is typically greater than in the general population, particularly among women (Fazel, Bains, & Doll, 2006; Mahoney, 2013; Pollock, 2008). There is not only an abundance of drugs available inside correctional facilities but arguably more drugs per capita than outside prisons.

Drug use and drug trafficking are a major part of prison life. However, securing and using drugs inside prisons remains difficult and complicated for most inmates, due to the high demand for these substances and, of course, the fact that they are prohibited. Therefore, trafficking in drugs has become a significant underground prison economy (Lines, 2002; Mjåland, 2014). The unfortunate reality is that although drugs may come into prisons via open access doors, those through which inmates and visitors may pass in and out, in many cases they are smuggled in by guards, visitors, volunteers, and inmates themselves. Efforts to keep drugs out, including searching visitors and using ion-scanning to detect trace residue of illicit drugs on skin and clothes, have not been overly successful. Detection methods used on prisoners are also problematic. In some cases prisoners have their cells regularly searched for drugs, and some may be subjected to random urinalysis. The threat of random testing means that injection drug use often becomes the method of choice as psychoactive drugs that are injected typically are metabolized faster than other drugs that are swallowed or smoked, particularly cannabis. The threat of random testing therefore translates into some non-injection drug users becoming injection drug users while incarcerated (Lines, 2002; Stöver & Michels, 2010).

Alcohol is also readily available within the prison system. Inmates are often able to make a mixture of fermented fruits and juice, then heating the mixture and hiding it in their cells for later use. As well, prescription drugs obtained from the prison's health care staff, licitly, are often used as a form of self-medication. The immediate emotional and psychological effects of the drugs provide a temporary escape from the negativity that inmates experience. To this end, some inmates may engage in drug use for the first time while imprisoned, while others continue their drug use, carrying their addiction with them from the community.

Inmates who are found to be using substances illicitly are punished and face substantive consequences including loss of prison privileges, higher security classification, and parole plan changes and even revocation. However, attempts to curb drug use in prisons do not address the fact that drugs continue to be used in dangerous ways throughout the correctional system. Historically, the zero tolerance approach to drug use in prison has failed, resulting in a need to access harm reduction tools and programs proven effective in the community (Lines, 2002). Recently, there has been a spate of overdose deaths within Canadian correctional facilities (Borden Colley, 2015; Dempsey, 2015; Hayes, 2015; O'Reilly, 2015). Research has also confirmed a high incidence of accidental deaths caused by overdoses in persons recently released from correctional settings (Binswanger, Blatchford, Mueller, & Stern, 2013; Wakeman et al., 2009).

Prison Subculture

Just as prison tattoos have become deeply enmeshed in prison subculture, so too have drugs and drug use. It is important to understand the power of this subculture over the lives of inmates in all correctional facilities, and in particular over those who are more vulnerable due to their addiction and mental health issues. The subculture that has evolved over time is one that supports and perpetuates violence, racism, homophobia, and classism. For those entering the system, it is often experienced as hostility, oppression, and fear. Exposure to it often results in a phenomenon called "prisonization," which involves taking on in greater or lesser degree the mores, customs, and culture of the penitentiary. This includes learning new values through associations and interactions that one has with other inmates who are already part of a deviant prison subculture. It may result in a severe alteration in one's self-concept, language, demeanor, and overall perspective (Terry, 2003; Zamble & Porporino, 2013).

This has many substantive ramifications for reintegration back into society. Most aspects of prison life that one must adhere to, for reasons related to survival and in order to avoid being preyed upon, are those which are likely to be considered antisocial and atypical within general society. This may include subscribing to racist values through the use of pejorative language, the devaluation of any type of vulnerability, and an overemphasis or effort to show oneself as extremely macho. However, prison subculture has changed drastically over the decades since it was first researched. In the past, it had been understood as having a few basic rules by which one was to abide, as well as several categories of identity into which individuals would fall. At the core of the prisoner's code were unwritten rules, including "...minding ones own business, playing it cool, never informing on another convict, never breaking your word, never showing weakness and communicating with guards as little as possible" (Terry, 2003, p. 64). Demonstrating these values allowed one to be seen as a person with integrity, as someone who was "solid." Prison subculture in the past provided a distinct hierarchy, a unique pattern of speech, and a variety of social roles. Prisoners were in charge of the prison, did most of the work, and often were left alone by prison staff. It also gave inmates a sense of self-respect (Terry, 2003).

Presently, prison subculture appears to be less concrete and static and much more fluid and dynamic. It differs from one geographic area to the next and from prison to prison. Claims have been made that prison subculture has been negatively impacted by the role of drugs and drug use, as people tend not to stay honest or "solid" when they are engaged in drug-seeking behaviours. They also tend to break other unspoken rules associated with doing one's own time and not bothering other inmates (Crewe, 2005). As well overcrowding, increased sentence durations, ethnically based gangs, and younger inmates rooted in the informal economy have led to the emergence of a different subculture (Wacquant, 2002; Zamble, & Porporino, 2013).

Correctional Service Canada's Perspective

Federally, Correctional Service Canada (CSC) has been very clear about their stance regarding drugs. There is a zero tolerance for drugs and drug use within the federal criminal justice system, with harm reduction not even having been mentioned in *The Transformation of Federal Corrections for Women* (2008a), a document summarizing long-term strategic directions and goals. The initiative itself was the result of the findings and recommendations set out by an independent Blue Ribbon panel appointed in April of 2007 by then Minister Stockwell Day. The Chair of the Panel, Rob Sampson, was the former Ontario Minister of Correctional Services who had been forced to resign his position due to a leak of confidential information during his time as Minister. During his brief tenure Ontario became the first province to open a privately run prison. This first privatized Canadian prison has since been handed back to the province following the decision not to renew the contract that had been granted to an American prison corporation.

Within the document, eliminating drugs from prisons is the second of five areas of concentration. Recommendations focus upon strengthening CSC's interdiction initiatives on all fronts with a focus on some "quick wins," or immediate successes that can be achieved, providing energy and support for the remaining goals within the proposal. As far as eliminating drugs from prison is concerned, it is recommended that Correctional Service Canada works towards increasing consistency at principal entrance, implementing scheduled visits, developing a national visitors database, and increasing the number of Security Intelligence Officers and the detector dog teams across the country (Correctional Service Canada, 2008b).

The Ongoing Criminalization of Addiction

Rates of Incarceration

Junkies and drug pushers don't belong near children and families. They should be in rehab or behind bars. The Conservative Government will clean up drug crime.

—NATIONAL CAMPAIGN FLYER, JAMES BEZAN, MP, SEPTEMBER 2008

Seven years later and on the cusp of another federal election, the ongoing belief in addicts as criminals was again evident with the introduction in 2015 of the Royal Assent of Bill C-12, the *Drug-Free Prisons Act*, by the Honourable Steven Blaney, Minister of Public Safety and Emergency Preparedness. This bill amended the Conditional and Corrections Release Act to provide the Parole Board of Canada (PBC) with explicit legislative tools to reconsider the release of criminals who have been granted parole, but refused or failed a drug test prior to being released in the community (Government of Canada, 2015b).

While Canadian politicians and the media regularly talk about our country as being soft on crime, particularly during elections, describing our prison system as one that is humane and progressive, the reality is that Canadian prisons can be barbaric. Despite decreasing crime rates, with Canada's crime rate reaching its lowest point in 25 years in 2006, Canada's incarceration rate remains similar to other Organisation for Economic Co-operation and Development (OECD) nations (Contenta & Rankin, 2008; Statistics Canada, 2014).

While drug offences constitute a major proportion of all criminal offences in Canada, most of the criminal charges that are handed down each year are the result of actions that took place due to drug-seeking behaviours. This has resulted in primarily property offences which seem unavoidable as long as drugs are illegal, since those who use illicit drugs will steal and re-sell items to supplement their income in order to allow for the purchase of substances made costly because they are illegal. When people with addiction issues cannot obtain their substances legally, they will do what they have to in order to obtain them illegally, and this often entails resorting to crime (Parnenon, Cousineau, Brochu, & Sun, 2002). However, in 2010-2011, it was impaired driving that accounted for more convictions (12%) than drug-related offences (4%), though theft types of offences, including theft of a motor vehicle, which can be associated with drug use, resulted in 11% convicted cases (Statistics Canada, 2014).

Historically, there has been the appearance of a political drive to ensure that the number of drug charges continues to be laid, despite the plethora of research that exists to show that treatment rather than incarceration is the best option for those dealing with addiction issues (Drug Rehab Referral, 2008). Under the Harper government mandatory minimum sentencing practices were introduced despite the fact that they were proven to be failures in other jurisdictions (Canadian HIV/AIDS Legal Network, 2006). The legislation took away the discretion judges had when determining sentences for drug-related offences.

Discriminatory Impacts of Drug Charging and Over-Incarceration

Generally, individuals in marginalized groups who end up in custody tend to have higher rates of illiteracy, unemployment, past abuse, drug and alcohol addiction, mental illness, poverty, and homelessness than the general population. Some may also come from backgrounds that involve family violence, have been socially isolated, lack self-esteem, and feel powerless and hopeless.

Just as marginalized groups are overrepresented in the populations that struggle most often with addiction, so too are they overrepresented in both the provincial and federal correctional systems. Large numbers of inmates from racialized groups and other minority populations, including those with mental health issues and those who are homeless, are found in every jail and detention centre across the country. Canadian prisons are populated with disproportionately high percentages of First Nations people relative to the general population. Overall Indigenous peoples account for only 4% of the Canadian population, but represent 23.2% of the incarcerated federal population, an increase of 56.2% from 2000-2001. In 2013 there were approximately 3,400 Aboriginal offenders in federal penitentiaries, 71% First Nation, 24% Metis, and 5% Inuit. At Stony Mountain Institution in Manitoba, 389 out of 596 inmates, 65.3% of the population, were Indigenous; at Saskatchewan Penitentiary, 63.9%; at the Regional Psychiatric Centre in Saskatoon, 55.7%; and at the Edmonton Institution for Women, 56.0% of the population was First Nations, Metis, or Inuit (Government of Canada, 2013).

However, it is women that account for the fastest-growing prison population world-wide. Although population-forecasting models are still under development for this group, numbers of women in custody are expected to continue to increase (Correctional Service Canada, 2008b; Pollock, 2008). Women who go to jail are usually racialized, poor, and face mental health issues. Most women in prison are seen as having high needs and to be of "higher risk" than their male counterparts. It is much more costly to incarcerate women than men, and the required specialized programs needed by this population are often absent in correctional facilities. More than half of the offences that federally sentenced women are convicted of are non-violent, property, and drug offences with 43% of federally sentenced women having substance abuse or addiction concerns and 69% indicating that drug and/or alcohol use played a major role in their criminalization (Canadian Association of Elizabeth Fry Societies, 2004; Pollock, 2008).

The Canadian Association of Elizabeth Fry Societies (2004) reported that First Nations women make up about 29% of the federally sentenced women in Canada, with 85% of criminalized First Nations women indicating that they used substances on the day of the offence for which they were incarcerated. Some of these women discussed their substance abuse as a method of self-medication. They also often disclosed personal pain with interpersonal relationships as the source of their difficulties. Abusive families and violent relationships were also strong themes in their lives.

Poverty, Addiction, and Criminal Justice

Poverty is linked not only to drugs and drug addiction, but also to crime and criminal behaviour. Simply, poor people are more likely to be involved in the criminal justice system and be incarcerated. Crime and incarceration further contributes to poverty, while broader social issues are associated with both poverty and decreased community safety across the province.

Research has consistently shown a link between poverty and violent crime, as well as between poverty and youth crime. In addition, strong correlations have been shown in the literature between income disparity and all types of criminal behaviour. The experience of the John Howard Society (2006) affiliates across Ontario also shows that poverty decreases a person's ability to avoid incarceration or be diverted from the criminal justice system earlier on in the process. For example, poverty decreases one's capacity to pay fines, provide financial restitution, or meet bail conditions.

Social science research has also long shown that poverty, crime, and other social issues are intimately related. Poverty contributes to crime by creating need (Reiman, 1990). While not all inmates commit crimes to be able to obtain drugs, generally, the price of the drug compared to a user's income and the level of the user's dependence would be a factor in these instances. Drug users who become imprisoned generally did not make enough money to be able to pay for the amount of substances that they required due to their addiction, and so they found other illegal means to obtain them. In fact, while some criminality is associated with drug addiction, most of the crimes are of an acquisitive nature (Brochu, Cousineau, & Gillet, 2001; Bukten et al., 2011). The fact that so many inmates are impoverished prior to incarceration suggests that prisons play a role in ensuring the effectiveness of drugs in controlling the poor. The frequent arrest of low-level drug dealers and users and the various tactics used to accomplish this goal contribute to the further immiseration and control of the poor (Singer, 2008).

Treatment Issues

Barriers to Treatment

Since virtually the inception of the modern criminal justice system, a persistent response to the question of what to do with lawbreakers has been to change them into law-abiders—that is, to rehabilitate them.

—DE BEAUMONT AND DE TOCQUEVILLE 1964 [1833]

The delivery of substance abuse programs for incarcerated persons in Canada has historically been impeded by issues of institutional/correctional security and enforcement that have taken priority over any rehabilitative treatment for offenders. While imprisonment provides an excellent opportunity for marginalized populations to engage with treatment services, there is a gross lack of these available to inmates across Canada (Fazal, Bains, & Doll, 2006). Government employees throughout the correctional system, as well as staff at community agencies, may often share an intention to deliver substance abuse programs; however, it is challenging to deliver programs that meet the specific requirements of the prisoner and ex-prisoner population, as funding is lacking, with money for security far outweighing money for treatment and being of greater priority. While treatment advocates acknowledge that security for some persons is important, based upon histories that include causing extreme physical harm to others, the value of treatment for all those charged with criminal offences, particularly those with histories of violent assaults on vulnerable members of our society including children, is even more imperative.

The addiction treatment programming that does exist in our correctional facilities is most often targeted only at those who have been sentenced. In Canada, this affords assistance to only a minority of inmates since the majority of prisoners are in fact on remand (Public Health Agency of Canada, 2012). For those dealing with an addiction problem, there are minimal services available, if any, and the services that are provided are often abstinence based, despite the confirmed value of harm reduction approaches with this population (Fazel, Bains, & Doll, 2006; Leukefelt, Tims, & Farabee, 2002).

Of utmost importance when delivering a successful program to individuals in custody is the ability to work with the correctional staff and prison administration to elicit their support. This is often taxing, especially at the onset of any new program, as once again, the focus is upon security. Social workers and other helping professionals working in the criminal justice system are frequently perceived as being "bleeding hearts," "naive" or "do-gooders." However, more often than not, once the correctional staff identify that the programs are being delivered professionally, and that they do make a difference in terms of improving the behaviours of prisoners, they tend to become more supportive (Early, 1996).

Barriers in delivering programs in correctional institutions once staff are onside, however, continue. Program delivery is frequently interrupted by security issues, which lead to periods during which community representatives are not permitted into the institutions and all visits are cancelled. These periods are referred to as lockdowns. Such program cancellations also include those offered through in-house programs. It is not unheard of for a community professional anywhere in Canada to call an institution prior to leaving their office to be advised that it is open for programming only to arrive to find it has just been locked down due to a security issue. Community practitioners who have not experienced these types of obstacles may at first feel that they are overwhelming (Yates & Rowdy, 2001). However, because of the obvious need for treatment and support it is imperative to the wellness of those incarcerated and those within the community that they persevere. Nearly all of these individuals will be released at some point and in order for them to achieve any measure of success and to reduce any harm to the community, they must learn the skills necessary to make positive changes. However, even with appropriate treatment during custody, a person's success is reduced without proper community supports in place upon release. Without proper housing, employment, and prosocial connections, the risks for reoffending are increased (Andrews & Bonta, 2006; Birgden & Grant, 2010).

Another treatment barrier that occurs within the prison system relates to the general ill health within the inmate population. Although prisoners are generally more likely to have access to ongoing medical treatment, the level of service is typically less than adequate. This is of grave concern for many reasons including the fact that drug use is associated with death from drug overdose, complications arising from HIV, hepatitis C, and other communicable pathogens. A variety of other health problems are also associated with excessive drug use including abscesses, infections, poor nutrition and malnourishment, endocarditic problems, and adverse drug interactions (Csiernik, 2014; Lines, 2002).

The health care of prisoners is substandard when compared to health care in the community. The Public Health Agency of Canada reported that in 2008 almost 2% of the federal prison population were living with HIV, and another 30% were known to be infected with hepatitis (Public Health Agency of Canada, 2012). During their lifetime 95.1% of male federal inmates consumed alcohol and 80.5% had used at least alcohol, cannabis, and cocaine on a daily or weekly basis (Brochu et al., 2001). Consumption of alcohol and drugs during incarceration is higher among men than women with length of incarceration, security level, pre-incarceration drug use, and prior drug use all being risk factors associated with substance use during their incarceration (Plourde, Brochu, Gendron, & Brunelle, 2012).

The cutback in many short-term residential community treatment programs from 28 to 21 days has led to decreased prison visitation and treatment. Qualifying criteria for such programs now generally excludes individuals on remand. Most centres simply do not have the resources to visit prisoners to provide assessments, especially as many do not show up for treatment upon release. It is also no longer financially feasible for treatment providers to leave beds vacant in case an individual is granted bail. However, the exclusion of treatment planning is a serious threat to community reintegration efforts of individuals and to the distribution of justice, since the submission of an addiction treatment plan to the courts can alter sentencing outcomes (Sims, 2005).

Providing Assistance in Remand

Through the provision of therapeutic intervention, criminal justice agencies have a unique opportunity to identify and rehabilitate, or habilitate, drug-involved prisoners or ex-prisoners who are likely, if untreated, to return to personally and socially destructive patterns of drug use and criminal activity following release from prison. Research has indicated that focused rehabilitation-oriented treatment services can lead to favourable outcomes following incarceration (Andrews et al., 1990; Cullen & Gendrou, 2000; Gendreau, Little, & Goggin, 1996; Leukfelt, Tims, & Farabee, 2002). Traditionally the most effective and efficient method to deliver substance abuse programs to those in custody are in group settings (Sims, 2005). On average, group sessions for those in remand run a standard 60 minutes, and include as many prisoners as possible to ensure time is used to benefit a number of people. Visual aids such as DVDs that focus on recovery and treatment are used for working with this population due to time constraints.

Treatment assessments can be completed more easily with those who have been sentenced. Since their criminal matter has already been before the courts, the individual can discuss in a more open manner the details of the crime and any involvement with substance use as there is no fear of further sanction. However, for those held in remand, counsellors are limited in the specific questions they can ask the individual as their trial dates are pending and anything they say could be held against them in court. As well, those being held on remand are only eligible for programs offered by external community providers. These are mostly peer support programs such as Alcoholics Anonymous and related 12-step groups, though in some jurisdictions agencies such as the John Howard or Elizabeth Fry societies may offer additional programming options. Many treatment programs have ceased to accept referrals from those with outstanding charges because of the inability to fully engage with this population pending court outcomes.

Also, when interviewing persons in remand, counsellors need to caution their clients regarding disclosures in the event that the client pleads not guilty. If open dialogue was to be encouraged regarding a charge still before the courts, an individual may say something that could put the counsellor in a position to have to testify against the client. For example, if the person being interviewed were to tell the counsellor that he or she did indeed commit the crime but is pleading not guilty to the charge, the professional could be called to testify against the individual. Therefore, in remand, helping professionals should not be asking for the details of the crime. These matters should be left to judges and lawyers. In these instances, the role of the counsellor should be only to discuss a treatment plan for addiction.

Time frames available to deliver programs are also typically minimal. Due to over-crowding, multiple court appearances, and court delays, prisoners are frequently transferred from one institution to another while being held in remand. Therefore, any treatment time with these individuals must be maximized and well structured in order to share as many therapeutic tools and as much resource information as possible.

As well, it is not recommended to offer programs to individuals in remand that might include psychotherapy or any therapy that would surface emotional discomfort. To engage in treatment that is intensive and could cause extreme emotions should be conducted in a safe environment with significant support. To do otherwise would be negligent as these individuals have nowhere to process these emotions after these sessions end, as they return to their living units in the prison where there are no counsellors (Yates & Rawlings, 2001).

Provincial Correctional Programs

Once provincial inmates are sentenced they are classified in order to determine at which correctional centre they should serve their sentence. Inmate classification is a continuous process that starts on admission and concludes when the individual's sentence has been completed. Classification officers at each remand and correctional centre are employed to complete these assessments. The information required to complete this process include previous correctional records; judicial reasons for the sentence; clinical reports; previous classification documents; Crown briefs; police synopses; and a release summary from the last known institution.

Should classification and the prisoner both agree that treatment would be the best intervention there are various treatment centres available within most provincial systems. In Ontario the criteria is that any prisoner may be considered for admission to one of these facilities, though it is preferable that he/she has a sentence of at least 16 months and/or a minimum of four to six months remaining in sentence. This provides for sufficient time for adjustment to the treatment environments (Ontario Ministry of Safety and Correctional Services, 2015).

Institution-based treatment programs tend to be closed therapeutic environments for prisoners who have been sentenced to receive psychotherapy and cognitive-behavioural treatment from educated professionals. The recognition of the fact that so many prisoners have substance abuse issues has meant several innovations in terms of harm reduction practices from needle exchange programs to methadone maintenance. However, these are in direct contrast to the options available within the federal system.

Ideally, any treatment program should begin with an extensive assessment that determines the individual's specific needs and individual objectives. It is during this process that issues such as concurrent disorders would also be identified to determine what other services are required to enhance treatment outcomes. A risk assessment tool is included to determine specific risk factors for the individual that require attention (Leukefelt, Tims, & Farabee, 2002).

The best models of delivery for treatment programs for this population, both during custody and in the community, are those that are based upon relapse prevention principles, and take place in a group setting (Marques & Formingoni, 2001). Such pro-grams provide individuals with the opportunity to identify their own high-risk cycles and behaviours (Sims, 2005). Relapse prevention is a cognitive-behavioural program in which the prisoner or ex-prisoner practices alternative responses to high-risk situations such as refusing a drink and planning, for example, an alternative activity for Saturday night. The relapse prevention model has considerable appeal and research on its effectiveness is promising. Relapse prevention techniques can reduce high-risk behaviours associated with this population. The objective of this approach is to assist the individual to identify behaviours, thoughts, feelings, people, places, and things that lead to substance abuse, otherwise known as triggers. They are encouraged and assisted to find alternative methods of dealing with these triggers that have a positive outcome. A meta-analysis of 26 studies (n=9,504) found relapse prevention strategies generally effective for alcohol problems (Irvin, Bowers, Dunn, & Want, 1999). It has become an essential component in treatment not only for addiction behaviours but also for sexual deviance (Hanson, 1996; Marlatt & Donovan, 2005; McCrady, 2000; Ward & Hudson, 1996) and general offending (Andrews & Bonta, 2006; Dowden, Antonowicz, & Andrews, 2003).

Anger is the emotion that substance-abusing prisoners and ex-prisoners are most often triggered by, which turns to aggression, often leading to relapse. This is the emo-tion that prisoners/ex-prisoners are often the most comfortable expressing, albeit in a negative manner. That is why any program working with prisoners and ex-prisoners should also include sessions that focus specifically on anger management strategies and stress reduction (Leukefelt, Tims, & Farabee, 2002).

Community Treatment

One of the major obstacles that newly released prisoners face is the stigma, both real and perceived, that is directed towards them. Being released can entail a severe sense of alienation (Terry, 2003). Readjusting to independence in the community is especially challenging for this population since incarceration affords few opportunities to be able to grow in a self-reliant, adult way. When it comes to issues of addiction and recovery, the issue of control is integral. However, individuals cannot learn to control themselves responsibly if they have spent years having every aspect of their lives, including the hour they wake; the number of minutes they wash; the time and content of eating, working, and exercising; and the hour at which lights go out regulated by someone else (Reiman, 1990).

Few addiction-specific residential programs take referrals from prisoners while they are in custody, as historically this population does not attend for scheduled treatment upon release and it is difficult for treatment centres to leave treatment beds open as they are in demand by other people who are both ready and available. As well, it has been identified by the John Howard Society of Toronto's addiction counsellors that another reason many recently released inmates do not pursue treatment is that almost all residential programs are abstinence based. Individuals who do follow-up with a residential treatment plan are often mandated to attend and thus are more motivated to be abstinent. While in custody, an individual may have this goal of abstinence in mind. However, once released, if they begin to use again, they would receive greater benefit from a harm reduction program (Leukefelt, Tims, & Farabee, 2002).

While abstinence may be the ultimate goal, not every inmate returning to the community may be able to achieve this goal and thus harm reduction becomes a viable alternative to minimize the risk of reoffending due to excessive or uncontrolled substance use. This approach can assist in minimizing risk as the individual is monitoring their intake of substances and doing so by accessing various harm reduction tools, which may include the use of clean needles and safe use of crack kits. Methods of tapering and reducing substances used are frequently addressed in harm reduction practice with the substance user (Thomas, 2005). Another initiative being strongly advocated for is the wider availability of naloxone, an opioid antagonist that can reverse overdoses long enough to be able to keep someone alive until emergency services can arrive. This would include teaching high-risk inmates how to use naloxone to prevent overdoses upon release (Municipal Drug Strategy Coordinator's Network of Ontario, 2015; Wakeman et al., 2009).

It has also been demonstrated that this population can benefit from being taught mindfulness meditation. This approach has proven useful to individuals in community treatment programs and also to those still in custody. The central idea is that 15 minutes of meditation before a group session calms the mind and assists the individual to be present and in the moment. Being present is extremely difficult for many chemically dependent people as there is a tendency to externalize and compartmentalize, making it difficult for them to focus and fully benefit from the treatment experience (Insight Prison Project, 2008). Since these persons used substances to escape uncomfortable feelings, strategies such as meditation can help them to relax. "Mindfulness practice will not by itself cool the addiction-heated mind, but, addicted or not, it is an invaluable adjunct to whatever else we do. It's a way of working with the most immediate environment, the internal one" (Mate, 2008, p. 351). Many counsellors working with this population acknowledge that spending this quiet time at the beginning of each session is well worth every minute, as afterwards the participation level is much more rich and engaging. In addition, the prison environment brings with it constant noise and tension, so to have 15 minutes of absolute quiet time to relax is invaluable. This tool, once learned, can also help individuals to deal with other stressful situations, including coping with daily custodial incapacitation (Insight Prison Project, 2008).

Drug Treatment Court

Drug treatment courts have been implemented as a diversion measure for those who have come into conflict with the law primarily due to their drug use. Participation can result in allowing an individual who would normally be sentenced to custody to remain in the community to receive formal treatment. The use of community sanctions is supported by evidence-based research findings that identify best practices in the areas of reducing recidivism.

Diversion is a pre-trial procedure where crown attorneys can, at their discretion, decide not to prosecute when the charge is minor and an illness or addiction is determined as the underlying cause of offence. Instead, the accused person is referred to appropriate mental health or addiction services in the community, professional treatment, and support to reduce the chances of reoffending (Canadian Mental Health Association, 2008).

The first Mental Health Court in Canada was initiated in Toronto, Ontario, on May 11, 1998 (Psychiatric Patients Advocate Office, 2003). This court and those that followed it were put in place to address the fact that Canadian prisons and penitentiaries are ill equipped to handle the growing number of prisoners with serious mental illnesses. The recently released Correctional Investigator's Report, studying mental health and illness of persons who are under the supervision of the Correctional Service Canada, suggests that our prisons have become "warehouses" for the mentally ill due, in part, to funding cuts and closures in community psychiatric facilities.

Advocates claim that this is an inhumane and unsafe way to care for people with mental illnesses, particularly for those who have been charged with relatively minor, non-violent crimes due to the limited availability or absence of treatment or support in the community. Therefore, there continues to be significant support for increases in treatment availability for this population, both within the community and within government. This has been reflected in funding increases over the past few years specifically for mental health and justice. However, these initiatives continue to fall short of being able to accommodate all those in need.

Likewise, drug treatment courts also exist as diversion options. They provide an alternative to incarceration and aim to reduce crimes committed as a result of substance dependency through court-monitored/mandated treatment and community service support for people with drug addictions (Department of Justice Canada, 2008). Beginning with the Dade County Florida program in June 1989 (Finn & Newlyn, 1993), the current generation of treatment drug courts has established an important presence in the criminal justice system. In many jurisdictions, drug courts have become the preferred mechanism for linking drug- or alcohol-involved persons in conflict with the law to community-based treatment and related clinical interventions to reduce recidivism (Somers, Rezansoff, & Moniruzzaman, 2014; Leukefelt, Tims, & Farabee, 2002; Mitchell, Wilson, Eggers, & MacKenzie, 2012; Somers et al., 2012).

Drug treatment court participants attend individual and group counselling sessions, receive appropriate medical attention such as methadone treatment, and are subjected to random urine screens, all while living in the community. To qualify for these programs individuals must be addicted to a substance and have been charged with one or more of the following offences: possession, trafficking of small quantities of crack/cocaine or heroin, property offences that they have committed in order to support their drug use, or prostitution-related crimes.

There are now drug treatment courts across Canada including Vancouver, Edmonton, Calgary, Regina, Winnipeg, London, Guelph, Hamilton, Toronto, Oshawa, Ottawa, Montreal, Quebec City, and Kentville, Nova Scotia. The principles and objectives of these courts are to:

- increase public safety,
- help participants reduce or eliminate drug use,
- help participants reduce or eliminate criminal behaviour,
- help reunite participants with their families, and
- help participants become productive members of society and experience overall improvements in personal well-being (Barnes, 2009).

Only recently has support for the effectiveness of these programs begun to emerge. Gliksman and colleagues (2003) found that 95.8% of the drug treatment court's graduates attributed overcoming their addiction directly to participating in the program and 59.5% who did not complete the program still acknowledged that the program helped them decrease their substance use. In meta-analyses of 66 drug treatment courts in Canada, the United States, and Australia it was found that the courts were 14% more effective in reducing recidivism, and 57% of the participants versus 43% of the comparison group were not charged with a subsequent criminal offence during follow-up (Latimer, Morton-Bourgon, & Chretien, 2006).

The key to the success for drug treatment court participants is that they must be honest with the judge in reference to their using activities. They need to advise the court as to whether or not they have been using. If they advise they have not been using in court, yet test positive in a urine screen, they will likely be reincarcerated and re-evaluated. If while in the program individuals commit another offence, they would also be reincarcerated. To be eligible, individuals in the program cannot have charges of violence on their records.

Many drug court participants have long-term histories of chemical abuse with previous unsuccessful attempts at recovery. Many participants have been frequently in conflict with the law though rarely involved with a useful treatment program. This court intervention provides a new opportunity to be successful. However, for some, obstacles such as homelessness and poverty, associated with the chronic nature of the addiction, preclude success through a drug court program. These individuals thus require more formalized and structured 24-hour community support services.

Significant to the success of all diversion programs, including mental health and drug treatment, is the experience of court worker staff and legal representatives to ensure that participants have access to the most accurate assessments of their treatment needs. In addition, it is important that throughout these processes of utilizing community options that every effort is made to ensure that the safety of the community is the priority in order to decrease the risk of incarceration and further charges.

Conclusion

The more vulnerable our clients, the more judicious we must be. Along with all of their other issues, those suffering with addictions also struggle with the judgments of society and their own fragility. Therefore, this group needs ethical, competent advocates working on their behalf. Further, experience suggests that the best course of action to address oppression, drug use, and the criminal justice system should be a government focus upon what will reduce the costs of crime in the long-term, rather than on immediate and short-sighted societal fears and moral outrage. The judgment of the Honourable Justice Barry Stuart regarding Marcellus Jacob that opened this chapter speaks to needing both compassion and concern and for offenders to take responsibility for their criminal behaviours. Simultaneously, practices, policies, legislation, and political will must allow for the creation of initiatives that will educate the community on the root causes of crime including poverty, income disparity, and unemployment.

In addition, other methods of reducing prison overcrowding should be explored. Possible solutions may include the provision of affordable housing options and housing supports; the implementation of programs/services/processes that encourage family involvement with prisoners, especially those who use substances; and allowing for appropriate resources to improve high-risk communities where many who have addiction problems will end up in custody and are likely to return. Encouragement and support is necessary for the utilization of the best practices that have been identified by research and that indicate they will actually reduce crime. Such initiatives should include a variety of treatment models, increased access to addiction and mental health screening, combined with treatment throughout the criminal justice system. Our governments must take on a positive leadership role towards a fair, humane, research-based and balanced approach to the justice system. To do so would reduce harm, racism, oppression, crime, and create safer communities and a more just society.

NOTE

1. *Regina* v. *Marcellus Norman Jacob* 2002, YKTC 15 at paras, 7 and 8.

REFERENCES

Andrews, D.A., & Bonta, J. (2006). *The psychology of criminal conduct* (4th ed.). Albany, NY: Matthew Bender & Company.

Andrews, D.A., Zinger, I., Hoge, R.D., Bonta, J., Gendreau, P., & Cullen, F.T. (1990). Does correctional treatment work? A clinically relevant and psychologically informed meta-analysis. *Criminology, 28*(3), 369–404.

Barnes, K. (2009). *Drug treatment courts: Basic principles.* Presented at the Canadian Criminal Justice Association Conference, Halifax, Nova Scotia. Retrieved from http://www.ccja-acjp.ca/cong2009/kofi-barnes.ppt

Bean, P. (2014). *Drugs and crime.* New York: Routledge.

Binswanger, I., Blatchford, P., Mueller, S., & Stern, M. (2013). Mortality after prison release: Opioid overdose and other causes of death, risk factors, and time trends from 1999 to 2009. *Annals of Internal Medicine, 159*(9), 592–600.

Birgden, A., & Grant, L. (2010). Establishing a compulsory drug treatment prison: Therapeutic policy, principles, and practices in addressing offender rights and rehabilitation. *International Journal of Law and Psychiatry, 33*(5), 341–349.

Borden Colley, S. (2015). Mother suing over son's death in jail. Retrieved from http://thechronicleherald.ca/metro/1291989-mother-suing-over-son%E2%80%99s-death-in-jail

Brochu, S., Cournoyer, L.G., Motiuk, L., & Pernanen, K. (1999). Drugs, alcohol, and crime: Patterns among Canadian federal inmates. *Bulletin on Narcotics, 51*(1 & 2), 57–73.

Brochu, S., Cousineau, M., & Gillet, M. (2001). Drugs, alcohol, and criminal behaviors: A profile of inmates in Canadian federal institutions. *Forum on Corrections Research: Focus on Alcohol and Drugs, 13*(3), 20–24.

Brochu, S., Cousineau, M., & Gillet, M., Cournoyer, L.G., Pernanen, K., & Motiuk, L. (2001). Les drogues, l'alcool et la criminalite: profil des detenus federaux canadiens. *Forum, 13*(3), 22–26.

Bukten, A., Skurtveit, S., Stangeland, P., Gossop, M., Willersrud, A.B., Waal, H., ... Clausen, T. (2011). Criminal convictions among dependent heroin users during a 3-year period prior to opioid maintenance treatment: A longitudinal national cohort study. *Journal of Substance Abuse Treatment, 41*(4), 407–414.

Canadian Association of Elizabeth Fry Societies. (2004). Human and fiscal costs of prison from the DAWN Ontario's issue based voter education and awareness campaign. Retrieved from http://dawn.thot.net/election2004/issues32.htm

Canadian Centre on Substance Abuse. (2004). *Substance abuse in corrections.* Ottawa, ON: Canadian Centre on Substance Abuse.

Canadian HIV/AIDS Legal Network. (2006). *Mandatory minimum sentences for drug offences: Why everyone loses.* Ottawa, ON: Canadian HIV/AIDS Legal Network.

Canadian Mental Health Association. (2008). *Mental health courts.* Retrieved from http://www.cmha-lg.ca/Court

Contenta, S., & Rankin, J. (2008, July 20). Politicians can't resist being tough on crime. *Toronto Star.*

Correctional Service Canada. (2008a). *The transformation of federal corrections for women.* Ottawa, ON: Correctional Service Canada.

Correctional Service of Canada. (2008b). *The changing federal offenders population: Profiles and forecasts.* Ottawa, ON: Correctional Service Canada.

Crewe, B. (2005). Prisoner society in the era of hard drugs. *Punishment and Society, 7*(4), 457–481.

Csiernik, R. (2014). *Just say know: A counsellor's guide to psychoactive drugs.* Toronto, ON: Canadian Scholars' Press.

Cullen, F.T., & Gendrou, P. (2000). Assessing correctional rehabilitation: Policy, practice and prospects. *Criminal Justice, 3*, 109–175.

de Beaumont, G., & de Tocqueville, A. [1833] 1964. *On the penitentiary system in the United States and its application in France*. Reprint. Carbondale: Southern Illinois University Press.

Dempsey, A. (2015, February 17). Toronto superjail sees second inmate death in a week. *Toronto Star*. Retrieved from http://www.thestar.com/news/crime/2015/02/17/toronto-superjail-sees-second-inmate-death-in-a-week.html

Department of Justice Canada. (2008). *Expanding drug treatment courts in Canada*. Retrieved from http://www.justice.gc.ca/eng/news-nouv/nr-cp/2005/doc_31552.html

Dowden, C., Antonowicz, D., & Andrews D.A., (2003). The effectiveness of relapse prevention with offenders: A meta-analysis. *International Journal of Offenders Therapy and Comparative Criminology, 47*(5), 516–528.

Drug Rehab Referral. (2008). *Prison is not a drug treatment centre: It might be the opposite*. Retrieved from http://blog.drugrehabreferral.com/views/2008/07/21/prison-is-not-a-drug-addction-treatment-centre-it-might-be-the-opposite

Early, K.E. (1996). *Drug treatment behind bars: Prison based strategies for change*. Washington, DC: Library of Congress.

Fazel, S., Bains, P., & Doll, H. (2006). Substance abuse and dependence in prisoners: A systematic review. *Addiction, 101*(2), 181–191.

Fazel, S., & Danesh, J. (2002). Serious mental disorder in 23,000 prisoners: A systemic review of 62 surveys. *Lancet, 359*(9306), 545–550.

Finn, P., & Newlyn, A. (1993). *Miami's "drug court": A different approach*. Washington, DC: National Institute of Justice.

Gendreau, P., Little, T., & Goggin, C. (1996). A meta-analysis of the predictors of adult offender recidivism: What works! *Criminology, 34*(4), 575–607.

Gliksman, L., Newton-Taylor, B., Greenaway, M., Patra, J., & Samant, D. (2003). *Toronto drug treatment court evaluation project: 2003 interim evaluation report*. Toronto, ON: Centre for Addiction and Mental Health.

Government of Canada. (2013). *Aboriginal offenders: A critical situation*. Ottawa, ON: Office of the Correctional Investigator.

Government of Canada. (2015a). *Controlled Drugs and Substances Act (S.C. 1996, c. 19)*. Retrieved from http://laws-lois.justice.gc.ca/eng/acts/C-38.8

Government of Canada. (2015b). *Harper government highlights Royal Assent of the Drug-Free Prisons Act*. Retrieved from http://news.gc.ca/web/article-en.do?mthd=index&crtr.page=1&nid=988999&_ga=1.7800754.1068561201.1389620396

Hanson, R.K. (1996). Evaluating the contribution of relapse prevention theory to the treatment of sex offenders. *Sexual Abuse: A Journal of Research and Treatment, 8*(3), 201–208.

Hayes, M., (2015, May 20). Inmate found dead in Barton St. jail cell. *Hamilton Spectator*. Retrieved from http://www.thespec.com/news-story/5633191-inmate-found-dead-in-barton-st-jail-cell

Insight Prison Project. (2008). *Mindful meditation*. Retrieved from http://www.insightprisonproject.org

Irvin, J.E., Bowers, C.A., Dunn, M.E., & Want, M.C. (1999). Efficacy of relapse prevention: A meta-analytic review. *Journal of Consulting and Clinical Psychology, 67*(4), 563–570.

John Howard Society of Ontario. (2006). *First report to the board: The super jails in Ontario*. Toronto, ON: John Howard Society.

Johnson, S., MacDonald, S.F., Cheverie, M., Myrick, C., & Fischer, B. (2012). Prevalence and trends of non-medical opioid and other drug use histories among federal correctional inmates in methadone maintenance treatment in Canada. *Drug and Alcohol Dependence, 124*(1–2), 172–176.

Latimer, J., Morton-Bourgon, K., & Chretien, J. (2006). *A meta-analytic examination of drug treatment courts: Do they reduce recidivism?* Ottawa, ON: Department of Justice. Retrieved from http://www.justice.gc.ca/eng/rp-pr/csj-sjc/jsp-sjp/rr06_7/index.html

Leukefelt, C.G., Tims, F., & Farabee, D. (2002). *Treatment of drug offenders, policies and issues.* New York: Springer Publishing.

Lines, R. (2002). A *guide to creating successful community-based HIV/AIDS programs for prisoners.* Toronto, ON: Prisoner's HIV/AIDS Support Action Network.

Mahoney, T.H. (2013). *Women and the criminal justice system.* Statistics Canada. Retrieved from http://www.statcan.gc.ca/pub/89-503-x/2010001/article/11416-eng.htm.

Marlatt, A.G., & Donovan, D.M. (2005). *Relapse prevention: Maintenance strategies in the treatment of addictive behaviors.* New York: Guilford Press.

Marques, A.C., & Formingoni, M.L. (2001). Comparison of individual and group cognitive behavioral therapy for alcohol and/or drug dependent patients. *Addiction, 96*(6), 835-846.

Mate, G. (2008). *In the realm of hungry ghosts: Close encounters with addiction.* Toronto, ON: Random House.

McClelland, G., & Teplin, L.A. (2001). Alcohol intoxication and violent crime: Implications for public heath policy. *American Journal on Addictions, 10*(suppl.), 70-85.

McCrady, B.S. (2000). Alcohol use disorders and the Division 12 Task Force of the American Psychological Association. *Psychology of Addictive Behaviors, 14*(3), 267-276.

Mitchell, D., Wilson, O., Eggers, A., & MacKenzie, D. (2012). Drug courts' effects on criminal offending for juvenile and adults. *Campbell Systematic Reviews, 4,* DOI: 10.4073/csr.2012.4

Mjåland, K. (2014). "A culture of sharing": Drug exchange in a Norwegian prison. *Punishment & Society, 16*(3), 336-352.

Municipal Drug Strategy Coordinator's Network of Ontario. (2015). *Prescription for life.* Retrieved from http://www.drugstrategy.ca/uploads/5/3/6/2/53627897/docs_admin-1886313-v1-final_rx_for_life_june_1__2015.pdf

Ontario Ministry of Safety and Correctional Services. (2015). *Inmate information guide for adult institutions.* Retrieved from: http://www.mcscs.jus.gov.on.ca/sites/default/files/content/mcscs/docs/ec167925.pdf

O'Reilly, N. (2015, February 18). Barton jail inmates are overdosing: Who's watching? *Hamilton Spectator.* Retrieved from http://www.thespec.com/news-story/5343112-barton-jail-inmates-are-overdosing-who-s-watching-

Parnanen, K., Cousineau, M., Brochu, S., & Sun, F. (2002). *Proportions of crime associated with alcohol and other drugs in Canada.* Ottawa, ON: Canadian Centre on Substance Abuse.

Ploude, C., Brochu, S., Gendron, A., & Brunelle, N. (2012). Pathways of substance use among female and male inmates in Canadian federal settings. *Prison Journal, 92*(4), 506-524.

Pollock, S. (2008). *Locked in, locked out: Imprisoning women in the shrinking and punitive welfare state.* Waterloo, ON: Faculty of Social Work, Wilfrid Laurier University.

Psychiatric Patient Advocate Office. (2003). *Mental health and patients' rights in Ontario: 20th anniversary special report.* Toronto, ON: Queen's Printers for Ontario.

Public Health Canada. (2001). *Profile of hepatitis C and injection use in Canada.* Retrieved from http://www.phac-aspc.gc.ca

Public Health Agency of Canada. (2012). *Fact sheet: People in prison.* Retrieved from http://www.phac-aspc.gc.ca/aids-sida/pr/sec4-eng.php

Reiman, J. (1990). *The rich get richer and the poor get prison: Ideology, crime and criminal justice.* Boston: Allyn and Bacon.

Sims, B. (2005). *Substance abuse treatment with correctional clients.* New York: Haworth Press.

Singer, M. (2008). *Drugging the poor: Legal and illegal drugs and society inequalities.* Long Grove, IL: Waveland Press.

Somers, J.M., Currie, L., Moniruzzaman, A., Eiboff, F., & Patterson, M. (2012). Drug treatment court of Vancouver: An empirical evaluation of recidivism. *International Journal of Drug Policy, 23*(5), 393–400.

Somers, J., Rezansoff, S., & Moniruzzaman, A. (2014). Comparative analysis of recidivism outcomes following drug treatment court in Vancouver, Canada. *International Journal of Offender Therapy & Comparative Criminology, 68*(6), 655–671.

Statistics Canada. (2014). *Correctional services key indicators, 2012/2013.* Retrieved from http://www.statcan.gc.ca/pub/85-002-x/2014001/article/14007-eng.htm#wb-tphp

Stöver, H., & Michels, I.I. (2010). Drug use and opioid substitution treatment for prisoners. *Harm Reduction Journal, 7*(1), 17.

Terry, C. (2003). *The fellas: Overcoming prison and addiction.* Toronto, ON: Wadsworth/Thomas.

Thomas, G. (2005). *Harm reduction for special populations in Canada: Harm reduction policies and programs for persons in the criminal justice system.* Ottawa, ON: Canadian Centre on Substance Abuse.

Vollmer, A. (1936). *The police and modern society.* Berkeley, CA: University of California Press.

Wacquant, L. (2002). The curious eclipse of prison ethnography in the age of mass incarceration. *Ethnography, 3*(4), 371–397.

Wakeman, S., Bowman, S., McKenzie, M., Jeronimo, A., & Rich, J. (2009). Preventing death among the recently incarcerated: An argument for naloxone prescription before release. *Journal of Addictive Diseases, 28*(2), 124–129.

Ward, T., & Hudson, S. (1996). Relapse prevention: Critical analysis. *Sexual Abuse: A Journal of Research & Treatment, 8,* 177–200.

Yates, R., & Rawlings, B. (2001). *Therapeutic communities for the treatment of drug users.* London, UK: Jessica Kingsley Publishers.

Zamble, E., & Porporino, F.J. (2013). *Coping, behavior, and adaptation in prison inmates.* Berlin, Germany: Springer Science & Business Media.

CHAPTER 19

The Experiences of Chinese Youth in Drug Treatment Programs in Vancouver, British Columbia

Siu Ming Kwok and Dora M.Y. Tam

Introduction

Drug treatment programs are disproportionately under used by racialized groups in Canada and other Western countries (Committee on Multiculturalism and Mental Health Treatment and Education, 1988a, 1988b; Fountain, 2009; Ja & Aoki, 1993). Lower rate of treatment program usage by racialized groups does not mean that there is no need for such programs and services among these populations. Rather, a growing body of literature suggests that drug abuse problems in Chinese communities are becoming a concern in North America (Liu & Iwamoto, 2007; Naegle, Ng, Barron, & Lai, 2002; Nakamura, Ilomiteanu, Rehm, & Fisher, 2011; So & Wong, 2006). Chinese-Canadians are the second largest racialized group in Canada and are expected to be greater than 1.8 million by 2017 (Statistics Canada, 2010). Nonetheless, there have been few studies on drug abuse in Chinese communities in this country (Nakamura, Ialomiteanu, Rehm, & Fischer, 2011). The lack of research in this area arises from a ban on the release of race-based crime statistics (including drug use) in Canada (Owusu-Bempah & Wortley, 2014) and the challenges related to collecting field data from racialized groups (Kwok & Tam, 2006). Nonetheless, a lack of sufficient data in this area hampers the development of policy, programs, and practices in the criminal justice system for these youth (Government of Ontario, 2008). As such, this paper reports on a qualitative study on the experiences of five Chinese youth in treatment programs in Vancouver, British Columbia, as a way to fill the current void in literature and provides empirical data for making informed policy and practice for this population. The study was conducted in 1998. But the findings of this first and only study on Chinese youth in drug treatment programs in Canada are still relevant and useful when relating to existing literature in the second decade of the 21st century.

Literature Reviews

Literature on interventions for Chinese-Canadians with drug abuse problems is very sparse. Still, there are literatures aimed at Chinese youth in conflict with the law, including the crime related to their drug abuse problem, which reveal valuable information about this population (Kwok & Tam, 2010; Pih & Mao, 2005; Sim & Wong, 2008).

First, Chinese youth perceive that there is structural discrimination against them as a racialized group. In a survey (n=128) in southern California, Tsunokai (2005) found that Chinese youth were more likely to be labelled by the school and police as Asian gang members and to be involved in illicit drug trade. In studies in Vancouver and Toronto, Chinese youth were also found to be less likely to get extrajudicial measures (diversion from court sanction) under the Youth Criminal Justice Act (Kwok, 2009).

Second, there is a lack of cultural sensitivity in current treatment programs. In terms of help-seeking behaviours, research suggests that Chinese people were more hesitant to turn to professional assistance; however, ethnicities of the professional helpers were not the determining factors in their consideration for asking for assistance. This holds true for those parents who speak limited English. Nevertheless, the intervention programs are not culturally sensitive enough for serving this population (Fountain, 2009; Kwok & Tam, 2010).

Third, literature documents that delinquency and drug abuse problems by youth from racialized groups can be explained by economic and social marginalization (Wortley & Tanner, 2006); nevertheless, the Chinese community has some unique responses that are different from other racialized groups. Zhang (1993) found that Chinese parents were more emotionally upset than Black parents concerning their children's conflict with the law and deviations from societal norms. Moreover, Chinese youth have the propensity to internalize social problems. For example, Chinese parents are found to be more likely to blame themselves for the misbehaviours of their children due to their inadequate parenting rather than attributing the issue to systemic discriminations (Kwok & Tam, 2009). Additionally, Chinese youth have a very close tie with the family regardless of their level of crime and drug involvements. In fact, such strong family connection and support is one of the main motivators for them to stop reoffending and abusing drugs again (Kwok & Tam, 2010; Pih & Mao, 2005).

Still, we do not have much knowledge regarding the pathway of Chinese youth to drug abuse in North America nor their pathways to reduce use or cessation. By understanding the experiences of Chinse youth in drug treatment programs in Canada, this study aims to fill the void of the literature in this area and provide information for more evidence-based policy making and identifying promising practices for this population.

Methodology

Sampling

Five Chinese males who have used drug treatment programs and services in British Columbia before were successfully interviewed in 1998 for this study. All of them were young immigrant Chinese males between the ages of 20 to 24 at the time of interview. Demographic information of the five participants is listed in Table 19.1. Semi-structured interviews were conducted and an interview guide was used to provide for the direction of the conversation. Each interview lasted around two hours. Four participants preferred to use Cantonese[1] in the interview and one participant used English. All interviews were audiotaped and transcribed.

Table 19.1   Background of Respondents

Name*	Home country	Age	Years of residence in Canada	Years of addiction	Currently involved in treatment	Time not using drugs
Ah Wai	China	24	4	7	detox	2 months
Ah Leung	China	20	4	5	detox	still using
Tony	Vietnam	24	12	5	detox	3 months
Mati	China	20	13	2	no	still using
Peter	Hong Kong	21	8	3	detox	14 months

Pseudonyms used throughout

Data Analysis

Data were analyzed by using the categorizing strategy. Though treatment programs are designed to serve all with substance abuse problems, people may have different experiences in the programs. Since themes are the structure of experience, the categorizing strategy was considered the best way to identify themes from which people construct their own experience (Manen, 1990).

During an interview, the interviewer needs to interpret and clarify data with the interviewee in order to establish a mutual understanding of the latter's life experience (Kvale, 1996). Such co-understanding helps the interviewer to code the data precisely. During the first interview, participants were assisted in reflecting upon the meaning of their experiences. After obtaining basic ideas through transcribing the interview, those tentative categories were listed and practice knowledge was used to interpret and transform coded data into different categories (Coffey & Atkinson, 1996). Categories were then grouped into major themes to allow the pieces to be placed in context. The aim of the entire process was to understand the entire phenomenon beyond each individual's experience. All materials relating to these themes were extracted from the data and grouped together.

Analysis of Emerging Themes

Family connection is the overarching theme found in this study, with two other subthemes: sense of belonging and shame. Additionally, three phases were identified along these Chinese youth's involvements with drug treatment programs. They are:

1. Before the treatment: drug use and drift away from family
2. During the treatment: tug of war with drugs and struggle to reconnect with family
3. After the treatment: say goodbye to drugs and reconnect with family

The pathway of drug treatment program involvements of Chinese youth is illustrated in Figure 19.1.

Before the Treatment: Drug Use and Drifting Away from Family

The themes in this phase serve as a background for understanding participants' later experiences in treatment programs. All participants started using drugs as they felt the distance between themselves and their families grow. As they became more regular users, they had stronger feelings of shame and felt increasingly distant emotionally from their families. The themes of rejection, worthlessness, feelings of guilt, and indifference to outside help are prevalent in this initial stage.

Rejection

There is a strong stigmatization associated with drug use in Chinese communities and people in the community look down on all drug abusers.

> People regard you as carrying a contagious disease. They walked away when they spotted you. (Tony)

Worthlessness

All participants thought that they were worthless to society because of their drug dependency. They felt that they were a lost cause in the society.

> Once you are using drugs, there is a sign hung over your neck. You are garbage. Your name is drug addict or failure. (Tony)

This kind of feeling appears to be stronger for a participant like Ah Wai, who frequented Chinatown, and was known by many in the community.

No one trusts you. When you go into a shop the staff would keep a watch-ful eye on you. They always thought that you were planning to shoplift even though I really wanted to buy something. (Ah Wai)

Figure 19.1   The Pathway of Drug Treatment Program Involvements of Chinese Youth

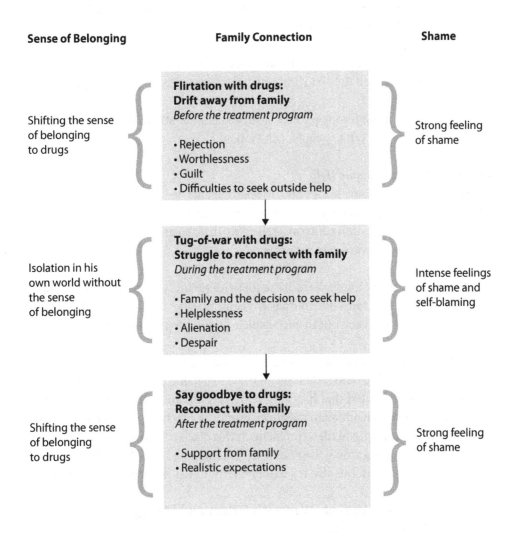

Sense of Belonging   **Family Connection**   **Shame**

Shifting the sense of belonging to drugs

**Flirtation with drugs:
Drift away from family**
Before the treatment program

• Rejection
• Worthlessness
• Guilt
• Difficulties to seek outside help

Strong feeling of shame

Isolation in his own world without the sense of belonging

**Tug-of-war with drugs:
Struggle to reconnect with family**
During the treatment program

• Family and the decision to seek help
• Helplessness
• Alienation
• Despair

Intense feelings of shame and self-blaming

Shifting the sense of belonging to drugs

**Say goodbye to drugs:
Reconnect with family**
After the treatment program

• Support from family
• Realistic expectations

Strong feeling of shame

Guilt

A strong sense of guilt was commonly found among all participants. They thought of themselves as a burden, bringing shame to their families.

> We [Chinese-Canadians] believe that we do not bring shame to the doorstep of our families ... I will keep this [drug use] as a secret away from my parents for the rest of my life. (Mati)

The guilt feeling became more intense when they broke the law in order to support their drug using habit.

> The only way to get money is to steal. How can you tell your parents that you have become such a kind of person? You are now not only a drug addict; you are also a criminal. (Ah Leung)

In addition to feeling indebted to their parents, these youth become very conscious of their ethnicities. They felt they had brought great disgrace to the Chinese community.

> I am now a burden for my parents, I am an insult to all Chinese ... loss of face by Chinese to the White people. (Ah Wai)

Difficulties Seeking Outside Help

Despite having been in Canada for years, the participants had limited knowledge about the existing drug treatment programs and services. They regarded withdrawal management centres (detoxification centres) as the only drug treatment programs available for them and were unaware of other options.

> At that time I only know there are detoxes [detoxification centres], I have no idea of other programs likes outpatient centre.... They are not publicized on TV nor does anyone reach out to us to explain [these programs]. (Peter)

However, they also resisted the idea of going to a detoxification centre for treatment as they did not think it would be helpful. Mati, who had not previously used any drug treatment program, stated that his Chinese friends told him that the detoxification centre was not very welcoming to racialized groups. As such, he would rather use his own resources to deal with his drug problem. At this phase, the participants developed a strong sense of guilt regarding their families, and this guilt not only further distanced them from their families, but also made them hesitant to ask for outside assistance.

During Treatment: Tug-of-War with Drugs and Struggle to Reconnect with Family

The second phase was dominated by the theme of participants' struggles to reconnect with their families. The participants used their participation in a treatment program as an attempt to re-connect with their families. However, this phase of the process was characterized by helplessness, alienation, and despair.

Family and the Decision to Get Help

After discovering the participants' drug abuse problems, their parents with no exception mobilized their own resources to aid their children. Some measures taken by the parents included locking the participants up, buying herbal medicine for them, and even taking them back to their home country for treatment.

> My father ... though angry (after discovering my use of drugs) ... tried to help me by locking me up to deny me access to drugs ... and bought herbal medicine for me. (Ah Leung)

Peter's father even took him to Hong Kong for treatment.

> My father did not know the services here, I was sent to Hong Kong. (Peter)

Additionally, they did not rule out the option of seeking help from mainstream agencies. In fact, it was the parents, rather than the participants, who were more willing to get outside help.

> I resisted the idea [of going to a treatment program]; however, my mother cried in front of me, I owed them [parents] too much. I had to go [to the detoxification centre]. (Ah Wai).

Although parents assumed that the drug treatment programs could help their children, experience of the participants with the treatment programs was far from positive.

Helplessness

All participants had feelings of helplessness when they were in the treatment programs. This was due to the sense of being not in control of the process of their treatment.

> On the first day of coming to the centre, I was so weak and my body craved drugs. I had no appetite for any food ... I only want sleep, however, the staff in there insisted upon waking me up for dinner. (Tony)

Moreover, all participants said that they were frustrated and did not get respect from the staff. They felt that they were regarded as making use of the detoxification centre as a hideout when they had nowhere to go and ran out of money.

> I sense that the staff did not believe that I could change. I was treated as a panhandler making use of the detoxification centre as a hostel for free meals and shelter. (Tony)

However, it should be noted that the attitude of staff did make a difference in how the participants felt in the treatment programs. For example, Tony had a totally different experience in a detoxification centre in Calgary.

> The staff [in the detoxification centre] cared about me ... they would ask if anything was wrong when I frequently visited the bathroom on the first day. (Tony)

Alienation

Moreover, all participants said that the drug treatment programs were not designed for someone from a racialized group. For instance, language was a major problem for those who could not communicate well in English.

> I can only say sick, sick, and sick to a medical doctor ... I cannot express myself other than that. (Ah Wai)

Even Peter, who speaks English very well, preferred to speak in Cantonese (a dialect in southern China) at a vulnerable moment in his life.

> You cannot express some very delicate feelings in your second language. That moment [the first day of admission] is important when I can communicate with my mother tongue; I feel safer and understood. (Peter)

Failing to get emotionally connected with staff, participants tried to seek emotional support from other residents; however, that proved to be another disappointment. They found no one with whom they could speak their own language.

> I talk to no one, no one cares about me. Even though I want to talk, I cannot express myself clearly in English ... I was an isolated island without connection. (Ah Wai)

All participants agreed that they found more social support when being in jail than being in a detoxification centre. They even preferred going to jail for getting off their drug dependency.

> Jail is a good detox [detoxification centre], and more effective, you have no choice but to stay in it ... and all your friends are in there. (Mati)

Moreover, all these young people mentioned that food has important meaning to them and that this was something to which detoxification centres did not respond. At a time when they were feeling sick and vulnerable, they desired to have something familiar. Food had powerful symbolic meaning for them.

> At that time [the first day of admission], I craved hot rice. ... However, when I was in the dining hall, my heart went down ... everything in my dish is cold ... it is a sandwich but not rice. (Ah Wai)

The sense of alienation made them feel that the treatment program was not a good choice and further reminded them that they are immigrants and a racial minority in Canada. It is interesting to note that despite having a sense of alienation from the mainstream treatment programs, all participants did not support the idea of having an ethno-specific treatment facility.

> The key point is a good and caring program. (Peter)

> A caring attitude by staff is very important. It is very different when you feel you are welcomed and respected. I would stay longer in such a caring atmosphere even though I might be the only Chinese in that agency. However, I would definitely leave without a second thought if a Chinese drug treatment program treats me like garbage. (Leung)

Self-Blame and Despair

The process of treatment was painful for both participants and their parents. All participants had been in treatment more than once with all but one in a treatment program at the time of the study. Each failure sank the participants to a lower level of despair and led to more self-blaming.

> Each time I left a detox [detoxification centre], I felt I was useless. I was nothing ... I was rejected by my [Chinese] community ... let alone by the mainstream society ... I am a liar to my parents. I cannot keep my promise [to stay in the program] and I bring further shame to the family. (Ah Wai)

They found themselves stuck in the "revolving door" of a drug abuse problem. The cycle of going to drug treatment programs and relapsing afterwards is repeated continually. Frequently they ended up in jails and their families gradually withdrew support to them due to their repeated failure in giving up the drug habit. Finally, they felt they were rejected by both the mainstream and their own ethnic community.

After Treatment: Goodbye to Drugs and Reconnection with Family

The themes in this phase, support from family and realistic expectations, help us to understand the importance of family support for participants to make a turnaround in their lives. The focus on interdependency between family members also has important implications for program design.

Support from Family
Family support to these young people was critical for them to reconnect with their family.

> When I stay clean, I contact again my parents ... they decide to support if I keep on staying clean.... It's good that you are forgiven by the people to whom you owe so much. (Peter)

Realistic Expectations
The key to success at this stage is to have realistic expectations. Trust is not built in one day.

> When there is a black spot on a white paper, people tend to see the spot only ... you must accept this because you cannot remove the spot. The only thing you can do is to convince people to see the clear part of paper rather than the spot. (Peter)

Even though some participants claimed that their sense of shame diminished after they stopped using drugs, their sense of sadness continued. One could tell from their body language in the interview that it was very difficult to talk about their experience with drugs.

Discussion

The pathway to drug treatment program involvement of Chinese-Canadians found in this study provides empirical data for policy-makers and practitioners to address the needs of this population in the areas of structural discrimination against Chinese drug abusers, institutional barriers to access to services, and cultural considerations when it comes to working with this population.

First, structural discrimination of racialized groups should be addressed. It is well-documented in the literature that there is structural discrimination against racialized groups in Canada (Commission on Systemic Racism in the Ontario Criminal Justice System, 1995; Government of Ontario, 2008). In addition to structural discrimination, youth from racialized groups with a drug abuse problem would be stressed even more (Sheu, 1996). In this study, participants were very conscious of their ethnic background, as they believed their drug problem would bring disgrace to the Chinese community. Additionally, participants' internalization of structural problems was an additional oppressive barrier. Their fear of being further discriminated against and the guilt they felt about their own ethnic community sank them further into despair and became a substantive hindrance in addressing their drug problem.

Second, institutional barriers for accessing services should be taken into consideration. It is found from this study that mainstream drug treatment services for ethnic communities are not adequately culturally sensitive to them. For example, there is a need to provide services in more languages. In this study, some participants had limited English skills and knowledge about drug treatment programs even though they had been in Canada for a while. Even worse, parents of the participants knew even less about the existing resources. Most parents of the participants did not speak English at all. Another example is the lack of provision of ethnic foods. It might not always be practical and feasible to provide a variety of ethnic foods in a program; however, program staff could still show more consideration and understanding of the dietary needs of service users, especially when they are in a very vulnerable moment. In fact, this finding corroborates existing literature. Recent reports from the governments of Ontario and British Columbia also said that most program initiatives for youth services in ethnic communities in the two provinces are based on intuition and imposed from a top-down manner without the support of research evidence or community consultations, even though there is compelling data to support the need for culturally sensitive models of intervention and prevention (Government of Ontario, 2008; Totten, 2008).

Moreover, without obtaining the cultural accommodations from mainstream treatment programs, the participants might seek protection from their own ethnic community (Cheung, 1991; Naegle, Ng, Barron, & Lai, 2002). Four of the five respondents in this study proposed an ethnic treatment centre. They believed that it is especially important for those who cannot speak English very well. However, a cautious note needs to be observed. Even Ah Leung, who could not communicate well in English, agreed during the follow-up interviews that a caring program is more important than an ethno-specific program. Research studies in Chinese communities in other Western countries also stress the importance of working with ethnic organizations and communities in order to make the programs more culturally sensitive and accommodating to this population (Fountain, 2009).

Third, other cultural factors found in this study have implications for intervention practices with this population. This study found that Chinese families use their own resources prior to seeking any outside help. At the same time, Chinese families do not rule out the option of seeking help from mainstream services. Contrary to general belief, Chinese parents are eager to attain help from mainstream treatment agencies after they exhaust their own resources. In fact, all participants in this study went to the drug treatment programs under the encouragement of their families. Although participants were reluctant to use the service, they still went to the programs with the hope of bonding again with their family. This discovery has significant implications for drug treatment programs working with Chinese-Canadians. The family should be included in the whole process of treatment. This finding is consistent with literature regarding favourable outcomes of including family in the drug treatment process with Chinese youth (Fong & Lam, 2007; Sim, 2007; Sim & Wong, 2008).

Conclusion and Further Research

This study is focused on Chinese-Canadians. However, the findings on structural discrimination, institutional barriers, and cultural factors to inform practice could also be relevant to other racialized groups who face similar difficulties. Drug abuse is a multi-faceted problem that should be examined in a social context. Structural discrimination against racial groups is well documented in Canada (Government of Ontario, 2008). Youth from racialized groups are more likely to get arrested and are less likely to get extrajudicial measures (diversion from court sanction) under the Youth Criminal Justice Act (Kwok, 2009). In addition to experiencing a disjunction of culturally defined goals, a drug abuser from a racialized group will add another layer of complexity in relation to drug problems in this society. Thus, all drug treatment policies proposed should take into account the difficulties and challenges faced by members of racialized groups at the structural level.

Institutional barriers for accessing treatment programs found in this study are relevant to other racialized groups as well. Most program initiatives for youth services were based on empirically based and informed culturally sensitive practice models of intervention and prevention (Government of Ontario, 2008; Totten, 2008). Racialized groups are then expected to accommodate the mainstream service rather than the other way around.

Last, the unique cultural factors of each racialized groups should call for mainstream services to work with ethnic communities to improve and enhance their services to these populations. A number of studies show that the best way to engage ethnic communities to deal with a drug problem is to form a partnership with ethnic community organizations (Fountain, 2009; Nakamura, Ialomiteanu, Rehm, & Fischer, 2011).

There are some distinct limitations of this study. Homogeneity of the sample is one of them. All participants were young immigrant Chinese males. Their experiences in treatment programs may be different from those of females or second-generation individuals. Moreover, there are a variety of treatment services in Canada, and the participants were involved in detoxification programs only. For future research, interviews with the parents would provide valuable information and a more comprehensive picture of the entire phenomenon. As family connection is important in Chinese culture, it is worthwhile trying to understand the experiences of the parents involved in the whole process.

NOTES

1. Cantonese is a dialect in Southern China widely spoken by the Chinese communities in North America.

REFERENCES

Cheung, Y.W. (1991). Ethnicity and alcohol/drug use revisited: A framework for future research. *International Journal of the Addictions, 25*(5A & 6A), 581–605.

Coffey, A., & Atkinson, P. (1996). *Making sense of qualitative data.* Thousand Oaks, CA: SAGE.

Commission on Systemic Racism in the Ontario Criminal Justice System (1995). *Report of the Commission on Systemic Racism in the Ontario Criminal Justice System.* Toronto, ON: Queen's Printer.

Committee on Multiculturalism and Mental Health Treatment and Education. (1988a). *Report of the Task Force on Chinese-Canadians.* Vancouver, BC: Greater Vancouver Mental Health Services.

Committee on Multiculturalism and Mental Health Treatment and Education. (1988b). *Report of the Task Force on Indo-Canadians.* Vancouver, BC: Greater Vancouver Mental Health Services.

Fong, S.F., & Lam, C.W. (2007). The paternal involvement of Chinese drug abusers: An exploratory study in Hong Kong. *Journal of Social Work Practice in Addictions, 7*(3), 87–98.

Fountain, J. (2009). *Issues surrounding drug use and drug services among the Chinese and Vietnamese communities in England.* London, UK: National Treatment Agency.

Government of Ontario (2008). *The review of the roots of youth violence.* Toronto, ON: Author.

Ja, D., & Aoki, B. (1993). Substance abuse treatment: Culture and barriers in the Asian American community. *Journal of Psychoactive Drugs, 25*(1), 67–71.

Kvale, S. (1996). *Interviews: An introduction to qualitative research interviewing.* Thousand Oaks, CA: SAGE.

Kwok, S.M. (2009). How Asian youth cope with the criminal justice system in Canada: A grounded theory approach. *Asian Pacific Journal of Social Work and Development, 19*(2), 21–37.

Kwok, S.M., & Tam, D.M.Y. (2006). Methodological challenges in studying Asian gangs in Canada. *Asia Pacific Journal of Social Work & Development, 16*(2), 43–52.

Kwok, S.M., & Tam, D.M.Y. (2010). Chinese immigrant youth and the justice system in Canada. *Canadian Social Work Journal, 12*(2), 114–122.

Liu, W.M., & Iwamoto, D.K. (2007). Conformity to masculine norms, Asian values, coping strategies, peer group influence and substance use among Asian American men. *Psychology of Men and Masculinity, 8*(1), 25–39.

Manen, V.M. (1990). *Researching lived experience: Human science for an action sensitive pedagogy.* London, ON: Althouse Press.

Naegle, M., Ng, A., Barron, C., & Lai, T. (2002). Alcohol and substance abuse. *Western Journal of Medicine, 76*(4), 259–263.

Nakamura, N., Ialoniteanu, A., Rehm, J., & Fischer, B. (2011). Prevalence and characteristics of substance use among Chinese and South Asians in Canada. *Journal of Ethnicity in Substance Abuse, 10*(1), 39–47.

Owusu-Bempah, A., & Wortley, S. (2014). Race, crime, and criminal justice in Canada. In S.M. Bucerius & M. Tonry (Eds.), *The Oxford handbook of ethnicity, crime, and immigration* (pp. 281–320). New York: Oxford University Press.

Pih, K.K.H., & Mao, K. (2005). Golden parachutes and gangbanging: Taiwanese gangs in suburban and Southern California. *Journal of Gang Research, 12*(4), 59–72.

Sheu, C.J. (1986). *Delinquency and identity: Juvenile delinquency in an American Chinatown.* New York: Harrow and Heston.

Sim, T. (2007). Structural family therapy in adolescent drug abuse: A Hong Kong Chinese family. *Clinical Case Studies, 1*(6), 79–99.

Sim, T., & Wong, W. (2008). Working with Chinese families in adolescent drug treatment. *Journal of Social Work Practice, 22*(1), 103–118.

So, D.W., & Wong, F.Y. (2006). Alcohol, drugs, and substance use among Asian-American college students. *Journal of Psychoactive Drugs, 38*(1), 35–42.

Statistics Canada. (2010). *Projection of the diversity of Canadian population 2006–2031.* Ottawa: Author.

Totten, M.D. (2008). *Promising practices for addressing youth involvement in gangs.* Vancouver, BC: Ministry of Public Safety and Solicitor General of British Columbia.

Tsunokai, G.T. (2005). Beyond the lenses of modern minority myths: A descriptive portrait of Asian gang members. *Journal of Gang Research, 12*(4), 37–58.

Wong, H.Z. (1985). *Substance use and Chinese American youths: Preliminary findings on an interview survey of 123 youths and implications for services and programs.* San Francisco, CA: Youth Environment Services.

Wortley, S., & Tanner, T. (2006). Immigration, disadvangtage, and urban youth gangs: Results of a Toronto study. *Canadian Journal of Urban Research 15*(2), 1–20.

Zhang, X.D. (1993). Coping with delinquency in a cultural context: The perceptions and coping behaviors of Black and Asian parents of juvenile delinquents. Doctoral dissertation, University of Southern California. *Dissertation Abstracts International, 55*(12), 4001.

CHAPTER 20

Understanding the Ultimate Oppression: Alcohol and Drug Addiction in Native Land

Kelly Brownbill and Mavis Etienne

Canada faces a crisis when it comes to the situation of Indigenous Peoples of the country. The well-being gap between Aboriginal and non-Aboriginal people in Canada has not narrowed over the last several years, treaty and Aboriginals claims remain persistently unresolved, and overall there appear to be high levels of distrust among Aboriginal peoples toward government at both the federal and provincial levels. Canada consistently ranks near the top among countries with respect to human development standards, and yet amidst this wealth and prosperity, Aboriginal people live in conditions akin to those in countries that rank much lower and in which poverty abounds. At least one in five Aboriginal Canadians live in homes in need of serious repair, which are often also overcrowded and contaminated with mold. The suicide rate among Inuit and First Nations youth on reserve, at more than five times greater than other Canadians, is alarming. One community I visited has suffered a suicide every six weeks since the start of this year. Aboriginal women are eight times more likely to be murdered than non-Indigenous women and Indigenous peoples face disproportionately high incarceration rates. For over a decade, the Auditor General has repeatedly highlighted significant funding disparities between on-reserve services and those available to other Canadians. The Canadian Human Rights Commission has consistently said that the conditions of Aboriginal peoples make for the most serious human rights problem in Canada.

    —JAMES ANAYA, UNITED NATIONS SPECIAL RAPPORTEUR ON THE RIGHTS
      OF INDIGENOUS PEOPLES, STATEMENT UPON CONCLUSION OF THE VISIT
      TO CANADA, OCTOBER 15, 2013

Introduction

Substance abuse among First Nations peoples in North America was virtually unknown until colonizing Europeans introduced different types of intoxicating beverages and later, psychoactive substances. The reason for this was that clearly defined codes of behaviour were established among the different nations. Elders, adults and children, and men and women all knew their roles and responsibilities. The reliance on the strong community created by the relationships between these roles meant that the consequences of not fulfilling a role were severe to both the individual and to the entire community. The value of respecting the plants, roots, and trees that the Creator made meant that these were not created for an individual to use in an unhealthy manner. In the past, one of the ways tobacco was used was in the spiritual context to commune with the Creator. Tobacco was also used in rituals and ceremonies where covenants were made with other peoples for peaceful purposes. The use and significance of tobacco changed for Native peoples because of the influence of Europeans and the need for capital. Today, many First Nations people are so addicted to tobacco products such as cigarettes and chewing tobacco that their health is compromised, with the prevalence of smoking among Indigenous youth being more than double that among non-Native youth (24.9% vs. 10.4%) (Elton-Marshall, Leatherdale, & Burkhalter, 2011).

The First Nations of North America were not used to ingesting the different intoxicants that were introduced by newcomers to this land, and they quickly became dependent upon the different substances. The main intoxicant was liquor, which was first introduced as a commodity for trading for valuable fur pelts. Liquor was also used for illegal transactions concerning land transfers from Native nations to non-Aboriginal individuals and also to colonial governments, which remains a contentious issue still today. The Natives became addicted quickly and soon lost many of their values as well as their teachings and traditions. The value of the family and the care and protection of the family became less important because individuals became so involved with their chemical addiction, a legacy that unfortunately has carried on to today.

The number of Natives who are now addicted to drugs and alcohol has been steadily rising in North America. The Royal Commission on Aboriginal Peoples (1996) concluded that alcoholism was the factor creating the greatest problem for Indigenous individuals and communities throughout Canada. Alcohol use is of great concern to people in First Nations, Innu, and Inuit communities, with surveys indicating that three-quarters of Indigenous peoples believe that alcohol use is a problem in their community with one-third stating it was a problem in their own family or household. Interestingly, First Nations, Innu, and Inuit use of alcohol is below the national average with only 66% of those living on reserve consuming alcohol compared to 76% of the general population. However, medical records from western Canada indicate that First Nations people, especially men, are admitted to hospital for problem substance use more often than other residents of these provinces. The cause of death due to alcohol use is 43.7 per 100,000 in the Indigenous Canadian population, almost twice the rate of the general population, which is 23.6 per 100,000. This suggests that those who do drink, drink heavily, consuming five or more drinks on one occasion on a regular basis (Khan, 2008). In Indigenous communities pre-adolescent youths are two to six times more likely to have already been exposed to alcohol-related problems compared to their non-Indigenous peers (Cotton & Laventure, 2013).

Death rates arising from illicit drug use are approximately three times that of the general Canadian population. Indigenous peoples who use illicit drugs have higher HIV incidence and prevalence when compared to their non-Indigenous drug-using peers (Khan, 2008). Indigenous street youth and female sex workers were also found to have higher HIV prevalence (Duncan et al., 2011). Also, one in five Indigenous youth reported having used solvents and of these one in three were under the age of 15 with half beginning sniffing or huffing before the age of 11. Cannabis is also commonly used among both First Nations adults (27%) and youth (32%) (Aboriginal Healing Foundation, 2007).

Understanding the Context

In addressing addiction in First Nations communities, it is important to recognize that Canadian history has affected these communities and community members in ways that differ dramatically from the rest of the country. Mainstream service providers are often at a loss to reach the core issues of historical trauma and pain that play such a significant role in how Indigenous people view the world and their own health. Anyone wishing to work effectively with Indigenous clients must endeavour to understand that any path First Nations, Inuit, Innu, and Metis people walk cannot move forward without coming to terms with the past.

It is vital to understand that the relationship between Indigenous people and the first visitors from Europe did not start out as destructive or damaging. Fish, furs, the chance to explore new horizons and an entire continent of people with whom to share the word of God were intoxicating lures for explorers. As those first boats arrived in the "New World," one in which human beings had been living and thriving for at least 15,000 years, the initial relationship between hosts and visitors was mutually beneficial. None of the European pursuits would have been possible without the wholehearted support of the current residents of the land. In return for welcoming the newcomers and ensuring that they did not perish from ignorance of the world around them, the First Peoples received iron axes, knives, and cooking vessels. These new tools and technology all improved the lives of those already living on the land, but without fundamentally altering their way of life.

To truly understand the path of the next few hundred years, it is important to devote some study and reflection to the differences between the predominant cultures of the time. Vast generalizations are necessary, but even so a picture can be painted with commonly held knowledge that demonstrates the relationship of Indigenous people with the newcomers and its devolution from beneficial to obstructive of European concerns. As this devolution severely impacts the perspective of Indigenous people, most particularly in their struggle for sobriety, caregivers must acquaint themselves with it in order to assist in an empathetic manner.

Although there are myriad factors to consider, a clear picture of the situation can be gleaned by examining the differing views of First Nations peoples, knowing that they were not a homogeneous group and that traditions varied between groups and Europeans in terms of:

- land usage,
- government structure,
- family structure, and
- spirituality.

This very preliminary and surface examination is meant as an introduction to these very complex concepts, and not as a comprehensive or complete analysis, and relates primarily to First Nations groups from the Maritimes to the Prairies.

Land Usage

To pre-contact First Nations people, the land on which they lived was sacred. Mother Earth was a gift from the Creator to cherish and protect, not to exploit. The commonly held belief that humans were just one part of Creation, not more or less important than any other, shaped their relationship with the world. All beings, be they plant, animal, or human, had gifts from the Creator that enabled them to fulfill their responsibility. Humans, with their increased brain capacity and opposable thumbs, were given gifts that made them able to fulfill their role as caretaker to Creation and Mother Earth.

The issue of ownership was simply not translatable. Native peoples did not have any concept regarding land ownership any more than we today believe we own our children. It sounds possessive among First Nations peoples to say our land, or my children, when in fact the possessive is meant to describe the relationship. Indigenous people firmly believed that they had a relationship with and a responsibility to the natural world around them, and that as stewards of the land they were tasked with its care. Compound this view with the relationships First Nations people had with the rest of Creation, as in the birds, animals, trees, and rocks, and the taking of resources became a matter of great forethought and ceremony. Simply cutting down a tree meant that great care was taken to understand the consequences of that action, followed by a ceremony of thanksgiving to celebrate the life of the tree and its gift to the people.

Conversely, in Europe, land was power. The rigidly structured class system of the pre-contact era was based upon land ownership and dictated standing in the community, wealth, and privilege. Natural resources were to be exploited as quickly and completely as possible. Any grade school history text will paint a picture of early contact with new worlds as simply a mechanism through which to provide more wealth and power to the ruling parties in Europe. Could these visitors understand a culture that conducted ceremony, or gave thanks, every time they cut down a tree, harvested berries, or took an animal for food? Thus, there was such a mammoth chasm in terms of world view between these two cultures with respect to this fundamental issue that a common understanding was unfathomable.

Government Structure

Most of the First Nations in Canada were governed through the clan system. Different nations would have different numbers and names of clans, but the common thread was the idea of a plurality of knowledge. In the Ojibway or Anishinaabe nations, seven clans shared leadership. Each clan was given the responsibility of a certain aspect of life and thus was designated but not limited to a role, be it warrior, teacher, negotiator, or healer. When decisions affecting the entire community were considered, all clans with their individual areas of expertise were consulted. Every voice would be heard in council, from the very old to the very young. Discussions would literally last days as each opinion was expressed and considered. Not until all perspectives were heard and a decision reached in consensus was the outcome considered to be appropriate for the entire community.

As each clan was recognized as having specific gifts, they were suited to different tasks. When it came to engaging with the newcomers, different people from different clans may have been sent to interact. For example, initially a member of the Crane Clan, known for their prowess at affairs between different groups, would have been sent to talk. If, because of the language barriers, the interaction was difficult, perhaps the next day a member of the Fish Clan, known as the teachers, would have been sent. If that did not go well, the community may have resorted to sending a member of the Marten or Warrior Clan.

In Europe, monarchies reigned. There was absolute authority, to be carried out without question. When ships left Europe, they carried a King or Queen's representative who was imbued with the same ultimate authority. Nothing in their history or experience would have prepared them for a culture that recognized the need for full community participation in any decision-making. It is completely understandable that they would have concluded the people in this new world had no formal governance structure. They were asked to send a leader and sent three different people on three different days, after all.

Family Structure

Even accounting for the many diverse nations occupying the territory now called Canada, the structure of family life was significantly different from European norms. The Anishinaabe Nations, for example, understood a life cycle of eight different and distinct periods. From birth to death, each stage of life had a significant role to play in the health of the entire community.

Infants brought and still bring the gift of unconditional love. They teach the community the importance of love in a happy and healthy life. Toddlers, as they start to walk and explore their environment, bring the gift of safety. As the rest of the community provides for their safety as the toddlers tear around with no understanding of consequence, the importance of ensuring safety for all is emphasized. Children bring the gift of learning, heralding in the era of "Why is the sky blue? Why is the grass green?" Perhaps the most difficult stage of all, youth brings the gift of questioning.

Adult stages of life also bring gifts. The young adults bring the gift of child-bearing. They start to find partners and to raise children of their own. Adults, when their children are old enough not to need them constantly at their side, can bring the gift of providing. They go out on the hunt and do their best to ensure the community does not go hungry. The grandparent stage sees a weakening physically, but brings the gift of teaching. And the Elders, who have lived through all stages of life, bring the gift of wisdom.

In Native culture, gift and responsibility often mean the same thing. A person would never be given a responsibility within the community without the recognition that they carried the requisite gifts needed to fulfill that responsibility. By the same token, a person would never carry a gift that did not come with the absolute responsibility of utilizing that gift for the entire community. In this way, each stage of life brings a gift that is needed in order for life in the community to be happy, healthy, and in balance. From the moment of birth until the moment of death, each human being is considered to be a functioning, necessary part of the community.

Just as important as the various gifts brought by each stage of life are the relationships that form between the stages. Traditional teachings tell us that the fire was at the centre of our life. As life stages are arranged around the fire, natural partnerships are formed across the fire. The infants sit across from the young adults. Just as young adults are forming relationships and learning to be responsible for more than just themselves, they are linked with that gift of unconditional love that is so important to healthy relationships. As the young adults bring more new life into the community, they are restocking the supply of love. The toddlers sit across from the adults that bring with them the gift of safety. As the adults provide for the safety of the toddlers, they too learn how important safety is to the life of the community. It is much more important to the community that a hunter returns home after each hunt, than to have him take risks that endanger himself to the point where he may never hunt again. The children, with their bright minds hungry to be filled with knowledge, sit across from the grandparents who have the time, patience, and learning to serve as teachers. And it takes the wisdom of the Elders to help the youth through that most difficult stage of life (Figure 20.1).

This model was the foundation of family and community prior to contact with European cultures. Not only was each stage of life valued for its contribution to the wellness of the entire community, but each stage of life was reliant on another for its own health. The system was completely integrated and balanced across blood relations, clan relations, and the entire population of a community.

Figure 20.1   Family Roles across the Fire

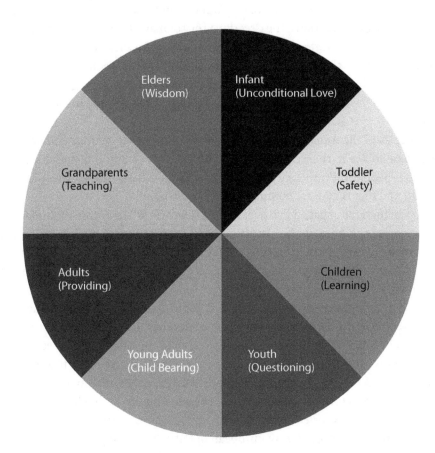

The system in Europe at the time did not recognize the contributions of anyone except the adult male ruling class. Decisions were made by a select few and women and children were never to be seen or heard, let alone asked for an opinion. Introducing the concept of having a five-year-old girl address the community in council was totally incomprehensible. This integrated approach to family and community would have been completely unrecognizable to the European visitors, who again would have ample demonstration that these new people were completely without structure or civilization.

Spirituality

When considering the spirituality of the Indigenous peoples of Canada, it is important to understand that spirituality was ingrained into every single part of life. It was their spirituality that told them where to live, who to marry, and when and what to hunt. Not resigned to any specific high and holy days, the oneness with the spirits around them gave the original people not just peace and balance, but an unshakeable under-standing of their place in Creation.

Perhaps the most significant aspect of the world view of the Indigenous people of North America lies in the teachings of the Four Colours of Man. Handed down through oral traditions for generations, the Creation Story of many Indigenous cultures speaks of the creation of four different races of human being. To each race the Creator gave original instructions that incorporated their own spirituality. Each race was also given their own place in the world to live and their own Sacred Gift. Each gift was different from those received by the other races, making each race or colour of man unique and special.

Prophecies of the Anishinaabe people talk of a time when all four colours of man would come to live in their traditional territory. From a traditional perspective, the Indigenous people knew there were other races in the world, that they would be very different, and that they were coming to visit, and to stay.

European nations engaged in travel to the "New World" had strong foundations in Catholicism. At this point in the history of the Church, the predominant teaching was "Ours is the only true path to Salvation." If one did not follow exactly the dictates of the Church, one was condemned to Hell for all eternity with their eternal soul living in perpetual agony.

Thus, consider how these two world views of spirituality would have interacted. The original people of this land knew that there were other nations of man in the world. The original people knew the other nations had different teachings. These teachings were viewed as being as valuable and sacred as their own, because all the teachings came from the same Creator. The European perspective was that any conflicting spiritual or religious path was wrong and in fact sacrilegious, and thus had to be changed according to the teachings of the one Holy Roman Catholic Church, otherwise the sinners would literally burn in Hell forever. Any European of Catholic upbringing, having even the slightest amount of compassion for these new people, would have been compelled to teach them the ways of their Church and save them from eternal damnation. In contrast, the original people of North America would have been eager to see another example of the wisdom of the Creator, and would have been anxious to listen to the new teachings. The original people, however, would have no comprehension of the need to give up their old ways in exchange for these new teachings.

A complete lack of understanding of the other's perspective was the foundation to the process of assimilation and colonization that would ensue in Canada for generations to come (De Leeuw, Greenwood, & Cameron, 2010). As the Europeans tried to instill the teachings of their church, they would become frustrated with the Indigenous perspective of listening to, but not adopting, these new ways. Eventually, the teachings would become more and more fervent. For example, if these "savages" don't understand that they can't come to Church and then return to their sweat lodge, perhaps we should burn down their sweat lodge. Benevolent intentions became subverted by frustration as "the others," native to the land, demonstrated that they had no concept of and thus obviously no interest in "conversion."

The Outcome

Taken from a contemporary perspective, it is not difficult to see that the course of destruction was preordained. Neither culture was equipped to understand the perspective of the other. First Nations people had a view of the world that encompassed a plurality of perspectives that honoured the individual gifts of each community member. The European perspective was based upon a rigid hierarchical system that saw human beings as the ultimate life form in the universe. It is completely understandable how, from today's view, the first visitors to this land saw nothing of value or consequence in the ways of the existing population. Convinced of their own right, only complete assimilation of the Indigenous people made sense, and with advanced technology and increasing numbers, inevitable—almost.

A Legacy of Trauma

The Royal Proclamation of 1763 outlined the relationship England intended for the residents of Canada. Citing the need for compensation for land, and a nation-to-nation relationship with the Crown, it would have paved the way for a much different history. Recognizing the autonomy of the First Nations while maintaining control of negotiations would have allowed the British Crown to ensure retention of Indigenous lands and rights while ensuring all citizens participated in the growth of a new nation.

Unfortunately, this proposed relationship would not come to pass. England, who by this time had become the ultimate power in North America, was simply too distant and communication took too long to meet the immediate needs of the colonists. As a result, a representational government started to form, imbuing some with the authority and the obligation to care for their neighbours. As the colonists' goal was to create a better life for themselves, and that included good land and access to resources, it became abundantly apparent that the First Peoples were now no longer allies but rather were getting in the way. From a mutually beneficial relationship at the instant of contact, to allies during war, Indigenous people quickly moved from irrelevant to obstructive to the pursuits of the European immigrants flocking to Canada. There was a brief respite during the War of 1812 when First Nations were useful, again in a time of war, but it was all too clear that something had to be done about "the Indian Problem."

Perhaps the most significant event to affect the relationship between the First Peoples and the colonists was not political but rather biological in nature. During the early years of settlement, thousands and perhaps tens of thousands of Indigenous people died. Diseases, namely small pox, brought over on ships from Europe, devastated the population. The effect was not merely linked to virgin soil epidemics. As these new diseases were introduced into a world with no immunity or medicine to treat them, the lives of the First Peoples were already being altered in such a way as to ensure the spread. Rather than existing in their smaller communities, Indigenous people were now gathering at trading posts and ports as they became dependent upon the new colonial economy, and began to drift away from their centuries-old traditions. As First Nations peoples travelled along river systems in search of ever more furs, they spread disease through contact with other groups with whom they would previously not have interacted. While the population of Indigenous people was dramatically falling, the population of colonists grew exponentially. It is estimated in the Royal Commission on Aboriginal Peoples report (1996) that by 1812 the non-Native people living in Upper Canada already outnumbered the Indigenous People by as much as ten to one.

Many accounts of the process of assimilation of Canada's First Peoples exist (Aboriginal Affairs and Northern Development Canada, 2013; Anderson & Denis, 2003; Dickason, 2010; Dussault, 2007; Haig-Brown, 1988). It was a concerted effort on behalf of the Canadian government to remove any vestige of Indigenous people from the landscape. When looked at from the current day, it is almost impossible to believe that the process from start to finish was not orchestrated as a whole. So efficient and effective were the numerous policies put in place to eliminate Indians that it is amazing that any Indigenous cultures exist today. The plans were brilliant in their inception and their execution and have left an irremovable impact on today's Indigenous people. The four aspects of traditional culture addressed previously were systematically attacked and all but eliminated through government policy and practice. Able to write laws to enforce their views, the Government of Canada had a free hand in how it chose to deal with Aboriginal people.

The creation of reserves served to sever the link between the First Nations and their land. Moved from traditional hunting and fishing territories, many communities were impoverished with no sustainable alternative to feed and clothe themselves. Moved over and over again, the First Peoples could no longer consider themselves stewards of the land and witnessed any direct relationship to Mother Earth deteriorate into a front row seat for observing the exploitation of Her resources. In 1885, the Department of Indian Affairs instituted a pass system, barring Indigenous people from moving outside of the boundaries of their reserve without written permission. To a people who had survived for generations with a personal and real relationship with the natural world around them, this effectively turned reserves into penal colonies, and into a system upon which South Africa's subsequent apartheid would be premised. Apartheid of course has been abolished, but Canada's reserve system remains.

The separation from the land and the displacement of Indigenous people onto reserves seriously jeopardized the continuation of the culture. Men in the Cree communities of Northern Ontario, for example, would participate each year in the spring goose hunt. When communities were moved away from migratory paths of the geese, and their travel across the land was restricted, significant parts of the culture were lost. If the men were not out on the land, the teachings were not shared from the old men. How to read the ice in the river, how to know how many geese to harvest, how to survive a spring blizzard; these teachings were cultural anchors no longer set fast in the younger generation.

The balanced approach to community government encapsulated in the clan system was now replaced by an election system dictated by the federal government through the Indian Act (1876). Even as it outlined who could and who could not run for chief or council, the act also gave the "Indian Agent," the non-Native government official placed upon reserves to oversee the government's interest, power to remove any elected Indian official from office. The vaguely defined reasons for removal from office were "dishonesty, immorality, or intemperance." No longer were all perspectives considered in council. In fact, as the Indian Agent chaired all Chief and Council meetings, governance was effectively limited to a perspective of one.

The family structure of the First Peoples had all but been destroyed. Women, once holding honoured positions in a community, were relegated to second-class status. In fact, while traditional teachings of finding partners and mates were forgotten, the Government of Canada decided who an Indian woman could or could not marry. The Gradual Enfranchisement Act of 1869 was a clear indication of the power of the Canadian government over Indian women. Removing Indian status from any woman who married a non-Indian, the act removed not just one generation of women from band membership, but all subsequent generations as well.

Arguably the most heinous and the most successful system instituted in the name of assimilation was the residential school system (Aboriginal Healing Foundation, 2007; Dickason, 2010; Mosby, 2013). Created to "educate the Indian out of the child," the schools were responsible for destroying a family structure as old as time. Residential school was traumatic for many Indigenous people because children were removed from their parents at an early age, taken far away from their homeland and mistreated. Much has been written about the individual consequences of the residential school system (Bombay, Matheson, & Anisman, 2011; Elias et al., 2012; Fournier & Crey, 1997; Grant, 1996; Milloy, 1999). The schools systematically removed a child's identity by removing language and culture and substituting an institutional life devoid of any attempt to nurture. Five year olds, literally ripped from their parents' arms, were housed in dormitories and taught that being an Indian was wrong. A female Elder who survived the residential school experience said that, as a five-year-old girl, she was told that if she did not go to residential school her "daddy" would be put in jail. The onus was put on her, as a child, whether her father would be free or locked away in prison. In addition, the children were punished for speaking their native language. They were moved great distances from their homes so that they would lose their language and culture, and they adapted by learning the mother tongue of the children in the area. Their braids were cut off and they were ridiculed because of the colour of their skin.

The schools were also magnets for predators looking for a captive supply of young boys and girls to prey upon. Some children were treated as if they were slaves and were often abused physically, sexually, emotionally, and/or mentally. Many of those children are now adults who have still not fully dealt with those issues and are continuing to do what they were taught—to abuse others including their immediate, extended, and community families. Not only were they not nurtured, they felt that they had been abandoned by their parents and missed out on having the support of extended families. Any attempt to reconcile or compensate for this period of history on the individual lives ruined by this system, while necessary, will be woefully inadequate regardless of the financial compensation. The systemic destruction of the traditional structure of the Indigenous family continues on well beyond the past school survivors.

Some survivors still carry resentment and bitterness because they were deprived of growing up in a family setting, and use drugs and alcohol to forget the pain, even if it is just for a short time. When people turn to alcohol and other psychoactive drugs to numb their pain, it can also result in other major problems, in particular fetal alcohol spectrum disorder. If a woman abuses alcohol and continues drinking throughout her pregnancy, the baby may be born with fetal alcohol effects. These children may have a lifetime of being misunderstood, and experience problems with comprehension, relationships, and the law, along with having a greater likelihood of experiencing their own addiction issues. These mothers also have the added stress and frustration of trying to find the required assistance for their children, assistance necessary because of their drinking. Siblings may be affected by the feeling that they are not given the same amount of attention as their brothers or sisters who suffer from the effects of fetal alcohol spectrum disorder, and families thus often experience additional guilt and shame.

For centuries, the spirituality of the Indigenous people of North America was the foundation of their lives. Religion was not designed around the dictates of one higher being, but was based upon the assumption that all of Creation, including humankind, was sacred. As the trauma experienced by Native people escalated through the process of assimilation, their traditional coping mechanisms, namely their spirituality, were removed. In the midst of colonization, how could the world be considered sacred? Superimposing a new religion onto this desolation does not provide strong enough roots to withstand the tempest of contemporary reality. When a people have had their identity stripped away, when they experience addiction, poverty, unemployment, violence, mental illness, and illiteracy at levels far surpassing the rest of the population, there is no quick fix. The history of alcohol misuse among Indigenous peoples is inextricably linked to colonialism, historic injustices, and the paternalistic relationships that have been in place between state and Indigenous groups (Davison, Ford, Peters, & Hawe, 2011).

Thus, Native peoples come to treatment programs, particularly residential programs, with great trauma in their individual and collective past. The trauma stems from a number of sources such as racism, residential schools, abuse, abandonment, loss of rights, and other significant losses including the loss of culture, language, land, spirituality, freedom, rights, and identity. These losses are a major contributing factor for the high rates of drug and alcohol abuse and suicide in Indigenous communities. Some Indigenous people experience flashbacks when they come into a residential addiction treatment program and feel as if they are back in school. The requirements and duties of the facility remind them of the structure of the residential school system that held them captive as children.

Responding to the Oppression: Onen'to:Kon Healing Lodge

There are now 59 drug and alcohol treatment centres specifically for Indigenous Peoples in Canada, including short- and long-term residential treatment programs as well as outpatient counselling centres. Some of these centres specialize in solvent abuse, and others work with the family as well as with the addicted individual (Health Canada, 2008).

Overview

In the Mohawk community of Kanehsatake on March 23, 1987, the Onen'to:kon Healing Lodge opened its doors to help Native people who are addicted to drugs and alcohol. The centre's main clients are primarily from the Mohawk communities of Kanehsatake, Kahnawake, Akwesasne, and Montreal. However, Indigenous peoples from other Nations are also welcome to utilize the Onen'to:kon Healing Lodge as well as affiliated outpatient services in the community of Kanehsatake and the city of Montreal. The program in this centre, described below, is representative of many of the 59 Native treatment centres across Canada.

The residential program, which is six weeks long, has a number of components including one-on-one counselling, talking circles, healing circles, lectures on a variety of issues such as defence mechanisms, 12 steps of AA, along with a prominent cultural component. The program is tailored to meet the client's individual needs. Not only is the chemical dependency addressed, but also the specific issues that the client identifies as her[1] own including anger, resentment, grieving, refusal skills, abuse, and low self-esteem.

There are two goals when an individual comes to the centre for treatment. The first is to have the individual love himself so that he will not destroy his body, dreams, relationships, career, and opportunities by continuing to drink and use drugs. The second is to rid clients of all the excuses they use for why they continue drinking or using drugs. Forgiveness is an important issue for people to deal with while in recovery from their drug and alcohol addiction because holding on to resentments may be a very good excuse or trigger for returning to drinking or using drugs. When an individual continues to be resentful because of past abuses or losses, it becomes difficult to make a decision to "let go and forgive." The person does not forgive an abuser because she deserves it, but because the injured party needs to set herself free.

Circles

In the residential program there are "talking circles" as well as "healing circles." Talking circles are a form of group therapy where a person talks about the issues that are causing pain. The other members of the circle give them individual feedback as well as confront behaviours that are not helpful in the individual's recovery program. In contrast, healing circles are conducted without confrontation unless an individual behaves in a manner that is disruptive. Individuals may choose to smudge prior to joining the circle. The act of smudging has a deeply spiritual significance for most First Nations peoples. The smoke from sage is used to cleanse oneself of evil spirits and the smoke from sweet grass is used to invite positive influences to help the individual engage in the event in a more positive, integrated, spiritual way that respects the Creator, ancestors, and the other participants. People use smudging to find calmness from negative feelings by using the medicines of sweet grass, sage, and cedar. There are also sweet grass braids and sage available for people who smudge as a way of communicating with their higher power.

Once the circle begins, the one who wishes to speak and share holds an eagle feather. The person who holds the feather has the right to speak. After that person has finished speaking, the eagle feather is passed on to the next individual. It has been witnessed that individuals reveal much more in the healing circles when men and women have their own individual circles. When a person discloses information about the abuse that he was subject to, it can easily start a chain reaction of disclosures as others realize that they are not the only ones who had been abused. The clients frequently mention how they enjoy and greatly benefit from the healing circles.

During the fifth week of a person's treatment program at Onen'to:kon, an "affirmation circle" takes place in one of the talking circles. Each individual is placed in the centre of the circle and the other circle members whisper words of affirmation in his ear, such as, "I am so happy that you were born," "I love you," "You are so special," "You are precious to me," and "I am so proud of you." This activity has a profound effect on the client because for some it may be the first time someone has said those positive words to her. The treatment program is geared to help people rid themselves of negative thinking and negative "self-talk." The affirmation circle is one of the opportunities for a client to experience hearing positive statements made about him.

Cultural Component

The culture component is vital to the program because it celebrates the individual's identity as a Native person and reconnects them with the traditions that assimilation attempted to eradicate. When an individual does not know where she belongs, it helps to discover her roots and origins. Learning about the traditions that her nation carries on today is also helpful. For example, individuals can develop great pride in learning that their ancestors were great hunters who fed their families with the wildlife that they trapped.

The program recognizes the importance of enjoying the language that the Creator gave to the Mohawk people. Natives from other nations also share their language with those in the program. Indigenous languages are very descriptive, so individuals are encouraged to translate written materials into their own language so that it is more meaningful to them.

The residents are taught about the values and beliefs that have sustained the First Nations in the past. There are discussions on the medicines that are taken from the land, the way the medicine is chosen, how it is used, and in what season it is to be picked.

In the past, Indigenous people learned about the medicines by watching the bears and other animals when they were ill and seeing what herbs, bushes, roots, and tree bark they ingested to feel better. Individuals are also taught the importance of replacing what you take from the land as well as gratitude for what the Creator provides. Berries, medicine plants, and the seeds for planting food are all necessary for sustaining life.

Music is also an important component in the healing process from drug and alcohol addiction. The drum music represents several things and also accompanies the healing that occurs by using the voice. The beating of a rhythm represents the beating of the human heart. Songs provide teachings and are a celebration of life and mourning for the ones who have passed on. When the drum is used to respect someone who has passed on, the implements that were created for the event are burned after the singing is completed.

Making the water drum, which represents life, is a large part of the cultural component at Onen'to:kon. The water represents all the life-giving waters and the minerals in the earth such as gas, salt, iron, gold, oil, rocks, and coal. The hide represents all the animals that run, fly, and swim such as bears, deer, moose, wolves, birds, and fish. The ring represents the universe known to humankind and creation itself. The plug is how humans are connected to the drum. This relationship is demonstrated by placing approximately three mouthfuls of water into the drum. Finally, the trees used in making the drum are the same trees that are used for building materials and for making tools.

The creation of beadwork is another important part of the treatment program's cultural component. Individuals learn patience by separating the different-coloured beads for selected projects. Program participants often achieve a great deal of pride when they produce a beautiful beaded article that they made either for themselves or for a family member.

Sweat lodges are also available for people who want to do a sweat during the week that they complete treatment. A sweat takes place in an enclosure with hot rocks where people can pray to their Higher Power. The sweat is used as a healing circle, a peaceful and calm place. It is a safe place to let go of issues.

There is a great deal of diversity in sweats, though many follow similar structures. Often there are four rounds to a sweat. The first round can be for praying, thanksgiving, and acknowledging the Creator. The second round is for the medicines, plants, and other items that help one cope when they have problems. The third round is for acknowledging all the women in an individual's life and the women who are companions and caregivers during illness. It is also a time for acknowledging and praying for the little children who are going through difficulties, as well as acknowledging the children who are doing good deeds. There is also a discussion of the Mohawk's three major foods: corn, squash, and beans. The fourth round is for discussing an individual's personal needs, difficult time, and pain. The person also talks about how he can help someone else. At that time, the individuals acknowledge each other in the circle and there is closure. Whoever conducts the sweat explains what the focus of each round is. Some sweats are one long round, while others have three rounds: one for communities/lands/

natural world, one for men and boys, and one for women and girls. Some sweats are only for women or only for men, and others are conducted for both sexes.

Some clients attend traditional Mohawk ceremonies like "mid-winter" and "strawberry." These clients are encouraged to participate as a way of learning what ceremonies are important for the Mohawk Nation. Spirituality, an important part of an individual's life, is usually neglected when a person drinks and uses drugs. In treatment, the clients are taught to balance their lives physically, emotionally, mentally, and spiritually. Clients who wish to attend church, to honour the Creator in this way, may do so on Sunday mornings. Onen'to:kon has a "Recovery Bible" that clients can utilize, as well as the four gospels in the Mohawk language.

The residents are also taught Native games such as lacrosse, snow snakes, and an activity where an eagle feather is picked up with the teeth. These activities help participants instill pride in themselves when they realize that their ancestors devised ways of acquiring skills, building strength, and having fun without using chemicals or alcohol.

New people come into the residential treatment program every three weeks. The new residents are called Pathfinders because they have just started to discover that there is a path of recovery from drug and alcohol addiction. Those who have been in the program for three weeks are called Pathwalkers because they are already walking on the path towards healing. Before their orientation to the program, new residents are given a welcoming ceremony patterned after the Mohawk condolence ceremony. The three items used in the ceremony are water, white doeskin (replaced in the ceremony by tissue for hygienic reasons), and the eagle feather. The water is used to symbolize a method of opening up the throat when a person is choking back words that she finds difficult to say. The doeskin (tissue) is used to wipe the tears that are caused by the sadness in a person's life. The eagle feather is used to dust in front of the ears so that the person will be able to hear what needs to be heard. The group of newcomers then forms a circle back to back, and an honour song is played on the drum. The staff and the Pathwalkers greet the Pathfinders, and at the end of the ceremony the Pathfinders are given a medicine pouch with sage, tobacco, and sweet grass.

The Anishinaabe Seven Sacred Teachings

Many First Nations cultural traditions speak of seven gifts or teachings that were given to the people by the Creator. Following these teachings would ensure the survival of all living things. While there are variations between the various First Nations in the way the teachings are recounted, for First Nations historically followed an oral tradition, the core principles are the same. These teachings, essential for healing, are also a gift to help guide daily behaviour and activities towards oneself, others, and all of creation.

1. Love is wanting the best for oneself, others, and all of creation.
2. Respect is honouring all in creation, past, present, and future.
3. Humility is knowing one's place in the circle of life, not above or below any others.

4. Wisdom is using one's gifts in a way that benefits oneself, family, community, nation, and all of creation.
5. Courage is confronting problems with integrity to resolve them in a good way.
6. Honesty is speaking well of oneself and others.
7. Truth is knowing all of these things and living by them.

Table 20.1 provides an application of these teachings to addiction counselling.

Table 20.1 Application of the Anishinaabe Seven Sacred Teachings to Addictions Prevention and Intervention Programming

Seven Teachings	Practical Application
Love: Commit to a lifelong vision	Love enters the work of recovery when the vision is lifelong and holistic, integrating physical, emotional, mental, and spiritual aspects of health, and creating places of belonging and hope that strengthen individuals, families, and communities.
Respect: Face up to the problem and own the solution	By acknowledging all aspects of the problem in an honourable way, how it came about (the past), and what it looks like (the present), not by shaming and blaming but by creating a vision for change, respect for self and others enters the process.
Humility: Build a circle of care	Humility enters the recovery process when everyone is welcomed into the circle as equally respected members in a continuum of care: clients, Elders, community leaders, families, addictions specialists, and stakeholders from other sectors.
Wisdom: Create a strategic plan	By cherishing traditional knowledge and valuing the experience of everyone in the circle, a full range of holistic healing options is developed that match the unique healing needs of each individual, family, and community.
Courage: Carry out the plan	Integrity enters the process when individuals, families, and communities have the courage to carry out their plans in the face of barriers such as denial, lateral violence, and unanticipated barriers, and when community leaders mobilize resources in support of family and community health.
Honesty: Evaluate, monitor, and readjust the plan	Honesty in recovery and prevention requires ongoing, rigorous monitoring and evaluation, the capacity to readjust plans based on a forthright assessment of what works and what does not work, as well as emerging obstacles and unforeseen impacts.
Truth: Live, share, and pass along what is learned	Knowing all of these things and living by them means role modelling healthy behaviours; sharing resources, lessons learned, and best practices; and empowering every Inuit, Metis, and First Nations community to self-manage their own recovery from addictive behaviours.

Source: Aboriginal Healing Foundation, 2007

Other Aspects of the Program

Videos are important teaching tools that assist in giving clients with an addiction insight into the phenomenon. The treatment centre produced a video entitled "Recovering Spirit," which features young Mohawk people and treatment staff. It has a great impact upon clients. In the video, staff speak about their own previous abusive behaviour. The staff also speak about how their past actions affected their families. The clients relate strongly to what is in the video because of their own chemical dependency experiences. Another effective video concerns an absent parent. It shows the clients how they might have been abandoned by a parent or how they may now be abandoning their own family because of an alcohol or drug dependency. This video is used as one component of the grieving lecture.

There is also a weekend program involving interactive activities, which covers topics that include thinking of hope, self-esteem, assumptions, and conversation, some of which are also presented during the week. The clients learn new skills and practice new ways of communicating. Unaccustomed to socializing without drugs or alcohol, some of the residents are uncomfortable with social interactions. They are told that this is a safe place to learn and practice new social skills.

During the time an individual is in treatment, the family has an opportunity to obtain help either by participating in the family program or by using the Outreach Office for significant other counselling. Attendance at the family program is necessary if the family wishes to visit their loved one who is in the residential treatment program. It is also an opportunity for families to interact with other families and discuss how they are feeling about their loved one's chemical dependency. The family program also helps the family members examine their own addiction and behaviours. Sometimes the family is more ready for help than is the addicted individual, and thus the program provides the necessary support to begin the process of healing.

Within the family program, which takes place every three weeks, the family is taught about enabling behaviours. Enabling behaviours in Native land is alive and flourishing. The nuclear family as well as the extended family, grandparents, aunts, and uncles, are often unaware that giving money to a person who is addicted does not enable him or her to take responsibility for his or her own life, but rather enables the person to continue drinking and using drugs. Bailing loved ones out of jail and providing child care while the individual is partying are two other significant ways that family members enable alcohol and drug users to continue their destructive lifestyles. The outreach counsellor can also make referrals to other professionals for family members who have not dealt with specific issues such as sexual abuse, violence, and other trauma-related issues.

Native communities are often small, and it seems as if everyone is related. Thus, confidentiality is a major concern for program participants. In small communities news spreads fast and people seem to know everyone else's business and history. That is why the Onen'to:kon Healing Lodge informs clients that there are only three situations where confidentiality will be broken: when someone threatens to harm himself; when someone threatens to harm others; and when there is abuse or neglect of children. Clients feel comfortable using the services provided by the Onen'to:kon Healing Lodge because they know that their information and the stories that they share will remain confidential and that clear boundaries exist.

At the conclusion of the six-week residential treatment program there is a graduation ceremony where individuals obtain certificates of achievement. This is a very important occasion where the participants' loved ones and friends are invited to help in celebrating each person's accomplishment. The graduates usually feel great pride in having completed the treatment program. For some clients it is the first time that they have completed something that they have started. When the clients complete the six-week residential program, there is a graduation day lunch. It is a traditional meal of corn soup, corn bread and, when available, wild meat such as moose, deer, or goose, though if wild meat is not available, beef is served.

During the graduation ceremony, the clients participate through drumming and singing. There is also a greeting circle that, for the Mohawks, proceeds counterclockwise. The only time it goes clockwise is if there has been a death in the community. The leader starts the greeting with the graduates and continues on to the guests and staff members. The circle gives each individual an opportunity to say the words that need saying, because those in the circle may not cross paths again for a long time.

Conclusion

The good news is that more people are accessing the services that are available through Native residential treatment centres. There is also more awareness among Indigenous peoples of the extent and severity of the problem and more prevention programs are now in place. Further, Health Canada (2010) reported that most National Native Alcohol and Drug Abuse Program centres operated on an extremely cost-effective basis with an average per-day cost of approximately $100 per client, representing good value for money. Sadly, young people are still becoming involved in drug and alcohol addiction. While there is more awareness of the destructiveness of chemical addiction, people tend to think it will happen to someone else. The easy access to alcohol and other psychoactive drugs creates an enticing activity for young people who feel like being part of a group. Some of them become trapped by an addiction to alcohol and drugs, which ruins their and their loved ones' lives. In Native land, there is a teaching that the seven coming generations need consideration when looking to the future. Thus, it is important to help Indigenous people of all ages find the recovery path from drug and alcohol addiction to ensure they will nurture and cherish their children in the way the Creator intended.

There was a wisdom that pertained to providing services for diverse populations. Born from a time when we needed to learn not to see the colour or the gender or the age or the sexual orientation but rather the person, it was summed up by the phrase, "Treat everyone the same." Unfortunately, treating everyone the same actually creates inequity. In order to provide equity in care, it is important to treat Indigenous clients according to the different history they have experienced. By not incorporating the trauma resulting from this historical persecution of Indigenous people by the government of Canada into a plan of care, caregivers run the risk of never reaching their client.

Assimilation has left an almost insurmountable legacy behind in Indigenous communities—the inability to choose. The government of Canada began by imposing control over almost all aspects of life. This taught Indigenous people about power and control, which were seen as the ticket out of misery. So now chief and council have control, or the Board of Directors of an off-reserve agency does. For so long First Nations people have had so little control over their lives that they simply cannot see free choice as an option. There is no use providing healthier choices if people really cannot conceive of their own ability to alter their destiny. Before any work can be done to address healthy choice, Indigenous people first need to have their right to choose re-established.

It is also important in any therapeutic relationship to recognize the power of community for Indigenous people. Even when dysfunctional, community has been the backbone of life for generations. If Indigenous people are removed from their communities, perhaps because they stop going to the local bar, they will need to re-establish community around them. If that does not happen, the draw of the bar will not just be about alcohol, but about fulfilling a deep need for community.

History is an interesting thing; it defines us, and yet does not need to have a direct correlation to the future. Our Elders tell us that it took 500 years for Indigenous people to arrive at the difficult position we now find ourselves in. It is not going to become fixed overnight. And yet, 500 years in the life of a people is really insignificant when viewed from the perspective of evolution. So the First Peoples in Canada find themselves adapting to severe changes in lifestyle and diet that usually take centuries for the appropriate evolution to take place. At the same time, they have suffered through control and assimilation tactics almost insurmountable for today's generation. A concerted effort to embrace the past, recognize the effects of the journey, accept the future, and devise meaningful, sustainable planning for the future is needed to affect real change in the lives of First Nations peoples in Native land.

NOTE

1.   Masculine and feminine pronouns will be used interchangeably throughout this chapter.

REFERENCES

Aboriginal Affairs and Northern Development Canada. (2013). *First Nations in Canada*. Retrieved from https://www.aadnc-aandc.gc.ca/eng/1307460755710/1307460872523

Aboriginal Healing Foundation. (2007). *Addictive behaviours among Aboriginal people in Canada*. Ottawa, ON: Aboriginal Healing Foundation.

Anderson, C., & Denis, C. (2003). Urban Natives and the nation: Before and after the Royal Commission on Aboriginal Peoples. *Canadian Review of Sociology and Anthropology, 40*(4), 373–390.

Bombay, A., Matheson, K., & Anisman, H. (2011). The impact of stressors on second generation Indian residential school survivors. *Transcultural Psychiatry, 48*(4), 367–391.

Cotton, J., & Laventure, M. (2013). Early initiation to cigarettes, alcohol and other drugs among Innu preadolescents of Quebec. *Canadian Journal of Native Studies, 33*(1), 1–15.

Davison, C., Ford, C., Peters, P., & Hawe, P. (2011). Community-driven alcohol policy in Canada's northern territories, 1970–2008. *Health policy, 102*(1), 34–40.

De Leeuw, S., Greenwood, M., & Cameron, E. (2010). Deviant constructions: How governments preserve colonial narratives of addictions and poor mental health to intervene into the lives of Indigenous children and families in Canada. *International Journal of Mental Health and Addiction, 8*(2), 282–295.

Dickason, O. (2010). *A concise history of Canada's First Nations*. Toronto, ON: Oxford University Press.

Duncan, K., Reading, C., Borwein, A., Murray, M., Palmer, A., Michelow, W., ... Hogg, R. (2011). HIV incidence and prevalence among Aboriginal peoples in Canada. *AIDS and Behavior, 15*(1), 214–227.

Dussault, R. (2007). Indigenous peoples and child welfare: The path to reconciliation. *First Peoples Child and Family Review, 3*(3), 8–11.

Elias, B., Mignone, J., Hall, M., Hong, S., Hart, L., & Sareen, J. (2012). Trauma and suicide behaviour histories among a Canadian Indigenous population: An empirical exploration of the potential role of Canada's residential school system. *Social Science & Medicine, 74*(10), 1560–1569.

Elton-Marshall, T., Leatherdale, S.T., & Burkhalter, R. (2011). Tobacco, alcohol and illicit drug use among Aboriginal youth living off-reserve: Results from the Youth Smoking Survey. *Canadian Medical Association Journal, 183*(8), E480–E486.

Fournier, S., & Crey, E. (1997). *Stolen from our embrace: The abduction of First Nations children and the restoration of Aboriginal communities*. Vancouver, BC: Douglas & McIntyre.

Grant, A. (1996). *No end of grief: Indian residential schools in Canada*. Winnipeg, MB: Pemmican Publications.

Haig-Brown, C. (1988). *Resistance and renewal: Surviving the Indian residential school*. Vancouver, BC: Arsenal Pulp Press.

Health Canada. (2008). *First Nations, Inuit and Aboriginal health treatment centre directory*. Ottawa, ON: Health Canada.

Health Canada. (2010). *National Native Alcohol and Drug Abuse Program (NNADAP) review*. Retrieved from http://www.hc-sc.gc.ca/fniah-spnia/pubs/substan/_ads/nnadap_rev-pnlaada_exam/index-eng.php

Khan, S. (2008). Aboriginal mental health: The statistical reality. *Visions, 5*(1), 6–7.

Milloy, J. (1999). *A national crime: The Canadian government and the residential school system, 1879 to 1986*. Winnipeg, MB: University of Manitoba Press.

Mosby, I. (2013). Administering colonial science: Nutrition research and human biomedical experimentation in Aboriginal communities and residential schools, 1942–1952. *Histoire Sociale/Social History, 46*(1), 145–172.

Royal Commission on Aboriginal Peoples. (1996). *Report of the Royal Commission on Aboriginal Peoples*. Ottawa, ON: Indian and Northern Affairs Canada.

CHAPTER 21

From Benzos to Berries: Treatment Offered at an Aboriginal Youth Solvent Abuse Treatment Centre Relays the Importance of Culture[1]

Colleen Anne Dell, Maureen Seguin, Carol Hopkins,
Raymond Tempier, Lewis Mehl-Madrona, Debra Dell,
Randy Duncan, and Karen Mosier

This is why I tell these stories over and over again. And there are others. I tell them to myself, to friends, sometimes to strangers. Because they make me laugh. Because they are a particular kind of story. Saving stories, if you will. Stories help keep me alive. But help yourself to one if you like. It's yours. Do with it what you will. Cry over it. Get angry. Forget it. But don't say in the years to come that you would have lived your life differently if only you had heard this story. You've heard it now.

—THOMAS KING (2003, P. 3)

Introduction

In the 19th and well into the 20th century, Indigenous ceremonies, traditions, and activities were discouraged and at times criminalized through Canadian government legislation, policy, and practice, as highlighted by the Indian Act (Frideres, 2002). This response was part of a comprehensive attempt to assimilate Indigenous Peoples into the contemporary Canadian mosaic, and resulted in the erosion of their traditional ways of life (Dickason, 2006; Morrision & Wilson, 2004). Consequently, the health and well-being of First Nations and Inuit were and remain negatively affected, demonstrated by their marginalized social and economic status, poor nutrition, and high rates of violence and substance abuse (Dell & Lyons, 2007). Traditional Indigenous understandings and approaches to addressing problematic substance use and mental health issues have historically been at odds with conventional biomedical approaches (Marbella et al., 1998; Morrisseau, 1998). Specific to substance-related diagnoses, Health Canada's First Nations and Inuit Health Branch, in partnership with First Nations and Inuit communities and organizations, moved towards closing this gap with the development of 56 Native substance abuse treatment programs in the 1970s. Most of these treatment centres were developed with an emphasis on Indigenous understandings of healing in conjunction with conventional approaches to substance use treatment. As well, a network of nine youth solvent-abuse-specific residential treatment centres have been established, beginning in 1996.

This chapter begins by comparing the conceptualization of mental health and substance abuse from Western and Indigenous world views. Next the serious gap in understanding and practice between these two world views is explored. Using a traditional Indigenous method of knowledge translation—storytelling—front-line experiences from people working in a culture-based youth solvent abuse treatment centre in Canada relay the difficulties with imposing conventional mental health diagnosis-based responses onto First Nations and Inuit youth. This leads into a discussion of how mental health counselling can better respond to the role of culture in care offered to First Nations and Inuit youth who abuse substances. The chapter concludes by reviewing the significant need for increased peer-reviewed, culturally responsive, and research specific treatments for Indigenous youth who abuse substances, including solvents. A health promotion perspective is suggested as a possible beginning point for attaining this understanding. It situates counselling's individualized approach to treating mental disorders within the etiology for First Nations and Inuit.

Treating Solvent Abuse among First Nations and Inuit Youth in Canada

Solvent abuse is the deliberate inhalation of fumes or vapours given off from a substance for its intoxicating and mind-altering effects (National Drug Abuse Information Centre, 1988). Solvents are a large and diverse group of chemical compounds located in hundreds of household and industrial products, including paint thinner, glue, gasoline, and correction fluid (Dell & Beauchamp, 2006). The health effects of inhaling can be acute, and include frostbite and burns (Janezic, 1997), brain and nerve cell damage (Dewey, 2002), and sudden heart failure (Ballard, 1998; Wille & Lambert, 2004). The social effects are equally destructive, and include poor academic performance (Carroll, Houghton, & Odgers, 1998), decreased mental wellness (Kurtzman, Otsuka, & Wahl, 2001), and problem behaviour, such as conflict with the law (White & Hayman, 2004).

The 2004 Canadian Addiction Survey found that 1.9% of males and 0.7% of females aged 15 years and older reported the use of an inhalant in their lifetime. The majority of people (67%) reported first using inhalants between the ages of 12 and 16 (Adlaf, Begin, & Sawka, 2005). Research and practice have indicated higher rates of solvent abuse among youth experiencing disenfranchised life conditions and at younger ages. This has been documented among street youth, inner-city youth, and some First Nations and Inuit youth living in select rural and remote areas of the country (O'Brien, 2005; Research Group on Drug Use, 2004). Solvent abuse among First Nations and Inuit youth has been linked to high rates of poverty, boredom, loss of self-respect, unemployment, family breakdown, and poor social and economic structures (Dell, Hopkins, & Dell, 2005).

Most youth who enter into the residential solvent abuse treatment centres in Canada have extensive histories of mental, physical, social, and spiritual abuse and disconnection (Coleman, Charles, & Collins, 2001; Youth Solvent Addiction Committee, 2008). These are the same youth who, in the conventional biomedical view, would most likely receive psychiatrist-supervised care. In contrast, the network of solvent treatment centres focuses on a culture-based model of resiliency, which is a strength-based approach to treatment. This holistic model of resiliency is understood as "balance between the ability to cope with stress and adversity [that is, inner spirit] and the availability of community support [that is, relations with the collective community]" (Dell, Hopkins, & Dell, 2005, p. 7).

Key in this model is recognition that a person's inner spirit and community cannot be disentangled from one another, as is commonly done within a Western world view. A person's inner spirit is intertwined with their family, community, and the land and cannot be understood apart from them. For example, among the Dene people, a person's addiction is seen as shared by all community members. Everyone in the community shares the responsibility and has a duty to contribute to the person's healing (Francis, 2004).

Other work on Indigenous youth resilience also supports this holistic understanding (Chandler & Lalonde, 1998; Ledogar & Fleming, 2008). Iarocci, Root, and Burack (2009) propose that understanding of resiliency needs to move beyond an individualized interpretation of the concept and include an understanding of families, communities, and broader society to account for culture, social context, and ecological environment. Numerous non-Western cultural traditions assume a sociocentric concept of self, which likewise views the individual as a relational, interdependent entity (Manson, 2000), which is in sharp contrast to the conventional biomedical view of an egocentric self that characterizes people as unique, separate, and autonomous beings (Beiser, 2003). Gladwell (2008) has criticized this individual-centred view with numerous examples of the ways in which individual behaviour is better explained by social networks and forces than the common assumptions of individual effort or blame. Within an Indigenous world view, people cannot be conceptually separated from their community.

The stories shared in this article originate from the Nimkee NupiGawagan Healing Centre in Muncey, Ontario. The centre opened in 1997 and is a four-month residential, gender-based treatment program for First Nations and Inuit adolescents. Its 12 treatment beds are funded through Health Canada's First Nations and Inuit Health Branch. As a cultural program, assessments, counselling, and programming begin from a place of respect that focuses on the strengths of Indigenous youth, families, and communities. The centre's name translates in English into "Thunderbird's Necklace." The Thunderbird's Necklace is a rainbow of colours, and the rainbow symbolizes the aura of a cleansed Creation that comes from the cleansing waters of the Thunderbeings. The cleansing work of the Nimkee NupiGawagan Healing Centre (2008) is to promote the true colours of the spirit of the youth to allow them to shine.

Traditional Psychiatric Responses to Aboriginal Peoples' Mental Health and Substance Abuse

The Diagnostic and Statistical Manual of Mental Disorders (DSM) in its various renditions has come under regular scrutiny for being conceptually Western based and laden with value judgments (Dalrymple, O'Doherty, & Nietschei, 1995; Lewis-Fernandez, 1998). A foremost example is psychiatry's historical recognition of Indigenous peoples as "primitive" and "inherently opathological" (Waldron, 2004, p. 105). Within Canada this is possibly most notable in that "mental health research has paid scant attention to the role culture plays" (Beiser, 2003, p. 48).

A debate within psychiatry that illustrates its reliance on an individual medicalized model of understanding is the efficacy of a categorical, compared with a dimensional, classification system of disorders. Discussions about adding a dimensional component to the DSM have been ongoing for many years (Kraemer, 2007), with dimensional measures gaining influence since the publication of the DSM-III-R in 1987 (Helzer, Bucholz, & Gossop, 2007; Regier, 2007). A categorical diagnosis is based on a binary distinction; an individual is either positive (has the disorder) or negative (does not have the disorder). Although there is recognition that there may be overlap between disorders, the focus is on diagnosing specific mental disorders. In contrast, a dimensional diagnosis is based on three or more categories or traits, with people placed on a continuum of traits from minimal to extreme.

Despite psychiatry's individualistic traditions, there has been movement away from focusing strictly on the reduction of psychiatric symptoms and towards greater understanding of individual experiences of meaningful living (Davidson et al., 2008; Goering, Boydell, & Pignatiello, 2008). This included discussing the role of culture in preparation for the DSM-V (Regier, 2007), though the DSM-IV did for the first time include a section on cultural variations for DSM disorders. For example, clinicians were advised to explore cultural explanations for the diagnosable illness. Scholarly reaction to this shift has been mixed. Whereas Manson (2000) identifies it as a step forward in acknowledging the role of culture in defining and treating mental illness, Kirmayer and Minas (2000) counter this with concern over the implied universality of the DSM categories. They state that the DSM-IV "introduces cultural considerations as just minor qualifications to what are presumed to be culture-free diagnostic categories" (p. 439).

Just as there has been little attention paid to culture within the DSM specifically, and psychiatry generally, there too has been minor attention allotted to the abuse of solvents. In 2000 an article in the Canadian Psychiatric Association Bulletin, describing a solvent-using client, only mentioned that "solvent abuse had contributed to his intellectual problems as well as exacerbating his psychotic disorder" (Haggarty & O'Reilly, 2000, p. 88). Similar to the medicalization of substance abuse within psychiatry generally, the documentation of solvent abuse that exists likewise focuses on diagnosing the individual, with little attention towards broader etiological factors or cultural context. For example, the case illustration presented by Duggal, Sinha, and Nizamie (2000) examines a male aged 18 years, referred to as P, who started sniffing gasoline at the age of six. Although the authors briefly mention the desirability of a holistic approach, including family history and premorbid temperament, their psychiatric-informed response was dominated by pharmacological interventions. In contrast, the story of a client's experience at the Nimkee NupiGawagan Healing Centre, presented below, relays a first-hand account of the need for cultural understanding in supporting First Nations youth who abuse solvents.

Story from the Treatment Centre

Cory is typical of many of the youth admitted to Nimkee's Healing Centre. She is 14 years old and has been abusing solvents for nearly three years as a way of coping with pain and trauma in her life. Within 72 hours of arriving at Nimkee, like all youth, Cory was sent for a mandatory physical and psychological assessment within the Western medical system. This is the first time Cory has travelled away from her land, territory, language, and people; naturally she is very quiet and shy. She is also experiencing the physical manifestations of detoxifying from the solvents she used before her admittance. As often happens with the youth at Nimkee, Cory's assessment identifies her as high risk and depressed, and consequently she receives a prescription. This was a common occurrence for youth at Nimkee ten years ago. Today, with mutual co-operation between Nimkee and the Western health services system, beginning with a sharing of Indigenous and Western world views, the general practitioner and the psychiatrist do their assessments at the treatment centre. They attempt to address assessment issues through Nimkee's cultural ways (for example, with an Elder) before any medication is prescribed.

Adopting a Holistic Approach

A prevalent finding within the Canadian literature is a significant gap in understanding and practice between Western-based and Indigenous-based approaches to treatment and healing, specifically for substance abuse, including solvent abuse, and in general for mental health issues. This result centres on disparate understandings of mental health and wellness. Very little literature exists specific to solvent abuse but three dominant themes were identified within the literature: connection with self, community, and political context. Each is examined from the two distinct world views and each provides an illustrative story based on the front-line experiences of workers at the Nimkee NupiGawagan Healing Centre. The transformative power of storytelling is well documented among Indigenous scholars and Elders alike (King, 2003; Mehl-Madrona, 2005). The stories presented here were collected, verbally, by the executive director of the centre, who has had direct contact with the staff and youth since it opened in 1997. Stories were later verified with staff. The stories are provided to help the reader better understand the key components of the two world views, as well as relay the limitations of imposing strictly Western psychiatric-based diagnosis and treatment responses onto First Nations and Inuit youth.

Connection to Community

Western orientations towards health concentrate on the absence of disease (Adelson, 1998). By extension, mental health, including substance abuse, is defined as the absence of mental disorder. As earlier discussed, psychiatry concentrates on diagnoses based on a system of classification. This system, whether categorical or dimensional, emphasizes an individual's healthy mind (Kraemer, 2007; Regier, 2007). Conversely, an Indigenous

---

Story from the Treatment Centre

Many of the communities from which the youth who attend the Nimkee NupiGawagan Healing Centre are characterized by pain and trauma from the impacts of colonization. Most of these communities have little knowledge of their traditional cultural practices and beliefs. From one community in particular, a young boy by the name of Joseph attended Nimkee and learned of his cultural heritage. He learned and adopted spiritual beliefs. This spiritual connection facilitated a connection to his true identity. A part of Nimkee's programming is involvement of the immediate family, parents, or guardians in one week of the youth's residential treatment process. This is done in a sensitive manner such that the parents or guardians are not insulted, or rejected outright, through the traditional teachings their children are learning. Joseph's family attended the centre and also learned about their cultural heritage, which made it possible for them to practice their beliefs as a family when they returned to their home community. It followed in this case, and frequently in other cases, that once Joseph returned home, other children from the family, and extended family, requested to attend the centre. The youth are very connected through their place in the community, and this transfers to the healing of not only the youth who attended treatment but also their families and communities.

---

world view of mental health asserts a holistic approach that accounts for cultural context and considers the person and the community (relations among the person and community) and their past, present, and future intersections (Kirmayer, Simpson, & Cargo, 2003; Mehl-Madrona, 2005; Morriseau, 1998; Waldram, 2000). Community is composed of the land, people, the non-physical world, and their interconnections (Frideres, 2002). Wieman, referenced on the Anishnawbe Health Toronto website (2008), explains that an Indigenous culture-based understanding of mental wellness includes "having good social relationships ... [and] having a sense of connected-ness to the community." This is further illustrated by the language of the Whapmagoostui Cree of Northern Quebec, who do not have a Cree translation for the Western word *health*, but rather refer to *being alive well—wiyupimaatisiiun—*which emphasizes community, history, identity, and resistance. It follows that to not be alive well may not mean a pathological condition of the individual, but instead, something pathological in society (Adelson, 1998).

Connection to Self

Indigenous conceptions of mental health do not assume the mind/body dichotomy or dualism that frames Western psychiatric beliefs about mental health (Beiser, 1985; Manson, 2000). Waldram (1997) explains that an Indigenous world view focuses more on developing an understanding of the body and mind as a whole, and on how illness is symptomatic of an imbalance between the individual, the society, and the spiritual realm. As such, the term mental wellness is more appropriate, as it incorporates physical,

---

Story from the Treatment Centre

A traditional teaching offered to the youth at Nimkee is that their identity, values, and language are innate within their inner spirit but may be dormant. They are taught that they have a genetic memory. The cultural environment at Nimkee helps to nurture the youth's inner spirit. For example, the youth are able to quickly participate in a sweat lodge once at Nimkee because their spirit is awakened and this is what motivates the youth to do what they do. This is what happened for Jamie. He was afraid of the dark, of taking off his shirt in front of others, and of sitting close to others. Because the sweat lodge is a cultural activity, the youth are motivated by their inner spirit to participate. Jamie did. This is different from a decision to play floor hockey, for example, just because it is something to do. The spiritual part of the youth's being needs to be in balance with the emotional, mental, and physical aspects of their self, and so they are internally motivated to take part in cultural activities to achieve this. A person's spirit causes their heart to beat, their blood to flow, and the movement of energy. Youth like Jamie become quickly attuned to this once in the healing centre environment.

mental, cultural, and spiritual elements of health (Chaimowitz, 2000). This is evident in the work of Health Canada's First Nations and Inuit Health Branch Mental Wellness Strategic Action Plan for First Nations and Inuit (n.d.). The framework conceptualizes mental health as a lifelong journey to achieve wellness and balance of body, mind, and spirit. Mental wellness includes self-esteem, personal dignity, cultural identity, and connectedness in the presence of a harmonious physical, emotional, mental, and spiritual wellness. Aboriginal health practices attempt to restore a sense of balance, harmony, and coherence for a person and nurtures their inner spirit (Buchwald, Beals, & Manson, 2000; Thatcher, 2004).

Connection to Political Context

Health, in particular for First Nations and Inuit in Canada, is imbued with social, political, and economic influences and must be viewed within historical and continually shifting parameters (Adelson, 1998; Frideres, 2002; Vicary & Bishop, 2005). The impacts of intergenerational trauma, owing to assimilation policies and practices in Canada, must be considered when addressing the current mental health and coping strategies for substance abuse of First Nations and Inuit. A historical perspective is necessary to avoid "psychologizing" political issues. To illustrate, issues such as secure attachment and trust, belief in a just world, a sense of connectedness to others, and a stable personal and collective identity are all particularly relevant to the history of colonization of Indigenous peoples in Canada, but are not accounted for in psychiatry's diagnosis

Story from the Treatment Centre

The impacts of residential schooling are evident in the generation of today's Indigenous youth who are having strained relationship issues with their parents and extended care-givers. When Janice completed the Nimkee program, she, like many of the other youth in the program, said one of the greatest things to come from it was her ability to communicate better with her parents, and to trust that she will be heard. While in the program Janice spoke on a regular basis with her parents by telephone, and her family was brought to the treatment centre for a week to participate alongside her in her treatment journey. Her family learned how important it was that they communicate effectively with Janice and that they encourage and speak positively with her and their other kids. Her parents also learned about the stages of youth development and cultural understandings of parenting. Janice also relayed, again as most other youth do, that the most meaningful part of her time at Nimkee was participating in cultural programming. This includes, traditionally, learning about parenting. Healthy parenting skills have been critically impacted, owing to the history of colonization of Indigenous peoples in Canada, especially residential schooling.

of post-traumatic stress disorder (Kirmayer, Simpson, & Cargo, 2003). McCormick (2009) elaborates:

> [C]ounseling grounded in Aboriginal values and perspectives ... start[s] with the recognition that substance use and related mental health problems are not only symptoms of individuals' distress but also efforts to cope with untenable social situations brought on by a history of collective oppression. (p. xix)

Discussion

The Nimkee NupiGawagan Healing Centre's adoption of a culture-based model of resiliency is loosely akin with a Western approach to health promotion; that is, it does not focus solely on the eradication of an illness or a disease. From a health promotion perspective, health is understood to be a state of unity or balance across the physical, mental, social, and spiritual components of a person's well-being, rather than merely the presence or absence of disease. This parallels the World Health Organization's holistic definition of health. Connection to self, community, and political context, including the determinants of health, can be accounted for within a health promotion framework. The historical drawback of the disease-based approach has been the placement of substance abuse outside the context of this understanding, thus creating a lack of recognition of the impacts of the determinants of health. The underlying assumption of a determinants-of-health perspective is that "reductions in health inequities require reductions in material and social inequities (Public Health Service of Canada, 2001, p. 60). Quite simply, "[t]he conditions in which people grow, live, work and age have a powerful influence on health. Inequalities in these conditions lead to inequalities in health" (World Health Organziation, 2007, p. 2). There is increasing acceptance of this approach within Canadian health care generally, and within the fields of substance abuse and mental health specifically.

The Assembly of First Nations (2006) have added to this understanding of the determinants of health, and propose Indigenous-specific indicators of well-being. In addition to the determinants of health commonly applied within the mainstream—such as income, social status, education, and literacy—Indigenous-specific indicators include not only health care, but also lands, resources, language, heritage, and culture. Health Canada's current Mental Wellness Framework for Culturally Appropriate Mental Health Services in First Nations and Inuit Communities likewise places mental health and addictions issues in the context of the broad determinants of health. Simply stated, "[t]he social origins or prevailing mental health problems require social solutions" (Kirmayer, Simpson, & Cargo, 2003, p. S21).

Nowhere is the need for this holistic understanding more evident than within the realm of solvent abuse among First Nations and Inuit youth. Research has shown that chronic solvent abusers are disproportionately located in impoverished social environments and are more likely to use solvents as a coping mechanism to suppress, among other things, emotional pain (Howard & Jensen, 1999; Perron & Loiselle, 2002). Solvent abuse cannot be understood in isolation from the relationship between large social issues and individual people. The whole person, alongside social and political processes and structures, needs to be accounted for in understanding and responding to any health issue, including solvent abuse. A health promotion approach, with its focus on the determinants of health, offers an opportunity for synthesis between Western and Indigenous world views, including a culture-based model of resiliency. In the attempt to apply a more inclusive model of service and health promotion, conventional approaches must be fundamentally rethought so that they are consistent with Indigenous realities, values, and aspirations.

The work of Wieman (2009) at Six Nations Mental Health Services relays the importance, and challenge, for mental health practitioners to respect local values and traditions and connect with community networks when providing care. John's experience at the Nimkee NupiGawagan Healing Centre illustrates the simultaneous reliance both on Indigenous (traditional medicine) and on Western (behaviour modification) approaches to treatment and healing.

Story from the Treatment Centre

When John started at Nimkee he learned that he had to take part in a spiritual "assessment" with an Elder. The Elder does a type of reading through which he is able to see negative energy blocks in a person. The Elder can tell from this whether the youth needs certain medicines, for example, or a feast. Many youth like to participate in the assessment because it is a time when they can have their name, clan, and colours identified to them. When John arrived at Nimkee it was quickly evident that he used his size to intimidate, control, and bully others, including Elders. In John's assessment, the Elder said he saw a trauma near John's neck, and John responded that he had never tried to commit suicide. The Elder continued to see this energy at John's neck, and John eventually relayed that his father tried to stab him in the neck when he was a young boy. The Elder told John that this block needed to be moved because John could not express himself with his voice, and as a consequence, he was compensating by being physical. The Elder held a spiritual intervention; he sang traditional healing songs, used his hands to move the energy block, prayed, and used traditional medicines. They included blueberries and unshelled peanuts. The Elder told John that when he felt himself getting angry, he needed to ask the staff for his medicine. Blueberries are a sacred traditional medicine as they are the first food to be offered by the earth. They will assist John in reconnecting with his internal energy and strength. Shelling peanuts gave John an activity to occupy himself with and time to reflect on his emotions and return to a calmer state of being. The Elder also encouraged John to speak with his counsellors each time he finished his medicine.

A fundamental shift in thinking will require both the discipline of Western medicine, especially psychiatry and those who work within it, to question their own sense and placement of self, community, and political context. Vicary and Bishop (2005) and Haggarty and O'Reilly (2000) suggest that mental health professionals need to educate themselves in traditional Indigenous approaches to treating mental illness and the role of culture in mental well-being to be able to consider their relevance to mainstream psychiatry practices. Reflecting on how to accomplish this type of education, Pazaratz (2005) draws on his experiences with training staff at a residential treatment centre for Northern youth, and suggests that "staff need to be versant with their own experiences or socialization acculturation. They must understand the basis of their own beliefs, mindsets, and assumptions" (p. 24). They must also be willing to take up the challenge of doing this. The consequence, according to Chaimowitz (2000), can be recognition that "Aboriginal concepts of problem-solving, reparative justice, and healing can contribute to [a mental health practitioner's] ... own set of experiences and knowledge base" (p. 606).

Acknowledgements

This study was funded by the Saskatchewan Health Research Foundation (grant number 407876) and the College of Medicine, University of Saskatchewan, Research Group Development Grant (grant number 407878).

NOTE

1. This chapter was originally published as Dell, C., Seguin, M., Hopkins, C., Tempier, R., Mehl-Madrona, L., Dell, D., & Mosier, K. (2011). From benzos to berries: Treatment offered at an aboriginal youth solvent abuse treatment centre relays the importance of culture. *Canadian Journal of Psychiatry, 56*(2), 75–83.

REFERENCES

Adelson, N. (1998). Health beliefs and the politics of Cree well-being. *Health, 2*(10), 5–22.

Adlaf, E., Begin, P., & Sawka E. (2005). *Canadian Addiction Survey (CAS): A national survey of Canadians' use of alcohol and other drugs. Prevalence of use and related harms. Detailed report*. Ottawa, ON: Canadian Centre on Substance Abuse.

Anishnawbe Health Toronto. (2008). *About Anishnawbe Health Toronto*. Retrieved from http://www.aht.ca/about-anishnawbe-health-toronto

Assembly of First Nations. (2006). First Nations' wholistic approach to indicators: Meeting on Indigenous peoples and indicators of well-being. Aboriginal Policy Conference, Ottawa, ON.

Ballard, M. (1998). Inhalant abuse: A call for attention. *Journal of Addictions and Offender Counselling, 19*(1), 28–32.

Beiser, M. (1985). The grieving witch: A framework for applying principles of cultural psychiatry to clinical practice. *Canadian Journal of Psychiatry, 30*(2), 130–140.

Beiser, M. (2003). Why should researchers care about culture? *Canadian Journal of Psychiatry*, *48*(3), 154–160.

Buchwald, B., Beals, J., & Manson, S. (2000). Use of traditional health practices among Native Americans in a primary care setting. *Medical Care*, *38*(12), 1191–1199.

Carroll, A., Houghton, S., & Odgers, P. (1998). Volatile solvent use among western Australian adolescents. *Adolescence*, *33*(132), 877–889.

Chaimowitz, G. (2000). Aboriginal mental health: Moving forward. *Canadian Journal of Psychiatry*, *45*(7), 605–606.

Chandler, M., & Lalonde, C. (1998). Cultural continuity as a hedge against suicide in Canada's First Nations. *Transcultural Psychiatry*, *35*(2), 191–219.

Coleman, H., Charles, G., & Collins, J. (2001). Inhalant use by Canadian Aboriginal youth. *Journal of Child and Adolescent Substance Use*, *10*(3), 1–20.

Dalrymple, A., O'Doherty, J., & Nietschei, K. (1995). Comparative analysis of Native admissions and registrations to Northwestern Ontario treatment facilities: Hospital and community sectors. *Canadian Journal of Psychiatry*, *49*(8), 467–473.

Davidson, L., Ridgway, P., Kidd, S., Topor, A., & Borg, M. (2008). Using qualitative research to inform mental health policy. *Canadian Journal of Psychiatry*, *53*(3), 137–144.

Dell, C., & Beauchamp, T. (2006). *Youth volatile solvent abuse: Frequently asked questions.* Ottawa, ON: Canadian Centre on Substance Abuse.

Dell, C., Hopkins, C., & Dell, D. (2005). Resiliency and holistic inhalant abuse treatment. *Journal of Aboriginal Health*, *2*(1), 4–12.

Dell, C., & Lyons, T. (2007). *Harm reduction and persons of Aboriginal descent.* Ottawa, ON: Canadian Centre on Substance Abuse.

Dewey, S. (2002). Huffing: What parents should know about inhalant abuse. *Reclaiming Children and Youth*, *11*(3), 150–151.

Dickason, O. (2006). *A concise history of Canada's First Nations.* Toronto, ON: Oxford University Press.

Duggal, H., Sinha, B., & Nizamie, S. (2000). Gasoline inhalation dependence and bipolar disorder. *Australian and New Zealand Journal of Psychiatry*, *34*(3), 531–532.

First Nations and Inuit Health Branch. (n.d.). *Mental wellness framework for culturally appropriate mental health services in First Nations and Inuit communities [internal report].* Ottawa, ON: FNIHB.

Francis, S. (2004). The role of dance in a Navajo ceremonial. In U. Gielen, J. Fish, & J. Draguns (Eds.), *Handbook of culture, therapy, and healing* (pp. 135–150). New York: Routledge.

Frideres, J. (2002). Overcoming hurdles: Health care and Aboriginal people. In B. Bolaria & H. Dickinson (Eds.), *Health, illness and health care in Canada* (pp. 144–166). Scarborough, ON: Thomson Learning.

Gladwell, M. (2008). *Outliers: The story of success.* New York: Little, Brown, and Company.

Goering, P., Boydell, K., & Pignatiello, A. (2008). The relevance of qualitative research for clinical programs in psychiatry. *Canadian Journal of Psychiatry*, *53*(3), 145–151.

Haggarty, J., & O'Reilly, R. (2000). Native mental health: More questions than answers. *Canadian Psychiatric Association Bulletin*, *32*(3), 88–89.

Helzer, J., Bucholz, K., & Gossop M. (2007). A dimensional option for the diagnosis of substance dependence in DSM-V. *International Journal of Methods in Psychiatric Research*, *16*(Suppl. 1), S24–S33.

Howard, M., & Jenson, J. (1999). Inhalant use among antisocial youth: Prevalence and correlates. *Addictive Behaviours*, *24*(1), 59–74.

Iarocci, G., Root, R., & Burack, J. (2009). Social competence and mental health among Aboriginal youth: An integrative developmental perspective. In L. Kirmayer & G. Valiskakis (Eds.), *Healing traditions: The mental health of Aboriginal Peoples in Canada* (pp. 80-106). Vancouver, BC: University of British Columbia Press.

Janezic, T. (1997). Burns following petrol sniffing. *Burns, 23*(1), 78-80.

King T. (2003). *The truth about stories: A Native narrative.* Toronto, ON: House of Anansi Press.

Kirmayer, L., & Minas, H. (2000). The future of transcultural psychiatry: An international perspective. *Canadian Journal of Psychiatry, 45*(5), 438-446.

Kirmayer, L., Simpson, C., & Cargo M. (2003). Healing traditions: Culture, community and mental health promotion with Canadian Aboriginal Peoples. *Australasian Psychiatry, 11*(Suppl. 1), S15-S23.

Kraemer, H. (2007). DSM categories and dimensions in clinical and research contexts. *International Journal of Methods in Psychiatric Research,* 16(Suppl. 1), S8-S15.

Kurtzman, T., Otsuka, K., & Wahl, R. (2001). Inhalant abuse by adolescents. *Journal of Adolescent Health, 28*(3), 170-180.

Ledogar, R., & Fleming, J. (2008). Social capital and resilience: A review of concepts and selected literature relevant to Aboriginal youth resilience research. *Pimatisiwin: A Journal of Aboriginal and Indigenous Community Health, 6*(2), 25-46.

Lewis-Fernandez, R. (1998). A cultural critique of the DSM-IV dissociative disorders section. *Transcultural Psychiatry, 35*(3), 387-400.

Manson, S. (2000). Mental health services for American Indians and Alaska Natives: Need, use, and barriers to effective care. *Canadian Journal of Psychiatry, 45*(7), 617-626.

Marbella, A., Harris, M., Diehr. S., Ignace, G., & Ignace, G. (1998). Use of Native American healers among Native American patients in an urban Native American health centre. *Archives of Family Medicine, 7*(2), 182-185.

McCormick, R. (2009). Aboriginal approaches to counselling. In L. Kirmayer & G. Valiskakis (Eds.), *Healing traditions: The mental health of Aboriginal Peoples in Canada* (pp. 337-354). Vancouver, BC: University of British Columbia Press.

Mehl-Madrona, L. (2005). *Coyote wisdom: The power of story in healing.* Rochester, VT: Bear & Company.

Morrison, R., & Wilson, C. (2004). *Native Peoples: The Canadian experience.* Toronto, ON: Oxford University Press.

Morrisseau, C. (1998). *Into the daylight: A wholistic approach to healing.* Toronto, ON: University of Toronto Press.

National Drug Abuse Information Centre. (1988). *Deaths due to volatile solvent abuse. Stat Update, Number 8.* Bethesda, MD: National Drug Abuse Information Centre.

Nimkee NupiGawagan Healing Centre. (2008). *Historical background.* Retrieved from http://www.nimkee.ca/background

O'Brien. D. (2005). Babies that smell like gas. Retrieved from: http://www.winnipegfreepress.com/historic/31604259.html

Pazaratz, D. (2005). Maintaining cultural integrity in residential treatment. *Residential Treatment for Children and Youth, 22*(4), 16-31.

Perron, B., & Loiselle, J. (2002). *Où en sont les juenes face au tabac, à l'alcool, aux drogues et au jeu? Enquete quebecoise sur le tabagisme chez lese eleves du secondaire (2002).* Montreal, QC: Institute de la Statistique du Quebec.

Public Health Agency of Canada. (2001). *What is the population health approach?* Ottawa, ON: Public Health Agency of Canada.

Regier, D. (2007). Dimensional approaches to psychiatric classification: Refining the research agenda for DSM-V: An introduction. *International Journal of Methods in Psychiatric Research, 16*(Suppl. 1), S1–S5.

Research Group on Drug Use. (2004). *Drug use in Toronto, Ontario.* Toronto, ON: Toronto Public Health.

Thatcher, R. (2004). *Fighting firewater fictions: Moving beyond the disease model of alcoholism in First Nations.* Toronto, ON: University of Toronto Press.

Vicary, D., & Bishop, B. (2005). Western psychotherapeutic practice: Engaging Aboriginal people in culturally appropriate and respectful ways. *Australian Psychologist, 40*(1), 8–19.

Waldram, J. (1997). *The way of the pipe: Aboriginal spirituality and symbolic healing in Canadian prisons.* Peterborough, ON: Broadview Press.

Waldram, J. (2000). The efficacy of traditional medicine: Current theoretical and methodological issues. *Medical Anthropology Quarterly, 14*(4), 603–625.

Waldron, J. (2004). Revenge of the Windigo: *The construction of the mind and mental health of North American Aboriginal Peoples.* Toronto, ON: University of Toronto Press.

White, V., & Hayman, J. (2004). *National Drug Strategy monograph series no 56.* Canberra, AU: Australian Government Department of Health and Ageing.

Wieman, C. (2009). Six Nations mental health services: A model of care for Aboriginal communities. In L. Kirmayer & G. Valiskakis (Eds.), *Healing traditions: The mental health of Aboriginal Peoples in Canada* (pp. 401–418). Vancouver, BC: University of British Columbia Press.

Wille, S., & Lambert, W. (2004). Volatile substance abuse: Post-mortem diagnosis. *Forensic Science International, 142*(2–3), 135–156.

World Health Organization. (2007). *Achieving health equity: From root causes to fair outcomes.* Commission on Social Determinants of Health interim statement. Retrieved from http://www.who.int/social_determinants/resources/csdh_media/cdsh_interim_statement_final_07.pdf

Youth Solvent Addiction Committee. (2008). *Saskatoon (SK): Youth Solvent Addiction Committee.* Retrieved from http://www.members.shaw.ca/ysac

CHAPTER 22

I Have Kept Too Many Secrets

Thomas Miller

Editor's Note: Thomas Miller's chapter is the only contribution to the book that is not authored or co-written by a social worker. Mr. Miller's personal narrative arose from reading the second edition of this book. It led him to recall a past that had been hidden away by him from himself for his protection. Its inclusion in the third edition of Responding to the Oppression of Addiction *is intended to move you beyond the theoretical, the empirical, and the brief case study, all of which are vital to knowing, yet still removed from the lived reality of the oppression of addiction. Thomas's story is not an easy one to read. Parts are graphic, unsettling, and fragmented, and there are gaps in the narrative, yet this is the individualized reality produced by government policy and practice in Canada. "I Have Kept Too Many Secrets" has also been included in the holdings of the Truth and Reconciliation Commission of Canada, which arose out of the Canadian Indian Residential Schools Settlement Agreement.* http://www.residentialschoolsettlement.ca/english.html

Part I: Issues of Oppression and Addiction

As a Native of Canada I have personal experience of the effects of oppression and drug dependency. It is present throughout my family history. The furthest back in my family tree that I can trace is to my great-great-grandparents. They lived on a small farm in the late 1800s. Their family consisted of eight children. Alcohol was a small problem at this time mostly because there was no money to purchase any. The family lived in extreme poverty. The farm did not meet the family's needs. The Canadian army would drop off food and clothing to the reserve. Neighbours would help each other. It was forbidden for alcohol to be consumed, bought, or sold at that time on the reserve yet people still drank. It is said that the Elders would police family homes during this time. The Elders, who were greatly respected, would say, "The mind changer is for the white people. It is not meant for us."

The concept of residential schools began to be discussed during this time. At first this idea was welcomed. Many leaders felt that education could provide a future for the children. It was unforeseen by the leaders of the time what the true outcome of this institution would be. They were led to believe that the children would learn "white ways" yet still retain our culture. It was the belief that Natives must learn how to function in white society. Many family farms failed during this time because the children who helped on the farms were forcibly removed. My great-great-grandparents had to totally rely on the government and the church to survive.

I have read that the most heinous and most successful system instituted in the name of assimilation was the residential school system. I totally agree with this statement. My great-grandparents and grandparents attended this institution. There are stories of sexual and physical abuse. My grandmother was sexually assaulted by the priest. She watched her friend die from appendicitis while at school. Many children ran away. Most of these children were returned home to the reserve having died from the elements. Children were expected to work in the morning and attend school in the afternoon. Native language was forbidden. My grandmother was fortunate as she did run away but managed to return to Curve Lake safely. I asked her how she got home safely while others died. She would not say. She did tell me that during her time at school many of her friends were beaten to unconsciousness.

After my great-grandfather, Eddie T., returned from the residential school he married my great-grandmother Maye. They had three boys. The Hill family was totally reliant on government support. During this time he was asked to sell his status if he wished to continue to receive support from the government. I do not know what Eddie T. experienced in residential school. He ignored me and I am actually happy he did so. He was alcohol dependent his entire life. I have been told he began drinking when he returned home from the school. Considering the stories I have heard from my grandparents, it would be safe to say his experiences at the residential school were not good. He was abusive. He often would beat his sons and wife. Eventually he beat his wife to death in front of my grandfather, his son.

My grandfather, Sam, also attended the residential school. He would never share his stories in regard to the school. He was also alcohol dependent. His two brothers both met untimely ends. One was shot and the other was beaten and drowned. My grandfather was also very abusive, not unlike his father. He physically and sexually abused his sons and daughters. He was abusive to my grandmother as well. She gave birth to a son named Johnny who suffered serious brain damage when he was struck by Sam and had his head caved in. I know that Sam tried try to kill my grandmother at least once. He held a gun to her head with black gloves on. Fortunately her sisters walked into the house and removed and emptied the gun. I asked my grandmother why she stayed with him. Her response was she tried to leave but the police just brought her back. Both my grandparents suffered from PTSD. Alcohol was their medicine of choice.

My mother also suffered from mental disorders. She experienced years of abuse from her father. She was sexually and physically abused by her father. Her mother suffered from what at the time was called a nervous breakdown. My mother always wanted normality. She wanted a stable family life and tried to create it. She would not use alcohol because it had always been present during the traumatic events in her life.

My mother attempted to create a stable family structure, however, her past trauma did not allow for it. She did love me and my biological father. However, he chose to leave at the time of my birth. I was told his family did not approve of me or my mother due to our Native heritage. My childhood was full of trauma. I inherited the PTSD. I did not escape the last 200 years of oppression.

Government-run organizations are not trusted by present-day Natives for these reasons. History has demonstrated the government has always put their goals ahead of the needs of Natives. I do believe many people had their heart in the right place, but were doing the wrong things. The Native issues on dependency could be argued for ages. We could argue about what came first, the substance abuse or the oppression. For me that is like arguing what came first, the chicken or the egg. Many present-day Natives all across Canada abuse substances to escape from the oppression, the trauma we as Natives inherited from our families.

But there is still hope. I believe that this trauma can be combated. It is not a hopeless cause. Natives need both addiction and mental health facilities on every major reserve. Now most Natives travel off the reserve to attend a centre to ensure confidentiality. Trust is given to centres that are run by competent, educated Natives fully versed in traditional teachings. Transportation to any facility must be made more easily available. If both the oppression and substance abuse is treated in the right facilities that serve all the needs of the client I believe that we can combat these phenomena effectively.

I am tired of talk that comes to nothing. It makes my heart sick when I remember all the good words and all the broken promises. There has been too much talking by men who had no right to talk. It does not require many words to speak the truth.

—CHIEF JOSEPH, NEZ PERCE

Part II: My Life Growing Up

I think I have kept too many secrets in my life. Secrets that have hid me, clothed me. What I fear is that if anything should ever happen to me my children will never really know who I am. One thing I have learned is that around the corner almost anything can happen. You never know, you might live to a hundred or go tomorrow. If you need to judge me, judge me for who I am, not what you think I should be. Until I wrote this, I never talked about my experiences with anyone, so how can anyone really know who I am? We are the sum of our experiences. The best way to explain who I am is to start at the earliest memory.

My real dad never wanted me. My parents dated, then got married. I think this was one of those happy times in my mom's life but it's hard to be sure. My father left my mother and me just before I was born. I have had the chance to talk to him on the phone before but all he has to say is that there were too many painful memories—not much of an explanation. How can you know yourself if your parents don't know themselves? My mom often talked about him. She always had a candle in the window for him right until the day of her death.

The earliest memory I have of myself is when I believe I was one. The order of early memories is hard to determine, they are unclear. I do remember being a happy baby for the most part. My mom and stepdad and I lived at the house next to my grandma's. In that first memory I was in a playpen outside on the front lawn at my grandma's house. I was not happy. There was a huge world outside my cage and I wanted to explore it. The next thing I remember it was my first birthday. My mom put a cake in front of me. I had no idea what it was. It definitely needed to be explored, unfortunately my arms were not working. A few years later I saw a picture of my first birthday and my stepdad holding my arms, and that explained to me why my arms weren't working that day. In my early years, I was a tremendously happy boy. My older brother lived with grandma and grandpa and I was, for a while, an only child who received attention from everyone.

The next real memory I have was sitting on the dining room table. My stepdad had already left for work. I cannot recall if my sister was born yet or not, but she was not with me that day. We lived at the apartments on Albright Street. Mom was dressing me, putting my shoes on. She was in a really good mood and so was I. I had everything a little boy could want. I had the best mom ever and a really good stepdad with all the toys I could want. I remember that it was a little cold out that day. My mom was putting layers and layers of clothes on me. She would always hug me and I was always hugging her back. We left the apartment to go for a walk. The sun was just rising. I did not know where we were going and did not care. I had everything and now I was going out to explore the world with my mom. We stopped at a bench on the street and waited there for a little while. This big huge bus pulled up. I was really excited. This looked like fun. The door opened and this nice man who looked a little like my stepdad opened the door. No one was on the bus. I was allowed to run anywhere I wanted, explore any secret places. The bus did not go anywhere. That made me a little disappointed. My mom sat in the front seat and talked to the nice man. He gave me candy, the best way to earn my respect I suppose. Then we left and I don't remember seeing that nice man again, but it was awesome.

When my sister was born we were still living at the apartments on Albright. I always had to get diapers for my mom. My little sister was annoying, as younger siblings always seem to be. She always interrupted my fun, but I got used to her after a while. Here is the strange thing. That annoying little baby sister meant so much to me. I had nightmares that something happened to her. My mom would get me up and I had to check on her almost every night in her crib. Then my sister started becoming more interesting. Samantha was an obedient sister. She played everything I played and always played the part I asked her to. I wanted to explore the world. This is when I started learning about my mother's wrath. I had several times gotten up early and sneaked out of the apartment while she was sleeping, but always returned before she woke up. I had mastered the locking mechanism on the door. I wanted to explore the whole building—I think it had 19 floors in total. This one time I took my sister with me. She only had her diaper on. It was great having a little sister to explore with. We went anywhere I wanted. Then I got caught. The superintendent spotted my sister and me. We had to run but Samantha was really slow and she got caught. I ran all the way back to the apartment and woke my mom up. It had happened, my worse fear had been realized, someone had actually stolen my sister. I was really upset. I told my mom everything. She was angry at me. She slapped me in the face she was so angry. That had never happened before. She took me with her and found my sister at the superintendent's apartment. Wow, she was angry at me. I felt really bad about it. I was never going to take my sister exploring again. I got caught because she was too slow and now I was in trouble. However, the next time to explore never came. My mom put more sophisticated locks on the door and on top of the door and she started to get up earlier. I never got the chance to decipher the new locking mechanisms. Well, she still was a good sister.

As I got older I was more of a happy brat. My aunts, uncles, and cousins always played with me. I was learning how to count: "What comes after 60 ... 61?" No one refused to answer any of my questions. I remember my grandma bathing me outside in a galvanized tub before she got running water. She was the best grandma. Not very often did she say no. I lived with her almost as much as I lived with my mom. I would play trucks with my older brother for hours when he was not picking on me. My grandma and grandpa wanted to take me to Fantasy Island in New York. There were mysterious Yankees and lots of fun rides there. I was excited. My mom called. She asked me to come home because she really missed me. We had not seen each other in a few days. My mom was more important to me than mysterious Yankees and fun rides, so I went home instead of visiting my fantasy place.

I have a few bad memories from that time. I saw my mom fighting with my Uncle Bill. She was crying, holding a bat, though I don't know why. This happened a few times, but I was still a truly happy brat. Once when both mom and I were at grandma's house I saw a dead fluffy rabbit—roadkill. It was too much for me to ignore; it was so soft. I took my new fluffy rabbit to the house to show mom and grandma. They freaked. My mom and grandma started arguing about the best way to disinfect me. My mom said bleach and then to a hospital, my grandma said rubbing alcohol, and soon after I got a live fluffy rabbit to play with. Eventually the rabbit got away and my brother said the wolves ate it.

My grandma's family wasn't as nice as my mom and grandma were, not that it mattered much to me. I remember that my evil Aunt Irene was visiting one day. My mother said, "Now just stay away from her and everything would be fine." However, I did not listen very well. My grandma and Aunt Irene were going for a walk. They had sneaked out without me knowing. Not much got past me so I ran after my grandma and caught up to them. Aunt Irene called me "a little bastard" so I ran back to the house and told my mom. She said, "I told you to stay away from her."

At this time things were changing for me. I was around three or four years old. We lived in Hamilton Side Street. We did not live there too long, only about two months. There were many neighbourhood kids for me to play with; most were around my age. They did not call their mothers mommy, just mom. This must have been an older thing to do. I'd have to speak to my mother about it. "Mommy I need to talk to you." Okay what is it?" "Well the other kids call their mommy mom because they are older, and I think it's time to call you mom now. Is that okay"? She seemed a little hurt but smiled at me. She gave me a hug told me she loved me and that was okay for her to be mom.

Next I remember living on Barton Street. I was almost old enough to go to school. My younger brother was born. He was a little scary at first as he had longer hair than me that stood straight up and had big black eyes. But I was happy to have a new baby brother anyway. At this time I was glued to my stepdad when I was not with my mom. I often travelled around with him in the transport truck. One place we stopped to unload was the best. The guys working there were always giving me treats. They went into their lunch boxes and found anything they thought I might enjoy. We stayed in the area for a couple of days.

I used to help my stepdad fix the family car. One day while helping I slipped and fell off, cutting my chin. My mom was not too impressed with him. It was around that time that things started changing with mom and stepdad. They started arguing more. Then the physical fighting began. My mom turned the stove on and tried to put my dad's head on it. I was scared. I thought it must have been his fault, but why would she do that?

I was in bed and I could hear mom and dad arguing. I grew afraid. I did not want to see my mom hurt. My bedroom door opened to the hallway, which in turn led into the kitchen. I could see him standing there. I needed to do something to help her. Well the hardest thing on my body was my head so I started from my door, put my head down, and ran at him as fast as I could; before he knew it I banged into him. He let out a little air. They were both surprised at me. I was supposed to be asleep. Mom asked me what I was doing and I said I thought they were fighting and that she needed my help. She told me they were just talking and gave me a hug. I don't remember saying I was sorry as I remember I wasn't completely sold they were just talking.

I had many nightmares at that age. I was always afraid someone would steal my sister or hurt my brother. I don't know why I had these nightmares but I woke up screaming and crying. Mom was always there every time.

Mom and dad were going on a trip to Quebec. They were going for three days. The babysitter we had left us after the first day. The three of us were alone. Samantha and I were arguing about how to feed baby Jamie. He got cereal as that was the only thing we knew. At this time Jamie only knew how to crawl. I am not sure how we did it but we cared for Jamie and changed his diapers hoping mom and dad would return. Eventually they did.

I was now old enough to go to school. I was so excited. This was going to be a whole new way to learn about the world. I loved school. I was allowed to walk to school all by myself. Every day I would wake my mom: "Is it time yet?" Life was pretty good for the most part. Mom and dad fought a lot but then they seemed close too. The next two years went well except my mom was short-tempered with my dad and, well, actually with most people.

It was going to be my seventh birthday. We lived on Cannon Street. This was my vegetarian time period. I asked my mother where hamburger came from. She told me a cow. This was unacceptable to me. That meant I was as bad as the wolves that ate my fluffy bunny when I was younger. At the end of this phase I was tricked into being a carnivore by my Uncle Tom. He was watching me cooking my dinner. I specifically said I did not want any meat from some poor animal. He cooked me ravioli, which I consumed. After I was finished I remarked how yummy it was. He then informed me it had cow in it. That was the end of my vegetarian days.

School was awesome. It was so exciting, I could not wait. I was going to be seven. I would be old enough to explore and learn new things that a seven year old could learn better than a six year old. This was going to be a whole new chapter in my life. I was like a sponge that wanted water. The more water the sponge got, the bigger the sponge, the more water it needed. There was no satisfying me. I had energy like the sun, endless and bright. There were a lot of kids at my birthday party and most were my friends and cousins. I received tons of presents. This was the best. I do not remember too many birthdays after this. Things started to change soon after. Mom became a little different. We still said "love ya" every night. She was always there whenever I needed her, but something was different.

I cannot remember how this happened. We were at home. Samantha was only six and I was only seven. What I remember next changed me, changed us. It was after Christmas. My mother grew very angry and was chasing my sister and me with a claw hammer. I am not sure if Samantha ran with me or I grabbed her but we ran under the dining room table as it was more difficult for mom to hit us with the hammer. We thought this was the end. We begged our mother to forgive us. Told her we loved her. She kept swinging the hammer and we kept dodging it screaming and screaming. I was on the right side of my sister. The table had steel legs with fake wood as a top. Then she got my sister. Hit her on her right thigh not far from my head. Then my mother fell over crying. Samantha was sobbing. I was quiet, unable to understand what just happened. I think my sister and I were in shock. Something changed in me that day. I became different.

A few days later the Children's Aid Society came to get us. Mom said she was having a nervous breakdown and needed time away from us kids. I was losing my mom.

The foster home was a jail. We were forced to live in the basement. We were warned not to cross the yellow lines. Our bedrooms were upstairs and only at bedtimes were we allowed up. The only other time we were allowed upstairs was when it was time to eat. At no time could we sit on any furniture other than at the table. These rules did not apply to the other children. My sister and brother were complacent. I was not. I resisted. I was a dirty little Indian who needed a few good beatings to put me in my place. My sister would cry and pleaded with the man in the house every time. I continued my resistance. Then it was time to attend a new school. I did not want to go. I was scared. I felt different and did not want anyone to know. I was different although at the time I did not know how. We were there three months. At the end of those months I finally learned to be complacent. I cried everyday for my mom.

We returned home early spring. My mother hugged Samantha and Jamie, but I was angry at her. It took me 20 minutes before I hugged her and started crying. I did not understand it at the time but I had unconditional love for her and still do to this day. Our daily lives almost returned to normal even though I was different and she was different. The love for each other was the only thing that remained the same.

We were now living in Alberton. It was a nice house with a lot of yard to play in. My sister and I where always playing together. We would ride our bikes together and make snowmen. Our snowmen needed to get bigger. We created a huge snowball. My sister and I were trying to roll on top of it but she fell off and hit her head on the concrete steps. I immediately took her to our mother but she was cross. When my dad came home we then took her to the hospital to get stitches. She screamed. I found myself crying for her.

My next memory is about Christmas time. It was mom's and my favourite time of the year. It was so hard to go asleep. I heard bells and jumped out of bed and ran to the Christmas tree. There was my mom moving presents around. I asked her what she was doing and she replied Santa was in a hurry and she wanted to straighten the presents out. I was sold on that one. Looking back now I realize there were never any presents for her under the tree.

We were now living on Wellington Street. There were lots of hiding places. This is when we started going to Sunday school at the Salvation Army. I barely passed grade three. Things were very different with my mom. One day she was cross. On those days she was having problems with her nerves. The next day it was my mom I had always known. As time passed the "problem nerves" days increased. School was not much fun. I found myself struggling. I felt different from the other kids and they sensed it as the started picking on me. This is when I started the violin lessons. I loved it. It was a way to forget. I could sense or feel the composer, the rise and fall of the notes. It was almost like a dream.

The summer preceeding grade four my best friend's 16-year-old brother moved in with us. My mother always felt compelled to help people she thought needed help. She could not have known how this was going to affect us.

I don't remember my eighth or ninth birthday but I clearly remember New Year's 1980. It was just mom and me looking out the front window watching the fireworks and people celebrating New Year's. It was my mom I had always known. I felt so close to her that day. We were talking about what the new year would bring. She seemed so optimistic and made me feel the same. There are times when I wished I could just live in that moment. We gave each other a big hug. I loved my mom.

The new year was anything but positive. My mother's nerve problems increased to almost daily. Then she said she had cancer and was not going for the operation. She was arguing with dad almost daily and all of our family. She went back to school. There she met her new friend. I found out about it. I was becoming lonely. My mother's attention towards me was now very rare. Her new friend brought all kinds of troubles. I was also becoming angry at her as it seemed I did not matter as much. I knew we still loved each other but it was not the same. Not only was she my mother but she was my best friend too. I had always told her everything, but now nothing. Schoolwork was extremely difficult now, but I continued to try. I was vulnerable. That's when "HE" struck. The sexual assault began. At first it was nice. "HE" showed me the same attention as my mom had. Then he made me feel sick. I wanted the attention from him but not the attention I received. I told no one as I felt ashamed, sad, and small. I went to school watching the other kids doing their everyday thing, yet I could not. I was more different now and did not want anyone to know. Things got worse with my mom as she would sometimes not be home for several hours. I did not see her daily as I once did. My dad became more cross with me. I went to bed crying many times when "HE" was not there.

It was my 10th birthday, maybe 12th. I was somewhat excited. Mom made arrangements for me to have my birthday at McDonald's. Every kid loves McDonald's. She did not keep her promise. She was going to spend the day with me. Instead I was dropped off. It was hard to blow out candles with tears in your eyes.

May 13th. I did not want to be angry with my mom anymore. I asked my mom to get that operation for her cancer. She asked my why and I said I did not want people to know I did not have a mom. I gave her a big hug. There were tears in my eyes.

May 14th. Mom was making supper. I started to lash out at my mom. She pinned me to the floor. I was crying and told her I hated her. Then I looked at "HIM," wanted "HIM" to help me. "HE" pulled my mom off me and started fighting with her. My dad came into the kitchen and he began fighting with her. The chicken and dumplings on the stove went flying onto the wall. Then the fighting stopped. My mom ran out of the house crying.

My mom is dead. She committed suicide. I was numb. Jamie had woken up the night before crying. My mom, my best friend was gone. The last thing I said to her was I hated her, when in fact I loved her more than anything in the world. It was the last straw. Because of me she was gone. I went to my bedroom and cried and cried. I did not want anyone to see me.

My mom had a beautiful casket. It was dark blue with gold handles. She looked so beautiful. She was smiling with her eyes closed and her hands together with her beautiful long black hair. It was entirely my fault. I let down my mom and best friend. We were staying with the people from the Salvation Army so dad could make arrangements. They asked me to say my prayers at night. "God, please look after my mom and let her know I love her."

Today is the funeral. I had my little blue suit on. The same colour as her casket. My grandma and grandpa came down the aisle, both were holding each other up crying. We sat in a room attached to the parlor. It was time to close the casket. The funeral people pulled a screen across us so we could not see them close it. My grandpa tried to tear it down. The family grabbed him and held him back. What have I done?

The next few days were a party. Everybody was drinking. I was invisible. I wanted to be invisible. I felt the change in me.

It was time to go back to school. I hated it. My grandma was not allowed over anymore. My dad, who became stepdad, hung around with us for a little while. Then he was around once or twice a week. "HE" was always around though. Sometimes we had nothing to eat. We would go to the grocery store and steal food. "HE" always gave me attention.

My sister and brother went to school early that day. I was running late. "HE" jumped on me, knocked me to the floor. I begged "HIM" to stop and let me go to school. I eventually got to school late. I told my teacher I slept in. The whole world was heavy. The very air had weight.

Three months had passed and we meet stepdad's new girlfriend. She had three kids, a girl and boy our age and a boy Jamie's age. Stepdad gave her mom's clothes. For three months I went into my mom's closet just to smell her clothes. Now they were gone and she was wearing them. Sometimes when we were there we had to stay in the basement.

We did not go over to Sandy's (my stepdad's new girlfriend) house that much. My sister and I learned how to do laundry, cook, and clean, plus look after our five-year-old brother. I did get a lot of attention from "HIM."

I got into a fist fight with a kid on the front lawn. He was on the ground and I was jumping on him. I felt like a real loser. He was picking on me but I was inflicting pain on someone else. I know what that feels like. I never did it again.

It seemed like I cried every night when "HE" was not around. Then I had this most amazing moment. I dreamt my mom and I were in this little room. She did not look well. She asked me how she looked and I said beautiful. She smiled at me, we had some small talk and told each other how much we loved each other, and then she gave me a big hug. She said she had to go now. I said "no mom, stay with me" but she could not. I asked her to let me go with her but she said no. She left the room and I chased after her. I was crying and crying, calling for her but there was only darkness. Then I saw him, the Great Spirit, when I turned right. He saw me. I felt like one person in billions. He was—no, He is a great light. So bright, He is brighter than the sun and fills every space. Even though I was one person in billions, I felt special. All my fear, grief, and anger was gone. All I felt was a happiness I never felt before. I was to have my own family. I needed to hang in there. Then a Christmas tree appeared. It was the most beautiful thing I had ever seen. There were presents everywhere and little animals all over the tree. I had never felt this kind of happiness before. Then I thought, hoped the biggest present was mine, and then wham it was gone and I was in my bedroom. The sun was shining and it felt like a wonderful day. But that day was soon over.

One day my grandma and Aunt Sandy were at the door. They took a few swings at "HIM" and pushed passed him. There was no way they knew what he had done or what he was doing. My grandma gave me this wonderful winter coat. Now I can go outside and not be cold. It was nicer than what Samantha and Jamie had.

Six months later my stepdad's mom moved in. She had a lot of cats and dogs. They made a mess. We saw a lot more of stepdad and his girlfriend. But this did not change the attention I received from "HIM." We learned how to be good children. We cooked, cleaned, did laundry, served coffee and tea at meal times. We needed to be grateful. One day "HIS" dog got away and was hit by a car and died. A few weeks later "HE" was gone. He left me feeling unwanted. About three years of sexual assaults had ended but the mental and physical abuse was accelerated.

If we were not with stepdad at home then we were at his girlfriend's house with him. The only girlfriend he had I liked was Cookie; she was really nice. We were grateful children. However, it seemed that I was not as grateful as the other children, as I needed old-fashioned correction. I often received the strap on "the bare ass." Other days a good old-fashioned beating was good for my attitude. Sometimes I needed this correction if I did not scrub the floor well enough. My "lazy ass" would sometimes do a "half ass job." The red-and-white squares on the floor revealed everything. "Your mother would roll over in her grave if she had seen this," he often said. I was "good for nothing."

I was very different from the other kids in school. Some of them would pick on me. In grades six, seven, and eight I concentrated on school and my violin lessons. Mrs. Wolven, my violin teacher, was always trying to do things for me. Mrs. Barbie from the Salvation Army would pick me up to take me places and give me clothes all the time. The clothes she gave me were always too big. This is when I learned how to sew by hand. Then I had clothes like the other children. Sometimes I went to school during hot days with winter boots on because that was all I had. The other children stopped picking on me. My best friend was Bobby. We always played together in the alleyway. He had a way of allowing me to forget things. I know I had birthdays but I don't remember them.

Grade six. My uncle Stanley (my stepdad's brother) moved in. Sometimes he was nice but most times he was cross. I helped him a lot. I would travel around with him picking up scrap cars and fetching whatever he needed. However, I was not grateful enough for the things he did for me so stepdad had to correct me.

Samantha was playing violin now. It was hard to practice with her as she was not that good at it. Mrs. Wolven had bought me a violin. Samantha and I played in an orchestra. It was awesome. The music seemed to take me away. If stepdad came to any of my concerts I could hear him snoring. It was better if he did not come. Then came the day where Samantha and I were going to play in an orchestra and travel around Hamilton to lots of schools. The first day was so much fun. Uncle Stanley was going to give us a ride to the first school the next day due to a city bus strike. The next day came; I was so excited I was up before the sun. It was going to be a warm sunny day. When it came time to leave Uncle Stan refused to give my sister and me a ride because we did not say "good morning" to him. I was crushed and started crying. I could not help it. Samantha was not going to accept this. She saw how crushed I was. She went to the school and told Mr. Thompson, the principal, what happened and how crushed I was. He came over, picked me up, and took Samantha and me to the first school.

I tried to stop crying before we got there. He told Mrs. Wolven what happened. Later on she gave me a hug.

We had no hot water or heat. We hung our laundry outside in the wintertime. Afterwards we would hang the clothes up in the house. If they had not dried, as it usually took two days, we would use an iron to finish them.

In grade eight my teacher's name was Mrs. Harris. My grades were almost straight A's. I don't think she liked me. At the end of the year she made fun of my clothes, shoes, and book bag. My book bag I made in home economics and sometimes my hand-sewn clothes did not turn out well and my shoes—I had what I had. I was very different from the other kids and she pointed that out to me in front of the class.

Mrs. Wolven I saw every day. She tried not to give me any more attention than the other kids. When they were not around she liked to talk to me. I never told her anything other than I was fine and she never pressed me. At my grade 8 graduation the other kids were shocked when I received the music award. Mrs. Wolven tried not to cry when she handed it to me. Her eyes were red. She had been my teacher since grade 5. I miss her.

The first semester of grade nine I attended school in Westdale. I delivered news-papers to pay for my bus fare, school supplies, and shoes. I bought one new pair of shoes. I would wipe them down everyday so that they would feel like new. I was in the Westdale symphony. It was the best in Ontario. It was beautiful. The way the notes came together from all the instruments. It was amazing. But it did not seem like enough anymore. I received more beatings than before. The world was so crushing. My grades fell. My French teacher tried to talk to me about what was wrong. She drove me to places but I could not tell her anything. I made up excuses but she did not buy any of it. I can't remember her name but obviously my act needed polishing. Some people could read me.

It was my plan. I had to run away. I was 15 now. The beatings got worse. He left bruises upon bruises where you could not see them. I ran away to my grandma's house. My younger brother years later remarked, "You did not have the balls to stick around." I could not stay. It was better at my grandma's. She seemed happy I was there.

I saw the other side of my grandma. It was not the grandma I had known. Time had tarnished her. She would start yelling at me for something I did not understand. After she told me that sometimes she gets that way. I did not have to do laundry, wash the floors and dishes, or cook. I offered to do so but she would not hear of it. Instead I would cut the grass. My high school years went by fast. My grandma was always yelling at me about my older brother Richard. She felt I was not looking out for him. He was always in trouble with the police. He smashed up cars, stole things like transport trucks. He was always angry at me. His jealously was maintained because he feared grandma might love me more but that was hardly the case. Whenever he did something wrong grandma would call me a little bastard for not looking out for him—after all, he was my brother. It hurt when she did. She even called me a little bastard in front of my friends and I did not want them to know why I was different, not even a clue. He had a lot of drug and alcohol problems. He took too many "magic mushrooms" and went schizophrenic. He was hospitalized for a couple of months. It was very peaceful in the house during that time. Almost peaceful, anyway, as there always seemed like trouble around.

I got my first real job working on a horse farm. I love horses; it was hard work but at times a lot of fun. During hay and straw season it was not so much fun. I would go out to the fields and pick up as many wagons as I could. Jack, my boss, asked me to slow down on the wagons or I would lose my help. I said they never complained, but he said they would not complain to me because I had out-worked them, they would just quit instead. So I slowed down a bit. I thought it was better to get as much done today, then there would be less tomorrow. I guess not everyone thinks like that.

I felt the predator in the shadows. Always there, taking little bites out of me. I found a way to keep it away. I loved to party. I never partied alone. It was a lot of fun. I always knew this was a short-term solution to the predator. Eventually it would not work anymore. I think I missed more high school classes than anyone in history. I was always skipping class. When exam time came up I would borrow the smart girl's books, study all night, get 80% on the exam, and pass the course with 50%. I patted myself on the back for it but really I cheated myself. I just could not go to school on a regular basis. If I did it seemed like the predator was gaining on me. It was better to be out having fun or be at work than at home. I was different. My friends knew I was different. I was always laughing. Give me a few and I forgot everything but the fun. I wondered if I had had a normal life like everyone else if I would still need a few to be happy. High school life was fun. Nearing the end of my high times the predator was getting closer.

This is when I met Micki. She was a blast. She had her own pad and there was always a party there. There also was a cute three-year-old girl who lived there, Micki's daughter. At first it was fun but then something unexpected happened. Usually I run away when I suspect this, but this time I did not. I saw something in Micki that intrigued me. I saw a spirit with such beauty. Her little girl was intelligent with a quest for knowledge, not unlike me at that age. Then I changed again. The party had to stop. I was going to be this pretty, wonderful little girl's dad. I was not going to be a stepdad. I would protect her from the grief, pain, fear, hurt, abuse, shame, all the physical, mental, and sexual abuse as I understood it. I would give her and all the children after her unconditional love. She and my future children would be able to reach their potential. Go to college or university uninhibited, without fear from the predator that still stalks me. I would love her mother with unconditional love. I would always be there for her. I would keep the predator at bay and remember.

I later learned why my mother broke down. Her father continuously sexually abused her. His excuse was his kids aren't perfect either. I often wonder what his childhood was like.

My great-grandfather murdered my grandfather's mother and stuffed her under the floor. I remembered him as an unkempt alcoholic. Who knows what he suffered in life to drive him to what he became.

My grandmother had a lifetime of abuse—from stealing cabbage from cows to having your baby die in your arms while your husband chatted with the gas bar attendant. She also gave birth to a boy who had his head smashed in by her husband.

This family tradition of abuse will end with me. Although the painful memories will always be there I must overcome them. I started out my life as a happy boy. All the people who should have protected me failed. My drive for something better given to me by the Great Spirit continues within me. There is a lot more to be said but I am afraid it would end up as a book and would not add anything relevant. The physical, mental, and sexual abuse was in abundance. This is who I am. We are the sum of our experiences. Now I am as naked. I have to put my faith in the Great Spirit as He guides me down my path. May I find happiness.

We were taught to believe that the Great Spirit sees and hears everything, and that he never forgets, that hereafter he will give every man a spirit home according to his deserts; if he has been a good man, he will have a good home; if he has been a bad man, he will have a bad home. This I believe and all my people believe the same.

— CHIEF JOSEPH, NEZ PERCE

A very great vision is needed and the man who has it must follow it as the eagle seeks the deepest blue of the sky.

— CRAZY HORSE/TASHUNKEWITKO, OGLALA

Part III: The Abuse

A lot has happened to me. At times I asked, "Why me?" My counsellor has asked me to do a journal and only talk about what I can. The day she asked me to imagine "HIM" walking towards me, but I did not have too, I remember. I was immobilized. I could not reason, I could not talk. The fear and panic rose up inside my chest like it was going to explode. It felt like it was happening at the moment. I wanted to run. It took me 30 minutes to recover from it. I was taken by surprise and so was she. Although she apologized, she did me a favour, as I have over and over again suppressed it. I discovered that this was a major problem. If I am going to be free of this I need to express it.

First I need to go over the recent past. I begin the day before Iroqrafts. The stress of the separation was apparent. What I have previously described as the predator, all the emotions and memories, was trying to resurface. Although the last few years the predator was gaining on me I was successful in partially being able to suppress it. My ability to do so was fragile. It was like a leaky dam—only the smaller, less traumatic things were surfacing.

The morning of Iroqrafts I had a dentist appointment. I went to get a coffee at Micki's cousin Alsea's. She treated me like I was from Mars. In my already fragile state the dam broke. Every traumatic event in my life was being experienced like I was there. I can't remember if I called Micki before the dentist appointment or after. She agreed to meet me at her work. I am not sure how I was at the dentist but I know I was really quiet. Something was happening to me and I did not understand. Eventually the memories were gone but all the emotions that came with them had made themselves over-whelming. When I reached Iroqrafts I was completely overwhelmed. The confusion, the emotions, and the need to run were beyond my understanding. At this time I had no idea what was wrong. Everything was running through me like water over a dam. I tried to talk to Micki about the gossip but I was unsuccessful. The gossip I could have discussed with her over the phone. The real reason why I was there was I needed Micki's help. She was the only person I trusted. My cognitive abilities were greatly diminished but I did not realize this at the time. My behaviour was erratic. Although I knew what I was trying to say, it would have been impossible for Micki to understand. I kept asking her to help me understand. I was completely lost. It would appear like I had been drinking, talking in circles. At the time I did not know I was like a crazy man. The fear, grief, hurt, panic, and so many other emotions were quite apparent to me. However, I did not know how to communicate this as I did not understand it myself at the time. I did not want to hurt Micki that day, I only wanted her help. Instead I frightened and hurt her. I am sure if I was watching from the outside I would have felt the same thing as this was not normal behaviour.

Eventually the police came. I had just returned from the beer store. I was going to have a few as this would put me to sleep. My mental state had not improved. The police arrested me and took me to the hospital. It felt like an attack. Everyone was attacking me and I had no way to defend myself. Eventually I was admitted. They strapped me to the bed. They needed to do so as I was in defence mode. They then medicated me. This put me to sleep. The next day I missed breakfast and lunch. When I awoke it was suppertime. I felt the effects of the drugs administered to me. I was calm and depressed. After dinner the psychologist assessed me. I did not show any symptoms that I was a danger to myself or anyone else. He noted that my cognitive abilities were at 50%, a rather generous number as I look back. I was suffering from anxiety and stress. He also noted that there was much more going on—that a separation had occurred within me.

For the next six months I operated on fear, anxiety, and anger. The anger was my way of protecting myself from the damaging effect of the traumatic events I had experienced. It gave me strength and allowed me to forget and re-establish my ability to suppress. For six months people were trying to talk to me but I could not understand. It was like trying to explain the theory of relativity to a three year old.

I cannot say when my cognitive abilities returned. I am sure it was slow in returning. After the six months, although I did not understand what had happened, I became extremely remorseful. I desperately needed to understand what happened. Eventually with my counsellor's help I regained my cognitive abilities and somewhat accidentally stumbled onto the problem. Again with her help, with a lot of phone calls to mental health offices in Ontario plus hours of research on the Internet, I found the answer: post-traumatic stress disorder. I did not take anyone's word on it. I had to confirm it from several different sources. I was a textbook case of PTSD. I do feel ashamed of this mental illness I experienced. For me it feels like weakness. I take full ownership of it. All these years I was able to partially suppress it. I thought I had dealt with it. I was wrong.

During all of this my employment was suffering. I was only at 50% of my capacity. Concentration was difficult. I was breaking under the stress. They had to let me go.

Now I need to talk about one of the traumatic events in my life. It is most likely the trauma that carries the most weight to this day and is also one of the things I experienced again that day.

I was nine years old. My best friend's brother moved in. My mother always felt the need to help someone, especially if she could relate to them. As my mother's nerve problem progressed she gave me less and less attention. My stepfather was becoming crueler as my mother failed to protect me. I was alone. Then he took advantage of my situation. It was quite easy for him as he lived with us. I had no understanding of what he was going to do. The sexual abuse began. At first I welcomed it. It felt like I was receiving parental love that I was lacking. I felt protected. The sexual act itself was very uncomfortable. I did not understand at the time but it felt like an invasion of my space. It seemed like it was a small price to pay for what I was lacking.

Three months later my mom died. This was devastating. The unwelcome sexual abuse continued as he was becoming more aggressive and more and more uncomfortable.

Three more months had passed. It was a nice fall sunny day. My sister and brother were off to school. I was running late. I must have only weighed about 60 pounds. He asked me to go into the bedroom with him. I asked him to leave me alone. At first he was compliant. As I was coming out of my bedroom he jumped on me, pinning me to the wood floor. I felt him on top of me. He started to kiss me on my left side then my right. I begged him to stop. I would have screamed but no one would hear me anyway. I also thought it would make things worse. Before this happened his behaviour was becoming more aggressive. I was terrified. I screamed in my head for my mom even though she was gone. I am not sure how to express how I felt, as it was a mix of fear and panic. My life felt like it was in danger. He easily out matched me and continued. I had no way of defending myself. Then it was over. I felt completely numb. I then progressed to clean myself up. I went to school. I told the teacher I had slept in. The very air was thick. It weighed me down like an anchor to a boat, pulling me down.

I am not sure if this happened the next day. I am sure it happened shortly after. I was in class. The terror of what happened to me crept up on me. I wanted to tell someone. If I did tell anyone he would come after me. My stepdad would beat me. No one was there to protect me. I think I was becoming agitated. Several classmates asked me what was wrong. I told them I was thinking of my mom. I had to try and control myself. If anyone found out I would be dead or severely beaten. I thought I would explode. I was terrified in that class that day. I wanted to be invisible. Although the teacher did not notice other classmates noticed and started to tease me. I felt like this was my fault for some reason that I did not understand. I was the lowest form of life. I am not sure how I managed to get through that day.

I did not resist him again no matter how painful it was. Every time he was on top of me I felt the panic, the fear, the guilt. When he was not around I would cry. For about a year and a half, I'm not completely sure, maybe even longer, I felt him on top of me on what appeared to be a regular event. Every time the emotions felt the same over and over again. Eventually he left but I was and I am always in fear of his return.

Although I managed to survive, it left many mental scars. I am to this day afraid of anyone who might resemble him in any way, whether it is the way he moves or the way he carries himself or any physical features. At most times I am uncomfortable in small crowds even though I might know everyone there. The panic sets in, and then I need to leave. The most important thing of all is the trauma itself and the implications it carries.

I cannot talk about this abuse. The only way I can communicate it is to write it down. It does not feel as real but it was extremely difficult to do so. I had to leave my computer several times. The emotions generated by this trauma are unbearable. I needed to do a little at a time. At times I wanted to jump in my van and go. Looking back I am surprised I did not turn into a carrot. I think my inner strength was a gift from the Great Spirit as I am sure I could not have survived on my own.

November 2012

CHAPTER 23

Examining the Intersection of Addiction and Issues of Ability[1]

Rick Csiernik and Melissa Brideau

Introduction

Over the past decade, two intersecting topics have gained increased attention within the profession of social work: addiction issues, whereby professionals have advocated that substance use is a multi-faceted process, not only affected by physical and psychological factors, but also environmental and societal factors (Csiernik, 2016; Csiernik & Rowe, 2010); and ability issues (Smart & Smart, 2007; West, Graham, & Cifu, 2009a, 2009b, 2009c, 2009d, 2009e). In this area of social work, professionals are helping to change perceptions in regards to the experience of living with an ability issue. Substantive efforts are being made to reduce isolation and oppression of those living with disabilities by providing education and awareness regarding the many barriers that people with ability issues are forced to contend with on a daily basis (Barnes & Mercer, 2010; Priestley, 2001). Recent legislative changes in Canada such as the Accessibility for Ontarians with Disabilities Act (2011) and Quebec's Act to Secure Handicapped Persons in the Exercise of their Rights with a View to Achieving Social, School and Workplace Integration (2014) have been designed with the goal of eliminating barriers commonly experienced by many individuals in the areas of physical accessibility, customer service, transportation, and employment, as well as information and communication (Ontario Ministry of Community & Social Services, 2011). In addition, research such as the 2012 Canadian Survey on Disability (Statistics Canada, 2013) has provided an overview of the number of Canadians living with a wide range of disabilities.[2] It reported that nearly 14% of the Canadian population, 3.8 million individuals, has some form of ability issue. However, despite the notable progress that has been made in both the disability and addiction fields, there remain significant gaps not only in the treatment continuum in instances where the two intersect, but also in general knowledge.

Traumatic Injury

Traumatic injury in the rehabilitation literature is an umbrella term used to describe a number of disabling conditions that are acquired as a result of an accident or disease (Bombardier & Turner, 2010). Although there are various forms of traumatic injury, the most prominent are those pertaining to brain and spinal cord injuries. The Ontario Brain Injury Association's impact report (2012), which was developed in an effort to provide a statistical snapshot of acquired brain injury and its effect on survivors/ caregivers, states that there are currently half a million Canadians living with the effects of an acquired brain injury, and it is estimated that within the province of Ontario alone, more than 18,000 individuals will suffer from a brain injury in a year. Further, this report indicates that acquired brain injury is 15 times more common than spinal cord injury, 30 times more common than breast cancer, and 400 times more common than HIV/AIDS. In addition, Spinal Cord Injury Ontario (2015) reports that there are currently 33,000 people in Ontario living with a spinal cord injury, and 86,000 individuals in the rest of Canada, with approximately 11 new cases each week. Unfortunately, there is no discussion in the impact report regarding the substance use, misuse, and abuse patterns of this population.

Survivors of brain and spinal cord injuries experience a number of challenges not only related to the physical effects of the injury but also to their psychological, social, and emotional levels of functioning (Bombardier & Turner, 2010; Kreutzer et al., 1996; Smedema & Ebener, 2010). In order to cope with these difficulties, many individuals use alcohol or drugs to reduce the feelings of anxiety, stress, anger, and isolation that are often associated with sustaining such injuries (Elliott, Kurylo, Chen, & Hicken, 2002; Smedema & Ebener, 2010; Saunders & Krause, 2011) with suggestions that more than half of traumatic injury survivors face additional issues related to substance use and abuse (Smedema & Ebener, 2010; West, Graham, & Cifu, 2009d). The literature focuses upon three areas of intersection: pre-injury, time of injury, and post-injury substance use. There are a multitude of implications that rehabilitation professionals must take into consideration in order to assist those contending with the effects of brain and spinal cord injury and co-existing substance use issues in the most efficient manner, beginning with when the injury occurred.

Pre-injury Substance Use

Although researchers have only begun to examine the incidence of pre-injury substance abuse among those with brain and spinal cord injury within the last two decades, it is evident that the rate of pre-injury substance use experienced by both of these groups is alarmingly high. An examination of the pre-injury substance use patterns among patients at a level one trauma centre who had experienced a traumatic brain injury (TBI) or spinal cord injury (SCI) found that 81% with TBI and 93% with SCI reported pre-injury alcohol use. In addition 42% of patients with TBI and 57% of those with SCI were classified as heavy drinkers, while abstinence in the year before injury was reported by only 19% of those living with TBI and only 4% of those living with SCI. Illicit drug use was also reported by 30% of the participants with TBI and approximately one-third of participants with SCI (Kolakowsky-Hayner et al., 1999).

Bombardier, Rimmele, and Zintel (2002) assessed the alcohol and drug use patterns of 142 patients with traumatic brain injury at an inpatient rehabilitation program by examining alcohol consumption and drug use, physical dependency, lifetime alcohol-related problems, readiness to change, preferred change strategies, blood alcohol levels and toxicology test results, and what the authors termed "attributions regarding the cause of injury," whereby subjects were asked to rate the extent to which they felt alcohol or drug use contributed to the cause of their injury. Results revealed that 59% of participants met the criteria for at-risk drinkers, as there was a high degree of pre-injury alcohol and drug use reported, including 34% reporting illicit drug use.

Additional research also suggests that pre-injury substance use patterns may be associated with poorer outcomes for those living with brain and spinal cord injury. For example, individuals living with TBI who have a history of alcohol abuse may be at an increased risk of experiencing emotional and behavioural problems as well as suffering a recurrent brain injury (Bombardier & Turner, 2010; Kolakowsky-Hayner et al., 1999). Similarly, individuals living with spinal cord injuries who abused alcohol prior to their injury have also been shown to have higher rates of depression and suicide (Bombardier & Turner, 2010). Thus, by obtaining information related to pre-injury substance abuse patterns, rehabilitation professionals may be better equipped to respond to individuals in achieving optimal recovery.

Substance Use at the Time of the Injury

Although several studies have documented the rates of pre- and post-injury substance use among those living with brain and spinal cord injuries, fewer studies have examined the prevalence of substance use at the time of injury for this population. It has been estimated that as many as 36% to 51% of TBIs occurred while individuals were intoxicated (Ponsford, Whelan-Goodinson, & Bahar-Fuchs, 2007). Kreutzer, Witol, and Marwitz (1996) found that of 51 patients with TBI, 32 (57.1%) had positive blood alcohol levels upon admission to hospital, with half meeting the criteria for intoxication.

Similar to the literature on TBI, individuals with SCI have also been found to have high rates of substance use at the time of injury with estimates of alcohol or drug intoxication at the time of injury ranging from 17% to 62% (Kolakowsky-Hayner et al., 1999; Tate et al., 2004). However, due to the limited literature in this area, it is difficult to discern whether or not substance use at the time of injury affects post-injury outcome. While some studies reveal that there is a correlation between substance use at the time of injury and poorer recovery outcomes, others have found no significant relationship between these two variables (Corrigan, 1995). Thus, additional recent research is still required to ascertain if a relationship between intoxication at the time of injury and post-injury outcomes exists.

Post-Injury Substance Use

Studies examining post-injury substance use patterns of those living with brain and spinal cord injuries demonstrate that a number of individuals are contending with serious substance abuse issues (Bombardier & Turner, 2010; Elliot, Kurylo, Chen, & Hicken, 2002; Kolakowsky-Hanyner et al., 1999; Kolakowsky-Hayner et al., 2002; Ponsfort, et al., 2004; Taylor, Kreutzer, Demm, & Meade, 2003). Kolakowsky-Hayner and colleagues (2002) compared the post-injury substance use patterns among 30 individuals living with spinal cord injury and 30 with traumatic brain injury. There were notable comparisons between both groups of individuals with respect to substance use patterns, with the majority who had consumed alcohol after injury categorized as moderate or heavy drinkers. Those who were considered to be moderate drinkers living with SCI reported drinking on average once or twice per week (23.3%), while those moderate drinkers contending with the effects of TBI reported drinking two to three times per month (33.3%). In contrast, those who were considered to be heavy drinkers living with spinal cord injury were more likely to report drinking on a daily basis (16.7%), whereas individuals with TBI who were classified as heavy drinkers reported drinking three to four times per week (10.0%). However, the most significant differences were identified when examining the illicit drug use patterns of both groups post-injury, where 20.7% of persons with SCI versus only 3.3% of those with TBI reported using illicit drugs, which included marijuana, cocaine, and opioids within the past 6 to 12 months. In addition, several studies documenting post-injury substance use indicate that while substance use does decline in the first year following injury, two and three year follow-ups show that substance use has often returned to pre-injury rates (Bombardier, Temkin, Machamer, & Dikmen, 2003; Kolakowsky-Hayner et al., 1999; Ponsford, Whelan-Goodinson, & Bahar-Fuchs, 2007; Tate et al., 2004).

Of further concern is that post-injury recovery can be significantly impacted by the use of psychoactive substances including the risk of re-injury, seizures, frustration/aggressiveness, decreased life satisfaction, as well as being at an increased risk for depression and suicide (Bombardier & Turner, 2010; DeLambo, Chandras, Homa, & Chandras, 2009; Kolakowsky-Hayner et al., 2002; Smedema & Ebener, 2010). In addition, using drugs after a traumatic brain injury can greatly exacerbate the effects of such injuries, as individuals may experience a number of other challenges in relation to the development of coping, problem solving, and social skills. Additional side effects of TBI such as deficits in memory, fatigue, and heightened sensitivity to stimulation can intensify with the use of substances and impede rehabilitation efforts (DeLambo, Chandras, Homa, & Chandras, 2009). Thus, while rehabilitation professionals typically have little education and training with regards to addiction issues these professionals have a unique opportunity and responsibility to offer critical assistance and support with regards to those with co-existing substance use issues in order to work towards optimal recovery.

Sensory Disabilities

Individuals Living with Low Vision or Blindness

According to the Canadian National Institute for the Blind (2015), there are approximately half a million Canadians currently living with visual impairments and it is estimated that more than 50,000 Canadians will lose their sight every year. Generally, visual impairment can be thought of in terms of a continuum ranging from modest low vision to total blindness (Jutai et al., 2005). While there has been increased awareness and insight regarding the specific needs of this population, research suggests that substance abuse issues remain higher among this group than within the general population (Koch, Nelipovich, & Sneed, 2002; Koch, Shearer, & Nelipovich, 2004; Nelipovich, Wergin, & Kossick, 1998).

Professionals have long recognized the negative effects of stereotyping and discrimination on the lives of those with visual impairments. However, professionals in both the disability and addiction fields need to understand that those who are visually challenged may experience various psychosocial effects, which may be directly related to their substance use or as a result of the negative public and professional attitudes towards those who are visually challenged and experiencing issues with substance use. Individuals contending with such issues face an additional amount of stigma, which can lead to distrust and resistance to working with helping professionals. Many within this population remain hesitant to disclose substance use as they are aware that doing so may lead to consequences, such as being ineligible for certain services that may be vital sources of support necessary to maintaining well-being, as well as experiencing direct discrimination, which in turn only serves to further oppress and isolate individuals within this population (Koch, Nelipovich, & Sneed, 2002; Koch, Shearer, & Nelipovich, 2004).

In addition, lack of professional preparation also contributes to negative attitudes as people living with the effects of low vision/blindness and a co-existing substance use issue do not fit into a specialized service delivery system. As a result, professionals from both the disability and addiction fields are typically unable to provide comprehensive services. For professionals who lack formal education and cross-training, visual challenges are often viewed as a barrier to treatment for substance abuse issues. Such compartmentalized thinking only serves to further define a person in terms of his or her disability, rather than as an individual with interrelated and integrated abilities and disabilities (Koch, Nelipovich, & Sneed, 2002; Koch, Shearer, & Nelipovich, 2004).

Along with attitudinal barriers, individuals with visual impairments can also experience a multitude of barriers when faced with the task of acquiring appropriate supports from substance abuse treatment programs. Too often substance treatment programs have policies and procedures that neglect to take into account the unique needs of those with visual impairments with the "one size fits all" approach failing to meet the needs of those with disabilities in culturally responsive ways. First and most obvious is that almost all substance abuse treatment programs provide participants with educational materials or written exercises designed to increase one's understanding and insight related to the nature of substance use, as well as to outline important agency policies. For those with visual challenges, however, this method of practice presents a significant barrier as these types of materials are rarely provided in alternate formats such as an audio version, braille, large print, or via a computer using assistive technologies (Koch, Nelipovich, & Sneed, 2002; Koch, Shearer, & Nelipovich, 2004). Even when material has been translated into braille, such as Alcoholics Anonymous (2001) Big Book, few agencies have this type of resource on hand. These barriers in service impede an individual's therapeutic process because they may not get the opportunity to participate in crucial components of substance abuse treatment. Second, the common empirically supported use of group therapy can create problems for those with visual impairments as some find it difficult to track the flow of conversation and miss out on many of the visual cues that are an integral part of the group therapy process (Sales, 2000). Further, treatment agencies often experience other systemic barriers, including lack of specific screening and referral procedures; failure to create formal system linkages, such as written understanding of policies and procedures regarding work with other agencies; and a lack of communication or collaboration among addiction professionals and those who specialize in assisting people with visual disabilities. Professionals may find it difficult to work in collaboration with other agencies in order to determine the most effective/appropriate intervention due to the fact that there is often a lack of written understanding with regard to case management procedures and specific processes for providing services to this unique population. As a result, confusion often arises across the ability and addiction fields as to whether one's substance abuse is considered to be the primary issue or a symptom of a co-existing ability issue. Thus, the lack of communication and collaboration across disciplines comes at a high cost to the individuals who are trying to access services, as they are shuffled through the addiction and disability service delivery systems only to experience further oppression and isolation as a consequence of unmet needs and unsuccessful treatment strategies (Koch et al., 2002; Koch et al., 2004).

Finally, in addition to considering the impact of attitudinal and programmatic barriers on the lives of those living with visual challenges and co-existing substance use issues, it is equally important to remove any architectural barriers that may interfere with a person's ability to access appropriate substance abuse treatment (Substance Abuse and Health Administration [SAMHSA], 1998). For instance, it is important to keep pathways clear, raise low-hanging lights, use large print, and include braille labels on all signs and elevator buttons within addiction treatment agencies and facilities. It is also crucial for individuals working at agencies to ensure that verbal announcements are made instead of using the traditional method of flyers or bulletin boards. In addition, efforts should be made to aid those individuals who require assistance in orienting themselves with the layout of a building or room by explaining where doors, furniture, and other important features are located (SAMHSA, 1998).

Individuals Who Are Deaf or Hard of Hearing

In Canada, the most recent census found over 700,000 people who are either deaf or hard of hearing (Statistics Canada, 2006). Unfortunately, there have been no subsequent updates partially due to the Harper government cutbacks in research. According to the Canadian Hearing Society, the term *deaf* is usually used to describe those individuals with a severe to profound hearing loss who primarily depend upon visual means of communication, which can include the use of sign language, speech reading, and reading and writing (Canadian Association of the Deaf, 2007; Canadian Hearing Society, 2008). In contrast, the term *hard of hearing* is used to describe those individuals who are able to communicate through the use of spoken language. Individuals who are hard of hearing can understand varying degrees of spoken language either with or without the use of assistive devices such as hearing aids. It is also important to note that while the use of this terminology is often used to describe the extent of one's disability, hearing loss occurs on a continuum ranging from moderate to severe (Canadian Hearing Society, 2008). Although substance use is prevalent among this group, little is known about the exact numbers of Canadians who are deaf or hard of hearing and contending with co-existing substance use issues, as these individuals are often isolated and hidden within deaf communities due to barriers related to communication and lack of under-standing of intercultural attitudes (Moore & McAweeney, 2006).

It is crucial to understand the unique culture that exists for many deaf individuals, for this group does not place significance upon the foundation of the counselling professions: hearing and speaking. Rather it is sign language that unites members of this community in a manner that is not experienced by others, including those who are living with other issues of ability. The use of sign language influences psychosocial development as it often serves various functions—as a bearer of culture and a transmitter of information—while also being the primary means through which those who are deaf present their own self-image to others. It is important to understand that for many individuals who are deaf, they do not only have a sensory disability, but they are also part of a unique and distinct culture (Lipton & Goldstein, 1997). Being part of deaf culture entails limited exposure to discussions regarding substance use, decreased access to formal prevention programs, and enabling behaviours by those around the individual, who feel that substance use is a justified method of coping given the disability-related challenges that the individual may experience on a daily basis. Concerns also arise as those who are deaf or hard of hearing often have limited access to informal support networks of family and close friends, which can lead to further the isolation and oppression that is already experienced by many individuals. As a result of this isolation, there is increased emotional distress as individuals may struggle to connect with those around them—for example, when youth who are deaf and hard of hearing have difficultly communicating with parents who are not dealing with hearing loss about basic needs, let alone contentious issues like drug use (Berman, Streja, & Guthmann, 2010; Titus & White, 2008). It is imperative that professionals be aware of such factors in order to begin to address specific barriers that impede an individual's access to substance abuse treatment.

I came to realize that I had a problem with drugs and alcohol just after turning 30. I had been using since I was 18—daily usage which I considered a normal part of my lifestyle.... I was missing work at an alarming rate.... My supervisor gave me a verbal warning ... as a last resort, I went to an employment counselor. The counselor at the Employment Service Agency for the Deaf ... told me I had alcohol-related problems whether I thought so or not and that it was nothing to be ashamed of.... The first four-and-a-half years, I was slipping and falling all over the place. In and out of therapy, 12-step programs, hospitals, jails, and near brushes with death. Being deaf created special problems. Each and every time I went to a 12 step meeting, I had to make a telephone call to arrange for interpreters.... It is hard not to feel the unfairness of things, knowing there are 800 different 12-step meetings per week in the Bay Area, and I can't choose any in my own neighbourhood because they have no sign language interpretation.

[...] I tried to achieve sobriety with the means available to me in the community, since no treatment programs were accessible to me. Looking back, I do feel that if a community based, social model program had been accessible, it might have been beneficial for me, as recovery from chemical dependency is such a difficult task done alone.... I found it much easier to share with another disabled person.... I still have to work to maintain my sobriety. It's still a hassle to get interpreters for meetings, but I believe that will get easier as people realize the dynamics involved in accommodating the hearing impaired. (Rendon, 1992, p. 104)

For any individual struggling with the effects of addiction, beginning substance abuse treatment is a very daunting and challenging task. However, as the above narrative illustrates, this task is made more difficult for those who are deaf or hard of hearing, as many people often face significant communication barriers (Alexander, DiNitto, & Tidblom, 2005; Guthmann & Blozis, 2001; Guthmann & Graham, 2004; Guthmann & Sandberg, 1998; Lipton & Goldstein, 2010; Moore & McAweeney, 2006; Titus & Guthmann, 2010; Titus & White, 2008). Individuals typically experience the first of many barriers when trying to obtain an assessment as there are no formalized assessment tools designed to meet the unique needs of this population (Guthmann & Graham, 2004; Guthmann & Sandberg, 1998). Due to a lack of cross-training, professionals are unfamiliar with how to effectively work with members of the deaf and hard of hearing community, and may be even less familiar with alternate modes of communication such as American Sign Language (ASL). Unfortunately, this lack of professional preparation only leads to further obstacles, as substance use is already a difficult issue for many to discuss (Guthmann & Graham, 2004). However, those who are deaf or hard of hearing are often less likely to be forthcoming about such issues, as communication barriers not only impede the therapeutic process, but often lead to misunderstandings among professionals and their clients (Alexander, DeNitto, & Tidblom, 2005; Guthmann & Graham, 2004).

Although sign language interpreters may be seen as an appropriate means of reducing such barriers, recent studies suggest that problems may still arise when using this method of communication (Guthmann & Graham, 2004). For example, Alexander, DiNitto, and Tidblom (2005) asked 26 deaf individuals about their understanding of two widely used screening tests: the CAGE and the AUDIT. Interviews were conducted by examining each assessment tool sentence by sentence while having an interpreter sign so that participants could understand and respond to the questions being asked. The results indicated only 4 out of the 26 participants involved in the study had a clear understanding of the items on both screening tests. In addition, the researchers found that there were a number of critical words identified on these screening tests, such as hangover and blackout, that had several different signs to convey their meaning, which only served to further contribute to the confusion and frustration experienced by participants. As a result, the validity of these assessments was compromised. Additional issues that can be encountered when relying on the use of interpreters include such challenges as contending with interpreter availability, locating interpreters that are properly qualified, and finding the funding to hire experienced professionals in order to limit the enormous financial burden that is often placed upon a client or agency. Furthermore, when using an interpreter for individual work, the clinician must carefully consider the impact of adding a third party to the situation, as this will inevitably affect the dynamics of the clinician/client relationship (Guthmann & Graham, 2004; Guthmann & Sandberg, 1998). In contrast, if a treatment provider wishes to use an interpreter for group therapy there are other critical factors that must be considered, including the fact that interpreting is very tiring and the interpreter's effectiveness will decrease over time. Therefore, in these situations it is essential to plan breaks to ensure that the interpreter can maintain the level of skill needed to keep track of what everyone in the group is saying, or, depending upon group size and length of session, hiring two interpreters to ensure effective communication and interactions among all members of the group (Guthmann & Graham, 2004).

It is also well established that within residential settings much of the treatment takes place outside of groups or one-to-one settings. Thus, clients need to have the opportunity to communicate with other peers in treatment as well as to be able to develop an element of trust and rapport with the professionals with whom they are working. However, this cannot occur if culturally sensitive assessment tools and education materials have not been developed (Guthmann & Graham, 2004). However, these issues are slowly being addressed, with the recent validation of a substance use screen in ASL (Guthmann, Moore, Lazowski, & Heinemann, 2012). In addition to this computer-based interactive assessment, there has also been the recent implementation of a web-based 12-step meeting run by deaf substance users who are in recovery that allows participants to interact with one another, as they are able to see each other in individual boxes on the computer screen where images are large enough to communicate (Titus & Guthmann, 2010).

Mobility Impairment

Statistics Canada (2006) reported that there are over 200,000 Canadians living with mobility impairments, whereas the Canadian Survey on Disability (Statistics Canada, 2013) reported 7.2% of Canadians aged 15 and over had some type of mobility impairment, which, given a national population of 35 million, represents a far greater number (Statistics Canada, 2006). The term *mobility impairment* is used when discussing individuals who have difficulty using their extremities or those individuals who demonstrate a lack of strength to walk, grasp, or lift objects. As a result, the use of devices such as a wheelchair, crutches, cane, or walker may be required to assist with mobility. This type of disability can be caused by a number of factors including disease, accident, congenital disorder, or aging (Colorado State University, 2010). Due to increased awareness and recent legislative changes, attempts have been made to reduce many of the barriers commonly experienced by this population on a daily basis. However, as with other groups discussed earlier, many barriers remain for those with mobility challenges who are attempting to access appropriate treatment for substance use issues as evident in the low rate of treatment participation among this group. For example, West, Graham, and Cifu (2009e) found that within the province of Ontario treatment providers indicated that, while they had served 235 individuals with various disabilities, this is a small percentage of the population given the estimated number of individuals living with such disabilities. In addition, they had only assisted a total of six with mobility impairments, five individuals with traumatic brain injuries, and one individual with a spinal cord injury within the year prior to the survey.

This low rate of treatment participation among this population is primarily due to the fact that many treatment centres are often inaccessible to those with mobility impairments (see Chapter 12). Pritzlaff Voss, Wargolet Cesar, Tymus, and Fieldler (2002) assessed the perceptions of managers at various substance abuse treatment centres regarding physical accessibility for those with spinal cord injuries. They found that while 30 of 32 facilities reported being wheelchair accessible, upon actual site visits only half actually were.

West, Luck, and Capps (2007) examined the impact of physical inaccessibility of various substance abuse treatment programs. They found that only 13% of the treatment professionals participating in the study had been approached by individuals with a spinal cord injury. However, of those only 39% indicated that they were able to provide service to this population due to inaccessibility of their treatment service. Similarly, 36% of the respondents revealed that they had previously been approached by those with traumatic brain injury seeking substance abuse treatment, yet 44% were unable to provide services to this population.

West, Graham, and Cifu's (2009d) study of those living with other types of mobility impairments found treatment denial rates based upon those impairments ranging from 67% for those with muscular dystrophy to rates as high as 91% for individuals with multiple sclerosis. Of particular interest was the fact that while previous studies have indicated that there was no association between the number of service refusals and type of treatment, results of this study suggested that those seeking treatment in outpatient settings experience less service refusals as opposed to those seeking treatment in residential treatment programs. This difference is attributed to the nature of outpatient services and the interactions that treatment providers have when working with those living with physical disabilities. For example, while outpatient service providers must ensure that all waiting areas and meeting rooms are accessible, those working in residential settings may find it increasingly difficult to accommodate individuals with physical disabilities; those with physical disabilities may often experience barriers related to bathing, sleeping, eating, and recreational activities, which are an essential part of one's daily routines.

Future Directions

This review has served to highlight a significant gap in the addictions treatment continuum for those with ability issues and co-existing substance misuse and abuse. Individuals with ability issues continue to face a multitude of attitudinal (Koch, et al., 2002; Robertson et al., 2009) programming (Guthmann & Graham, 2004; Koch, et al., 2002), and environmental barriers (West, Graham, & Cifu, 2009b, 2009c; West, Luck, & Capps, 2007; SAMSHA, 1998; Pritzalaff et al., 2002) when attempting to access appropriate substance abuse treatment. In order to reduce such barriers, professionals in both the disability and addiction fields need to place a priority on examining practices at the individual, agency, and policy levels of service to identify both existing and potential barriers that may inhibit the ability of those with disabilities to access care that is both holistic and supportive in nature. At the individual level of practice, professionals must make every effort to reduce attitudinal barriers to allow for the client and clinician to work as a team in identifying individual needs and making appropriate referrals. Without doing so, those with ability issues and co-existing substance abuse issues risk becoming "lost" in the very systems that many depend on for adequate treatment, guidance, and support. As a result, individuals contending with such issues become a part of a vicious cycle of unmet needs and unsuccessful treatment strategies, which only serves to further perpetuate the isolation and oppression that is already experienced by members of this population. It is also paramount that post-secondary institutions include a focus upon this oppression hiding in plain view in a range of academic disciplines, including but not limited to social work, disabilities studies, health sciences, psychology, and of course addiction studies.

In order to prevent further isolation and oppression of this group, it is crucial for staff working in agencies that specialize in issues related to disability or addiction to receive adequate cross-training and education to increase professional preparation and competency, so that clinicians can be better equipped with the knowledge and tools necessary to serve this population in the most effective and efficient manner. In particular, the high incidence of refusal rates among those with physical disabilities attempting to access treatment (West, Graham, & Cifu, 2009d; West et al., 2007), lack of appropriate substance abuse screening tools (Ashman et al., 2004; Bombardier, Kilmer, Ehde, 1997) and misunderstandings about what it means for a service to be truly accessible to all individuals no matter their ability or disability (Pritzlaff Voss et al., 2002) all serve as indications that professionals from across respective disciplines must unite together to increase collaboration and communication. Strengthening human relationships and creating a professional dialogue of this nature will pave the way for the critical examination of current policies and procedures in terms of how effective they are in meeting the needs of such a diverse group. For example, substance abuse treatment programs that retain an abstinence mission adhere to a "no psychoactive substance use" rule that may inadvertently impact the ability of those with disabilities to participate in treatment, as they may need to take medications due to other conditions and ceasing to do so would further compromise their health and well-being. In addition, it is important for treatment facilities to explore the benefits of utilizing assistive technologies and the assistance of skilled professionals, such as a personal support worker, to effectively work towards the removal of environmental and programmatic barriers. Yet, in 2010, after the Canadian Centre on Substance Abuse and the National Advisory Group on Workforce Development published an extensive national consultation including the technical and behavioural competencies for addiction counsellors, not one competency related to issues of ability or to those with disabilities.

While it is evident that those with disabilities experience a greater incidence of substance use than those within the general population, further research is required to examine the incidence of this issue within the Canadian population, as the current information is extremely limited. Specifically, future research studies should attempt to explore the first-hand experiences of those who have been forced to endure many attitudinal, programming, and environmental barriers when trying to access services within the addiction treatment continuum, as little is known about how dealing with such barriers has impacted the lived experiences of those with disabilities. As awareness and professional preparation increase, it will become increasingly imperative for policy-makers to take note and develop more up-to-date legislation to ensure that those with ability issues and addictions are no longer ignored, but instead given equal access to resources that provide comprehensive treatment options, support, and guidance that reflects each individual's unique needs and goals, regardless of the nature of their abilities or disabilities.

NOTES

1. This chapter was originally published as Csiernik, R. & Brideau, M. (2013). Examining the intersection of addiction and issues of ability in Canada. *Journal of Social Work Practice in the Addictions, 13*(2), 163–178.

2. The Canadian Survey on Disability (CSD) (Statistics Canada, 2013) utilizes concepts and measures that differ significantly from those used in previous research dedicated to documenting rates of disability in Canada, such as the 2006 Participation and Activity Limitation Survey. The most important difference noted in these surveys is that they each have distinct definitions of disability. The new set of screening questions employed by the CSD not only reflect a more fuller implementation of the social model of disability, but they also allow for increased consistency in disability identification by type, and enhanced coverage of the full range of disabilities Canadians are currently contending with.

REFERENCES

Alcoholics Anonymous. (2001). Alcoholics Anonymous, 4th Edition. New York: A.A. World Services.

Alexander, T., DiNitto, D., & Tidblom, I. (2005). Screening for alcohol and other drug use problems among the deaf. *Alcoholism Treatment Quarterly, 23*(1), 63–78.

Ashman, T., Schwartz, M., Cantor, J., Hibbard, M., & Gordon, W. (2004). Screening or substance abuse in individuals with traumatic brain injury. *Brain Injury, 18*(2), 191–202.

Barnes, C., & Mercer, G. (2010). *Exploring disability.* Cambridge, UK: Polity Press.

Berman, B.A., Streja, L., & Guthmann, D. (2010). Alcohol and other substance use among deaf and hard of hearing youth. *Journal of Drug Education, 40*(2), 99–124.

Bombardier, C., Kilmer, J., & Ehde, D. (1997). Screening for alcoholism among persons with recent traumatic brain injury. *Rehabilitation Psychology, 42*(4), 259–271.

Bombardier, C., & Rimmele, C.T. (1998). Alcohol use and readiness to change after spinal cord injury. *Archives of Physical Medicine & Rehabilitation, 79*(9), 1110–1115.

Bombardier, C., Rimmele, C., & Zintel, H. (2002). The magnitude and correlates of alcohol and drug use before traumatic brain injury. *Archives of Physical Medicine & Rehabilitation, 83*(12), 1765–1773.

Bombardier, C., Temkin, N., Machamer, J., & Dikmen, S. (2003). The natural history of drinking and alcohol-related problems after traumatic brain injury. *Archives of Physical Medicine & Rehabilitation, 84*(2), 185–191.

Bombardier, C., & Turner, A. (2010). Alcohol and other drug use in traumatic disability. In R. Frank, M. Rosenthal, & B. Caplan (Eds.), *Handbook of rehabilitation psychology* (2nd ed.), (pp. 241–258). Washington, DC: American Psychological Association.

Canadian Association of the Deaf. (2007). *Definition of "deaf".* Retrieved from http://www.cad.ca/definition_of_deaf.php

Canadian Centre on Substance Abuse (2010). *Competencies for Canada's substance abuse workforce.* Ottawa, ON: Canadian Centre on Substance Abuse.

Canadian Hearing Society. (2008). *Get connected to deaf, deafened and hard of hearing people: A guide for service providers and businesses.* Retrieved from http://www.psncorp.com/Downloads/CHS:Guide_To_Service_Providers_And_Businesses.pdf

Canadian National Institute for the Blind (2015). *Fast facts about vision loss.* Retrieved from http://www.cnib.ca/en/about/media/vision-loss/pages/default.aspx

Colorado State University. (2010). *The access project: Mobility impairments definition.* Retrieved from http://accessproject.colostate.edu/disability/modules/MI/tut_MI.cfm

Corrigan, J. (1995). Substance abuse as a mediating factor in outcome from traumatic brain injury. *Archives of Physical Medicine & Rehabilitation, 76*(4), 302–309.

Csiernik, R. (2016). *Substance use and abuse: everything matters* (2nd ed.). Toronto, ON: Canadian Scholars' Press.

Csiernik, R., & Rowe, W. (Eds.). (2010). *Responding to the oppression of addiction: Canadian social work perspectives* (2nd ed.). Toronto, ON: Canadian Scholars' Press.

DeLambo, D., Chandras, K., Homa, D., & Chandras, S. (2009). Traumatic brain injuries and substance abuse: Implications for rehabilitation professionals. *Proceedings from the 2009 American Counseling Associations Annual Conference and Exhibition*. Charlotte, NC: American Couselling Association.

Elliot, T., Kurylo, M., Chen, Y., & Hicken, B. (2002). Alcohol abuse history and adjustment following spinal cord injury. *Rehabilitation Psychology, 47*(3), 278-290.

Frank, R., Rosenthal, M., & Caplan, B. (2010). *Handbook of Rehabilitation Psychology* (2nd ed.). Washington, DC: American Psychological Association.

Guthmann, D., & Blozis, S. (2001). Unique issues faced by deaf individuals entering substance abuse treatment and following discharge. *American Annals of the Deaf, 146*(3), 294-303.

Guthmann, D., & Graham, V. (2004). Substance abuse: A hidden problem within the deaf and hard of hearing communities. *Journal of Teaching in the Addictions, 3*(1), 49-64.

Guthmann, D., Moore, D., Lazowski, L., & Heinemann, A. (2012). Validation of the substance abuse screener in American sign language. *Rehabilitation Psychology, 57*(2), 140-148.

Guthmann, D., & Sandberg, K. (1998). Assessing substance abuse problems in deaf and hard of hearing individuals. *American Annals of the Deaf, 143*(1), 14-21.

Jutai, J., Hooper, P., Cooper, L., Hutnik, C., Sheidow, T., Tingely, D., & Russell-Minda, E. (2005). *Vision rehabilitation: Evidence-based review*. London, ON: CNIB Baker Foundation for Vision Research.

Koch, S., Nelipovich, M., & Sneed, Z. (2002). Alcohol and other drug abuse as coexisting disabilities: Considerations for counselors serving individuals who are blind or visually impaired. *Review: Rehabilitation and Education for Blindness and Visual Impairment, 33*(4), 151-159.

Koch, S., Shearer, B., & Nelipovich, M. (2004). Service delivery for persons with blindness or visual impairment and addiction as coexisting disabilities: Implications for addiction science education. *Journal of Teaching in the Addictions, 3*(1), 21-48.

Kolakowsky-Hayner, S., Gourley, E., Kreutzer, J., Marwitz, J., Cifu, D., & Mckinley, W. (1999). Pre-injury substance abuse among persons with brain injury and persons with spinal cord injury. *Brain Injury, 13*(8), 571-581.

Kolakowsky-Hayner, S., Gourley, E., Kreutzer, J., Marwitz, J., Meade, M., & Cifu, D. (2002). Post-injury substance abuse among persons with brain injury and persons with spinal cord injury. *Brain Injury, 16*(7), 583-592.

Kreutzer, J., Witol, A., & Marwitz, J. (1996). Alcohol and drug use among young persons with traumatic brain injury. *Journal of Learning Disabilities, 29*(6), 643-651.

Kreutzer, J., Witol, A., Sander, A., Cifu, D., Marwitz, J., & Delmonico, R. (1996). A prospective longitudinal multicenter analysis of alcohol use patterns among persons with traumatic brain injury. *Journal of Head Trauma, 11*(5), 58-69.

Lipton, D., & Goldstein, M. (1997). Measuring substance use among the deaf. *Journal of Drug Issues, 27*(4), 733-754.

Moore, D., & McAweeney, M. (2006). Demographic characteristics and rates of progress of deaf and hard of hearing persons receiving substance abuse treatment. *American Annals of the Deaf, 151*(5), 508-512.

Nelipovich, M., Wergin, C., & Kossick, R. (1998). The macro model: Making substance abuse services accessible to people who are visually impaired. *Journal of Visual Impairment and Blindness, 92*(8), 567-570.

Ontario Brain Injury Association. (2012). *The OBIA impact report 2012: A statistical snapshot of acquired brain injury and its effects on survivors and caregivers.* Retrieved from http://obia.ca/wp-content/uploads/2013/01/ImpactReportOnline-Dec2012.pdf

Ontario Ministry of Community & Social Services. (2011). *Accessibility for Ontarians with disabilities act.* Retrieved from http://www.eaws.gov.on.ca/html/source/regs/english/201/elaws_src_regs_r11191_e.htm

Ponsford, J., Whelan-Goodinson, R., & Bahar-Fuchs, A. (2007). Alcohol and drug use following traumatic brain injury: A prospective study. *Brain Injury, 21*(13-14), 1385-1392.

Priestley, M. (2001). *Disability and the life course: Global perspectives.* Cambridge, UK: Cambridge University Press.

Pritzlaff Voss, C., Wargolet Cesar, K., Tymus, T., & Fiedler, I.G. (2002). Perceived versus actual accessibility of substance abuse treatment facilities. *Topics in Spinal Cord Injury Rehabilitation, 7*(3), 47-55.

Rendon, M.E. (1992). Deaf culture and alcohol and substance abuse. *Journal of Substance Abuse Treatment, 9*(2), 103-110.

Robertson, S., Davis, S., Sneed, Z., Koch, D., & Boston, Q. (2009). Competency issues for alcohol/ other drug treatment counselors. *Alcoholism Treatment Quarterly, 27*(3), 265-279.

Sales, A. (2000). *Substance abuse and disability.* Retrieived from: http://files.eric.ed.gov/fulltext/ED440352.pdf

Saunders, L., & Krause, J. (2011). Psychological factors affecting alcohol use after spinal cord injury. *Spinal Cord, 49*(5), 637-642.

Smart, J., & Smart, D. (2007). Models of disability. Implications for the counseling profession. In A. Dell Orto & P. Power (Eds.), *Psychological and social impact of illness and disability* (5th ed., 75-100). New York: Springer Publishing.

Smedema, S., & Ebener, D. (2010). Substance abuse and psychosocial adaptation to physical disability: Analysis of the literature and future directions. *Disability and Rehabilitation, 32*(16), 1311-1319.

Spinal Cord Injury Ontario. (2015). *What is an SCI?* Retrieved from http://www.sciontario.org/what-is-an-sci

Statistics Canada. (2006). *Participation and activity limitations survey.* Ottawa, ON: Statistics Canada.

Statistics Canada. (2013). *Canadian survey on disability.* Ottawa, ON: Statistics Canada.

Substance Abuse and Mental Health Service Administration. (1998). *Substance use disorder treatment for people with physical and cognitive disabilities.* Rockville, MD: Substance Abuse and Mental Health Service Administration.

Tate, D., Forchheimer, M., Krause, J., Meade, M., & Bombardier, C. (2004). Patterns of Alcohol and substance use and abuse in persons with spinal cord injury: Risk factors and correlates. *Archives of Physical Medicine & Rehabilitation, 85*(11), 1837-1847.

Taylor, L., Kreutzer, J., Demm, S., & Meade, M. (2003). Traumatic brain injury and substance abuse: A review and analysis of the literature. *Neuropsychological Rehabilitation, 13*(1/2), 165-188.

Titus, J., & Guthmann, D. (2010). Addressing the black hole in substance abuse treatment for deaf and hard of hearing individuals: Technology to the rescue. *Journal of the American Deafness and Rehabilitation Association, 43*(2), 92-100.

Titus, J., & White, W.L. (2008). Substance use among youths who are deaf and hard of hearing. *Student Assistance Journal, 20*(3), 14-18.

West, S., Graham, C., & Cifu, D. (2009a). Alcohol and other drug problems and persons with disabilities: A new light on an often overlooked problem. *Alcoholism Treatment Quarterly, 27*(3), 238-241.

West, S., Graham, C., & Cifu, D. (2009b). Physical and programmatic accessibility of British alcohol/other drug treatment centers. *Alcoholism Treatment Quarterly, 27*(3), 294–304.

West, S., Graham, C., & Cifu, D. (2009c). Prevalence of persons with disabilities in alcohol/other drug treatment in the United States. *Alcoholism Treatment Quarterly, 27*(3), 242–252.

West, S., Graham, C., & Cifu, D. (2009d). Rates of alcohol/other drug treatment denials to persons with physical disabilities: Accessibility concerns. *Alcoholism Treatment Quarterly, 27*(3), 305–316.

West, S., Graham, C., & Cifu, D. (2009e). Rates of persons with disabilities in alcohol/other drug treatment in Canada. *Alcoholism Treatment Quarterly, 27*(3), 253–264.

West, S., Luck, R., & Capps, F. (2007). Physical inaccessibility negatively impacts the treatment participation of persons with disabilities. *Addictive Behaviors, 32*(7), 1494–1497.

CHAPTER 24

Concurrent Disorders and Social Work Intervention

Dennis Kimberley and Louise Osmond

Historical Context

Since the beginnings of the profession, social workers have been concerned with mental disorders and addiction problems, both as separate issues and as confounding issues. An example of the latter might include when child protection social workers have concerns with the mental health and/or substance abuse of parents (Cleaver, Unell, & Aldgate, 1999; Webb, 2006; Kimberley, 2016; Straussner, 2011). Social workers, along with early leaders of mental health movements, referred to as mental hygiene in the early 1900s, were among the first to redefine substance use compromised personal and social functioning as being more representative of social problems rather than of a moral weakness. This represented the changing social context when J.W. Langmuir established the first inebriate hospital at 999 Queen Street in Toronto, Ontario, during the 1880s (Grinker et al., 1964; Richmond 1917/1944; Timms, 1964). While early health literature recognized substance abuse problems in mental health populations as well as mental health problems in addicted populations, the clinical focus was often upon which disorder to assess as the primary problem and which may have caused the other (Watkins, Lewellen, & Barrett, 2001; Young, Mcafee, & Dziegielewski, 2005). In contrast, the social work literature in both addiction and mental health appeared less concerned with primary psychiatric diagnoses and more concerned with each problem domain becoming part of a complex nexus of interactions that compromised personal and social functioning, including collective family functioning (Cork, 1969; Markowitz, 2014; Mowbray et al. 1999; Richmond, 1917/1944).

Straussner (2001) discussed Mary Richmond's recognition of interactions among substance use and mental health issues. Richmond created a social diagnostic question-naire for inebriety that assessed: current drinking patterns and duration of problems; family history of drinking; drug problems as well as "mental and nervous trouble," going back four generations; medical and psychiatric histories; current social, work, and family situation; and "causal factors," which included the client's "own analysis of the cause or causes of his drinking." Of significance is that this instrument had distinct questions for women at risk. These themes, found as early as 1917, are still reflected in modern social work with co-occurring disorders (Scheffler, 2014; Watkins, Lewellen, & Barrett, 2001).

A Canadian social worker, Dr. H. David Archibald, attracted attention in his work with individuals dependent upon alcohol, which led to the establishment of the Ontario Alcoholism Research Foundation in 1949; the foundation evolved into the Alcoholism and Drug Addiction Research Foundation in 1961 (Rankin, 1976) and eventually the Centre for Addiction and Mental Health in 1998. Archibald, in his role as director, signalled a respect for multiple factors contributing to problems, risks, needs, and resolution. His efforts included but went beyond the medical model by balancing organ-izational foci on: biomedical-biochemical concerns; psychological-psychosocial risks, contributing factors, and harm-needs; and opportunities for risk-harm control such as the controversial controlled drinking as early as the 1970s. Under his leadership issues such as therapeutic amelioration, respect for human potential to change and thrive, personal and social change through public and professional education, community development concerns and social action, and associated research undertakings in the interests of both individuals and society were a focus for the organization. Thus, social work interventions, from early case finding to psychotherapy, have been undertaken while respecting the paradox that what appears to be dysfunctional often serves a personal and social function such as modulating some sequelae of trauma through self-medication or disassociation, or helping to generate a sense of self-empowerment or self-regulation—even when some patterns may be maladaptive in the end.

Multiple Interactions and Concurrence

There are diverse concurrent disorder literatures in professional practices and human services. The notion of duality appears in this broad literature with respect to mental health problems and developmental delays co-occurring; two addiction problems co-occurring; addiction and mental health problems co-occurring; two mental health problems co-occurring; as well as addiction and sex abuse survivor problems co-occurring (Health Canada, 2002; Ryglewicz & Pepper, 1996; Stohler & Rossler, 2005; Watkins, Lewellen, & Barrett, 2001). We prefer the terms concurrent or co-occurring disorders, referring to the co-occurrence and mutual impact, one on the other, of sub-stance use/abuse problems and mental health disorders, as well as otherwise clinically significant mental health symptoms or patterns (Health Canada, 2002; Kimberley & Osmond, 2010; Skinner, 2005).

In the context of this analysis, the co-occurring convergences and interactions are conceptualized more broadly to include both substance use and compulsive behaviours.

The latter would include, but not be limited to, problems of compulsive gambling, compulsive sexual behaviours including excessive viewing and use of pornography, compulsive Internet viewing, as well as gaming, social networking, and sexting, the latter referring to the sending and receiving of explicit personalized sexualized-eroticized messages including written, audio, and photo-video (Calvert, 2014; Kimberley & Scheltgen, 2013; Yau, Derevensky, & Potenza, 2016). In the current context it is important that social workers not succumb to habitual binary thought in their ideological positions. They must respect that the complex experiences and sequelae in life involve much more complexity than can be accounted for by only medicalized models (abstinence), behavioural models (harm reduction), developmental models (childhood experiences or familial trauma), or socio-political models (poverty, race, sexuality). A critical attitude of respecting "both-and" realities and socially constructed meanings, reflected in biopsychosocial interactional thinking and integrative supports and therapies, may be more beneficial to social workers and their clients, as well as to community needs (Kimberley & Bohm, 1999). Abstinence and harm reduction, developmental insight and present influences, strengths and vulnerabilities, resilience enhancement, and potential actualization may all serve to optimize effective treatment-intervention-support-help, and as social supports and treatments unfold, holistic, integrated, and relational common factors approaches are most promising (Sprenkle, Davis, & LeBow, 2009). These approaches emphasize the repeated findings that interpersonal relationship factors in the helping process, such as trust and empathy, have more personal and social change impacts than do specific therapeutic techniques such as cognitive-behavioural therapy (CBT).

Compromised mental health may best be broadly defined to encompass sub-clinical patterns of expression such as sadness, as well as clearer disorders such as depression. These are currently framed within clinically significant dimensional boundaries and medicalized paradigms in DSM-V (American Psychiatric Association, 2013), including sexual disorders and sex offence patterns of expression. This chapter does not analyze prescribed medication induced disorders like toxic psychoses that are not clearly related to the client having evidenced patterns that fit the addiction paradigm. For this analysis, concurrent disorders refer to problems of the person that fall within a general addiction paradigm, including behavioural and developmental patterns, as well as a general mental health–mental disorder paradigm. Furthermore, addiction and mental health problems are considered concurrent if they impact the person at relatively the same time, including often being mutually, reciprocally, and dynamically interactive, as well as influential in ways that compromise personal and social functioning, both adaptive and maladaptive, in both individuals and social collectives.

Additionally, family members and close supportive friends most likely experience the multiplicity of problems, risks, and interactions in life as lived, with some express-ing clinically or functionally significant transgenerational sequelae (Kimberley, 2016; Markowitz, 2014; Wilson, Bennett, & Bellack, 2013). What is most clinically significant, and what increases the complexity and uncertainty for the client, social supports, and the counsellor, is that co-occurring disorders and associated compromised personal and social functioning are:

1. Not expressed or experienced simply as being in parallel.
2. Not expressed or experienced simply as sequential.
3. Experienced as having mutual and reciprocal influence one on the other.
4. Likely compounded when two or more mental health problems are also operating (depression and complex trauma).
5. Most likely compounded when drug use is occurring with a compulsive behaviour (alcohol abuse/XTC use alongside compulsive sexual behaviour/pornography viewing).
6. Able to transcend binary, duality, and "either-or biases" in assessment and thus support attending to multiple relevant factors that pose challenges for client systems. In parallel dynamic, mutual, and reciprocal influences of strengths, protective factors, resiliencies, risks, and vulnerabilities add to the complexity of the client's situations and challenges while also creating opportunities for sustained changes as desired, required, or needed (Al-Krenawi & Kimberley, 2016).

Biopsychosocial Interactional Assessment of Complex Interactions

Screening and Early Intervention

Assessments of persons, including families, wishing psychosocial services may be conducted in venues that are not directly related to addiction or mental health services, such as post-incarceration services provided by the John Howard Society. Within these contexts, one of the best indicators of mental health, addiction, and compounding concerns are repeated direct observations by a case manager with whom a client has developed a trusting relationship (Barry et al., 1995). Canadian best practices processes suggest brief screening to determine "whether the individual may have a mental health or substance abuse problem that warrants more comprehensive assessment" (Health Canada, 2002, p. 28). A Canadian expert panel recommended use of the Dartmouth Assessment of Lifestyle Instrument (DALI) to screen persons with severe mental illnesses for substance abuse risks (Rosenberg et al., 1998). The panel recommended screening for both addiction in the generic sense and basic indicators of mental health concerns. However, there appeared to be more of a challenge in screening for mental health risks in an addicted population than the reverse. There are a variety of valid and reliable tools to use with the addicted or mentally ill populations. In the clinical work of the authors, the following screening questions, based upon extensive case experience, have been used to explore the likelihood of a clinically significant mental health–mental risk in a person known to have an addiction risk (Kimberley & Osmond, 2001, 2016). A client would be asked to respond to each of the 10 screening questions (see Table 24.1).

Table 24.1   Screening Questions

	Yes, recently, in the past year	Yes, in the past	Never	Can't remember
1. Has anyone personally close to you suggested that you might have a mental health problem?				
2. Has a professional counsellor or therapist suggested that you might have a mental health problem?				
3. Have you "worried" that you might have a mental health problem, risk, or a need for mental health assessment?				
4. Have you ever been professionally assessed for a troublesome mental health or psychiatric problem?				
5. Have you felt emotionally unstable to the point where you worried that you would lose control—sometimes referred to in self-talk as "losing it"?				
6. Have you felt emotionally unstable to the point that you experienced a troublesome "loss" of self-control of your emotions, thinking, and/or behaviour?				
7. Have you felt mentally unstable to the point that you feared not regaining emotional stability?				
8. Have you felt that your personality, identity, or sense of self was becoming disturbingly fragile or unstable?				
9. Have you behaved or acted unstable to the point that you feared that you would have difficulty regaining self-control of your actions?				
10. Have you experienced a significant loss of ability in personal and social functioning to the point that you felt fearful that you would fail in a social role (e.g., parent, employee, student, partner, family member, friend)?				

Respecting the high proportion of persons with addiction problems who report mental health concerns, if the client responds positively (Yes) to three or more of the ten questions, then a more comprehensive mental health assessment is likely needed, one that explores the likelihood of co-occurring mental health and social functioning challenges being present, interactive, and mutually influencing.

Beyond screening, an early decision in assessment is the range of considerations to which the counsellor might pay attention in arriving at an assessment of suspected concurrent disorders and related problems, risks, impacts, needs, resiliencies, strengths, and potentials. As well, it is important to recognize that the observed and reported patterns of dynamic influences are going to shift over time. Practitioners are encouraged to consider the following dimensions of personal and social functioning when assessing concurrence and interactional influences.

Common Biochemical and Bio-neurological Considerations

In assessing the biological dimension, it is wise for the social worker to be attentive to the direct psychopharmacological effects of the substance used, and to addiction patterns and dynamics, including on the alliance between the counsellor and client. Issues that can arise include increased agitation and increased heart rate with cocaine use to impaired perception produced by alcohol, plus the development of tolerance and experiences of withdrawal from any substance used in a chronic manner. The direct effects of psychoactive substances must always be considered within the context of their interactions with the symptoms and patterns associated with mental health concerns, such as the compounded effect of central nervous system depression, associated with alcohol ingestion, interacting with clinically significant depression as well as compounded suicide risks for a client. For the person living with a diagnosed mental illness, a moderate or low dose of any psychoactive substance may have serious impacts, direct and indirect, upon the expression of the mental health concerns, as well as upon personal and social functioning dimensions such as family functioning and parenting capacity (Pilat & Boomhower-Kresser, 1992; Kimberley, 2008, 2016). Other considerations are the impact of age and gender factors in interaction with drug effects and the expression of mental health problems, as well as confounding effects of polydrug use (Doweiko, 2015; Dziegielewski & Lupo, 2005).

Current scholarship alerts the clinician to become aware of potential changes in neurological functioning (not to be misinterpreted as linearly causal), associated with:

a. *mental health issues*: (i) maternal stress or maternal substance abuse often influences the neurological development of the fetus and neonate (Begun & Brown, 2014; Davies, 2011; Pomeroy & Parish, 2011); (ii) biopsychosocial histories may offer important insights into current concerns.

b. the *use-abuse of prescribed medications*: (i) some medications are designed to target neurological receptors while others impact neurological functioning by default of use; (ii) drug-induced neurologic syndrome; (iii) neurolepsis, or serotonin syndrome, which impact both physical well-being and social functioning (Begun & Brown, 2014; Csiernik, 2014). Thus, knowledge of amounts, types, strengths, and duration of substance administration/use patterns is important in estimating risk and harm.

c. the *non-medical use-abuse of substances*: methamphetamine use has associated stroke-paralysis risks and harm, and both inhalants and ketamine reactions may cause permanent damage to the brain (Csiernik, 2014; McKim & Hancock, 2013). Given the impurities in street drugs, risk may be higher than suspected based on unreliable client self-reports.

d. *compulsive behaviours*: compulsive gaming and Internet use, including compulsive pornography viewing, are associated with neurological processes, and may share similar neurobiological abnormalities (Hou et al., 2012; Kuss & Griffiths, 2012; Love et al., 2015).

e. *developmental trauma*: changes in neurological structure associated with parental attachment deficits with children are overrepresented among children whose mothers used or abused psychoactive substances while pregnant, who had a parent with one or more addiction risk, and/or who were exposed to an psychoactive drug using lifestyle (Brisch, 2012; Davies, 2011; Silberg, 2013; Straussner, 2011).

f. *generational effects*: offspring of addicted parents processing the interaction of parental mental health and addiction are considered to be at greatest risk (Kimberley, 2016; Straussner 2011; Tarter & Horner, 2016).

g. *interactions of factors*: the intersection of any of the previously stated factors increases the likelihood of influences that can significantly compromise personal and social functioning and parenting capacity. (Back et al., 2015; Kimberley, 2008)

Affect, Emotions, Feelings

Included in a psychological and psychosocial frame within a biopsychosocial paradigm are affect, cognition, and cognitive functioning, as well as behaviour or actions. With respect to affect, a social worker must assess and address the patterns of feelings: as experienced (sensation of warmth and well-being associated with many psychoactive substances); repressed (unconscious hurt associated with parental addiction); suppressed (fear associated with one's own mental disorder); and/or expressed (anger associated with exploitation to support a parent's addiction) by the client experiencing a concurrent disorder as an adult (Dziegelewski & Lupo, 2005; McKim & Hancock, 2013). As well, it needs to be recognized that the experience and expression of affect and the management of intense feelings within the context of concurrent disorders are filtered through gender, cultural, and sexual orientation differences (Leahy, 2015; Vohs & Baumeister, 2016).

Habitual Behaviours and Conscious Action Patterns

Assessment of behaviour, including relatively unconscious habitual patterns and substance-impaired awareness, consciously chosen actions, and especially repeated clinically significant patterns of activity based on problem, risk, harm, maladaptations, and failures with respect to desired or required personal and social functioning and change, should address the complex interaction of:

a. *addictive behaviour patterns* involving the pattern of drug administration, frequency, dose, strength, and duration, including patterns of problematic or compulsive gambling, compulsive sexual behaviour, and/or impulsive use of pornography;
b. *actions or patterns of expression that more directly trigger or maintain drug using behaviour,* among which are included keeping alcohol or drugs in the home, or personal strategies for managing anger that include the use of substances as "permission givers," which might contribute to risks such as disinhibiting aggression;
c. *behaviour patterns that are directly related to mental health problems* and disorders, including developmental damage, such as not paying attention in a classroom, which can be associated with dissociation, experienced as zoning out, related to trauma experiences, and related "flashbacks," as well as to Fetal Alcohol Spectrum Disorder;
d. *activities that are more directly related to treatment* or other ameliorative interventions such as failing to use prescribed medication properly, or using the label "addiction" strategically to excuse socially unacceptable and unjustifiable actions;
e. *non-addictive related, and non-disorder related, actions* that are interactive with addiction or mental health problems, including resistance to using available positive alternatives and non-substance using or pro-sobriety peers to replace activities defined as "boring" or no longer desired;
f. *addiction and mental health associated problems interacting with personal and social role functioning* such as parenting activities or management of aggressive behaviour (Kimberley and Osmond, 2016; Rush & Koegl, 2008);
g. *addiction lifestyle choices that reinforce mental health risks* such as hanging out with the group-sex gang where availability of street drugs is high and unprotected sex is all too common among people who have otherwise practiced safe sex, but feel less inhibited (Andrasik & Lostutter, 2012); and
h. *interactions over time* among any of the preceding behaviour-action patterns, including between them, mental health compromises, and other significant dimensions of social interaction and social functioning.

The above factors may be addressed in interaction with other biopsychosocial dimensions, but focusing primarily upon behaviour change is very limiting in terms of assessments, service-care plans, and therapy. For example, behaviourally oriented models run the risk of reducing addictions interventions to abstinence goals or harm reduction goals, which are more logically framed as the beginnings of supportive treatment rather than as being the end-goals of interventions. Also, behavioural habits and risks, including selective use of protective action patterns, as impacted by social learning and adaptations to social situations, vary with age, gender, sexual orientation, cultural background, and the life experiences of persons of diverse racial and ethnic backgrounds. As one example, the justified distrust felt by Indigenous persons, or persons of colour, directed at persons of privilege in positions of service authority, too often dissuade such marginalized persons from seeking needed and desired psycho-social supports and interventions (Menzies & Lavallée Jr., 2014).

Cognitive Functioning and Cognitive Scripts

The social worker must also assess cognitive functioning and the influence of cognitive scripts, which are interactive with addiction and mental health risks, as well as explore pathways for needed personal and social change in the directions of harm reduction, abstinence, symptom management, recovery, and progress, including optimizing resilience and strengths. Cognitive functioning can be complicated by serious mental health problems such as those leading to disorientation of time, place, and self (Gold & Elhai, 2008). A client's dissociation from physical reality, for example, may be reinforced where the substance of choice is associated with hallucinogenic effects (LSD, MDMA). As well, ketamine may reinforce a client's dissociation from physical reality, and alcohol may contribute to impaired judgment and disinhibition of affect, thought, and actions (Doweiko, 2015; Dziegielewski & Lupo, 2005). Antipsychotic treatment medications, even when used as prescribed, can impair attention, perception, memory, reasoning, judgment, and problem solving; a person living with schizophrenia, for example, may become confused by the middle of a standard 50-minute interview. Dangerous use of some substances, such as "crack" cocaine, crystal methamphetamine, MDMA (ecstasy), and their related lifestyles, are associated with long-term effects such as confusion, difficulty reasoning, and problems with memory and attention, with some clients experiencing hallucinations, psychotic disorders and paranoidal fears (Rush, Stoops, & Ling, 2008; Tang, Martin, & Cotes, 2014). Cognitive functioning assessment may also benefit from an exploration of unconscious determinates of affect and behaviour. An example of unconscious dynamics may be the client who has likely been sexually abused and has blocked the event from current recall, but still depends upon alcohol or other drugs to control anxiety in situations where intimacy and sexual expression are desirable like committing to a long-term relationship (Maltz, 1991).

Cognitive content, such as information, beliefs, attitudes, values, social expecta-tions, interpretations of reality, assignment of meaning to situations, and cognitive scripts about life—which influence a person's observations, judgments, reasoning, and decisions—should be assessed as experienced before, during, and after use of a substance (VanGilder, Green, & Dziegielewski, 2005). The cognitive-content assessment should include significant points during the occurrence or expression of symptoms of mental disorder, as well as those expressed in the client's accounts/narratives describing problems, risks, harm, and needs, as well as potential strengths and resilience, includ-ing motivation for change. For example, analysis of thought patterns, in the form of self-talk or interpersonal communication, could provide insight, congruent with mindfulness therapies, such as in a situation where an anxious and agitated person using cocaine has an increased risk for paranoidal ideation, cognitive distortion, and delusional conclusions.

Of special interest are thought patterns and convergences that a client applies in either finding solutions and enabling effective coping such as avoiding street subculture, or in adapting through reinforcing "pathological" or relatively maladaptive responses or self-expression such as permitting the effects of cocaine to support disinhibitions for having unprotected sex. Patterns can include clients who believe that no level of self-medication is worth the risk, juxtaposed with those who believe more alcohol will give a "lift" out of depression. Such patterns of thought may be further articulated as defensive routines that enable the person to exaggerate, deny, minimize, or project their problems, risks, needs, and impacts associated with addiction, mental health, and related sequelae, as well as their interactions. Cognitive-affective defensive routines may also help the client to delude him- or herself that he or she has "progressed so much ... in two weeks that I can do one line for old times' sake ... no problem." Such cognitive scripts may be reflective of *delusional thinking*, sometimes more broadly termed *cognitive distortions*, involving self-deception in the expression of false and unreasonable beliefs, often exacerbated by *compromised reality-testing*: "Alcohol caused me to beat my wife ... she was asking for it ... she wants me back because she agrees that she caused the problem."

Social Relationships and Social Bonds

Biological-biomedical behaviours, and cognitions associated with both addiction and mental health issues, often filtered through support and counselling decisions, interact with diverse and intersecting social-relational dimensions of the client's life. In a study by Bergly, Gräwe, and Hagen (2014), 92% of concurrent disordered respondents defined improving family and significant-other relationships as a key treatment goal. Social workers commonly address interpersonal relationship dynamics throughout the life cycle, with due respect to social bonds, especially as they contribute to problems, risks, and harm, as well as support resiliencies, solutions, recovery, healthy development, and needed fulfillment (Van Hook, 2014; Walsh, 2015). Intrapersonal conflict (conflicting feelings and thoughts), interpersonal conflict, and less-than-optimal quality of social support are among the major motivators for substance misuse and relapse (Marlatt & Witkiewitz, 2005; Potter-Efron & Potter-Efron, 1992). Interpersonal conflict dynamics can also contribute to the risks associated with drug and/or mental illness-influenced disinhibition, such as with bipolar disorder challenges (McKim & Hancock, 2013; Weiss & Connery, 2011). Primary relationships such as partnerships, marriage, and family must be assessed in terms of how they contribute to addiction and/or mental health problems and risks, and how they contribute to maintaining risk, as well as how they may effectively support strengths enhancement, reinforcing adaptive resiliencies (Van Hook, 2014; Walsh, 2015), and solution building (Berg & Reuss, 1997). Additionally, assessment must include how these primary relationships can help meet client needs in ways that support recovery and reduce or otherwise help to control maladaptive habits (Skinner, 2005; Watkins, Lewellen, & Barrett, 2001).

Social workers have a history of attachment-informed practice, and recognize that attachment and bond problems are overrepresented in, and interactive for, addicted populations, compulsive behaviours, populations with mental health challenges, and persons who have experienced PTSD and complex trauma (Brisch, 2012; Padykula & Conklin, 2010). Those experiencing complex trauma, addiction, and mental health issues are overrepresented among those who struggle with attachment difficulties throughout the life cycle, including in therapeutic relationships (Back et al., 2015; Flores, 2004; Ruisard, 2015). Those who have experienced sexual, physical, and emotional maltreatment and exploitation are overrepresented among those who have addiction, mental health, and complex trauma problems, confounded by compounded interactions with developmental damage, identity, and self-regulation challenges, evidenced in interpersonal attachment difficulties (Briere & Scott, 2015; Mikulincer & Shaver, 2016; Steele & Malchiodi, 2012). This complex nexus is associated with many avenues to exacerbate and sustain concurrent disorder risks, as is reflective of many marginalized groups for whom social workers provide social care, mental health services, addictions services, and victim, corrections, and protection services (Farley, 2003; Miller, 2002).

Another sub-dimension of interpersonal concerns, which are too often avoided in addiction and mental health assessment and treatment are patterns of intimacy and sexual expression (Andrasik & Lostutter, 2012; Sharpe, 2005). It is not uncommon for issues linked with intimacy and sexual expression to be precipitated by, or compounded with, compromised functioning, associated with addiction such as heavy use of alcohol or opioids that often reduce sex drive, sexual interest, and sexual functioning. Persons who are depressed often experience reduced sex drive (Clayton & Montejo, 2006; James, 2012) while persons with manic symptoms have been observed to be at considerable risk for self-destructive indiscriminate sexual actions (Weiss & Connery, 2011). Of major concern in both addiction and mental health services are those persons who have had experiences of sexual trauma regardless of age, including the impacts of such life experiences on partnerships and marriages (Dayton, 2000; Osmond & Kimberley, 2010; Mikulincer & Shaver, 2016). As well, sex offenders may evidence significant problems with substance use (Sheldon & Howitt, 2007) and/or mental health issues as part of their problem nexus (Booth & Gulati, 2014; Wheeler, George, & Stephens, 2005). It is also not uncommon for there to be a history of substance abuse or mental health problems, or both, in the problem-risk sets associated with persons who have been assessed as exhibiting compulsive sexual activity, sex trade activities, or high-risk sexual behaviour, including those who have been exploited (Carnes, 2001; Farley, 2003).

Social Dimensions Signaling Intersecting Oppressions

As part of social workers' commitments to social justice, human services, and anti-oppressive practice, they attend to complex social factors, many of which intersect with oppression. Related risks are amplified when addictions struggles, mental health challenges, and associated human sufferings all converge. Concerns in concurrent disorder literature and practice include:

a. *Socio-economic concerns* including manic persons and problem gamblers who are at risk for insolvency and loss of material goods, while those with a concurrent diagnosis are, in general, at high risk of living a life of chronic poverty and homelessness (Cooper et al., 2010). Intersections are clinically significant in that those managing concurrent disorders and those who are homeless are also overrepresented among persons who have experienced trauma as children and youth, those who are at high risk for repeated trauma, as well as military and other first responder personnel who have experienced operational trauma (Kerfoot, Petrakis, & Rosenheck, 2011).

b. *Socio-legal issues*, for in North America persons with mental health and addiction problems are at risk for being treated as criminals more so than as being ill or otherwise functionally challenged. North American governmental-bureaucratic culture has constructed more long-term correctional institutions and has reduced optimal mental health and addiction services, with those provided operating on short-term or "time-sensitive" programmatic models. A large increase in criminalization is found in sub-populations of women, persons of colour, and Indigenous persons. Rudin (2014) writing within the Canadian context of addiction, mental health, concurrent disorder, transgenerational trauma, and colonialism sequelae concluded, "more recent 'tough on crime' legislation has severely impinged the ability of the courts to address Aboriginal overrepresentation through the sentencing process" (p. 352).

c. *Social situational concerns* for those with an affect disorder are compounded. The combination of heavy medication and an addiction problem are likely to contribute to alienation and social isolation from family, friends, school, the workplace, and the community, leaving many to struggle without benefit of required social supports.

d. *Social-structural and other social environmental, social situation, and social context interactions*, highlighted by social stigmatization, oppression, social exclusion, and marginalization of addicted persons who have mental health problems, especially for the seriously mentally ill, persons of colour, First Nations persons, and LGBTQ subgroups.

Social policies and programs have increasingly criminalized the concurrent disorder population, with large increases of incarceration of Indigenous persons and women. Within this population, social justice, structural, and social situational dynamics converge to compound deprivation and oppression. Ryglewicz and Pepper (1996) noted that as psychiatric hospital beds have decreased, prison beds have increased, and the problem of the social control of mentally ill people has thereby been transferred to the criminal justice system, conceptualized as transinstitutionalizational patterns. While not all homeless people are mentally ill, deinstitutionalization has forced a considerable number of people onto the streets, many of whom are at risk for becoming transferred to criminalizing institutions, including some who have made false confessions.

Spirituality often acts as a paradoxical dimension of life experience that contributes to both risk and recovery for this group. On the risk side, spirituality, morality, meaning in life, and personal connection with the metaphysical may be associated with guilt related to misusing or abusing a chemical, feelings of being demonized in terms of being addicted and/or mentally ill, and relapse triggered in part by feelings of moral failing and deviant identities. Some substance use and abuse effects, and mental health effects, may distort the experience of spirituality so that it is expressed as part of pathology, such as hearing voices of angels or God and responding to their commands, or taking LSD because it gives one an experience of being "connected with the cosmos." On the other hand, spirituality in the sense of spiritual strength and support for resilience in the face of personal suffering, attaching to a more adaptive and hopeful meaning to life, or putting oneself in the hands of a higher being have been associated with both recovery and being able to cope with chronicity, including the client who, paradoxically, feels empowered to self-control by putting himself or herself in the hands of a higher being (Diamond, 2000; Witkiewitz, McCallion, & Kirouac, 2016). Given that persons with concurrent disorders, and those who have experienced significant trauma, are at increased risk for suicide attempts, and given that drug effects could further disinhibit suicidal behaviour (Esposito-Smythers, Perloe, Machell, & Rallis, 2016), enabling more spiritual or existential growth to establish more meaning in life, hope in the future, and sustaining strengths and resilience may help reduce risks of self-harm.

Converging and Intersecting Complexities

All of the above biopsychosocial factors, along with the spiritual dimension of individuals, converge to help develop and maintain personality contributing to self-concept, self-worth, self-esteem, and grounded self-confidence. These attributes support integration and relative stability of an adaptive self-identity while also supporting some fluidity in terms of stable and integrated identity transformations. Alternately, identity issues may contribute to disintegration and instability when a person is impacted by the interaction of developmental, addiction, mental health, and associated problems, especially post-trauma effects (Kimberley & Parsons, 2016). Impacts upon self and upon the path of self-development in the face of concurrent disorders may be addressed from the point of view of the professional observer—adopting a self-analysis model such as that of Denzin (1987), which could guide exploration of the addicted and disordered self—or from the point of view of a client's diverse self-narratives (McAdams, 1993). Working upon complex and sustained self-change may enable persons with concurrent disorders to move beyond simple desirable behavioural and cognitive changes to more substantive improvements in personal stability leading to an integration of a more healthy self. Substantive, complex, and uncertain self-changes support sustained improvements. This in turn supports resiliencies that enable the development of strengths beyond problem or symptom management, without unrealistic expectations of a "cure."

In addressing all of the above, it may be in the best interest of some clients to also explore developmental history, transgenerational history, developmental strengths, biopsychosocial pathways to addiction, mental health difficulties, and their dynamic interaction within the contexts of compromised personal and social functioning. Such an exploration of both historical-developmental facts and experiences and related personal narratives are not intended to discover any singular cause or even clear multiple causes of problems. Historical-developmental information (a biopsychosocial-spiritual history) may identify contributing factors, help reduce a sense of personal blame, support a grounded taking of responsibility and enable the identification of past, current, and potential strengths and resiliencies, which may support sustained recovery. For some clients, to be understood in his or her biopsychosocial developmental context, such as recognizing previous sexual exploitation and understanding complex trauma sequelae, is affirming and equally important to knowing potential causes or contributing factors.

In addition to the above considerations, the following questions may help ensure effective differential assessment:

a. Do the mental health problems, while concurrent, appear to have arisen out of addictive experiences, such as alcohol hallucinosis or depression associated with gambling-related losses?

b. Do the addiction problems, while concurrent, appear to have arisen out of coping with mental health problems, such as those persons managing complex trauma who use excess alcohol to "relax and numb out," or use cocaine "so I can feel again"? (Kimberley & Parsons, 2016).

c. Do concurrent addiction and mental health problems appear to have developed in parallel, in dynamic interaction, as is often the case with persons with personality disorders or bipolar disorders (Hunter, Rosenthal, Lynch, & Linehan, 2016; Rush & Koegl, 2008; Watkins, Lewellen, & Barrett, 2001)?

d. Is the amplification of symptoms of a serious mental illness, such as schizophrenia, related to the move from experimentation with drugs to heavier or continuous drug use (Green, Drake, Brunette, & Noordsy, 2007)?

e. Are there more than two concurrent problem domains in mutual interaction? For example, it is not unusual to find those managing PTSD or complex trauma also complaining of depression and also presenting with polydrug use (Back et al. 2015; Briere & Scott, 2015; Kimberley & Parsons, 2016).

f. Does the use of any substance at a low dose interact with addiction risks and/or mental health risks, or does such use impact the client's treatment regime, including prescribed medications? For example, disinhibition related to low levels of alcohol consumption may be associated with risks of indiscriminate sexual behaviour for persons experiencing a manic phase of an affect disorder (Weiss & Connery, 2011), violence, or sex offence relapse. One paradox of both substance use and compulsive behaviours is that the patterns may be pursued to soothe loneliness yet increase loneliness, and in turn increased loneliness may contribute to increased pursuit of negative solutions to felt loneliness (Flores, 2004; Milulincer & Shaver, 2016; Young, Yue, and Ying, 2011).

g. Are compulsive behaviours such as Internet use significant co-occurring factors that may be interacting with either substance use risks or other mental health problems? For example, it appears that those experiencing compulsive Internet use are overrepresented among those who have, or who are recovering from, substance use problems, as well as those who have had chronic attachment difficulties—often confounded with challenges in terms of trust, empathy, and affect-regulation (Mikulincer & Shaver, 2016).

h. Is there a paradoxical effect where the symptoms and patterns of co-occurring problems are mediated by the presence of another interactive co-occurring problem? For example, the use of crystal methamphetamine may not only increase a sense of well-being for persons who feel depressed (a self-medication theory), but there may be an associated improvement in the subjective experience of intimacy and sex (a relationship enhancement theory).

i. Is there a compounding effect of attachment insecurities, disorganized attachments, and affect regulation challenges within co-occurring disorders? Given the complex interactions of attachment issues with trauma, addiction, and serious mental illnesses, attachment-informed assessment and treatment is imperative (Mikulincer & Shaver, 2016; Padykula & Conklin, 2010; Schore & Schore, 2007).

In bringing closure to some of the dimensions of assessment for a counsellor to consider, one must recognize that the paths to detection and screening may vary and that the bias in assessment often varies according to the function of the agency and management's attraction to treatment models that fit their management paradigms, such as time-sensitive treatments encoded with efficiency language. When time and other resource restrictions support only minimum intervention versus optimal supportive actions and provision, one side of a concurrence to either addiction or mental health will likely be missed, at best, and dismissed, at worst.

Also, there are gender differences that have significance for both assessment and treatment. Among the most significant are that women are more likely to enter treatment through mental health services and are overrepresented among the users of prescription drugs (Doweiko, 2015). Also, while women are more likely to attempt suicide, males, often masquerading as resilient, are three times more likely to be successful in their attempts (Lester, 2000; Navaneelan, 2009).

Personal and Social Functioning

Regardless of what mental health assessments or psychiatric diagnoses are formulated, no matter what the substance uses, abuses, or other compulsive activities and risks are observed, and no matter what interactions among clinically significant biopsychosocial-spiritual dimensions are attributed to the person and her or his social situation, the social worker, the client, and the community must understand the dynamic interactions with problems/risks and resiliencies/strengths, associated with both adaptive and maladaptive personal and social functioning. In the best interest of the individual, family, and society, the goals of intervention and co-discovering paths to recovery should include empowering the client to develop capacities, improve strengths, and sustain gains in personal and social functioning, with due consideration to culturally sensitive prosocial self-determination. The knowledge, skills, and practice wisdom of social workers, in the assessment of personal and social functioning integration into a dynamic and responsive case plan, and the application of empowerment and resilience-enhancing strategies in care and recovery, are significant contributions to any multidisciplinary effort with the client (Skinner, 2005; Watkins, Lewellen, & Barrett, 2001). An assessment model with a known reliability and validity that respects the complexities and uncertainties associated with personal and social functioning is the person-in-environment system, the PIE classification system for social functioning problems (Karls & O'Keefe, 2008; Walsh & Ramsay, 1994). Biopsychosocial models guide the integration of observations and judgments with respect to social functioning, environmental factors, mental health, and physical health in interaction. They consider risks, vulnerabilities, needs, resiliencies, and strengths holistically (Kimberley & Osmond, 2016).

Considerations for Case Management and Treatment with Concurrent Disorders

Integrated Treatment: Co-occurring Addictions and Mental Health Challenges

Hilarski and Wodarski (2001) and Watkins, Lewellen, and Barrett (2001), consistent with the Canadian expert panel on concurrent disorder (Health Canada, 2002), concluded that the scholarship in the area of concurrent disorders suggests integrated treatment is the preferred treatment approach. The evolution of integrated treatments (Daley & Zuckoff, 2000; Evans & Sullivan, 2000; Kimberley & Osmond, 2010; Skinner, 2005; Nace, 1995; Scheffler, 2014) is in part supported to reduce the risk of clients not being served, being only partially served, or having to revolve through multiple treatments and multiple services. From a clinical point of view, the client can actually feel disintegrated if not helped to integrate various aspects of themselves and their life situations, as experienced, socially defined, and expressed.

A wide range of interventions are needed to improve services and support for persons experiencing co-occurring disorders, as significant proportions of mental health and psychiatric populations experience problems with substance use and related compulsive behaviours (Back et al., 2015; Rush, Stoops, & Ling, 2008). Persons with concurrent disorders are still often *not* assessed as such. Because of the intransigence of their complex problems, early detection and case finding are needed that span many human services. Early detection and case finding can reduce the likelihood of mentally ill and addicted clients being defined as primarily criminal or untreatable, and may enable a client to retain more strengths as well as benefit from treatment programs to help acknowledge vulnerabilities and foster resiliencies (Kimberley & Osmond, 2010; Skinner, 2005).

Intake and case management interventions present unique opportunities for screening, assessment, engagement and referral, and the establishment of an integrated service team, with some assurance of integrated treatment within an integration-informed service. In contrast to the ideal of addressing both the addiction problems and the mental health problems in an integrated and holistic fashion, with due respect for individual differences, those with concurrent disorders are most likely to have one side of the duality ignored or minimized. Effective case management must not only monitor harm, risk, capacity, progress, and treatment integration, but must also ensure that concrete social and economic supports are in place to sustain strengths and to promote resilience and recovery. A holistic synthesis is required, congruent with biopsychosocial-spiritual thinking in social work, as client's needs are likely to be pervasive and typically go well beyond counselling and therapy to include other forms of community-based care (Cooper et al., 2010; Nelson, Aubry, & LeFrance, 2007; Neumiller et al., 2009). Interagency partnerships in service planning are necessary to support optimal care, within the context of clients who may likely need long-term social supports and counselling, or who are anticipated to leave services prematurely, then return and, throughout their life cycle, be repeat users of multiple services.

Beyond the issue of service integration is the recommendation that an integrated approach be taken for individual counselling and therapy (Health Canada, 2002; Hilarski & Wodarski, 2001; O'Connell & Beyer, 2002; Scheffler, 2014) with due respect to the client's "readiness for change" (Watkins, Lewellen, & Barrett, 2001). The following synthesis covers many of the initial treatment issues faced by social workers and other mental health and addiction professionals. Within this context, the Canadian expert panel concluded that "clinicians/support workers in an integrated program or system should provide specific services concurrently or sequentially, depending on the particular combination of concurrent disorders and other individual factors" (Health Canada, 2002, p. 14).

Co-occurring Addiction and Mood and Anxiety Disorders

Problems with substance use are highly associated with mood and anxiety disorders. The expert group concluded that

> With the exception of post-traumatic stress syndrome (PTSD) ... a sequencing of the specific intervention (beginning with substance abuse) is recommended ... and an adjustment of the treatment/support if the mood and anxiety disorder does not improve following an improvement in the substance use disorder. (Health Canada, 2002, p. 53)

The report recommends integrated treatment of PTSD, as does more recent scholarship addressing the link between substance use risks and concurrent post-trauma concerns, including developmental sequelae of trauma (Back et al., 2015). The interactions among substance use and abuse and mood disorders, anxiety or PTSD, are complex and change over time. While social workers do apply transtheoretical paradigms to addiction (Watkins, Lewellen, & Barrett, 2001), counsellor-therapists need to be aware that some rather linear motivation and change models derived from effective addiction treatment (Prochaska, DiClemente, & Norcross, 1992; Velasquez, Crouch, Stephens, & DiClemente, 2016) may not be successfully generalized to some concurrent disorder situations where convergence is observed. For example, a client may be enthusiastic about setting change goals in a manic phase, but feel hopeless, helpless, and less motivated about change when depressed. Applying common factors within the context of influencers of success, the clinical rule of beginning where the client is and moving at a pace that is comfortable, while still supporting motivations and actions in the direction of efficacious change, remains best (Sprenkle, Davis, & LeBow, 2009). The exceptions are when there are imminent life-threatening risks, or when mental health symptoms are associated with the client not progressing to settling on needs and personal and social change intentions and paths. Mood and anxiety challenges are also associated with compulsive behaviours such as uninterrupted Internet use (Rosen, 2012).

Co-occurring Addiction and Persistent Mental Disorders

Treatment and support with this group is quite complex. Interventions generally require a wide range of integrated supports, some of which may be concurrent and some of which may be sequential, depending upon the unique developmental factors and current situations in each case. Both harm reduction and extensive psychosocial interventions will likely be needed—on a long-term and repeated basis for those clients who have a persistent and serious mental illness. Advocacy with this group can prevent unnecessary criminalization of clients and may also ensure social supports that are beyond the minimums mandated under modern managerialism based human services. Too frequently clients, while living in a supported community setting, have meagre accommodation, typically one-room bed/sitting arrangements, and receive limited supportive social contact (Nelson, Hall, & Forchuk, 2003). Many have experienced homelessness. Constructive and concrete care, with extensive social supports and medication, and more directive therapies, may offer a level of integration sufficient to provide a feasible beginning point for substantive change with this group (Cooper et al., 2010).

Co-occurring Addiction and Personality Disorders

Persons diagnosed with personality disorders, or with associated serious interpersonal relationship challenges, are overrepresented among persons with co-occurring disorders (Rush & Koegl, 2008; Watkins, Lewellen, & Barrett, 2001). An integrated approach with this group may best follow a concurrent treatment model as a first choice, with the exception of persons diagnosed with anti-social personality disorder. With the latter, it may be wise to address the substance use problem first, as substance use may disinhibit or potentiate aggressive behaviour and erode adaptive impulse control. The Canadian expert group suggested that dialectical behaviour therapy, a psychosocial model, holds promise with the borderline personality group (Health Canada, 2002, p. 64), a view that continues to be supported (Hunter, Rosenthal, Lynch, & Linehan, 2016).

The authors recommend individual therapy until clients are group ready. Entering prematurely into a psychiatric, addiction, or concurrent disorder groups or attempting to address concurrence may harm both the individual and the group. Preventable conflicts may be anticipated, such as when a person with narcissistic tendencies, common among persons with personality disorders, dominates educational or therapeutic group transactions and is insistent upon monopolizing attention from group leaders. Those suspected of some form of personality disorder are often a very demanding subgroup to treat, as with some subclasses such as borderline personality, evidencing unpredictability, lability, inflexibility maladaptive patterns, and rapid regression are not uncommon (Burckell & McMain, 2009; Goldstein, 2004). Assessment and intervention is even more complex and uncertain with those diagnosed with personality disorders, sometimes described as relational disorders. This group is overrepresented among those who have experienced significant life traumas and evidenced developmental damage associated with attachment difficulties (Briere & Scott, 2015; Brisch, 2012; Flores, 2004; Mikulincer & Shaver, 2016). Sadly, those with such attachment problems may find that their favourite bottle or their favourite video lottery terminal remain their best friends.

Co-occurring Addiction and Eating Disorders

Associations between eating disorders and substance use disorders have been observed in many studies (Cohen & Gordon, 2009). The dynamics of the interaction are not clear and the findings are not consistent. One possibility is that both are interactive with problems of regulating painful affect (Freeman, 1992; Krahn, 1991). It is common for social workers to explore developmental influences and painful affect in assessing both eating disorders and addiction (Baker, Metzger, & Bulik, 2016).

> In addition, when evaluating ... both disorders, one must consider not only common substances abused ... but also substances that are associated with eating disorders. Laxatives, diuretics, diet pills, emetics, unregulated supplements, and anabolic steroids.... (p. 279)

Eating disorders have been found to be comorbid with anxiety and affect disorders. When alcohol use disorder and anorexia nervosa interact, then "there is a substantial mortality in women with this presentation" (Baker, Metzger, & Bulik, 2016). Also, non-medical use of psychostimulants may be used to control weight. The conclusion of the Canadian expert panel was that treatment be concurrent unless the eating disorder presents imminent risks such as threat to life, in which case one disorder may have to be addressed first (Health Canada, 2002). For clinicians, exploratory questions could be, "What substances have you used, or contemplated using, to control weight? How are you feeling before, during, and after over-eating?" We have observed clients with eating disorders that are relatively compulsively involved with Internet, social networking, and sexting.

Co-occurring Addiction and Problems of Intimacy and Sexual Expression

Within this broad theme, the first clinically significant issues are experiences of sex anxiety, the fear of physical sharing or fear of embarrassing performance, or sexual dysfunction such as impotence, anorgasmia, and delayed orgasm, associated with substance use and abuse, as well as interacting mental health issues such as depression or bipolarity. If the sexual dysfunction predates the substance abuse or mental health problem, then often concurrent treatment is in order. If the sexual dysfunction appears to have been precipitated by substance abuse or a mental disorder such as depression, then treatment for the sexual dysfunction may follow in sequence but still in an integrated manner. For those who exhibit more disinhibition sexually, associated with mental health and/or addiction problems including compulsive sexual behaviour, the risk of HIV infection is increased (Health Canada, 2002). Blocks in effective assessment and treatment are often related to helpers who avoid addressing problems of intimacy and sexual expression out of their own sensitivities and discomfort, or out of using a client's discomfort as a signal that sexuality and intimacy matters can't be explored. Questions might include How do the substances you use, prescribed and not, help and interfere with intimacy and sex in your life? How do your mental health symptoms help and interfere with your patterns of being intimate and being sexual?

Sexual abuse survivors are at substantial risk for issues with intimacy and sexual expression, as they often exhibit problems with both substance use and significant mental health risks such as PTSD (Briere & Scott, 2015; Hien, 2009; Pilat & Boomhower-Kresser, 1992). Even within integrated treatment and survivor issues, often trauma treatment must demonstrate progress before the addiction problems are likely to be reduced, suggesting sequencing. Improvements in safe social bond, interpersonal trust, and affect regulation, as supporters of a gradual reclaiming of one's intimacy and sexual expression, may be the third nexus in the sequencing of therapy within this context, with due respect to needed periods of therapeutic integration. Persons who have been sexually abused have been found to use substances and mental health symptoms to enable them to feel sexual and erotic (alcohol, MDMA, manic phase); to use substances (heroin, ketamine) and mental health symptoms (dissociation) to "numb out" while having unwanted sex; and to use compulsive activities to avoid sexual interactions (gaming, gambling, Internet use).

Sex offenders are primarily dealt with by the criminal justice system where effective optimal treatment may be rare for mental health problems, addiction problems, or mental health risks. Integrated individual, group, and family therapy, where active bonds are still feasible, as well as engaging prosocial supports such as pro-abstinence friends, may be key to reduction of re-offence risks. Actively addressing offender mental heath problems (complex trauma treatment) and addiction problems (cocaine abuse therapy), which may contribute to relapse prevention, makes clinical sense. Some sex offenders may likely need a term of individual therapy before they are ready to be effective group participants. For the sex offender, substance use at even very low amounts, as little as two standard drinks of alcohol, or one use of crystal meth, may dramatically increase sex offence relapse risk (Kimberley & Osmond, 1999; Pilat & Boomhower-Kresser, 1992).

A subgroup within those experiencing problems with intimacy and sexual expression are those who have been assessed as engaging in compulsive sexual behaviours which have been conversationally, and inaccurately, labelled as sexual addiction (Carnes, 2001) and love addiction (Briggie & Briggie, 2015; Logan, 1992). It is not unusual for those within this population to experience problems with substance use or abuse as well. There also appears to be a number of expressions of mental disorder such as borderline personality disorder, and bipolar disorder, which may elevate risks for indiscriminate and frequent sexual activity. Compulsive Internet use may also be linked to compulsive sexual behaviour and pornography use. As well, sex offenders are overrepresented among those who compulsively use pornography. As such risks may vary and converge over time, and addiction and mental health treatment should periodically revisit the risks of compulsive sexual behaviour, compulsive pornography viewing, and compulsive Internet use with due respect to how co-occurring substance use or mental health issues, including disturbed attachments, increase associated risks.

Co-occurring Addiction and Attention Deficit Hyperactivity Disorder (ADHD)

There is an increased risk of obsessive-compulsive disorder and substance use-abuse problems in those with ADHD (Goldstein & Goldstein, 1998). Wilens and Zulauf (2016) have analyzed findings and have concluded that the prevalence of ADHD co-occurring with substance abuse disorders are significant in studied populations and that both are associated with challenges in personal and social functioning, including learning difficulties and psychiatric problems. As ADHD and substance abuse problems are both associated with impulse control issues, their interactions present unique challenges; as well, substance use disorders "are among the most problematic disorders that co-occur with ADHD," including early onset of substance use in this population (Wilens & Zulauf, 2016, p. 107). The symptoms of the ADHD must be moderated, and the client must learn some degree of self-monitoring and self-regulation of the expression of ADHD, often supported by medication, if he or she is to be able to optimize personal and social change, or build strengths to ameliorate addiction and other mental health risks, with the hope of sustained gains. Substance use with associated disinhibition or euphoria may pose compounded threats such as further disinhibition of risk-taking behaviour associated with ADHD, or amplifying agitated behaviour; thus there may be a good argument to sequence treatment beginning with non-medical use of substances. As well, for persons experiencing ADHD, there appears to be a preference for drugs over alcohol, with marijuana and stimulants being dominant in the teen group (Wilens & Zulauf, 2016). Clinically, it is more difficult to evaluate the role of ADHD in a client's struggles when non-medical substance use continues.

Co-occurring Addiction and Anger Disorders

Anger and aggression are reflected in the literature in terms of significant and damaging links with addiction and personality disorders, and may be overrepresented in post-trauma populations, those involved with the criminal justice system, and concurrent disorder services. Often the link is considered within the context of anti-social personality disorders and associated substances use and misuse. There is a growing argument that a category of anger disorders was needed in DSM-V, and that at times the interaction of anger disorders and substance use may be independent of anti-social personality symptoms (Kassinove, 1995). The link between anger and addiction can be quite complex and requires a holistic approach that addresses anger management and addiction in an integrated fashion (Potter-Efron, 1991; Korman, 2005). As well, relapse prevention models have been adapted to include anger management risks (Clancy, 1996). A therapeutic contract to cease aggressive acts, with a verifiable control of interpersonal violence, such as partner abuse, enables the client and the therapist to address anger, violence, and addiction interactions concurrently. The authors have also observed cases where risk of aggression is increased by caffeinism, which is becoming more of an issue with the proliferation of energy/power drinks, or the use of other more powerful stimulating chemicals such as cocaine or amphetamines, or perception modifiers such as ketamine. The clinician must also be aware that there may be an interactive effect of anger and aggression issues with other expressions of mental disorder such as mania, borderline personality disorder, or complex trauma, and that even moderate substance use often is sufficient to increase risk of decreasing inhibitions and increasing irritability for the client who is managing co-occurrence, with due respect for interactive effects.

Crises, Trauma, and Co-occurring Substance Use

Crisis intervention and trauma-informed practice-based services also need to address concurrent disorder risks, harm, and needs. Those who have experienced PTSD and complex traumas are overrepresented by persons who also have experienced or developed addiction problems and other co-occurring mental health struggles (Kimberley & Parsons, 2016; Wiechelt, 2014). Many concurrent disorder clients are likely to be suicidal at some point (Esposito-Smythers, Perloe, Machell, & Rallis, 2016), difficult to get along with, rejected by family and friends, marginalized and oppressed by society, including being defined as personally and socially dysfunctional (Csiernik, Forchuk, Speechly, & Ward-Griffin, 2007; Rush & Koegl, 2008). Crisis and trauma-informed services create opportunities to mediate links among mental health and addiction concerns, with more complex and comprehensive assessment and treatment services than the person struggling with concurrent disorders may have experienced. Early intervention is important in terms of both risk-reduction and helping a person at a point where he or she may be able to develop more resiliencies and tap into more personal and relational strengths, as well as be more personally and socially functional than might be the case as the concurrent disorder progresses (e.g., more efficacious in parent roles, partner roles, student roles, employee roles). We believe that integrated concurrent disorder services require both trauma-informed services and attachment-informed services.

Other Co-occurring Addiction and Mental Health Disorders

There is very little information or practice wisdom available in some areas where concurrence may appear. Among the most notable links in the practice of the authors has been addiction and/or other mental disorders linked with tic disorders, dementia and self-prescription, inhalant-linked disorders, hypochondria, dissociative disorders, sleep disorders, and adjustment disorders. In our experiences with Indigenous persons, inhalants are used for dissociative purposes, and they reinforce dissociative defences associated with complex trauma, and vicarious and transgenerational trauma, including transgenerational influences akin to residential school syndrome (Kimberley, 2016). As clinical wisdom and knowledge progresses in these areas, it is safe to conclude that integrated assessment and treatment must be considered as a leading option.

Co-occurring Compulsive Behaviours and Mental Health Problems

The addiction paradigm has been applied successfully to help understand compulsive problems such as gambling (Gaudia, 1992), Internet use (Young, 1999; Young & de Abreu, 2011), compulsive sexual activity (Carnes, 2001), and gaming and social networking (Ascher & Levounis, 2015; Calvert, 2014; Young & de Abreu, 2011). In these areas, as with substance use and abuse, clients have been observed to exhibit patterns of obsession, compulsivity, development of psychological tolerance, withdrawal, dependence, and pervasive impacts on personal and social functioning, as well as co-occurrence with other mental health issues. When co-occurrence exists, integrated and concurrent treatment should be attempted first. One clinical presumption is that the lack of progress in one area could threaten progress made in the other(s).

Other Therapies and Interventions

The focus of this chapter has been upon assessment and individual treatment. Concurrent disorder clients with substance use and mental health problems may need residential treatment or institutional care for a period of time before they are sufficiently stable to sustain gains through outpatient therapy and community support arrangements. While social support may enable recovery and more sustained progress, family therapy that includes a client with serious problems of personal and social functioning may increase family frustration and rejection of the client (Ward-Griffin, Schofield, Vos, &

Coatsworth-Puspoky, 2005). As well, the client must be assessed carefully for group readiness and not placed in a group merely because that is the only addiction or mental health therapy service readily available. With regard to both group and family therapy, the client's readiness for integration into the collective is likely to vary with regression and relapse, as well as with sustained, verifiable, and contextually relevant progress.

Of concern is the finding that those with substance- and mental illness–based concurrent disorders "were higher in terms of overall problem severity and ... lower on the overall strengths index," with high need for a significant level of concrete, structured, and long-term interventions, such as represented by Assertive Community Treatment (ACT) (Rush & Koegl, 2008, p. 813–814). Included in the ACT model of intensive support and intervention are: assertive outreach with a proactive orientation to service; integrated mental health and addiction counselling; motivational treatment strategies and active support in the clients' environments; continuity of care with no time limit; advocacy; and behavioural support and interventions, including social skills training aimed at improved personal and social functioning, symptom management, improved quality of life, and recovery, as well as intensive integrative case management. Also, with concurrent disorders, due to the intractable nature of problems and risks, illness management and recovery models may be promoted in the interest of improved personal and social functioning and concrete gains in quality of life such as housing, training, and/or peer supports. Simple CBT or other short-term therapies are typically not likely to meet the needs or reduce risk and harm in a sustained fashion. Integrative therapies consider a broad range of influences, including attachment, trauma, affect regulation, and developmental damage; they apply common relational factors accounting for impacts in therapy (relationship building and empathy), and apply holistic and dialectic biopsychosocial-spiritual, interactional, and personal and social change oriented assessment and interventions. These therapies hold promise because the complexity of the client's life as lived is respected.

Conclusion

Since the turn of the 20th century, social work practice has included a considerable history of concerns with addiction risks and mental disorders as they contribute to problems in personal and social functioning, particularly as addiction and mental health problems are affected by factors and dynamics in the social environment.

The challenge in biopsychosocial-spiritual assessment is to understand the complexities of the concurrence of addiction and mental health problems, and the implications for service planning in the interest of enabling improved personal and social functioning elements that evidence adaptive strengths. We propose a broader paradigm that also includes compulsive gambling, sexual behaviour, Internet use, viewing of pornography, and gaming, as often persons within these classes of compromised functioning also have exhibited other mental health and/or substance use problems. The challenge for case management and supportive and more in-depth treatment is addressing a seemingly intractable and recurring nexus of problems. In most instances, a flexible and relevant client-centred form of integrated services program delivery, integrated treatment, and continuity of care is recommended for those suffering with concurrent disorders. Some non-chemical issues may also require residential programs. The diversity of client subgroups requires flexibility and patience, including concurrent disorder-informed service systems, in the development of treatment plans to meet unique needs. "Cure" and complete recovery may be unrealistic goals, but sufficient symptom management to support improved and somewhat satisfying personal and social functioning may be well grounded. At an organizational level, programmatic offerings must be flexible in policy, process, and content, or there is a risk of further oppressing the clients and blaming them for "not fitting the program," when it is the responsibility of the program to fit the client's risks and needs.

There remains a great need in the community for early detection, screening, and comprehensive assessment to ensure that persons experiencing concurrent disorders are identified and placed in services that are integrated and treatments that are integrative. The problems, needs, and risks for such clients may contribute to rejection by support systems, including health, addiction, and social services. Strong advocacy is needed to ensure a team approach that is integrated, timely, in the best interest of the client, and sufficiently flexible to meet diverse needs and to nurture resiliencies, diverse strengths, and capacities. While this analysis has attempted to synthesize research, practice wisdom, and the experience of a range of clients, more pilot projects and in-depth study are still needed, particularly in the Canadian context.

REFERENCES

Al-Krenawi, A., & Kimberley, D. (2016). Palestinian youth and their families: Paradoxes of resilience in the cultural and sociopolitical context of, conflict, stress and trauma in the Middle East. In J. Merrick (Ed.), *Public health: Some international aspects*, pp. 81-96. Hauppauge, NY: Nova Publishing.

American Psychiatric Association (2013). *Diagnostic and statistical manual of mental disorders* (5th ed.). Washington, DC: American Psychiatric Association.

Andrasik, M.P., & Lostutter, T.W. (2012). Harm reduction for high-risk sexual behavior and HIV. In G.A. Marlatt, M.E. Larimer, & K. Witkiewitz (Eds.), *Harm reduction: Pragmatic strategies for managing high-risk behaviors* (pp. 201-228). New York: Guilford Press.

Ascher, M., & Levounis, P. (2015). *The behavioural addictions.* Arlington, VA: American Psychiatric Publishing.

Back, S.E., Foa, E.B., Killeen, T.K., Mills, K.L., Teesson, M., Cotton, B.D., Carroll, K.M., & Brady, K.T. (2015). *Concurrent treatment of PTSD and substance use disorders using prolonged exposure (COPE).* New York: Oxford University Press.

Baker, J.H., Metzger, L.M., & Bulik, C.M. (2016). Eating disorders and substance use disorders. In Y. Kaminer (Ed.), *Youth substance abuse and co-occurring disorders* (pp. 279-306). Arlington, VA: American Psychiatric Association Publishing.

Barry, K.L., Fleming, M.F., Greenley, J., Widlack, P., Kropp, S., & McKee, D. (1995). Assessment of alcohol and other drug problems in the seriously mentally ill. *Schizophrenia Bulletin, 21,* 315-321.

Begun, A., & Brown, S. (2014). Neurobiology of substance use disorders and implications for treatment. In S.L.A. Straussner (Ed.), *Clinical work with substance abusing clients* (3rd ed., pp. 47–49). New York: Guilford Press.

Berg, I.K., & Reuss, N. (1997). *Solutions step by step: A substance abuse treatment manual.* New York: W.W. Norton and Company.

Bergly, T.H., Gräwe, R.W., & Hagen, R. (2014). Domains and perceived benefits of treatment among patients with and without co-occurring disorders in inpatient substance abuse treatment. *Journal of Dual Diagnosis, 10*(2), 91–97.

Blankertz, L.E., Cnaan, R.A., & Freedman, E. (1993). Childhood risk factors in dually diagnosed homeless adults. *Social Work, 38*(5), 587–596.

Booth, B.D., & Gulati, S. (2014). Mental illness and sexual offending. *Psychiatric clinics of North America, 37*(2), 183–194.

Briere, J.N., & Scott, C. (2015). *Principles of trauma therapy: A guide to symptoms, evaluation, and treatment* (2nd ed.). Thousand Oaks, CA; Sage Publications.

Briggie, A., & Briggie, C. (2015). Love addiction: What's love got to do with it?" In M.S. Ascher and P. Levounis (Eds.), *The behavioural addictions* (pp. 153–174). Arlington, VA: American Psychiatric Publishing.

Brisch, K.H. (2012). *Treating attachment disorders: From theory to therapy* (2nd ed.). New York: Guilford Press.

Burkell, L.A., & McMain, S. (2009). Concurrent personality disorders and substance use disorders in women. In K.Y. Brady, S.E. Back, & S.F. Greenfield (Eds.), *Women and addiction: a comprehensive handbook* (Chapter 16, pp. 269–279). New York: The Guilford Press.

Calvert, C. (2014). Youth-produced sexual images, "sexting" and the cellphone. In F.M. Saleh, A.J. Grudzinskas, and A.M. Judge (Eds.), *Adolescent sexual behavior in the digital age: Considerations for clinicians, legal professionals, and educators* (pp. 89–116). New York: Oxford University Press.

Carnes, P. (2001). *Out of the shadows: Understanding sexual addiction* (3rd ed.). Centre City, MN: Hazelden Information & Educational Services.

Clancy, J. (1996). *Anger and addiction: Breaking the relapse cycle.* Madison, CT: Psychosocial Press.

Clayton, A.H., & Montejo, A.L. (2006). Major depressive disorder, antidepressants, and sexual dysfunction. *Journal of Clinical Psychiatry, 67*(Suppl. 6), 33–37.

Cleaver, H., Unell, I., & Aldgate, J. (1999). *Children's needs—parenting capacity: The impact of parental mental illness, problem alcohol and drug use, and domestic violence on children's development.* London, UK: Her Majesty's Stationary Office.

Cohen, L.R., & Gordon, S.M. (2009). Co-occurring eating and substance use disorders. In K.Y. Brady, S.E. Back, & S.F. Greenfield (Eds.), *Women and addictions: A comprehensive handbook* (Chapter 13, pp. 236–245). New York: Guilford Press.

Cooper, R.L., Seiters, J., Davidson, D.L., MacMaster, S.A., Rasch, R.F.R., Adams, S., & Darby, K. (2010). Outcomes of integrated assertive community treatment for homeless consumers with co-occurring disorders. *Journal of Dual Diagnosis, 6*(2), 152–170.

Cork, M. (1969). *The forgotten children.* Toronto, ON: Ontario Alcoholism & Drug Addiction Research Foundation.

Csiernik, R. (2014). *Just say know: A counsellor's guide to psychoactive drugs.* Toronto, ON: Canadian Scholars' Press.

Csiernik, R., Forchuk, C., Speechly, M., & Ward-Griffin, C. (2007). De "myth"ifying mental health—findings from a community university research alliance (CURA). *Critical Social Work, 8*(1), 1–15.

Daley, D.C., & Zuckoff, A. (2000). *Improving treatment compliance: Counseling and systems strategies for substance abuse and dual disorders*. Centre City, MN: Hazelden Information & Educational Services.

Davies, D. (2011). *Child development: A practitioner's guide* (3rd ed.). New York: The Guilford Press.

Dayton, T. (2000). *Trauma and addiction*. New York: The Guilford Press.

Denzin, N.K. (1987). *The alcoholic self*. Newbury Park, CA: Sage.

Diamond, J. (2000). *Narrative means to sober ends: Treating addiction and its aftermath*. New York: The Guilford Press.

Doweiko, H.E. (2015). *Concepts of chemical dependency* (9th ed.). Stamford, CT: Cengage Learning.

Dziegielewski, S.F., & Lupo, S. (2005). Polysubstance addiction. In S.F. Dziegielewski (Ed.), *Understanding substance addictions: Assessment and intervention* (pp. 239–254). Chicago: Lyceum Books.

Earle, R.H., & Earle, M.R., with Osborne, K. (1995). *Sex addiction: Case studies and management*. New York: Brunner/Mazel.

Esposito-Smythers, C., Perloe, A., Machell, K., & Rallis, B. (2016). Suicidal and nonsuicidal self-harm behaviors and substance use disorders. In Kaminer, Y. (Ed.), *Youth substance abuse and co-occurring disorders* (pp. 227–252). Arlington, VA: American Psychiatric Association Publishing.

Evans, K., & Sullivan, J.M. (1994). *Treating addicted survivors of trauma*. New York: The Guilford Press.

Evans, K., & Sullivan, J.M. (2000). *Dual diagnosis: Counseling the mentally ill substance abuser* (2nd ed.). New York: The Guilford Press.

Farley, M. (Ed.). (2003). *Prostitution trafficking, and traumatic stress*. New York: Haworth Press/ Routledge.

Flores, P. (2004). *Addiction as an attachment disorder*. New York: Jason Aronson.

Freeman, E.M. (1992). *The addiction process: Effective social work approaches*. New York: Longman.

Gaudia, R. (1992). Gambling: Reframing issues of control. In E.M. Freeman (Ed.), *The addiction process: Effective social work approaches* (pp. 237–248). New York: Longman.

Gold, S.N., & Elhai, J.D. (2008). *Trauma and serious mental illness*. Binghamton, NY: Haworth Maltreatment & Trauma Press.

Goldstein, E. (2004). Substance abusers with borderline disorders. In S. Straussner (Ed.), *Clinical work with substance-abusing clients* (2nd ed., Chapter 17, pp. 370–391). New York: The Guilford Press.

Goldstein, S., & Goldstein, M. (1998). *Managing attention deficit hyperactivity disorder in children: A guide for practitioners*. New York: John Wiley & Sons.

Green, A.I., Drake, R.E., Brunette, M.F., & Noordsy, D.L. (2007). Schizophrenia and co-occurring substance use disorder. *American Journal of Psychiatry, 164*(3), 402–408.

Grinker, R., MacGregor, H., Selan, K., Klein, A., & Kohrman, J. (1964). *Psychiatric social work: A transactional case book*. New York: Basic Books.

Health Canada (2002). *Best practices: Concurrent mental health and substance use disorders*. Ottawa, ON: Health Canada.

Hien, D. (2009). Trauma, posttraumatic stress disorder, and addictions among women. In K.Y. Brady, S.E. Back, & S.F. Greenfield (Eds.), *Women and addictions: A comprehensive handbook* (Chapter 14, pp. 246–256). New York: Guilford Press.

Hilarski, C., & Wodarski, J.S. (2001). Comorbid substance abuse and mental illness: Diagnosis and treatment. *Journal of Social Work Practice in Addictions, 1*(1), 105–119.

Hou, H., Jia, S., Hu, S., Fan, R., Sun, W., Sun, T., & Hong, Z. (2012). Reduced striatal dopamine transporters in people with Internet addiction disorder. *Journal of biomedicine and biotechnology*, vol. 2012, Article ID 85424.

Hunter, D., Rosenthal, M.Z., Lynch, T.R., & Linehan, M.M. (2016). Dialectical behavior therapy for individuals with borderline personality disorder and substance use disorders. In A. Mack, K.T. Brady, S.I. Miller, and R.J. Frances. (Eds.), *Clinical textbook of addictive disorders* (4th ed., pp. 648–667). New York: The Guilford Press.

James, R.L. (2012). *Sexuality and addictions: Making connections, enhancing recovery*. Santa Barbara, CA: Praeger.

Karls, J.M., & O'Keefe, M. (2008). *Person-in-Environment system manual* (2nd ed.). Washington, DC: NASW Press.

Kassinove, H. (Ed.). (1995). *Anger disorders: Definition, diagnosis, and treatment*. London, UK: Taylor & Francis, Ltd.

Kerfoot, K.E., Petrakis, I.L., & Rosenheck, R.A. (2011). Dual diagnosis in an aging population: Prevalence of psychiatric disorders, comorbid substance abuse, and mental health service utilization in the Department of Veterans Affairs. *Journal of Dual Diagnosis, 7*(1–2), 4–13.

Kimberley, D. (2008). *Assessing the consequences for children and families when a parent has a problem with substance use and abuse—considerations for social workers and other helping professionals*. Presented at Substance Abuse: Exploring Consequences and Remedies: An Interdisciplinary Perspective, March 9–14, 2008, Oxford Round Table at Lincoln College, Oxford University, UK.

Kimberley, D. (2016). Compromised cognitive functioning in concurrent disordered parents: Implications for Aboriginal children, foster care, mental health and addictions. In R. Neckoway & K. Brownlee (Ed.), *Child welfare in rural remote areas with Canada's First Nations peoples: Selected readings* (pp. 16–43). Thunder Bay, ON: Lakehead University, Centre of Eduction and Research for Positive Youth Development.

Kimberley, M.D., & Bohm, P. (1999). Drug addiction: a BPSI model. In F.J. Turner (Ed.), *Adult psychopathology: A social work perspective* (2nd ed., pp. 611–637). New York: The Free Press.

Kimberley, M.D., & Osmond, M.L. (1999). *Male-female co-therapy with treated sex offenders*. London, UK: 8th European Group Work Symposium, August 20.

Kimberley, M.D., & Osmond, M.L. (2001, revised 2016). *An index of self-reported mental health concerns*. St. John's, NL: Advanced Therapy & Consulting Services.

Kimberley, M.D., &. Osmond, M.L. (2010). Concurrent disorders and social work intervention. In R. Csiernik & W. Rowe, *Responding to the oppression of addiction: Canadian social work perspectives* (2nd ed., pp. 274–293). Toronto, ON: Canadian Scholars' Press.

Kimberley, D., & Osmond, M.L. (2016). Role theory and concepts applied to personal and social change. In F.J. Turner (Ed.), *Social work treatment* (6th ed., in press). Toronto, ON: Oxford University Press.

Kimberley, D., & Parsons, R. (2016). Complex trauma and trauma-informed social work treatment. In F.J. Turner (Ed.), *Social work treatment* (6th ed., in press). Toronto, ON: Oxford University Press.

Kimberley, D., & Scheltgen, M. (2013). *Sexting: The game changer in psychosocial development—transformed communication with global challenges*. Paper presented at the Annual Guelph Sexuality Conference, June.

Korman, L.M. (2005). Concurrent anger and addictions treatment. In W.J.W. Skinner (Ed.), *Treating concurrent disorders: A guide for counsellors* (pp. 215–233). Toronto, ON: Centre for Addictions and Mental Health.

Krahn, D.D. (1991). The relationship of eating disorders and substance abuse. *Journal of Substance Abuse, 3*(2), 239–253.

Kuss, D.J., & Griffiths, M.D. (2012). Internet and gaming addiction: A systematic review of neuroimaging studies. *Brain Science, 2*(3): 347–374.

Leahy, R.L. (2015). *Emotional schema therapy.* New York: Guilford Press.

Lester, D. (2000). Alcoholism, substance abuse and suicide. In R.W. Maris, A.L. Berman, & M.M. Silverman (Eds.), *Comprehensive textbook of suicidology* (Chapter 15, pp. 341–356). New York: Guilford Press.

Logan, S.M. (1992). Overcoming sex and love addiction: An expanded perspective. In E.M. Freeman (Ed.), *The addiction process: Effective social work approaches* (pp. 207–221). New York: Longman.

Love, T., Laier, C., Brand, M., Hatch, L., & Hajela, R. (2015). Neuroscience of Internet pornography addiction: A review and update. *Behavioral Sciences, 5*(3), 388–433.

Maltz, W. (1991). *The sexual healing journey: A guide for survivors of sexual abuse.* New York: Harper Perennial.

Markowitz, R. (2014). Dynamics and treatment issues with children of individuals with substance use disorders. In S.L.A. Straussner (Ed.), *Clinical work with substance abusing clients* (3rd ed., pp. 348–368). New York: Guilford Press.

Marlatt, G.A., & Witkiewitz, K. (2005). Relapse prevention for alcohol and drug problems. In G.A. Marlatt & D.M. Donovan (Eds.), *Relapse prevention: Maintenance strategies in the treatment of addictive behaviours* (2nd ed., pp. 1–44). New York: Guilford Press.

McAdams, D.P. (1993). *The stories we live by: Personal myths and the making of the self.* New York: William Morrow.

McKim, W.A., & Hancock, S.D. (2013). *Drugs and behavior: An introduction to behavioural pharmacology* (7th ed.). Upper Saddle River, NJ: Pearson.

Menzies, L., & Lavallée Jr., P. (2014). *Journey to healing: Aboriginal people with addiction and mental health issues: What health, social service and justice workers need to know.* Toronto: Centre for Addiction and Mental Health.

Mikulincer, M., & Shaver, P.R. (2016). *Attachment in adulthood: Structure, dynamics and change* (2nd ed.). New York: The Guilford Press.

Miller, D. (2002). Addictions and trauma recovery: An integrated approach. *Psychiatric Quarterly, 73*(2), 157–170.

Mowbray, C.T., Jordan, L.C., Ribisl, K.M., Kewalramani, A., Luke, D., Herman, S., & Bybee, D. (1999). Analysis of post-discharge change in dual diagnosis populations. *Health and Social Work, 24*(2), 91–101.

Nace, E.P. (1995). The dual diagnosis patient. In S. Brown (Ed.), *Treating alcoholism* (pp. 163–196). Toronto, ON: Jossey-Bass Publishers.

Navaneelan, T. (2009). *Suicide rates: An overview.* Catalogue no. 82-624-X. Ottawa, ON: Statistics Canada.

Nelson, G. Aubry, T., & LeFrance, A. (2007). A review of the literature on effectiveness of housing and support, assertive community treatment, and intensive case management interventions for persons with mental illness who have been homeless. *American Journal of Orthopsychiatry, 77*(3), 350–361.

Nelson, G., Hall, B., & Forchuk, C. (2003). Current and preferred housing of psychiatric consumer/survivors. *Canadian Journal of Community Mental Health, 22*(1), 5–19.

Neumiller, S., Bennett-Clark, F., Young, M.S., Dates, B., Broner, N., Leddy, J., Kendall, D., Richards, S., & De Jong, F. (2009). Implementing assertive community treatment in diverse settings for people who are homeless with co-occurring mental health and addictive disorders: A series of case studies. *Journal of Dual Diagnosis, 5*(3 & 4), 239–263.

O'Connell, D.F., & Beyer, E.P. (2002). *Managing the dually diagnosed patient: Current issues and clinical approaches* (2nd ed.). New York: Haworth Press.

Osmond, M.L., & Kimberley, M.D. (2010). Patterns of intimacy and sexual expression. In R. Csiernik & W.S. Rowe (Eds.), *Responding to the oppression of addiction* (2nd ed., pp. 151–166). Toronto, ON: Canadian Scholars' Press.

Padykula, N.L., & Conklin, P. (2010). The self-regulation model of attachment trauma and addiction. *Clinical Social Work Journal, 38*(4), 351–360.

Pilat, J., & Boomhower-Kresser, S. (1992). Dynamics of alcoholism and child sexual abuse: Implications for interdisciplinary practice. In E.M. Freeman (Ed.), *The addiction process: Effective social work approaches* (pp. 65–78). New York: Longman.

Pomeroy, E.C., & Parrish, D.E. (2011). Prenatal impact of alcohol and drugs on young children: Implications for interventions with children and parents. In S.L.A. Staussner & C.H. Fewell (Eds.), *Children of substance abusing parents: Dynamics and treatment* (pp. 77–100). New York: Springer Publishing.

Potter-Efron, P.S., & Potter-Efron, R.T. (1992). *Anger, alcoholism, and addiction: Treating individuals, couples, and families.* New York: W.W. Norton.

Prochaska, J.O., DiClemente, C.C., & Norcross, J.C. (1992). In search of how people change: Applications to addictive disorders. *American Psychologist, 47*(4), 1102–1114.

Rankin, J.G. (1976). Alcoholism and Drug Addiction Research Foundation of Ontario: Research goals and plans. *Annals of the New York Academy of Sciences, 273,* 87–97.

Richmond, M.E. (1917/1944). *Social diagnosis.* New York: The Free Press.

Rosen, L. (2012). *iDisorder: Understanding our obsession with technology and overcoming its hold on us.* New York: St. Martins Griffin.

Rosenberg, S.D., Wolford, G.L., Mueser, K.T., Oxman, T.E., Vidaver, R.M., Carrieri, K.L., & Luckoor, R. (1998). Dartmouth Assessment and Lifestyle Instrument (DALI): A substance use disorder screen for people with severe mental illness. *American Journal of Psychiatry, 155*(2), 232–238.

Rudin, J. (2014). The criminal justice system: Addressing Aboriginal overrepresentation. In P. Menzies & L.F. Lavallee (Eds.), *Journey to healing: Aboriginal people with addiction and mental health issues* (pp. 343–356). Toronto, ON: Centre for Addiction and Mental Health.

Ruisard, D.J. (2015). Transformation through attachment: The power of the relationship in clinical social work. *Clinical Social Work Journal, 44*(3), 279–292.

Rush, B., & Koegl, J. (2008). Prevalence and profile of people with co-occurring mental and substance use disorders within a comprehensive mental health system. *Canadian Journal of Psychiatry, 53*(12), 810–821.

Rush, C.R., Stoops, W.W., & Ling, W. (2008). Behavioural pharmacology and psychiatric consequences of methamphetamine. In J.M. Roll, R.A. Rawson, W. Ling, & S. Shoptaw (Eds.), *Methamphetamine addiction: From basic science to treatment* (Chapter 5, pp. 92–116). New York: The Guilford Press.

Ryglewicz, H., & Pepper, B. (1996). *Lives at risk: Understanding and treating young people with dual disorder.* New York: The Free Press.

Scheffler, S. (2014). Assessment and treatment of clients with co-occurring psychiatric and substance use disorders. In S. Straussner (Ed.), *Clinical work with substance-abusing clients* (3rd ed., pp. 371–394). New York: The Guilford Press.

Schore, J.R., & Schore, A.N. (2007). Modern attachment theory: The central role of affect regulation in development and treatment. *Clinical Social Work Journal, 36*(1), 9–12.

Silberg, J.L. (2013). *The child survivor: Healing developmental trauma and dissociation.* New York: Routledge.

Sharpe, T.T. (2005). *Behind the eightball: Sex for crack cocaine exchange and poor black women.* New York: Haworth Press.

Sheldon, K., & Howitt, D. (2007). *Sex offenders and the Internet.* Chichester, UK: John Wiley and Sons.

Skinner, W. (2005). *Treating concurrent disorders: A guide for counsellors*. Toronto, ON: Centre for Addiction and Mental Health.

Sprenkle, D.H., Davis, S.D., & Lebow, J.L. (2009). *Common factors in couple and family therapy: The overlooked foundation for effective practice*. New York: The Guilford Press.

Steele, W., & Malchiodi, C.A. (2012). *Trauma-informed practices with children and adolescents*. New York: Routledge.

Stohler, R., & Rossler, W. (2005). *Dual diagnosis: The evolving conceptual framework*. Basel, Switzerland: S. Karger.

Straussner, S.L.A. (2001). The role of social workers in the treatment of addictions: A brief history. *Journal of Social Work Practice in Addictions, 1*(1), 3–9.

Straussner, S.L.A. (2011). Children of substance abusing parents: An overview. In S.L.A. Straussner & C.H. Fewell (Eds.), *Children of substance abusing parents: Dynamics and treatment* (pp. 1–27). New York: Springer.

Tang, Y., Martin, N.L., & Cotes, R.O. (2014). Cocaine-induced psychotic disorders: Presentation, mechanism, management. *Journal of Dual Diagnosis, 10*(2), 98–105.

Tarter, R.E., & Horner, M.S. (2016). Developmental pathways to substance use disorder and co-occurring psychiatric disorders in adolescents. In Y. Kaminer (Ed.), *Youth substance abuse and co-occurring disorders* (pp. 1–20). Arlington, VA: American Psychiatric Association Publishing.

Timms, N. (1964). *Psychiatric social work in Great Britain (1939–1962)*. London, UK: Routledge & Kegan Paul.

VanGilder, I.J., Green, C., & Dziegielewski, S.F. (2005). Inhalants. In S.F. Dziegielewski (Ed.), *Understanding substance addictions: Assessment and intervention* (pp. 225–235). Chicago: Lyceum Books.

Van Hook, M.P. (2014). *Social work practice with families: A resiliency-based approach* (2nd ed.). Chicago: Lyceum Press.

Velasquez, M.M., Crouch, C., Stephens, N.S., & DiClemente, C.C. (2016). *Group treatment for substance abuse: A strategies of change therapy manual* (2nd ed.). New York: Guilford Press.

Vohs, K.D., & Baumeister, R.F. (2016). *Handbook of self-regulation: Theory and applications* (3rd ed.). New York: Guilford Press.

Walsh, F. (2015). *Strengthening family resilience* (3rd ed.). New York: Guilford Press.

Walsh, K., & Ramsay, R. (1994). The PIE system: A Canadian field test with a multidisciplinary mental health team. In J.M. Karls & K.E. Wandrei (Eds.), *Person-in-Environment system: The PIE classification system for social functioning problems* (pp. 129–142). Washington, DC: NASW Press.

Ward-Griffin, C., Schofield, R., Vos, S., & Coatsworth-Puspoky, R. (2005). Canadian families caring for members with mental illness: A vicious cycle. *Journal of Family Nursing, 11*(2), 140–161.

Watkins, T.R., Lewellen, A., & Barrett, M.C. (2001). *Dual diagnosis: An integrated approach to treatment*. Thousand Oaks, CA: Sage Publications.

Webb, N.B. (Ed.) (2006). *Working with traumatized youth in child welfare*. New York: Guilford Press.

Weiss, R.D., & Connery, H.S. (2011). *Integrated group therapy for bipolar disorder and substance abuse*. New York: The Guilford Press.

Wheeler, J.G., George, W.H., & Stephens, K.A. (2005). Assessment of sexual offenders: A model for integrating dynamic risk assessment and relapse prevention approaches. In D.M. Donovan & G.A. Marlatt (Eds). *Assessment of addictive behavior* (2nd ed., pp. 392–424). New York: Guilford Press.

Wiechelt, S.A. (2014). Intersection between trauma and substance misuse: Implications for trauma-informed care. In S. Straussner (Ed.), *Clinical work with substance-abusing clients* (3rd ed., pp. 179–201). New York: The Guilford Press.

Wilens, T.E., & Zulauf, C.A. (2016). Attention deficit/hyperactivity disorders and substance use disorders. In Y. Kaminer (Ed.), *Youth substance abuse and co-occurring disorders* (pp. 103-130). Arlington, VA: American Psychiatric Association.

Wilson, C.S., Bennett, M.E., & Bellack, A.S. (2013). Impact of family history in persons with dual diagnosis. *Journal of Dual Diagnosis, 9*(1), 30-38.

Winick, C. (1992). Substances of use and abuse and sexual behaviour. In J.H. Lowinson, P. Ruiz, R.B. Millman, & J.G. Langrod (Eds.), *Substance abuse: A comprehensive textbook* (2nd ed., pp. 772-733). Baltimore: Williams & Wilkins.

Witkiewitz, K., McCallion, E., & Kirouac, M. (2016). Religious affiliation and spiritual practices: An examination of the role of spirituality in alcohol use and alcohol use disorder. *Alcohol Research, 38*(1), E1.

Yau, Y.H.C., Derevensky, J.L., & Potenza, M.N. (2016). Pathological preoccupation with the Internet. In Y. Kaminer (Ed.), *Youth substance abuse and co-occurring disorders* (pp. 337-350). Arlington, VA: American Psychiatric Association, Publishing.

Young, K.S. (1999). Evaluation and treatment of Internet addiction. In L. Vandecreek & T.L. Jackson (Eds.), *Innovations in clinical practice: A source book* (pp. 19-32). Sarasota, FL: Professional Resource Press.

Young, K.S., & de Abreu, C.N. (Eds.) (2011). *Internet addiction: A handbook and guide to evaluation and treatment.* Hoboken, NJ: John Wiley and Sons.

Young, K.S., Yue, X.D., & Ying, L. (2011). Prevalence estimates and etiologic models of internet addiction. In K.S. Young and C.N. de Abreu (Eds.), *Internet addiction: A handbook and guide to evaluation and treatment* (pp. 3-19). Hoboken, NJ: John Wiley & Sons.

Young, V.B., McAfee, M., & Dziegielewski, S.F. (2005). Dual diagnosis: Mental health and substance addiction. In S.F. Dziegielewski (Ed.), *Understanding substance addictions: Assessment and intervention* (pp. 255-271). Chicago: Lyceum.

PART 4

POLICY

CHAPTER 25

Many Paths to Prohibition: Drug Policy in Canada

Rick Csiernik, Munish Bhakri, and Robin Koop-Watson

Introduction

Drug policy in Canada has historically not truly been about tobacco, narcotics, and alcohol, but rather about economic, employment, immigration, criminal justice, and even military policies. Canadian drug policy has also concerned issues of morality, racism, punishment, social control, discrimination, and oppression. The intention of social policy is to better social life and ameliorate social problems. However, there is limited consensus on the relationship between social policy and psychoactive drugs and addiction. The Canadian solution has consistently focused upon supply-side issues with criminalization and prohibition being the preferred approach, as has occurred in much of the world. Prohibition initiatives have entailed a variety of laws, sanctions, criminal justice practices, and some social evaluations that have limited and suppressed access, use, production, and sale of the continuum of psychoactive drugs.

The First Prohibition: Alcohol

There is virtually no aspect of Canadian society from the earliest colonial times to the present that has not been affected by alcohol. Alcohol is our most popular drug after caffeine, used by the majority of adults and many under the arbitrarily determined and regularly shifting legal drinking age. Brandy quickly became a fixture between First Nations groups and Europeans during the 16th century and was an integral part of the fur trade, with furs exchanged routinely for liquor. As early as the 1600s, the Roman Catholic Church in New France expressed concern about the consumption of alcohol by First Nations populations and the accompanying social problems. The first prohibition in North America occurred in 1657 when French king Louis XIV issued an edict prohibiting the sale of alcohol to First Nations groups with fines and public flogging as penalties. The initial prohibition and regulations pertaining to alcohol were implemented as a consequence of public disorder and cases of aggression and hostility, as well as an increase in crime rate with the First Nations people that culturally threatened to hamper the amicable relationships within various groups that resided in the area controlled by the French (Davis, 1988; Smart & Ogborne, 1996; Spencer, 1919; Warsh, 1993).

In 1660, Bishop Laval went further, issuing a sentence of excommunication for trading alcohol to First Nations people. The Church in New France spearheaded the first "Canadian" temperance campaign to increase the presence of Christianity in the "New World," decrease alcohol consumption among both Native Canadians and Europeans, and end the trade of fur for alcohol. However, First Nations groups in search of alcohol simply found new trading partners: non-Roman Catholic English traders who had no qualms about engaging in trading fur for liquor. The French eventually rescinded the first Canadian prohibition, primarily at the urging of military authorities, who protested that the trade in brandy was essential for keeping the allegiance with the First Nations groups against the English. It was not until the 19th century that corporate policy came to diminish the reliance on alcohol for trade. When the Hudson's Bay Company and the North West Company created the first major Canadian corporate merger, they also created a new corporate policy to decrease trade in alcohol, which resulted in a far greater impact than had any previous government policy. In numerous land and treaty negotiations between First Nations groups and colonizing Europeans, Native Canadians were typically given large gifts of alcohol prior to negotiations and treaty signings. Several historians claim that the primary cause of the decline of many First Nations groups in Eastern Canada who had contact with Europeans was the trade for alcohol (Davis, 1988; Smart & Ogborne, 1996; Spencer, 1919; Warsh, 1993).

In 1668, after the first Canadian prohibition was lifted, Jean Talon formally established the inaugural brewery in New France. A century later Molson's was established, and by 1786 was selling 9,000 gallons of beer a year in Montreal, whose population was approximately 9,000 persons. In the 1700s, commanders of both English and French garrisons openly complained to superiors of the problems with discipline as a result of excessive alcohol use by their troops. The military went as far as permanently closing shops that sold liquor to troops, though a comprehensive solution to the problem was never found (Davis, 1988; Spencer, 1919).

With increasing immigration from Europe came a variety of drinking traditions that were enhanced due to the harsh living and working conditions along with the social isolation that agrarian colonial life produced. With the eventual English conquest of northern North America, liquor became primarily an economic vehicle. The English lifted all prohibitions the French had imposed and replaced these with policies for the licensing and taxation of spirits. There was economic benefit in liquor, for the increasing number of taverns provided both new employment and also revenue from licences. As well, custom duties on alcohol legally imported from Britain and the West Indies produced over one-quarter of all custom duty, the primary form of taxation, during the 1830s (Davis, 1988; Smart & Ogborne, 1996).

On April 15, 1828, the first temperance meeting was held in Beaver River, Nova Scotia. The origins of the temperance movement were rooted in several sources. It was the agrarian evangelical Protestants and the emerging middle-class professionals who most supported the concept. Temperance agitation was strongest where rapid growth, urbanization, and the transformation to market agriculture was most evident. The temperance drive eventually became the most significant social movement of the 19th century in Canada. It was a grassroots undertaking with no government support that dramatically influenced social policy and changed living conditions. While modeled on both British and American initiatives, the Canadian effort was far more successful at instituting several short- and long-lived alcohol prohibitions. By 1832, there were 100 temperance groups with a membership of over 10,000, during a time when the per capita consumption of whisky for every man, woman, and child in Canada was estimated at 30 bottles. Prohibition groups varied in intent, however, with some promoting total abstinence and taking the "new pledge," while others tolerated drinking beer, cider, and wine but not spirits, and thus became members of "old pledge" societies. However, temperance societies were neither populist nor democratic, as African-Canadians and First Nations groups were typically not welcome within white-founded societies. There are historic records of black temperance groups, but none consisting exclusively of First Nations members. As well, some groups arose in direct response to the immigration of Orangemen, who had fled Ireland because of rebellions and famines, and who were perceived by many established colonists as the heaviest-drinking members of communities (Smart & Ogborne, 1996; Warsh, 1993).

The Maritimes and Ontario were the bastions of prohibition in Canada's early history. Between 1854 and 1859 five separate prohibition drives were sponsored in Nova Scotia and two in Prince Edward Island, though all petitions were defeated. However, in 1856 colonial prohibition was established in New Brunswick, though the law was openly ignored. Consumption did not decrease, though government revenues did. Sir Leonard Tilley's provincial government was quickly defeated in part due to the backlash against his party's prohibition policy. This second Canadian prohibition was repealed even faster than the first. After seven months the policy was abolished, with New Brunswick returning to liquor licensing as a means of controlling alcohol sale and consumption and, perhaps most importantly, obtaining revenue for the province. A similar fate would befall the first elected Farmer's Political Party of Ontario, which placed its 1923 re-election hopes on prohibition, only to be defeated and to never regain power (Smart & Ogborne, 1996; Warsh, 1993).

Between the beginning of the temperance movement and 1861, alcohol consumption among settlers decreased, with the number of distilleries dropping in Upper and Lower Canada from 217 to 58, with imports of whiskey falling by nearly half. One particularly notable group, the Women's Christian Temperance Union (WCTU), was so successful that it had courses and textbooks on scientific temperance added to school curriculum in Ontario, Alberta, and the Maritimes. However, as this movement evolved from rural agrarian evangelical Protestantism, it is not surprising that Quebec did not have as large a temperance initiative, despite earlier attempts of the Roman Catholic Church to prohibit and moderate drinking. Some prohibition leaders did arise in Quebec, though. The single most prominent figure was the diminutive, but charismatic, Father Charles Chiniquy. His interest in temperance was fueled by his belief, now empirically validated, that many of the sick in hospitals were there as a direct result of their intemperance. He became extremely influential in having many French-Canadian Roman Catholics take the pledge and refrain from drinking alcohol. Ignace Bourget, the bishop of Montreal, also promoted abstinence, though the message was better received in rural Quebec than in the more urban setting of Montreal. Support for abstinence was also intertwined with the message of the shrinking French presence in North America and the need for French Canadians to survive within the midst of the growing Anglophone presence (Noel, 1990).

Confederation and the formal creation of Canada in 1867 further muddled the prohibition issue. The British North America Act did not mention alcohol anywhere, and it was not until 1878 that the Canadian Supreme Court ruled that laws regulating the role of alcohol were a federal responsibility. However, the first national battle lines had already been drawn and were solidified by 1876, when the first national anti-alcohol lobby group, the Dominion Alliance for the Total Suppression of Liquor Traffic, was established. Their action was instrumental in having the Canada Temperance Act (the Scott Act) passed in 1879. The Scott Act led to 26 of 40 Maritime municipalities becoming dry by 1900. However, those residents living in dry areas needed only to go to a neighbouring wet community to obtain a drink (Davis, 1988; Spencer, 1919).

The first national attempt for prohibition occurred in 1898 when a plebiscite was held. The main theme of the prohibitionist movement was that alcohol was flagrantly abused and was the antecedent event to many of society's worst problems. As well, new Liberal Prime Minister Wilfrid Laurier had promised to hold a national plebiscite on prohibition if elected. However, Laurier and the Liberal party as a whole were not pro-temperance. A national plebiscite was eventually held, with Canada voting for prohibition by a slight 52% majority, though a significantly smaller proportion of Quebec voters supported the initiative. To avoid having to institute a policy clearly unwanted in an area where Liberals dominated politically, Laurier's response to the plebiscite was to invalidate it, as only 25% of eligible Canadian voters had voted (Davis, 1988; Spencer, 1919).

This then led some provinces to again attempt to establish provincial-based prohibition. Both Manitoba and Prince Edward Island brought in legislation, though the Manitoba Supreme Court ruled in 1901, one year after the policy's passage, that the Manitoba Liquor Act was unconstitutional. In yet another provincial plebiscite, in 1902, the majority of Manitoba voters rejected prohibition, though Prince Edward Island did institute alcohol prohibition on June 5, 1901. The Prince Edward Island Supreme Court, in a 1902 appeal, supported this legislation, though the act only applied to the provincial capital, Charlottetown. Over the next decade, other provincial governments became supportive of prohibition, primarily because of the ongoing work of temperance groups. However, it was World War I that finally moved the nation to institute this social policy. Messages that liquor stops soldiers from shooting straight, grain for alcohol takes food away from starving allies, and liquor is unpatriotic led alcohol use to become strongly associated with the German war effort (White, 1979). Thus, prohibition came to Manitoba (1916–1924), Alberta (1916–1924), Ontario (1916–1926), British Colombia (1917–1921), Saskatchewan (1916–1925), Nova Scotia (1916–1929), New Brunswick (1917–1927) and even Quebec for two years (1918–1919). In fact, the Canadian War Measures Act of 1917 mandated prohibition, but as soon as World War I ended, the act was rescinded in Quebec. As well, even though Newfoundland was not part of Canada at this time, prohibition existed there from 1915–1924. On top of these provincial restrictions, federal legislation, the Doherty Bill of March 1916, was enacted so that intoxicating beverages could not be imported into prohibition provinces, and as of March 1918, alcohol for beverage purposes could not be sold in Canada. This legislation was in place until one year after the completion of World War I (Davis, 1988; Hallowell, 1972; Hunt, 1995).

British Colombia soon followed Quebec and repealed its prohibition law in 1921, with all provinces overturning the legislation save Prince Edward Island. Provinces had different periods of prohibition and one could always travel across a provincial border to order an alcoholic beverage, which were of course often accidentally brought back to the buyer's home province, sometimes even in large enough quantities to share. One could also obtain temperance beer whose alcohol content was restricted to 2.5% or less throughout Canada. Locally produced wines and home-fermented products were also readily available during prohibition periods. As well, one could obtain a prescription for alcohol from one's doctor. Alcohol was still seen by the medical profession during the prohibition era as a legitimate therapeutic agent for a range of maladies such as improving appetite, convalescence, senile decay (dementia), malnutrition, wasting diseases and, of course, for nursing mothers. As well, it was legal for Canadian distilleries and breweries to export their products to the United States during this time, even when the United States had its own prohibition policy in place. Many distributors, such as Labatt's, merely went across a provincial border and established mail businesses to deliver alcohol to customers, though a few breweries did not even bother to leave the newly dry provinces to conduct their mail-order businesses (Hallowell, 1972; Hunt, 1995; Smart & Ogborne, 1996; Spencer, 1919; Warsh, 1993).

The time discrepancy between Canadian and American prohibition legislation was a key factor that undermined the success of alcohol prohibition. The failure of prohibition is linked to its evolution from a middle-class to a working-class movement. Once the policy initiative began to garner support among the working class, the middle class came to resent the initiative. Alcohol use was easier to put up as an example of moral failure when drunkenness was attributed to a marginalized group. However, when this outsider group embraced temperance, the movement became less appealing to those of status and privilege. There was also an early anti-Semitic element among some factions of the prohibition movement. Another contributing factor for the failure of prohibition was that drinking was an established tradition of the dominant class. Those of English, Scottish, Welsh, and Irish ancestry had long-standing drinking traditions and the behaviour of the majority was impossible to vilify for an extended period of time. As well, Catholic French Canadians all but ignored the Protestant-based attempts to prohibit alcohol during this era (Hunt, 1995; Warsh, 1993).

Maritime prohibition coincided with a regional economic depression that led to perhaps even greater rum running and bootlegging. In the Maritime provinces, the repeal of prohibition was more about money than alcohol, as the increasing short-age of provincial revenues to fund hospitals, schools, and public assistance became a persistent political problem. The unintended consequences of alcohol prohibition are well-known: fortunes were made in rum running and bootlegging, organized crime flourished, and corruption and perjury were commonplace, as were an increasing number of arrests and convictions for a behaviour that previously had not been con-sidered criminal (Davis, 1988; Hallowell, 1972; Warsh, 1993). This is a pattern that would repeat itself with other psychoactive drugs in the future.

In place of prohibition emerged provincial government monopolies on alcohol. Provincial liquor acts legalized and regulated liquor sales and had both a revenue fea-ture and an availability and control dimension. Profits from alcohol sale were directed towards public services (Davis, 1988; Hallowell, 1972). It was not until the Canadian centennial in 1967 that the Canadian Temperance Federation would finally formally disband. Remnants of prohibition organizations still exist, as does alcohol prohibition to a limited degree, as several Indigenous communities have banned the drug, the most recent coming in 2009 in the community of Tuktoyaktuk, Northwest Territories. While total enforcement is nearly impossible, social and health problems do decline with the implementation of this social policy. However, overall alcohol policies have become more liberal in Canada since World War II. By the 1990s, Canada was in the top five nations in the world with respect to taxes collected on alcohol consumption per capita. Though of course as taxation levels increased, so has smuggling (Smart & Ogborne, 1996).

A multitude of changes have been made to the policies and laws that regulate the usage and distribution of alcohol in Canada across time. Alcohol began as a simple com-modity in the fur trade between First Nations people and early colonizers, but quickly became an important factor contributing to the oppression of this group for centuries. With the formal end of alcohol prohibition attempts in the 20th century this drug became fully integrated into mainstream culture, with the assistance of advertising and marketing campaigns broadcasting its purported benefits to an increasingly younger audience (Gordon, Harris, Marie Mackintosh, & Moodie, 2011). It is now obvious that complete bans as occurred during both the Canadian and American alcohol prohibition eras are ineffective means of reducing problems despite having some positive health and community impacts. Whether by legal or illegal means, alcohol will continue to remain a commodity within our communities and for this reason there is a need for well-established policy and strategies to reduce alcohol-related harm. However, it seems that recent Canadian policy has become focused more on the economical profits that alcohol generates as opposed to the social welfare of its citizens. The gradual shift from government-run distributors towards private outlets moves us away from strict regulations. This leads not only to cheaper alcohol but also increased availability, and as density of private alcohol outlets increases so does the degree of alcohol-related harm, particularly among younger consumers (Stockwell et al., 2011).

The Second Prohibition: Opium, Heroin, and Non-narcotic Drugs

During the era of debate on alcohol prohibition, other psychoactive drugs slowly came under scrutiny for the first time. Prior to the 20th century, there were virtually no restrictions on psychoactive drugs in Canada and, unlike alcohol drug prohibition, drug prohibition was very much a social and political experiment of the 20th century. Opioids, cocaine, and cannabis were widely distributed. Drug abuse was not a criminal or social issue, but one of moral weakness and personal vice (Boyd, 1991; Solomon, Hammond, & Langdon, 1986). However, fear, social conflict, and racism created myths relating to drug use that led to specific policy initiatives. Opium particularly was labelled dangerous, and its use was restricted and criminalized due to its association with the Asian community in Canada (Giffen, Endicott, & Lambert, 1991).

Opioids were readily available and freely prescribed in Canada during the late 1800s and early 1900s. Opium shops where one could purchase and smoke the product were licensed and accepted. Individuals addicted to opium were generally not jailed but more typically viewed as individuals with a specific moral transgression, sometimes pitied, though just as likely to be despised depending upon their ethnicity. During this time opium consumption was also seen as an indulgence of the upper class and, to a lesser extent, the Canadian middle class. During this same era cocaine was sold in soft drinks, combined in alcoholic beverages, and was also often part of the formulation of patent medicines. Gradually, however, opium use became associated with the socially disadvantaged immigrant Chinese population.

At the beginning of the 20th century, concerns regarding the content of patent medicines led to the Adulteration Act of 1906. This policy prohibited changes to food, drug, and drink products sold for human consumption including alcohol, opium, Indian hemp (cannabis), and tobacco. Three years later, in 1909, the Patent Medicine Act came into effect. Supported by pharmaceutical companies, pharmacists, and physicians, the goal was to eliminate patent medicines as competition for medical practitioners. This legislation allowed Canadian health professionals and drug companies to take political, economic, social, and cultural authority of medicine in Canada. The Patent Medicine Act eventually evolved into the Canadian Food and Drug Act in 1920, prominent legislation still in effect today (Boyd, 1991; Chenier, 2001). While creating a safer health environment it also created a monopoly in terms of licit drug distribution.

In 1907, there was a huge racially motivated riot in Vancouver initiated by white labour activists who remained fearful of losing employment to Chinese labourers. Prime Minister Laurier dispatched then deputy minister of labour, William Lyon Mackenzie King, to British Colombia to investigate. The amount of economic activity associated with opium shocked and greatly influenced King when writing his brief to the House of Commons entitled *The Need for Suppression of the Opium Traffic in Canada* (1908). King wrote that opium smoking was increasing among young white women and men, and the profits were primarily accruing to Chinese opium merchants. There was also an underlying sentiment that use of opium by white women led them into lives of prostitution, servicing Chinese men. King's thoughts on simply placing further restrictions on the trade were further challenged by a delegation of affluent and powerful Chinese-Canadian Christian clergy and merchants who petitioned him to make opium an illegal substance. This presentation adequately swayed King so that he became an advocate for prohibition. This process would directly lead to the passing of the Opium Act, in 1908, which remains the foundation of Canada's current social policy pertaining to illicit psychoactive substances. This was the first instance of a psychoactive drug other than alcohol being criminalized in Canada. Three years later the act was amended to include cocaine and morphine. By 1929, the legislation had become an 11-page document and would be the foundation for Canadian drug policy for the remainder of the century (Boyd, 1983; Erickson, 1980; Giffen, Endicott, & Lambert, 1991; King, 1908).

The creation of the "dope fiend" stereotype, associated with people of Asian ancestry and lower status whites, made it possible to approach opium use and addiction as a moral crusade. In 1911, after a Royal Commission to investigate Chinese fraud and bribery of Canadian custom officials found no basis to the accusations, the opium laws were changed nonetheless. Mackenzie King, now minister of labour, introduced and then later expanded the Opium and Drug Act, in part as a reaction to the anti-opium movement, but also because after attending international conferences King felt Canada was a laggard when it came to drug control. Thus, in Canada, it became a criminal offence to be found in an opium den, or to possess opium, morphine, or cocaine, the latter of which is a central nervous stimulant, the opposite of a narcotic. The bill was left partially open-ended so that any other drug could be added at a later time, as has been done on several occasions. There was still an ongoing fear by the general public that opium smoking facilitated sexual contact between Chinese men and white women that could lead to unwanted "mixing of the races." A similar connection was made with cocaine, except its early use was associated with use by black men, even though cocaine is a product of South America. There was a general belief that cocaine use would lead to superhuman strength and sexual assaults against white women by black men (Giffen, Endicott, & Lambert, 1991).

From 1908 to the depression era, opium was transformed from an indulgence of a small minority of people to a great social danger, a pattern to be followed for other drugs (Boyd, 1991). More refined versions of opium, namely heroin, became the choice to import illegally. In 1922, Canadian drug policy was modified to allow for the deportation of convicted aliens, which, in a House of Commons debate, referred to assisting to deal with the "Oriental question" in Canada (Moser, 1998). The legislation was not only written with Chinese-Canadians in mind, it was also disproportionately enforced so that, between 1924 and 1936, 60% of the 3,096 convictions were against this minority group. What is surprising, however, is that there was no significant difference in sentencing length between visible minorities and whites convicted under the law. While minor amendments have been made, the racially motivated Narcotic Control Act of the 1920s remains the basis for much of contemporary Canadian illicit drug law. Canada also played a prominent role under the leadership of Mackenzie King in the international movement to criminalize the use and distribution of narcotics (Boyd, 1983; Crawshaw, 1978; Erickson, 1980).

Cannabis, like opioids and cocaine, was once a legal substance but became a demonized, illicit substance. Within a few years, cannabis went from being widely available and legal to being portrayed as a drug that produced sexual promiscuity, insanity, and certain death. In 1923, without any debate by parliament, marijuana became a narcotic under Canadian law and possession became a criminal offence (Crawshaw, 1978; Giffen, Endicott, & Lambert, 1991).

Debating Prohibition: From Le Dain to the War on Drugs to Harm Reduction

New initiatives after the 1920s were typically brought about through the lobbying of the Royal Canadian Mounted Police (RCMP) and related law enforcement interests. The United Nations treaty, the Single Convention on Narcotic Drugs (1961), along with the 1971 Convention on Psychotropic Substances and the 1988 Convention Against Illicit Traffic in Narcotic Drugs and Psychotropic Substances, coordinated through the Commission of Narcotic Drugs of the United Nations Economic and Social Council (ECOSOC), has set the tone for contemporary prohibitionist drug policy in Canada and much of the world (Bryan & Crawshaw, 1978; Giffen, Endicott, & Lambert, 1991).

The next significant domestic event in drug policy development did not occur until the end of the 1960s when the Pierre Trudeau government struck The Royal Commission of Inquiry into the Non-Medical Use of Drugs (the Le Dain Commission) to examine increasing drug use in Canada. The amount of marijuana that in 2000 would result in a simple possession fine could and often would, in the 1960s, lead to a charge of dealing and potential federal penitentiary time (Erickson, 1980; Gormley, 1970).

Members of the Le Dain Commission set up meetings and public hearings with many pop cultural figures and prominent musicians of the era that recreationally were known to use drugs, to discuss the impacts and future of marijuana legislation. This included meetings with the likes of Led Zeppelin, the Grateful Dead, Allen Ginsberg, and The Beatles. Aside from meeting celebrities, the commission travelled more than 80,000 kilometers to hold public hearings in 27 cities and 23 universities. The extensive reports filed by the Le Dain Commission were seen as groundbreaking in their recommendations, the most significant being the call for the decriminalization of possession of cannabis, though dealing would remain a criminal act (Le Dain Commission, 1972). Unfortunately, the commission's work did not lead to any major revisions in Canada's drug policy. Nonetheless, it did open up debate and provide the first broader, scientific perspective on drugs in Canadian drug policy history. The report articulated important definitions of non-medical drug use that encompassed both licit and illicit substances that are still in use today (Erickson, 1992).

The earliest significant attempt to decriminalize cannabis was brought forward by the Pierre Trudeau government in 1974, but the proposed legislation died at the committee level. Again, in 1980, some members of the Trudeau government, newly returned to power, attempted to move cannabis from the Narcotic Control Act to the Food and Drug Act, but this idea met resistance within the cabinet and was never included in a throne speech (Boyd, 1991). Two days after American president Ronald Reagan declared a War on Drugs, Conservative Prime Minister Brian Mulroney deviated from a prepared speech and publicly stated that drug abuse had become an epidemic in Canada, and it was undermining Canada's economic and social fabric. Mulroney's statement led to a renewed emphasis on alcohol and drugs in Canada. A new Canadian drug secretariat was formed, a new royal commission struck, and a new agency birthed to oversee policy initiatives (Erickson, 1992). The Canadian Centre on Substance Abuse was created by a federal act of parliament in 1988 as Canada's national non-governmental organization on addiction. Among its stated objectives was to promote and assist in the development of realistic policies and programs aimed at reducing the harm associated with alcohol and drug abuse.

Considering the impetus for this new emphasis upon psychoactive drugs, and the direction taken by the Canadian government, the outcomes were surprising. In 1987, the federal government study on substance abuse turned down the idea of introducing mandated drug testing programs. Rather, recommendations advocated the introduction of Employee Assistance Programs (EAPs), workplace-based counselling initiatives, as the primary mechanism for dealing with employees with the full spectrum of personal problems in the workplace, not only drug- and alcohol-related issues. All federal agencies were mandated to have such programs that federal civil servants and, in most cases, their family members could access. The Canadian strategy entitled "Action on Drug Abuse" allocated slightly over $40 million a year for five years with a minimum of 38% going towards treatment, 32% to education and prevention, and 20% going to enforcement (Canada, 1987, 1988). In 1989, Bill C-61 provided additional powers to enforcement and prosecution agencies along with new investigative tools to allow for the confiscation of any assets earned through the profits of drug trafficking. At that point in time Canada already had the fifth-highest rate of incarceration in the world, with an increasing proportion of Canadians being incarcerated for drug-related offences (Erickson, 1992) until we ranked second in the world per capita (Kellen & Powers, 2010).

Then came AIDS (acquired immune deficiency syndrome). One of the early acknowledged and accepted forms of acquiring HIV (human immunodeficiency virus) was through sharing contaminated needles for injecting psychoactive drugs, primarily heroin. Needle exchange initiatives were begrudgingly adopted in Canada, primarily through the activism and lobbying of people who had already acquired HIV and their supporters, along with some addiction professionals and social workers. Along with this came a resurgence of methadone treatment and methadone maintenance programs (Elliot, 1998) to be followed by needle exchanges and North America's first Supervised Injection Site (see chapter 3).

These harm reduction approaches were a dramatic leap from the typical Canadian historic response of prohibition. Thus, it was unsurprising that these initiatives faced and still face opposition, as there is a belief that these programs support criminal behaviour due to the illicit nature of the substances indirectly causing the health epidemic.

The intent of methadone and opioid harm reduction programs is not the elimination of the addiction. Rather, it is a public health initiative to stop the spread of the virus into uninfected users and people who directly or indirectly come into contact with them. However, attached to this public health approach is the underlying presence of social control. The programs that were eventually approved still had to overcome the bias and stigma leading to oppression that decision-makers and funders had against the perceived population in need. The irony of the need for and resistance to needle exchange programs is that it is legal to sell, exchange, or provide a syringe in Canada— no prescription is necessary to do so. Yet, special programs and policies needed to be put in place to ensure what was already legal was provided to people in need (Hankins, 1998). Despite the lifting of this discriminatory practice, many pharmacists initially remained very hesitant to sell syringes to customers that they believed to be drug users (Myers et al., 1995). Established needle exchange programs also often faced quotas for users. After special initiatives began to be introduced for intravenous drug users (IDU), many diabetics complained of preferential treatment and wanted similar pricing and access as the once-shunned group was now receiving (Hankins, 1998). At the end of the 20th century, IDUs and those with HIV had become the newly oppressed and deviant group, partially because of the anti-Chinese sentiment of a century ago.

Though Canada has never had an all-out War on Drugs as has and does the United States, a greater amount of prohibitionist sentiment did surface during the early 1990s, in a response to what was perceived as liberalization of drug policies over the previous two decades, and has become the sentiment in the 21st century under two successive federal Conservative minority governments. In the latter half of the 1990s, Bill C-8, the Controlled Drugs and Substances Act (CDSA), was tabled. The intent of the policy was the modernizing and consolidation of existing legislation, while providing law enforcement with greater tools to combat illicit drug activity. With the policy came Canada's Drug Strategy (CDS) document (Canada, 1998). Along with the $245 million dedicated to the CDS for the subsequent five years, the federal government renewed its commitment to a balanced approach, addressing both the demand for and supply of drugs and emphasizing the four pillars: prevention, treatment, harm reduction, and enforcement. In addition, it included a new focus on leadership, research and monitoring, partnerships and intervention, and promises for modernizing legislation and policy (Collin, 2006).

Among the programs supported under the CDS was the North American Opiate Medication Initiative (NAOMI) study to test controlled clinical trials of heroin maintenance treatment for individuals addicted to heroin, needle exchange programs, and the introduction of drug treatment courts as an alternative measure to sentencing and incarceration. Drug courts were specifically designed to assist in the treatment of non-violent, marginalized populations including Indigenous Peoples, sex workers, and injection drug users and to help these traditionally oppressed groups stay out of prison. In particular, the renewed CDS was the impetus for making national history with both its consideration of drug law reform with respect to cannabis decriminalization and with its introduction of a safer injection site in Vancouver, British Colombia.

In 2001, Canada became the first country to adopt a regulated system for medicinal marijuana through the development of Marihuana Medical Access Regulations (MMAR). Under the MMAR, a controlled amount of marijuana was provided to individuals with chronic and debilitating illness who have been unable to be treated by conventional methods. Although eligible individuals were given an authorization to possess medicinal marijuana (ATP), access to a legal supply remained an issue. Part of the CDS reform in 2003 included making amendments to the MMAR in order to provide greater access to a sanctioned supply as well as relaxing some of the previous prohibitions surrounding those with a licence to produce (Canada Gazette, 2003).

In response to the controversial 2002 Canadian Senate report that grew great interest as it proposed decriminalizing cannabis, the Minister of Justice proposed Bill C-38 in May 2003, an act to amend the Contraventions Act and the Controlled Drugs and Substances Act. The legislation proposed reduced penalties for possession of marijuana or cannabis resin (less than 15 grams) and when possession was between 15-30 grams, there would have been discretion to give either a reduced penalty or to prosecute as a criminal offence. The Senate study agreed with the Le Dain Commission's conclusions that the criminalization of cannabis had no scientific basis and that continued criminalization of cannabis remained unjustified based on scientific data (Library of Parliament, 2003, 2004).

However, when the Conservative government took power, drug policy took on a distinct criminal orientation, with substance use being conceptualized as an issue of public safety. The role of policy became to remove drug users from society. Bill C-10 is a classic example: included in the omnibus Safe Streets and Communities Act is manda-tory minimum jail terms, such as six months for growing six or more cannabis plants. The legislation established stricter sentences for drug-related convictions returning to a prohibitionist mindset. The Harper government used incarcerating drug users as an indicator of being tough on crime. However, there has never been any evidence that serving jail time lowers the prevalence of illicit drug use.

This theme of getting tougher on drug crimes was further emphasized in the Harper government's National Drug Strategy (Canada, 2015), which provided close to $170 million over a five-year period from 2010–2015 for law enforcement efforts to locate, investigate, and shut down organizations involved in the production and distribution of illicit drugs. The strategy allocated one-sixth of that amount in new funding to drug prevention and $100 million for drug treatment over the same five-year period. The policies enacted and attitudes towards drug problems expressed, by the Harper government signalled a retreat from the harm reduction principles established in the early 2000s. However, the ultimate showdown between the government's social conservative policy agenda and public health policy came in the decade-long legal battle over closing InSite, Canada's supervised safe injection site. Despite support from local and provincial government officials, the federal government attempted at every level to shutter the program. Finally, when the Supreme Court of Canada ruled that it would be a violation of human rights and freedoms to restrict access to a program that had demonstrated it served a health need of Canadian citizens, the government wrote new legislation making it extremely difficult to open any other such programs in Canada. Scientific evidence, the needs of the community, and provincial or federal justice systems could not curtail policy written to deny service to those who were dependent on psychoactive drugs during the term of this government.

Another piece of drug-related legislation that was successfully implemented during this time was Bill C-32. Bill C-32 proposed amendments to the Canadian Criminal Code and related acts to strengthen the enforcement of drug-impaired driving offences. Prior to Bill C-32, section 253(a) of the Criminal Code made it an offence to drive while one's ability to operate a vehicle was impaired by alcohol or a psychoactive drug, or a combination of alcohol and a drug. While section 253(b) contained a further offence for driving while one's blood-alcohol level was over the legal alcohol limit, no similar drug limit offence existed in Canada. Thus, although drug-impaired driving was a criminal offence, law enforcement officials had few legally designated means of con-trolling that offence, with drug tests being admissible as evidence in court only if the driver participated voluntarily. Bill C-32 expanded drug enforcement capabilities by giving police the authority to demand a physical sobriety test and bodily fluids to test for impairment produced by not only illicit psychoactive drugs but also over-the-counter and prescription substances. A driver's refusal to comply with an officer's request for a physical sobriety or bodily fluid sample test now constitutes a criminal offence punishable under the same provisions that are currently applicable for refusing to perform an alcohol breath or blood test (Barnett, 2007).

In 2015, the Liberal party came to power federally, and a small but key component of the Justin Trudeau government's election platform was the promise to legalize cannabis. At the time of writing, the anticipated new legislation has not yet been presented to parliament but is anticipated to be implemented in 2017. When this legislation is passed, it will be the most progressive change in drug policy since the lifting of alcohol prohibition nearly 100 years ago.

The Prohibition of Tobacco

Historically, tobacco has had its own unique policies, unaffiliated with those of alcohol or other licit and illicit psychoactive drugs. In Canada, tobacco is responsible for more premature death than all other psychoactive drugs combined. During colonization, tobacco became used as a recreational and social drug, but unlike alcohol it took several hundred years to discover the risks associated with its constant use.

In 1908, the federal government introduced the Tobacco Restraint Act prohibiting the sale of tobacco to persons under the age of 16, while in 1914 the Commons Select Committee considered a prohibition of cigarettes when nicotine was described during a submission as the narcotic poison of tobacco (Giffen, Endicott, & Lambert, 1991). However, the societal status of tobacco became firmly entrenched in North America when, during World War I, American general John Pershing decreed that cigarettes would be part of every soldier's ration kit, as it was a form of relaxation that could be easily provided to all troops (Boyd, 1991).

While historically less than 100 Canadians a year die of heroin overdose, there are upwards of 40,000 Canadians who die prematurely, annually, as a result of smoking tobacco—roughly 20% of all deaths. Contemporary anti-smoking forces are currently among the most successful prohibitionists. Their battles have led to the banning of cigarette vending machines, tobacco advertising, smoking within bars and restaurants, and now even immediately outside all public buildings. They have been successful in raising the smoking age to 19 from 16 and banning mini or "kiddie" packs of cigarettes. The government has also supported this by placing increasingly higher taxes on cigarettes, though with the inevitable increases in smuggling that accompany higher prices. In 1996, the Ontario Medical Association stated that parental tobacco use in the home, resulting in the inhalation of known carcinogens and asthmagens by children, should be considered a form of physical abuse (Chenier, 2001). This, along with ongoing advocacy from anti-smoking groups, has led several jurisdictions, including Nova Scotia and Ontario, to enact legislation banning smoking in automobiles when children and youth under the age of 19 are in the vehicle, though enforcement is rare.

In 1997, the Tobacco Act (Department of Justice Canada, 1997) was enacted to regulate the manufacturing, sale, labelling, and promotion of tobacco products in Canada, with a goal to discourage young people from beginning to smoke. The act allowed the advertising of tobacco products

- in publications delivered directly to an identified adult through the mail, or that have a known adult readership of not less than 85%;
- in places where young people aren't permitted by law, such as bars or taverns;
- by highlighting actual brand characteristics, rather than by "lifestyle" advertising that attempts to portray the product to consumers in a flattering light; and
- by providing factual information about the characteristics, availability, or price of the product.

As well, tobacco companies were not allowed to:

- attempt to convince young people of the desirability of their product by associating it with glamour, recreation, excitement, vitality, risk, daring, or sexuality;
- depict in any manner any tobacco product, or its package or brand;
- sponsor youth-oriented activities or events; and
- include the name of a tobacco product or manufacturer as part of the name of a permanent sports or cultural facility.

However, the Act's definition of "promotion" did not include tobacco products or brands that are used or depicted in a literary, dramatic, musical, cinematographic, scientific, or educational way, or in artistic works, productions, or performances, as long as the tobacco company was not paying for the inclusion of the tobacco product or brand. Interestingly, the frequency in smoking in top-grossing American movies has doubled since 1990 with nine out of ten Hollywood movies showing characters smoking, over a quarter of which had specific brand designations (Thorpe, 2004).

In 2012, changes were made so that almost all tobacco packaging is required to outline warnings on at least 75% of the front and back of box, as well as have a toll-free "quit-line" number made accessible to all. Canada is a world leader in many dimensions of effective tobacco control including implementing bylaws and provincial legislation that include restricting smoking, funding cessation programs, aggressive pricing, taxation of tobacco products, and policies that restrict sales to minors. Thus, prohibition sentiment towards tobacco remains alive, well, and pervasive in Canada. However, as occurred during the major alcohol prohibition, this decrease in use has not affected production, for Canada continues to produce billions of cigarettes annually, though now primarily for export to overseas markets, primarily in the developing world. As well, smuggling has returned to being a significant issue, particularly along some Indigenous territories that span the Canadian-American boarder.

Conclusion

Perception rather than reality shaped early Canadian drug policy. The inaugural anti-opium, anti-Chinese laws have created many unintended long-term social problems. While alcohol prohibition was rescinded because the social policy was unworkable, other psychoactive agents have retained their illicit status and remain prohibited substances. Like most industrialized societies, Canada has come to rely heavily upon criminal law to control drug supplies and to punish offenders. Canada's social policy regarding drugs has been almost exclusively supply-side orientated with prohibition being the tool and criminalization being the outcome. Prohibition is premised upon the belief that drug taking is a social evil that ought to be suppressed (Inglis, 1975). Drug policy took a leap backwards to an overt, unbalanced emphasis upon prohibition and enforcement under the rule of Prime Minister Stephen Harper. It appears, however, that Prime Minister Justin Trudeau will be taking on his father's legacy in this policy area and promoting more progressive policy.

The Harper government's prohibition-flavoured approach followed in the footsteps of the United States' long standing War on Drugs approach, a tactic that has been demonstrated to be ineffective in this policy area. Despite the priority and financial resources enforcement and supply-side policies have been given, there has been little evidence to suggest their effectiveness in reducing drug use or harm (Canadian HIV/AIDS Legal Network, 2006; Gabor & Crutcher, 2002; Strang et al., 2012). Canadian research has suggested that enforcement measures such as police crackdown and large heroin seizures in core drug areas have done little to impact drug use or public health in a positive way (Wood et al., 2004; Wood et al., 2003) while Caulkins and Reuter (2010) reported that as drug-related incarceration rates rose in the United States so did drug availability. In fact, despite the disproportionate financial investment in prohibition and enforcement, United Nations Office on Drugs and Crime (2002, 2008, 2014) has regularly estimated that law enforcement agencies seize only about 5% of illicit drugs worldwide. In reality, these measures create an opposite, unintended effect by increasing the price for illicit drugs and giving organized crime the monopoly on the black market. This contributes to the social harms that have traditionally been ascribed to drug use and users themselves such as violence, crime, and the increased transmission of HIV (Haden, 2002).

The impact of prohibition, regardless of the drug, is that it does not deal with demand. As long as there is demand, there will be product. The act of prohibition simply led to increases in both price and profit, though as Caulkins and Reuter (2010) discussed, now even increasing incarceration is not having an impact on drug availability.

Most of Canadian drug policy has been a result of economic, racial, and political will intermingled with the moral model. Canada's reaction to substance misuse has historically been strict law enforcement and punitive sanctions abetted by broad police powers, with treatment and prevention being an afterthought and a secondary financial consideration (Erickson, 1991). Rather than on health educators, social workers, and other helping professionals, we spend our limited funds on police and correctional and probation officers. In our society we still remain unsure of how to characterize those with an addiction: as a victim or as a villain.

As stated in the opening chapter, as long as there is longing, pain, suffering, loneliness, and spiritual and economic poverty, there will be a desire by some people to escape using psychoactive drugs. Once we can prohibit those characteristics of human existence, it will become much easier to successfully prohibit psychoactive drugs. The question to be asked is: do we have the political and economic will to pursue a new social policy that is client centred?

> If there is an answer (to drug use) it would be found in consistent law enforcement, reasonable legislation and a sound educational program.
>
> —Alex C. Thompson, Chair, Board of Education, City of Toronto, in his address to the Le Dain Commission (Gromley, 1970, p. 152)

REFERENCES

Barnett, L. (2007). *Bill C-32: An act to amend the criminal code (impaired driving)*. Ottawa, ON: Legislative Summaries, Library of Canada.

Boyd, N. (1983). The dilemma of Canadian narcotics legislation: The social control of altered states of consciousness. *Contemporary Crises, 7*, 257–269.

Boyd, N. (1991). *High society: Legal and illegal drugs in Canada*. Toronto, ON: Key Porter Books.

Bryan, C., & Crawshaw, P. (1978). *Core knowledge in the drug field: Law and social policy*. Ottawa, ON: Minister of Supply and Services Canada.

Canada. (1987). *Booze, pills and dope: Reducing substance abuse in Canada*. Ottawa, ON: Queen's Printer for Canada.

Canada. (1988). *Action on drug abuse: Making a difference*. Hull, QC: Ministry of Supply and Services.

Canada. (1998). *Canada's drug strategy*. Ottawa, ON: Minister of Public Works and Government Services Canada.

Canada. (2015). *National anti-drug strategy evaluation*. Ottawa, ON: Department of Justice.

Canada Gazette (2003). *Controlled drugs and substances act: Regulation amending the marihuana medical access regulations*. Ottawa, ON: Minister of Public Works and Government Services Canada.

Canadian HIV/AIDS Legal Network. (2006). *Mandatory minimum sentences for drug offences: Why everyone loses*. Toronto, ON: Canadian HIV/AIDS Legal Network.

Caulkins, J.P., & Reuter, P. (2010). How drug enforcement affects drug prices. *Crime and Justice, 39*(1), 213–271.

Chenier, N. (2001). *Substance abuse and public policy*. Ottawa, ON: Minister of Public Works and Government Services Canada.

Collin, C. (2006). *Substance abuse issues and public policy in Canada: Canada's federal drug strategy*. Ottawa, ON: Parliamentary Information and Research Service.

Crawshaw, P. (1978). *Core knowledge in the drug field: Historical aspects and current developments*. Ottawa, ON: Health and Welfare Canada.

Davis, C.M. (1988). Rum and the law: The maritime experience. In J.H. Morrison & J. Moreira (Eds.), *Tempered by rum: Rum in the history of the maritime provinces* (pp. 40-52). Porters Lake, NS: Pottersfield Press.

Department of Justice Canada. (1997). *Tobacco act*. Ottawa, ON: Department of Justice Canada.

Elliott, L. (1998). Ten years of needle exchange provision, but do they work? In M. Bloor & F. Wood (Eds.), *Addictions and problem drug use: Issues in behaviour, policy and practice* (pp. 139-154). Philadelphia: Jessica Kingsley Publishers.

Erickson, P. (1980). *Cannabis criminals: The social effects of punishment on drug users*. Toronto, ON: Addiction Research Foundation.

Erickson, P. (1991). Past, current and future directions in Canadian drug policy. *The International Journal of the Addictions, 25*(3A), 247-266.

Erickson, P. (1992). Recent trends in Canadian drug policy: The decline and resurgence of prohibitionism. *Daedalus, 121*(Summer), 239-267.

Gabor, T., & Crutcher, N. (2002). *Mandatory minimum penalties, their effects on crime, sentencing disparities, and justice system disparities*. Ottawa, ON: Justice Canada.

Giffen, P., Endicott, S., & Lambert, S. (1991). *Panic and indifference: The politics of Canada's drug laws*. Ottawa, ON: Canadian Centre on Substance Abuse.

Gordon, R., Harris, F., Marie Mackintosh, A., & Moodie, C. (2011). Assessing the cumulative impact of alcohol marketing on young people's drinking: Cross-sectional data findings. *Addiction Research & Theory, 19*(1), 66-75.

Gormely, S. (1970). *Drugs and the Canadian scene*. Toronto, ON: Pagurian Press.

Haden, M. (2002). Illicit IV drugs: A public health approach. *Canadian Journal of Public Health, 93*(6), 431-434.

Hallowell, G. (1972). *Prohibition in Ontario, 1919-1923*. Toronto, ON: Ontario Historical Society.

Hankins, C. (1998). Syringe exchange in Canada: Good but not enough to stem the HIV tide. *Substance Use and Misuse, 33*(5), 1129-1146.

Hunt, C. (1995). *Whisky and ice: The saga of Ben Kerr, Canada's most daring rumrunner*. Toronto, ON: Dundurn Press.

Inglis, B. (1975). *The forbidden game: A social history of drugs*. Toronto, ON: Hodder & Stoughton.

Kellen, A., & Powers, L. (2010). Drug use, addiction and the criminal justice system. In R. Csiernik & W.S. Rowe (Eds.), *Responding to the oppression of addiction* (2nd ed., pp. 215-234). Toronto, ON: Canadian Scholars' Press.

King, W.L.M. (1908). *The need for the suppression of the opium traffic in Canada*. Ottawa, ON: S.E. Dawson.

Le Dain Commission. (1972). *The study of non-medical use of drugs in Canada*. Ottawa, ON: Information Canada.

Library of Parliament. (2003). *37th Parliament, 2nd session*.

Library of Parliament. (2004). *37th Parliament, 3rd session*.

Moser, C.J. (1998). *Discrimination and denial: Systemic racism in Ontario's legal and criminal justice systems, 1892-1961*. Toronto, ON: University of Toronto Press.

Myers, T., Cockerill, R., Millson, P., Rankin, J., & Worthington, C. (1995). *Canadian community pharmacies HIV/AIDS prevention and health promotion: Results of a national survey*. Toronto, ON: LB Publishing.

Noel, J. (1990). Dry patriotism: The Chiniquy crusade. *Canadian Historical Review, 71*(2), 189-207.

Smart, R., & Ogborne, A. (1996). *Northern spirits: A social history of alcohol in Canada*. Toronto, ON: Addiction Research Foundation.

Solomon, R., Hammond, T., & Langdon, S. (1986). *Drug and alcohol law for Canadians*. Toronto, ON: Addiction Research Foundation.

Spencer, R. (1919). *Prohibition in Canada*. Toronto, ON: Dominion Alliance.

Stockwell, T., Zhao, J., Macdonald, S., Vallance, K., Gruenewald, P., Ponicki, W., ... Treno, A. (2011). Impact on alcohol-related mortality of a rapid rise in the density of private liquor outlets in British Columbia: A local area multi-level analysis. *Addiction, 106*(4), 768–776.

Strang, J., Babor, T., Caulkins, J., Fischer, B., Foxcroft, D., & Humphreys, K. (2012). Drug policy and the public good: Evidence for effective interventions. *The Lancet, 379*(9810), 71–83.

Thorpe, R. (2004). Monkey see, monkey do. *AADAC Developments, 24*(1), 3.

United Nations Office on Drugs and Crime. (2002). *Global illicit drug trends 2002*. New York: United Nations.

United Nations Office on Drugs and Crime. (2008). *2007 world drug report*. New York: United Nations.

United Nations Office on Drugs and Crime. (2014). *2013 world drug report*. New York: United Nations.

Warsh, C. (1993). *Drink in Canada: Historical essays*. Kingston and Montreal: McGill-Queen's University Press.

White, W. (1979). *Themes in chemical prohibition: Drugs in perspective*. Rockville, MD: National Drug Abuse Center/National Institute on Drug Abuse.

Wood, E., Spittal, P., Small, W., Kerr, T., Li, K., Hogg, R., Tyndall, M., Montaner, J., & Schechter, M. (2004). Displacement of Canada's largest public illicit drug market in response to a police crackdown. *Canadian Medical Association Journal, 170*(10), 1551–1556.

Wood, E., Tyndall, M., Spittal, P., Li, K., Anis, A., Hogg, R., Montaner, J., O'Shaughnessy, M., & Schechter, M. (2003). Impact of supply-side policies for control of illicit drugs in the face of AIDS and overdose epidemics: Investigation of a massive heroin seizure. *Canadian Medical Association Journal, 168*(2), 165–169.

CHAPTER 26

Addiction Intervention, Employability, and Welfare

Rick Csiernik, Carolyne Gorlick, and Joe Antone

Introduction

In the 1980s, during the Reagan administration, the American government seemingly ran out of wars to fight outside the United States and turned its attention inwards. It rediscovered an old enemy lying somewhat dormant since the Nixon administration and began a new war against it—a War on Drugs. This war has been fought on several fronts leading to a historic number of Americans being incarcerated, with a disproportionate number being young men of colour, with black people 3.73 times more likely to be arrested for marijuana possession than white people (American Civil Liberties Union, 2015). The war has also been enthusiastically fought in the workplace. In September 1986, President Ronald Reagan signed an executive order requiring all federal American agencies to establish compulsory drug testing for current and prospective employees, a campaign that quickly spread to the private sector (Blackwell, 1994; Hayashida, 2001).

The Canadian government's response to this conflict and to the "Just Say No" era was to strike an all-party committee to scrutinize the issue of drug use in Canada. The committee did not recommend the drug testing of federal employees. Instead, access to Employee Assistance Programs (EAPs) for all federal employees and their family members was mandated to provide assistance with not only alcohol and other drug-related problems, but with any type of personal or work-related issues (Standing Committee on National Health and Welfare, 1987). However, when Canada entered into a free trade pact with the United States, Canadians working for Canadian companies in the United States were forced to participate in drug testing schemes. In turn, Canadian branch plant companies such as Esso/Exxon and Canadian organizations such as the Toronto Dominion Bank began testing employees. However, various judiciary bodies such as the Ontario Law Reform Commission (1992) and the Canadian Human Rights

Commission (2002) publicly opposed the idea of drug testing employees as quickly as new initiatives were proposed. Unfortunately, presently there is virtually no federal or provincial legislation in Canada to guide decisions. Instead, a combination of human rights legislation, court decisions, and labour arbitrations are used to define guidelines relating to drug testing (Bomhof, 2005; Holmes & Richer, 2008).

Not content to focus solely upon employed Americans, a different political, ethical, and legal level of drug testing action soon emerged. Several jurisdictions proposed that persons wishing to receive welfare benefits should first have to pass a drug test to qualify for assistance (Harrison & Simpler, 1989; Metsch & Pollack, 2005; Parker, 1995; Zimmer, 1999). This sentiment has returned with a vengeance since the protracted economic downturn extended into 2009, and as of 2015, at least 13 states have passed legislation regarding drug testing/screening of some sort, including Alabama, Arkansas, Arizona, Florida, Georgia, Kansas, Michigan, Mississippi, Missouri, North Carolina, Oklahoma, Tennessee, and Utah (National Conference of State Legislatures, 2015). The legislation ranges from applying to all applicants, to needing reasonable suspicion, to requiring a specific screening process. Specific assistance programs that involved passing a drug test before receiving support include recipients of food stamps, unemployment bene- fits, Supplemental Nutrition Assistance Program (SNAP), Employment and Training program, Temporary Assistance for Needy Families (TANF), and Women, Infants and Children (WIC) programs.

This linkage between employability and drug testing also appeared in the Canadian social welfare arena, with the neo-conservative government of Ontario articulating an action plan that attempted to link employability, mandatory drug testing, and welfare exiting in 2000. Although initial statements proclaimed that "this policy isn't about kicking people off welfare," it was also announced that individuals who refused treat- ment or who would not take tests on demand would be ineligible for welfare assistance (Ontario Ministry of Community and Social Services, 2000). The same ministry later issued a statement that, along with screening for alcohol, drugs, and prescription medication addictions, welfare recipients would undergo mandatory literacy testing. Critics maintained that this additional plan was "mean-spirited and indicative of an appalling ignorance of the complexity of addictions" (Boyle & Mallan, 2001). However, by 2006, with a Liberal provincial government in place, "helping social assistance recipients with substance abuse problems to tackle their addictions head-on" became the focus of the new Addiction Services Initiative (ASI) (Ontario Ministry of Community and Social Services, 2009). Introduced slowly by focusing upon a few communities at a time, the program language and intent was not to punish welfare recipients by, for example, mandatory drug testing, but to offer individualized support and a range of support services. What did not change though was the primary goal to move welfare recipients off social assistance as quickly as possible through employment. As of 2013, the Addiction Services Initiative was declared a "best practice" based on a review of the program in the city of Hamilton, as it keeps with the "vision and recommendations of the Social Assistance Review report 'Brighter Prospects: Transforming Social Assistance in Ontario'" (City of Hamilton, 2013, p. 2).

Compared to the United States, where addiction intervention legislation has led to the spawning of an entire new profession, substance abuse professionals (SAPs), Canadian social workers have been less affected by drug testing issues. Those who work in addiction treatment facilities generally have not had contact with individuals forced to seek assistance due to failing a drug test, while few social workers are employed by organizations who use their Employee Assistance Program as a mechanism to fight the War on Drugs (Macdonald, Csiernik, Durand, Rylett, Wild, & Lloyd, 2006). In Ontario's Addiction Services Initiative, those most involved are specialized caseworkers and health professionals in community-based addiction treatment agencies, though some of these are social workers.

Addiction intervention has differentiated between two groups, one employed and one not. In the workplace, environment drug testing has been almost universally deemed unacceptable (Holmes & Richer, 2008). Employed Canadians who experience work-related issues are typically provided access to counselling and treatment before they are even disciplined, let alone terminated, thereby losing their income. In the workplace, an addiction is viewed as simply another health condition that requires treatment (Macdonald, Csiernik, Durand, Rylett & Wild, 2006). For people on assistance, addiction is increasingly being viewed as a punishable offence. This chapter provides an overview of the key issues and concerns associated with addiction intervention to assist social workers in familiarizing themselves with this contentious matter. Specifically, it addresses the types, complexities, and efficacy of drug testing; debates over public safety, privacy, and individual rights; the outcomes of drug testing policy attempts; the targeting of substance abuse in the welfare-to-work context; issues associated with implementing addiction intervention; and concludes with a discussion of future considerations.

Drug Testing: Types, Complexities, and Efficacy

Each of the four primary mechanisms of drug testing has its own strengths and weaknesses. One key criterion in evaluating the various options is the relative ease of obtaining and the accessibility of the targeted body fluid required by the specific test. A second factor to consider is the validity and reliability of the test. A third consideration is if the testing process involves one step or if follow-up procedures are also required after a preliminary positive result. Fourth, drug tests are only as good as the sample from which they are drawn, and not all tests can assess all drugs equally. Finally, and associated with all of these issues, is the actual time and cost of conducting and analyzing each individual test result.

The most familiar instrument for drug testing is the breathalyzer. The human body processes and eliminates alcohol in a manner such that the amount of alcohol in our breath is closely related to the actual concentration of alcohol in our blood. In turn, the level of alcohol in our blood is correlated with one's level of central nervous system impairment. Blood alcohol concentration (BAC) is an accurate indicator of the level of intoxication produced by the consumption of alcohol, regardless of its form: beer, wine, or spirits. The breathalyzer provides a general BAC result. The result is used to assess impairment, which is dependent upon how the reading compares with the individual province's definition of intoxication, ranging from a 0.05 to 0.10 ml blood alcohol level. However, the breathalyzer is not as precise as other measurement methods (Kapur, 1994).

Until recently, breath testing was only possible when testing for alcohol impairment. However, in 2010 a new breath test was developed that was able to detect methamphetamines (Beck, Leine, Palmskog, & Franck, 2010), which opened the door to the possibility of testing for other substances in this manner. Five years later a commercial sampling device using spray from the breath and a tandem set of lab tests called chromatography and mass spectrometry was validated. The combined test was able to test for marijuana, cocaine, heroin, amphetamine, methamphetamine, and various benzodiazepines. Again, while it is possible with this test to measure impairment, it is not able to measure whether or not the person is substance dependent (Stephanson, Sandqvist, Shafaato, & Beck, 2015). There has also been a portable breathalyzer device patented to detect the use of cannabis (Cannabix, 2015).

Blood tests are more specific and can provide more precise results, but require a skilled professional to procure the sample. Blood tests are also the most intrusive and painful method of drug testing and again provide only a measurement of recent use and not dependency let alone addiction.

The least used of the four drug testing options is radioimmunoassay of hair. This rather expensive but quite precise testing option uses a single strand of hair from a suspected user. Human hair provides a history of drug use over the length of time the hair has been grown, as drug molecules remain detectable for the life of the hair shaft. Thus, this method can provide a history of the person's drug use, both licit and illicit, over an extended period of time, such as if you smoked crack cocaine several months ago and then again in the past week. However, radioimmunoassay of hair is not effective in detecting current alcohol or other drug use (Gupta & Dhingra, 2012; Macdonald, 1997).

This leaves urine sampling, which is the most common method of testing for drugs. Urine testing is typically conducted in two stages: immunoassay and gas chromatography. Immunoassay is similar to a breathalyzer in that it provides a gross estimation of drug use. It can indicate if you have taken a drug from within a family of psychoactive substances such as opioids. Thus, you may test positive for an opioid, but the test cannot indicate if the drug ingested was heroin, methadone, or Dilaudid, or some combination of the three. The test also does not indicate if the Dilaudid was prescribed by a doctor or bought from a street dealer. Immunoassay is also the least reliable method of testing, with some individuals testing positive for cannabis after ingesting ibuprofen, an anti-inflammatory drug with pain-masking properties (Alberta Alcohol and Drug Abuse Commission, 1997). As in the Olympics, when a person provides a urine specimen, it is divided into two distinct samples. If a person tests positive on an immunoassay of their urine, the second sample should be analyzed to rule out false positives using a more sophisticated and also much more expensive confirmation technique, gas chromatography/mass spectrometry (GC/MS). This chemical process provides a precise indication of which drug the person has ingested. An added feature of this testing method is that the provision of the sample typically requires direct observation while the specimen is produced (Kapur, 1994; McNair & Miller, 2011).

Also critical to note is that the body processes different psychoactive drugs at different rates. This process of elimination is also affected by the subject's age, sex, physical health, how long the person has been taking the drug(s), and if the person is ingesting other licit or illicit substances. Typically, alcohol is metabolized within hours, while amphetamines, short-acting barbiturates, tranquilizers, cocaine, methadone, heroin, and other opioids are eliminated within one to three days. The drugs that are easiest to detect through blood tests and urinalysis, as they or their metabolites remain in the body the longest, are long-acting barbiturates, PCP, and cannabis. The first of these is usually taken for medical reasons such as epilepsy. The second, PCP, is characteristically taken by mistake, as few people actively chose to use it due to its harsh negative side effects. Cannabis is the most intriguing drug of the three. Its use is the easiest to detect because of its pharmacological properties, and while somewhat benign in small quantities, it is not a harmless psychoactive drug.

Finally, a distinction needs to be made between the three types of testing: mandatory, random, and for reasonable cause. Mandatory drug testing (MDT) is the process where everyone in a population is tested, such as all new recruits to the armed forces or all welfare recipients. Random drug testing (RDT) is what theoretically occurs to all Olympic-calibre amateur athletes and those in the US transportation industry, with everyone eligible to be tested at any time. Last, reasonable cause testing occurs in situations when it is believed alcohol or other psychoactive drugs are the reason behind the occurrence of an event, such as a workplace injury or automobile collision.

The Drug Testing Debate

Drug testing was initially proposed for employed persons. Among the most prominent arguments in favour of adopting this approach was that drug testing would benefit public safety. There was limited dissent against testing persons *with reasonable cause* in safety-sensitive positions, such as railroad engineers, bus drivers, pilots, transport truck drivers of hazardous materials, or operators of nuclear power plants. The crash of the Exxon Valdez in 1989 further intensified this argument in combination with the belief that drug testing would enhance employee safety, assist with determining fitness for duty, and in general enhance the public trust. Drug testing has also been recommended for those who work unsupervised, as it is one means for management to oversee those employees with whom they do not have regular contact. Finally, there are those who believe drug testing is a means to eliminate problematic employees from a workforce. Ironically, this last rationale would lead some people, perhaps many, to rely on welfare (Karch, 2007; Keay et al., 2010; Spencer, Muroff, & Delva, 2000).

Among the key arguments against mandatory and random drug testing is the belief that any form of testing is an invasion of privacy and a violation of civil rights (American Civil Liberties Union, 2000; Beaudoin, 2007; Ontario Law Reform Commission, 1992). As well, there is a belief and supporting documentation that drug tests are open to abuse and mistakes, and uncertainty remains regarding the validity of testing proced- ures. As well, the costs associated with the entire enterprise could be better spent on proactive initiatives such as health promotion, education, and prevention programs, particularly when there is now evidence that drug testing is a waste of taxpayer dol- lars, such as in Tennessee where only 37 people out of 16,017 tested positive (WBIR. com, 2015). The implementation of drug testing also sets the foundation for a negative and adversarial work environment. It is a punitive process, indicating a lack of faith in supervisors' and administrators' abilities to manage, and certainly has a negative impact upon employee morale and undermines the intent of voluntary Employee Assistance Programs. Workplace drug testing also raises this important philosophical question: What rights do employers have to inquire, let alone know, what employees do on their own time, outside of the work environment, especially if it does not interfere with work performance?

Most importantly, though, is the fact that drug testing does not and cannot dis- tinguish between use and misuse, let alone abuse, dependency, or addiction. Tests, including the breathalyzer, which tends not to be used with welfare recipients, have arbitrarily selected cut-off points. Thus, a drug test result cannot indicate if you per- sonally smoked three or four joints before engaging in an activity, or if you were merely in a small room with five or six other people who were inhaling cannabis, and all you ingested was second-hand smoke. Drug testing also does not take into account the antecedent events that led to the consumption of a drug, such as underemployment, unemployment, or poverty. MDT and RDT place no consideration on environmental factors. In both Canada and the United States, testing laboratories have been sued over providing false positives that caused the loss of employment and loss of children to child welfare authorities. In one prominent case, a male employee lost his job when the decongestant in an over-the-counter cold remedy he was taking was identified as a methamphetamine (crystal meth) by the laboratory's immunoassay analysis of his urine specimen (Texas Supreme Court, 1995). In Canada, the Motherisk Drug Testing Laboratory at Toronto's Hospital for Sick Children was suspended, and shut down, after issues arose regarding the reliability of its hair-testing method used in criminal and child protection cases between 2005 and 2010 (Mendelson, 2015).

As well, there have been no statistically significant linkages made between drug testing results and the ability to work (Macdonald, 2005). Neuhaus, Jr. and Caplan (1992) were the first to discuss how there had been no link made between a positive drug test and the ability to perform an assigned work task. Later, Zimmer (1999) reported that workplace drug testing has been ineffective in reducing drug use and absenteeism or in improving productivity, despite increasingly more American companies taking part in the practice. It is also valuable to note that the Canadian Human Rights Commission (2002) stated that the general use of drug testing resulting in dismissal of employees who test positive was potentially discriminatory and contrary to the Canadian Human Rights Act. This is unless the employer can show that the requirement to be free of drug dependency is a bona fide occupational qualification (Pinsonneault, 1994). An example of the ongoing legal struggle was a loss by Imperial Oil in November 2000. The case entailed an eight-year legal battle that witnessed Imperial Oil's attempt to demote an employee for a previously undetected alcohol-related problem that an employee had successfully sought treatment for and which had never affected the individual's ability to perform his job (Law Society of Upper Canada, 2000).

On February 8, 2009, at 7:30 a.m. a Coach Canada bus was stopped by an Ontario Provincial Police officer on the Queen Elizabeth Way, one on Canada's busiest highways. The driver of the bus, which had 20 passengers on board, was charged with having a blood alcohol concentration over the legal limit. Coach Canada had recently won a protracted two-year battle with the Canadian Human Rights Commission to implement a drug testing policy for its drivers. Prior to the policy no employee had ever had a reported on-road incident involving alcohol or other drugs. It was only after this policy was implemented to rid the organization of a problem that had never occurred that a bus operator for the company was ever charged with an alcohol-related offence (Johns, 2009).

The essence of this debate hinges on balancing the right to privacy versus public safety, and largely it has been determined that unless there is reasonable cause, random or mandatory drug testing is deemed an unsuitable practice for employers. The current state of arbitral case law is such that some consistencies have developed with respect to decisions around this matter: a) if a workplace is considered dangerous, workplaces can test their employees if there is reasonable cause to believe an employee is impaired while on duty, has been involved in a workplace accident, or is returning to work after drug and alcohol treatment; and b) a workplace does not have just cause to implement unilateral mandatory random drug testing, even if a workplace is determined to be unsafe. Both of these points were concretized in Canada by a Supreme Court ruling on June 14, 2013, on the matter of Irving Pulp and Paper versus the Communications, Energy and Paperworkers Union of Canada, where the court judged that mandatory random drug testing is "an unjustified affront to the dignity and privacy of employees" (Supreme Court of Canada, 2013).

We also need to ask what the implications are if a welfare recipient does test positive. By doing so there is no indication that there is a dependency to a drug (Macdonald et al., 2001; Pollack, Danziger, Seefeldt, & Jayakody, 2002), so why initiate a treatment protocol that may not be necessary when there are already extensive waiting times for those who have an addiction issue and who want assistance to resolve it? Historically, attempts at prohibition have been most successful at criminalizing what social work views as a social issue. However, if a person tests positive and refuses treatment, or refuses to be tested, and loses his or her welfare benefit, the choices for survival become quite limited and the social issue can quickly become a criminal justice issue. To paraphrase Neuhaus, Jr. and Caplan (1992), drug testing is a simplistic solution for dealing with a complicated problem, and is neither empirically sound nor humanistic.

Targeting Substance Abuse in the Welfare to Work Context

On November 14, 2000, in support of Ontario's proposed drug testing initiative, a provincial government press release listed five American states that had instituted drug testing into their welfare-to-work programs: Oregon, Maryland, Nevada, North Carolina, and Illinois. However, several of these states did not have drug testing as their exclusive, let alone primary, focus. Oregon had a standardized screening and assessment tool, the American Society of Addiction Medicine screening test, to assess if addiction was a barrier to employment. Oregon did not engage in mass or random testing, but rather focused upon selected clients who were having difficulty with employment or in participating in job opportunity or basic skills programming. Some counties did try pilot drug testing programs, but opted out of this as it was discovered that this invasive procedure was no more effective at detecting drug abuse than less intrusive assessment procedures. Not surprisingly, drug testing also created more resistance and resentment among clients than did a typical assessment process. In fact, one Oregon county opted out of the entire program. Likewise, Nevada employed social workers to deal with multiple barriers to finding employment, including substance abuse, though its focus was not primarily on drug use. North Carolina hired SAPs for every social service office in the state to provide on-site counselling and support. However, Ontario initially appeared to be following the lead of Maryland. That state was using legislation to link managed medical care and welfare. In Maryland, all adults and teen parents on social assistance are screened for substance abuse by law, with any person testing positive receiving a mandatory referral for addiction counselling. The refusal of welfare recipients to go for treatment led to their immediate removal from social assistance (Etsten & Ballon, 2001).

Interestingly, the initial Ontario government's mandatory drug testing announcement did not discuss the situation in Michigan, the first state that attempted to implement mandatory drug testing of welfare recipients. A month prior to Ontario's announcement, a federal district judge in Michigan blocked mandatory drug testing as a "dangerous precedent" under the American Constitution, as it allows for random, unsuspicious testing. The state argued that drug testing was necessary because substance abuse and child neglect are highly correlated. The American Civil Liberties Union (2000) countered, claiming that if the state is allowed to drug test welfare recipients by virtue of its advocacy on behalf of minors there was the risk that testing could be expanded to access other core services such as Medicaid, State Emergency Relief, educational grants or loans, or even access to public education.

Further, a federal district judge noted that the objective of the Temporary Assistance for Needy Families (TANF) programs is not to prevent child abuse or neglect, but to provide financial support for families. A punitive and fear-based approach to social assistance poses a real danger to the children of parents that do use drugs. Whether they are substance-dependent or just occasional users, some pregnant women or parents with children are afraid to apply for benefits, fearing that if they test positive their children may be taken. In these cases, the fear of being tested means that these children may not have access to the food and shelter they require (Player, 2014). According to the American Civil Liberties Union (2008), at least 21 states concluded that mandatory drug testing may be unlawful, 17 states cited cost concerns, 11 states had not considered drug testing at all, and 11 gave a variety of practical/operational reasons.

In a review of welfare-to-work programs at the close of the 20th century in Canada, it was discovered that substance abuse counselling, but not mandatory drug testing, had already been integrated to some extent with these programs (Gorlick & Brethour, 1998a). Given objectives to cut welfare costs by reducing rates and increasing welfare recipients' departure from social assistance, provincial and territorial welfare-to-work programs have from the outset incorporated responses to substance abuse. Across the country, substance abuse has been defined as an impediment of employability and subsequently an inability to leave welfare. The process is similar for most jurisdictions, with substance abuse assessment overlapping and intertwined with the "negotiated plan" for exiting welfare by gaining employment. The idea of a mutually agreed upon plan of action between a welfare recipient and the welfare agency is carried out within the welfare recipient assessment process. This is the same context within which the initial identification of substance abuse is made. In most cases, those with a substance abuse issue are referred to a community agency for assistance.

What remains difficult to ascertain is the extent to which the welfare recipient views this referral as mandatory, and indeed the extent to which the welfare agency implies the same understanding. Manitoba's Bill 40, the Employment and Income Assistance Amendment Act (1999), maintains in sections 5.5(1) and 5.5(2) that if a welfare recipient or applicant fails to satisfy the social welfare agency director that he or she is participating in an addiction treatment program then the director (or municipality) may "deny, reduce, suspend or discontinue the income assistance, municipal assistance or general assistance." Thus, the issue of implied and actual mandatory drug testing from the perspective of the welfare recipient is significant. Real or imagined, the perceived loss of privacy is a significant issue, especially if the welfare recipient believes that a refusal to participate in substance abuse counselling may lead to the loss of social assistance.

Implementing Substance Abuse Screening, Case Management, Assessment, and Treatment

For substance abuse assessments being made within the welfare-to-work program context, who is making these assessments and in what manner? Case workers and employment counsellors, increasingly third parties involved in welfare-to-work programs, are in most cases not SAPs and thus are not always trained in substance abuse assessment, and there appears to be no significant initiative to address this training issue. An American report noted that the most common detection methods of substance abuse included recipients' self-declarations and behavioural and appearance cues (American Public Human Services Association, 1999).

Substance abuse detection methods were occurring as the field of Canadian social work was being de-credentialized in some areas, with the outsourcing of social work activities to third parties such as employment counsellors and social assistance case-workers who spend little time with the people they serve due to an abundance of administrative processes. We are witnessing the replacement of a social care model with a "shortest route to employment" for welfare recipients' orientation, with an emphasis upon clerical functions over case management processes. These activities have occurred with the restructuring of social assistance and the emergence of an "exiting" bureaucracy with new ways of "doing business" (Gorlick & Brethour, 1998b). In sum, the objectives of welfare assistance are to identify the barriers to welfare independence and employability, and once identified, eradicate them. This identification and eradication of barriers, however, is selective. Accessible and suitable child care, housing, and transportation are examples of those clearly defined barriers, yet these have not been effectively addressed. The question becomes, Why would we target those with substance abuse rather than, or in addition to, addressing an issue such as the welfare recipients' need for child care services?

Along with its selective nature, the "shortest route to employment" approach, in the case of addiction, is not grounded in research, which tells us an abstinence orientation is not typical with respect to a person's recovery journey, given that 70% of people experience at least one relapse (Centre for Addiction and Mental Health, 2012). Given the complex nature of substance abuse, which is often a primary method of coping for people experiencing social, psychological, biological, spiritual, and cultural discord, inequality, and/or trauma, simply removing this from a person's coping repertoire overnight is not reasonable, and usually does not happen no matter what the social or personal cost. This is also a valid argument for diverting funds from testing to prevention efforts, or developing harm-reduction approaches to service people on social assistance, that are free of sanctions and the fear associated with those sanctions.

What is also quite selective is why drug testing occurs with people on social assistance programs like Ontario Works, and not on other provincial assistance programs such as the Ontario Disability Support program or any of the many assistance programs provided for farmers in Ontario. Governments claim it is a cost saving measure;

however, several states that have tried drug testing social assistance recipients have yielded little to no savings, and in some cases, have cost the state money. Another argument is that drug use is rampant in people that access social assistance. Out of all the American states that have implemented drug testing for people on social assistance, not one has found that people on social assistance test higher than the national average, and typically far below (Stone, 2015). For example, Arizona tested 87,000 people and yielded one (0.001%) positive result (USA Today, 2012); Missouri tested 38,970 in 2014 and yielded 48 (0.01%) positive results (Think Progress, 2015); and in Utah the rate was 0.2% of the entire population tested (Stone, 2015). Given that the average cost of a drug test in 2002 was approximately $42 per person (Dupont, Campbell, & Mazza, 2002), adjusting for inflation this would mean each basic test cost $61, not including the costs of hiring personnel to administer the tests, to ensure confidentiality of results, and to run confirmatory tests to guard against false positives resulting from passive drug exposure and cross-identification with legal prescription. This additional expense would conservatively imply a cost of $70 per person per test. Thus, Arizona spent $6 million to identify one drug user receiving social assistance, whereas Missouri used $2.75 million tax dollars to identify 48 people who used drugs while on welfare. So if the rationale for drug testing welfare assistance is not about the money, or providing treatment to a high substance-abusing population, than what is it about? From an anti-oppressive standpoint it can be argued that this is about punishing a class of people that has no social power for an issue that is seen as a medical and mental health concern in the workplace, or in any other class of people for that matter. No statistical analysis is required to prove this is not a good use of tax dollars, especially given that social assistance rates provide an income below the poverty line.

Also significant to the link between assessing substance abuse and employability is the emergence of public health as a definer of employability. Jayakody, Danziger, and Pollack (2000) noted that program implementers have turned to clinical language and findings to determine who is employable. Past attempts to pathologize the poor have been critiqued, raising the question of what role more formalized clinical language and direction plays in deciding the end of welfare support and employability.

Another question is how to implement addiction intervention in the context of welfare to work. It is critical to begin by noting the different mandates of the two systems. Each agency's organizational culture has different objectives, normative and value understandings, professional and occupational interpretations, and organizational missions. For the welfare agency, the emphasis is upon a very particular outcome: ensuring the recipient is no longer welfare dependent. The goal of most social assistance services is to make employment a priority and thus they have developed programs that emphasize "the shortest route possible to employment" and "any job is a good job" orientations. Agencies whose primary mandate is to assist individuals with addiction issues must, because of the nature of their work, be more process focused, with a different time perspective than that of a welfare agency regarding a welfare recipient's progress. Thus, organizational conflict between the systems is inevitable, accompanied by distorted objectives, altered time frames, and frustrated professionals, which in turn leaves welfare recipients vulnerable to sanctions (Gorlick, 2002). There appears to be a view that addressing addictions does not require a new service delivery system (Kirby, Pavetti, Kauff, & Tapogna, 1999).

As well, it is most important to be aware that each system does not come from an equitable place of power. Addiction Services Initiatives and similar programs are products of outsourcing funded by the government. Frequently, funding and length of time to conduct satisfactory and sufficient addiction intervention is a concern of addiction treatment agencies. Thus, both government and addiction treatment agencies are left to seek common understandings but without sufficient program implementation resources.

In addition to a lack of professional supports, organizational confusion, and change, the implementation of substance abuse assessment and treatment may threaten the privacy of welfare recipients. For example, the lack of safeguards surrounding confidential medical information may impact a welfare recipient's employability. Employers may decide not to hire those with an addiction, as was seen in the case of Entrop versus Imperial Oil (Law Society of Upper Canada, 2000). With the primary objective to cut social assistance costs by moving welfare recipients into the labour force, this is an interesting paradox for welfare-to-work and addiction intervention programs. Furthermore, the implementation of these programs fails to incorporate the heterogeneous nature of the population such as gender differences (Suffet, 1999), the impact of educational and previous employment experiences (Wicker, Campbell, Krupski, & Stark, 2000), and the lack of program accountability measures through comprehensive database tracking. Research findings in the United States noted that illicit drug use among welfare recipients nationally decreased between 1990 and 1998, and that mental health disorders such as major depression and post-traumatic stress disorder were more common than illicit drug dependence among welfare recipients (Pollack, 2002). With a homogeneous policy view of the targeted population, few organizational resources and supports, and an emphasis upon employability without appropriate outcome tracking and analysis, it is questionable whether addiction intervention and accompanying support services for the welfare recipient are being implemented effectively and fairly.

A significant element often missing in discussions on this topic is the economy. If all of the individual, program, and employability criteria are met, will there be employment available or that is suitable? This question, which is always appropriate to ask, seems particularly pertinent during economic recessionary periods. Analyzing employment data during a booming economy, Danziger (2002) observed:

> ... the percentage of current and former (welfare) recipients who worked in any month was never above 70 percent. Even women with few barriers to employment are unlikely to work 40 hours per week year round during an economic boom. Women with substance abuse problems and other barriers

to employment are unlikely to work full-time, year round. Many will not find jobs that offer 40 hours of work per week; others will have difficulty working in every week during the year. The women are likely to obtain and lose several jobs during the year, with periods of unemployment between jobs. (p. 5)

Finally, there is the question of social work ethics. Addiction intervention in the welfare-to-work context underscores the dilemma between social work as a helping profession and social workers as agents of social control. Cossom (1992) wrote of the increasing vulnerability and powerlessness of a client who seeks social work services. Historically, the intent of social work has been treatment of substance abusers, including finding financial supports for them and not creating additional financial hardships. Yet everything about contemporary "welfare reform" has been about taking away citizens' rights, as was highlighted by the initial mandatory drug testing initiative, and to a lesser extent by current addiction intervention services. Social workers are challenged on many ethical levels—not only the duty to aid, but also the equitable distribution of services and resources and the principles of equality, need, compensation, and contribution (Loewenberg & Dolgoff, 1992).

Concluding Thoughts

There are dozens of recorded attempts at prohibition in human history, some of which date back over 4,000 years. The current ongoing North American attempt to prohibit the use of psychoactive drugs has been as effective as the Pharaohs' attempts to stop their soldiers from drinking, Pope Urban VIII's and Pope Innocent X's attempts to ban smoking among the clergy in the 1600s, the Ontario Temperance Act of 1916, and the 18th Amendment of the US Constitution (Csiernik, 2016). Thus, if we cannot win the War on Drugs in society, perhaps we can win it against the "undeserving poor."

As a series of legal battles continue to be lost in Canada's private sector (Holmes & Richer, 2008), as well as by the Harper government at the Supreme Court level, it is interesting that attention has turned to welfare recipients who are perceived by some tiers of society to have fewer rights. It appears that the issues of privacy and freedom from unreasonable search and seizure may not apply to recipients of social assistance. While there is no doubt that a percentage of individuals receiving social assistance have an addiction, the number has not been shown to be greater than that of the general population. In April 2001, Toronto's Daily Bread Food Bank conducted a survey of food bank users, asking the same questions the Centre for Addiction and Mental Health does in ascertaining drug use in Ontario. The results were surprising to many, but reflected those found in similar American studies (Rodriguez & Chandra, 2006). The Daily Bread Food Bank survey found that welfare recipients drank less frequently and less often than the "average" Ontario taxpayer, and used cannabis and other psychoactive drugs less often and in lesser amounts than an average adult living in Toronto (Slosser, 2001).

There are also far greater and more prominent barriers to employability than drug use, including a lack of appropriate skills, illiteracy, lack of child care, lack of housing, depression, and other mental health issues (American Civil Liberties Union, 1999; Grant & Dawson, 1996; Macdonald et al., 2001; Shawna & Vinokur, 2007). What, then, is the value in a government portraying welfare recipients as a group of drug addicts, further adding to their stigmatization and oppression?

REFERENCES

Alberta Alcohol and Drug Abuse Commission. (1997). *Employment-related drug testing.* Edmonton, AB: Alberta and Drub Abuse Commission.

American Civil Liberties Union. (1999). *Marchwinski v. Family Independence Agency.* Washington, DC: ACLU.

American Civil Liberties Union. (2000). *Citing dangerous precedent, federal judge blocks Michigan's plan to drug test welfare recipients.* Washington, DC: ACLU.

American Civil Liberties Union. (2008). *Drug testing of public assistance recipients as a condition of eligibility.* Washington, DC: ACLU.

American Civil Liberties Union. (2015). *The war on marijuana in black and white.* Retrieved from https://www.aclu.org/report/war-marijuana-black-and-white

American Public Human Services Association. (1999). *Building bridges: States respond to substance abuse and welfare reform.* Washington, DC: The Substance Abuse Research Program of The Robert Wood Johnson Foundation.

Beaudoin, C. (2007). Random drug testing in the workplace: All but universally rejected by Canadian arbitrators." *Employment and Labour Law Reporter, 16*(12), 101–106.

Beck, O., Leine, K., Palmskog, G., & Franck, J. (2010). Amphetamines detected in exhaled breath from drug addicts: A new possible method for drugs-of-abuse testing. *Journal of Analytical Toxicology, 34*(5), 233–237.

Blackwell, J. (1994). Drug testing, the war on drugs, workers, and the workplace: Perspectives from sociology. In S. Macdonald & P. Roman (Eds.), *Drug testing in the workplace* (pp. 319–334). New York: Plennum Press.

Bomhof, K.J. (2005). Addressing substance abuse in the workplace: The legal challenges to implementing a drug and alcohol testing program. Vancouver: Lawson Lundell, LPP.

Boyle, T., & Mallan, C. (2001). Read and write test for welfare. *Toronto Star,* May 4, A1 & A17.

Canadian Broadcasting Corporation. (2013). Canadian police chiefs propose ticket system for pot. Retrieved from: http://www.cbc.ca/news/canada/manitoba/canadian-police-chiefs-propose-ticket-system-for-pot-1.1335493

Canadian Human Rights Commission. (2002). *Policy on alcohol and drug testing.* Ottawa, ON: Canadian Human Rights Commission.

Cannabix. (2015). *Cannabix technologies partners with University of Florida to develop marijuana breath test devices.* Retrieved from http://www.cannabixtechnologies.com/news-releases.html

Centre for Addiction and Mental Health. (2012). *Mandatory drug testing and treatment of welfare recipients position statement.* Retrieved from http://www.camh.ca/en/hospital/about_camh/influencing_public_policy/public_policy_submissions/Pages/manddrugtesting.aspx

City of Hamilton. (2013). Information report: Ontario Works Addiction Services Initiative evaluation (CS10086(b)) (City Wide). Retrieved from http://www2.hamilton.ca/NR/rdonlyres/C0468829-A6E6-4815-8567-0CA604B72907/0/Oct2253CS10086b.pdf

Cossom, J. (1992). What do we know about social work ethics? *The Social Worker, 60*(3), 165-171.

Csiernik, R. (2016). *Substance use and abuse: Everything matters.* Toronto, ON: Canadian Scholars' Press, 2nd edition.

Danziger, S. (2002) *Policy relevancy of research findings, policy briefing on substance abuse, families and welfare reform for the substance abuse policy research program.* Washington, DC: Robert Wood Johnson Foundation.

Dupont, R., Campbell, T., & Mazza, J. (2002). *Elements of a successful school-based student drug testing program.* Washington, DC: United States Department of Education.

Etsten, D., & Ballon, D. (2001). Forcing welfare recipients into drug testing and treatment: The North American experience. *Journal of Addiction and Mental Health, 4*(2), 4.

Grant, B., & Dawson, D. (1996). Alcohol and drug use, abuse, and dependency among welfare recipients. *American Journal of Public Health, 86*(10), 1450-1454.

Gorlick, C., & Brethour, G. (1998a). *Welfare to work programs in Canada: A national inventory.* Ottawa, ON: Canadian Council on Social Development.

Gorlick, C., & Brethour, G. (1998b). *National welfare to work programs: From new mandates to exiting bureaucracies to individual and program accountability.* Ottawa, ON: Canadian Council on Social Development.

Gorlick, C. (2002). *Policy expectations and program realities: Welfare to work programs in Canada.* Ottawa, ON: Human Resources Development Canada.

Gupta, S., & Dhingra, V. (2012). Hair: An evidence for drug of abuse. *Indian Internet Journal of Forensic Medicine & Toxicology, 10*(2), 41-48.

Harrison, B., & Simpler, L. (1989). Antidrug rules and regulations. *EAP Digest, 9*(6), 19-24.

Hayashida, S. (2001). Suspicionless drug testing. *Municipal Lawyer, 41*(2), 16-18.

Holmes, N., & Richer, K. (2008). *Drug testing in the workplace.* Ottawa, ON: Library of Parliament, Parliamentary Information and Research Service.

Jayakody, R., Danziger, S., & Pollack, H. (2000). Welfare reform, substance abuse and mental health. *Journal of Health Politics, Policy and Law, 25*(4), 623-651.

Johns, E. (2009). Wild bus ride on QEW ends in driver's arrest. *The Hamilton Spectator,* February 9, A1.

Kapur, B. (1994). Drug testing methods and interpretations of test results. In S. Macdonald & P. Roman (Eds.), *Drug testing in the workplace* (pp. 103-120). New York: Plennum Press.

Karch, S. (2007). *Workplace drug testing.* Boca Raton, FL: CRC Press.

Keay, E., Macdonald, S., Durand, P., Csiernik, R., & Wild, T.C. (2010). Reasons for adopting and not adopting: Employee assistance and drug testing programs in Canada. *Journal of Workplace Behavioral Health, 25*(1), 65-71.

Kirby, G., Pavetti, L., Kauff, J., & Tapogna, J. (1999). *Integrating alcohol and drug treatment into a work oriented welfare program: Lessons from Oregon.* Paper prepared for Mathematica Policy Research, Inc., June 1999.

Law Society of Upper Canada. (2000). Entrop et al. v. Imperial Oil Limited et al.; Canadian Civil Liberties Association, intervenor. *Ontario Reports, 50 O.R. (3d),* 18-64.

Loewenberg, F., & Dolgoff, R. (1992). *Ethical decisions for social work practice.* Itasca, IL: F.E. Peacock Publishers.

Macdonald, S. (1997). Workplace alcohol and other drug testing: A review of the scientific evidence. *Drug and Alcohol Review, 16*(3), 251-259.

Macdonald, S. (2005). Drug testing in the workplace: Issues, answers, and the Canadian context. In R. Csiernik (Ed.), *Wellness and work: Employee assistance programming in Canada* (pp. 57-72). Toronto, ON: Canadian Scholars' Press.

Macdonald, S., Bois, C., Brands, B., Dempsey, D., Erickson, P., Marsh, D., Meredith, S., Shain, M., Skinner, W., & Chiu, A. (2001). Drug testing and mandatory treatment for welfare recipients. *International Journal of Drug Policy, 12*(3), 249–257.

Macdonald, S., Csiernik, R., Durand, P., Rylett, M., & Wild, T.C. (2006). Prevalence and factors related to Canadian workforce health programs. *Canadian Journal of Public Health, 97*(2), 121–125.

Macdonald, S., Csiernik, R., Durand, P., Rylett, M., Wild, T.C., & Lloyd, S. (2006). Organizational characteristics related to the adoption of employee assistance and drug testing programs in Canada. *Canadian Journal of Community Mental Health, 25*(2), 159–171.

McNair, H., & Miller, J. (2011). *Basic gas chromatography*. New York: John Wiley & Sons.

Mendleson, R. (2015). *Sick Kids suspends Motherisk's hair drug testing*. Retrieved from http://www.thestar.com/news/gta/2015/03/05/sick-kids-suspends-motherisks-hair-drug-testing.html

Metsch, L., & Pollack, H. (2005). Welfare reform and substance abuse. *Milbank Quarterly, 83*(1), 65–99.

National Conference of State Legislatures. (2015). *Drug testing for welfare recipients and public assistance*. Retrieved from http://www.ncsl.org/research/human-services/drug-testing-and-public-assistance.aspx

Neuhaus, Jr., C., & Caplan, R. (1992). Employee drug testing: Complicated problems defy simplistic solutions. *Employee Assistance Quarterly, 7*(4), 35–49.

Ontario Law Reform Commission. (1992). *Report on alcohol and drug testing in the workplace*. Toronto, ON: Ontario Law Reform Commission.

Ontario Ministry of Community and Social Services. (2000). *News releases*. Retrieved from http://www.gov.on.ca/css

Ontario Ministry of Community and Social Services. (2009). Ontario Works Policy Directives: 8.4 Addiction Services Initiative (ASI). Retrieved from: http://www.mcss.gov.on.ca/documents/en/mcss/social/directives/ow/0804.pdf

Parker, C. (1995). BATs, SAPs, and MROs. *EAPA Exchange, 25*(4), 18–20.

Pinsonneault, M. (1994). Some legal aspects of drug testing in the Canadian workplace: Human rights, collective bargaining and labour arbitration, and the Canadian Charter of Rights and Freedoms. In S. Macdonald & P. Roman (Eds.), *Drug testing in the workplace* (pp. 165–184). New York: Plennum Press.

Player, C. (2014). Public assistance, drug testing, and the law: The limits of population-based legal analysis. *American Journal of Law and Medicine, 40*(1), 26–84.

Pollack, H.A. (2002) *Substance abuse trends among welfare recipients, policy briefing on substance abuse, families and welfare reform for the substance abuse policy research program*. Washington. DC: Robert Wood Johnson Foundation.

Pollack, H., Danziger, S., Seefeldt, K., & Jayakody, R. (2002) Substance use among welfare recipients: Trends and policy responses. *Social Service Review, 76*(2), 256–274.

Rodriguez, E., & Chandra, P. (2006). Alcohol, employment status, and social benefits: One more piece of the puzzle. *American Journal of Drug and Alcohol Abuse, 32*(2), 237–259.

Shawna, L., & Vinokur, A. (2007). Work barriers in the context of pathways to the employment of welfare-to-work clients. *American Journal of Community Psychology, 40*(3/4), 301–312.

Slosser, C. (2001). *Government fails the test: Most welfare recipients aren't using drugs*. Toronto, ON: Daily Bread Food Bank.

Spencer, M., Muroff, J., & Delva, J. (2000). Conditional welfare: A family social work perspective on mandatory drug testing. *Journal of Family Social Work, 4*(4), 3–14.

Standing Committee on National Health and Welfare. (1987). *Booze, pills and dope: Reducing substance abuse in Canada*. Ottawa, ON: Health and Welfare Canada.

Stephanson, N., Sandqvist, S., Shafaato, M., & Beck, O. (2015). Method validation and application of a liquid chromatography-tandem mass spectrometry method for drugs of abuse testing in exhaled breath. *Journal of Chromatography*, *985*, 189–196.

Stone, J. (2015). The sham of drug testing for benefits: Walker, Scott and political pandering. *Forbes*, February 17. Retrieved from http://www.forbes.com/sites/judystone/2015/02/17/the-sham-of-drug-testing-walker-scott-and-political-pandering

Suffet, F. (1999). Some sex-neutral and sex-specific factors related to employment among substance abuse clients. *American Journal of Drug and Alcohol Abuse*, *25*(3), 517–527.

Supreme Court of Canada. (2013). *Supreme court judgments: Communications, Energy, and Paperworkers Union of Canada, Local 30 v. Irving Pulp & Paper, Ltd*. Retrieved from https://scc-csc.lexum.com/scc-csc/scc-csc/en/item/13106/index.do

Texas Supreme Court. (1995). *Willis v. Roche Biomedical Laboratories*. Fifth Circuit United States Court of Appeals, 92-2361, August 2.

Think Progress.org. (2015). *What 7 states discovered after spending more that $1 million drug testing welfare recipients*. Retrieved from http://thinkprogress.org/economy/2015/02/26/3624447/tanf-drug-testing-states

USA Today. (2012). *Editorial: Drug testing welfare applicants nets little*. Retrieved from http://usatoday30.usatoday.com/news/opinion/editorials/story/2012-03-18/drug-testing-welfare-applicants/53620604/1

WBIR.com. (2015). *Drug testing of welfare applicants yields few positives*. Retrieved from http://www.wbir.com/story/news/politics/2015/02/08/drug-testing-of-welfare-applicants-yields-few-positives/23086333

Wicker, T., Campbell, K., Krupski, A., & Stark, K. (2000). Employment outcomes among AFDC recipients treated for substance abuse in Washington state. *Milbank Quarterly*, *78*(4), 585–608.

Zimmer, L. (1999). *Drug testing: A bad investment*. Washington, DC: American Civil Liberties Union.

PART 5

COMPULSIVE BEHAVIOURS

Adolescent and Youth Gambling: Current Knowledge, Clinical Perspectives, and Concerns

Jeffrey Derevensky, Renée A. St-Pierre, and Rick Csiernik

Introduction

The landscape of gambling has changed dramatically over the past three decades. The widespread legalization of gambling activities around the world and the impressive growth of existing and new forms of gambling remains unprecedented. The glitz, glamour, and excitement of gambling, once relegated to major international gambling destinations such as Las Vegas, Atlantic City, Monte Carlo, and Macau, has transcended borders with the development of multi-billion-dollar mega resorts. Today, there are 984 casinos currently operating in 39 US states (American Gaming Association, 2014), approximately 883 casinos operating in multiple European countries (European Casino Association [ECA], Gambling Compliance, & Herzfeld Consulting, 2014), and a growing number of large casinos throughout Asia and Australasia.

The growth of the gambling industry, however, has not been limited to casinos. Gambling is now omnipresent, from the corner convenience store where individuals can purchase lottery or scratch tickets, to enhanced race tracks ("racinos") that combine race track betting, electronic gambling machines, and certain types of casino games, to poker playing, and multiple opportunities for online wagering. In 2013 alone, gambling revenues in Macau, China, surpassed those of Las Vegas by sevenfold (Liu, Chang, Loi, & Chan, 2015). Televised poker tournaments are abundant nationally and internationally, with celebrities and athletes endorsing a variety of Internet gambling sites. In Europe, Australasia, Asia, and North America, a burgeoning highly profitable industry has emerged.

Gambling throughout Canada continues to expand and has become a multi-billion-dollar business with revenues playing an important role in funding provincial government budgets. While not recession-proof, the industry continues to grow at a rapid rate. Even in jurisdictions where gambling in general or certain types of gambling is prohibited, multiple opportunities exist as technological advances have brought gambling into the home via the Internet. Today, in many Canadian jurisdictions one can legally place a wager on lottery products, bingo, keno, casino games, horse racing, poker, and on provincially owned and operated online gambling sites. While for most individuals gambling remains a form of entertainment and a socially acceptable recreational pastime, as with substance abuse an identifiable minority of individuals experience significant gambling-related problems. What begins as an enjoyable, relatively benign behaviour can escalate into a problem with serious social, emotional, interpersonal, physical, financial, and legal problems.

Gambling in Canada

A number of landmark events have been related to the legalization of gambling in Canada, which has resulted in its widespread proliferation (Campbell, Hartnagel, & Smith, 2005). Gambling is regulated under the Criminal Code of Canada, a federal statute, originally enacted in 1892. Over the past century a variety of amendments have been added, all of which have liberalized gambling from its prohibition contained in the early legislation. Gambling regulation is, for the most part, unless prohibited by the Criminal Code, under the jurisdiction of each province, which decides licensing, regulatory statutes, types of games offered, and enforcement. As a result of subsequent amendments, most notably the 1969 revision of the Criminal Code, almost all forms of gambling can be found in Canada, although there are some distinct differences between the provinces (Hargreave & Csiernik, 2003). Currently there are 70 casinos, over 96,000 Electronic Gambling Machines (slots or VLTs), 222 venues for racetrack pari-mutuel wagering, and in excess of 30,000 lottery ticket outlets currently available to the Canadian population (Alberta Gaming Research Institute, 2015; Smith, 2014). While gambling has historically followed a pendulum from prohibition at one extreme to widespread availability and accessibility at the other (Yorke, 2003), there remains little doubt that the huge revenues being generated for provincial governments will not result in a more conservative, restrictive approach in the foreseeable future. The most recent available data suggests that revenues from government-operated lotteries, video lottery terminals (VLTs), casinos, and slot machines (excluding those in casinos) rose from $2.7 billion in 1992 to approximately $13.1 billion in 2012–2013, over a 400% increase (Responsible Gambling Council, 2014; Statistics Canada, 2009). Areas with new casino developments have been shown to experience large, positive growth in earnings and employment within one to five years following the opening of the casino, particularly in the gambling and hospitality industries (Humphreys & Marchand, 2013).

With the widespread use of new emerging technologies such as Internet wagering, the environmental landscape of gambling possibilities is further undergoing a momentous and unparalleled growth. Although still in its infancy, there is a selection of Internet gaming options now legally available to gamblers in seven provinces, including online lottery or instant-win/scratch tickets, bingo games, casino slot and table games, player-banked poker games, sports betting, and video poker games (Responsible Gambling Council, 2014). Further, recent reports suggest that Internet gambling is a viable source of revenue for provincial governments. Within Canada alone, revenues were estimated to have exceeded $38.1 million in 2012–2013 (Responsible Gambling Council, 2014).

Adult Gambling Behaviour and Problems

Gambling behaviour can best be conceptualized on a continuum ranging from non-gambling to social/occasional/recreational gambling to problem gambling and finally disordered gambling, the term that has now replaced compulsive gambling, pathological gambling, and Level III gambling. Disordered gambling is currently conceptualized as a behavioural addiction in the fifth edition of the *Diagnostic and Statistical Manual of Mental Disorders* (DSM-V; American Psychiatric Association [APA], 2013), and is characterized by persistent and recurrent dysfunctional gambling behaviour that typically leads to significant impairment and/or distress for the individual. It is also important to note that individuals with disordered gambling have a negative impact on peers, family members, and employers. Several negative consequences associated with problem gambling have been identified, including

- substantial financial problems, such as high debt and personal bankruptcy;
- strained family relationships and violence;
- employment and/or academic-related problems including absenteeism, loss of employment, poor academic performance, and high dropout rates; and
- concomitant mental health disorders.

With most Canadian adults and a large percentage of adolescents having gambled, it is not surprising that an early meta-analysis of studies carried out in the United States and Canada between 1975 and 1997 found that past-year disordered gambling rates among adults averaged between 1.3% and 8.0% in prevalence surveys (Shaffer, Hall, & Vander Bilt, 1999). Other more recent Canadian studies report adult past-year prevalence rates of disordered/pathological gambling ranging between 0.4% and 1.4% (Responsible Gambling Council, 2014). It is interesting to note that research conducted in jurisdictions where VLTs and other electronic gambling machines (EGMs) are legal tend to find higher prevalence rates, as VLTs and EGMs are considered by many to lead to the most disordered gambling activity (St-Pierre, Walker, Derevensky, & Gupta, 2014). Interestingly, almost all adult prevalence studies of gambling behaviour report that the youngest adults, those between the ages of 18 and 25, have the highest preva-lence rates for severe problem gambling (Temcheff, St-Pierre, & Derevensky, 2013). It is also important when examining prevalence rates to note the time frame for problem gambling, as lifetime prevalence rates are generally higher than past-year reports and significant changes to opportunities and gambling activities have changed.

While there still exist significant gaps in our knowledge, there is a growing body of evidence suggesting that governmental policies increasing ease of access to EGMs, VLTs, and other types of continuous forms of gambling are most likely to generate increases in problem gambling, with concomitant rising social costs to the individual, their families, and society (Abbott, Volberg, Bellringer, & Reith, 2004). The National Research Council (1999) concluded that certain groups may in fact be more vulnerable to the risks associated with problem and excessive gambling. Adolescents, seniors, women, and individuals from ethnic cultural minorities, namely populations more likely to suffer oppression, seem to be at greatest risk.

There remains little doubt that the changing attitudes towards gambling in general, and in particular in Canada, have moved from one of stigmatized criminal activity to general acceptance. The general social acceptability of gambling has likely increased as a result of the more liberal stance held by the public, religious institutions, and gov-ernment legislatures, who need to seek increased sources of revenue and job creation. In spite of the fact that most adults gamble in a responsible manner, those individuals gambling excessively not only have significant individual personal costs to their wellness but also negatively impact their families and the larger community.

Over the past decade there has been increased research aimed at understanding this complex behaviour. Individuals with significant gambling problems, in general, score high on measures of impulsivity, risk-taking, compulsivity, psychoticism (aggression, aloofness, anti-social behaviour, and impulsive actions), and neuroticism. They tend to experience a wide variety of personality disorders, such as obsessive-compulsive, anti-social, and avoidant personality disorders, mood disorders, particularly anxiety and depression, along with comorbid alcohol and drug use, cognitive distortions, and erroneous beliefs (Abbott, Volberg, Bellringer, & Reith, 2004; Dowling et al., 2015; Lorains, Cowlishaw, & Thomas, 2011; Shaffer & Martin, 2011). There is also strong empirical evidence that disordered gambling occurs predominantly among males, although female prevalence rates of disordered gambling are increasing. Ethnic, cul-tural, and racial differences have also been found to exist (Barry, Steinberg, Wu, & Potenza, 2008). These risk factors, coupled with suggested neurological indices, point to the complexity of the issues surrounding disordered gambling.

Measuring Problem Gambling among Adults

From a clinical perspective, a number of gambling screening instruments are available today. These screening instruments serve as a critical first step in identifying potential gambling problems (Brown et al., 2015). The vast majority of these instruments have been adapted from past editions of the APA's *Diagnostic and Statistical Manual of*

Mental Disorders (DSM-III, DSM-III-R, DSM-IV, DSM-IV-TR), or are related to the Gamblers Anonymous 20 Questions (GA-20). Such scales include the South Oaks Gambling Screen (SOGS), Diagnostic Interview for Gambling Severity (DIGS), the Canadian Problem Gambling Index (CPGI), the National Opinion Research Center DSM-IV Screen for Gambling Problems (NODS), the Massachusetts Gambling Screen (MAGS), and the Lie/Bet Questionnaire (Brown et al., 2015; Stinchfield, Govoni, & Frisch, 2007).

However, there remain significant disagreements and criticisms about the utility of many of these screening scales. Such criticisms have included that

- non-problem gamblers (social gamblers) often equally endorse some of the items on the scales;
- the time frames vary between scales, with some incorporating only the past year and others using lifetime rates; and
- many of the screens appear to be insensitive to cultural diversity and context.

The DSM-V remains the primary classification system for diagnosis of psychiatric disorders in North America, including gambling disorder (Petry et al., 2014). Although it is acknowledged that the current and previous versions of the DSM fail to represent an exhaustive list of symptoms of disordered gambling (Gebauer, LaBrie, & Shaffer, 2010), they are nevertheless thought to include symptoms that are sufficiently relevant to provide an accurate diagnosis (Brown et al., 2015). Following initial identification of potential gambling problems via screening instruments, formal diagnosis of a gambling disorder requires meeting four (or more) of the following nine criteria in the DSM-V (APA, 2013, section 312.31) over a 12-month period:

1. Needs to gamble with increasing amounts of money in order to achieve the desired excitement.
2. Is restless or irritable when attempting to cut down or stop gambling.
3. Has made repeated unsuccessful efforts to control, cut back, or stop gambling.
4. Is often preoccupied with gambling (e.g., having persistent thoughts of reliving past gambling experiences, handicapping or planning the next venture, or thinking of ways to get money with which to gamble).
5. Often gambles when feeling distressed (e.g., helpless, guilty, anxious, or depressed).
6. After losing money gambling, often returns another day to get even ("chasing" one's losses).
7. Lies to conceal the extent of involvement with gambling.
8. Has jeopardized or lost a significant relationship, job, or educational or career opportunity because of gambling.
9. Relies on others to provide money to relieve desperate financial situations caused by gambling.

There are also exclusion criteria, such as that these behaviours cannot be better accounted for by a manic episode. Further, diagnosis can involve specification of the course of the disorder—episodic, persistent, or in remission—as well as the severity of the disorder—mild, moderate, or severe.

The DSM-V includes several revisions of the DSM-IV. These include

- a reclassification from Impulse Control Disorders to Substance-Related and Addictive Disorders;
- reduction of the number of criteria needed to be met for diagnosis from five to four;
- elimination of the illegal acts criterion; and
- specification that symptoms occur within a past-year time frame (Brown et al., 2015).

It is important to note that while the illegal acts criterion has been removed, assessment of illegal acts can be achieved under the criterion about lying to others: "these instances of deceit may also include, but are not limited to, covering up illegal behaviors such as forgery, fraud, theft or embezzlement to obtain money with which to gamble (Criterion A7)" (APA, 2013, p. 586).

Adolescent Gambling Behaviour and Problem Gambling

There is a growing body of literature suggesting that gambling remains a popular form of recreation among adolescents. Although most jurisdictions prohibit children and adolescents from accessing government-regulated or government-sponsored gambling activities including lottery draws, instant scratch card play, casino venues, horse or dog racing, EGMs, or Internet wagering, there remains little doubt that vast numbers of adolescents manage to gamble on a variety of unlicensed as well as regulated activities (Derevensky, 2012; Stinchfield, 2011; Volberg et al., 2010).

On an international scale, survey findings and reviews of prevalence studies examining youth gambling behaviour have been remarkably consistent in their findings. Generally, adolescents begin gambling for money informally with family members and peers (Derevensky, 2012; Volberg et al., 2010). As they get older and gain access to other regulated forms of gambling their preferences typically change. The most popular adolescent gambling activities typically include wagering on non-casino card and dice games, playing bingo, participating in sports wagering and sports pools—particularly fantasy sports wagering, which has increased dramatically in the last few years—and betting on the outcomes of games of personal skill including pool, bowling, golf, and even competitions playing video games (Derevensky, 2012; DiCicco-Bloom & Romer, 2012; Stinchfield, 2011; Turner, Macdonald, Bartoshuk, & Zangeneh, 2008; Wickwire, Wheelan, & Meyers, 2010). However, it is important to note that in addition to gambling with family and peers, adolescents have also been shown to participate in other forms of regulated and provincially sanctioned gambling activities (Derevensky, 2012;

DiCicco-Bloom & Romer, 2012). The most common regulated forms of gambling that adolescents participate in are instant scratch card play (Delfabbro, King, & Griffiths, 2014; Felsher, Derevensky, & Gupta, 2004; Stinchfield, 2011; Turner, Macdonald, Bartoshuk, & Zangeneh, 2008). Although some adolescents report participating in other regulated forms of gambling, gambling at casinos, gambling on EGMs, pari-mutuel wagering, and wagering via Internet gambling sites, these are much less frequent or common (Delfabbro, King, & Griffiths, 2014; Stinchfield, 2011; Turner, Macdonald, Bartoshuk, & Zangeneh, 2008; Wickwire, Whelan, & Meyers, 2010). This is primarily because accessibility is clearly age-related. As youth approach the legal age to access certain venues, namely casinos and VLTs, their engagement in these activities increases.

A number of factors have been associated with the incidence of youth gambling. Gambling remains more popular amongst males than females (Abbott, Volberg, Bellringer, & Reith, 2004; Stinchfield, 2011; Volberg et al., 2010). Adolescent males tend to prefer sports wagering whereas adolescent females report more often engaging in lottery purchases (Delfabbro et al., 2014) and bingo (Derevensky, 2012). As well, older adolescents and underage young adults are more likely to engage in electronic gaming machines and casino playing (Abbott, Volberg, Bellringer, & Reith, 2004; Ellenbogen, Gupta, & Derevensky, 2007; National Research Council, 1999; Stinchfield, 2011). There has also been speculation that the availability and accessibility of gambling opportunities in a jurisdiction also gives rise to a greater incidence of gambling among youth. However, few studies have actually explored the significance of availability of gambling opportunities for adolescent gambling involvement. The findings from this small body of research suggest that the relationship between gambling availability and youth gambling is not a straightforward one, and that restrictions on potential opportunities and venues in which to wager, as well as enforcement of legal age limits, likely play an important role (Abdi, Ruiter, & Adal, 2015; Stinchfield, 2011; Welte, Barnes, Tidwell, & Hoffman, 2009b).

Gambling behaviour among youth, like their adult counterparts, can also be conceptualized along a continuum, ranging from non-gambling to social/recreational gambling to problem and disordered gambling. In general, prevalence rates suggest that most adolescents who engage in gambling do so in a responsible manner, by setting and generally maintaining both money and time limits. However, there is a large body of research suggesting that adolescents also constitute a population that is particularly vulnerable to the development of gambling problems, as is the case with substance using youth.

The results of most international prevalence studies, large-scale meta-analyses, and reviews have been remarkably consistent in their conclusion that adolescents, as a group, constitute a high-risk population for gambling problems (Derevensky, 2012; Jacobs, 2004; National Research Council, 1999). Although these figures represent only a general approximation of gambling involvement, estimates of adolescent past-year and lifetime gambling range between 35% and 92%, depending on the year in which the data was collected, methodological differences, the ages of the adolescents surveyed, and the jurisdiction in which the surveys were completed (Temcheff, St-Pierre, & Derevensky, 2013; Volberg et al., 2010). Nevertheless, while most teens can be described as social, recreational, or occasional gamblers, there is ample evidence that between 0.9% and 8.1% of adolescents, internationally, meet diagnostic criteria for disordered gambling (Volberg et al., 2010), with another 8% to 14% at risk for developing or returning to a severe gambling problem (Derevensky, 2012; Jacobs, 2004).

Assessing Adolescent Gambling Problems

Similar to adults, screening instruments represent the first critical step in the assessment for disordered gambling among youth. Presently, there exist four instruments that are commonly used to screen and identify potential adolescent gambling problems:

1. South Oaks Gambling Screen Revised for Adolescents (SOGS-RA; Winters, Stinchfield, & Fulkerson, 1993);
2. DSM-IV-Juvenile (DSM-IV-J; Fisher, 1992) and its revision, the DSM-IV-Multiple Response-Juvenile (DSM-IV-MR-J; Fisher, 2000);
3. Massachusetts Gambling Screen (MAGS; Shaffer, LaBrie, Scanlan, & Cummings, 1994); and
4. Canadian Adolescent Gambling Inventory (CAGI; Tremblay, Stinchfield, Wiebe, & Wynne, 2010).

Of the four, the CAGI alone was not derived and/or adapted from an adult instrument but rather was designed explicitly for adolescents. This is important to note, because the classification system for diagnosing gambling disorder in DSM-V (as well as previous editions of the DSM) have not specifically addressed adolescents. A number of studies of older adolescents also employed the Gamblers Anonymous 20 Questions (GA-20) scale (Blinn-Pike, Worthy, & Jonkman, 2010).

Independent of instrument, a number of constructs are common amongst adolescent problem gambling survey instruments (see Stinchfield, 2010, for a comprehensive discussion and critical review of adolescent problem gambling assessment instruments). These constructs include both psychological factors as well as the negative financial and behavioural costs associated with excessive gambling. Some of the more common constructs examined among these instruments include:

- stealing money to support gambling
- school- and/or employment-related problems
- chasing to recoup gambling losses
- lying or use of deception to conceal the extent of gambling problems
- strained familial relationships
- tolerance or a need to gamble with greater frequency and/or increasing amounts of money

- thinking about or preoccupation with gambling; and
- gambling-related concerns or criticism from others.

With the exception of the CAGI, the underlying concern with these instruments is that they have been adapted from adult screening measures to make them more developmentally appropriate. This practice is considered particularly problematic as youth problem gambling is hypothesized to have different characteristics than adult disordered gambling (Stinchfield, 2010). An additional concern with the adapted screening instruments is that they have little information available regarding their psychometric properties, reliability, validity, and classification accuracy, and they frequently use varying cut-off scores to indicate problem gambling, with cut-off scores being typically lower than those established for their corresponding adult screen (Blinn-Pike, Worthy, & Jonkman, 2010; Derevensky, 2012; Stinchfield, 2010).

These criticisms notwithstanding, a comparison of instruments revealed that the DSM-IV-MR-J remains a more conservative measure (Derevensky, Gupta, & Winters, 2003). The DSM-IV-MR-J has nine criteria, and endorsement of four or more criteria is needed to classify an individual as having potential gambling problems (Fisher, 2000). The scale includes the following questions:

a. In the past year, how often have you found yourself thinking about gambling or planning to gamble?
   ( ) Never ( ) Once or Twice ( ) Sometimes ( ) Often
b. During the course of the past year have you needed to gamble with more and more money to get the amount of excitement you want?
   ( ) Yes ( ) No
c. In the past year have you ever spent *much* more than you planned to on gambling?
   ( ) Never ( ) Once or Twice ( ) Sometimes ( ) Often
d. In the past year have you felt bad or fed up when trying to cut down or stop gambling?
   ( ) Never ( ) Once or Twice ( ) Sometimes ( ) Often ( ) Never tried to cut down
e. In the past year how often have you gambled to help you escape from problems or when you are feeling bad?
   ( ) Never ( ) Once or Twice ( ) Sometimes ( ) Often
f. In the past year, after losing money gambling, have you returned another day to try and win back money you lost?
   ( ) Never ( ) Less than half the time ( ) More than half the time ( ) Every time
g. In the past year has your gambling ever led to lies to your family?
   ( ) Never ( ) Once or Twice ( ) Sometimes ( ) Often
h. In the past year have you ever taken money from the following *without permission* to spend on gambling:
   1. School dinner money or transportation money?
      ( ) Never ( ) Once or Twice ( ) Sometimes ( ) Often

2. Money from your family?
   ( ) Never ( ) Once or Twice ( ) Sometimes ( ) Often
3. Money from outside the family?
   ( ) Never ( ) Once or Twice ( ) Sometimes ( ) Often

i. In the past year has your gambling ever led to
1. Arguments with family/friends or other?
   ( ) Never ( ) Once or Twice ( ) Sometimes ( ) Often
2. Missing school?
   ( ) Never ( ) Once or Twice ( ) Sometimes ( ) Often

In an examination of the DSM-IV-MR-J, Fisher (2000) observed that all of the items were more frequently endorsed by adolescent disordered gamblers than non-disordered gamblers, with the exception of the "chasing losses" item.

Correlates and Risk Factors Associated with Disordered Gambling

A number of correlates and risk factors for adolescent problem gambling have been recognized and reported (Derevensky, 2012; Shead, Derevensky, & Gupta, 2010). It appears that participation in gambling rises steadily as adolescents get older, peaking in young adulthood (Delfabbro, King, & Griffiths, 2014; Stinchfield, 2011; Turner, Macdonald, Bartoshuk, & Zangeneh, 2008; Welte, Barnes, Tidwell, & Hoffman, 2011). There also seems to be a more rapid progression from social or recreational gambling to more problematic gambling among adolescents compared to adults (Derevensky & Gupta, 2004; Gupta & Derevensky, 1998). As well, adolescent problem gamblers generally report initiating gambling at an early age, between 9 and 12, compared to peers who report gambling at a later age but experience fewer gambling-related consequences (Abbott, Volberg, Bellringer, & Reith, 2004; Derevensky & Gupta, 2001; Productivity Commission, 2010; Rahman et al., 2012), and onset of gambling behaviour in pre-adolescence and adolescence is shown to be associated with later development of gambling problems (Vitaro et al., 2004).

Almost universally, prevalence studies reveal that more male than female adolescents engage in gambling and exhibit disordered gambling behaviours (Abbott, Volberg, Bellringer, & Reith, 2004; Derevensky, 2012; Derevensky & Gupta, 2004; Jacobs, 2004; Productivity Commission, 2010; Stinchfield, 2011; Volberg et al., 2010; Welte, Barnes, Tidwell, & Hoffman, 2011). In general, males have been found to make larger gross wagers (Derevensky, Gupta, & Della-Cioppa, 1996), gamble on more diverse activities (Jackson et al., 2008), gamble more frequently (Donati, Chiesi, & Primi, 2013; Welte, Barnes, Tidwell, & Hoffman, 2008), and spend more time and money on gambling than females (Jacobs, 2004). However, there is some recent evidence that indicates girls are starting to engage in Internet wagering in greater numbers (Derevensky &

Gupta, 2007; McBride & Derevensky, 2009), and some focus groups have indicated a rise in adolescent girls engaged in poker playing.

While there is a general paucity of research examining cultural differences, findings suggest that gambling involvement and gambling problems in adolescence may be closely associated with cultural traditions. Stinchfield (2000) and Arndt and Palmer (2013) observed that cultural grouping had a noticeable effect on the weekly gambling involvement of adolescents, with Caucasian and Asian adolescents reporting the lowest rates of gambling involvement compared to other cultural groupings. Additionally, Ellenbogen, Gupta, and Derevensky (2007) reported that adolescents of Allophone origin (i.e., those whose first language is neither English nor French) gamble more and have more gambling-related problems than either adolescents of Anglophone or Francophone origin.

From a psychological perspective, adolescent problem gamblers tend to be more excitable, are greater risk-takers, and have greater difficulty conforming to societal norms, as well as maintaining self-discipline (Gupta, Derevensky, & Ellenbogen, 2006; Nower, Derevensky & Gupta, 2004). Also, similar to adults, impulsivity is acknowledged as an important clinical feature of adolescent problem gambling, as well as a risk factor for early gambling involvement in childhood (Pagani, Derevensky, & Japel, 2009, 2010; Vitaro & Wanner, 2011), and for frequent gambling and gambling problems in later adolescence (Liu et al., 2013; Vitaro, Arseneault, & Tremblay, 1999; Vitaro, Brendgen, Ladouceur, & Tremblay, 2001; Vitaro et al., 2004).

Adolescent problem gamblers have been shown to have greater mental health problems, including depressive or dysphoric symptoms (Hammond et al., 2014; Rahman et al., 2012; Yip et al., 2011), higher levels of anxiety (Ste-Marie, Gupta, & Derevensky, 2002, 2006), and greater suicidal ideations and suicide attempts (Cook et al., 2015; Gupta & Derevensky, 1998; Nower, Gupta, Blaszczynski, & Derevensky, 2004). This is especially true among adolescent girls (Desai, Maciejewski, Pantalon, & Potenza, 2005; Martins, Storr, Ialongo, & Chilcoat, 2008). Further, there is evidence that adolescent gambling problems are associated with externalizing behaviour problems such as conduct disorder and attention deficit/hyperactivity disorder (Barnes, Welte, Hoffman, & Tidwell, 2011; Derevensky, Pratt, Hardoon, & Gupta, 2007; Faregh & Derevensky, 2011; Welte, Barnes, Tidwell, & Hoffman, 2009a), and that externalizing behaviour problems in childhood or early adolescence are a risk factor for the development of later gambling problems (Hayatbakhsh et al., 2006; Martins et al., 2013).

Besides individual characteristics, early exposure to gambling via parental or peer gambling is reported to be associated with youth gambling problems. Specifically, adolescent problem gamblers are more likely to have parents and/or peers that engage in risky and addictive behaviours, including gambling and/or excessive substance use, or parents and/or peers that are problem gamblers themselves (Dickson, Derevensky, & Gupta, 2008; Hardoon, Gupta, & Derevensky, 2004; Vitaro, Wanner, Brendgen, & Tremblay, 2008; Volberg et al., 2010; Wickwire, Whelan, Meyers, & Murray, 2007).

Other studies have also indicated parental gambling and affiliations with peers who engage in high risk behaviours to be additional risk factors for early gambling involvement and later adolescent gambling problems (Scholes-Balog, Hemphill, Dowling, & Toumbourou, 2014; Vachon, Vitaro, Wanner, & Tremblay, 2004; Vitaro, Brendgen, Ladouceur, & Tremblay, 2001; Vitaro & Wanner, 2011; Winters, Stinchfield, Botzet, & Anderson, 2002).

It is widely acknowledged that adolescents with gambling problems experience a range of serious economic, health, psychological, legal, and social problems. Indeed, adolescent gambling problems are found to be associated with greater frequency of play and greater gambling expenditures (Hansen & Rossow, 2008) and youth problem gamblers report consistently chasing their losses, to win back money previously lost (Hardoon, Derevensky, & Gupta, 2001). In addition, gambling problems in adolescents have been shown to be correlated with academic difficulties, poor or disrupted family and peer relationships, risky sexual behaviours, alcohol and substance use problems, and delinquency (Blinn-Pike, Worthy, & Jonkman, 2010; Cook et al., 2015; Derevensky, 2012; Shead, Derevensky, & Gupta, 2010; Volberg et al., 2010). Gambling problems in adolescence are further observed to be associated with criminal behaviour (Wanner, Vitaro, Carbonneau, & Tremblay, 2009) later in early adulthood.

Is Disordered Gambling an Enduring Disorder?

While gambling problems are generally perceived to be progressive and enduring, there is emerging evidence that adolescent gambling behaviour may be transitory, and that gambling problems during adolescence may not persist into adulthood (Delfabbro, King, & Griffiths, 2014; Delfabbro, Winefield, & Anderson, 2009; Winters, Stinchfield, Botzet, & Slutske, 2005). In contrast to traditional conceptualizations of disordered gambling, Nower and Blaszczynski (2003) have hypothesized the existence of a distinct subgroup of episodic binge gamblers. As such, these individuals would display behaviour characterized by a history of intermittent bouts of severe dyscontrol and excessive gambling and these behaviours would be accompanied by intervening and longer periods of abstinence. Binge gamblers have been suggested to experience a rapid escalation of intense uncontrolled gambling binges that consequently results in both short-term and long-term chronic negative consequences. However, these binges are perceived to be time-limited, followed by periods of abrupt cessation after peaking. Preliminary research suggests that most adolescent problem gamblers do not necessarily fit these criteria (Gupta, Derevensky, Shead, & Nower, 2009). However, focus group data with youth who have significant substance and alcohol disorders suggests that their gambling behaviours may fit this pattern, following the lines of binge drinking and binge psychoactive substance abuse (Sklar, Gupta, & Derevensky, 2010).

The Importance of Understanding Cognitive Decision-Making

Why is it that bright, intelligent people believe they can beat the odds associated with games of chance? The gaming industry not only produces highly seductive advertisements for their products, but also tries to foster an illusion of control. For example, within most modern casinos, attached to the roulette wheel there is an electronic board that provides information on the last 16 or so spins of the wheel. Observing players will study the board (data) so as to arrive at some magical mathematical formula enabling them to predict the outcome. If the players observe that the past five or more winning numbers were black, given their knowledge that there is a 50-50 chance of either red or black they are likely to place a bet on red "because it's due." Today's sophisticated roulette tables have video images actually showing the past percentages of red/black wins, "hot numbers," and a wide variety of statistical information for future betting, all useless given that the little white ball cannot remember where it landed previously and has no memory. This notion, referred to as the lack of understanding of the laws of independence of events, is symbolic of some of the erroneous cognitions employed by all gamblers, but in particular problem gamblers. Casinos will often brazenly advertise in bold neon lights that their slot machine payouts are 96%, 97%, or 98%. What they are saying is that, based upon millions of spins, for every dollar you place in the machine you will get less money than inserted. Unfortunately, rubbing one's lucky rabbit foot has not been shown to be a solution to success. To understand games based purely upon chance and randomness, one has to discard previous knowledge and superstitious beliefs.

There is a substantial body of literature examining differences in cognitive processing between individuals with and without gambling disorders. Toneatto (1999), in a review of the cognitive behaviours associated with gambling, has provided a comprehensive compendium of the gambling-related cognitive distortions endorsed by adult disordered gamblers. Such findings relate to the erroneous beliefs, cognitive thinking displaying a lack of utilization of independence of events when making judgments, and an exaggeration of perceived skill involved in gambling. Toneatto contends that these cognitive distortions play an important role in the development and maintenance of gambling problems, in spite of repeated, persistent, and escalating losses. It is suggested that most of these erroneous cognitions perpetuate problem gamblers' irrational beliefs that they can predict the outcome of random events.

As individuals mature, the general manner in which they think, rationalize, and problem solve becomes increasingly sophisticated and differentiated (Derevensky, Gupta, & Della-Cioppa, 1996). Therefore, following Piaget's theory of cognitive development, we can expect that younger children's limited cognitive understanding of abstract concepts such as probability, independence of events, and outcome may predispose them to a greater number of errors in reasoning (Derevensky, Gupta, & Della-Cioppa, 1996). While cognitive maturation is proposed to play a significant role in the gambling decision-making process, there is a dearth of empirical literature that has examined developmental differences in gambling-related cognitions. Nevertheless, available research evidence suggests that younger children's thinking during gambling involvement is actually more "rational" and less prone to cognitive distortions than is older children's and adolescents' reasoning (Derevensky, Gupta, & Della-Cioppa, 1996; Herman, Gupta, & Derevensky, 1998). Further, findings from studies indicate that, similar to adults, adolescent and young adult disordered gamblers tend to be more irrational in their perceptions of gambling, as evidenced by a stronger belief in their ability to predict the outcome and an exaggerated level of skill involved in games of chance (Delfabbro, Lahn, & Grabosky, 2006; Moore & Ohtsuka, 1999; Tang & Wu, 2012; Turner, Macdonald, Bartoshuk, & Zangeneh, 2008).

Situational and Environmental Factors

Is gambling equally problematic across all contexts and situations? Are all gambling activities equally problematic? Social scientists have long recognized the importance of environmental impact upon adolescent behaviour and development (Kulis, Marsiglia, Sicotte, & Nieri, 2007; Leventhal & Brooks-Gunn, 2000). Consequently, researchers have begun to stress the need for greater attention to the environmental context in which gambling behaviour arises and evolves (Blinn-Pike, Worthy, & Jonkman, 2010; Savard, Tremblay, & Turcotte, 2015). This, nevertheless, remains an underexplored area of research in the adolescent gambling field. Preliminary findings with youth (Barnes, Welte, Tidwell, & Hoffman, 2013; Lussier, Derevensky, Gupta, & Vitaro, 2014; Martins, Storr, Lee, & Ialongo, 2013) suggest that higher levels of neighbourhood disadvantage are associated with a greater likelihood of past-year gambling problems. This research also reveals that the association between neighbourhood disadvantage and problem gambling holds even when socio-economic status, race/ethnicity, and accessibility of gambling venues are controlled for (Barnes, Welte, Hoffman, & Tidwell, 2013). Also, given that gambling has been shown to occur on school grounds (Foster et al., 2015) and that disorganized school context has previously been linked with substance use outcomes for adolescents (Mayberry, Espelage, & Koenig, 2009), researchers have begun to examine school contextual issues as a potential risk factor for adolescent gambling problems. In a large-scale study of Maryland high school students, Lee, Martins, Pas, and Bradshaw (2014) observed that student suspension rates and the percentage of African-American students attending school were inversely related to lifetime gambling involvement.

In the last decade, there has been significant "convergence" of gambling activities with digital technology (Griffiths & Parke, 2010; King, Delfabbro, & Griffiths, 2010; King, Delfabbro, Kaptsis, & Zwaans, 2014). Despite continued prohibitions in some jurisdictions such as China, Japan, South Korea, and many American states, the online gambling market represents one of the fastest growing segments of the industry

(Gainsbury, 2015; KPMG International, 2010). Online gambling remains an attractive choice for consumers, given individuals can gamble on a multitude of games easily and conveniently from the comfort of the home or workplace, can place multiple types of wagers, and can engage in gambling privately and in isolation (Gainsbury, 2015; Griffiths & Parke, 2010). Moreover, unlike their land-based counterparts, online gambling websites allow for greater experimentation with small bets, as well as offer "practice" or "free play" modes where gamblers engage in a variety of games of chance without having to spend actual money (Derevensky, Gainsbury, Gupta, & Ellery, 2013; Gainsbury et al., 2013). Not surprisingly, there is growing empirical evidence to suggest that underage adolescents are gambling online at higher rates than adults (Gainsbury, 2012, 2015). Research findings also reveal a possible relationship between Internet gambling and problem gambling severity among adolescents, with adolescent Internet gamblers more likely to be identified as problem gamblers than non-Internet gamblers (Brunelle et al., 2012; McBride & Derevensky, 2009; Olason et al., 2011; Wong & So, 2014). Further, there appears to be a trend towards greater youth involvement in Internet gambling, with the increased availability of online gambling opportunities over the past decade (Gainsbury, 2012, 2015). Olason and colleagues (2011) observed that the prevalence of adolescent Internet gambling had increased from 2% to 20% between 2003/2004 and 2006, and rose again to 24% in 2007/2008. There is great concern that age prohibitions set by corporations or governments have not been followed (Derevensky, 2012).

A less recognized area of concern relates to simulated forms of gambling via social media games for virtual currency, in spite of the lack of possibility of monetary reward (King et al., 2010). Simulated gambling includes any digitally interactive gambling activity simulation that does not result in monetary gain but is otherwise structurally identical to the standard format of gambling activity, due to its wagering features and chance-determined outcomes of play (King, Delfabbro, Kaptsis, & Zwaans, 2014). These include "free play" and "demo" games using virtual credits, as used by *DoubleDown Casino*, *Slotomania*, and *Zynga Poker*, as well as hybrid video game/gambling activities with monetization features including *World of Warcraft*, *RuneScape*, and *Red Dead Redemption* (Griffiths, King, & Delfabbro, 2012; Griffiths & Parke, 2010). Whether individuals playing such games will view their behaviour as normalized and migrate to actual online gambling is a real concern (Derevensky, 2012). There appears to be growing popularity for simulated gambling among adolescents, with 25–50% of teens reporting having played "free play" or "demo" modes of online gambling websites (Griffiths, Derevensky, & Parke, 2012; Griffiths & Parke, 2010). Additionally, King, Delfabbro, Kaptsis, and Zwaans (2014) reported that while one quarter of adolescents reported having engaged in simulated video game gambling features, another 9.6% indicated having participated in simulated gambling via Facebook apps, and 6.3% engaged in simulated gambling via smartphone apps. Of particular interest, King and his colleagues suggested that a history of involvement in all types of simulated gambling was significantly more prevalent among adolescent problem gamblers than non-problem gamblers. While these simulated gambling activity modes cannot technically be considered gambling given the absence of monetary reward, adolescents have reported using them to "learn to manage risk, to improve their skills at gambling, and enhance their confidence about gambling for real money" (Meerkamper, 2010). Such simulated gambling games potentially provide adolescents with unrestricted access to realistic gambling and gambling-like experiences, since these games typically have no age restrictions or age verification procedures, and may represent a gateway for teens towards online gambling for actual money.

Gambling as a Form of Psychological Coping and Escape

As previously noted, individuals with gambling problems are reported to have a wide range of concomitant psychological, emotional, behavioural, employment/academic, personal, and interpersonal problems. These individuals have also been shown to exhibit limited or maladaptive general coping skills (Abbott, Volberg, Bellringer, & Reith, 2004). It has been suggested that this maladaptive coping may be a mediating factor for disordered behaviour (Bergevin, Derevensky, Gupta, & Kaufman, 2006; Gupta, Derevensky, & Marget, 2004). As a result, when faced with adversity or daily problems, disordered gamblers use their gambling as a form of psychological escape for unlike an addiction there is no biological component. When gambling, individuals frequently report going into a dissociative state, an escape from reality highlighted by losing track of time and forgetting about responsibilities and commitments. According to Jacobs (2004), fostering a dissociative state enables the gambler to forget, albeit for a short period, their problems in the same way psychoactive drugs allow users to escape temporarily from reality, though in the case of drugs, both biologically and psychologically. A recent finding pertaining to post-secondary students found that many of these young adults are engaged in Internet wagering as a form of escape from boredom (McBride & Derevensky, 2009).

Treating Disordered Gamblers

Given that there is no single identifiable cause for adolescent gambling problems, there too is no single therapeutic approach that universally works for helping all adolescents. The treatment paradigms currently being employed for adults as well as adolescents are varied and have generally been predicated upon diverse theoretical approaches and models. These approaches and models include (Brown et al., 2015; Carlton & Goldstein, 1987; Comings, 1998; DeCaria, Hollander, & Wong, 1997; Lesieur & Blume, 1991; McCormick & Taber, 1988; Rosenthal, 1987; Rugle & Rosenthal, 1994; Saiz, 1992; Yakovenko & Hodgins, 2014):

- psychoanalytic or psychodynamic
- behavioural
- cognitive and cognitive-behavioural
- pharmacological, with and without concurrent traditional forms of therapy
- brief treatments
- self-help programs
- motivational interviewing
- family
- physiological
- biological/genetic
- addiction-based models.

The lack of empirically sound scientific studies examining the long-term efficacy of each of these approaches has resulted in a failure to establish Best Practices or Empirically Validated Treatment (EVT) approaches for treating both adolescents and adults with gambling problems (Nathan, 2005; Toneatto & Ladouceur, 2003; Toneatto & Millar, 2004). Whether or not all individuals with gambling problems should be treated as a homogeneous group has also been seriously questioned (Blaszczynski & Nower, 2002, Gupta & Derevensky, 2004; Nower & Blaszczynski, 2003). Further, questions still remain about the efficacy of specific treatment models, the role of natural recovery, and whether certain individuals experiencing gambling problems require complete abstinence from gambling or whether controlled gambling—maintaining pre-established time and money limits—is a viable option.

There is ample evidence suggesting that gambling behaviour involves a complex and dynamic interaction between ecological, psychophysiological, developmental, cognitive, and behavioural components. As well, there is a growing body of new evidence and acceptance suggesting that problem gamblers, like substance abusers, are not a homogeneous group, but rather come with distinct behavioural, personal, and social difficulties. Given these assumptions, in the absence of empirically validated treatment programs, Gupta and Derevensky (2008) argued for a dynamic interactive approach assuming a multiplicity of interacting factors that need to be addressed and accounted for in any treatment paradigm for individuals experiencing significant gambling problems. Other factors that need to be considered in developing a treatment program include the type of game the individual engages in, which means that machine players require different treatment strategies than sports gamblers; gender, with males requiring different interventions than females; self-help (Gamblers Anonymous) versus professional therapy; and group versus individual treatment. As well, to make matters more complicated, we know that disordered gamblers exhibit evidence of abnormal physiological resting states, report significantly greater emotional distress and anxiety, display depressive symptomatology, and are more likely to have higher rates of comorbidity with other substances and other mental health problems (Kimberley & Osmond, 2010). While alternative and customized approaches may be required, we strongly contend that while treating gambling problems in isolation of other presenting social, physiological, developmental, cognitive, emotional, and mental health difficulties may lead to limited short-term success, this ultimately increases the risk for relapse. Derevensky (2012) has strongly argued for the necessity to address those underlying problems concomitant with the gambling problems.

Work by Hodgins and his colleagues (Hodgins, 2005; Hodgins & el-Guebaly, 2000; Hodgins, Currie, & el-Guebaly, 2001) have argued that Prochaska and DiClemente's (1982) transtheoretical model may be a useful framework in helping to understand treatment and natural recovery of disordered gamblers. Another approach focuses upon the use of short-term brief motivational enhancement therapy and telephone counselling, with and without manuals. The results of Hodgins and his colleagues suggest that brief telephone counselling and the use of a home-based manual may be an effective approach, especially for individuals with less severe and persistent gambling problems (Hodgins, 2005; Hodgins & el-Guebaly, 2000).

A pilot project by McGill's International Centre for Youth Gambling Problems and High-Risk Behaviors suggests that a web-based interactive chat line (www.gamtalk4teens.org and www.gamtalk.org) may be an effective tool for reaching adolescents unable or initially not willing to seek professional assistance. This real-time chat line, staffed by graduate students and monitored by supervising psychologists, operated daily for a one-year period for four hours per evening allowing youth to discuss pertinent issues via interactive software similar to MSN messenger. While not empirically evaluated, with follow-ups limited to user self-reports, those adolescents and young adults participating reported very much appreciating the service provided. A similar model for adults was implemented and is continuing in the United Kingdom after receiving a positive evaluation. The use of chat lines, telephone counselling, and self-guided manuals that can be completed remotely, while not ideal, may represent an important innovative and promising approach to helping individuals with gambling problems by reducing some of the traditional barriers to seeking treatment.

The field of psychopharmacology and pharmacotherapy may further provide a promising complementary strategy for working with individuals experiencing significant gambling problems. Current pharmacological treatment approaches to disordered gambling suggest the use of selective serotonin reputake inhibitor (SSRI) antidepressants, mood stabilizers, and opioid antagonists (Brown et al., 2015; Grant, Kim, & Potenza, 2003). The data reveal that opioid antagonists show the most promise in treating the symptoms associated with gambling disorder (Brown et al., 2015; Grant, Odlaug, & Schreiber, 2014; van den Brink, 2012; Yip & Potenza, 2014). Available research also suggests positive short-term effects of other pharmacological treatments, although many of these studies have methodological challenges and the results, while promising, are not yet conclusive (Achab & Khazal, 2011; Blanco, Petkova, Ibáñez, & Sáiz-Ruiz, 2002; Grant, Chambers, & Potenza, 2004; Hollander et al., 2005). Nevertheless, there are important cautions. Some medication currently used to treat patients with Parkinson's disease have been reported to stimulate urges to gamble, with a number of individuals developing significant gambling problems.

Abbott, Volberg, Bellringer, and Reith (2004), in their review of treatment outcome studies, concluded that there is sufficient evidence suggesting that individuals who have received treatment for a wide variety of mental health disorders, including addiction and disordered gambling, generally do better than individuals not receiving any treatment. They concluded that irrespective of the particular type of therapy, most clients who show initial improvement maintain either abstinence or controlled gambling, albeit the probability of relapse increases with time.

Currently, the numbers of individuals seeking help for gambling problems remain minute compared to the prevalence estimates of disordered gamblers, which is approximately 10% of the adult population. Some have argued that this may be related to the lack of available specialist treatment providers or gambling-specific treatment centres, and in the United States a lack of insurance companies accepting treatment for disordered gambling under traditional health policies (Gainsbury, Hing, & Suhonen, 2014; Mee-Lee, 2015; Pulford et al., 2009). However, even in jurisdictions and countries where treatment is provided without cost to the individual, such as Canada, the number of individuals seeking help remains small. In addition to service-level barriers, other psychological barriers to treatment have been consistently identified in the literature. These include the desire or motivation to make a change oneself; feelings of shame, embarrassment, pride, and/or fear of stigma; and a reluctance to admit the existence or magnitude of the problem (Gainsbury, Hing, & Suhonen, 2014; Pulford et al., 2009; Suurvali, Cordingly, Hodgins, & Cunningham, 2009; Suurvali, Hodgins, Toneatto, & Cunningham, 2012). As such, new techniques of outreach have been employed, including having counsellors available in casinos, enhanced self-exclusion programs, greater commercial advertising of available services, and public service announcements.

Industry Initiatives

Other approaches to minimize the potential harms are being tried. Smart card technology and player protection keys incorporating biometric identity solutions are being used to prevent underage gambling from occurring and allowing player pre-commitment loss and duration limits to be established outside the gambling venue. Some of these new innovations also have the capability to restrict Internet gambling, while software is also being used to block access to Internet wagering sites. Evidence suggests using smart card technology may be a promising approach for limiting play for individuals with gambling problems (Schrans, Schellinck, & Walsh, 2000). However, a large-scale implementation of this project was viewed as a dismal failure, with the Australian government removing this smart card technology as patrons refused to use their cards. There are also some promising findings regarding the effectiveness of responsible gambling "bank" features, which prevent winnings from being re-gambled by depositing them into a quarantined credit meter that can be collected only upon termination of a gambling session (Blaszczynski, Gainsbury, & Karlov, 2014).

From the gambling industry's perspective, most land-based casinos have now instituted self-exclusion programs enabling individuals to place themselves on lists prohibiting their entry into casinos, though implementation remains an issue. Some jurisdictions, because of government regulations, notably in Singapore, has third-party exclusion where a spouse, parent, or even possibly a teenager may request that a family member be barred from gambling at the casino because of a gambling problem. Other casinos provide huge impediments to local residents, attempting to focus their revenue generation on tourists, thus keeping social costs down or at least limiting the amounts that local citizens can gamble in a given time period.

Concluding Remarks

Disordered gambling is a serious, and often neglected, public health issue and concern. Balancing the revenues and benefits of regulated gambling against the social costs is raising issues about its expansion. More research into better understanding the dynamics, risks and protective factors, and the efficacy of alternative treatment models for adult and youth problem gamblers is still necessary before any definitive best practices can be empirically established. However, some existing treatment models hold great promise for helping individuals with gambling problems, given the significant comorbidity of other addictive and disordered behaviours and the overlap in risk factors.

Research into disordered gambling among adolescents and adults is comparatively new. As a result, there remain significant gaps in our knowledge. The landscape of gambling is continually changing, with technological changes leading the way. As provincial governments become more dependent upon the revenues being generated, few are likely to restrict or curtail their gambling operations. On the contrary, they are more likely to expand gambling options and opportunities. On the horizon is likely full online and remote wagering. Merely 10 years ago few individuals would have predicted the unprecedented growth of Internet wagering, poker playing, and mobile gambling. Legalized single-sports wagering in Canada is on the horizon, with fantasy sports wagering gaining momentum. The reality is that more and more governments view this as a lucrative source of revenue generation and employment. The fact that most Canadians view gambling as a socially acceptable form of entertainment, in spite of acknowledging its risks, will likely result in increased availability. While our provincial governments have generously contributed to research, treatment, and to a lesser degree prevention of gambling problems, greater accessibility in combination with more potentially risky games may possibly result in more problems. Today's youth will spend their entire lives in a society where gambling is not only legal but provincially endorsed, supported, and owned, and where they are actively encouraged to participate.

It has been argued that many other more highly visible adolescent mental health problems, like cigarette smoking, alcohol consumption, substance abuse, increased rates of suicide, risky sexual behaviour, and suicidal behaviours have prompted social policy interventions (Messerlian, Derevensky, & Gupta, 2004). Problem gambling is just now getting on the radar screen of legislators and the public. While the prevalence rates are relatively small, it is nevertheless important to note that each problem gambler directly negatively impacts 7 to 10 significant others. The economic, legal, mental health, and personal fallout resulting from gambling problems negatively impacts individuals and their family, friends, and society (Petry, Blanco, Stinchfield, & Volberg, 2013; Temcheff, St-Pierre, & Derevensky, 2013). Given that it takes several years to go from the onset of gambling and occasional/recreational gambling to a significant gambling problem, its true social impact and long-term consequences will likely take years to realize and be a challenge for mental health professionals in upcoming decades.

REFERENCES

Abbott, M., Volberg, R., Bellringer, M., & Reith, G. (2004). *A review of research on aspects of problem gambling*. Report prepared for the Responsibility in Gambling Trust, United Kingdom.

Abdi, T.A., Ruiter, R.A., & Adal, T.A. (2015). Personal, social and environmental risk factors of problematic gambling among high school adolescents in Addis Ababa, Ethiopia. *Journal of Gambling Studies, 31*(1), 59-72.

Achab, S., & Khazaal, Y. (2011). Psychopharmacological treatment in pathological gambling: A critical review. *Current Pharmaceutical Design, 17*(14), 1389-1395.

Alberta Gaming Research Institute (2015). *Canada casinos*. Retrieved from http://abgamblinginstitute.ca/resources/reference-sources/canada-casinos

American Gaming Association. (2014). *Get to know gaming*. Retrieved from http://www.gettoknowgaming.org/stats-and-facts#national

American Psychiatric Association. (2013). *Diagnostic and statistical manual of mental disorders* (5th ed.). Washington, DC: American Psychiatric Publishing.

Arndt, S., & Palmer, J. (2013). *Iowa youth gambling using the 2012 Iowa Youth Survey: Who, what, where and what else?* Iowa City, IA: Iowa Consortium for Substance Abuse Research and Evaluation.

Barnes, G.M., Welte, J.W., Hoffman, J.H., & Tidwell, M.-C.O. (2011). The co-occurrence of gambling with substance use and conduct disorder among youth in the United States. *The American Journal on Addictions, 20*(2), 166-173.

Barnes, G., Welte, J., Tidwell, M.C., & Hoffman, J. (2013). Effects of neighborhood disadvantage on problem gambling and alcohol abuse. *Journal of Behavioral Addictions, 2*(2), 82-89.

Barry, D., Steinberg, M., Wu, R., & Potenza, M. (2008). Characteristics of black and white callers to a gambling helpline. *Psychiatric Services, 59*(11), 1347-1350.

Bergevin, T., Derevensky, J., Gupta, R., & Kaufman, F. (2006). Adolescent gambling: Understanding the role of stress and coping. *Journal of Gambling Studies, 22*(2), 195-208.

Blanco, C., Petkova, E., Ibáñez, A., & Sáiz-Ruiz, J. (2002). A pilot placebo-controlled study of fluvoxamine for pathological gambling. *Annals of Clinical Psychiatry, 14*(1), 9-15.

Blaszczynski, A., Gainsbury, S., & Karlov, L. (2014). Blue Gum gaming machine: An evaluation of responsible gambling features. *Journal of Gambling Studies, 30*(3), 697-712.

Blaszczynski, A., & Nower, L. (2002). A pathways model of problem gambling and pathological gambling. *Addiction, 97*(5), 487–499.

Blinn-Pike, L., Worthy, S.L., & Jonkman, J. (2010). Adolescent gambling: A review of an emerging field of research. *Journal of Adolescent Health, 47*(3), 223–236.

Brown, J., Stinchfield, R., Hesse, M.L., Krasowski, M.D., Harris, B., Von Eschen, J., … Burger, P. (2015). Problem gambling: A beginner's guide for clinical and forensic professionals. *Behavioural Health, 2*(2). Retrieved from http://jghcs.info/index.php/bh/article/view/398

Brunelle, N., Leclerc, D., Cousineau, M.M., Dufour, M., Gendron, A., & Martin, I. (2012). Internet gambling, substance use, and delinquent behavior: An adolescent deviant behavior involvement pattern. *Psychology of Addictive Behaviors, 26*(2), 364–370.

Campbell, C.S., Hartnagel, T.F., & Smith, G.J. (2005). *The legalization of gambling in Canada.* Ottawa, ON: Law Commission of Canada.

Carlton, P., & Goldstein L. (1987). Physiological determinants of pathological gambling. In Y. Galski (Ed.), *The handbook of pathological gambling* (pp. 111–135). Springfield, IL: Charles C. Thomas.

Comings, D. (1998). *The genetics of pathological gambling: The addictive effect of multiple genes.* Presented at the 12th National Conference on Problem Gambling, June, Las Vegas.

Cook, S., Turner, N.E., Ballon, B., Paglia-Boak, A., Murray, R., Adlaf, E.M., … Mann, R.E. (2015). Problem gambling among Ontario students: Associations with substance abuse, mental health problems, suicide attempts, and delinquent behaviours. *Journal of Gambling Studies, 31*(4), 1121–1134.

DeCaria, C., Hollander, E., & Wong, C. (1997). *Neuropsychiatric functioning in pathological gamblers.* Paper presented at the 11th National Conference on Problem Gambling, August, New Orleans.

Delfabbro, P., King, D., & Griffiths, M.D. (2014). From adolescent to adult gambling: An analysis of longitudinal gambling patterns in South Australia. *Journal of Gambling Studies, 30*(3), 547–563.

Delfabbro, P., Lahn, J., & Grabosky, P. (2006). It's not what you know, but how you use it: Statistical knowledge and adolescent problem gambling. *Journal of Gambling Studies, 22*(2), 179–193.

Delfabbro, P., Winefield, A., & Anderson, S. (2009). Once a gambler–always a gambler? A longitudinal analysis of gambling patterns in young people making the transition from adolescence to adulthood. *International Gambling Studies, 9*(2), 151–163.

Derevensky, J.L. (2012). *Teen gambling: Understanding a growing epidemic.* Lanham, MD: Rowman & Littlefield Publishers.

Derevensky, J.L., Gainsbury, S., Gupta, R., & Ellery, M. (2013). *Play-for-fun/social-casino gambling: An examination of our current knowledge.* Winnipeg, MB: Manitoba Gambling Research Program.

Derevensky, J., & Gupta, R. (2001). Le probleme de jeu touche aussi les jeunes. *Psychologie Quebec, 18*(6), 23–27.

Derevensky, J.L., & Gupta, R. (Eds.) (2004). *Gambling problems in youth: Theoretical and applied perspectives.* New York: Kluwer Academic/Plenum Publishers.

Derevensky, J., & Gupta, R. (2007). Internet gambling amongst adolescents: A growing concern. *International Journal of Mental Health and Addictions, 5*(2), 93–101.

Derevensky, J., Gupta., R., & Della-Cioppa, G. (1996). A developmental perspective of gambling behaviour in children and adolescents. *Journal of Gambling Studies, 12*(1), 49–66.

Derevensky, J., Gupta, R., & Winters, K. (2003). Prevalence rates of youth gambling problems: Are the current rates inflated? *Journal of Gambling Studies, 19*(4), 405–425.

Derevensky, J.L., Pratt, L.M., Hardoon, K.K., & Gupta, R. (2007). Gambling problems and features of Attention Deficit Hyperactivity Disorder among children and adolescents. *Journal of Addiction Medicine, 1*(3), 165–172.

Desai, R.A., Maciejewski, P.K., Pantalon, M.V., & Potenza, M.N. (2005). Gender differences in adolescent gambling. *Annals of Clinical Psychiatry, 17*(4), 249–258.

DiCicco-Bloom, B., & Romer, D. (2012). Poker, sports betting, and less popular alternatives: Status, friendship networks, and male adolescent gambling. *Youth & Society, 44,* 141–170.

Dickson, L., Derevensky, J.L., & Gupta, R. (2008). Youth gambling problems: Examining risk and protective factors. *International Gambling Studies, 8*(1), 25–47.

Donati, M.A., Chiesi, F., & Primi, C. (2013). A model to explain at-risk/problem gambling among male and female adolescents: Gender similarities and differences. *Journal of Adolescence, 36*(1), 129–137.

Dowling, N.A., Cowlishaw, S., Jackson, A.C., Merkouris, S.S., Francis, K.L., & Christensen, D.R. (2015). The prevalence of comorbid personality disorders in treatment-seeking problem gamblers: A systematic review and meta-analysis. *Journal of Personality Disorders, 29*(6), 735–754.

Ellenbogen, S., Gupta, R., & Derevensky, J. (2007). A cross-cultural study of gambling behavior among adolescents. *Journal of Gambling Studies, 23*(1), 25–39.

European Casino Association, Gambling Compliance Research Services, & Herzfeld Consulting. (2014). *ECA's European casino industry report.* Retrieved from http://www.europeancasinoassociation.org/fileadmin/user_upload/Home_About_ECA/ECA_2014_European_Casino_Report.pdf

Faregh, N., & Derevensky, J. (2011). Gambling behavior among adolescents with Attention Deficit/Hyperactivity Disorder. *Journal of Gambling Studies, 27*(2), 243–256.

Felsher, J., Derevensky, J., & Gupta, R. (2004). Lottery participation by youth with gambling problems: Are lottery tickets a gateway to other gambling venues? *International Gambling Studies, 4*(2), 109–126.

Fisher, S. (1992). Measuring pathological gambling in children: The case of fruit machines in the U.K. *Journal of Gambling Studies, 8*(3), 263–285.

Fisher, S. (2000). Developing the DSM-IV criteria to identify adolescent problem gambling in non-clinical populations. *Journal of Gambling Studies, 16*(2–3), 253–273.

Foster, D.W., Hoff, R.A., Pilver, C.E., Yau, Y.H., Steinberg, M.A., Wampler, J., ... Potenza, M.N. (2015). Correlates of gambling on high-school grounds. *Addictive Behaviors, 56,* 57–64.

Gainsbury, S. (2012). *Internet gambling: Current research findings and implications.* New York: Springer.

Gainsbury, S.M. (2015). Online gambling addiction: The relationship between Internet gambling and disordered gambling. *Current Addiction Reports, 2*(2), 185–193.

Gainsbury, S., Hing, N., & Suhonen, N. (2014). Professional help-seeking for gambling problems: Awareness, barriers and motivators for treatment. *Journal of Gambling Studies, 30*(2), 503–519.

Gainsbury, S.M., Russell, A., Hing, N., Wood, R., & Blaszczynski, A. (2013). The impact of Internet gambling on gambling problems: A comparison of moderate-risk and problem Internet and non-Internet gamblers. *Psychology of Addictive Behaviors, 27*(4), 1092–1101.

Gebauer, L., LaBrie, R., & Shaffer, H.J. (2010). Optimizing DSM-IV-TR classification accuracy: A brief biosocial screen for detecting current gambling disorders among gamblers in the general household population. *The Canadian Journal of Psychiatry/La revue canadienne de psychiatrie, 55*(2), 82–90.

Grant, J.E., Chambers, R.A., & Potenza, M. (2004). Adolescent problem gambling: Neurodevelopment and pharmacological treatment. In J. Derevensky & R. Gupta (Eds.), *Gambling problems in youth: Theoretical and applied perspectives* (pp. 81–98). New York: Kluwer Academic/Plenum Publishers.

Grant, J.E., Kim, S.W., & Potenza, M.N. (2003). Advances in the pharmacological treatment of pathological gambling. *Journal of Gambling Studies, 19*(1), 85–109.

Grant, J.E., Odlaug, B.L., & Schreiber, L. (2014). Pharmacological treatments in pathological gambling. *British Journal of Clinical Pharmacology, 77*(2), 375–381.

Griffiths, M., Derevensky, J., & Parke, J. (2012). Online gambling among youth: Cause for concern? In R. Williams, R. Wood, & J. Parke (Eds.), *Routledge international handbook of Internet gambling* (pp. 125–143). New York: Rutledge.

Griffiths, M.D., King, D.L., & Delfabbro, P.H. (2012). Simulated gambling in video gaming: What are the implications for adolescents? *Education and Health, 30*(3), 68–70.

Griffiths, M.D., & Parke, J. (2010). Adolescent gambling on the Internet: A review. *International Journal of Adolescent Medicine and Health, 22*(1), 59–75.

Gupta, R., & Derevensky, J.L. (1998). Adolescent gambling behavior: A prevalence study and examination of the correlates associated with problem gambling. *Journal of Gambling Studies, 14*(4), 319–345.

Gupta, R., & Derevensky, J.L. (2004). A treatment approach for adolescents with gambling problems. In J. Derevensky & R. Gupta (Eds.), *Gambling problems in youth: Theoretical and applied perspectives* (pp. 165–188). New York: Kluwer Academic/Plenum Publishers.

Gupta, R., & Derevensky, J. (2008). Gambling practices among youth: Etiology, prevention and treatment. In C.A. Essau (Ed.), *Adolescent addiction: Epidemiology, assessment and treatment* (pp. 207–230). London, UK: Elsevier.

Gupta R., Derevensky J.L., & Ellenbogen S. (2006). Personality characteristics and risk-taking tendencies among adolescent gamblers. *Canadian Journal of Behaviour Science, 38*(3), 201–213.

Gupta, R., Derevensky, J., & Marget, N. (2004). Coping strategies employed by adolescents with gambling problems. *Child and Adolescent Mental Health, 9*(3), 115–120.

Gupta, R., Derevensky, J., Shead, N.W., & Nower, L. (2009). *Bingeing behaviour in youth: An exploratory study of gambling patterns.* Guelph, ON: Ontario Problem Gambling Research Centre.

Hammond, C., Pilver, C., Rugle, L., Steinberg, M., Mayes, L., Malison, R., … Potenza, M. (2014). An exploratory examination of marijuana use, problem-gambling severity, and health correlates among adolescents. *Journal of Behavioral Addictions, 3*(2), 90–101.

Hansen, M., & Rossow, I. (2008). Adolescent gambling and problem gambling: Does the total consumption model apply? *Journal of Gambling Studies, 24*(2), 135–149.

Hardoon, K., Derevensky, J., & Gupta, R. (2001). Social influences involved in children's gambling behavior. *Journal of Gambling Studies, 17*(3), 191–215.

Hardoon, K.K., Gupta, R., & Derevensky, J.L. (2004). Psychosocial variables associated with adolescent gambling. *Psychology of Addictive Behaviors, 18*(2), 170–179.

Hargreave, C., & Csiernik, R. (2003). An examination of gambling and problem gambling in Canada. In R. Csiernik & W.S. Rowe (Eds.), *Responding to the oppression of addiction* (1st ed., pp. 313–333). Toronto, ON: Canadian Scholars' Press.

Hayatbakhsh, M.R., Najman, J.M., Aird, R., Bor, W., O'Callaghan, M., Williams, G., … Heron, M. (2006). *Early life course determinants of young adults' gambling behaviour.* Brisbane, Australia: University of Queensland.

Herman, J., Gupta, R., & Derevensky, J.L. (1998). Children's cognitive perceptions of 6/49 lottery tickets. *Journal of Gambling Studies, 14*(3), 227–244.

Hodgins, D. (2005). Implications of a brief intervention trial for problem gambling for future outcome research. *Journal of Gambling Studies, 21*(1), 13–19.

Hodgins, D.C., Currie, S.R., & el-Guebaly, N. (2001). Motivational enhancement and self-help treatments for problem gambling. *Journal of Consulting and Clinical Psychology, 69*(1), 50–57.

Hodgins, D.C., & el-Guebaly, N. (2000). Natural and treatment-assisted recovery from gambling problems: A comparison of resolved and active gamblers. *Addiction, 95*(5), 777–789.

Hollander, E., Sood, E., Pallanti, S., Baldini-Rossi, N., & Baker, B. (2005). Pharmacological treatments of pathological gamblers. *Journal of Gambling Studies, 21*(1), 101–110.

Humphreys, B.R., & Marchand, J. (2013). New casinos and local labor markets: Evidence from Canada. *Labour Economics, 24,* 151–160.

Jackson, A., Dowling, N., Thomas, S., Bond, L., & Patton, G. (2008). Adolescent gambling behaviour and attitudes: A prevalence study and correlates in an Australian population. *International Journal of Mental Health and Addiction, 6*(3), 325–352.

Jacobs, D.F. (2004). Youth gambling in North America: Long-term trends and future prospects. In J.L. Derevensky & R. Gupta (Eds.), *Gambling problems in youth: Theoretical and applied perspectives* (pp. 1–24). New York: Klewer Academic/Plenum Publishers.

Kimberly, M., & Osmond, M. (2010). Concurrent disorders and social work intervention. In R. Csiernik & W.S. Rowe (Eds.), *Responding to the oppression of addiction: Canadian social work perspectives* (2nd ed., pp. 274–293). Toronto, ON: Canadian Scholars' Press.

King, D., Delfabbro, P., & Griffiths, M. (2010). The convergence of gambling and digital media: Implications for gambling in young people. *Journal of Gambling Studies, 26*(2), 175–187.

King, D.L., Delfabbro, P.H., Kaptsis, D., & Zwaans, T. (2014). Adolescent simulated gambling via digital and social media: An emerging problem. *Computers in Human Behavior, 31,* 305–313.

KPMG International. (2010). *Online gaming: A gamble or a sure bet?* Zurich, Switzerland: KPMG International.

Kulis, S., Marsiglia, F.F., Sicotte, D., & Nieri, T. (2007). Neighborhood effects on youth substance use in a southwestern city. *Sociological Perspectives, 50*(2), 273–301.

Lee, G.P., Martins, S.S., Pas, E.T., & Bradshaw, C.P. (2014). Examining potential school contextual influences on gambling among high school youth. *American Journal on Addictions, 23*(5), 510–517.

Lesieur, H.R., & Blume, S.B. (1991). Evaluation of patients treated for pathological gambling in a combined alcohol, substance abuse, and pathological gambling treatment unit using the Addiction Severity Index. *British Journal of Addictions, 86*(8), 1017–1028.

Leventhal, T., & Brooks-Gunn, J. (2000). The neighborhoods they live in: The effects of neighborhood residence on child and adolescent outcomes. *Psychological Bulletin, 126*(2), 309–337.

Liu, M., Chang, T.T.G., Loi, E.H., & Chan, A.C.H. (2015). Macau gambling industry: Current challenges and opportunities next decade. *Asia Pacific Journal of Marketing and Logistics, 27*(2), 499–512.

Liu, W., Lee, G.P., Goldweber, A., Petras, H., Storr, C.L., Ialongo, N.S., & Martins, S.S. (2013). Impulsivity trajectories and gambling in adolescence among urban male youth. *Addiction, 108*(4), 780–788.

Lorains, F.K., Cowlishaw, S., & Thomas, S.A. (2011). Prevalence of comorbid disorders in problem and pathological gambling: Systematic review and meta-analysis of population surveys. *Addiction, 106*(3), 490–498.

Lussier, I.D., Derevensky, J., Gupta, R., & Vitaro, F. (2014). Risk, compensatory, protective, and vulnerability factors related to youth gambling problems. *Psychology of Addictive Behaviors, 28*(2), 404–413.

Martins, S.S., Liu, W., Hedden, S.L., Goldweber, A., Storr, C.L., Derevensky, J.L., ... Petras, H. (2013). Youth aggressive/disruptive behavior trajectories and subsequent gambling among urban male youth. *Journal of Clinical Child & Adolescent Psychology, 42*(5), 657–668.

Martins, S.S., Storr, C.L., Ialongo, N.S., & Chilcoat, H.D. (2008). Gender differences in mental health characteristics and gambling among African-American adolescent gamblers. *American Journal on Addictions, 17*(2), 126–134.

Martins, S.S., Storr, C.L., Lee, G.P., & Ialongo, N.S. (2013). Environmental influences associated with gambling in young adulthood. *Journal of Urban Health, 90*(1), 130–140.

Mayberry, M.L., Espelage, D.L., & Koenig, B. (2009). Multilevel modeling of direct effects and interactions of peers, parents, school, and community influences on adolescent substance use. *Journal of Youth and Adolescence, 38*(8), 1038-1049.

McBride, J., & Derevensky, J. (2009). Internet gambling behaviour in a sample of online gamblers. *International Journal of Mental Health and Addiction, 7*, 149-167.

McCormick, R.A., & Taber, J.I. (1988). Attributional style in pathological gamblers in treatment. *Journal of Abnormal Psychology, 97*(3), 368-370.

Mee-Lee, D. (2015). Getting real about gambling disorder: How the ASAM criteria can help. Presented at the 29th National Conference on Problem Gambling, July, Baltimore, MD.

Meerkamper, E. (2010). Youth gambling 2.0: Decoding the rapidly changing world of youth gambling. In *Annual Nova Scotia Gambling Conference, Halifax.*

Messerlian, C., Derevensky, J., & Gupta, R. (2004). A public health perspective for youth gambling. *International Gambling Studies, 4*(2), 147-160.

Moore, S.M., & Ohtsuka, K. (1999). Beliefs about control over gambling among young people, and their relation to problem gambling. *Psychology of Addictive Behaviors, 13*(4), 339-347.

Nathan, P.E. (2005). Commentary, special issue, Journal of Gambling Studies. *Journal of Gambling Studies, 21*(3), 355-360.

National Research Council. (1999). *Pathological gambling: A critical review.* Washington, DC: National Academy Press.

Nower, L., & Blaszczynski, A. (2003). Binge gambling: A neglected concept. *International Gambling Studies, 3*(1), 23-35.

Nower, L., Derevensky, J.L., & Gupta, R. (2004). The relationship of impulsivity, sensation seeking, coping and substance use in youth gamblers. *Psychology of Addictive Behaviors, 18*(1), 49-55.

Nower, L., Gupta, R., Blaszczynski, A., & Derevensky, J. (2004). Suicidality and depression among youth gamblers: A preliminary examination of three studies. *International Gambling Studies, 4*(1), 69-80.

Olason, D.T., Kristjansdottir, E., Einarsdottir, H., Haraldsson, H., Bjarnason, G., & Derevensky, J.L. (2011). Internet gambling and problem gambling among 13 to 18 year old adolescents in Iceland. *International Journal of Mental Health and Addiction, 9*(3), 257-263.

Pagani, L.S., Derevensky, J.L., & Japel, C. (2009). Predicting gambling behavior in sixth grade from kindergarten impulsivity. *Archives of Pediatrics & Adolescent Medicine, 163*(3), 238-243.

Pagani, L.S., Derevensky, J.L., & Japel, C. (2010). Does early emotional distress predict later child involvement in gambling? *Canadian Journal Of Psychiatry, 55*(8), 507-513.

Petry, N.M., Blanco, C., Auriacombe, M., Borges, G., Bucholz, K., Crowley, T.J., ... O'Brien, C. (2014). An overview of and rationale for changes proposed for pathological gambling in DSM-5. *Journal of Gambling Studies, 30*(2), 493-502.

Petry, N.M., Blanco, C., Stinchfield, R., & Volberg, R. (2013). An empirical evaluation of proposed changes for gambling diagnosis in the DSM-5. *Addiction, 108*(3), 575-581.

Prochaska, J., & DiClimente, C. (1982). Stages and process of self-change in smoking: Towards an integrative model of change. *Psychotherapy, 20*(2), 161-173.

Productivity Commission. (2010). *Gambling: Productivity Commission inquiry report.* Report No. 50. Canberra, Australia: Commonwealth of Australia.

Pulford, J., Bellringer, M., Abbott, M., Clarke, D., Hodgins, D., & Williams, J. (2009). Barriers to help-seeking for a gambling problem: The experiences of gamblers who have sought specialist assistance and the perceptions of those who have not. *Journal of Gambling Studies, 25*(1), 33-48.

Rahman, A.S., Pilver, C.E., Desai, R.A., Steinberg, M.A., Rugle, L., Krishnan-Sarin, S., & Potenza, M.N. (2012). The relationship between age of gambling onset and adolescent problematic gambling severity. *Journal of Psychiatric Research, 46*(5), 675-683.

Responsible Gambling Council. (2014). *Canadian gambling digest 2012–2013.* Toronto, ON, Canada: Canadian Partnership for Responsible Gambling.

Rosenthal, R.J. (1987). The psychodynamics of pathological gambling: A review of the literature. In T. Galski (Ed.), *The handbook of pathological gambling* (pp. 41–70). Springfield, IL: Charles C. Thomas.

Rugle, L.J., & Rosenthal, R.J. (1994). Transference and countertransference reactions in the psychotherapy of pathological gamblers. *Journal of Gambling Studies, 10*(1), 43–65.

Saiz, J. (1992). No hagen juego, senores (Don't begin the game). *Interviu, 829,* 24–28.

Savard, A.-C., Temblay, J., & Turcotte, D. (2015). Problem gambling among adolescents: Toward a social and interactionist reading. *International Gambling Studies, 15*(1), 39–54.

Scholes-Balog, K.E., Hemphill, S.A., Dowling, N.A., & Toumbourou, J.W. (2014). A prospective study of adolescent risk and protective factors for problem gambling among young adults. *Journal of Adolescence, 37*(2), 215–224.

Schrans, T., Schellinck, T., & Walsh, G. (2000). *Technical report: 2000 regular VL players follow up: A comparative analysis of problem development and resolution.* Focal Research Consultants, Ltd. Retrieved from http://www.gov.ns.ca/health/downloads/VLPlayers_Technical_Report.pdf

Shaffer, H., Hall, M., & Vander Bilt, J. (1999). Estimating the prevalence of disordered gambling behavior in the United States and Canada: A research synthesis. *American Journal of Public Health, 89*(9), 1369–1376.

Shaffer, H., LaBrie, R., Scanlan, K., & Cummings, T. (1994). Pathological gambling among adolescents: Massachusetts Gambling Screen. *Journal of Gambling Studies, 10*(4), 339–362.

Shaffer, H.J., & Martin, R. (2011). Disordered gambling: Etiology, trajectory, and clinical considerations. *Annual Review of Clinical Psychology, 7,* 483–510.

Shead, N.W., Derevensky, J.L., & Gupta, R. (2010). Risk and protective factors associated with youth problem gambling. *International Journal of Adolescent Medicine and Health, 22*(1), 39–58.

Sklar, A., Gupta, R., & Derevensky, J. (2010). Binge gambling behaviors reported by youth in a residential drug treatment setting: A qualitative investigation. *International Journal of Adolescent Medicine and Health, 22*(1), 153–162.

Smith, G. (2014). The nature and scope of gambling in Canada. *Addiction, 109*(7), 706–710.

Statistics Canada. (2009). *Perspectives on labour and income: Gambling.* Catalogue No. 75-001-X. Ottawa, ON, Canada: Statistics CAnada.

Ste-Marie, C., Gupta, R., & Derevensky, J.L. (2002). Anxiety and social stress related to adolescent gambling behaviour. *International Gambling Studies, 2*(1), 123–141.

Ste-Marie, C., Gupta, R., & Derevensky, J. (2006). Anxiety and social stress related to adolescent gambling behavior and substance use. *Journal of Child & Adolescent Substance Abuse, 15*(4), 55–74.

Stinchfield, R. (2000). Gambling and correlates of gambling among Minnesota public school students. *Journal of Gambling Studies, 16*(2), 153–173.

Stinchfield, R. (2010). A critical review of adolescent problem gambling assessment instruments. *International Journal of Adolescent Medicine and Health, 22*(1), 77–93.

Stinchfield, R. (2011). Gambling among Minnesota public school students from 1992 to 2007: Declines in youth gambling. *Psychology of Addictive Behaviors, 25*(1), 108–117.

Stinchfiled, R., Govoni, R., & Frisch, G.R. (2007). A review of screening and assessment instruments for problem and pathological gambling. In G. Smith, D.C. Hodgins & R.J. Williams (Eds.), *Research and measurement issues in gambling studies* (pp. 179–213). Burlington, MA: Academic Press.

St-Pierre, R.A., Walker, D.M., Derevensky, J., & Gupta, R. (2014). How availability and accessibility of gambling venues influence problem gambling: A review of the literature. *Gaming Law Review and Economics*, *18*(2), 150–172.

Suurvali, H., Cordingley, J., Hodgins, D.C., & Cunningham, J. (2009). Barriers to seeking help for gambling problems: A review of the empirical literature. *Journal of Gambling Studies*, *25*(3), 407–424.

Suurvali, H., Hodgins, D.C., Toneatto, T., & Cunningham, J.A. (2012). Hesitation to seek gambling-related treatment among Ontario problem gamblers. *Journal of Addiction Medicine*, *6*(1), 39–49.

Tang, C.S., & Wu, A.M.S. (2012). Gambling-related cognitive biases and pathological gambling among youths, young adults, and mature adults in Chinese societies. *Journal of Gambling Studies*, *28*(1), 139–154.

Temcheff, C.E., St-Pierre, R.A., & Derevensky, J.L. (2013). Gambling among teens, college students and youth. In D.C.S. Richard, A. Blaszczynski, & L. Nower (Eds.), *The Wiley-Blackwell handbook of disordered gambling* (pp. 306–326). Chichester, UK: John Wiley & Sons Ltd.

Toneatto, T. (1999). Cognitive psychopathology of problem gambling. *Substance Use and Misuse*, *34*(11), 1593–1604.

Toneatto, T., & Ladouceur, R. (2003). Treatment of pathological gambling: A critical review of the literature. *Psychology of Addictive Behaviors*, *17*(4), 284–292.

Toneatto, T., & Millar, G. (2004). Assessing and treating problem gambling: Empirical status and promising trends. *Canadian Journal of Psychiatry/La Revue canadienne de psychiatrie*, *49*(8), 517–525.

Tremblay, J., Stinchfield, R., Wiebe, J., & Wynne, H. (2010). *Canadian Adolescent Gambling Inventory (CAGI): Phase III final report*. Ottawa, ON: Canadian Centre on Substance Abuse.

Turner, N., Macdonald, J., Bartoshuk, M., & Zangeneh, M. (2008). Adolescent gambling behaviour, attitudes, and gambling problems. *International Journal of Mental Health and Addiction*, *6*(2), 223–237.

Vachon, J., Vitaro, F., Wanner, B., & Tremblay, R.E. (2004). Adolescent gambling: Relationships with parent gambling and parenting practices. *Psychology of Addictive Behaviors*, *18*(4), 398–401.

van den Brink, W. (2012). Evidence-based pharmacological treatment of substance use disorders and pathological gambling. *Current Drug Abuse Reviews*, *5*(1), 3–31.

Vitaro, F., Arseneault, L., & Tremblay, R.E. (1999). Impulsivity predicts problem gambling in low SES adolescent males. *Addiction*, *94*(4), 565–575.

Vitaro, F., Brendgen, M., Ladouceur, R., & Tremblay, R.E. (2001). Gambling, delinquency, and drug use during adolescence: Mutual influences and common risk factors. *Journal of Gambling Studies*, *17*(3), 171–190.

Vitaro, F., & Wanner, B. (2011). Predicting early gambling in children. *Psychology of Addictive Behaviors*, *25*(1), 118–126.

Vitaro, F., Wanner, B., Brendgen, M., & Tremblay, R.E. (2008). Offspring of parents with gambling problems: Adjustment problems and explanatory mechanisms. *Journal of Gambling Studies*, *24*(4), 535–553.

Vitaro, F., Wanner, B., Ladouceur, R., Brendgen, M., & Tremblay, R. (2004). Trajectories of gambling during adolescence. *Journal of Gambling Studies*, *20*(1), 47–69.

Volberg, R.A., Gupta, R., Griffiths, M.D., Ólason, D.T., & Delfabbro, P. (2010). An international perspective on youth gambling prevalence studies. *International Journal of Adolescent Medicine and Health*, *22*(1), 3–38.

Wanner, B., Vitaro, F., Carbonneau, R., & Tremblay, R.E. (2009). Cross-lagged links among gambling, substance abuse, and delinquency from mid-adolescence to young adulthood: Additive and moderating effects of common risk factors. *Psychology of Addictive Behaviors*, *23*(1), 91–104.

Welte, J.W., Barnes, G.M., Tidwell, M.-C.O., & Hoffman, J.H. (2008). The prevalence of problem gambling among US adolescents and young adults: Results from a national survey. *Journal of Gambling Studies, 24*(2), 119–133.

Welte, J.W., Barnes, G.M., Tidwell, M.-C.O., & Hoffman, J.H. (2009a). Association between problem gambling and conduct disorder in a national survey of adolescents and young adults in the United States. *Journal of Adolescent Health, 45*(4), 396–401.

Welte, J.W., Barnes, G.M., Tidwell, M.-C.O., & Hoffman, J.H. (2009b). Legal gambling availability and problem gambling among adolescents and young adults. *International Gambling Studies, 9*(2), 89–99.

Welte, J.W., Barnes, G.M., Tidwell, M.-C.O., & Hoffman, J.H. (2011). Gambling and problem gambling across the lifespan. *Journal of Gambling Studies, 27*(1), 49–61.

Wickwire, E.M., Whelan, J.P., & Meyers, A.W. (2010). Outcome expectancies and gambling behavior among urban adolescents. *Psychology of Addictive Behaviors, 24*(1), 75–88.

Wickwire, E.M., Whelan, J.P., Meyers, A.W., & Murray, D.M. (2007). Environmental correlates of gambling behavior in urban adolescents. *Journal of Abnormal Child Psychology, 35*(2), 179–190.

Winters, K.C., Stinchfield, R.D., Botzet, A., & Anderson, N. (2002). A prospective study of youth gambling behaviors. *Psychology of Addictive Behaviors, 16*(1), 3–9.

Winters, K.C., Stinchfield, R.D., Botzet, A., & Slutske, W.S. (2005). Pathways of youth gambling problem severity. *Psychology of Addictive Behaviors, 19*(1), 104–107.

Winters, K., Stinchfield, R., & Fulkerson, J. (1993). Toward the development of an adolescent gambling problem severity scale. *Journal of Gambling Studies, 9*(1), 63–84.

Wong, I.L.K., & So, E.M.T. (2014). Internet gambling among high school students in Hong Kong. *Journal of Gambling Studies, 30*(3), 565–576.

Yakovenko, I., & Hodgins, D.C. (2014). Treatment of disordered gambling. In F. Gobet & M. Schiller (Eds.), *Problem gambling: Cognition, prevention and treatment* (pp. 221–251). New York: Palgrave Macmillan.

Yip, S.W., Desai, R.A., Steinberg, M.A., Rugle, L., Cavallo, D.A., Krishnan-Sarin, S., & Potenza, M.N. (2011). Health/functioning characteristics, gambling behaviors, and gambling-related motivations in adolescents stratified by gambling problem severity: Findings from a high school survey. *The American Journal on Addictions, 20*(6), 495–508.

Yip, S.W., & Potenza, M.N. (2014). Treatment of gambling disorders. *Current Treatment Options in Psychiatry, 1*(2), 189–203.

Yorke, W.M. (2003). Gambling in Canada: History, economics, and public health. In H.J. Shaffer, M.N. Hall, J. Vander Bilt, & E. George (Eds.), *Futures at stake: Youth, gambling, and society* (pp. 49–62). Reno, NV: University of Nevada Press.

CHAPTER 28

Compulsive Internet and Cyber Use

Dennis Kimberley and Louise Osmond

Social Context

Internet networks and search engines are pervasive in the worlds of military and security forces; education and teaching; government services and communications; marketing, commercial information, and product exchanges; non-government services; arts and letters; play, gaming, and gambling; entertainment; personal, populist, and organized political information and social action forums; historical and archival records; and private activity, personal public activity, and interactive social discourse. Depths of endless information and activity support relatively continuous searches for information, activity, product-monetary exchange, social exchange, and new cyber platforms such as 3D virtual reality games, which have not only purposeful interests but also have come to serve impulsive interests associated with serendipitous discoveries such as child pornography and live-streaming sex acts. These net activities, processes, and contexts enable stimulation and reinforcement of old or novel obsessions as diverse as grooming exchanges with underage children, war games, and presentations, such as a male of 40 self-presenting as a 12-year-old female or a 40-year-old woman self-presenting as "sextoy40." The dynamic interplay of compulsions, impulses, and obsessions are parallel to expected patterns of psychological dependency in substance addiction.[1] The onset of substance misuse and addiction is very seldom observed before teen years, possibly with the exception of children subjected to sex trafficking. In contrast, in the online universe there is a vast capacity for pre-teens to compulsively use the Internet for bottomless information, purchasing, play, and premature eroticization. This presents some positives, such as searching for information on puberty in a non-embarrassing environment, but also some substantive risks and harms, ranging from online seduction to personal exposure through sexting images that live in cyberspace. Early onset child-youth compulsive cyber use is most likely in gaming (Taneli, Guo, & Mushtaq, 2015) and texting (Zaman & Lache, 2015). Early onset of content exposure risks such as cyberbullying and sexual exploitation in the current cyber culture pose significant public health and social concerns that social workers and other counselling professions face (Judge & Leary, 2014; Saleh et al., 2014).

Initial concerns about the net were often focused on pornography and the exploitation of women and children; since the 1990s helping professionals have been aware of the inherent risks of compulsive, impulsive, and obsessive Internet use, which could fit a modified DSM disorder paradigm (Rosen, 2012; Scheiber, Potenza, & Grant, 2016; Young, 1999). We take the position that behavioural assumptions are too narrow to address the Internet phenomenon, especially given the significance of attachment and social bond issues across behaviours (Brisch, 2012; Crocker, 2015; Mikulincer & Shaver, 2016). Likewise, a traditional medical pathology model is far too limited given the paradox that some compulsive Internet use may be associated with resiliencies, strengths, and empowerment of marginalized groups such as transgender persons (Kimberley & Scheltgen, 2013). A paradox exists in the cyberspace realm, with some expressions of net use serving an anti-oppressive function and supporting relatively healthy self-determination such as assisting individuals in exploring their sexuality, while notions of webphilia—or hyper-attractions to web content and processes—require targeted assessment and treatment as they can create substantive life disruption (Kimberley & Osmond, 2000; Kimberley & Scheltgen, 2013; Sheldon & Howitt, 2007). Beginning assessment questions to pose are: What is it about the net and cyber activity that you find so exciting? What does engaging in that activity do for you?

No matter what differential classification schemas evolve from practice-based evidence, the clinical reality is that biological changes, psychological changes, psychosocial changes, social changes, techno-contextual progress (devices with higher speed and resolutions), and spiritual-existential issues are part of the complex nexus of compulsive Internet and associated compulsive cyber use that social workers need to be aware of in the 21st century. As well, there is a need to be cognizant of precursors related to net use and abuse, particularly social isolation, social alienation, marginalization, social exclusion, and attachment issues, which create challenges to personal and social functioning (Rosen, 2012). These may manifest as loss of a partner (Whitty, 2010), workplace conflict (Kimberley & Osmond, 2003), exploitation in a sexting exchange (Kimberley & Scheltgen, 2013), or only having cyber social contacts (Rosen, 2012; Scott, 2014). Any of these factors may motivate a person to approach addiction and mental health services. However, compulsive Internet issues can often be overlooked as many individuals also present with co-occurring substance or mental health issues (Rosen, 2012). A question to be considered in exploring this topic is: What was your life like before your use of cyber content and activities?

Internet and related compulsive cyber use transcends national boundaries and may have more common presentations than not across cultures and between men and women. Accelerated cyber linking spawns cyber-engaged virtual communities (Kimberley & Scheltgen, 2013; Sheldon & Howitt, 2007; Taneli, Guo, & Mushtaq, 2015) that range from normative (diabetes support), to prosocial (political advocacy), to deviant (sharing images of bestiality), to anti-social (child pornography exchange), to anarchistic (dumping, sharing, and plumbing secret state and corporate information). As with substance-using communities, cyber communities present positive opportunities (peer support/mutual aid groups) as well as risks (compromised personal and social functioning). Internet servers and cyber platforms provide a medium for information exchange via text, audio, photos, and video, as well as real-time interactive and social engagement exchanges such as gaming, texting, and sexting. They work through multiple devices—computer, tablet, smartphone, and virtual reality simulators—making information, activities, social exchanges, and economic exchanges accessible through search engines and cyber links that provide access to a bottomless reservoir of information, like museum collections, and real-time engagement activities including role-playing games and virtual sex chat rooms (Blinka & Smahel, 2011). They also work through computer applications that enable interactive processes, emails, texting, and streaming, and include real-time engagement from gaming to smartphone sexting.

Thus, it is not surprising that Internet issue incidence projections may rise along with concomitant sequelae (Rosen, 2012; Young & de Abreu, 2011) due to the following social conditions:

- Accelerating increase in Internet service revenues/profits for governments and organizations
- Increased societal, educational, and employment demands for computer and cyber literacy
- Increased demands for skills in managing web-based information and cyber content
- Increasing exposure to unsolicited web commercialization, including deceptive presentations
- Increased personalization of web relationships from cyber "friending" to cybersex
- Increased net user capacity to cover sensitive cybertracks
- Increased likelihood of sensitive and criminal cyber-tracks being discovered by police or cyber-spies, either of which may be unauthorized and operating against privacy laws
- Increasingly exciting cyber technologies (virtual reality) and cyber processes (sexting)
- Increased cyber-inclusion opportunities in everyday life (coffee shop web access)

Such patterns have some parallels in the realm of substance use and addiction, such as drinking buddies, illegal access to substances, increasingly exciting and potent substances, and even simple business lunches and dinners. Thus, as part of your assessment, questions to pose are: How does the Internet and cyber activity work for you emotionally and socially? and What concerns you the most about your use of your phone/the net?

Potential Internet and cyber use and abuse issues presented by clients parallel the psychological dimension of addiction, including:

- Compulsive attention to, and use of, the Internet and cyber surfing: high frequency, high interest; difficulty averting attention from access sources and content; long duration; and difficulty ceasing a cyber session.
- Impulsive attention to, and use of, the Internet and cyber surfing: a strong reactivity to cue stimuli in the environment, such as the sound of keyboarding; high emotional arousal, especially excitement, when anticipating cyber activity; rapid redirection of energy to the web at "the urge" to use; and anxiety over loss of access to the net or smartphone.
- Obsession with Internet use, cyber surfing, and World Wide Web content, processes, and equipment: experiencing intrusive thoughts about the Internet when doing other needed or required activities; consistent and intense interest and desire for cyber activity; and becoming irritated when interrupted from cyber activities.
- Exhibiting defensive routines to account for, and support, continued use and abuse of the net, as well as cyber information or virtual social exchanges: minimization, rationalization, and projection.
- Attention to deviant, perverse, or other unacceptable content that may reflect socially unacceptable actions, at best, and a pathology, at worst.
- Cyber seduction and infidelity.
- Premature sexualization-eroticization of children and youth.
- Personal and social problems directly associated with Internet use, including criminal activity.
- Personal and social problems, such as loss of a partner or cyber bullying.

Questions to be posed to a client in assessing this area of concern are To what extent do you see net interest and cyber activity taking over your life? What does your online life give you that your offline life does not?

Differential Assessment and Treatment Considerations

Besides the exploratory questions articulated above, a biopsychosocial-spiritual framework, familiar to social workers operating within person-in-environment, ecological, interactional, and integrative transtheoretical frames, may help clinicians and their clients reduce the complexity of the many facets of Internet misuse to manageable proportions for purposes of assessment, intervention, and recovery.

Biological Considerations

One of the markers of substance addiction is the strong association with biological processes at points of use, immediately post-use, and post-abstinence. One of the arguments for including compulsive use of non-substance activities within a larger addiction paradigm is that biochemical and neurological changes in persons living with compulsive behaviours also occur. Some scholars, such as Love and colleagues (2015), argue that the general diagnostic class should be Internet addiction with related addiction approached as a subset, such as compulsive pornography use, recognizing that all appear to be associated with neurological processes influencing "reward, motivation and memory circuitry" (p. 388). However, this view minimizes and negates the fact that all human action activates neurological processes involved with learning and retention. Nevertheless, Laier, Schulte, and Brand (2013) found that repeated pornography exposure was associated with the same compromised working memory that occurs with excessive psychoactive drug consumption. Similar themes were raised by Kuss and Griffiths (2012), who argued that those who game compulsively should be called addicts because they show compromised cognitive functioning due to their excessive gaming. However, they did not discuss the effect of the behaviour on peripheral nervous system functioning, particularly the autonomic nervous system.

Calm, stable, accepting, and safe environments, along with active therapies including exercise, deep breathing, relaxation, meditation, music, play, dance, movement, sports, and expressive art, have all been found to help reset some neurological and biochemical balances of clients, further indicating that all human activity alters brain chemistry. The interactions of clinically significant biophysical, biochemical, and bio-neurological dimensions with other biopsychosocial dimensions are important in guiding integrative interventions. Thus, the biological dimension must always be considered when working with individuals with compulsive Internet use. One paradox with regard to bioneurological and biochemical dynamics is that net and cyber activities may help with issues of affect regulation, some even overcoming developmental damage associated with attachment failures and trauma, a theme of functionality in what otherwise is primarily dysfunctional behaviour.

Affect Expression, Suppression, Repression, and Regulation

As with addiction to psychoactive drugs, compulsive net use may be associated with strong emotions, felt urges, and affect regulation issues, influenced by developmental precursors (child abuse, compromised attachments, anxieties); contiguous precipitants (fear or stresses associated with unemployment); real-time triggers (irritability and aggressiveness when a web session is interrupted); active mood modification associated with use of cyber processes and content (relaxing with escapist information such as art gallery collections, moving out of numbness and starting to feel again with safe social networking under the viewer's control[2]); attempting to alter mood through social-sexual networking; and purposeful numbing from exhaustive net lurking with random-serendipitous and seemingly purposeless surfing. Intense use of the web can lead to a host of altered affects:

- improved mood through social networking ("This is where I belong and feel worthwhile ... I am master of the war game!");
- a feeling of defeat ("I've been lurking for five hours but only felt better for five minutes.");

- a sense of self-loathing ("Six fucking hours surfing kiddy shit ... I feel like a pervert.");
- confirmed feelings of worthlessness ("I showed myself (exhibitionism) but I got no (few) lookers (voyeurs) ... nobody texted me back (no personalized engagement).");
- intense emotions associated with wins and loses (net games with winner and loser identities, with perceptions distorted towards the recall of wins, as with compulsive gambling); and
- physical sensations and congruent affect that parallel the tolerance-withdrawal dynamic in the substance addictions paradigm, such as irritability, agitation, and impaired cognitive functioning, sometimes with a sense of panic when one's access to the net has been thwarted (Greenfield, 2011).

Attachment issues with compulsive Internet use are associated with feelings of "not belonging" and a sense of being disconnected; feelings of rejection, alienation, and exclusion; fears of separation, abandonment, and loss of social connections and supports; aloneness and feeling lonely, even in the presence of primary supports; feeling a loss of desired intensity of emotional connection in relationships; and feeling overwhelmed by the chaos, disturbance, and disorganization in past and existing social relationships.

Consistent with substance addiction on the psychological level, there is much shame, guilt, remorse, and regret associated with some patterns of compulsive Internet use. These include the shame associated with "dehumanizing" persons online; guilt associated with "objectification or depersonalization" of other persons, their avatars, hentai, and cyber-selves; remorse for letting down significant others in primary relationships; and regret at violating rules of the workplace or educational institutions. Mood disorders that parallel addiction have also been documented including anxiety, depression, and bipolar disorder (Delmonico & Griffin, 2011; Rosen, 2012). A pattern may emerge where the person never feels fulfilled, satiated, or a sufficient intensity of relational connections, which may lead to longer and more frequent Internet sessions that do not quite satisfy; this can be viewed as being parallel to a substance user who must "drink until there is none left or until it makes me pass out." The psychological theme of not being able to stop is shared between addiction and compulsive cyber activity. Rosen coined the term iDisorder to signal the influence of technology in "inducing ... moods swings ... from high highs down to low lows," paralleling bipolar patterns (2012, p. 78). As well, "instant messaging, texting, playing video games, and watching television" are all associated with depression and dysthymic disorder (p. 79). The client may be confused by the paradox of a felt desire for social connections and fearing the very attachment desired, often acted out as approach-avoidance behaviours. It is not surprising then that the net may be found to be both a negative influence and emotionally supportive (Rosen, 2012).

To the extent that the social worker can provide a safe and stable environment, as well as continuity in a face-to-face relationship involving trust, genuine empathy, and support, then intense and overwhelming emotions derived from net use may be tempered. Once this affect is moderated, the client's feelings of safety and stability may increase, allowing further exploration of emotionally sensitive issues (Mikulincer & Shaver, 2016). Social workers may find emotional schema therapy of interest as it respects both biologically determined as well as cognitively and culturally constructed emotions, as well as transtheoretical considerations (Leahy, 2015). The interactions of clinically significant expression, suppression, and repression of affect, with other biopsychosocial and spiritual dimensions, are important in guiding integrated and holistic assessment and therapy. A question to include in the counselling process based on these concpets is how might you express your emotions on the net and in cyberspace that is different from your life as lived offline?

Cognitive Processes, Content, and Unconscious Determinates

Interactive with intense and often overwhelming emotions are beliefs, attitudes, values, expectations, and meanings associated with one's compulsive net use and one's life offline. Consider the following client cognitive scripts and their counterpoints:

- Web needs: "I need Web buddies—I feel lost without them."
- Internet as an imperative: "I require net time and space, to keep sane—cyberspace is my life; my real life is online."
- Cyber preferences: "I wish to be with people who are excited by showing and looking (exhibitionism and voyeurism)—I've become perverted in what I do in cyberspace; that is not me."
- Reinforcing a cyber lifestyle: "I prefer my cyber community and the way they are—I should leave cyberlife but have tried and failed."
- Web-related habits of thought: "My web buddies understand the real me—I'm not sure having a new best friend every week is good."
- Wish for social connection and confirmation: "I must answer texts so my people will keep connecting—I'm sick that my life is reduced to messaging."

These are all scripts that can be reinforced in counselling-therapy with potential to support abstinence (cessation of net use), harm reduction (reduction of net use and control of risky cyber activities), healthy recovery, building on past strengths, and increasing resiliencies ("I'm spending increased quality time with family while being consciously in the moment").

With compulsive Internet use there are unconscious processes, such as defensive routines to block attention to alternative beliefs, attitudes, values, expectations, and interpretations, as well as rationalizations supporting net life. There are also habitual patterns of thought supporting web activity: cognitive scripts, such as "my best friends are on the web." Maladaptive patterns of thought—"I'll only stay online another 20 minutes"—may gain more strength than either espoused abstinence or harm reduction intentions. Before effective challenges to unconscious patterns and expressed cognitive scripts are likely to be effective, treatment requires substantive relationship building, trust building, emotional support, listening, and empathetic understanding. Such relational gains will set the stage for ameliorative education, suggestive or directive therapies, or reframed narratives. Additionally, assessment and therapy may be sensitive to compromised cognitive functioning based on (a) precursors (trauma and associated dissociation, organic impacts of past substance abuse, and mental disorder compromised delusions, as with borderline personality disorder); (b) current cyber activity (perceptual dysmorphology such as perceiving an 11-year-old child in the physical form expected of an 18 year old); (c) habitual minimization regarding surfing, texting, and email-compromised personal and social functioning; and (d) anticipated future cyber expectations and rationalizations ("I can stop gaming any time I want to!").

Assessment and intervention must also consider obsessive and intrusive thoughts about net content (endless facts about cars), net processes (surfing for auto pictures, videos, and narratives), and a compulsive orientation to achieve complete, encyclopedic knowledge and affirmed expertise (knowing everything about 1961 Chevy trucks). These patterns may converge to become personally and socially overwhelming and all-consuming. Part of therapy is aimed at empowering the client in the direction of more self-control, which in current language is framed as self-regulation (Mikulincer & Shaver, 2016; Schore, 2003).

Reliable interpretations of reality may be compromised and fantasy thinking may be amplified and reified, such as where the client's alter ego in role-playing games begins to be internalized as the "real self," and elements of the role continue to be played in real life scripts. The client may also discover or co-create cyberspaces and identities of cyber-place. Cyber-fantasies and cyber-realities may cohere to become more satisfying than the client's real world life; these may be experienced as empowering, but maladaptive patterns such as disingenuous empathy may be cognitively and emotively processed as strengths. Non-sexual surfing may default into spontaneous sex interest including serendipitous and surprising attraction to child pornography or sexting.* Defensive scripts could signal dynamics of minimization ("She decided to show [exhibitionist] and I decided to direct [voyeur asking for particular self-presentations of the real-time "model"] ... can't hurt."). Scripts could also signal supports for a search for affirmation of questionable interpretations of reality ("There was no real child there ... only pictures ... so I harmed no one—right?"). The latter is similar to the alcohol-dependent individual who concludes, "I am hurting no one but myself with my drinking."

The patterns described above and below have some parallels with the psychological dimension of psychoactive drug addiction, including

- Compromised attention, tracking, concentration, and observations: not attending to child care, concentrating on gaming, or not tracking a child's needs, resulting in the child's failure to thrive.

---

* When sexting involves minors and the images involve nude photos, it is considered child pornography under Canadian law regardless of who the sender is or his/her age.

- Distorted sensations and related interpretations: interpreting erotic sensations to "hot avatars" or "sexy hentai" as if they have real personalized relational significance.
- Compromised memory: content memory (not recalling what day it is or who has been home, as the net activity was a distraction continuously for days), having procedural memory and recalling how to get to one's child's school, but then forgetting to pick up the child.
- Distorted perceptions and compromised judgment: "That is a young adult ... not a child."
- Distorted interpretations of reality and compromised reasoning: "This is not exploitive ... she consented to sext me ... she was into it (teen was 14)."
- Disinhibited thinking and related affect: often associated with web creep and accelerated cyber activity; for example, moving from two hours per day to four to six, because "my friends are on for seven or more hours a day."
- Compromised problem solving and adaptations: "I have started to only look at porn sites that say 18-plus."
- Compromised decision-making: "It won't hurt that I did not join my husband in bed ... he was already asleep ... he understands that I'm less of an ogre when I get my cyber-friends and cyberspace fix ... they are more sexy."

In integrated treatment, which attends to cognitive content, processes, and changes, the clinician must take care with pacing, the timing and depth of insight explorations, as well as controlling the intensity of challenges to distortions, delusions, deceptions, fantasy, and maladaptive cognitive scripts. An uncritical and broad application of "the client is expert" treatment ideology may be unjustified when beliefs, attitudes, values, expectations, and interpretations of reality are likely subject to clinically significant distortions and defensive routines, at best, and to delusions at worst. In the extreme, a therapist will not wish to reinforce the perception of a pedophile that he/she "loves children ... and society unfairly oppresses me." A paradoxical analysis of the function of protecting distorted, delusional, defensive, deceptive, and otherwise clinically significant compromised thinking may help in treatment as the functional school of social work has taught us that there is function in apparent dysfunctional thinking and associated actions. Questioning styles could include What functions may be served by your excessive net interests/activities/content viewing? What meaning do you attach to your cyber life?

Within personalized social bonds and other relational contexts, clients' shifting beliefs, attitudes, values, expectations, and assignment of meanings, as well as declared or espoused intentions ("My children and wife are first in my life") may be a source of confusion, disbelief, distrust, or at least skepticism. Clients may become masters of double messaging to protect their net habits, often expressed in the form "You know I want to help with your homework *but* I must finish this or I will let my game buddy down" or "I know I am neglecting you but *you* know that you are the most important person in my life ... you should not feel abandoned." As well as distrust, social-relational alienation themes may come to dominate primary group narratives. The interactions of clinically significant patterns of cognitive functioning and memory, related cognitive content ("I live in cyberspace"), and related cognitive social processes (cyber identity transformation), are important to assess in informing integrated and holistic therapies. Interventions should avoid unjustified privileging of cognitive-behavioural intervention models when issues of affect regulation and social bonds may require more affect-oriented (Leahy, 2015) and relation-oriented social work interventions (Maltz & Maltz, 2008; Schore & Schore, 2008). The use of mindfulness-based therapies provide added depth in dealing with heightened awareness of self and context, self-reflection, and insight, in real time, such as while one is surfing (Pollak, Pedulla, & Siegel, 2016). Critical to consider when working with clients is the why—why is this cyber life better than the real world?

Habitual Behaviours and Action Patterns

Affect and cognition, mediated through bioneurological and biochemical realities, and interacting with conscious actions and habitual behaviour patterns, are the hallmark of various cognitive-behavioural, rational-emotive behavioural therapies, community reinforcement, and dialectic behaviour therapies. Of first note is that few people appear for service with their first statement of problem being compulsive Internet use; the result is that presenting problems may expand to be co-occurring issues (Young, 2011). Once compulsive Internet use is suspected, in considering clinically significant properties, attention is paid to the content of actions (war games versus sexualized social networking), duration of the net sessions, habitual behaviour patterns associated with onset, and frequency of sessions (compulsive checking for text messages). Assessments may include the intensity associated with the cyber activity, ranging from rapid and continuous movement (such as surfing through 3,000 pornography images in a sitting) to multi-platform simultaneous cybering (involving live streaming, real-time text messaging on the net, and personalized sexting).

Applied cognitively oriented therapies may focus on abstinence, harm reduction, or intervening in behaviour and thinking patterns before, during, and following the heavy use of net processes, content, and platforms. The attention may not just be to the behavioural and cognitive content of action sets, but also to the processes of thinking as well as self-expression transitions before, during, and after. As this is primarily a psychological process, emphasis is on understanding patterns of compulsive, impulsive, obsessive, and adaptive-maladaptive cyber activities. Attention may also focus on net creep where one not only stays online longer than intended but also repeatedly adds "just five more minutes" until 15 minutes turns into another two hours spent gaming, looking at pornography, or social networking.

Attention also needs to be paid to cue stimuli that often trigger compulsive actions as part of the cyber process. Sensory and cognitively generated revivification cues, which stimulate net action.

Any one of these sensory cues may be sufficient to trigger imminent interest or strong impulses for cyber thinking and associated net activity, as well as sensate and affective arousal—the anticipatory excitement and cognitive imagery associated with cybersex. An analysis of a client's action patterns would normally examine socially acceptable, unacceptable, deviant, and criminal actions, including:

- web gambling;
- compromised social functioning associated with surfing, gaming, or social networking;
- sharing confidential web file information on diverse websites (dark web);
- live obscene talk, often with underaged persons (scatologia);
- voyeuristic lurking, with or without sexual intent;
- posting of activities captured on spy cameras;
- real-time and online prostitution services; and
- extorting money or favours from persons who are threatened with sexual exposure based on web/phone activities (sextortion).

When sexual stimulation, pleasure, and/or sexual release are part of the cyber sex process, whether or not any of these have any association with sexual dysfunctions such as latency to orgasm, the clinician may need to shift the focus to examining compulsive sexual behaviour rather than compulsive Internet use (Hall, 2011, 2013; Kimberley, 2014; Riemersma & Sytsma, 2013).

Social Relational Considerations (Attachment, Social Isolation, and Anxiety): The "Social" in Social Work

One of the hallmarks of social work is the theme of social-relational considerations, which transcend simplistic biological or psychological knowledge. At an ideological level there is a belief in the fundamental interdependence of humans, one with the other. This begins with theories (person-in-environment theories, interactional theories, ecosystems theories, humanistic philosophies of human agency) positing that the interface between the individual and multiple bounded social groups is influenced by, and in turn influences, their environments. Social work has long attended to ideologies of equal rights and social justice (the rights of a client oppressed by addictions), as well as mutuality and reciprocity of shared social responsibility, one for the other (social support, social interventions, and the client's responsibility to undertake paths towards needed and required personal and social change). As Doweiko stated (2015, p. 394): "Self-awareness brings with it the right of self-determination, but also carries with it the responsibility for making choices."

Notions of the relational and the social converge in the conclusion that social systems cohere around social narratives, based in part on:

- common beliefs and interests, often reflected in societal, cultural, religious, ethnic group, language group, and family values, and common human needs such as social supports;
- diverse expressions of social expectations, needs, risks, harm, strengths, and a shared identity, in varied social groupings;
- relatively unique expressions of self, risks, desires, needs, harm, strengths, resiliencies, and potential within specific social contexts; and
- ethno-cultural imperatives, traditions, and contextual adaptations.

Social work attention to social factors, social forces, and social influences assumes that social structures (family, social agencies), social processes (family support for control and recovery), and social content (meanings assigned to written or visual imagery)—as well as beliefs, attitudes, values, expectations, knowledge, and assignment of meaning—are formulated and applied in social interaction both conscious and unconscious. Understanding the influence of social factors and processes includes attending to differentials in social position (child pornography viewers are highly stigmatized within already stigmatized groups); social roles (the gamer being disordered versus the therapist who represents society's health); social power and influence (the power differential power between client and social worker who can alter family relations by involving societal authorities such as child welfare and the police); social inclusion-exclusion (excluding a cyberbully from a net support group); and social privilege (those interested in heterosexual relationships with opposite-sex children defining gay males interested in sex with male children as being more deviant). Thus, a general question to ask arising from this domain would be What does the social network of the web offer you? What do you offer the web?

Social and Relation Factors

Social work's consideration of what might be assessed and addressed for required and desired interpersonal changes makes more sense if contextualized by the above-described social factor/social forces considerations. However, in addiction, a paradox of social influences is found in the reality that therapists attend to social factors that influence risks and harm of addiction, while at the same time promoting client strengths, self-determination, and self-agency by supporting resilience and recovery through relational supports. Some argue that if the latter were carried to its extreme, then society might hold the client fully and solely responsible for "causing" themselves to be addicted, or "causing" themselves to be pedophiles, as well as for "sustaining" their compulsive Internet use.

As with those who have a substance addiction there is an overrepresentation among those who are compulsive net users in regards to having

- suffered maltreatment, including neglect, abuse, and relational trauma (Briere & Scott, 2015);
- experienced compromised parenting, including attachment-bond deficits that impact interpersonal functioning (Kimberley, 2015);
- convergent influences of maltreatment, parenting deficits, and attachment deficits, which compromised their biopsychosocial-spiritual development (Dayton, 2000; Doweiko, 2015);
- exposure to parental or significant other addiction and concurrent disorder patterns (Kimberley, 2015);
- family relationship dynamics that required adaptations (the empowered parentified child) and maladaptations (the scapegoated child) associated with living with an addicted and/or concurrent disordered member in the family (Kimberley, 2015); and
- experienced social stigma first-hand on a personal level, including those who have lived in a family with a stigmatized and socially marginalized identity or label (e.g., pervert, druggie).

Social workers have expressed a particular sense of concern for those whose risks and needs nexus is interactive and intersecting with marginalization, stigma, disempowerment, and social rejection.

Given the inherent risk factors associated with compulsive net and cyber use it is not surprising that in terms of relational factors the following issues emerge:

- a sense of social isolation and social alienation;
- a sense of not belonging anywhere, or with or to anyone;
- profound loneliness as a precursor to and as a consequence of the behaviour;
- feelings of aloneness and loneliness, often even in the presence of others;
- unfillable voids in terms of emotional connection, social bond, and attachment;
- paradoxical avoidance of, or premature ending of, much-desired social bonds;
- a sense of distrust in relationships and cognitive construction of internalized fantasy models of desired relationships;
- paradoxical distrust of those trustworthy, juxtaposed to trusting the less than trustworthy;
- underdeveloped social skills at the level of genuine relationships, accurate and other-centred empathy, mutuality, reciprocity, and co-operation;
- defining children as safer social peers than adults, most common among pedophiles and sexters;
- a sense of overwhelming family, school, or work-related distress, anxiety, or dissatisfaction;
- rapid social bonding and rapid detachment, often linked with illusions of genuine and lasting cyber-friends;
- defining cyber-relationships as more "real" than are person-to-person bonds in life as lived; and

- non-contiguous but "real time" cyber-relating, defined as more safe than relating through live face-to-face relationships ("you can end/unfriend with a click") (Crocker, 2015; Doweiko, 2015; Morahn-Martin, 1999).

Too often, online superficial relationships become defined as "real" and "deep," in part due to their novelty and emotional intensity. In turn, established face-to-face relationships may become defined as unreal and superficial. Sadly such patterns may take place in a context where the client claims to "need more intense connection" and to desire "real and genuine" social bonds.

Social work counselling arises from a strong tradition of attending to common social relational factors and social processes that account for most influences in therapy, which supports client stabilization, personal and social change, and sustained recovery (Ruisard, 2015; Shulman, 2015). In providing counselling to clients with these issues in a social-relational, integrative, and holistic manner, the social worker should consider: (a) bioneurological change/biochemical change, providing active deep relaxation and creating contextual calmness and safety to construct a social place and relational space where interpersonal therapeutic work may be expanded; (b) emotional experience and affect expression change, expressing empathy, creating relational security, engendering trust feelings, and co-building relational safety and hopefulness; (c) cognitive changes, using language of respect, and encouraging beliefs in self-agency and an attitude of being ready for an alliance engaged in personal, social-relational, spiritual, and con-textual changes; (d) behavioural and action pattern changes, including social-relational action pattern changes through assessment of relational dynamics and through using self and the helping relationship to change relationship patterns and internal mod-elling of working relationships; and (e) by behavioural modelling of safe, supportive, encouraging, genuine, and shared effort, even when the client has lapsed or relapsed or is being reactive to the social worker through transference responses such as "You will get tired of me just as everyone has, ... other than net friends, because we are all in the geek-space together."

Among the compulsive net patterns that may confound and compromise social relationships are:

- increased frequency and duration of net use while reaching out for relationship and social affirmation;
- increased net session time and frequency to sustain life satisfaction and a sense of relational "belonging with," and online places to "belong to";
- decreased attached, shared leisure time, and instrumental time with family and significant others;
- online or other relationship patterns characterized by superficiality and illusions of genuineness;
- relationship patterns characterized by secretiveness and deception associated with surfing and exchanges;

- live expression of self or of a cyber-persona, including more risky net activities such as exhibitionism and sexting, in a range of net relationships that could be unsafe or could be exited to safety with one click;
- atypical activities, including sexual acts, which may be validated and affirmed in cyber communities with common and diverse interests and where unique desires may be affirmed;
- relying on cyber-buddies for emotional support, empathy, encouragement, and acceptance; and
- risking loss of valued and significant relationships.

Such indictors of clinically significant Internet dynamics imply directions for change at a relational level, which can be addressed through a variety of traditional counselling formats, including individual therapy, couple and family therapy, and group therapy. *Individual therapy* uses the therapeutic relationship as part of the therapeutic process and explores issues related to development, co-occurring mental health or addiction issues, trauma experiences, and attachment challenges (Schreiber, Potenza, & Grant, 2016). *Couple and family therapy* uses couple and family relational structure as a part of the therapeutic process (and relational process), and relational exchange and communication (Kaufman, 2016; Maltz & Maltz, 2008; Whitty, 2010; Young et al., 2000). *Group therapy* uses the therapeutic relationship and mutual aid relationships, with desired treatment effects, as a part of the therapeutic process, to address a full range of biopsychosocial and spiritual issues. This is accomplished through group structure, group process, and group content (Woods, 2013).

In short, part of integrated social work methods is to heal relationships through relationships, and through changing relationship patterns and associated interpersonal transactions. The expectation is that changes in the social-relational elements and social supports, in life as lived in real-world social contexts, will help sustain changes in affect, behaviour, and thinking associated with desired, needed, and required changes in addictive Internet patterns of expression.

Social-Relational Considerations in Terms of Intimacy and Sexual Expression

A major consideration in terms of the place of relational dynamics associated with compulsive Internet use is to differentiate relational dynamics associated with intimacy and sexual expression. Part of the function of intimacy and sexual expression is reinforcing attachments, social support, emotional connection and commitment, a sense of belonging, and life satisfaction.

Cyber sex patterns of surfing, viewing, and/or hearing sexual content and processes, including creating and sharing sexual content, may include active sexting, verbal sex exchange without images; transactions that include a reality image of a person named Harry or a fantasy image of self as an avatar named Goth4; live interactive streaming of cyber relational and cyber sexual transactions (Harry with Heather); and presentations of self ranging from real (Harry) to imaginary identities, often with extensive fantasy narratives to support that monicker (e.g., toy boy, hot chic) (Christy & Fox, 2016). Cyber-friend relationships can be framed by messages of an actual social bond and attitude of respect, feelings of empathy, valid affirmation, extensive trust, and predictable continuity, at least in the short term, with sexual interest and erotic exchange only being part of what sustains the cyber connection, enabling some genuineness in social-emotional intimacy (Kimberley & Scheltgen, 2013). In cases of presentations of self as an image or in real-time digital video, the viewer may experience an image where some physical elements are unconsciously but perceptually modified, often with the function of the presentation of the objectified "other self" being morphed into the desired fantasy (the online sex partner who starts looking like a husband who has died). With pedophiles it would not be uncommon that a 12-year-old child will be, perceptually, physically morphed into an 18 year old, or the 18 year old morphed into the child; then either way the viewing may be framed as "not really looking at child porn," a complex defensive routine (Kimberley & Osmond, 2000). It is vital to acknowledge that it is not uncommon during a one-hour cyber exchange for more social relationship exchanges to occur than sexual or eroticized relational exchanges. However, whether a contact consists of a single one-hour session or is conducted over six continuous hours that ends at 5 a.m., primary partnerships and marriages usually suffer from some crisis of confidence, and the excuse of net "addiction" may carry little credibility as the cause (Maltz & Maltz, 2008). Lurking on reality sites and sex sites without identifying oneself or engaging a person in live streaming may be evidence of high degrees of social isolation and social alienation, a pattern that can also affect the primary relationship. Paraphilic net interests typically bring other emotional shocks and relational-bond threats to otherwise lasting relationships, beyond a disgust and disapproval of voyeurism and exhibitionism, and these may include adult pornography; child pornography; zoophila; bondage and sadomasochism; group sex; and cyber-spying. However, here too paradoxical patterns can arise when this behaviour allows primary relationships to be sustained because one partner understands that the couple bond does not meet all of the justified needs of the other partner (a lack of ability to engage in intercourse due to illness).

Societal factors that increase the attractiveness of sexual cyber relationships include:

- decreased ease, acceptability, and safety of partner-mate selection in the workplace;
- increased marital and family stress, disturbed relationships, and dissolution;
- loss of established and valued non-cyber close relationships;
- a modern ethos of friends with benefits including "sexting booty calls"; and
- social location and social marginalization, which renders cyberspace as a primary source of social inclusion, intimacy, and sexual relations (for example, for a gay Muslim woman) (Champion & Pedersen, 2015; Leiblum, 2001; Wang & Chang, 2010).

Motivational Considerations from Onset to Sustained Impulses and Compulsions

Social workers have long been aware of motivational dynamics, including interaction with addiction issues, and have focused their practice to attend to compromised biopsychosocial precursors to addiction and recovery including trauma and attachment issues, developmental damage, and dissociation (Brisch, 2011; Dayton, 2000; Flores, 2004; Kimberley, 2015). While therapists can't change the past we may be able to help reduce the influence of the past on the present. Client's narratives may be of the form: "The thing I wanted the most is a good relationship and my relationships have been fucked up since I was born ... I escaped into booze since I was 12, ... and now that I am 45, I escape in the web." One of the themes in both compulsive behaviours and addiction is that both substances and non-substances provide means to dissociate from the realities of daily life, and many engage in them in order to regulate intense emotions related to neglect, maltreatment, failures to protect, and other human sufferings and their developmental sequelae. Affect regulation and supports in life as lived are tasks that effective attachment and bonds help to mediate. In competition with self-regulation are stimulus cues, and impulsive, compulsive, and obsessive patterns dominate the motives to use the net. Part of the clinician's role is to influence motivation for change in one's relationship with the Internet that has yet to be contemplated, to progress to actively contemplated desired, needed, and required changes in personal and social functioning, and to aid the person in the action stage.

A client may be aware of some motives for engaging in compulsive net use, but motivation may also be based on unconscious processes such as distrust of desired relationship intensity. This can influence a client's net use and how it relates to current motivational accounts and narratives, because whether based on reality (achieving an orgasm) or social construction ("I *am* perverse scum"), both influence recovery. Narratives can include, "I can get lost in the net ... when I get lost in a game with my buddies, I'm gone, nothing else exists." Integrating those concerns with developmental sequelae and behavioural, emotive, affect, relational, and contextual changes is part of the counselling process. These foci are in the interests of personal and social change with respect to reducing risky net use patterns in the form of harm reduction, expanding strengths, and reaching for resiliencies, while recognizing that complete abstinence from the web is unlikely in contemporary society especially for those attending a post-secondary institution.

There will be supportive and protective factors, along with risk factors, which will either support or compromise the client's desire for personal and social change. The social worker must explore the client's motivational accounts and narratives, as well as their felt commitment to support personal and social change to help increase protective factors. Accounts may take the form of: "I know I need to change my net and gaming patterns; I need my family's support; I don't want to lose them or my job." Counsellors must also explore, in the client's motivational accounts and narratives, any felt commitment to reduce and control risk factors. One motivational narrative might take the form: "I can't stand conflict ... it makes me scared ... I avoid people; I need to learn to live with conflict, not just work out frustrations in war games and then get off with a one-night stand online." If interacting dynamics associated with developmental damage, attachments, affect regulation, and dissociation are significant, then motivations for primarily behaviour change, be it abstinence or harm reduction, will not likely be sufficient to sustain recovery.

In respecting the complexities of compulsive Internet use, social workers need to help clients enhance their motivations for desired, required, and needed changes. For example:

- Pre-Contemplation: "Yes, I wish I could talk with my wife without exploding ..."
- Contemplation: "Yes, I must change how I handle stress and anger if I'm going to keep my wife."
- Action: "Yes, I talked to her about what *we* need (note language beyond "I")— we plan on doing more together while we both practice communicating more openly, rather than me escaping into cyberspace when we disagree."

One reason why cognitive-behavioural methods are effective in the early stages of change is that they are relatively simple to understand and to undertake, and both the client and social worker can see changes. Most of the early changes represent action-oriented and thought-change beginnings of treatment rather than insight, affect regulation, relationship building, and identity-self change—the more complex integration ends of treatment. "Failures" in treatment are less likely when clients and primary support systems are putting efforts into sustaining early gains, enhancing resiliencies, and building strengths, including sustaining motivation for personal and social change. Also, workers are aware of their supportive counselling role in instilling hope, even when there are lapses. As with substance addiction, relapse to Internet misuse may be triggered by intense negative emotions, interpersonal conflict, a sense of failure, rejection, and a loss of, or reduction in, pro-recovery supports. Also, in parallel with substance addiction, clients needing support may return to peer support from cyber-friends or find a sense of belonging in cyberspace through returning to known equipment (my special keyboard), favourite surfing sites ("I've really missed lurking")[3], or favourite interactive sites or 5G communication (sexualized chat rooms, gaming communities, sexting friends).

In reaching for motivations to sustain desired, required, and needed changes, the therapist would be remiss to not explore motivations to return to past net behaviours. Such counter-themes could arise out of a felt sense of loss, while not having sufficient insight that relapse is not just behavioural but dynamic, in the sense that retuning to negative net using patterns may help the client meet needs to dissociate, to support affect regulation, and, when in cyberspace, feel a sense of belonging while reducing intrapsychic conflicts or transactional conflicts. Clients may signal motivation to change: "We want to talk with you next week about how to handle situations where I feel the loss of my net-buddies, without my partner fearing abandonment." Motivations supporting returning to previous behaviour may be so strong that part of sustaining progress requires challenging counterpoint motivations. Among the changes that may be difficult to sustain, within the context of counselling, are those defined as "required" (partner demands, court imperatives) as they rely on external motivators that may be more committed to the change than is the client.

Dynamics of net activity may create new needs that, once experienced, are difficult to give up. One possible narrative might be "I need continuous activity that's not boring, and novelty of information, content, process ... within a space where I belong, and where others accept me even when I don't talk ... all so I feel normal, connected, and fitting in; my real world is the net; my real me is my cyber-self." If one's place on the net is in sex chats, and your "watcher stats" are indicating that you have 1,000 active viewers, then it can give a boost to your self-esteem. In short, the web creates new markets for itself and attracts persons who become excited by novelty and self-confirmation ("it's better than depression and loneliness")—sexual self-confirmation is a strong aphrodisiac ("there is something uplifting about doing sex in front of 1,000 people"). As with one's favourite psychoactive substance, hypersexual behaviour may potentiate the value of the net to the client (Zmuda, 2014), much as does a "win" in gambling, or a "superbuzz" potentiated by mixing different psychoactive drugs. Thus, social workers should always consider employing motivational therapies as part of their intervention with clients experiencing compulsive Internet usage (Del Giudice & Kutinsky, 2007).

Identities: Convergence, Integration, and the Cyber-Me

Therapists respect the complexity of identity. Even though "self" or "self-concept" are grounded and show some stability and integration, identity also evidences plastic and malleable elements. Complex dynamics of identity present the counsellor and the client with the paradox that what appears stable is a self that is constantly in flux, and what is experienced as integrated is a self that may be disintegrated at varied points of human development and in diverse contexts (real, virtual, cyber). In the Internet context the worker must explore the meanings assigned by the client, significant others, and social networks to identity interactive self-definitions, including

- **Self-esteem**: internalized esteem, based on social-relational messages of low value and negative attitudes, and messages of high value and positive attitudes, signalled by others verbally and non-verbally, to a person as presented socially in the real world and in cyber networks. ("Others see me as a loser; on the net, I can be a winner.")
- **Self-worth**: the felt worth of self and an emotionally experienced sense of self, as positive and negative, that a person experiences, which may be relatively congruent with how others value them, or may be incongruent. ("I like myself as a gamer ... I am useless as a father and as a husband.")

- **Self-concepts**: the beliefs, attitudes, expectations, and meanings of identity that one applies to one's self. ("I am a loser in real life ... I am a winner in cyber life ... Why lose that?")
- **Self-confidence**: the attitude that one presents in terms of knowledge, capacities, and self-agency, in networks online and in daily life. ("I really don't feel as confident as I present when I express myself to others ... getting confirmation that I am great at war games gives me an emotional boost and a place (the Internet) where I need to belong.")
- **Cyber-self Identity**: temporal integration of various dimensions of self as presented and self as identified in cyberspace; some of the presentations may be based on suggestive monikers. ("I don't see myself as a sexy thing, but in the chat room I have friends and thousands of lookers who say that I am sexy and that they get off on me.")
- **Stable self-identities**: self-identities are often diverse and may also form a relatively stable nexus (father, employee, brother, husband) of self-identities and personas; those online may be new, exciting, uncertain, and potentially unstable (sexy thing, sexy friend, sexy Girl Toy-5G, or Boy Toy-5G).[4]
- **Self-agency**: a sense of self as an actor within social and physical environments, one who may observe, apply knowledge, make judgments, apply skills, reflect and problem solve, and decide and act with anticipated influence. ("As a black woman who is over 40 and a bit overweight for a tranny (transsexual), in a sex chat room, before I do anything sexual online, I make it clear ... 'no directors' ... 'no beggars' ... 'no disrespect,' I only do what I am comfortable with ... they want to feel good ... I want to feel good.")
- **Identity formation and re-formation**: counsellors may wish to explore the developmental history and dynamics in the stabilization of a net identity as it formed (perverted lurker) and re-formed (e.g., an "out" online sexual participant).

Therapists and clients would do well to explore the level at which cyber-identities are internalized and become integrated into presentations of self in daily life, that is, outside of the net and cyberspace. The cyber-selves may carry layers of suffering, pain, and developmental damage; counsellors may wish to explore the extent to which net surfing and social life on the net help in sustaining hope, building active resilience, enabling empowerment, and contributing to the formation of a revised identity as felt and as narrated (Baker, 2008; Fink, 1999; Rosen, 2012), similar to reinventing oneself when moving away to university. Some identities have delusional elements of clinical significance, such as the pedophile who defines self as "lover of children" and does not differentiate between genuinely loving children and being child-centred and grooming the child in the interest of the adult's agenda. Other identities may reflect personality disorders, which are overrepresented among those who are compulsive net users (Kimberley & Scheltgen, 2013). On the other hand, cyber identities of some marginalized persons reflect important empowered selves (Kimberley & Scheltgen, 2013), such as the gay Iranian female who may "be herself" in a cyber chat and show room, where she obtains positive confirmation and social support from global participants. A paradox is that cyber identity is associated with a sense of empowerment, confirmation, and belonging in persons whose identities include social skill deficits, rejection, and social exclusion. For those experiencing net dependency, especially associated with socially disapproved and deviant identities, the therapist will likely have to reach into the depths of identities, the "true me," typically the prosocial, and the "not me," the deviant. Caution must be taken in these actions, for in cyber exchanges, the distance between the exploited and the exploiter may be as thin as a sheet of paper.

Developmental Convergences and Influences

Human development continues throughout the life cycle and impacts compulsive behaviours, and is in turn impacted by exposure to parents with dependency issues (Kimberley, 2015). Biopsychosocial development may become fixated or may regress due to negative cyber behaviours and may confound clients' development, as well as those of significant others. As with substance addiction, compulsive cyber activity has been linked with dissociation, trauma, attachment issues, and affect regulation. There may also be traumas experienced in extreme cyber content production (live child sex abuse) as well as in the surfer's exposure to traumatic net content. Many children and adolescents view net images that represent premature but otherwise normative sexual activity that is meant for "entertainment" rather than being realistic. Child and adolescent exposure to sexual material on the web may provide relatively healthy sex education but can easily distort sex interest, attraction, and arousal, while members of the aging population may find shared interests, social support, and sexual exchange networks that support vital involvement in old age.

Spirituality and Existential Issues

Social workers and other counselling professionals may be called upon to help clients explore spiritual and existential issues associated with the functions of excessive negative cyber activity, virtual living online, belonging in virtual community, and the meaning of escape from life-as-lived offline. Therapists need to be sensitive to clients who share existential issues of social bond, discomfort with detachment, and feelings of disconnection or not fitting. As Doweiko (2015, p. 394) states, "we strive to join or merge with something beyond the 'self,' be it another person, a Higher power, or a chemical that holds the promise of existential anesthesia ... the promise of endless joy and peace." Therapists may wish to explore with a client the existential power of the net in filling vacuums of meaning and relationship, as well as in creating more existential angst and suffering. Recovery may be enhanced by spiritual beliefs and meanings attached to existence, relatedness, and growth.

There are many questions about the meaning of life and existence that clients may explore within the context of Internet use that can easily become all absorbing: Who am I? Why am I here? What is life all about? Where do I belong? Why is my cyber-self more meaningful than my offline self? Why is my net-life more real and meaningful than is my real life? Why are my cyber relationships more meaningful than are my primary relationships? When surfing, the client might ask Where am I? What am I doing here? Why am I doing this? Why do I let myself be enslaved by the net and cyberspace? Is my virtual life real or fantasy? Does God live in cyberspace? Can I really control this behaviour? Can I be honest with myself, let alone others? Why do I want to abstain or to reduce harm ... does it really matter? What else must I change?

When a therapist is being supportive in the exploration of these issues and signalling hopefulness, the discourse is reflective of the importance given to hopefulness in many religions and faith practices. Meditative approaches may help the client to both live in the moment and to reflect, which may influence personal and social functioning.

Conclusion

Expansion of the Internet, the World Wide Web, and cyberspaces, including 5G communications, is globally pervasive, accelerating, and will only grow in magnitude as we become an increasingly technologically driven species. These forms of information sharing, communication, and real-time social engagement have the capability to empower persons and organizations, but just as readily can exploit not only individuals but also entire social systems. Paradoxically, even in cases of negative Internet and cyber behaviours, anti-oppressive, social justice, and empowerment goals may be met.

There are a range of Internet-cyber processes that parallel those of substance addiction, which has led to the terms *Internet addiction* and *cyber addictions* becoming widely used, as they are easy conceptualizations; yet there are distinct differences between these addictions and excessive and negative psychoactive drug use regarding how the central and peripheral nervous systems are stimulated and altered (Csiernik, 2016). This in turn necessitates the development of distinct treatment, treatment systems, and policies. Regardless, compulsive Internet and cyber use themselves lead to extensive suffering, social challenges, and compromised social functioning. Beyond attempting to create simple disorder classifications and checklists that better assist clients in the change process, a biopsychosocial-spiritual interactional model should be applied to offer a change-oriented approach to clients that respects the complexities and paradoxes of their lives as experienced in their physical and their cyber worlds.

NOTES

1. Editor's Note: This similarity has led many in the popular, clinical, and academic spheres to label this an addiction, despite physical and social differences leading to the need for distinct treatment, treatment systems, and policies.

2. The dynamics of numbness have been linked to dissociation and associated with imminent threat or trauma sequelae, common with many social work clients; compulsive patterns may both increase numbness and also elevate a client out of numbness (Brisch, 2011; Briere & Scott, 2015).

3. One motivation for lurking is similar to people who find meaning in "people watching" and excitement in being "let in" to private space and to watch "games people play." Such patterns create a sense of social space without imperatives for social engagement. These patterns may be of value to marginalized persons who exhibit disorders such as Autism Spectrum Disorder or social phobia, and lack adequate social engagement skills. However, these patterns may also be deviant and pathological, such as streaming spy cameras.

4. While someone in the cyber world may have used such monikers, they are applied here as metaphoric, representing a set of potential net identities.

REFERENCES

Baker, A.J. (2008). Down the rabbit hole: The role of place in the initiation and development of on-line relationships. In A. Barak (Ed.), *Psychological aspects of cyberspace: Theory, research, applications* (pp. 163-184). New York: Cambridge University Press.

Blinka, L., & Smahel, D. (2011). Addiction to online role-playing games. In K.S. Young & C.N. de Abreu (Eds.), *Internet addiction: A handbook and guide to evaluation and treatment* (pp. 73-90). New York: John Wiley & Sons.

Briere, J., & Scott, C. (2015). *Principles of trauma therapy: A guide to symptoms and treatment.* Thousand Oaks, CA: Sage.

Brisch, K.H. (2012). *Treating attachment disorders: From theory to therapy.* New York: Guilford Press.

Calvert, C. (2014). Youth-produced sexual images, "sexting" and the cellphone. In F. Saleh, A. Grudzinskas, and A. Judge. (Eds.) *Adolescent sexual behavior in the digital age: Considerations for clinicians, legal professionals, and educators.* New York: Oxford University Press.

Champion, A.R., & Pedersen, C.L. (2015). Investigating differences between sexters and non-sexters on attitudes, subjective norms, and risky sexual behaviours. *Canadian Journal of Human Sexuality, 24*(3), 205-214.

Christy, K., & Fox, J. (2016). Transportability and presence as predictors of avatar identification within narrative video games. *Cyberpsychology, Behavior and Social Networking, 19*(4), 283-287.

Crocker, M. (2015). Out-of-control sexual behavior as a symptom of insecure attachment in men. *Journal of Social Work Practice in the Addictions, 15*(4), 373-393.

Csiernik, R. (2016). *Substance use and abuse: Everything matters* (2nd ed.). Toronto: Canadian Scholars Press.

Dayton, T. (2000). *Trauma and addiction.* New York: The Guilford Press.

Del Giudice, M., & Kutinsky, J. (2007). Applying motivational interviewing to the treatment of sexual compulsivity and addiction. *Sexual Addiction & Compulsivity, 14*(4), 303-319.

Delmonico, D., & Griffin, E. (2011). Cybersex addiction and compulsivity. In K. Young & C. de Abreu, (Eds). *Internet addiction: A handbook and guide to evaluation and treatment.* Hoboken: John Wiley & Sons.

Doweiko, H. (2015). *Concepts of chemical dependency.* Stamford, CT: Cengage.

Fink, J. (1999). *Cyberseduction: Reality in the age of psychotechnology*. New York: Prometheus Books.

Flores, P. (2004). *Addiction as an attachment disorder*. New York: Jason Aronson.

Greenfield, D. (2011). The addictive properties of Internet usage. In K. Young & C. de Abreu, (Eds.), *Internet addiction: A handbook and guide to evaluation and treatment* (pp. 135-171). Hoboken, NJ: John Wiley & Sons.

Hall, P. (2011). A biopsychosocial view of sex addiction. *Sexual and Relationship Therapy, 26*(3), 217-228.

Hall, P. (2013). Sex addiction—an extraordinarily contentious problem. *Sexual and Relationship Therapy, 29*(1), 68-75.

Judge, A., & Leary, M. (2014). From the streets to cyberspace: The effects of technology on children and adolescents in the United States. In F. Saleh, A. Grudzinskas, & A. Judge (Eds.), *Adolescent sexual behavior in the digital age: Considerations for clinicians, legal professionals and educators* (pp. 180-214). New York: Oxford University Press.

Kaufman, E. (2016). Family therapy approaches. In A. Mack, K. Brady, S. Miller, & R. Frances (Eds.), *Clinical textbook of addictive disorders* (pp. 612-628). New York: Guilford Press.

Kimberley, D. (2014). Many faces of Internet addictions. Presented at the 55th Institute on Addiction Studies, Kempenfelt, Ontario, July 13.

Kimberley, D. (2015). Compromised cognitive functioning in concurrent-disordered parents: Implications for Aboriginal children, foster care, mental health and addictions. In R. Neckoway & K. Brownlee (Eds.), *Child welfare in rural remote areas with Canada's First Nations Peoples: Selected readings* (pp. 16-43). Thunder Bay, ON: CERPYD, Lakehead University.

Kimberley, D., & Osmond, L. (2000). *Assessment and treatment of persons sexually addicted to child pornography and sex exploitation within the context of Internet addiction*. Presented at From Answers to Action: A Conference on Healing Sexual Exploitation and Prostitution, Grant MacEwan College, Edmonton, Alberta, May 4-6.

Kimberley, D., & Osmond, L. (2003). *Internet addiction: The personal and organizational problem for the new millennium*. Presented at Input 2003, 15th Biennial Symposium on Employee and Family Assistance Programs in the Workplace, Ottawa, Ontario, November 16.

Kimberley, D., & Scheltgen, M. (2013). Sexting: A game changer in sexual development, intimacy and sexual expression. Presented at the 35th Annual Sexuality Conference, Guelph, Ontario, June.

Kuss, D.J., & Griffiths, M. (2012). Internet and gaming addictions: A systematic literature review of neuroimaging studies. *Brain Science, 2*(3), 347-374.

Laier, C., Schulte, F., & Brand, M. (2013). Pornographic picture processing interferes with working memory performance. *Journal of Sex Research, 50*(7), 642-652.

Leahy, R. (2015). *Emotional schema therapy*. New York: The Guilford Press.

Love, T., Laier, C., Brand, M., Hatch, L., & Hajela, R. (2015). Neuroscience of Internet pornography addiction: Review and update. *Behavioral Science, 5*(3), 388-433.

Leiblum, S.R. (2001). Women, sex and the Internet. *Sexual and Relationship Therapy, 16*(4), 389-405.

Maltz, W., & Maltz, L. (2008). *The porn trap: The essential guide to overcoming problems caused by pornography*. New York: Harper.

Mikulincer, M., & Shaver, P. (2016). *Attachment in adulthood: Structure, dynamics, and change*. New York: Guilford Press.

Morahan-Martin, J. (1999). The relationship between loneliness and Internet use and abuse. *Cyber Psychology and Behaviour, 2*(5), 431-439.

Pollak, S., Pedulla, T., & Siegel, R. (2016). *Sitting together: Essential skills for mindfulness-based psychotherapy*. New York: Guilford Press.

Riemersma, J., & Sytsma, M. (2013). A new generation of sexual addiction. *Sexual Addiction & Compulsivity, 20*(4), 306–322.

Rosen, L. (2012). *iDisorder: Understanding our obsession with technology and overcoming its hold on us*. New York: St. Marin's Griffin.

Ruisard, D. (2015). Transformation through attachment: The power of the relationship in clinical social work. *Clinical Social Work Journal, 44*(3), 1–14.

Saleh, F., Feldman, B., Grudzinskas, A., Ravven, S., & Cody, R. (2014). Cybersexual harassment and suicide. In F. Saleh, A. Grudzinskas, & A. Judge (Eds.), *Adolescent sexual behavior in the digital age: Considerations for clinicians, legal professionals and educators* (pp. 139–160). New York: Oxford University Press.

Scheiber, L., Potenza, M., & Grant, J.E. (2016). Gambling disorder and other "behavioral" addictions. In A. Mack, K. Brady, S. Miller, & R. Frances (Eds.), *Clinical textbook of addictive disorders* (4th ed., pp. 327–349). New York: Guilford Press.

Schore, A.N. (2003). *Affect regulation and the repair of the self*. New York: W.W. Norton.

Schore, J., & Schore, A. (2007). Modern attachment theory: The central role of affect regulation in development and treatment. *Clinical Social Work Journal, 36*(1), 9–20.

Scott, C. (2014). Chat rooms and social networking sites. In F. Saleh, A. Grudzinskas, & A. Judge (Eds.), *Adolescent sexual behavior in the digital age: Considerations for clinicians, legal professionals and educators* (pp. 117–139). New York: Oxford University Press.

Sheldon, K., & Howitt, D. (2007). *Sex offenders and the Internet*. Chichester, UK: John Wiley and Sons.

Shulman, L. (2015). *The skills of helping individuals, families, groups and communities*, (8th ed.). Belmont, CA: Cengage.

Taneli, T., Guo, Y.H., & Mushtaq, S. (2015). Internet gaming disorder: Virtual or real? In M. Ascher & P. Levounis (Eds.), *The behavioral addictions* (pp. 67–80). Washington, DC: American Psychiatric Press.

Wang, C.C., & Chang, Y.T. (2010). Cyber relationship motives: Scale development and validation. *Social Behavior and Personality: An international journal, 38*(3), 289–300.

Whitty, M.T. (2010). Internet infidelity: A real problem. In K. Young & C. de Abreu (Eds.), *Internet addiction: A handbook and guide to evaluation and treatment* (pp. 191–204). New York: John Wiley & Sons.

Woods, J. (2013). Group analytic therapy for compulsive users of Internet pornography. *Psychoanalytic Psychotherapy, 27*(4), 306–318.

Young, F.S. (2011). Clinical assessment of Internet addicted clients. In K. Young & C. de Abreu, (Eds.), *Internet addiction: A handbook and guide to evaluation and treatment* (pp. 19–34). Hoboken, NJ: John Wiley & Sons.

Young, K. (1999). Evaluation and treatment of Internet addiction. In L. Vandecreek & T. Jackson (Eds.), *Innovations in clinical practice: A source book* (pp. 19–31). Sarasota, FL: Professional Resource Press.

Young, K., & de Abreu, C. (Eds.) (2011). *Internet addiction: A handbook and guide to evaluation and treatment*. Hoboken, NJ: John Wiley & Sons.

Young, K., Griffin-Shelley, E., Cooper, A., O'Mara, J., & Buchanan, J. (2000). Online infidelity: A new dimension in couple relationships with implications for evaluation and treatment. In A. Cooper. (Ed.), *Cybersex: The dark side of the force* (pp. 59–74). New York: Brunner/Routledge.

Zaman, T., & Lache, D. (2015). Texting and e-mail problem use. In M. Ascher & P. Levounis (Eds.), *The behavioral addictions* (pp. 101–112). Washington, DC: American Psychiatric Press.

Zmuda, N. (2014). Assessment and treatment of co-occurring substance use disorders and process addictions. In S. Straussner (Ed.), *Clinical work with substance abusing clients* (pp. 520–536). New York: Guilford Press.

Rick Csiernik

Rick is a professor in the School of Social Work at King's University College, Western University. He holds a BSc, BSW, MSW, PhD, and RSW, and has written and edited 10 books, including *Substance Use and Abuse: Everything Matters*, *Just Say Know: A Counsellor's Guide to Psychoactive Drugs*, and *Workplace Wellness*, authored over 150 peer reviewed articles and book chapters, and has been an invited presenter to over 200 national and international conferences, workshops, and seminars. He has been part of research teams that have received over 3 million dollars in funding and has been on the King's University College Honour Roll of teaching 16 consecutive times. Rick was the co-developer of the McMaster University addiction studies program where he has taught for 30 years and where he was the inaugural recipient of the McMaster University Instructor Appreciation Award.

William S. Rowe

William is a professor of social work at Southern Connecticut State University, New Haven, and professor emeritus of social work at the University of South Florida, Tampa. He has held professorships at McGill University, Memorial University of Newfoundland, and King's College at Western University. He has worked extensively in the fields of social work education, child welfare, corrections, health, and HIV, serving on numerous boards and committees at local, national, and international levels. William has authored more than 150 academic and professional publications and provided lectures and trainings at agencies and universities in more than 30 countries. He has led the development of social work education in Canada, USA, and Indonesia and is currently working to develop and expand social work education in China at the Beijing University of Civil Engineering and Architecture and Central China Normal University in Wuhan. He is a co-investigator on a brief intervention for addictions project with the Yale School of Emergency Medicine and serves on the editorial board of *Best Practices in Mental Health* and the *Journal of Evidence-Based Practice*. William's most recent book co-authored with Francis Turner is *101 Clinical Social Work Techniques* (2013).

Ramona Alaggia

Ramona earned her MSW and PhD at the University of Toronto where she is an associate professor and holds the Factor-Inwentash chair in children's mental health. Coming from an ecological orientation she uses her considerable practice experience in family systems work to inform her clinical teaching and research. Her work also focuses on gender and violence in families including child sexual abuse, intimate partner violence, and understanding the effects of exposure to violence on children's mental health and important resilience factors. Ramona works closely with agencies serving families experiencing violence and abuse to evaluate and improve services. She has co-edited a book, *Cruel but Not Unusual: Violence in Canadian Families*, in its second edition.

Joe Antone

Joe is a First Nations social worker whose home community is Oneida Nation of the Thames. He has recently completed his Master of Social Work, and also holds a Bachelor of Social Work degree and a diploma in fish and wildlife. Joe has several years of experience doing direct addictions practice and writes academically in the field of addiction. Joe has worked with Indigenous people in a variety of contexts including Indigenous mental health, addiction, and community development. Joe has presented at national and international conferences on First Nations issues. Other areas of expertise include youth leadership, program development, and research. Joe is a proud new parent who is excited about fatherhood.

Laura Béres

Laura is an associate professor in the School of Social Work at King's University College, Western University. She received her MSW from the University of Toronto and completed her PhD at the Ontario Institute of Studies in Education. She trained as a narrative practitioner with Michael White at the Dulwich Centre in Adelaide, Australia. She is author of *The Narrative Practitioner* (2014) and co-author of *Innovations in Narrative Therapy: Connecting Practice, Training, and Research* (2011) and *Practicing Spirituality: Reflecting on Meaning-Making in Personal and Professional Contexts* (2016).

Munish Bhakri

Munish is an international medical student of Windsor University currently completing the clinical component of his Doctor of Medicine (MD) degree in the United States. He attended the University of Toronto for undergraduate studies in life sciences and later continued his educational pursuit at McMaster University, where he developed a keen interest and advocacy in the field of mental health, addictions, and primary health care. He has been actively involved with non-profit organizations over the years to raise funds and awareness for causes he holds close to heart. His interests include research projects studying the various techniques in mental health and neurosciences, particularly music therapy and applications in treating PTSD, individuals with schizophrenia, and addiction patients in clinical environments.

Rachel Birnbaum

Rachel is a professor cross-appointed in childhood & social institutions (interdisciplinary studies) and social work at King's University College, Western University. She has over 20 years of clinical practice experience working with children and families of separation and/or divorce. Her research focus is on interdisciplinary scholarship with colleagues in law, social work, medicine, and psychology. Rachel has presented and published both nationally and internationally on child custody and access assessments, child legal representation, access to justice issues, children's participation in family law, and working with high conflict families post-separation. Rachel is the 2014 recipient of the Stanley Cohen Distinguished Research Award presented by an international interdisciplinary organization for research in family justice. She was the president of the Ontario College of Social Workers and Social Service Workers for four years, the president of the Canadian Council of Social Work Regulators for two years, and the president of AFCC-Ontario 2015–2017, and has been elected to the Royal Society of Canada.

Melissa Brideau

Melissa completed her BSW and MSW degrees at King's University College, Western University. She works as a social worker/advocate assisting those individuals having difficulty navigating various social benefit systems. Her research interests focus on disability issues, addiction/substance use, and the many barriers that are often insurmountable to those individuals with ability issues who wish to access appropriate and comprehensive treatment.

Kelly Brownbill

Kelly's spirit name, *Wabunnoongakikwe*, means "Woman Who Comes from the East," and she is proud to be Wabizhashi Dodem, Marten Clan. She is a member of the Flat Bay community of the Mi'kmaq Nation in Newfoundland and a member of the Three Fires Midewin Lodge. Kelly believes that addressing the complexities of Aboriginal health and wellness must include participation of mainstream agencies in delivering culturally competent and culturally safe services. To that end, much of her career has been focused on providing safe, pertinent, and appropriate training on cultural competency. She believes that it is important to provide balanced understanding of historical issues and is adept at enhancing the learner's knowledge in a manner that utilizes humour, kindness, and compassion. Kelly has conducted countless cultural awareness training sessions across a broad range of service sectors for both Native and non-Native participants. She has also worked with Aboriginal communities both on and off reserve to develop healthy agency models and to further develop counselling skills with Aboriginal clients.

Tara Bruno

Tara is a PhD graduate of the University of Toronto's collaborative program in addiction studies and sociology. Her dissertation compared the substance use patterns of street youth with high school youth living in Toronto. She is currently an assistant professor at King's University College at Western University, where she teaches Introduction to Sociology, Introduction to Criminology, Youth in Conflict with the Law, and Drugs in Society. Her current research and scholarly interests include substance use and misuse in Canadian society, media representations of illegal drugs, youth and families, crime and victimization, and drug policy.

Nicole Dedobbeleer

Nicole has completed her PhD studies and is currently professor at the Faculty of Medicine, Université de Montréal, in the Department of Health Administration. Her research program focuses on the concept of WHO "Health Promoting Hospital" with a first project, funded by CIHR, being conducted in Montérégie. It was designed to examine the possible extension of the concept "hospital health promoter" in the concept "CSSS health advocate."

Colleen Anne Dell

Colleen is a professor and the research chair in substance abuse at the University of Saskatchewan in the Department of Sociology and School of Public Health. She is also a senior research associate with the Canadian Centre on Substance Abuse, Canada's national addiction agency. Her research is grounded in an empowering community-based participatory approach and is specific to Aboriginal populations, criminalized women, and drug-using populations. Her research interests focus on healing and wellness, and include identity, animal-assisted interventions, treatment programming, self-harm, and evaluation. She has worked extensively at the community and national levels, including with the Elizabeth Fry Society and the Senate of Canada.

Debra Dell

Debra, who holds a Master of Arts in counselling psychology, is the executive director of the National Youth Solvent Addiction Committee in Saskatoon, Saskatchewan, and co-author of "Resiliency and Holistic Inhalant Abuse Treatment." Through her organization RCW Consulting, she offers contracted writing and researching services in the addictions field.

Jeffrey Derevensky

Jeffrey is a professor and director of Clinical Training in School/Applied Child Psychology, Department of Educational and Counselling Psychology, and a professor in the Department of Psychiatry at McGill University. He has published widely in the fields of child development, developmental psychopathology, gambling studies, and education and is on the editorial board of numerous journals. Since 1992 he has developed a comprehensive research program investigating many facets of gambling, is actively involved in treating young people with severe gambling problems, and has been a consultant to gaming corporations and governments throughout the world. He is the director of the McGill University Youth Gambling Research and Treatment Clinic and the International Centre for Youth Gambling Problems and High-Risk Behaviors. Jeff is a recipient of numerous awards, is considered an international expert in the field of gambling studies, and has testified before legislative committees in North America, Europe, Asia, and Australasia.

Randy Duncan

Randy is an educational psychologist affiliated with the Department of Sociology at the University of Saskatchewan. He specializes in applied measurement and program evaluation with primary research interests in instrument construction and validation. His research is grounded in equine assisted learning (EAL) for at-risk populations. His focus on EAL research has been with Aboriginal populations and more recently with veterans and their families suffering from the effects of PTSD. He has an extensive background in program evaluation with Saskatchewan organizations providing mental health and addictions services.

Mavis Etienne

Mavis is a Mohawk woman of the Wolf Clan from Kanehsatake Mohawk Territory. She has been married to her husband, James, for over 40 years. They have one son, Rycki. Mavis is the clinical supervisor at the Onen'to:kon Treatment Centre. She has been in the drug and alcohol addictions field for over 20 years. Mavis is an international certified alcohol and drug counsellor (ICADC) and has also earned a certificate in Aboriginal social work practice at McGill University. Mavis does presentations on issues such as abuse, addiction, and suicide prevention for universities, schools, churches and retreats. She is involved in Bible translation into the Mohawk language and hosts the Mohawk Gospel Program on the Kanehsatake community radio station CKHQ.

Anna Francis

Anna received her MSW from the University of Toronto and works as a social worker in a children's mental health centre in Ontario, providing intensive community-based therapeutic services to children and their families. Anna was the principal investigator on a research project through the University of Toronto that examined the relationship between women's disclosure of intimate partner violence and their experiences of substance abuse and mental health.

Carolyne Gorlick

Carolyne retired as associate professor from the School of Social Work, King's University College, Western University, after 25 years of service. Her primary area of research interest was policy issues pertaining to poverty. As principal investigator, she completed a federally funded, four-year research project on welfare to work programs in Canada. Carolyne was also a member of the CURA/UWO research project on homelessness, community economic development, and mental health consumer-survivors.

Diane Hiebert-Murphy

Diane received her PhD from the University of Manitoba in 1995 where she is currently a professor in the Faculty of Social Work. Her research interests focus on issues of interpersonal violence with major projects including Power and Relationship Satisfaction in Couples with a History of Violence and Understanding Women's Perceptions of Risk for

Intimate Partner Violence with an Intersectionality Framework: The Case of Disabled, Separated and Lesbian women in Canada. Diane is also the co-editor of *Partnering with Parents: Family-Centred Practice in Children's Service.*

Carol Hopkins

Carol holds a MSW and is Wolf Clan from the Lenni Lenape Nation, otherwise known as the Delaware of the Thames First Nation located in southwestern Ontario. Carol is the mother of four and grandmother of six. She is the executive director of the National Native Addictions Partnership Foundation, whose mandate is to advocate on behalf of and support the National Native Alcohol and Drug Abuse Program and the National Youth Solvent Addiction Program for First Nations and Inuit people in Canada. Carol is also a part-time professor at King's University College, School of Social Work.

Cecilia M. Jevitt

Cecilia is the midwifery education coordinator for Yale University and practices within the Yale-New Haven Health system. She holds a CNM, PhD, and FACNM. Prior to coming to Yale in 2013, she practiced full-scope midwifery in the Tampa Bay area for 30 years. She taught women's health, health policy and economics, evidence-based practice, and qualitative research from 1999 to 2011 with the USF College of Nursing while jointly appointed to the Colleges of Medicine and Public Health. In 2012, she organized an academic division of midwifery within the USF Morsani College of Medicine, Department of Obstetrics and Gynecology. Her scholarship focuses on integrating obesity prevention and management into women's health. She was a Florida Nurses Association Great 100 Nurses in 2009, the 2010 Reviewer of the Year for the *Journal of Midwifery & Women's Health*, a 2014 Connecticut Nightingale Excellence in Nursing Award winner, and is an elected Fellow of the American College of Nurse-Midwives.

Blanka Jordanov

Blanka graduated with a Master of Social Work from King's University College, Western University. Her spectrum of work has included work with children, youth, and high-risk families in child protection and in the youth justice system. She is currently working in long term care facilities, as well as with a community health service to provide support for individuals and families impacted by illness or a disability.

Amber Kellen

Amber has a BA and a BSW from York University along with a master's degree in public policy and administration from Ryerson University. She has been with the John Howard Society of Toronto for 14 years where she has held a senior management position for the past 9. She has also co-facilitated a course called Homelessness in Canadian Society at Ryerson University through their continuing education program. In addition to developing and supervising a variety of front-line programs at the John Howard Society of Toronto, she occupies various leadership roles on local committees concerning mental health/justice, substance use/harm reduction, housing, and reintegration innovations. As well, Amber is responsible for local research and policy initiatives, and community engagement projects.

Dennis Kimberley

Dennis, a former director with the Addiction Research Foundation of Ontario, has nearly half a century of experience in addiction and mental health. Since 1985 he has been a professor at the School of Social Work, Memorial University. He has presented nationally and internationally on addiction issues and their links with mental health, sex abuse, sex offending, child maltreatment and exploitation, and aggression risks. He has appeared in various legal settings as an expert witness and was a member of the Canadian expert panel that addressed best practices for concurrent disorders and substance abuse. He has a special interest in concurrent disorders in Indigenous communities.

Robin Koop-Watson

Robin is a registered social worker who earned her BSW and MSW at King's University College, Western University. Her approach to counselling is client-centreed and grounded in mindfulness. She views the counselling process as one means to awaken this potential while addressing the barriers to growth and healing. Robin integrates a variety of therapeutic interventions with the unique needs of each client. Much of her experience has been with individuals who have experienced trauma or childhood abuse and she has specialized training in eye movement desensitization and reprocessing (EMDR).

Siu Ming Kwok

Siu Ming is professor with the Faculty of Social Work, University of Calgary, where he earned his PhD. He is a registered social worker and practiced in the field of youth criminal justice, drug addiction, and child protection. He has extensive research experience in the areas of social justice among racialized youth and youth in conflict with the law in Canada, and has engaged in multiple national and international studies and research networks. His broader research interests centre on youth justice, child welfare, social work education, social policy, and non-profit sector administration.

Lewis Mehl-Madrona

Lewis is the executive director of the Coyote Institute for Studies of Change and Transformation and holds an MD, MPhil, and PhD. The Institute is focused on transforming medicine and mental health through the integration of Indigenous wisdom into contemporary practice. He is the author of the *Coyote* trilogy. His work discusses healing practices from Lakota, Cherokee, and Cree traditions, and how they intersect with conventional medicine.

Thomas Miller

Thomas is an Anishinaabe Native from Curve Lake First Nations. Thomas was born in Hamilton, Ontario. Growing up, he was raised by his mother until her suicide in 1980. He was then raised by his maternal grandmother. Compounded by this childhood, traumas resulting from the ongoing effects of residential schooling resulted in Thomas being diagnosed with post traumatic stress disorder. He has lived on the Six Nations Reserve for several years and is currently residing in an old farmhouse in Jarvis, Ontario. He is the loving father of five beautiful children. In addition, Thomas has recently welcomed his first grandchild into the world. He is currently employed as a machinist with a company in Brantford, Ontario. Thomas hopes that through sharing his experiences he can educate and help others.

Pauline Morissette

Pauline is a social worker with a doctorate in community health from the Faculty of Medicine of the Université de Montréal. She is currently a professor in the School of Social Services at the Université de Montréal. She has written several articles on the use of alcohol and psychotropic drugs among working women and men.

Karen Mosier

Karen is a research facilitator at the Western College of Veterinary Medicine, University of Saskatchewan. In her current position, she works with faculty to find funding opportunities for them to do research, facilitates networking and partnerships with other colleges, universities, and industry partners, and assists in guiding new faculty through the grant writing process. In addition, she has a special mandate to promote international collaborations with universities outside Canada by assisting international students to apply for Government of Canada scholarships to come and do research with faculty at the Western College of Veterinary Medicine.

Tanielle O'Hearn

With the unyielding support of her family and son, Christian, Tanielle graduated with both her BSW and MSW from King's University College, Western University. Tanielle discovered her passion for educating others while attending King's and has held a variety of research and teaching positions. She recently moved to the beautiful city of Orillia, Ontario, where she will continue to invite further opportunities for both personal and professional growth and development. Although continuously engaging in lifelong learning and academic pursuits, she ensures that her life remains revolved around her favourite activity—being a mother.

Louise Osmond

Louise is a graduate of the MSW program at Memorial University School of Social Work with over 20 years of experience in social work, much of which has been in private practice. She has appeared in court as an expert witness in child protection cases, including cases where parents are suspected of having addiction and mental health risks. Her practice has included dual-disordered youth, women, Indigenous, and physically challenged persons. She has presented nationally and internationally on substance use and abuse and their links with mental health, sex abuse, sex offending, and aggression risks. She has worked extensively with women who have addiction risks and problems with intimacy and sexual expression associated with sexual trauma. One of her areas of scholarship is eroticized children and sibling incest.

Lois Powers

Lois is assistant executive director of the Toronto division of the John Howard Society. She has a degree in sociology and fine arts from York University and is a graduate of criminal justice studies at George Brown College. Lois has extensive counselling experience working with men who have been in conflict with the law. She has developed programs to address issues of anger management and substance abuse.

Lisa Rapp

Lisa received her MSW degree in social work from the University of Buffalo and worked as a psychiatric social worker in the areas of domestic violence, children and adolescent inpatient units and outpatient clinics, and in the juvenile justice system. She earned her PhD in social welfare in 1999 at the University of Buffalo and has taught at the University of Nevada Las Vegas, the University of South Florida, and is currently at Saint Leo University, Florida. Lisa was Co-PI of the Prodigy Cultural Arts Prevention Program. She has conducted numerous program evaluations, focus groups, and written grants and reports for profit and non-profit agencies. Her research expertise includes: juvenile crime and violence, children and adolescents with mental illness, prevention, and program evaluation. She is co-director of the Maribeth Durst Applied Research Institute at Saint Leo University.

Renée A. St-Pierre

Renée is a doctoral candidate in the School/Applied Child Psychology program at McGill University. As a graduate student member of the International Centre for Youth Gambling Problems and High-Risk Behaviors, she has participated in both basic and policy-related research in the area of youth and problem gambling. She has published several articles in international gambling and addiction journals on the topics of risk and protective factors for problem gambling, problem gambling prevention, and responsible gambling policies. She has won several awards for her research, including the 2009 National Council on Problem Gambling Award for Outstanding Master's Thesis. Her recent research has focused on using social cognition models of health behaviours to understand and prevent adolescent gambling and problem gambling.

Maureen Seguin

Maureen is a PhD candidate at the London School of Hygiene and Tropical Medicine with almost 10 years of research experience in the sociology of health, with particular expertise on the mental health of marginalized women and girls. She has experience contributing to projects in close collaboration with diverse stakeholders including leading academic institutions, policy-makers, and NGOs in low- and middle-income countries. Most prominently, she has focused on women's mental health in post-conflict settings and violence against women and girls in low- and middle-income countries. Maureen is a trained mixed-methods researcher, with strengths in regression analysis, respondent-driven sampling, qualitative thematic analysis, and systematic literature reviews.

Chris Stewart

Chris is an associate professor in the social work and criminal justice departments at the University of Central Florida. His research attempts to provide empirical evidence for improving community-based interventions. In particular, he is interested in the interaction of individual and environmental risk factors and the mechanisms through which these factors may contribute to behaviour. Because substance abuse is a significant factor for many populations, much of his research has included individuals struggling with addiction. His latest projects have focused upon the juvenile justice system and identifying those elements that might enhance adolescent re-entry into their communities.

Dora M.Y. Tam

Dora is an associate professor with the Faculty of Social Work, University of Calgary. Dora holds a PhD from the University of Calgary, is a registered social worker, and has practiced in the fields of family services, probation, hospital, and group home settings. Dora's program of research involves social work education, violence against women issues, youth delinquentcy, program evaluation, and scale development. As a social work educator, Dora strongly believes that social work programs should prepare graduates to become practitioner-researchers. To achieve such a goal, Dora has been actively involved in a number of research projects, which provide training opportunities to undergraduate and graduate students in terms of planning, implementation, analysis, and knowledge mobilization. Apart from research, Dora is a member of the board of directors of a number of social services and professional organizations as a way to keep on the pulse of clients' needs and advance social work practice, and to develop social work education.

Raymond Tempier

Raymond is a professor of psychiatry at the Faculty of Medicine, University of Ottawa. He is consultant in general psychiatry at the Montfort Hospital, Ottawa. He has been appointed senior researcher at the Institut de Recherche de l'Hôpital Montfort, heading a mental health research team. He holds a medical degree from the University of Aix-Marseille II, France, and psychiatry specialty diplomas from both France and Canada. He holds a master's degree in community health from the Université de Montréal. He was awarded Distinguished Fellow of the Canadian Psychiatric Association in 2012.

Jim Watkin

Jim is an instructor at Nunavut Arctic College in Iqaluit. He received both his BSW and MSW from King's University College, Western University. Jim has experience working with the AIDS Committees of London and Guelph, the London Harm Reduction Coalition, and as a member of Law Enforcement Against Prohibition (LEAP). He has also been instrumental in developing harm reduction strategies and materials in the Street Outreach program for at-risk individuals, including those involved with the sex trade in London, and coordinating a low threshold methadone clinic in London, providing support and counselling for individuals struggling with addiction.

Emma Wilson

Emma received both her BSW and MSW from King's University College, Western University. She has over 15 years of experience working with children/youth and their families. Presently, she works as a social worker and attendance counsellor in a high school in London, Ontario, with an interest in attachment issues and the implications on student success.

Lee Woytkiw

Lee received her BSW from the University of Calgary and her MSW from the University of Manitoba. She worked for 10 years at the Laurel Centre in Winnipeg, before moving on to become a therapy specialist at Rockyview Hospital in Calgary. She is currently serving as a social worker within the Alberta Health system.

COPYRIGHT ACKNOWLEDGEMENTS

INDEX